Juvenile Delinquency

NINTH EDITION

Clemens Bartollas

- University of Northern Iowa

Frank Schmalleger

- Emeritus, University of North Carolina at Pembroke

PEARSON

Boston   Columbus   Indianapolis   New York   San Francisco   Upper Saddle River
Amsterdam   Cape Town   Dubai   London   Madrid   Milan   Munich   Paris   Montreal   Toronto
Delhi   Mexico City   São Paulo   Sydney   Hong Kong   Seoul   Singapore   Taipei   Tokyo

Editorial Director: Vernon Anthony
Acquisitions Editor: Gary Bauer
Development Editor: Elisa Rogers at 4development
Editorial Assistant: Lynda Cramer
Director of Marketing: David Gesell
Marketing Manager: Mary Salzman
Senior Marketing Coordinator: Alicia Wozniak
Marketing Assistant: Les Roberts
Senior Managing Editor: JoEllen Gohr
Project Manager: Jessica H. Sykes

Senior Operations Supervisor: Pat Tonneman
Senior Art Director: Diane Ernsberger
Text and Cover Designer: Wanda Espana at Wee Design
Cover Art: ARTLIFE
Full-Service Project Management: Kelli Jauron, S4Carlisle
   Publishing Services
Composition: S4Carlisle Publishing Services
Printer/Binder: Courier/Kendallville
Cover Printer: Lehigh-Phoenix Color/Hagerstown
Text Font: ITC Century Light

10 9 8 7 6 5 4 3 2 1

ISBN 10:   0-13-298731-7

ISBN 13: 978-0-13-298731-8

This book is dedicated to our daughters,
Kristin Polatty, Nicole Schmalleger,
Cherie Nantz, and Michelle Lallos

Brief Contents

Contents

PART 2 *The Causes of Delinquency*

CHAPTER 3 **Individual Causes of Delinquency** 52

CHAPTER 4 Social Structural Causes of Delinquency 79

PART 3 *The Environmental Influences on and the Prevention of Delinquency*

CHAPTER 7 **Gender and Delinquency** 159

CHAPTER 10 **Gangs and Delinquency** 240

PART 4 *The Juvenile Justice System*

CHAPTER 12 **Juvenile Justice Process** 297

What's New in This Edition

The ninth edition has a number of features that make it quite different from previous editions:

- The chapters include more summary statements, line art, and tables to illustrate the chapter content and make the information more accessible.

- The chapter on prevention (Chapter 12 in the eighth edition) no longer appears in the book because prevention is now a focus in every chapter, addressed within the context of each chapter topic. Prevention is especially pertinent to the study of delinquency today because so many studies on effective prevention programs have recently been done.

- The chapter on juvenile corrections (Chapter 16 in the eighth edition) is now divided into two chapters, community-based corrections (Chapter 15) and juvenile institutions and aftercare (Chapter 16).

- Most chapters contain integrated materials on delinquency and social policy where a vital question is posed: What can be done about the delinquency issues raised in this chapter?

- A new boxed feature, *People In the Know*, contains interviews with individuals who have made significant contributions to our understanding of delinquency. Four interviews are with well-known criminologists—Albert K. Cohen, David Matza, Travis Hirschi, and Richard Quinney—and most contain updates about their classic theories. Five interviews focus on contemporary and ongoing developments in the delinquency literature, and include talks with John Laub, Terrie E. Moffitt, Karen Heimer, Meda Chesney-Lind, and Jorja Leap. The tenth interview features a former gang leader, Sam Dillon.

- Each chapter concludes with an ongoing hypothetical case study of a young woman's life, called *The Life Course of Amy Watters*.

- A number of chapters focus on evidence-based findings, and include evidence of best practices in prevention programs. Evidence-based findings form the core of another contemporary and exciting research initiative intended to understand and reduce delinquency in America.

- The ninth edition has been substantially updated, and every effort has been made to include the most recent studies and statistics of relevance to the study of juvenile delinquency. Updates have been made to juvenile court statistics, data on the co-occurrence of substance abuse behaviors in youth, juvenile offense data, statistics from the *Monitoring the Future* study, and statistical updates from the Federal Bureau of Investigation, the Bureau of Justice Statistics, and the Office of Juvenile Justice and Delinquency Prevention.

- A number of new exhibit boxes throughout the text highlight the changing nature of delinquency in America and the juvenile justice system's response. Two chapters now include exhibits on the use of technology that is designed to reduce the risk faced by youthful offenders in community-based corrections and juvenile institutions.

Chapter-Specific Changes

- Chapter 1 now includes a section on crossover youth and individuals, a discussion of resilience, an interview with John Laub, and (in the policy section) a brief introduction to model programs identified by the Office of Juvenile Justice and Delinquency Prevention (OJJDP).

- Chapter 2 now includes an added section on the victimization of children, including an exhibit on victimization and its results. The prevention of delinquency section now includes discussion of Positive Youth Development, a new approach to youth in trouble.

- Chapter 3 includes a new interview with Terrie E. Moffitt, which is part of a discussion of her theory and research. The delinquency and social policy section provides a discussion of evidence-based policy decisions, which has importance to all policy makers.

- Chapter 4 now contains an interview with Albert K. Cohen, who offers updates on his classic theory.

- Chapter 5 now includes interviews with two individuals who have made major contributions to the delinquency field, David Matza and Travis Hirschi.

- Chapter 6 now includes interviews with Karen Heimer and Richard Quinney, and there is a new exhibit on criminology and peacemaking.

- Chapter 7 contains new exhibits on the differences between girls and boys, the Amicus Girls Study, and the sexualization of girls. Also included is an interview with Meda Chesney-Lind, who explains her feminist theory of delinquency. In the prevention section, there is further a discussion of Girls, Inc., and the policy section examines the expansion of a gender-responsive policy and practice.

- Chapter 8 includes a new section on other expressions of family life—including the foster family, the adopted child, children with lesbian, gay, bisexual, and transgender parents, and cohabitating parents. The prevention section now examines parent training.

- Chapter 9 contains expanded material on bullying and suicide, the bullying of gay teens, bullying and school shootings, and bullying and student disabilities. A new exhibit entitled "Nine Adolescents Charged After Suicide of Classmate" focuses on the possible deadly consequences of bullying in an adolescent female's life. More emphasis is placed on school failure, as well as the inclusion of models of best practice and evidence-based education. Furthermore, the chapter now examines security measures at contemporary schools, including corporal punishment, out-of-school suspensions, and expulsions from school.

- Chapter 10 includes more emphasis on social, economic, political, and structural factors in the emergence of gangs. There are interviews with Sam Dillon, a former "Main 21" of the Black P-Stone Nation, and with Jorja Leap who is well known for her research on West Coast gangs. This chapter also contains additional information on terrorism and gangs; a discussion of Homeboy Industries and an exhibit on its founder, Father Greg Boyle, S.J.; a new exhibit on keeping gangs off the streets, and an exhibit on those who have made the biggest contributions to understanding gangs.

- Chapter 11 includes updated national data on drug use and a new table on legal drug classifications.

- Chapter 12 contains new sections on treatment, the use of graduated sanctions in juvenile justice, disproportionate minority confinement (DMC), and a discussion on the importance of early intervention.

- Chapter 13 contains new sections on the history of police, the police processing of juveniles, and the police and the prevention of delinquency, as well as a new discussion of racial issues.

- Chapter 14 includes a new section on juvenile court personnel, an updated and expanded section on transfer to an adult court, and a new section on the legal rights of juveniles during the adjudicatory stage of juvenile court proceedings.

- Chapter 15 includes new sections on the philosophy underlying community-based corrections, the administration of community-based corrections and probation, and an exhibit on technocorrections about reducing risk with youthful offenders sentenced to community-based corrections. It also addresses increased concerns about improving the effectiveness of probation and community-based programs.

- Chapter 16, while revealing what is wrong with juvenile institutions, now also provides directions and policy recommendations on how to improve juvenile facilities. The chapter also contains a new discussion of the characteristics of those on aftercare, a discussion of three model juvenile institutions, and an important evidence-based study about sexual victimization in our nation's training schools.

Organization of the Text

Clemens Bartollas and Frank Schmalleger, who were classmates and friends at The Ohio State University during their Ph.D. studies, have joined together to coauthor this ninth edition of Bartollas's well-known text, *Juvenile Delinquency*. The authors believe that students and instructors alike will find the following features especially helpful in understanding delinquency today and in preparing society to deal with it:

- *Strong sociological focus throughout the text.* The root causes of delinquency, along with the environments in which it either flourishes or is discouraged—including family, school, peers, and community—receive major emphasis. Each chapter includes a theme of delinquency across the life course, which is one of the most promising and exciting perspectives in the study of delinquency. This theme helps students understand how delinquent behavior originates and then either continues and evolves into adult criminality or terminates.

- *Special attention to desistance, which dovetails with the examination of behavior across the life course.* Some individuals persist in antisocial behavior throughout life, whereas others make the decision to end their involvement in antisocial behavior and become law-abiding citizens. This book helps to identify what young people in given circumstances are likely to do.

- *Emphasis on the important roles that gender, race, social class, and place of residence play in the formative adolescent years.* Specifically, Chapter 7 examines gender and delinquency while race and ethnicity receive attention in Chapter 12.

- *Discussion of gangs and gang activity.* Gangs, an increasingly important aspect of juvenile offending, are given special coverage, with significant discussion of groups such as Mara Salvatrucha, or MS-13, and 18th Street, or MS-18.

- *Emphasis on prevention throughout the text.* The book reveals what has been tried in the past as well as discloses exciting new ventures in the prevention of delinquency.

- *Substantial policy-oriented analyses.* In the midst of national soul-searching about what to do with serious and repeat juvenile offenders, nearly every chapter of this text offers evidence-based policy recommendations on prevention and suggests possible treatment interventions.

The Four Parts of the Text

This text is divided into four parts: (1) the nature and extent of delinquency, (2) the causes of delinquency, (3) the environmental influences on and the prevention of delinquency, and (4) the juvenile justice system.

- Part 1 explores how delinquent behavior affects the larger society and reports on the measurement of the nature and extent of delinquency by examining the available statistical tools.

- Part 2 looks at four types of explanations for delinquent behavior: (1) individual causes, ranging from free will to biological and psychological positivism; (2) social structural factors; (3) social process factors; and (4) social interaction theories.

- Part 3 examines the relationship between delinquency and gender; problems in the family, such as child neglect and abuse; experiences in the school; peer and gang delinquency; and drug abuse.

- Part 4 includes an overview of the juvenile justice process, including police–juvenile relations, the juvenile court, community-based corrections, juvenile institutions, and aftercare.

Special Features

This text contains a number of special features that students should find especially helpful in understanding juvenile delinquency, including its causes, consequences, deterrence, prevention, and treatment:

- *Themes and boxes.* This book builds on three exciting themes: (1) the prevention of delinquency, (2) delinquency across the life course, and (3) delinquency and social policy. Two types of boxes are also used in this text, including Juvenile Law boxes and individually titled exhibits.
- *The Life Course of Amy Watters.* This hypothetical case study appears at the end of each chapter. It is the continuing story that follows a young girl from childhood through her high school years. The problems and challenges that Amy faces as she matures are typical of many children, but eventually lead to her institutionalization and then successful release back into the community. The events of each segment in Amy's life are tied directly to the chapter concepts, and Internet links are provided at the conclusion of each story segment for further research into the issues raised.
- *Marginal glossary terms and a comprehensive end-of-book glossary.* Key terms and their definitions are found throughout the book in the margins, and a comprehensive end-of-book glossary makes it easy for students to learn the terminology used by professionals who work with delinquents. The glossary incorporates selected terms adapted from the FBI's *Uniform Crime Reporting Handbook*, the *Juvenile Court Statistics* report series, and the Census of Juveniles in Residential Placement. The National Center for Juvenile Justice's *State Juvenile Justice Profiles* was also influential in determining the content of selected definitions.
- *Web features.* An outstanding assortment of Web-based resources complements the text; they are found in the margins or at the end of chapters for ease of access. Included here are MyCrimeKit features such as *Library Extras* and *Web Extras*. Library Extras consist of documents found on the Web that are available as supplements to the discussions in the text. Library Extras include publications from the Office of Juvenile Justice and Delinquency Prevention (OJJDP), the National Institute of Justice (NIJ), the federal office of Community Oriented Policing Services (COPS), and the National Institute on Drug Abuse (NIDA), as well as articles from some of the field's most notable journals. Web Extras consist of websites of special relevance to the study of juvenile delinquency and include sites such as the Office of Juvenile Justice and Delinquency Prevention, the Child Trends Databank, the Child Welfare Information Gateway of the U.S. Department of Health and Human Services, the National Youth Gang Center, the American Bar Association, the National Library of Medicine, and the Centers for Disease Control and Prevention.

Student Resources Online

The following student resources are available at www.pearsonhighered.com/careers:

- *Juvenile Justice Video Case Studies* that appear at the end of each chapter featuring real-life cases of juveniles in contact with the justice system.
- *Web Extras*
- *Library Extras*

- *Voices of Delinquency* contains twenty-six real-life stories that range from those told by children who quickly turned their delinquent behavior around during their adolescent years and then lived exemplary lives as adults to those related by delinquents who committed serious crimes such as murder and who are now serving life in prison (one of these stories comes from an individual who is presently on death row). These fascinating and sometimes very sad stories reveal how the theoretical explanations in this textbook apply to the actual life experiences of delinquents.

Instructor Resources

- *eBooks. Juvenile Delinquency* is available in two eBook formats, *CourseSmart* and Adobe Reader. *CourseSmart* is an exciting new choice for students looking to save money. As an alternative to purchasing the printed textbook, students can purchase an electronic version of the same content. With a *CourseSmart* eTextbook, students can search the text, make notes online, print out reading assignments that incorporate lecture notes, and bookmark important passages for later review. For more information, or to purchase access to the *CourseSmart* eTextbook, visit **www.coursesmart.com**.
- *TestBank* and *MyTest*. These supplements represent a new standard in testing material. Whether you use the basic *TestBank* or generate questions electronically through *MyTest*, every question is linked to the text's learning objective, page number, and level of difficulty. This allows for quick reference in the text and an easy way to check the difficulty level and variety of your questions. *MyTest* can be accessed at **www.PearsonMyTest.com**.
- *Interactive Lecture PowerPoint presentation*. This supplement will enhance lectures like never before. Award-winning presentation designers worked with our authors to develop *PowerPoints* that truly engage the student. Much like the text, the *PowerPoints* are full of instructionally sound graphics, tables, charts, and photos that do what presentation software was meant to do: support and enhance your lecture. Data and difficult concepts are presented in a truly interactive way, helping students connect the dots and stay focused on the lecture. The *Interactive Lecture PowerPoints* also include in-depth lecture notes and teaching tips so you have all your lecture material in one place.
- *The Pearson Criminal Justice Online Community*. Available at www.mycriminaljustice community.com, this site is a place for educators to connect to exchange ideas and advice on courses, content, *CJ Interactive*, and so much more.

To access these supplementary materials online, instructors need to request an instructor access code at **www.pearsonhighered.com/irc**. Within 48 hours after registering, you will receive a confirmation e-mail that includes an instructor access code. When you receive your code, go to the site and log on for full instructions on downloading materials you wish to use.

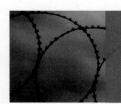

Acknowledgments

Many individuals have made invaluable contributions to this text. Foremost, we would like to thank our wives, Linda Dippolid Bartollas and Ellen Szirandi Schmalleger. A special thank you goes to Jeneve R. Brooks, at Troy University's Dothan, Alabama, campus for providing a detailed review of the manuscript and for making numerous helpful suggestions for improvement.

At the University of Northern Iowa, we would like to express our appreciation to Wayne Fauchier and Gloria Hadachek, who in various ways helped to keep the manuscript moving. Thanks to the following reviewers: Felix Brooks, Jr., Western Michigan University; Julia Glover Hall, Drexel University; Jeri Kirby, West Virginia University; Jiletta Kubena, Sam Houston State University; David Levine, Florida Atlantic University; Ruth X. Liu, San Diego State University; David Musick, University of Northern Colorado; John Paitakes, Seton Hall University; Beverly Quist, Mohawk Valley Community College; and Jennifer L. Schulenberg, Sam Houston State University.

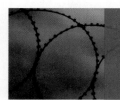

Clemens Bartollas, Ph.D., is Professor of Sociology at the University of Northern Iowa. He holds a B.A. from Davis and Elkins College, a B.D. from Princeton Theological Seminary, an S.T.M. from San Francisco Theological Seminary, and a Ph.D. in sociology, with a special emphasis in criminology, from The Ohio State University. Dr. Bartollas taught at Pembroke State University from 1973 to 1975, at Sangamon State University from 1975 to 1980, and at the University of Northern Iowa from 1981 to the present. He has received a number of honors at the University of Northern Iowa, including Distinguished Scholar, the Donald McKay Research Award, and the Regents' Award for Faculty Excellence.

Dr. Bartollas, like his coauthor, is also the author of numerous articles and more than 40 books, including previous editions of *Juvenile Delinquency* (Prentice Hall, 2014), *Juvenile Justice in America* (with Stuart J. Miller; Prentice Hall, 2014), and *Women and the Criminal Justice System* (with Katherine Stuart van Wormer; Prentice Hall, 2014).

Frank Schmalleger, Ph.D., is Distinguished Professor Emeritus at the University of North Carolina at Pembroke. He holds an undergraduate degree from the University of Notre Dame and both master's (1970) and doctoral (1974) degrees, with special emphasis in sociology, from The Ohio State University. From 1976 to 1994, he taught criminology and criminal justice courses at the University of North Carolina at Pembroke; for the last 16 of those years, he chaired the university's Department of Sociology, Social Work, and Criminal Justice. The university named him Distinguished Professor in 1991.

Dr. Schmalleger has taught in the online graduate program of the New School for Social Research, helping to build the world's first electronic classrooms in support of distance learning through computer telecommunications. As an adjunct professor with Webster University in St. Louis, Missouri, Dr. Schmalleger helped develop the university's graduate programs in administration of justice as well as security administration and loss prevention and taught courses in those curricula for more than a decade. A strong advocate of Web-based instruction, Dr. Schmalleger is also the creator of numerous award-winning websites.

Dr. Schmalleger is the author of numerous articles and more than 40 books, including the widely used *Criminal Justice Today* (Pearson, 2013), *Criminal Justice: A Brief Introduction* (Pearson, 2014), *Criminology Today* (Pearson, 2011), *Criminology: A Brief Introduction* (Pearson, 2013), *Criminal Law Today* (Pearson, 2014), and *Corrections in the Twenty-First Century* (with John Smykla; McGraw-Hill, 2013). He is also founding editor of the journal *Criminal Justice Studies* and has served as imprint adviser for Greenwood Publishing Group's criminal justice reference series. Visit the author's website at www.schmalleger.com.

Adolescence and Delinquency

Chapter Objectives

After reading this chapter, you should be able to:

1. Compare the treatment of adolescents in the past to the treatment of adolescents today.
2. Describe the youths most likely to become delinquent and their behaviors.
3. Define the terms *juvenile delinquency* and *adolescence*.
4. Describe status offenses and how status offenders are handled.
5. Summarize the treatment of delinquents.
6. Summarize the three themes of this text.

The future promise of any nation can be directly measured by the present prospects of its youth.

—President John F. Kennedy, February 14, 1963

Introduction

On Tuesday, February 28, 2012, T. J. Lane, a seventeen-year-old boy, took a knife and a twenty-two-caliber revolver into Chardon High School in Chardon, Ohio. Once inside the school's cafeteria, Lane began shooting. Three teenagers died and two others were seriously wounded. Local media soon identified the shooter as a student who attended a nearby school for at-risk youth. Lane, who was arrested wearing a T-shirt with the word "killer" emblazoned on it, later told a judge in Geauga County Juvenile Court that he had selected his victims randomly.[1]

Lane's family expressed shock over his actions, and the Lane family lawyer Bob Farinacci told local WKYC news, "This is something that could never have been predicted."[2] The lawyer described the young man as a "good kid" who had never been in trouble and had impressive grades. "He's a sophomore. He's been doubling up on his classes with the intent of graduating this May. He pretty much sticks to himself but does have some friends and has never been in trouble over anything that we know about," the attorney said.[3]

School violence, as in this story, is relatively infrequent. Many communities, however, are increasingly having to react to juvenile offenses that some experts say might have been effectively prevented. The Chardon school shooting raises a number of questions relevant to this study on juvenile delinquency: How serious is the problem of juvenile crime? Why do some youths commit serious or nonserious offenses, while others never do? How do family environments contribute to juvenile delinquency? What is the role of the school in juvenile offenses? How could such behaviors be prevented? Might the agencies of law enforcement have a more significant role to play in prevention? What should the punishment be for serious instances of delinquency, and for relatively nonserious law violations? Should punishment have a larger role in the juvenile justice system, and can it effectively prevent future delinquency?

The subject matter of this book is **juvenile delinquency**. The juvenile court codes in every state define what constitutes delinquency and the conditions under which the state can legitimately intervene in a juvenile's life. To bring the subject of delinquency into clearer focus, this chapter places it in the broader context of adolescence and the narrow context of those adolescents who are youths at risk. The discussion then turns to high-risk children who can be further divided into delinquents and status offenders. The chapter then examines how juvenile delinquents have been handled from the past to the present and concludes by presenting three themes that will be examined throughout the text.

The term **adolescence** refers to the life interval between childhood and adulthood. In fact, prior to the 1930s, the concept of an adolescent or teenager did not exist. The term has been used in the past few decades to mark a new stage of human growth and development, but there is no agreed-on way to pinpoint this period chronologically or to restrict it within physiological boundaries; for purposes of discussion in this chapter, however, adolescence is considered to be the years between ages 12 and 18. Within this transitional period, youngsters experience many biological changes and develop new attitudes, values, and skills that they will carry into their young adult years.

Delinquency and other problem behaviors increase during the adolescent years for several reasons. These years bring increasing freedom from parental scrutiny, and with this freedom come more opportunities to be involved in socially unacceptable behavior. Teenagers develop new, often expensive tastes for such things as sound systems, clothing, automobiles, and alcohol, yet legitimate means for satisfying these desires are often not available. The lengthening of adolescence in U.S. culture has further expanded the crises and struggles of this life period, thereby increasing the chance of problems with the law, at school, and in the home. In addition, there is often a mismatch between adolescents' needs and the opportunities provided them by their social environment.[4] Finally, in some cases, the unmet needs and frustrations of early childhood fester into socially unacceptable behavior in later years.

The Changing Treatment of Adolescents

Adolescence, as a term describing a particular stage of human growth and development, evolved out of the modern notion of childhood. The concept of childhood, as reflected in

juvenile delinquency
An act committed by a minor that violates the penal code of the government with authority over the area in which the act occurs.

adolescence
The life interval between childhood and adulthood; usually the period between the ages of twelve and eighteen years.

today's child-centered culture, is a relatively recent phenomenon.[5] Much of recorded history reveals abuse and indifference to be the fate of many children. Lloyd de Mause, an American social thinker known for his work in the field of psychohistory, depicted childhood historically as a time when children were "killed, abandoned, beaten, terrorized, and sexually abused"; he prefaced this statement by saying, "The history of childhood is a nightmare from which we have only recently begun to awaken."[6]

The end of child labor was one of the watershed events in the development of modern adolescence. Throughout history, children have worked, but until the Industrial Revolution their work was usually done within or around the house, often outdoors. As work moved from the home to the factory, children were considered a source of cheap labor. It was not unusual for them to work in the worst of conditions for sixteen hours a day, six days a week.[7] Until the child labor laws were actually enforced, children as young as ages 4 and 5 worked in mines, mills, and factories. There was a major battle between the U.S. Supreme Court and Congress over abolishing child labor. In 1916 Congress passed the Keating-Owen Act that attempted to end child labor throughout the United States by forbidding the sale of goods made with child labor through interstate commerce. Two years later, in 1918, the Supreme Court declared the law unconstitutional. In 1919, Congress tried again in 1919 with the Pomerene Act, but again the Supreme Court overturned it. In 1924, Congress tried a new tactic and attempted to get a constitutional amendment passed, but the states failed to ratify it. It was not until 1938 when President Franklin Roosevelt signed the Fair Labor Standards Act (FLSA) that child labor was finally made illegal.

Another important stage in the development of modern adolescence was compulsory public schooling. As Chapter 9 discusses, nineteenth-century U.S. schools were violent and chaotic places in which teachers attempted to maintain control over unmotivated and unruly children, sometimes using brutal disciplinary methods. The Progressive education movement arose partly because of the dissatisfaction of some elements of society with the schools. The influence of John Dewey and other Progressive educators encouraged individualism and personal growth in the classroom. Compulsory education laws also evolved from early-twentieth-century social and religious views, which held that adolescents should be kept in school because they needed guidance and control.

A further stage in the development of modern adolescence was the development in the twentieth century of the belief that raising children had less to do with conquering their spirits than with training and socializing them. In the middle of the twentieth century, around the end of World War II, many parents in the United States began to assume a helping role toward their children and attempted to meet their children's expanding needs in a democratic and supportive family environment. One of the leading voices of that era, psychologist Erik H. Erikson, became famous for his observation that "Childhood is the model of all oppression and enslavement, a kind of inner colonization, which forces grown-ups to accept inner repression and self-restriction."[8] A chief reason for the repression that characterized childhood, according to Erikson and others, was the lack of legal and social rights available to young people at the time. Consequently, the children's rights movement developed during the 1970s, creating a consensus about the needed components that would allow an adolescent to grow into responsible adulthood. Those components included:

- The facilitated development of personal identity
- An expedited search for a personal set of values
- The acquisition of competencies necessary for success in adulthood, such as problem solving and decision making
- The development of skills necessary for positive social interaction
- The attainment of emotional independence from one's parents
- The ability to negotiate between the need for personal achievement and the need for peer acceptance
- The need to experiment with a wide variety of behaviors, attitudes, and activities.[9]

Library Extra 1–1
National Institute of Justice (NIJ) publication: *A Century of Juvenile Justice*

▲ A young girl stands by a box containing bags of food as people receive a monthly food handout distributed from the Imperial Valley Food Bank in El Centro, California, where unemployment stands at 22.6 percent.
■ **What risk factors increase with lower income levels?**

Also in the 1960s and 1970s special legal protections for juveniles were established by the U.S. Supreme Court, highlighting the perception of adolescents as needing special attention, guidance, and support.

In sum, today's concept of adolescence centers on a set of beliefs that emerged during the late nineteenth and twentieth centuries. The result has been a lengthening of childhood and the delaying of adult responsibilities. Today's beliefs about the nature of adolescence have had the result of removing young people from the employment world and the mainstream of society. See Table 1–1.

Youth Culture

A youth culture, which has emerged in recent decades in the United States and other nations, builds on the unique beliefs, behaviors, and symbols that represent young people in society. How, when, what, where, and whom they interact with is part of this culture. A primary feature of today's youth culture is the use of social media and technology to interact with one's peers. Typically, youth culture also incorporates trends or fads.[10] Youth culture involves distinctive clothing styles, hairstyles, behaviors, footwear, and interests. Vehicles such as cars, motor scooters, motorcycles, skateboards, and surf boards, as well as video games, cell phones, computers, the Internet, and numerous other high-technology devices, have played central roles in the development of today's youth culture. As will be discussed in future chapters, the features of youth cultures vary by class, gender, race, and ethnicity.

Body art—involving multiple piercings for both males and females in literally every part of the body, including the tongue, eyebrows, lips, cheeks, navel, genitals, and breasts—and tattooing are widely found among some youth cultures today. Ritual scarification and 3D-art implants are popular, and so are stretching and cutting of the genitals, scrotal implants, transdermal implants, tooth art, and facial sculpture.[11]

Adolescents have always been connected to their peers, but they are now connected at all times of the day, texting in class, from home, and in the middle of the night. In addition to constant communication, adolescents are also joining online groups or communities,

---

TABLE 1–1
Treatment of Adolescents in the Past and in the Present

Past Treatment	Present Treatment
Were treated as small adults.	Adolescence is seen as preparation for adulthood.
Were expected to work in the home or outside the home at a young age.	Employment takes place after school or on weekends and usually is seen as a way to make extra money.
Education was considered to be of minor significance and usually extended only a couple years.	Education is compulsory and emphasis is spent on attending college has increased.
Adolescent girls were expected to marry and raise a family.	Female adolescents are experiencing growing equality.
Parents had minimal emotional attachment to children because of high infant death rates.	Parents have an emotional investment high in children from birth.
Children were punished like adults.	Children, especially those who commit minor crimes, are protected by the state in a separate system and are separated from adults.
Children were seen as having few rights.	Special legal protections were granted to children in the final decades of the twentieth century and continue into the twenty-first century.

posting numerous self-portraits, creating their own Facebook pages and Twitter accounts. The groups that some adolescents join include youth gangs or street gangs, and social or informal groups linked by common interests. Another component of some youth subcultures is hip-hop (technically, today's music is referred to as alternative hip-hop, and encompasses the work of artists such as Kanye West, Gnarls Barkley, and OutKast), which is made up of rapping, urban art/tagging (graffiti), and break dancing.[12]

Youths at Risk

The population of children in the United States is increasing and becoming more racially and ethnically diverse. In 2010, there were approximately 74.2 million children, ages newborn to 17 years, in the United States—and this was 1.9 million more than in 2000. There were approximately equal numbers of children in each age group: ages 0 to 5 (25.5 million), 6 to 11 (24.8 million), and 12 to 17 (24.8 million).[13] Since the 1960s, children have been declining as a proportion of the total population in the United States. In 2010, children made up 24 percent of the population, down from a peak of 36 percent at the end of the baby boom in 1964.[14] Children's share of the population is projected to remain basically the same through 2050.[15]

The **juvenile** population is also becoming more racially and ethnically diverse. In the 2010 census, 54 percent of children were white, non-Hispanic; 23 percent were Hispanic; 14 percent were African Americans; 4 percent were Asian; and 5 percent were "all other races." The proportion of Hispanic children has increased faster than that of other racial and ethnic groups; it grew from 9 percent of the population of children in 1980 to 23 percent in 2010. By 2050, if projections hold true, 38 percent of the U.S. population will be Hispanic.[16]

Of the 25 million adolescents (ages 12 through 17 years) in the United States, approximately one in four was at high risk of engaging in multiple problem behaviors. These behaviors, particularly committing delinquent acts and abusing drugs and alcohol, quickly bring adolescents to the attention of the juvenile justice system. Another 6 million youngsters, making up another 25 percent, practice risky behavior but to a lesser degree and, consequently, are less likely to experience negative consequences.[17]

In its publication, *The State of America's Children 2011,* the Children's Defense Fund (CDF) paints a devastating portrait of childhood across the nation. With unemployment, housing, foreclosures, and hunger still at historically high levels, children's well-being is in great jeopardy, says the CDF. Child poverty increased by almost 10 percent between 2008 and 2009, which was the largest single-year increase since data were first collected. As the country struggles to climb out of recession, children are falling further behind.[18] CDF, a nonprofit organization, seeks to educate the nation about the needs of children and to encourage preventive investment before youngsters become sick, get into trouble, drop out of school, or suffer family breakdown.[19]

High-Risk Behaviors

Researchers have identified several important insights into adolescents' problem behaviors. Those adolescents who have the most negative or problem-oriented factors in their lives are defined as "high risk." First, high-risk youths often experience multiple difficulties: They are frequently socialized in economically stressed families and communities, more often than not have histories of physical abuse and sexual victimization, typically have educational and vocational skill deficits, and are prone to become involved in alcohol and other drug abuse and forms of delinquency.[20] The more of these problem behaviors that are present, the more likely it is that a youth will become involved in socially undesirable behaviors (see Figure 1–1).[21]

Second, adolescent problem behaviors—especially delinquent acts such as being involved in drug and alcohol abuse, failing or dropping out of school, and having unprotected sex—are interrelated, or linked; that is, an involvement in one problem behavior is generally indicative of some participation in other socially undesirable behaviors.[22] Third, high-risk youths tend to become involved in behaviors that contribute to unintentional injury and

juvenile
A youth at or below the upper age of juvenile court jurisdiction in a particular state.

Web Extra 1–1
Office of Juvenile Justice and Delinquency Prevention (OJJDP) website

Web Extra 1–2
Youth Risk Behavior Surveillance System (YRBSS) website (part of the Centers for Disease Control and Prevention)

Library Extra 1–2
OJJDP publication: *Juvenile Offenders and Victims: 2006 National Report, Chapter 1*

Library Extra 1–3
OJJDP publication: *Risk Factors for Delinquency: An Overview*

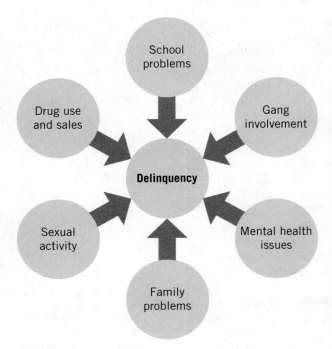

FIGURE 1–1
Problem Behaviors Leading to Delinquency

violence; some of these behaviors include carrying a weapon, driving when they have been drinking, riding with someone else who has been drinking, and rarely or never wearing a seat belt when driving or riding with someone else.[23]

The federally funded Program of Research on the Causes and Correlates of Delinquency (also known as the Causes and Correlates Program, which is described in more detail in Chapter 2) comprises three coordinated longitudinal projects: the Denver Youth Survey, the Pittsburgh Youth Survey, and the Rochester Youth Development Study. These three projects examined the co-occurrence or overlap of delinquent behavior with drug use, problems in school, and mental health problems. Across all three study sites, the prevalence of persistent problem behaviors was usually consistent: 20-30 percent of males were serious delinquents, 7 to 22 percent had school problems, 14 to 17 percent were abusing drugs, and 7 to 14 percent had mental health problems.[24]

Another study analyzed the prevalence and overlap of substance-related behaviors among youths. The central finding of this study is that given one substance-related behavior, other substance-related behaviors became much more likely. For example, among youths who reported drinking alcohol (23 percent of all youths ages 12 to 17), the level of marijuana use was 32 percent and the level of drug selling was 23 percent.[25] Table 1–2 illustrates that higher levels of problem behaviors and delinquency appear among substance abusers across all age groups.

Delinquency is one of the problem behaviors with which almost all high-risk adolescents become involved (see Chapter 2). *Delinquency*

TABLE 1–2
Substance Abuse, by Age

Behavior	Drank Alcohol (30 days)		Used Marijuana (30 days)		Sold Drugs (ever)	
	No	Yes	No	Yes	No	Yes
Youths Ages 12–14						
Suspension from school	18%	31%	19%	46%	19%	55%
Vandalize property	13	37	14	50	14	56
Major theft	2	11	2	20	2	27
Attack/assault	8	28	9	36	9	53
Belong to a gang	1	7	1	16	1	18
Carry handgun	4	12	4	20	4	25
Arrested	2	8	3	15	2	22
Youths Ages 15–17						
Suspension from school	27%	38%	27%	52%	27%	63%
Vandalize property	10	23	11	33	11	40
Major theft	3	10	4	17	3	23
Attack/assault	8	21	10	29	9	37
Belong to a gang	1	5	1	9	1	12
Carry handgun	4	10	5	15	5	18
Arrested	5	12	5	21	5	26

Note: The time frame for "Suspension from school" was ever; for the other items, it was the past 12 months. The value in the "Yes" column differs significantly ($p < 0.05$) from the value in the "No" column for all column pairs within substance behavior and age groups.

Source: Carl McCurley and Howard N. Snyder, *Co-Occurrence of Substance Use Behaviors in Youth* (Washington, D.C.: Office of Juvenile Justice and Delinquency Prevention, 2008), p. 3.

is a legal term initially used in 1899 when Illinois passed the first law on juvenile delinquent behavior. The age at which an individual is considered a minor varies among states, but it is sixteen or seventeen years and younger in most states.

Some evidence indicates that the nature of delinquency in U.S. society is changing. Beginning in the late 1980s and extending throughout the 1990s, adolescents participated widely in street gangs, some of which provided a base for trafficking narcotics; had rising rates of murder from 1989 through 1993; were more likely to own and use firearms than ever before; and were becoming increasingly involved in various forms of hate crimes. These trends continued into the first decade of the twenty-first century.

Yet today's average American delinquent is far more likely to shoplift, commit petty theft, use marijuana, violate liquor laws, or destroy property than to commit a violent or serious crime. In 2010, 239,170 juveniles between the ages of 10 and 17 years were arrested for property crimes, compared with 47,450 arrests for violent crimes. In other words, juveniles were arrested four and one-half times more often for committing property crimes rather than violent crimes.[26]

Besides committing many of the same crimes as adults, juveniles can also be arrested for truancy, incorrigibility, curfew violations, and runaway behavior—behaviors that would not be offenses when engaged in by adults. Such offenses are called **status offenses** because they are law violations only when committed by an underage person. (Status offenses are discussed in more detail below.) The legal separation between status offenses and delinquency is important because of the large number of arrests each year for acts such as being truant, disobeying parents, and running away from home. The Federal Bureau of Investigation's (FBI) *Crime in the United States 2010* (see Chapter 2) reveals that three times as many youths are typically arrested for status offenses as for violent crimes. This ratio between status offenses and violent crimes would be even greater if truancy and incorrigibility were included in the FBI statistics.

▲ A young man lights up a marijuana pipe during a pro-drug rally at Civic Center Park across from the Capitol in Denver, Colorado, on April 20, 2010. According to the Program of Research on the Causes and Correlates of Delinquency, drug use and other problem behaviors correlate with other forms of delinquency.

■ **What factors are likely to account for the relationship?**

status offense
A nondelinquent/noncriminal offense; an offense that is illegal for underage persons but not for adults. Status offenses include curfew violations, incorrigibility, running away, truancy, and underage drinking.

Juvenile Court Codes and Definitions of Delinquency

parens patriae
A medieval English doctrine that sanctioned the right of the Crown to intervene in natural family relations whenever a child's welfare was threatened. Under *parens patriae*, the state assumed the parental role over juvenile lawbreakers. The philosophy of the juvenile court is based on this legal concept.

Juvenile court codes, which exist in every state, specify the conditions under which states can legitimately intervene in a juvenile's life. State juvenile codes, as part of the **parens patriae** philosophy of the juvenile court (explained later in this chapter), were enacted to eliminate the arbitrary nature of juvenile justice beyond the rights afforded juveniles by the U.S. Constitution and to deal with youths more leniently because they were seen as not fully responsible

---

Juvenile Law 1–1
Definitions of Delinquency

- Violates any law or ordinance.
- Violates a juvenile court order.
- Associates with criminals or immoral persons.
- Engages in any calling, occupation, or exhibition punishable by law.
- Frequents taverns or uses alcohol.
- Wanders the streets in the night.
- Grows up in idleness or breaks curfew.
- Enters or visits a house of ill repute.
- Is habitually truant.
- Is habitually disobedient or refuses to obey reasonable and proper (lawful) orders of parents, guardians, or custodians.
- Engages in incorrigibility or is ungovernable.

- Absents himself or herself from home without permission.
- Persists in violating rules and regulations of school.
- Endangers welfare, morals, and/or health of self or others.
- Uses vile, obscene, or vulgar language (in a public place).
- Smokes cigarettes (around a public place).
- Engages in dissolute or immoral life or conduct.
- Loiters or sleeps in alleys.
- Begs or receives alms (or is in the street for that purpose).

■ *These definitions are taken from various state codes. Which of these definitions is most surprising to you? Are these definitions especially favorable or unfavorable to any particular economic, racial, or ethnic group? Explain your response.*

for their behavior. The U.S. District Court for the District of Columbia's now-classic decision in the *In re Poff* decision established the logic of this argument in 1955, when the court held:

> The original Juvenile Court Act enacted in the District of Columbia was devised to afford the juvenile protections in addition to those he already possessed under the Federal Constitution. Before this legislative enactment, the juvenile was subject to the same punishment for an offense as an adult. It follows logically that in the absence of such legislation the juvenile would be entitled to the same constitutional guarantees and safeguards as an adult. If this is true, then the only possible reason for the Juvenile Court Act was to afford the juvenile safeguards in addition to those he already possessed. The legislative intent was to enlarge and not diminish those protections.[27]

Juvenile court codes usually specify that the court has jurisdiction in relation to three categories of juvenile behavior: delinquency, dependency, and neglect. First, the courts may intervene when a youth has been accused of committing an act that would be a misdemeanor or felony if committed by an adult. Second, the courts may intervene when a juvenile commits certain status offenses. Third, the courts may intervene in cases involving dependency and neglect; for example, if a court determines that a child is being deprived of needed support and supervision, it may decide to remove the child from the home for his or her own protection.

An examination of the various juvenile court codes, or statutes, shows the diverse definitions of delinquent behavior that have developed. Some statutes define a "delinquent youth" as a young person who has committed a crime or violated probation; others define a "delinquent child" in terms of such behaviors as "associating with immoral or vicious persons" (West Virginia) or "engaging in indecent or immoral conduct" (Connecticut).[28] A particular juvenile, then, could be considered a delinquent under some juvenile codes and not under others.

Some controversy surrounds the issue of how long juveniles should remain under the jurisdiction of the juvenile court. The age at which a youthful offender is no longer treated as a juvenile ranges from sixteen to eighteen years. In thirty-seven states and the District of Columbia, persons who, prior to their eighteenth birthday, are charged with a law violation are considered juveniles. In ten states, the upper limit of juvenile court jurisdiction is sixteen years (i.e., prior to the seventeenth birthday), and in three states, the upper limit is fifteen years (prior to the sixteenth birthday). See Figure 1–2 for the upper age of juvenile court jurisdiction across various states.[29]

FIGURE 1–2
Upper Age Limit for Defendants in Juvenile Court, 2011

Source: Howard N. Snyder and Melissa Sickmund, *Juvenile Offenders and Victims: 2006 National Report* (Washington, D.C.: Office of Juvenile Justice and Delinquency Prevention, March 2006), p. 103; and Sarah Alice Brown, *Trends in Juvenile Justice State Legislation, 2001–2011* (Denver, Colo.: National Conference of State Legislatures, 2012).

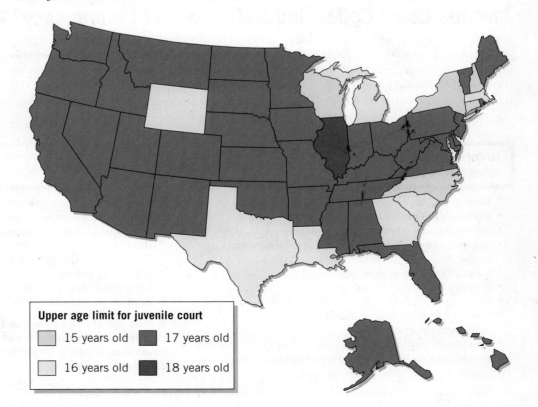

Upper age limit for juvenile court

- 15 years old
- 16 years old
- 17 years old
- 18 years old

What Is a Status Offender?

As mentioned previously, a status offense is behavior that is an offense only because the person committing it is a juvenile. In various jurisdictions, **status offenders** are known as minors in need of supervision (MINS), children in need of supervision (CHINS), juveniles in need of supervision (JINS), children in need of assistance (CHINA), persons in need of supervision (PINS), children in need of protection and services (CHIPS), or members of families in need of supervision (FINS). They also may be termed *predelinquent, incorrigible, beyond control, ungovernable,* or *wayward.* What these terms and acronyms have in common is that they view the status offender as being in need of supervision or assistance.

There are three important questions about status offenders: Why do they behave the way they do? Should status offenders be separated from delinquents in terms of institutional placements? Should the juvenile court have jurisdiction over status offenders?

▲ Teenagers drink alcohol on the beach. Status offenses involve acts that are illegal only because of a person's age, such as smoking, drinking, or running away from home. Very few youths who commit only status offenses come in contact with the juvenile justice system.

■ **Should status offenders be treated more harshly?**

Explanations for Status Offense Behavior

Generally speaking, status offenders, many of whom come from single-parent homes, place the blame for their problems on parental figures in the home and believe that fulfilling their need for a warm, accepting, and loving relationship with their parents is not possible. They want to be loved by a parent who may not have the capacity to provide that love. Although their needs for sustenance and shelter may have been met, some have been physically or sexually abused; at the least, they feel rejected and neglected. They become resentful and angry with their parents, who may have problems expressing physical affection, setting reasonable and consistent limits, and showing acceptance to their children. Many of these parents were abused as children, have limited parenting skills, or evince immature behaviors themselves.

The parents, in turn, often view status offenders as defiant, demanding, and obnoxious. Parents usually believe that they have no control over their children, who will not accept restrictions or limitations on their behavior, and a power struggle results. The struggle often climaxes in verbal altercations, and physical violence can erupt when the child strikes or pushes the parent. As a result, parents call the police to intervene with their abusive or unmanageable children. Sometimes a parent asks police to act because the youngster stays out very late, associates with older youths or delinquent friends, or responds to the parent with rage.[30]

Some status offenders commit both status offenses and delinquent acts, and it is not always easy to separate an offending population into delinquents and status offenders. Status offenses do vary in seriousness; however, no recent evidence exists that shows escalation in offense behavior for those who are solely engaged in status offenses. See Table 1–3 for a list of typical status offenses.

Some theorists argue that society's response to status offenders, especially female status offenders, is a major contributing factor in defining who has this legal status. Society believes that young males should behave in a certain way, typically granting leniency for the right of "boys to be boys." Society's expectations for young females, however, are still based on the notion that "Sugar and spice and everything nice, that's what little girls are made of." University of Hawaii Women's Studies Professor Meda Chesney-Lind and Lisa J. Pasko found during their examination of the judicial handling of female status offenders that the juvenile justice system discriminates against girls because of the fear of sexual activity.[31]

Deinstitutionalization of Status Offenders (DSO)

The **deinstitutionalization of status offenders (DSO)**, which refers to the removal of status offenders from secure detention facilities, has received considerable acceptance in the past few decades. The **Juvenile Justice and Delinquency Prevention (JJDP) Act of 1974**, and

status offender
A juvenile who commits a minor act that is considered illegal only because he or she is underage.

TABLE 1–3
Typical Status Offenses

Incorrigibility at home
Ungovernability at school
Running away from home
Truancy
Smoking cigarettes and using smokeless tobacco
Drinking alcohol

Web Extra 1–3
Child Trends Databank (with the latest national trends and research on over one hundred key indicators of child and youth well-being)

Deinstitutionalization of Status Offenders (DSO)
The removal of status offenders from secure detention facilities.

Juvenile Justice and Delinquency Prevention (JJDP) Act of 1974
A federal law that established a juvenile justice office within the then-existing Law Enforcement Assistance Administration to provide funds for the prevention and control of youth crime.

Office of Juvenile Justice and Delinquency Prevention (OJJDP)
A federal agency that works to provide national leadership, coordination, and resources to prevent and respond to juvenile delinquency and victimization.

its various modifications, have served as the most significant impetus for the nationwide deinstitutionalization of status offenders.[32] The JJDP act contained a DSO provision that requires status offenders to be kept separate from delinquents in secure detention facilities as a condition for states to continue receiving federal funding for their juvenile justice programs. The act also limited the placement of juveniles in adult jail facilities.[33]

The DSO provision has been successful in encouraging states to amend laws, policies, and practices that had previously led to the confinement of juveniles who committed no criminal act. The DSO core protection of the JJDP act is premised on the belief that juveniles who exhibit problematic behavior, but who have not violated criminal laws, are more properly served by social service, mental health, and other community initiatives, and may be damaged by placement in secure detention facilities or correctional institutions.[34] Soon after the adoption of the JJDP Act and its DSO requirement, the **Office of Juvenile Justice and Delinquency Prevention (OJJDP)** recorded approximately 171,581 violations of the federal DSO requirement. According to OJJDP's 2006 compliance monitoring reports, the number of annual DSO violations had dropped to 6,324.[35]

Jurisdiction over Status Offenders

Some experts have gone so far as to question the juvenile court's long-standing jurisdiction over status offenders. Critics present at least four arguments for the removal of status offenders from the jurisdiction of the juvenile court:

- The lack of clarity of many status offender statutes makes them unconstitutionally vague in their construction. Such laws, critics claim, are often discriminatory, especially with regard to gender.

- Although status offenders have not committed a criminal act, they are frequently confined with chronic or hard-core offenders, in defiance of the federal DSO mandate.

- The procedure of processing and confining status offenders is not in the child's best interests, and therefore violates the *parens patriae* principle that underlies the juvenile court system. Some theorists argue that the formal intervention by the juvenile court into the lives of status offenders promotes rather than inhibits unlawful behavior.

- It should be obvious that status offenders are a special class of youth who must be treated differently from delinquents in order to prevent them from becoming delinquents themselves.[36]

Juvenile court officials, not surprisingly, have often challenged the movement to strip the court of jurisdiction over status offenders. They argue that status offenders will have no one to protect them if they are removed from the court's jurisdiction. They also argue that other agencies would have to take over if the court relinquishes jurisdiction over status offenders, and that few options are presently available for providing status offenders with a nurturing or positive environment in lieu of the home.

Maine, New York, and Washington are among the states that have decriminalized status offenses, thus removing from the juvenile court's jurisdiction youthful behaviors that would not be chargeable offenses if committed by adults.[37] However, the status offense legislation initially passed in Maine and Washington was partly repealed to give juvenile courts in those states a continuing degree of jurisdiction, especially over abandoned, runaway, or seriously endangered children.[38] The most broad-based movement to strip the juvenile court of jurisdiction over all status offenders began in New York state in 1985 with passage of the 1985 PINS Adjustment Services Act. Under that law the eligibility age for persons in need of supervision (PINS) was raised to eighteen years (from what had been sixteen). The intent of this bill was to "prevent unnecessary and inappropriate out-of-home placements of children and youth" and to assist and support families seeking help with troubled older children.[39] In 2005, New York passed additional legislation requiring each county in the state and the city of New York to provide diversion services to youth at risk of becoming the subject of a PINS petition.[40]

It is unlikely that many more states will remove status offenders from the juvenile court's jurisdiction in the near future. Widespread resistance comes from those who feel that status offenders need the close supervision available through the juvenile court in order to prevent them from becoming involved in increasingly criminal behaviors. However, even in states that strongly support deinstitutionalization, the juvenile court frequently can still institutionalize status offenders by redefining them as delinquents. A truant, for example, may be charged with a minor delinquent offense and be brought before the court, or a court may require school attendance as a condition of probation for an act of delinquency thereby bringing continued acts of truancy under its purview.[41]

Crossover Youth

Juveniles in the child welfare system often cross over into the juvenile justice system. Because these youth are known to both the child welfare system and the juvenile justice system, they are frequently referred to as *crossover youth*. Other terms used to describe these youth are *dual-jurisdiction cases*, *dually adjudicated youth*, and *cross-system cases*.

Crossover youth often move back and forth between a child welfare system in which they are looked upon as underprivileged youth, and a juvenile justice system that sees them as youthful offenders. Yet, little integration and coordination take place between the two systems. In fact, in many jurisdiction, a common practice is for child welfare agencies to abruptly close the cases of children who become involved in the juvenile justice system.[42]

Many crossover youth experience co-occurring mental health and drug and alcohol abuse problems, which are often left unscreened and untreated in both systems. These youth frequently do poorly in school and end up being suspended or dropping out. Youth in the child welfare system who are placed in out-of-home settings are at greater risk of crossing over into juvenile justice jurisdiction. Child welfare placements in group home settings have been found to be especially predictive of future involvement in the juvenile justice system.[43]

Another matter of grave concern is the disproportionate number of crossover minority youth. The disproportionate involvement of minority children in the welfare system tends to produce disproportionate involvement in the juvenile justice system among crossover youth. Research sponsored by the Annie E. Casey Foundation reports that although minority children are not abused more often than other children, they are put into foster care faster, receive fewer services, stay there longer, and are reunited with their families less often than white children.[44]

Consequently, professionals in the juvenile justice system have been led to ask "What can be done to help crossover youths, and to avoid their future involvement with juvenile court"? In a report released in 2010, the Federal Advisory Committee on Juvenile Justice (FACJJ) identified promising court-related practices through which family and juvenile court programs can work together to address at least some of the difficulties posed by crossover cases.[45] Among other things, the FACJJ proposed the routine screening of youth on intake in an effort to identify each youth's strengths and needs, as well as the clear coordination of all of the different agencies involved in serving youths involved with the juvenile justice system.

The Handling of Juvenile Delinquents

The philosopher George Santayana once wrote that "those who cannot remember the past are condemned to repeat it."[46] Many contemporary sociological interpretations of delinquency lack a sense of history. Such approaches have serious shortcomings

▲ Two boys play in the village stocks at St. Mary's Parish church in Cheshire, England. Throughout much of history, children were treated the same as adults for purposes of the law, and those who committed crimes were severely punished.

■ **Why are children treated differently today?**

because the history of how law-violating juveniles have been dealt with is important in understanding how delinquent youths are handled today.

The history of societal responses to juvenile delinquency in the United States can be divided into seven periods, as follows: (1) the colonial period, (2) the houses of refuge era, (3) the juvenile courts era, (4) the juvenile rights era, (5) the reform agenda era, (6) the social control and juvenile crime era, and (7) the contemporary period (Figure 1–3).

The Colonial Period (1636–1823)

The history of juvenile justice in the United States began in the colonial period. The colonists saw the family as the source and primary means of control over children. In colonial times the law was uncomplicated, and the family was the cornerstone of the community.[47] Town fathers, magistrates, sheriffs, and watchmen were the only law enforcement officials, and the only penal institutions were jails for prisoners awaiting trial or punishment. "Doing time for crime" had not yet been added to the stable of punishments available for offenders, and most punishments were corporeal in nature.

Juvenile lawbreakers did not face a battery of police, probation, or parole officers, nor would the juvenile justice system try to rehabilitate them; instead, most young offenders were sent back to their families for punishment. If they were still recalcitrant after whippings and other forms of discipline, they could be returned to community officials for more punishment, such as public whippings, public humiliation, or the stocks, and in more serious cases, expulsion from the community or even hanging.

The Houses of Refuge Era (1824–1898)

In the nineteenth century, reformers became disillusioned with the family as a form of social control for serious delinquency, and looked for a substitute that would provide an orderly, disciplined environment similar to that of the "ideal" family.[48] **Houses of refuge** were proposed as the solution; there, discipline was to be administered firmly and harshly. These facilities were intended to protect wayward children from "weak and criminal parents," "the manifold temptations of the streets," and "the peculiar weakness of [the children's] moral nature."[49] Houses of refuge, which were early residential facilities, reflected a new direction in juvenile justice. No longer were parents and the family the first line of control over children; instead the family's authority had been superseded by that of the state, and wayward children were placed in facilities presumably better equipped to reform them.

Houses of refuge flourished for the first half of the nineteenth century; but by the middle of the century, reformers were beginning to suspect that these juvenile institutions were not as effective as had been hoped. Some had grown unwieldy in size,

house of refuge
An institution that was designed by eighteenth- and nineteenth-century reformers to provide an orderly, disciplined environment similar to that of the "ideal" Puritan family.

FIGURE 1–3
Seven Historical Eras of Societal Response to Juvenile Delinquency

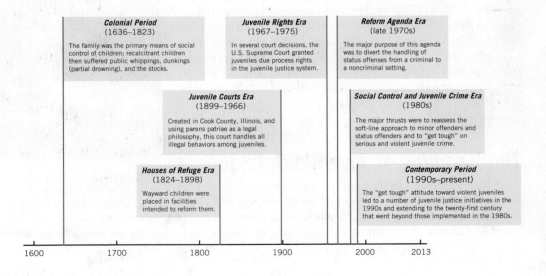

Colonial Period
(1636–1823)

The family was the primary means of social control of children; recalcitrant children then suffered public whippings, dunkings (partial drowning), and the stocks.

Juvenile Courts Era
(1899–1966)

Created in Cook County, Illinois, and using parens patriae as a legal philosophy, this court handles all illegal behaviors among juveniles.

Houses of Refuge Era
(1824–1898)

Wayward children were placed in facilities intended to reform them.

Juvenile Rights Era
(1967–1975)

In several court decisions, the U.S. Supreme Court granted juveniles due process rights in the juvenile justice system.

Reform Agenda Era
(late 1970s)

The major purpose of this agenda was to divert the handling of status offenses from a criminal to a noncriminal setting.

Social Control and Juvenile Crime Era
(1980s)

The major thrusts were to reassess the soft-line approach to minor offenders and status offenders and to "get tough" on serious and violent juvenile crime.

Contemporary Period
(1990s–present)

The "get tough" attitude toward violent juveniles led to a number of juvenile justice initiatives in the 1990s and extending to the twenty-first century that went beyond those implemented in the 1980s.

| 1600 | 1700 | 1800 | 1900 | 2000 | 2013 |

and discipline, high standards of care, and the desired level of order had disappeared from many. Reformers also were aware that many youths were being confined in adult institutions—jails and prisons—that were filthy, dangerous, degrading, and ill equipped to manage juveniles effectively. A change was in order, and reformers proposed the development of a separate juvenile court as a way to provide for more humane care of law-violating youths.

The Juvenile Courts Era (1899–1966)

First created in Cook County, Illinois, the juvenile court came into existence to handle all illegal behavior among people under a certain age. This new type of court, just for children, was based on the legal concept of *parens patriae*, a medieval English doctrine that sanctioned the right of the Crown to intervene in family relations whenever a child's welfare was threatened. The concept was explained by the committee of the Chicago Bar Association that created the juvenile court:

> The fundamental idea of the juvenile court law is that the state must step in and exercise guardianship over a child found under such adverse social or individual conditions as to encourage the development of crime. The juvenile court law proposes a plan whereby he may be treated, not as a criminal, or legally charged with crime, but as a ward of the state, to receive practically the care, custody, and discipline that are accorded the neglected and dependent child, and which, as the act states, "shall approximate as nearly as may be that which should be given by its parents."[50]

Proponents of the juvenile court promised that it would be flexible enough to pay individual attention to the specific problems of wayward children. Reformers believed that once the causes of deviance were identified accurately, specific problems could be addressed and cured. Thus, the hope was that juveniles would be kept out of jails and prisons, thereby avoiding corruption by adult criminals.

The juvenile court period did not see radical change in the philosophy of juvenile justice, because the family continued to be subservient to the state and children still could be institutionalized. What differed was the viewpoint that children were not altogether responsible for their behavior. They were seen as victims of a variety of factors, including poverty, the ills of city life, inadequate families, schools, and corrupt neighborhood influences. No longer regarded as criminals, youthful violators were defined as children in need of care, protection, moral guidance, and discipline. Accordingly, the juvenile court was established as an official agency to aid in controlling wayward children. Juvenile delinquents would continue to be under the control of the state until they were either rehabilitated or too old to remain under the jurisdiction of juvenile authorities.

Society extended its control over the young in several other ways. Police departments established juvenile bureaus. The notion of treating juveniles for their specific problems was evidenced by the implementation in the first part of the twentieth century of both probation and parole (aftercare) agencies. Commitment to training or industrial school, a carryover from the nineteenth century, was reserved for those whose needs became secondary to the protection of society.

The Juvenile Rights Era (1967–1975)

Mounting criticism of the juvenile court culminated in the 1960s when the court was widely accused of dispensing capricious and arbitrary justice. The U.S. Supreme Court responded to this criticism with a series of decisions that changed the course of juvenile justice: *Kent* v. *United States*, 1966; *In re Gault*, 1967; *In re Winship*, 1970; *McKeiver* v. *Pennsylvania*, 1971; and *Breed* v. *Jones*, 1975.[51] (See Chapter 14 for a discussion of these cases.) The *In re Gault* decision, a landmark case, stated that juveniles have the right to due process safeguards in proceedings in which a finding of delinquency could lead to confinement; that juveniles have rights to notice of charges, counsel, confrontation, and cross-examination; and that juveniles are privileged against self-incrimination. The intent of the Court decisions was to ensure that children would have due process rights in the juvenile justice system.[52]

Reformers also believed that inconsiderate treatment by the police, five-minute hearings in juvenile courts, and degrading and sometimes brutal treatment in training schools fostered rather than reduced juvenile crime. Lower-level federal courts responded to the curbstone justice dispensed by police and the repressive justice administered in training schools by handing down numerous decisions that brought more due process rights to juveniles at the time they were arrested and taken into custody and more humane conditions during their time of confinement.

Community-based programs received an enthusiastic response in the late 1960s and early 1970s as more and more states began a process of deinstitutionalization under which only hard-core delinquents were sent to long-term training schools. Enthusiasm for community-based corrections was so widespread in the early 1970s that many observers believed that training schools would soon become extinct.

The children's rights movement also gathered momentum during the 1960s. Interest groups began to examine children's special needs, and in the 1970s, the rights of children were litigated in the courts. That decade also saw progress in the areas of custody in divorce cases, guardianship for foster children, protection of privacy rights, independent access to medical care, and legislation on child abuse.

The Reform Agenda Era (Late 1970s)

para 5

The reform agenda of the middle to late 1970s emphasized reducing the use of juvenile correctional institutions, diverting minor offenders and status offenders from the juvenile justice system, and reforming the juvenile justice system. The major purpose of the reform agenda was to divert the handling of status offenses from a criminal to a noncriminal setting. Status offenders were accorded such an emphasis because of the mandate of the federal JJDP act of 1974 (discussed earlier). The principal objectives of this act were to promote the deinstitutionalization of status offenders as dependent, neglected, and abused children; to encourage the elimination of the practice of jailing juveniles; and to encourage the development of "community-based alternatives to juvenile detention and correctional facilities."[53]

However, noted gang researchers Ira M. Schwartz, Lloyd Ohlin, and others argue that proponents of this liberal agenda blundered by paying too little attention to the problem of serious juvenile crime. At a time when public concern about serious juvenile crime was running high, the federal government was emphasizing a very different agenda.[54] Less than 10 percent of the nearly $120 million in discretionary funds given out by the OJJDP between 1975 and 1980, for example, targeted the population of violent and serious juvenile offenders.[55] At that time, Ohlin predicted that the failure to address violent youth crime and repeat offenders would prove to be "the Achilles' heel of the reform process."[56] The failure of the reformers of the 1970s to provide meaningful programs and policies aimed at youthful offenders who committed serious crimes contributed to the wave of "get-tough" legislation that was to later sweep across the United States.[57]

Web Extra 1–4
U.S. Department of Health and Human Services (DHHS) Child Welfare Information Gateway

para 6

The Social Control and Juvenile Crime Era (1980s)

By the 1980s, the public had been alerted by the media to the chilling realities of youth crime and wanted something done to curb the serious problem of juvenile delinquency. Ronald Reagan was in the White House, and the hard-liners' formerly muted criticisms suddenly became public policy. The new federal agenda attacked the JJDP act as being "anti-family" and called for cracking down on juvenile law violators. Alfred S. Regnery, an OJJDP administrator, communicated this new federal perspective in a speech delivered on December 2, 1984:

> In essence, we have changed the outlook of the office from emphasizing the lesser offender and the nonoffender to one emphasizing the serious juvenile offender. We have placed less emphasis on juvenile crime as a social problem and more emphasis on crime as a justice problem. In essence, the office now reflects the general philosophy of President Reagan and his administration rather than that of President Carter and his administration.[58]

In 1984, the federal National Advisory Committee (NAC) for Juvenile Justice and Delinquency Prevention said that "the time has come for a major departure from the existing philosophy and activity of the federal government in the juvenile justice field."[59] The NAC recommended that the "federal effort in the area of juvenile delinquency should focus primarily on the serious, violent, or chronic offender."[60] The committee also recommended that federal initiatives be limited to research into carefully designed and evaluated demonstration projects, to the "dissemination of information," and to "training and technical assistance."[61]

The spirit of the era was about "getting tough" on serious juvenile offenders. Several factors led to a national reassessment of minor offenders and status offenders: Young people seemed to be out of control, drug and alcohol abuse were viewed as serious problems, teenage pregnancy had reached epidemic proportions, and teenage suicide was increasing at an alarming rate.[62] Nationwide, politicians assured their constituencies that the answer to youth problems was to crack down at all levels. Furthermore, "tough love" and other such movements evidenced a growing acceptance of the notion that parents must be stricter with their children. Finally, the Reagan administration made a concerted effort to show that the soft-line approach had had disastrous consequences in children's lives; government-sponsored studies, for example, showed that increasing numbers of middle-class runaway girls ended up as prostitutes.

The major thrusts of the Reagan administration's crime control policies for juveniles, then, were to "get tough" on serious and violent juvenile crime and to undermine the reform efforts of the 1970s. This new federal mandate encouraged the development of five activities: (1) preventive detention, (2) the transfer of violent juveniles to adult court, (3) mandatory and determinate sentencing for violent juveniles, (4) the increased confinement of juveniles, and (5) enforcement of the death penalty for juveniles who commit especially brutal murders.[63] These trends are described and evaluated elsewhere in this text.

Even though the federal government and the public favored a more punishment-oriented response to juvenile delinquency, the juvenile court continued throughout the 1980s to have three approaches to juvenile lawbreakers (see Figure 1–4). On one end of the spectrum, the court applied the *parens patriae* doctrine to status offenders and minor offenders. As in the past, these youths were presumed to need treatment rather than punishment, because their offenses were seen as caused by internal psychological or biological conditions or by sociological factors in their environment. On the other end of the spectrum, juveniles who committed serious crimes or continued to break the law were presumed to deserve punishment rather than treatment on the grounds that such youngsters possessed free will and knew what they were doing. That is, the court viewed serious delinquents' crimes as purposeful activities resulting from rational decision making in which youths weighed the pros and cons of their actions and undertook behavior that promised the greatest potential gains.[64] Consequently, juvenile delinquents during this historical period were seen as bad actors rather than as sick individuals, and delinquency was viewed as the culmination of a rational decision-making process. Given this perspective, it was only logical to treat delinquent youth in the juvenile justice system more like adult criminals than juvenile offenders.

Between these two groups fell young people who saw crime as a form of play and committed delinquent acts because they enjoyed the thrill of getting away with illegal behavior or because they wanted to overcome boredom. Although criminologists usually conclude that the crimes such juveniles commit represent purposeful activity, the courts in the 1980s did not consider the youths in this middle group to be as bad as serious delinquents, reasoning that even though these youths might be exercising free will, their behavior was mischievous rather than delinquent. The juvenile court today commonly continues to excuse such mischievous behavior.

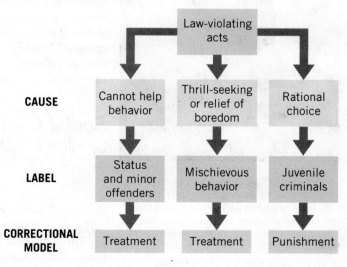

FIGURE 1–4
Three Approaches to Delinquency Control

The Contemporary Period (1990s–Present)

Several interrelated social trends emerged in the 1980s that influenced the nature and handling of delinquency in rather dramatic ways in the 1990s. Many of them continue into the present. In the mid-1980s, for example, crack cocaine became widely available in urban areas. A burgeoning crack epidemic soon led to the recruitment of young people as crack merchants. By the early 1990s, the crack epidemic had become a major impetus for the development and spread of drug-trafficking street gangs throughout the nation. By the start of the twenty-first century, street gangs were found in nearly every American city and in many small towns across the United States.

One of the consequences of the growing market for crack and the accompanying growth of street gangs was the arming of many young people on the fringes of society. Drug-involved juveniles began using guns to protect themselves from being robbed, and by the early 1990s the use of guns had spread from individuals involved in drug transactions to a relatively large number of young people. Soon, the availability and use of guns, the spread of the drug market, and the skyrocketing growth of street gangs all contributed to a dramatic rise in murder rates among young people.[65] Finally, beginning in the 1980s and continuing through the 1990s, young people became increasingly involved in various forms of hate crimes. Although many of these crimes were committed on the basis of gender and ethnic bias, they were given new life by the terrorist attacks of September 11, 2001, when a focus on Muslims provided a new outlet for hatred.

This changing nature of delinquency, as well as increased media coverage of violent juveniles who carried weapons and were typically involved in gangs, continued to harden public attitudes toward juvenile delinquents. The resulting "get-tough" attitude toward the violent juvenile led to a number of juvenile justice initiatives in the 1990s that went beyond those implemented in the 1980s. The urgency with which states responded could be seen in the fact that in the 1990s nearly every state enacted legislation changing the way juvenile delinquents were handled.[66] This legislation led to nine state initiatives in juvenile justice that continue in force today: (1) an expanded use of curfews, (2) innovative parental responsibility laws, (3) organized efforts to combat street gangs, (4) a movement toward graduated sanctions, (5) the creation of juvenile boot camps, (6) a focus on youths with guns, (7) changes in juvenile proceedings and record keeping, (8) a larger number of juvenile transfers to adult criminal court, and (9) enhanced sentencing options for dealing with serious youthful offenders. All of these initiatives will be discussed in future chapters.

Although many of these initiatives are still in place, a number of reforms are currently taking place in the nation's stance toward juvenile delinquency. Some people now question the get-tough approach to juvenile crime,[67] many advocate for the increased use of use of evidence-based programs, and others call for the implementation of a greater number of restorative justice programs (see the *Delinquency and Social Policy* section later in this chapter for more discussion of evidence-based programs).[68] Similarly, increased attention is being paid to juvenile reentry and aftercare (i.e., juvenile parole)[69] and the creation of federal mandates to reduce the victimization that sometimes takes place in institutional contexts.[70]

▲ Anthony and Susan Provenzino (shown here) were convicted of violating a parental responsibility ordinance when their sixteen-year-old son was charged with breaking and entering and possession of marijuana. Such laws make parents liable for the actions of their dependent children.

■ **Do you agree with the idea of holding parents responsible for the behavior of their underage children?**

Social Context of Delinquency

Delinquent behavior takes place in a social context. It is within this context that social and structural conditions influence the development of delinquency, the definition of delinquency, the reform and punishment of delinquents, and policy decisions about preventing delinquency. It is important to recognize that the social setting in which delinquency occurs is shaped by historical, legal, sociocultural, economic, and political contexts (Figure 1–5).

The *historical context* recognizes how juvenile delinquents were handled in the past and influences how they are perceived and handled in the present. A study of history also enables us to perceive previous cycles of juvenile justice and to understand the emergence and the eventual decline of the philosophies undergirding these cycles.

para 7

The *legal context* establishes the definition of delinquent behavior and status offense behavior. It is within this context that the roles and jurisdictions of the juvenile courts are determined. This context also determines the legal basis of juvenile court decisions and the constitutional procedure for dealing with youth in trouble.

The *sociocultural context* shapes the relationship between the delinquent and societal institutions, including the family, the school, and the church or synagogue. Sociocultural research investigates the extent to which peer groups, neighborhoods, urbanization, and industrialization contribute to delinquent behavior. Sociocultural forces also shape society's norms and values, including its attitudes toward youth crime.

The *economic context* sets the conditions under which delinquents live and determines the extent to which economic factors contribute to delinquent behavior. This context cannot be ignored in U.S. society because so many attitudes and behaviors are influenced by success goals and the means—whether legal or illegal—that people employ to achieve them. The economic context gains in importance in fiscally hard times, because high unemployment and tight budgets affect all institutions (including those for youth) in society.

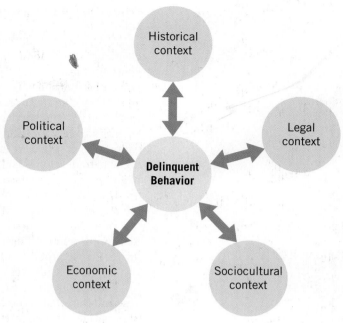

FIGURE 1–5
The Social Context of Delinquency

Finally, the *political context* influences local and national policy decisions that deal with youth crime. It is within this context that decisions are made to toughen or soften the approach to juvenile crime. Political factors have a direct impact on juvenile justice agencies, including budgets, policy, and the handling of adjudicated youth.

Some studies of delinquency use contextual analysis to understand how much the interrelationships among different contexts affect the interpretation and handling of delinquency. Interest in doing contextual analysis in examinations of delinquency increased during the 1980s and 1990s. We will describe some of these studies later in this text.

Themes in the Study of Delinquency

Before concluding this introductory chapter, it is important to discuss the three themes that flow through this text. The first theme focuses on *delinquency prevention*. The second theme, *delinquency across the life course*, examines risk factors that contribute to delinquent behavior and looks at how such behavior affects subsequent life experiences. *Delinquency and social policy* forms our third theme, and it is one that asks what can be done to improve the effectiveness of treatment, to reduce recidivism rates, and to elevate the quality of young people's lives.

Delinquency Prevention

The first of our themes is *delinquency prevention*. The prevention of delinquency is something that can be accomplished by effective social programs, or it may involve personal characteristics that shield young people from negative environmental influences. In terms of the individual level, one of the most important concepts in the area of delinquency prevention is **resiliency**. We know that many of today's youth face a host of negative influences in their lives—substance abuse, gang affiliations, teenage pregnancy, school violence, and many others. Despite these and other hardships, some youth remain resilient; that is, they are able to persevere in the face of difficulty and become productive community citizens. Why is it that some youth thrive despite inauspicious beginnings while others do not?[71]

A 2010 study by Duke University researcher Joanna Maselko and her colleagues found that the quality of a mother's interaction with her young child is crucial in determining levels of stress and anxiety as the child grows older. Specifically, Maselko found that providing high levels of maternal affection to children at eight months of age was associated

resiliency
The capacity to regain personal power and develop a strong core sense of self in the face of poverty, severe family hardship, and community devastation.[83]

with stress reduction and produced "long-lasting positive effects on mental health well into adulthood."[72]

Youth are generally considered resilient when they are able to rely on apparently innate characteristics to fend off or recover from life's misfortunes. Some proponents contend that youth best learn resiliency when they reside in environments that (1) offer caring and supportive relationships, (2) hold high expectations for behavior and attitudes (for themselves and others), and (3) provide opportunities for meaningful participation.[73] Others believe that children who survive risky environments benefit in large part from personal qualities such as strong self-confidence, coping skills, and the ability to avoid risky situations.[74] Some experts suggest that we are all born with an innate capacity for resilience through which we are able to develop social competence, problem-solving skills, critical consciousness, sense of autonomy, and a sense of purpose and accountability.[75]

The online publication *Voices of Delinquency*, which is a supplement to this text, contains stories of youth who became delinquent or experimented with delinquent behavior, but later chose to pursue other paths in life. Some of these people had friends who continued to move in a different direction, some to lives of crime and prison, and others to the grave. People profiled in *Voices*, however, escaped delinquency and went on to live productive and successful lives—largely due to their resiliency.

Throughout this text, we attempt to identify characteristic(s) that resilient youth possess and that enable them to realize successful life outcomes, notwithstanding the presence of other high-risk environmental situations.

◆ Delinquency across the Life Course

Our second theme, delinquency across the life course, examines risk factors that contribute to delinquent behavior and asks how such behavior affects subsequent life experiences. **Developmental life-course (DLC) theory** represents a major change in how we think about and study lives.[76] DLC theory is concerned with four main issues in the study of delinquency: (1) the development of offending and antisocial behavior, (2) protective factors, (3) the risk of offending at different ages, and (4) the effects of life events on the course of a person's social and personal development. DLC theory attempts to integrate what is known about the individual, family, school, peers, and the community with situational influences on offending. It also integrates key elements of preexisting theories that attempt to explain delinquency, such as strain theory, control theory, differential association theory, and social learning theory.[77]

Developmental Life-Course (DLC) theory

A framework suggesting that four key factors determine the shape of the life course: location in time and place, linked lives, human agency, and timing of lives.

DLC holds that human development and aging are lifelong processes, and that people are rational actors who make informed choices as they go through life. The choices that people make, however, can be influenced by "turning points," or life experiences (such as getting married), that change the nature or modify the strength of social ties. According to life-course criminology, crime is more likely to occur when an individual's ties to the wider society are disrupted, and the trajectory of the life course tends to be continuous.[78] Hence, it becomes important to explain why some young people experiment with acts of delinquency early on in life, but do not continue with criminal careers into adulthood.

An increased emphasis on the life course in both sociology and delinquency studies has been accompanied by a resurgence of interest in **human agency**. The principle of human agency recognizes that juveniles, like people everywhere, are influenced by social opportunities and structural constraints, and that they make personal choices and decisions based on the costs and benefits of alternatives that they believe they are facing. Life-course theory relates individuals to a broad social context, and it recognizes that within the constraints of their social world, individuals purposely plan and make choices from among the options facing them, and those decisions largely determine their life course.[79]

human agency

The active role juveniles take in their lives; the fact that juveniles are not merely subject to social and structural constraints but also make choices and decisions based on the alternatives that they see before them.

Studies of delinquency across the life course are reported in many chapters in this text. Another advantage of the *Voices of Delinquency* feature mentioned earlier is that many of the stories it record the lives of individuals across the course of their lives. A few stories describe how some individuals made decisions that ultimately resulted in their being placed on death row or being sentenced to prison for the remainder of their lives. Other stories are stirring and inspiring accounts of how other individuals used turning points in their lives to desist from crime and to alter their personal futures.

People In the Know
Interview with John H. Laub

Question: Psychologist Anne Colby has concluded that "the establishment of [the life-course] approach, which is widely shared internationally as well as across disciplines, is one of the most important achievements of social science in the second half of the twentieth century." How much do you believe the life-course approach will impact the study of juvenile delinquency/criminology in the twenty-first century?

Laub: I think that the life-course approach will greatly influence the study of juvenile delinquency and criminology in the twenty-first century. First, from a theoretical perspective, the importance of studying the unfolding of individual lives across the entire life course is becoming more prominent in criminology and the social sciences at large. It is well recognized now that crime does not just happen, but needs to be understood in a larger developmental and life-course framework. Secondly, and perhaps more practically, there are a number of longitudinal studies whose subjects are coming of age and entering adulthood. Thus, the challenge will be to assess how the diversity of life-course experiences across various groups (e.g., race/ethnicity, gender, socioeconomic status, and place) will affect the stability and change in criminal offending and deviance over the life course.

Question: Your concept that "adult life course matters" is certainly corrective to the deterministic message of "the child is father to the man," especially the antisocial child, found in so many studies. But does the persistent, chronic, or whatever this offender may be called have a different process of desistance from the other offenders?

Laub: In our analysis of the Glueck delinquents from age seven to seventy, we found that while all offenders eventually desisted from crime, some do so at different ages or at different rates. Thus, the age–crime curve is not invariant across all offenders. At the same time, we found no support for the idea of a life-course persistent offender; namely, someone whose rate of offending does not decline with age. In our study, we found that all offenders undergo a similar process of the desistance, albeit at different times in the life course.

Desistance results from strong social ties to family (typically the result of marriage), military service, or stable employment. Moreover, we see strong evidence that persistent offending and desistance from crime can be understood through a common theoretical lens; namely, a revised age-graded general theory of informal social control that emphasizes social ties, routine activities, and human agency.

Question: What best explains the behavior of those who zigzag back and forth between criminal behavior and noncriminal behavior?

Laub: Drawing on Dan Glaser's notion of zigzag offending, we find that this idea captures the true nature of criminal offending. Even the most persistent offender does not offend each minute of the day, and those that desist from crime may well relapse and commit minor crimes. In our work we see the propensity to offend as the result of a variety of individual, situational, and community factors. Offenders cease offending when they experience structural turning points (for example, marriage) that lead to a strengthening of their social support systems in conjunction with a resolve to change their life. They are thus better positioned situationally to respond to the monitoring and control and the love and social support around them.

Question: When I first read Matza, I was intrigued by his notion of "will." Interestingly, this concept of will or human agency until recently has been largely ignored by criminological studies. With the various contributions of life-course theorists (Clausen, "planful competence"; Maruna, "redemptive scripts"; Giordano et al., "cognitions of human agency," etc.), human agency is increasingly found in criminological publications. This human construction appears to be changing the perception of the delinquent from a reactor to a redactor. Do you believe this will have a long-term effect on delinquency and criminology research?

Laub: As David Matza said almost forty years ago, the missing element in traditional social control theory is human agency … and motivation has always been its weakest link. I think that our work underscores the point that individuals actively create their own life course as it is being shaped by larger structural forces. Perhaps the concept that best captures this idea is "situated choice." It is important then to reconcile the idea of choice or will with a structuralist notion of turning points, and that is one of the challenges for future research. In crucial ways, criminal persistence is more than a weakening of social bonds, and desistance is more than the presence of a social bond, as one might be led to conclude (mistakenly) from our earlier work, *Crime in the Making*. At a metatheoretical level, our long-term follow-up data direct us to insist that a focus purely on institutional, or structural, turning points and opportunities is incomplete, for such opportunities are mediated by perceptions and human decision making. Even if below the surface of active consciousness, as in the concept of desistance by default, actions to desist are in fundamental sense willed by the offender, bringing a richer meaning to the notion of commitment. Further supporting this idea is that the men who desisted from crime, and even those who persisted, accepted responsibility for their actions and freely admitted getting into trouble. They did not, for the most part, offer excuses. Tough times due to the Great Depression, uncaring parents, poor schools, discrimination based on ethnicity and class, and the like, were not invoked to explain their criminal pasts.

Question: By the way, how can human agency (choice, decision making, planning, resourcefulness, resilience, etc.) ever be measured or calibrated?

Laub: There is no easy answer to this question. In our book *Shared Beginnings, Divergent Lives*, our effort was to reposition human agency as a central element in understanding crime and deviance over the life course. We did not develop an explicit theory of human agency replete with testable causal hypotheses. This will be a first-order challenge for future work in life-course criminology. One strategy might be to unpack agency and begin to articulate the key elements—planfulness, self-efficacy, time orientation, etc. Regardless, in the end, I think some combination of quantitative and qualitative data is needed to measure agency in its fullest sense of the term.

(Continued)

Question: One of the damning things, as my in-service students like to remind me, is that the explanations of delinquent behavior do not work in the real world. The process model found in *Shared Beginnings, Divergent Lives* seems to present a much more multidimensional (and I think accurate) understanding of human behavior. How do you think the criminological community will respond to this process model?

Laub: The criminological research community has been very receptive to what you call "the process model," because it does add the complexity that is evident in the "real world." However, at the same time, there are elements of the model that seem out of control of policy makers—for example, marriage, human agency, and aging. However, objections to the model on this basis are short-sighted. Our theory provides a framework to understand continuity and change in offending over the life course. Also, our work reminds policy makers of the difficulty of predicting adult outcomes based solely on childhood characteristics. We found that while childhood prognoses are modestly accurate in predicting level differences, they simply do not yield distinct groupings that are valid prospectively for troubled kids. Not only is prediction clearly poor at the individual level; our data reveal the tenuous basis for the sorts of distinct groupings that dominate theoretical discussion (e.g., "superpredator," "life-course persistent offender"). These groupings wither when placed under the microscope of long-term observation.

Source: Reprinted with permission from John H. Laub. John H. Laub is director of the National Institute of Justice, and was formerly a professor of criminology at the University of Maryland. He and Robert J. Sampson have authored the award winning book, *Crime in the Making: Pathways and Turning Points through Life, Shared Beginnings, Divergent Lives,* and many other publications. This interview took place in August 2004.

Delinquency and Social Policy

Delinquency and social policy form our third theme—one that asks what can be done to improve the quality of young people's lives and provides ideas for effectively treating and controlling youth crime. The Children's Defense Fund's publication titled *State of America's Children 2011* is quick to remind us of the cost to society of letting vast numbers of young people grow up without realizing their full potential. To stay on the path to successful adulthood, the publication says, it is necessary to champion policies and programs that lift children out of poverty, protect them from abuse and neglect, and ensure their access to health care, quality education, and a solid moral and spiritual foundation. What this kind of success requires is healthy communities, constructive peer relationships, productive after-school and summer programs, and positive role models.[80] The pressing and exciting challenge for all of us is to design policy recommendations that provide helpful directions for dealing more effectively with adolescents in general and with delinquents in particular.

Effective policy will emerge when well-thought-out theoretical assumptions are supported by methodologically sound research. Another way to say this is that the two basic tools of social science are research and theory; each helps to guide and direct the other. Research identifies appropriate methods for collecting data, helps to identify variables to be studied, tests variables for their impact on the subject under study, analyzes related variables, and suggests new directions for theory development. Theory points the way to new research, helps derive new variables, builds interconnections among variables, interprets old and new ideas, builds systems of thought, and leads the way to new social and theoretical conclusions. Research collects and theory analyzes; research discovers and theory explains; research disproves and theory reorders.[81] Most importantly, policy recommendations will be taken more seriously by policy makers if they are based on research findings that are inextricably bound to sound theory.

When social programs are based on evidence derived from research, they are said to be **evidence based**. The OJJDP offers a model programs guide (MPG) of evidence-based prevention and intervention programs, which is available on the Web at http://www.ojjdp .gov/mpg. The MPG database of over 200 evidence-based programs covers the entire continuum of youth services from prevention through sanctions to reentry. The OJJDP says that the MPG "offers a database of scientifically-proven programs that address a range of issues, including substance abuse, mental health, and education programs."[82] The online guide can be used to assist juvenile justice practitioners, administrators, and researchers seeking to enhance accountability, ensure public safety, and reduce recidivism. See Figure 1–6 for a visual representation of the relationship between research, theory, and social policy.

Voices of Delinquency 1–1
Twenty-six stories written by former delinquents can be accessed on the MyCrimeKit website that supports this book under the *Voices of Delinquency* tab. The *Voices of Delinquency* resource is helpful in understanding delinquency across the life course as well as the influence of the social environment on delinquent behavior. Where appropriate, various *Voices of Delinquency* stories are cited throughout this book.

Web Extra 1–5
OJJDP PowerPoint presentation: "Juvenile Population Characteristics"

evidence based
The use of scientific research as the basis for determining the best practices in a field.

The Case

The Life Course of Amy Watters, Age 5

Until she was five years old, Amy Watters didn't know that she lived a life different from most children. Shortly after she was born her mother, Kassey, was killed in a car accident. Amy was only six months old at the time, and had no recollection of her mother as she started kindergarten. She had been raised by her father, Simon—a loving, but hard-working man—and by her older sister, Jordan. On her first day in kindergarten, however, she was unsettled to see the many doting mothers that accompanied the other children to school. Amy's father had dropped Amy off at the school, leaving her in the hands of a capable teacher, before rushing off to work. Jordan, a sixth grader, had taken the bus to school. Although Amy sensed on that first school day that something was different about her, she was unaware of recently published life-course research showing that the more mothers shower their young children with warmth and affection, the less anxious, hostile, and distressed those children will likely be as adults. Other studies, published at about the same time, revealed the important role of genetics in personality development, showing that children of parents with anxiety disorders are up to seven times more likely than other children to develop anxiety problems themselves. There had also been another significant event in Amy's life that happened even before she was born. When her mother was eight months pregnant, a category 3 hurricane struck southern Florida where the family lived. Although no one in the family was physically injured, the experience had been stressful for Amy's parents and sister, and had resulted in quite a bit of damage to their home and to the surrounding community. Again, although Amy didn't know it, studies have demonstrated that stressful events like hurricanes can have a lasting impact on fetal development.

What have been the most significant influences in Amy's young life?

What things might have happened differently, causing her life to take a different direction?

Follow the continuing Amy Watters saga in the next chapter.

Learn more on the Web:

- Fetal Distress Risk: http://usat.ly/aUj6R7
- Childhood Affection and Stress: http://usat.ly/bEknJB
- Learn more about the causes and correlates of girls delinquency from the Girls Study Group via http://justicestudies.com/girls_study_group.pdf.

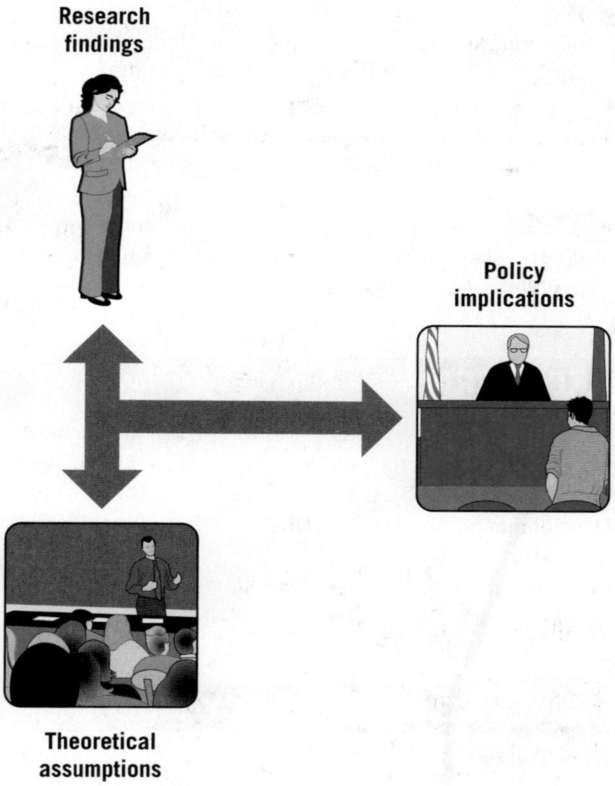

FIGURE 1–6
The Relationship between Research, Theory, and Social Policy

CHAPTER SUMMARY

This chapter has placed delinquent behavior within the wider context of adolescent problem behaviors and has emphasized the following points:

- Those adolescents most likely to become delinquents are high-risk youths who are involved in multiple problem behaviors.
- Characteristic problem behaviors include school failure and dropout, teenage pregnancy and fatherhood, and drug use and other forms of delinquency.
- About one in every four adolescents is at high risk of engaging in multiple problem behaviors.
- The history of responses to juvenile misbehavior displays a pattern in which society has taken authority away from the family and given it to juvenile authorities while simultaneously growing dissatisfied with the official handling of juvenile crime.
- The legal context for dealing with delinquency stems from the early philosophy of *parens patriae* and provides for the juvenile court to become a substitute parent for wayward children. Historically, the task of the juvenile court has been to reconcile the best interests of the child with the adequate protection of society.
- Although they sometimes commit the same crimes as adults, juveniles may also be apprehended for status offenses, behaviors that would not be defined as criminal if adults engaged in them.
- Although the public is child centered, there is a growing concern about serious juvenile crime, and a "get-tough" attitude has come to characterize recent public awareness.

- Policy makers are currently focused on serious and repeat juvenile criminals, and both the public and legislators want to make certain that these offenders are held accountable.

- One of our book's themes, the social context of delinquency, focuses on the environments in which young people find themselves and considers how these contexts influence the likelihood of delinquent behavior.

- Another theme of this text is delinquency across the life course, also called life-course theory, life-course criminology, or

life-course perspective, which examines the extent and causes of delinquency as well as the methods to control it.

- A third text theme is delinquency and social policy, which looks at the process of proposing and enacting means by which youngsters in our society can realize their potential and lead productive and satisfying lives while ensuring safety and security for all.

KEY TERMS

adolescence, p. 2
deinstitutionalization of status
    offenders (DSO), p. 9
Developmental Life-Course (DLC)
    theory, p. 18
evidence based, p. 20

house of refuge, p. 12
human agency, p. 18
juvenile, p. 5
juvenile delinquency, p. 2
Juvenile Justice and Delinquency
    Prevention (JJDP) Act of 1974, p. 10

Office of Juvenile Justice and Delinquency
    Prevention (OJJDP), p. 10
parens patriae, p. 7
resiliency, p. 17
status offender, p. 9
status offense, p. 7

JUVENILE DELINQUENCY VIDEOS

Kids Today

Kids Today focuses on the goals of the juvenile court and the ideology of working in the best interests of juvenile delinquents as well as juvenile victims. Based on the video and the readings from this chapter, discuss how the early juvenile justice system differs from the evolved juvenile justice system of today. How are the two systems similar? How does focusing on the best interest of the child impact the juvenile justice system? What are the pros and cons of this approach?

Status Offender

Status Offender looks at the intake process and the initial detention hearing for a seventeen-year-old female status offender. The juvenile was brought into the intake facility for running away. At both stages of the justice system, the court attempts to make decisions that would be in the best interest of the child. In the video two recommendations are made concerning whether or not the youth is mature enough to understand what is in her own best interests; the first was given at the youth's initial detention hearing, the other was given at the second hearing. Discuss both recommendations and the changes displayed by the youth between the two hearings. Based on the readings and

the videos, explain and discuss status offenses. What makes a behavior a status offense? How does the juvenile justice system handle status offenses? What treatment model best handles status offenses? Explain.

Delinquent Offender

Delinquent Offender displays a juvenile detention hearing. The judge discusses the proceedings with the delinquent juvenile, including his rights, the methods for determining probable cause for trying the offenses brought before the court, and the petition for the youth's delinquency. Throughout the case professionals within the juvenile court and juvenile care agencies recommend different proposals for dealing with the youth, all of which are intended to be in the best interest of the child. Based on the charges filed against the juvenile in the video, what options does the court have in treating the youth? What kinds of recommendations are made to the judge for dealing with the youth? How do these recommendations treat the juvenile's risk factors and delinquency? Based on your readings discuss other methods not mentioned in the video that could be used to treat a juvenile with a similar record.

REVIEW QUESTIONS

1. How has the role of the family changed throughout the history of juvenile justice in the United States?
2. What is the concept of parens patriae? Why is it important in the history of juvenile delinquency?
3. What are the three categories in which the juvenile court has jurisdiction over youth?

4. What are some of the factors that made juvenile delinquents a serious problem in U.S. society?
5. How have the juvenile justice initiatives of the 1990s affected the way delinquents are handled?

DISCUSSION QUESTIONS

1. What is meant by the phrase "the lengthening of adolescence"? What elements of U.S. culture have contributed to this phenomenon?
2. As we begin the twenty-first century, many American youths are significantly more mature than young people were at the beginning of the twentieth century. Therefore, should the age at which an offender is considered a minor be reduced? If so, what age would be appropriate today?
3. Is involvement in status offenses a progressive behavior that inevitably leads to delinquency and then criminality? What factors might dissuade a status offender from continued problem behavior? What factors might propel a status offender into more severe offenses?
4. Do you agree with the notion that juvenile offenses are a response by young people to being victimized by such life factors as poverty, broken families, and poor schools and neighborhoods? If such victimization can be used to defend criminal behavior in juveniles, why shouldn't it be used to defend criminal behavior in adults? For youths, at what point does victimization become outweighed by the requirements to accept responsibility for their decisions and actions?
5. Do you agree with or oppose parental responsibility laws? Explain your position. How do you feel about curfews in a community?

GROUP EXERCISES

1. Divide the class into two groups. Have the first group research child labor laws in the 50 U.S. states; have the second group research labor laws in the 30 most populous countries. Have each group present its findings.
2. Ask volunteers to relate personal "turning point" experiences that diverted them from delinquency and to describe the factors that helped them make the choices they made. How are their experiences related to those found in the *Voices of Delinquency* of those youngsters who turned their lives around?
3. Poll the class to determine how many hold the conservative view that using a "get-tough" approach to crime control is most effective and how many hold the more liberal view that solving social problems such as poverty and joblessness will reduce crime. Allow the students to debate/discuss their respective viewpoints.
4. Divide the class into two groups, the first consisting of those who believe status offenses result from normal youthful exuberance, irresponsibility, immaturity, and a tendency to challenge authority or test limits and the second consisting of those who believe such behavior is indicative of a tendency toward criminality. Ask members of each group to explain their reasoning, and allow the groups to debate/discuss the issue.

NOTES

1. "Ohio School Shooter Confesses as Death Toll Climbs," http://www.reuters.com/article/2012/02/28/us-shooting-ohio-urgent-idUSTRE81Q1AD20120228 (accessed December 22, 2012).
2. Ibid.
3. Ibid.
4. For an examination of the crises and strategies of adolescence, see David A. Wolfe, Peter G. Jaffe, and Claire V. Crooks, *Adolescence Risk Behaviors: Why Teens Experiment and Strategies to Keep Them Safe* (New Haven, Conn.: Yale University Press, 2006).
5. The concept of childhood is usually identified as beginning in the early decades of the twentieth century. For a good discussion of the social construction of adolescence, see Barry C. Feld, *Bad Kids: Race and the Transformation of the Juvenile Court* (New York: Oxford University Press, 1999), pp. 19–31.
6. Lloyd de Mause, ed., *The History of Childhood* (New York: Psycho-History Press), 1974, p. 1.
7. One of the exciting new areas of research is in relating adolescence to the life-course cycle or theory. See Silvia Bonimo, Elena Cattelino, and Silvia Ciairano, *Adolescent and Risk, Behavior, Functions, and Protective Factors* (New York: Springer-Verlag Italia, 2005), pp. 1–33.
8. Erik H. Erikson and Huey P. Newton, *In Search of Common Ground* (New York: W. W. Norton, 1973), p. 52.
9. Joy G. Dryfoos, *Adolescents at Risk: Prevalence and Prevention* (New York: Oxford University Press, 1990), p. 25.
10. Christopher R. Edginton, Christophere L. Kowalski, and Steven W. Randall, *Youth Work: Emerging Perspectives in Youth Development* (Champaign, Ill.: Sagamore Publishing, 2005).
11. See David Kupelian, "Why Today's Youth Culture Has Gone Insane," *WorldNew Daily Exclusive Commentary,* January 16, 2004.
12. See "In the Heart of Freedom, in Chains," *City Journal,* 2007, http://city-journal.org/html/173black.america.html.
13. *America's Children: Key National Indicators of Well-Being, 2011,* http://www.childstatstgov/americas/children/demo.asp (accessed May 18, 2012).
14. Ibid.

15. Ibid.
16. Ibid.
17. Ibid.
18. Children's Defense Fund, *The State of America's Children 2011: Highlights,* http://www.childrendefense.org.
19. Children's Defense Fund, "Mission Statement," http://www.childrensdefense.org.
20. Danice K. Eaton et al., "Youth Risk Behavior Surveillance: United States, 2007," *MMWR Surveillance Summaries* 57 (2008), pp. 1–131.
21. Michael A. Gusseri, Teena Willoughby, and Heather Chalmers, "A Rationale and Method for Examining Reasons for Linkages among Adolescent Risk Behaviors," *Youth Adolescence* 36 (2007), pp. 279–289.
22. Ibid.
23. Eaton et al., "Youth Risk Behavior Surveillance."
24. David Huizinga, Rolf Loeber, Terence P. Thornberry, and Lynn Cothern, *Co-Occurrence of Delinquency and Other Problem Behaviors* (Washington, D.C.: Office of Juvenile Justice and Delinquency Prevention, 2000), p. 1. For an examination of the prevalence and patterns of co-occurring mental health problem symptoms, substance use, and delinquency conduct in a sample of multiple-problem and detained youths, see Carolyn C. Potter and Jeffrey M. Jenson, "Cluster Profiles of Multiple Problem Youth: Mental Health Problem Symptoms, Substance Use, and Delinquent Conduct," *Criminal Justice and Behavior* 30 (April 2003), pp. 230–50.
25. Carl McCurley and Howard N. Snyder, *Co-Occurrence of Substance Use Behaviors in Youth* (Washington, D.C.: U.S. Department of Justice, 2008).
26. Federal Bureau of Investigation, *Crime in the United States 2010,* http://www.fbi.gov/about-us/cjis/ucr/crime-in-the-u.s/2010/crime-in-the-u.s.-2010/tables/10tbl38.xls.
27. *In re Poff,* 135 F. Supp. 224 (C.C.C. 1955).
28. Barry Krisberg and James Austin, *The Children of Ishmael: Critical Perspectives on Juvenile Justice* (Palo Alto, Calif.: Mayfield Publishing, 1978), p. 60.
29. Howard N. Snyder and Melissa Sickmund, *Juvenile Offenders and Victims: 2006 National Report* (Washington, D.C.: Office of Juvenile Justice and Delinquency Prevention, March 2006), p. 103.
30. Interviews with parents conducted in Illinois, Iowa, and Minnesota by Linda Bartollas.
31. Meda Chesney-Lind and Lisa J. Pasko, *The Female Offender: Girls, Women, and Crime,* 2d ed. (Thousand Oaks, Calif.: Sage, 2004).
32. U.S. Congress, Senate Committee on the Judiciary, Subcommittee to Investigate Juvenile Delinquency, 1973, *The Juvenile Justice and Delinquency Prevention Act,* S.3148 and S.821. 92d Cong. 2d sess.; 93d Cong. 1st sess.
33. National Council on Juvenile Justice, *National Juvenile Court Case Records 1975–1992* (Pittsburgh: National Center for Juvenile Justice, 1994).
34. Federal Advisory Committee on Juvenile Justice, *Annual Report 2008* (Washington, D.C.: Office of Juvenile Justice and Delinquency Prevention, 2008), p. 1.
35. Ibid., p. 2.
36. Charles W. Thomas, "Are Status Offenders Really So Different?" *Crime and Delinquency* 22 (1976), pp. 440–42.
37. Martin Rouse, "The Diversion of Status Offenders, Criminalization, and the New York Family Court," paper presented at the annual meeting of the American Society of Criminology, Reno, Nevada (November 1989), 1, 2, 10–11.
38. Thomas, "Are Status Offenders Really So Different?" pp. 438–455.
39. New York State Office of Children and Family Services, *PINS Reform Legislation,* http://www.ocfs.state.ny.us/main/legal/legislation/pins (accessed May 3, 2012).
40. Ibid. (accessed June 12, 2012).
41. Ibid.
42. Federal Advisory Committee on Juvenile Justice, *Annual Report 2010* (Washington, D.C.: U.S. Department of Justice, 2010), p. 3.
43. T. P. Thornberry, "Co-Occurrence of Problem Behavior among Adolescents," paper presented at Multi-System Approaches in Child Welfare and Juvenile Justice Wingspread Conference, Milwaukee, WI, May 7–9, 2008.
44. National Resource Center for Family Centered Practice, *Minority Youth and Families Initiative (MYFI)* (Baltimore, Md.: Annie E. Casey Foundation, 2005).
45. Federal Advisory Committee on Juvenile Justice, *Annual Report 2010,* p. 5.
46. George Santayana, *The Life of Reason* (London: Constable, 1905), p. 284.
47. David J. Rothman, *The Discovery of the Asylum* (Boston: Little, Brown, 1971).
48. Ibid.
49. Bradford Kinney Peirce, *A Half Century with Juvenile Delinquents* (Montclair, N.J.: Patterson Smith, 1969 [1869]), p. 41.
50. Roscoe Pound, "The Juvenile Court and the Law," *National Probation and Parole Association Yearbook* 1 (1944), p. 4.
51. *Kent* v. *United States,* 383 U.S. 541, 86 S.Ct. 1045, 16 L.Ed.2d 84 (1966); *In re Gault,* 387 U.S. 1, 18 L.Ed. 368 (1970); *McKeiver* v. *Pennsylvania,* 403 U.S. 528, 535 (1971); *In re Winship,* 397 U.S. 358, 90 S.Ct. 1928, 25 L.Ed.2d 368 (1970); and *Breed* v. *Jones,* 421 U.S. 519, 95 S.Ct. 1779 (1975).
52. *In re Gault.*
53. U.S. Congress, Juvenile Justice and Delinquency Prevention Act.
54. Ira M. Schwartz, *(In)justice for Juveniles: Rethinking the Best Interests of the Child* (Lexington, Mass.: Lexington Books, 1989).
55. National Advisory Committee for Juvenile Justice and Delinquency Prevention, *Serious Juvenile Crime: A Redirected Federal Effort* (Washington, D.C.: U.S. Department of Justice, 1984).
56. R. B. Coates, A. D. Miller, and L. E. Ohlin, *Diversity in a Youth Correctional System: Handling Delinquents in Massachusetts* (Cambridge, Mass.: Ballinger Publishing, 1978), p. 190.
57. Barry Krisberg et al., "The Watershed of Juvenile Justice Reform," *Crime and Delinquency* 32 (January 1986), pp. 5–38.

58. Alfred S. Regnery, "A Federal Perspective on Juvenile Justice Reform," *Crime and Delinquency* 32 (January 1986), p. 40. For an extensive examination of crime control in the 1980s, see Ted Gest, *Crime and Politics: Big Government's Erratic Campaign for Law and Order* (New York: Oxford University Press, 2001), pp. 41–62.

59. National Advisory Committee for Juvenile Justice and Delinquency Prevention, *Serious Juvenile Crime,* p. 9.

60. Ibid., pp. 9, 11.

61. Ibid., p. 11.

62. Schwartz, *(In)justice for Juveniles.*

63. Krisberg et al., "Watershed of Juvenile Justice Reform"; Barry C. Feld, "Legislative Policies Toward the Serious Juvenile Offender," *Crime and Delinquency* 27 (October 1981), pp. 497–521.

64. Edward Cimler and Lee Roy Bearch, "Factors Involved in Juvenile Decisions about Crime," *Criminal Justice and Behavior* 8 (September 1981), pp. 275–86.

65. For the development of these trends, see the interview with Alfred Blumstein in *Law Enforcement News* 21 (April 30, 1995), pp. 1–2 and 11–12.

66. National Criminal Justice Association, *Juvenile Justice Reform Initiatives in the States: 1994–1996* (Washington, D.C.: Office of Juvenile Justice and Delinquency Prevention, 1997).

67. *Roper* v. *Simmons,* 543 U.S. 551 (2005).

68. Mark W. Lipsey, James C. Howell, Marion R. Kelly, Gabrielle Chapman, and Darin Carver, *Improving the Effectiveness of Juvenile Justice Programs: A New Perspective on Evidence-Based Practice* (Washington, D.C.: Center for Juvenile Justice Reform, 2010).

69. Federal Advisory Committee on Juvenile Justice, *Annual Report 2010,* pp. 31–37.

70. Allen J. Beck, Paige M. Harrison, and Paul Guerino, *Sexual Victimization in Juvenile Facilities Reported by Youth, 2008–2009* (Washington, D.C.: Bureau of Justice Statistics, 2010).

71. Toney Bissett Ford, *A Glance Backwards: An Analysis of Youth Resiliency through Autoethniological and Life History Lenses,* Ed.D. dissertation, 2010.

72. J. Maselko, L. Kubzansky, L. Lipsitt, and S. L. Buka, "Mother's Affection at 8 Months Predicts Emotional Distress in Adulthood," *Journal of Epidemiology and Community Health* (July 2010), doi:10.1136/jech.2009.097873 (accessed June 24, 2012).

73. M. Rutter, "Psychopathological Development across Adolescence," *Journal of Youth and Adolescence* 36 (January 2007), pp. 101–10.

74. B. Rodman, "Reclaiming Youth: What Restorative Practices Add to the Thinking: Reclaiming Children and Youth," *Journal of Strength-Based Interventions* 16 (Summer 2007), pp. 48–51, 59.

75. Ibid.

76. Glen H. Elder Jr., Monica Kirkpatrick Johnson, and Robert Crosnoe, "The Emergence and Development of Life Course Theory," in *Handbook of the Life Course,* edited by Jeylan T. Mortimer and Michael J. Shanahan (New York: Kluwer Academic/Plenum Publishers, 2003), pp. 3–19.

77. David P. Farrington, "Introduction to Integrated Developmental and Life-Course Theories of Offending," in *Integrated Developmental & Life-Course Theories of Offending,* edited by David P. Farrington (New Brunswick and London: Transaction Publishers, 2005), pp. 1–14.

78. John H. Laub, "Edwin H. Sutherland and the Michael-Adler Report: Searching for the Soul of Criminology: Seventy Years Later," *Criminology,* 44 (May 2006), pp. 235–58.

79. Glen H. Elder Jr., "Time, Human Agency, and Social Change: Perspectives on the Life Course," *Social Psychology Quarterly* 57 (1994), pp. 4–15. For an excellent review of agency, see Mustafas Emirbayer and Ann Mische, "What Is Agency?" *American Journal of Sociology* 103 (January 1998), pp. 962–1023.

80. Children's Defense Fund, *The State of America's Children 2011,* http://www.childrensdefense.org.

81. Clemens Bartollas and Stuart J. Miller, *Juvenile Justice in America,* 7th ed. (Upper Saddle River, N.J.: Prentice-Hall, 2013), p. 49.

82. Office of Juvenile Justice and Delinquency Prevention, *OJJDP Model Programs Guide*, http://www.ojjdp.gov/mpg (accessed June 12, 2012).

83. Ford, *A Glance Backwards,* p. 2.

Chapter Objectives

After reading this chapter, you should be able to:

1. Summarize the types of information provided by each major source of delinquency statistics.
2. Describe the purpose, procedures, and findings of juvenile court statistics.
3. Compare official and unofficial statistics regarding the extent of juvenile delinquency.
4. Describe the purpose, procedures, and findings of victimization studies.
5. Explain how various social factors relate to delinquency.
6. Summarize the measurements used to explain individual changes in offending across the life course.
7. Explain the correlation between guns and youth violence and the efforts to curb gun use by juveniles.

Most juvenile crime does not come to the attention of the juvenile justice system.

—Juvenile Offenders and Victims: 2006 National Report

Introduction

In 2012, 17-year-old Matthew Brent was convicted by a Florida jury of the 2009 aggravated battery of Deerfield Beach Middle School student Michael Brewer.[1] Brewer, who was fifteen years old at the time he was assaulted by Brent and two other teenagers in a tree-lined parking lot, suffered burns over 65 percent of his body when he was doused with rubbing alcohol and set on fire. The assault came after Brewer threatened to identify one of the three alleged offenders as a bicycle thief.[2] Brent, who was also fifteen at the time of the assault, was charged as an adult under Florida's transfer law, but was cleared by the jury of the more serious charge of attempted second-degree murder, which prosecutors had sought to bring against him. Although he hasn't been sentenced as this book goes to press, he faces up to fifteen years in prison.

The same Deerfield Beach Middle School that Brent and Brewer attended made national headlines again after another fifteen-year-old student, Josie Ratley, was severely beaten at a bus stop in 2010 by a male classmate who was angry over a text message that she had sent.[3] Ratley, who was kicked in the head repeatedly by her attacker's steel-toed boots, suffered extensive brain damage. She underwent three brain surgeries and had part of her damaged brain removed. Her family is suing the city, claiming that they failed to provide adequate security to prevent the attack.[4]

Sensational crimes, like the attacks on Brewer and Ratley, have fueled public concern over juvenile crime. Some of the questions that we will address in the pages that follow include the following: Is juvenile crime more serious today than it was in the past? Is it increasing or decreasing? What do we know about violent and chronic delinquents? Is a major juvenile crime wave about to engulf our society? Are there more juvenile "monsters" now than there were before, or have the media merely sensationalized the violent acts of a few?

To determine answers to these questions, it is necessary to examine the extent of delinquent behavior, the social factors related to delinquency, the dimensions of delinquent behavior, and the various ways that are used today to measure delinquency.

Uniform Crime Reporting (UCR) Program data, **juvenile court statistics**, **cohort studies**, self-report studies, and victimization surveys are the major sources of data that researchers use to measure the extent and nature of delinquent behavior. Knowledge of both the prevalence and the incidence of delinquency is necessary if we are to understand the extent of youth crime. This chapter looks at these research efforts and their findings about youth in trouble. See Table 2–1.

The term **prevalence of delinquency** has to do with the proportion of members of a **cohort** or specific age category who have committed delinquent acts by a certain age[5]; **incidence of delinquency** refers to the frequency of offending or to the number of delinquent events.

Measurements of Delinquency
Uniform Crime Reports

New York, Massachusetts, and Maine were the first states to collect crime statistics, but for the most part, record keeping by states and localities during the early years of U.S. history was haphazard or nonexistent. Federal record keeping was authorized in 1870 when Congress created the Department of Justice. Initially, the states and local police establishments largely ignored the task of record keeping (either because of indifference or because of fear of federal control), but this tendency began to reverse in the early part of the twentieth century when the International Association of Chiefs of Police formed a Committee on Uniform Crime Reports. In 1930, the attorney general designated the Federal Bureau of Investigation (FBI) to serve as the national clearinghouse for data collected by the UCR Program. Beginning with the 2005 data set (posted in 2006), the UCR Program no longer publishes a printed copy of annual crime data. Instead, it is electronically posted to the FBI's website under the title *Crime in the United States (CIUS) XXXX*, where *XXXX* indicates the year represented by the data.

An examination of the *CIUS 2010* indicates that juveniles are arrested for the same kinds of offenses as adults, as well as for status offenses (see Chapter 1). For example,

Uniform Crime Reporting (UCR) Program
officially reported crime
The Federal Bureau of Investigation's program for compiling annual data about crimes committed in the United States.

juvenile court statistics
The data about youths who appear before the juvenile court, compiled annually by the National Center for Juvenile Justice.

cohort studies
Research that usually includes all individuals who were born in a specific year in a particular city or country and follows them through part or all of their lives.

prevalence of delinquency
The percentage of the juvenile population who are involved in delinquent behavior.

cohort
A generational group as defined in demographics, in statistics, or for the purpose of social research.

incidence of delinquency
The frequency with which delinquent behavior takes place.

Video 2–1 The Hearing Process

TABLE 2–1
Major Sources of Data in Delinquency

Data Source	Sponsoring Agency	Type of Information	General Findings
Uniform Crime Reporting Program	Federal Bureau of Investigation	Arrest statistics	Youth crime is widespread in U.S. society.
National Crime Victimization Survey	Bureau of Justice Statistics	Victimization data	The number of victimizations discovered is much higher than the number of offenses reported to the police.
Juvenile Court Statistics	Office of Juvenile Justice and Delinquency Prevention	Delinquency cases processed in federal courts	Most youths come into juvenile court as a result of the filing of a petition or complaint.
Self-report surveys	Universities/ academic researchers	Individual self-reports of involvement in delinquency and crime	A large amount of hidden delinquency occurs, and is not reported in official statistics.

---

although both adults and juveniles are arrested for serious offenses such as aggravated assault and murder and for less serious offenses such as simple assault and carrying weapons, only juveniles can be taken into custody for running away, violating curfew, or being truant from school.

The crimes for which the FBI collects information are divided into two classes: Part I and Part II offenses. Part I offenses include both crimes against the person (murder, rape, robbery, and aggravated assault), and crimes against property (burglary, larceny, auto theft, and arson). Taken together, Part I used to form what the FBI called a **crime index**, which was used to compare crime rates from one year to another. A few years ago, however, the FBI officially abandoned use of the term.

Juveniles who are arrested for violent Part I offenses are more likely to be held for trial as adults, whereas those who are arrested for less serious offenses usually are processed by juvenile authorities. The exceptions to this general rule are those juveniles who have lengthy records of crime, including violent offenses, and those who are held over for trial in adult court because they are believed to be a threat to society.

Each month, police departments across the United States report to the FBI the number of offenses that come to their attention and the number of offenses that the police were able to clear by arrest. **Clearance by arrest** indicates that a person was arrested because he or she confessed to an offense or was implicated by witnesses or by other criminal evidence. These monthly reports are summarized in year-end reports, which constitute our major official source of information about crime in the United States. The data are subdivided into many different statistical categories, including the backgrounds of alleged offenders and the types of crimes for which they are arrested.

In response to law enforcement's need for more flexible in-depth data, the UCR Program formulated the National Incident-Based Reporting System (NIBRS), which presents comprehensive and detailed information about crime incidents. One advantage of NIBRS is that, unlike the UCR Program, it reports all offenses committed during a crime event, not just the most serious offense. Although more law enforcement agencies are participating, the data still are not pervasive enough to make generalizations about crimes in the United States.

In evaluating the measurement of the extent and nature of delinquency in this chapter, one of the important considerations is the **validity** and **reliability** of the data sources.

crime index
A now-defunct but once-inclusive measure of the UCR Program's violent and property crime categories, or what are called *Part I offenses*.

clearance by arrest
The solution of a crime by arrest of a perpetrator who has confessed or who has been implicated by witnesses or evidence. Clearances can also occur by exceptional means, as when a suspected perpetrator dies prior to arrest.

validity
The extent to which a research instrument measures what it says it measures.

reliability
The extent to which a questionnaire or interview yields the same answers from the same juveniles when they are questioned two or more times.

CIUS data pose numerous problems. In terms of validity, one of the most serious complaints is that the police can report only crimes that come to their attention. Many crimes are hidden or are not reported to the police; therefore, the UCR Program vastly underestimates the actual amount of crime in the United States. Some critics also charge that because the police arrest only juveniles who commit serious property and personal crimes and ignore most of the other offenses committed by young people, these statistics tell us more about official police policy and practice than about the amount of youth crime. Moreover, youthful offenders may be easier to detect in the act of committing a crime than older offenders, with a resulting inflation of the rates for youths. Finally, there is the reliability issue: Do local police departments often manipulate the statistics that are reported to the FBI? The intent may be to make the problem appear worse or better, depending on the reporting agency's agenda.

▲ A mother, distraught over the arrest of her thirteen-year-old son, pleads police officers not to take her son away.

■ **What types of offenses are likely to be committed by juveniles?**

Crime by Age Groups

The UCR Program examines the extent of juvenile crime; compares youth crime to adult crime; considers gender and racial variations in youth crime; and presents urban, suburban, and rural differences in youth crime. Following are the chief findings of *CIUS* data as they relate to juveniles[6]:

1. Youth crime is widespread in U.S. society. For example, *CIUS* 2010 data revealed that 1,288,615 juveniles under age 18 were arrested in that year. While juveniles between ages 10 and 17 constituted about 24 percent of the U.S. population, youths in this age group were arrested for 13.7 percent of the violent crimes and 22.5 percent of property crimes.

2. The percentages of total arrests involving juveniles are highest in curfew breaking, disorderly conduct, liquor-law violations, drug-abuse violations, vandalism, larceny-theft, and runaways.

3. Juveniles are arrested for serious property offenses as well as violent offenses. As Figure 2–1 indicates, in 2010 juveniles were arrested for 22.7 percent of all burglaries, 24.1 percent of robberies, 19.8 percent of weapons offenses, 9 percent of murders, and 11.0 percent of aggravated assaults in 2010.

4. Juvenile murder rates increased substantially between 1987 and 1993. In the peak year of 1993, there were about 3,800 juvenile arrests for murder; between 1993 and 2003, however, juvenile arrests for murder declined, with the number of arrests in 2010 (784) averaging a drop of 11.7 percent from 2001. The number of female juveniles arrested in 2010 represented 14.5 percent of all female arrests that year.

5. Drug arrests increased by 3.7 percent from 2001 to 2010. During these years, arrests for male drug offenses dropped 14.1 percent, while arrests for females increased 14.7 percent.

6. Youth crime trends, according to these official statistics, comparing 2001 and 2010 data for all offenses involving juveniles under the age of eighteen declined 23.5 percent, in these years, the percentage of violent arrests declined 9.6 percent, but the percentage of property crimes increased 3.3 percent over 2001. Interestingly, motor vehicle thefts declined 48.3 percent between 2001 and 2010.

Juvenile Court Statistics

Most information about the number of children appearing before the juvenile court each year comes from the publication *Juvenile Court Statistics*, released annually by the Office of Juvenile Justice and Delinquency Prevention (OJJDP), an arm of the U.S. Department of Justice.

FIGURE 2–1
Juvenile Arrests

Note: Running away from home and curfew violations are not presented in this figure because, by definition, only juveniles can be arrested for these offenses.

Source: Data from FBI, *Crime in the United States*, http://www.fbi.gov.

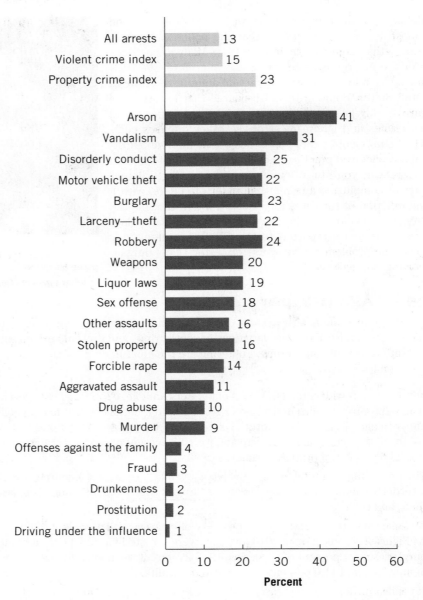

The number of children appearing before the juvenile court significantly increased from 1960 until the early 1980s, when it began to level off. It then started to rise again and continued to rise until the late 1980s, when it began to level off again. In 2009, juvenile courts in the United States handled an estimated 1.5 million delinquency cases: 38 percent of these cases were property cases, 24 percent were person offenses, 27 percent were public-order offenses, and 11 percent were drug offenses. The largest percentage of person offenses consisted of simple assaults, followed by aggravated assaults and then robberies; larceny-theft made up the largest number of property offenses, followed by vandalism and burglary, and obstruction of justice; and disorderly conduct comprised the largest percentages of public-order offenses (see Figure 2–2).[7]

The publication *Juvenile Court Statistics 2009* describes what happened to the cases brought into the system. For example, 55 percent of the delinquency cases were petitioned; that is, these youths came into the juvenile court as a result of the filing of a petition or complaint requesting the court to declare the youths either delinquent or dependent, or to transfer the youths to an adult court. In terms of nonpetitioned delinquency cases, 45 percent were informally handled cases in which authorized court personnel screened the cases prior to the filing of a formal petition and decided not to prosecute the offenders.[8] See Figure 2–3, which shows the processing of delinquency cases in juvenile court in 2009.

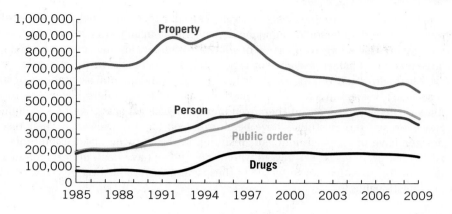

FIGURE 2-2
Delinquency Cases by Offense, 1985-2009

Source: OJJDP Statistical Briefing Book (Washington, D.C.: Office of Juvenile Justice and Delinquency Prevention, May 1, 2012), http://www.ojjdp.gov/ojstatbb/court/qa06205.asp?qaDate=2009 (accessed July 3, 2012).

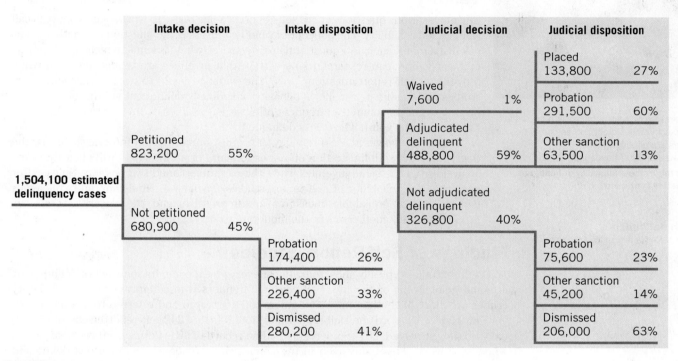

FIGURE 2-3
Delinquency Cases Processed in Juvenile Courts, 2009

Source: OJJDP Statistical Briefing Book Washington, D.C.: Office of Juvenile Justice and Delinquency Prevention, May 1, 2012), http://www.ojjdp.gov/ojstabb/court (accessed June 30, 2012).

The data from the *Juvenile Court Statistics series,* like the *CIUS* data, have some serious limitations. Their validity is compromised by the usual time lag between gathering and publishing these statistics and by the fact that the cases reported make up only a small percentage of the total number of juveniles handled by the justice system. Other data collected by the OJJDP also represent only an estimate of juvenile crimes that come to the attention of the juvenile court. Still, these national statistics, as well as statistics provided by local juvenile courts, offer ways for researchers to examine the characteristics of referred juveniles and to identify emerging trends in juvenile justice.

Self-Report Studies

In the late 1950s and 1960s, the use of delinquency studies that relied on official statistics on incarcerated populations declined, whereas self-report surveys using community or school samples rapidly increased.[9] Like other forms of measurements, **self-report studies** have

self-report study
A study of juvenile crime based on surveys in which youths report on their own delinquent acts.

▲ A handgun being purchased in a back alley. Studies show that violent crimes committed by juveniles are directly linked to the availability of handguns.

■ **How might the availability of handguns be better controlled?**

hidden delinquency
Any unobserved or unreported delinquency.

shortcomings, but criminologists generally consider them to be helpful tools in efforts to measure and understand delinquent behavior. The main justifications for self-report surveys are that a large proportion of youthful offenders are never arrested and that a large amount of **hidden delinquency** is not contained in official arrest statistics.

The logic of self-report studies is based on the fundamental assumption of survey research: "If you want to know something, ask."[10] Researchers have gone to juveniles themselves and asked them to admit to any illegal acts they have committed. However, self-report studies have been criticized for three reasons: Their research designs have often been deficient, resulting in the drawing of false inferences; the varied nature of social settings in which the studies have been undertaken makes it difficult for investigators to test hypotheses; and the studies' validity and reliability are questionable.[11]

Validity and Reliability of Self-Report Studies

The most serious questions about self-report studies relate to what social scientists call validity and reliability. The concept of validity addresses the question of whether a survey instrument, such as a questionnaire, measures what it claims to measure. In terms of validity, how can researchers be certain that juveniles are telling the truth when they fill out self-report questionnaires? The evidence seems to suggest that self-report studies underestimate the illegal behavior of seriously delinquent youths, because any juvenile who has committed frequent offenses is less likely to answer questions truthfully than is the youth who is less delinquent.[12]

Reliability gauges the consistency of a questionnaire or an interview, that is, the degree to which administration of a questionnaire or an interview will elicit the same answers from the same juveniles when they are questioned two or more times. After analyzing the reliability of self-report studies, Michael J. Hindelang and colleagues concluded that "reliability measures are impressive, and the majority of studies produce validity coefficients in the moderate to strong range."[13]

Findings of Self-Report Studies

Self-report studies typically show that almost every youth commits some act of delinquency at some point in his or her life.[14] Of course, offenders who commit violent or predatory crimes are more likely than minor offenders to be arrested and referred to juvenile court; yet Franklyn W. Dunford and Delbert S. Elliott found that of 242 self-reported career offenders who they surveyed, 207 (86 percent) had no record of arrest during a three-year period when they were actively involved in the commission of frequent and serious delinquent offenses.[15] (Figure 2–4 provides an example of a self-report questionnaire.)

Self-report studies conducted in the early 1990s in several locations, as part of the Program of Research on the Causes and Correlates of Delinquency, showed that a surprisingly large proportion of juveniles committed violent acts, as follows[16]:

• By the time they were tenth or eleventh graders, 54 percent of the Denver (Colorado) juveniles and 58 percent of the Rochester (New York) youths reported that they had been involved in a violent crime at some time in their lives.

• Chronic violent offenders, constituting 14 percent of the sample in Denver and 15 percent in Rochester, accounted for 82 percent of the violent offenses in Denver and 72 percent of the violent offenses in Rochester.[17]

According to these self-report studies, a large proportion of those who become involved in violent behavior at an early age later become chronic violent offenders. In Denver, chronic offenders reported a total of 4,134 violent crimes, an average of 33.6 per person, and in Rochester, chronic violent offenders reported 5,164 violent acts, an average of 51.7 person.[18]

David S. Kirk, in using official and self-report arrest data on a sample from the Project on Human Development in Chicago Neighborhoods, examined whether the life course of adolescent crime appears differently across self-report and official crime data and found that a sizable number of juveniles self-report being arrested without having a corresponding

Please indicate how frequently in the past twelve months you did each of the following (circle the best answer).

Stole something of little value	Never	Once	2–5 Times	6–10 Times	Over 10 Times
Stole something worth more than $100	Never	Once	2–5 Times	6–10 Times	Over 10 Times
Broke into a place to do something illegal	Never	Once	2–5 Times	6–10 Times	Over 10 Times
Beat up or hurt someone on purpose	Never	Once	2–5 Times	6–10 Times	Over 10 Times
Carried a gun or a knife	Never	Once	2–5 Times	6–10 Times	Over 10 Times
Took a car without the owner's permission	Never	Once	2–5 Times	6–10 Times	Over 10 Times
Took money by threatening someone with a weapon	Never	Once	2–5 Times	6–10 Times	Over 10 Times
Smoked marijuana	Never	Once	2–5 Times	6–10 Times	Over 10 Times
Used cocaine	Never	Once	2–5 Times	6–10 Times	Over 10 Times

FIGURE 2–4
An Example of a Self-Report Questionnaire

official arrest record, while a sizable proportion of those juveniles with an official arrest record failed to self-report that they had been arrested. Yet despite significant differences across the two arrest measures on many criminal career dimensions, parent–child conflict, effects of family supervision, and neighborhood disadvantage operated similarly across these two types.[19]

University of Alaska criminologist Andre B. Rosay and colleagues' examination of the validity of self-reported drug use found that African American offenders provide less accurate self-reports than white offenders because they are more likely to underreport crack/cocaine use than white offenders. At the same time, an African American offender who tests positive is not more likely to underreport crack cocaine use than a white offender who tests positive.[20]

The desire to uncover the true rate of delinquency and the recognition that official statistics on juvenile delinquency have serious limitations have led to a growing reliance on the use of self-report studies. Taken together, these studies appear to reveal the following:

1. Considerable undetected delinquency takes place, and police apprehension is low—probably less than 10 percent.

2. Juveniles in both the middle and lower classes are involved in considerable illegal behavior.

3. Not all hidden delinquency involves minor offenses; a significant number of serious crimes are committed each year by juveniles who elude apprehension by the police.

4. Youth who have lower socioeconomic status (SES) appear to commit more frequent delinquent acts, especially in their early years, and are more likely to be chronic offenders than are middle-class youth.

5. African Americans are more likely than whites to be arrested, convicted, and institutionalized, even though both groups commit offenses of similar seriousness.

6. Females commit more delinquent acts than official statistics indicate, but males still appear to commit more delinquent acts and to perpetrate more serious crimes than do females.

7. Alcohol and marijuana are the most widely used drugs among adolescents, but other drug use has decreased in recent years.

8. Annual surveys of high school youths have revealed that some drug offenses have increased but others have not. Overall crime trends, especially in the population of seventeen- to twenty-one-year-olds, failed to indicate any increased tendency toward criminality.[21]

Victimization Studies

National Crime Victimization Survey (NCVS)
An ongoing survey of crime victims in the United States conducted by the Bureau of Justice Statistics to determine the extent of crime.

Findings from the 2010 **National Crime Victimization Survey (NCVS)**, conducted annually by the Bureau of Justice Statistics and administered by the U.S. Census Bureau, showed that persons twelve years or older reported over 18 million criminal victimizations to surveyors in that year. Of the total, nearly 15 million were property crimes, 5.2 million were violent crimes, and more than 11 million were crimes of theft.[22] Overall, the number of victimizations uncovered by the survey was much higher than the number of offenses reported to the police. See Figure 2–5 for changes in reported violent crime victimization rates between 1973 and 2010.

NCVS's data showed that juveniles are highly overrepresented in comparison to other age groups in the population of those victimized. Juveniles between ages 16 and 19 experience the highest victimization rate of any age group for all violent crimes, and youths between ages 12 and 15 have the next highest rate, with rates dropping with the victim's increasing age. Data also showed that adolescents are more likely than adults to commit violent crimes against peers and to report knowing their assailants. Crimes against adolescents are also less likely to be reported to the police than are crimes against adults.[23]

Within the adolescent population, males are more likely than females to become victims of most violent crimes, but females are much more likely to be victims of rape and sexual assault (see Figure 2–6). The survey also revealed that African-Americans are several times more likely than whites to be victims of violence overall—including rape, sexual assault, aggravated assault, and robbery. Finally, the NCVS showed that persons ages 16 to 19 experienced overall violence, rape, sexual assault, and assault at rates at least slightly higher than rates for individuals in other age categories.[24]

Although victimization surveys have not been used as widely in analyzing delinquency as have the *Uniform Crime Reports, Juvenile Court Statistics,* cohort studies, and self-report studies, they add significantly to what is known about crime in the United States. Following are some of the principal findings of victimization surveys:

FIGURE 2–5
Self-Reported Violent Crime Victimization Rate per 1,000 Persons Ages 12 or Older

Note: Violent crimes include rape, robbery, and aggravated and simple assault. Property crimes include burglary, theft, and motor vehicle theft. The National Crime Victimization Survey redesign was implemented in 1993. The data before 1993 are adjusted to make them consistent with later years.

Source: Bureau of Justice Statistics, *Criminal Victimization, 2010* (Washington, D.C.: Bureau of Justice Statistics, 2011).

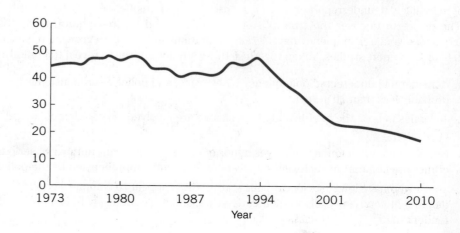

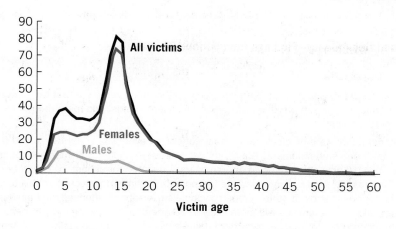

C
R
200

1. Much more crime is committed than is recorded, and the discrepancy between the number of people who say they have been victimized and the number of crimes known to the police varies with the type of offense.

2. The rank order of serious offenses reported by victims, with the exception of vehicle theft, is identical to that of the *Uniform Crime Reports*.

3. The probability of being victimized varies with the kind of crime and with where people live. The centers of cities are more probable sites of violent crimes.

4. Juveniles are more likely to commit crimes, especially property offenses, than any other age group; juveniles also are more likely to be victimized than any other age group.

5. African Americans are overrepresented both as perpetrators and as victims of serious personal crimes. Official arrest data indicate that a somewhat greater proportion of African American offenders is involved in forcible rape, aggravated assault, and simple assault than the victimization data indicate.[25]

NCVS data have similar problems with validity and reliability as do self-report studies. For example, individuals may define their personal victimization experiences differently than the official survey instrument (i.e., a woman may feel that she was raped, but her understanding of the term *rape* might not be the same as that used by NCVS researchers). Likewise, people who are queried more than once about a specific event, may give different answers to interviewees' questions. Another problem with the validity of NCVS data is that victimizations of people under age 12 are not included.

Web Extra 2–1
OJJDP PowerPoint presentation: "Juvenile Victims"

Social Factors Related to Delinquency

The first half of this chapter explored the extent of delinquency in the United States; the second half will focus on the nature of youth crime and understanding delinquency behavior. An examination of gender, racial and ethnic relations, and socio-economic status (SES) reveals much about the social factors affecting delinquency in America. The importance of gender in delinquency is examined in Chapter 7, the relationship of SES and delinquency is considered in Chapter 4, and the disproportionate handling of racial and ethnic groups is a major juvenile justice concern addressed in Chapters 13 and 16. Here, we focus on the measurement of these social factors.

Gender and Delinquency

Official arrest statistics show that adolescent males are involved in more frequent and more serious delinquent acts than are adolescent females. Table 2–2 details some of the findings

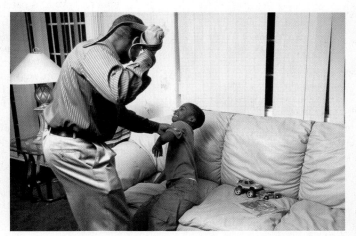

A child being beaten. Children are at risk for many kinds of violent victimization, some at the hands of their peers and some at the hands of their caregivers.

■ **Why do juveniles experience high rates of violent victimization?**

TABLE 2–2
Gender and Delinquency—Findings from Various Sources

Uniform Crime Reports

- *Crime in the United States 2010* data documented that male–female arrest ratios were five to one for drug violations, more than five to one for violent crimes, and more than three to one for property crimes.

- The gender ratios were much closer for some offenses, averaging about two to one for larceny-theft and embezzlement. The overall ratio between adolescent male and female arrests in 2010 was about three to one (females accounted for almost 30 percent of the total arrests).[1] Adolescent males are far more likely than adolescent females to be arrested for possession of stolen property, vandalism, weapons offenses, and assaults; in contrast, adolescent females are more likely to be arrested for running away from home and prostitution (arrests for running away from home account for nearly one-fifth of all female arrests).[2]

Cohort Studies

- Longitudinal research adds that males are arrested for more serious charges than are females.[3]

- Furthermore, males are more likely than females to begin their careers at an early age and to extend their delinquent careers into their adult lives.[4]

Self-Report Studies

- Female delinquency is more prevalent and more similar to male delinquency than official arrest statistics suggest.[5] For example, Hee-Soon Juon and colleagues, following a sample of African American children from first grade to age 32, found that females who were often punished as first graders were more likely to have later arrests for serious crimes and that males who were from mother-only families were at higher risk of having serious criminal arrests compared to those youths from two-parent families.[6]

Victimization Data

- Victimization data reveal that adolescent females are more likely to be victims than are adolescent males and that their victimization is shaped by their gender, race, and SES.[7]

- One study, using pooled NCVS data, found that the female-to-male offending rates for aggravated assault, robbery, and simple assault have increased over time rather than narrowed, and this study—consistent with studies of adolescent girls cited later—failed to reveal an increase in violent offending by females.[8]

- Gender differences in child abuse are particularly pronounced: Data from the federal Child Welfare Information Gateway (formerly the National Clearinghouse on Child Abuse and Neglect) showed that the rate of sexual abuse is significantly higher for girls (1.7 per 1,000) than for boys (0.4 per 1,000).[9]

Notes:

1. FBI, *Crime in the United States, 2010* (Washington, D.C.: U.S. Department of Justice, 2011).
2. U.S. Census Bureau, *Statistical Abstract of the United States, 2012: Law Enforcement, Courts, and Prisons*, http://www.census.gov/compendia/statab/2012/tables/12s0324.pdf (accessed June 14, 2012).
3. Peter E. Tracy, Marvin E. Wolfgang, and Robert M. Figlio, *Delinquency in Two Birth Cohorts: Executive Summary* (Washington, D.C.: U.S. Department of Justice, 1985).
4. Meda Chesney-Lind and Randall G. Shelden, *Girls, Delinquency, and Juvenile Justice*, 3d ed. (Belmont, Calif.: Wadsworth/Thompson, 2004).
5. For a review of these studies, see Chesney-Lind and Shelden, *Girls*, pp. 19–23.
6. Hee-Soon Juon, Elaine Eggleston Doherty, and Margaret E. Ensminger, "Prospective Study of African Americans," *Journal of Quantitative Criminology* 22 (2006), pp. 193–214.
7. Chesney-Lind and Shelden, *Girls*.
8. Janet L. Lauritsen, Karen Heijmer, and James P. Lynch, "Trends in the Gender Gap in Violent Offending: New Evidence from the National Crime Victimization Survey," *Criminology* 47 (May 2009), pp. 361–99.
9. Cited in Chesney-Lind and Shelden, *Girls*.

Web Extra 2–2
OJJDP PowerPoint presentation: "Juvenile Offenders"

obtained by the various data collecting strategies. See Figure 2–7 for trends in arrest rates by gender.

In sum, official arrest statistics and self-report studies all reveal that adolescent males are involved in more frequent and more serious delinquency than are adolescent females, but self-report studies have found that female delinquency is more similar to male delinquency than

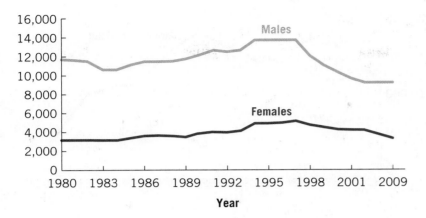

FIGURE 2–7
Arrest Trends, Ages 10–17, by Gender (per 100,000)

Source: Charles Puzzanchera and Benjamin Adams, *Juvenile Arrests 2009* (Washington, D.C.: Office of Juvenile Justice and Delinquency Prevention, Bureau of Justice Statistics, 2011).

official arrest statistics indicate. Victimization data also show that adolescent females are victimized more often than adolescent males and that, generally speaking, this victimization is influenced by their gender, race, and socioeconomic status (SES). Exactly what leads to such correlation, however, is not entirely clear. The Seattle Social Development Project's longitudinal survey of 808 youths, for example, in a 2010 report, found that gender differences in rates of court referral are unlikely to be attributable to gender biases in juvenile justice processing or in law enforcement activities.[26]

Racial/Ethnic Background and Delinquency

Studies based on official statistics have reported that African Americans are overrepresented in arrest, conviction, and incarceration relative to their population base. In contrast, most studies using self-report measures have found that African Americans are more likely to be adjudicated delinquent but are not significantly worse than whites in their prevalence or frequency of offending.[27] See Figure 2–8 for arrest rates by race.

One study, using data from the National Longitudinal Survey of Adolescent Health, compared involvement in serious violence for African Americans, Asians, Hispanics, Native Americans, and Caucasians. The results indicated that African American, Hispanic, and Native American adolescents were involved in significantly higher levels—and Asians in significantly lower levels—of serious violence than were Caucasians. The researchers explained the statistical differences between whites and minority groups by variations in community disadvantage (for African Americans), situational variables (for Asians), involvement in gangs (Hispanics), and social bonds (for Native Americans).[28]

A recent study found, using both official records and self-report data on samples of serious youthful offenders in Philadelphia and Phoenix, that racial differences of the kind usually seen in the delinquency literature were not evident in their sample of serious offenders.[29]

Another recent study, also using data from the National Longitudinal Survey of Adolescent Health, found that African American adolescents experience and are involved in higher rates of violence, especially armed violence. The same study found, however, that African American teenagers do not have higher rates of property or drug crime.[30]

A further study, this one using the Add Health data collected at the University of North Carolina and involving a nationally representative sample of adolescents, found that the combination of neighborhood context, SES, and social psychological processes can explain most of the relationship between race and violence as well as ethnicity and violence.[31]

A 2011 study found that African American children are more often cited for disciplinary infractions in schools than are children from other racial groups.[32] Classroom factors, school factors, and student behavior were not sufficient to account for this finding, leading the researchers to conclude that underlying social or community features, or racial bias, could explain the results.

Library Extra 2–1
OJJDP publication: *Disproportionate Minority Confinement: Year 2002 Update*

▲ A homeless girl on the sidewalk in the Soho District of Manhattan holds a sign that reads: "Traveling, Broke, Hungry." Self-reports seem to show that female delinquency is more prevalent and more similar to male delinquency than official statistics suggest.

■ **What kinds of delinquency are most likely to characterize girls?**

FIGURE 2–8
Juvenile Arrest Rates for All Crimes, Ages 10–17, by Race (per 100,000)

Source: FBI, *Crime in the United States, 2010,* http://www.fbi.gov.

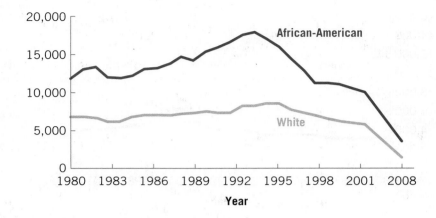

Another finding is that school-level characteristics (e.g., percentage of African American students) were related to overall discipline levels, which is consistent with a racial threat hypothesis. Such a hypothesis holds that a larger racial minority population causes the majority to feel more threatened by the minority, and consequently to prefer the use of stronger social control measures.[33] These findings may point to one explanation for why minority students fare less well in school, and are more likely to disengage from schools at a young age than white students.[34]

A 2012 presentation at the American Society of Criminology, which was part of a larger body of work, proposed that ethno-racial inequality in neighborhood crime rates is an outgrowth of racial residential segregation.[35]

In sum, official statistics and self-report data produce conflicting results. Official statistics show that African Americans tend to be overrepresented in rates of arrest, conviction, and incarceration, but self-report studies have found that African Americans are not significantly worse than whites in their prevalence or frequency of offending. There appears to be some evidence, however, that African Americans and some other minorities are involved in more serious and violent forms of delinquency than are whites, but such involvement may be influenced by neighborhood context and SES.

Library Extra 2–2
OJJDP publication: *Statistical Briefing Book (SBB)*

Socioeconomic Status and Delinquency

Decades of debate have still not produced a consensus on the relationship between socioeconomic status (SES) and delinquency. In particular:

- A review of 35 studies examining the relationship between socioeconomic status and crime concluded that very little support existed for the contention that delinquency is basically a lower-class phenomenon.[36]

- Self-report studies seem to show that delinquent involvement by middle-class and upper-class children is similar to those of lower SES. However, some people charge that self-report studies overload questionnaires with queries about trivial offenses, so that when middle- and upper-class youths record their participation in minor offenses such as swearing or curfew violations, they appear to be as delinquent as lower-class youths.[37]

- One study applied a new self-report measure deemed to be more representative of the full range of official acts for which juveniles could be arrested to a national probability sample of adolescents. These researchers reported class differences in the number of youth crimes in society (prevalence) and in the frequency of delinquent acts for serious offenses (incidence), and their study also revealed class differences in the incidence of nonserious offenses; class differences, according to these researchers, were more pervasive and stronger according to an incidence (as opposed to a prevalence) measure.[38]

In sum, research traditionally has been unable to find a firm relationship between SES and delinquency. It may be, however, that lower-class youngsters are not so different from middle- and upper-class youngsters in the frequency with which they commit delinquent acts, but that they are involved in more serious forms of delinquent behaviors (see Exhibit 2-1).

Exhibit 2–1
Socioeconomic Status (SES) and Delinquency

The middle-class youth whose interview appears below was never arrested or referred to juvenile court, even though she was involved in both status offenses and delinquent behaviors. This interview originally took place in 1995, although some information was updated in 2003, and again in 2010.

> I was a real mess as a teenager. I got into the party crowd in high school. My mother is a doctor, and I ran around with lawyers' and doctors' kids. We were looked upon as rich kids. But I had such low self-esteem at the time that I would do just about anything to make friends.
>
> Fourteen was a big turning point for me. I had my first beer [and] my first cigarette, had sex for the first time, and started to do drugs. I would sleep with guys just to make myself feel like I was liked. We would get high before school or skip classes and get high. It started out with marijuana, but by my junior year I started to do acid. We drank a lot. We got drunk every weekend and sometimes during the week. A lot of people I hung out with did cocaine, but I pretty much stayed away from it.
>
> I never got into the crime thing. I think the reason for this was I was a good student. I went to a Catholic school, made good grades, and didn't have to put any effort into it. I did run away from home my junior year and stayed with an abusive boyfriend for a week. I almost got kicked out of school for that.
>
> I came from the classic dysfunctional family. My father is an alcoholic. He controlled every aspect of my life. My father is incapable of loving anyone but himself. The turning point for me was when my parents divorced my senior year in high school.
>
> I got rid of my abusive boyfriend. I started to grow up and realize that I am not totally worthless. Now, I am a senior in college. It has been two years since I've done drugs. I have a boyfriend who loves me and wants to marry me. I've learned so much by everything I've been through. It makes me appreciate what I have and what I am now.
>
> I am now working with kids a lot like I was. The only difference is that I never got involved with the system, and these kids have been arrested, referred to the juvenile court, and sent to this residential facility.

Source: Interviewed by Clemens Bartollas.

Peers and Delinquency

One of the most consistent findings in delinquency research is the correlation between peer behavior and delinquency.[39] Yet other studies have found that peer influence on some specific forms of delinquency such as substance use depends on neighborhood context. In neighborhoods with greater opportunities for crime, the peer effect appears initially strong, but decreases as peer substance use increases. In neighborhoods with fewer opportunities for crime, the effects of peer behavior is initially small, but as delinquent peer association increases, so does the influence of the peers on the behavior of other youth.[40]

Considerable debate exists about the importance of closeness with delinquent others. Travis Hirschi, for example, believed that most delinquents have relationships with each other that can be described as "cold and brittle." Hirschi argued that "since delinquents are less strongly attached to conventional adults than nondelinquents they are less likely to be attached to each other"[41]

A recent study challenges the notion of delinquents having "cold and brittle" relationships with each other. As part of the first wave of the ongoing Toledo Adolescent Relationships Study (TARS) undertaken by researchers at Bowling Green State University, the connection between delinquency and the character of adolescent romantic ties was analyzed. Researchers looked at 957 teens with dating experience, and found that delinquent youth actually report more frequent contact with their romantic partners than other teens. The study also found that durations of romantic relationships did not differ according to the level of respondent delinquency, but more delinquent youths reported higher levels of verbal conflict with their partners.[42]

Prevention of Delinquency: Positive Youth Development

Positive Youth Development (PYD) is a comprehensive way of thinking about adolescence that challenges the traditional deficit-based perspective (which holds that adolescents become delinquent by virtue of some personal flaw) by pointing out that youths can sometimes

Positive Youth Development (PYD)
A comprehensive way of thinking about adolescence that challenges the traditional deficit-based perspective by pointing out that youths can sometimes thrive even in the presence of multiple risk factors.

thrive even in the presence of multiple risk factors. It provides an alternative model for approaching adolescents and their issues. Supporters of PYD claim that traditional approaches to the problems of young people and the societal interventions that are intended to address them are based on a deficit-based perspective. Instead, PYD advocates say that youth development activities and organizations should build on youths' resilience and competencies. PYD uses the term *resilience* (introduced in Chapter 1) to describe the qualities that support healthy adolescent development in the face of adversity. From the perspective of PYD, adolescents are seen not as objects that need to be acted upon, but as self-directed, independent individuals who may deserve special care and who merit the autonomy and dignity accorded to other members of the community. The concepts of PYD propose that youths will develop and flourish when they are connected to the right mix of relationships, opportunities, and social assets.[43]

The PYD approach has long been present in the field of juvenile justice and its influence can be seen in many prevention programs implemented throughout the nation. Recently, however, the principles of PYD were championed using federal resources and including the backing of the White House through the Helping America's Youth (HAY) initiative, launched by the Bush administration. The final report of the White House Task Force for Disadvantaged Youth highlighted research that shows that healthy adolescent development requires youth to have "caring adults in their lives, opportunities to learn marketable skills ... and opportunities to contribute meaningfully in their communities and society."[44]

The basic principles of PYD practice are:

- Youth development must strive to enhance individual and community capacities. One is not possible without the other.

- Youth development is predicated on youths exercising meaningful choices over the programs in which they participate.

- Youth development must break down racial/ethnic, gender, disability, sexual orientation, and class barriers and stereotypes.

- Youth development must build bridges between community-based organizations (formal and informal).

- Youth development activities must transform the environment in which youths live.

- Youth development must provide participants with an opportunity to learn and at the same time to have fun.

- Youth development must provide youths with opportunities to serve their community.

- Youth development must provide youths with the necessary knowledge and skills that can be converted into meaningful lifelong employment.

- Youth development must actively integrate as many core elements as possible into all activities.[45]

PYD seems to be a particularly desirable approach for prevention programs as well as for those youths accused of less serious and nonviolent offenses, who make up three-quarters of the youths referred annually to juvenile justice authorities in the United States.[46]

⟿ Delinquency across the Life Course: Length and Intensity of Juvenile Offending

One question we might ask is whether delinquency ends with adolescence or if offending behavior tends to continue throughout life. For some individuals, delinquency is strictly confined to their adolescent years; one story that illustrates this is "I Was a Chosen Child" in the *Voices of Delinquency*. Other individuals, however, make a transition from delinquency during adolescence to crime during their adult years (see Parts III and IV of *Voices of Delinquency*).

Developmental life-course criminology (see Chapter 1) is particularly concerned with documenting and explaining within-individual changes in offending across the life course. This paradigm has greatly advanced knowledge about the measurement of criminal career

Voices of Delinquency 2–1
Read "I Was a Chosen Child." In this story, the author relates all the illegal activities he was in before he decided to turn his life around. Why did the storyteller walk away from delinquency?

features such as (1) age of onset, (2) continuation or persistence, (3) escalation of offenses, (4) specialization of offenses, (5) tendency toward chronic offending, (6) length of criminal career, and (7) **desistance** or termination of offending. One of the reasons that developmental life-course criminology became important during the 1990s was the enormous volume of longitudinal research on offending that was published during that decade.[47]

desistance
The termination of a delinquent career or behavior.

Age of Onset

Several studies have found that the **age of onset** is one of the best predictors of the length and intensity of delinquent careers.[48]

The Seattle Social Development Project data, for example, showed that an early age of onset predicted a high rate of offending in both self-reports and court referrals. There was significant continuity of offending in both court referrals and self-reports, but continuity was greater in court referrals; the concentration of offending, as well as the importance of chronic offenders, was greater in self-reports.

Another study, examining the differences between early- and late-start youthful offenders in a sample of previously incarcerated youths in Oregon's juvenile justice system, determined that youths with foster care experience were four times more likely to be early-start offenders than those without foster care experience. Those youth who had family members convicted of a felony were two times more likely to be early-start delinquents than those with no family felons.[49]

Still another study revealed that the average age of onset for self-reported delinquency was 11.9 years, while the first court contact for a serious offense took place at an average age of 14.5 years.[50] Finally, Terrie Moffitt and colleagues' 2001 study further contended that "investigations that rely on official data to study crime careers will ascertain age of onset approximately 3–5 years after it has happened."[51]

age of onset
The age at which a child begins to commit delinquent acts; an important dimension of delinquency.

Library Extra 2–3
OJJDP publication: *Juvenile Offenders and Victims: 2006 National Report*, Chapter 2

Library Extra 2–4
OJJDP publication: *Juvenile Offenders and Victims: 2006 National Report*, Chapter 3

Escalation of Offenses

The findings on **escalation of offenses**, or the increase in the frequency and severity of an individual's delinquent offenses, are more mixed than those on age of onset. Official studies of delinquency have generally found that the incidence of arrest accelerates at age 13 and peaks at about age 17, but this pattern is not so clearly evident in self-report studies. A classic study, Rolf Loeber and colleagues' longitudinal study on the development of antisocial and prosocial behavior in 1,517 adolescent males in Pittsburgh, found numerous correlates of escalation in offending among the three samples. The across-age effects were low educational achievement and low school motivation; the age-specific effects were physical aggression, untrustworthiness, unaccountability, truancy, negative attitude toward school, school suspension, positive attitude toward problem behavior, single parenthood, and negative caretaker–child relations.[52] Using data from two community samples of boys, Loeber and colleagues identified three developmental pathways to a delinquent career:

escalation of offenses
An increase in the frequency and severity of an individual's offenses; an important dimension of delinquency.

1. An early "authority conflict" pathway, which consists of a sequence of stubborn behavior, defiance, and authority avoidance

2. A "covert" pathway, which consists of minor covert behaviors, property offenses, and moderate to serious forms of delinquent behavior

3. An "overt" pathway, which consists of fighting, aggression, and violence.[53]

They concluded that these pathways are interconnected; that is, youths may embark on two or three paths simultaneously. An implication of this research is that the youths' problem behaviors may escalate as youths become involved in more than one developmental

▲ Bullying behavior takes place on a Texas playground. Some studies have found that the age of onset is one of the best predictors of the length and intensity of delinquent careers.

■ **How might the findings of those studies help in delinquency prevention efforts?**

FIGURE 2–9
Pathways to Boys' Disruptive Behavior
and Delinquency

Source: Barbara Tatem Kelley, Rolf
Loeber, Kate Keenan, and Mary
DeLamatre, *Developmental Pathways
in Boys' Disruptive and Delinquent
Behavior* (Washington, D.C.: Office
of Juvenile Justice and Delinquency
Prevention, Bureau of Justice
Statistics, 1997), p. 9.

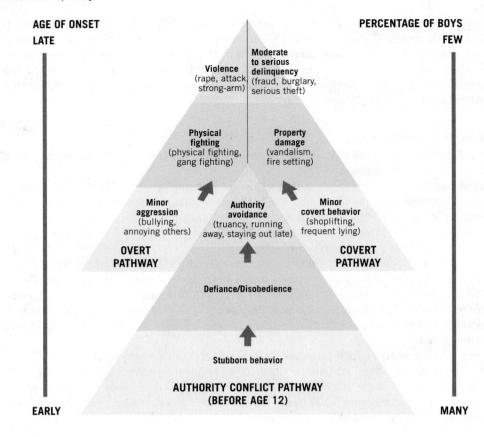

pathway. See Figure 2–9 for a diagrammatic representation of these three pathways to boys' disruptive behavior and delinquency.[54]

In 2007 Alex Piquero and colleagues, using data from the Baltimore portion of the National Collaborative Perinatal Project, tested Moffitt's hypothesis that offenders who persist in criminality throughout life (known as "life-course-persistent offenders") will be at high risk in midlife for poor physical and mental health, early disease morbidity, and cardiovascular disease. This study found that compared to adolescence-limited offenders, life-course-persistent offenders are more likely to experience adverse physical and mental health outcomes, and they explained these findings by saying that life-course-persistent offenders are more likely than their counterparts to be involved in the type of antisocial lifestyles that increase the chances of adverse health outcomes.[55]

Specialization of Offenses

specialization
The repeated involvement of a juvenile
in one type of delinquency during the course
of his or her offending.

The findings on **specialization**, or repeated involvement in one type of offense, have generally reached a greater consensus than those on escalation. The majority of early studies found little or no specialization among delinquent populations, but several recent studies have found some evidence of specialization.

One study examined the interaction between gender and age at onset of offending and asked how these factors relate to specialization. They determined that offenders who initiated offending earlier in the life course demonstrated more versatility in their offending patterns and that delinquents who began offending at a later age tended to be more specialized. Early-onset females tended more toward offending diversity than early-onset males, whereas among late-onset groups, males tended more toward offending diversity than females.[56]

Library Extra 2–5
Bureau of Justice Statistics (BJS) publication: *Juvenile Victimization and Offending*

Yet another study found that violent offenders are more likely to engage in additional violent offenses and that nonviolent offenders are more likely to continue nonviolent offense patterns.[57]

D. Wayne Osgood and Christopher J. Schreck, using 2007 data from three studies, further concluded that there are substantial levels of specialization in violence, that specialization remains considerably stable over time, and that the consistent relationships of specialization are partly explained by gender, parental education, and risk seeking.[58]

Chronic Offenders

Chronic offending is drawing increased attention for several reasons. Some believe that **chronic youthful offenders**, who constitute a small number of all offenders, account for a disproportionate share of all crimes. To understand chronic youthful offenders, researchers examine their social background and criminal history and analyze potential predictors of chronic offending. In terms of social background, the vast majority of chronic offenders are identified by most cohort studies as coming from the ever-growing minority underclass that finds itself permanently trapped. As to criminal history, cohort studies consistently report that chronic offenders are more frequently involved in violence than are other juvenile offenders and that they are more likely than other youthful offenders to use crack cocaine or other hard-core drugs or to traffic drugs to other juveniles at school and in the neighborhood.[59]

Predictors of Chronic Offending

One of the most important but controversial issues is whether chronic juvenile offending can be predicted. Several important studies have attempted to identify predictors of chronic offending within delinquent populations.

In a classic work, Alfred Blumstein and colleagues identified three population groups: (1) a group of "innocents" never involved with law enforcement, (2) a group of "amateurs" with a relatively low recidivism probability, and (3) a group of "persisters" with a relatively high recidivism probability. They also discovered seven factors that distinguished the persisters (or chronic offenders) from other convicted offenders: (1) conviction for crime before age 13, (2) low family income, (3) "troublesome" rating by teachers and peers at ages 8 to 10, (4) poor public school performance by age 10, (5) psychomotor clumsiness, (6) low nonverbal IQ, and (7) convicted sibling(s).[60]

Lila Kazemian and David P. Farrington's 2006 longitudinal study of a sample of British males and their fathers examined residual career length (i.e., average remaining number of years in criminal careers until the last offense) and residual number of offenses (i.e., average remaining number of offenses in criminal careers), and concluded that official records make it difficult to accurately predict criminal career outcomes.[61]

Youth Crimes and Adult Criminality

The experience of having been institutionalized as a juvenile seriously compromises multiple life domains in adulthood, especially for females. Research shows that institutionalization is strongly predictive of premature, unstable, precarious, and unsatisfied conditions in multiple life domains, but is much less predictive of behavior outcomes.[62]

In their well-received and now-classic book, *A General Theory of Crime*, Michael Gottfredson and Travis Hirschi concluded, for example, that competent research regularly shows that the best predictor of crime is prior criminal behavior.[63] Daniel S. Nagin and Raymond Paternoster, in examining the relationship between delinquency and adult criminality, suggested two interpretations of this relationship. The first is that "prior participation has a genuine behavioral impact on the individual. Prior participation may, for example, reduce inhibitions against engaging in delinquent activity."[64] Another explanation is that individuals have different propensities to delinquency and that each person's innate "propensity is persistent over time."

In a now-classic work, theorists Robert Sampson and John Laub sought to explain both the continuity of delinquency into

chronic youthful offender
A juvenile who engages repeatedly in delinquent behavior. The Philadelphia cohort studies defined chronic offenders as youths who had committed five or more delinquent offenses. Other studies use this term to refer to a youth involved in serious and repetitive offenses.

Web Extra 2–3
OJJDP PowerPoint presentation: "Law Enforcement and Juvenile Crime"

Voices of Delinquency 2–2
Read the story "My Father Was an Alcoholic," and identify this person's onset, escalation, specialization, and continuance into adult crime. Given the factors that made up his delinquency and adult criminality, are you surprised that he is on death row today?

▲ Teenage boys flashing gang signs in Brooklyn, New York.
■ **What kinds of prevention programs might successfully target chronic offenders?**

criminality and noncriminality (that is, a change) in adulthood for those who were delinquent as children using a threefold thesis:

1. Structural context mediated by informal family and school social control explains delinquency in childhood and adolescence.

2. In turn, there is continuity in antisocial behavior from childhood through adulthood in a variety of life domains.

3. Informal social bonds in adulthood to family and employment explain changes in criminality over the life span despite early childhood propensities.[65]

Using life-history data drawn from an earlier longitudinal study, Sampson and Laub found that although adult crime is connected to childhood behavior, both incremental and abrupt changes still take place through changes in adult social bonds. The emergence of strong bonds to work and family among adults deflects earlier established behavior trajectories. Laub and Sampson also posited that the events that trigger the formation of strong adult bonds to work and family often occur by chance or luck.[66] Their theory, known as the *age-graded life-course perspective*, holds that attachments or social bonds in adulthood increase the social capital (or the personal resources gained from quality social relationships) of some people, leading to desistance from most types of deviant behavior.

Length of Criminal Careers

The length of criminal career has been relatively neglected in empirical research until recently. Recently, British researcher Brian Francis and colleagues examined criminal career length using data from six different birth cohorts between 1953 and 1978 (totaling 58,000 males and females from England and Wales), and came up with four key findings: (1) It is possible to predict the length of criminal careers from variables available at the first court conviction, (2) the risk of desistance remains constant during a 20- to 25-year period if the offender does not immediately stop after the first conviction, (3) the most significant variable is the age at first conviction, and (4) gender differences and birth cohorts are of significant importance.[67]

In a somewhat earlier study, Alex Piquero and colleagues examined the career lengths of a sample of California Division of Juvenile Justice parolees released in the 1970s and followed them through early adulthood. They determined that the average career length of these serious offenders was 17.3 years, with white parolees having shorter careers than nonwhite parolees (16.7 versus 17.7 years). This study further revealed that age of onset, low cognitive abilities, and disadvantaged childhood environment significantly affected the length of their careers.[68]

Michael E. Ezell, who also used a random sample of offenders released from the California Youth Authority CYA in 1981–1982 and followed them into their thirties, examined the career length for five categories of offenses—serious, violent, serious violent, drug, and property—and reached five conclusions:

1. The overall mean career length for this sample was roughly 17 years.

2. The distribution of overall career lengths varied from a low of 0.01 year to a high of 34 years.

3. Violent careers tended to be slightly longer than property careers.

4. The mean residual career lengths (time remaining in career) peaked early in the life course and then strongly declined with age.

5. Several control variables, particularly age at first criminal arrest and ethnic/racial differences (African American offenders in the sample had the longest careers on average), were found to significantly affect the mean career length.[69]

In sum, this section addresses some key issues important in evaluating developmental life-course theory. These issues include why delinquents start offending, how onset sequences are explained, why there is continuity in offending from adolescence to adulthood,

TABLE 2–3
Dimensions of Delinquent Behavior

Dimension of Behavior	Finding	Consensus
Age of onset	It is the best predictor of length and continuity of delinquent behavior.	Strong
Escalation of offenses	Official studies have generally found that the incidence of arrest accelerates at age 13 and peaks at about age 17.	Mixed
Specialization	The majority of studies have found little or no specialization.	Fairly strong
Chronic offender	A small group of offenders commits the most serious offenses.	Strong
Youth crimes and adult criminality	Some childhood factors have been identified as contributing to the continuity of criminality.	Very mixed
Lengths of criminal careers	Careers tend to be longer for violent offenders, for those with early convictions, and for minority offenders.	More studies needed to determine outcomes

why early onset predicts a long criminal career, whether there is versatility in offending, what the main factors are in predicting chronic offenders, and what we know about lengths of criminal careers.[70] The studies revealed greater consensus on some of these dimensions of delinquent behavior than on others, but together, they do represent a helpful understanding of the nature of delinquent behavior. (See Table 2–3 for a summary of these dimensions of delinquent behavior.)

Library Extra 2–6
OJJDP publication: *Juvenile Offenders and Victims: 2006 National Report,* Chapter 5

Delinquency and Social Policy: Guns and Youth Violence

One of the most important issues facing juvenile delinquency at the present time is the continued reduction of youth violence. The national epidemic of youth violence began in the mid-1980s, peaked in the 1990s, and then began to decline (see Figure 2–10). There is common agreement that this outburst of youth violence was as deadly as it was because more guns were carried and used than ever before. Homicide death rates of males thirteen to seventeen years old tripled, primarily because of gun assaults.[71]

The studies also reported the following findings:

- Youths who carried guns were more likely to live in communities that had a high prevalence of gun ownership.
- Youths who lived in communities with high rates of violence were more likely to carry guns than were those who lived in communities with low rates of violence.
- Youths who carried guns were significantly more likely to engage in serious assaults and robberies than were those who did not carry guns.
- Youths who sold large amounts of drugs at every age were more likely to carry guns than were those who did not sell drugs.
- Youths who were dealing large quantities of drugs and money that could be stolen were more likely to carry guns because they believed that gun carrying was necessary to protect themselves and their investment.

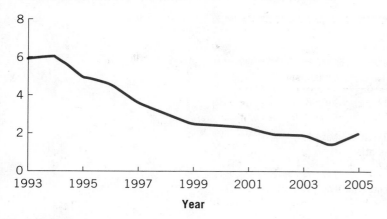

FIGURE 2–10
Nonfatal Firearm-Related Violent Victimization Rate (per 1,000 Persons Ages 12 and Older), 1993–2005

Source: Bureau of Statistics, *Nonfatal Firearm Crime Rates* (Washington, D.C.: U.S. Government Printing Office, 2007).

• Youths who were heavy drug users were also more likely to carry guns because they believed that buying drugs from armed dealers made it necessary for them to be armed themselves.

• Youths who were members of gangs had a higher probability of carrying a hidden gun than those who were not members of gangs.

• Youths who were chronic offenders and were involved in gangs played some part in most youth homicides, both as offenders and as victims.[72]

The police have played a major role in the decline of gun use by juveniles. Their efforts have resulted in a reduction of firearm violence in Atlanta, Boston, Detroit, Indianapolis, Los Angeles, and St. Louis. The Boston Gun Project has been one of the most successful projects; the two main elements of its Operation Ceasefire were a direct law enforcement attack on firearms traffickers supplying juveniles with guns, and an attempt to generate a strong deterrent to gang violence. Youth homicides decreased dramatically following the first gang intervention in May 1996 and have remained low to the present.[73]

The Office of Juvenile Justice and Delinquency Prevention (OJJDP) implemented the Partnerships to Reduce Juvenile Gun Violence Program to focus on gun violence and juveniles. Gun ownership, possession, and carrying have led to violence in drug transactions, schools, and gangs. After examining four hundred gun violence programs throughout the United States, it was decided that implementation of the seven strategies shown in Figure 2–11 would be required if the program is to achieve its goals.[74]

FIGURE 2–11
Seven Strategies to Reduce Juvenile Gun Violence

The Case

The Life Course of Amy Watters, Age 8

When Amy was eight years old she was in the third grade. One day, her teacher handed out a one-page questionnaire to all of the students in the class, and asked them to fill in circles with their pencils to answer the ten questions that it contained. Although Amy didn't know it, the anonymous questionnaire was actually a self-report social survey intended to give researchers at a local university insight into instances of early delinquent behavior. The researchers were attempting to identify situations in the lives of young children that might make them more crime-prone. They were also seeking to gain some understanding of the extent of unreported and undiscovered delinquency among the community's children in grades three through six. Question number four asked whether she had ever stolen anything. She answered "yes" to that question, and then circled "drug store" to provide more details as to where she had stolen from. Although she'd only done it twice, she'd taken items from the beauty section of a Walgreen's pharmacy that she'd visited with her father. One time it was glue-on nails, and the second time it was nail polish. She'd told a couple of friends about it, but her father never knew. Most importantly, she hadn't been caught. Survey question number nine asked if she was thinking of stealing again, to which she answered "yes."

What have been the most significant influences in Amy's young life?
What things might have happened differently, causing her life to take a different direction?

Follow the continuing Amy Watters saga in the next chapter.

Learn more on the Web:

- The Self Report Method for Measuring Delinquency and Crime: www.ncjrs.gov/criminal_justice2000/vol_4/04b.pdf

CHAPTER SUMMARY

Official and unofficial statistics reveal much of significance about youth crime in U.S. society today:

- Juveniles under the age of eighteen commit a disproportionate number of property and violent offenses.
- Juveniles today are committing more violent crimes than their counterparts did in the past, but juvenile rates of homicide have been decreasing since the middle 1990s.
- Juveniles are carrying far more guns than in the past. The good news is that law enforcement efforts in large urban areas have had some success in reducing juveniles' use of guns. Most youths are involved in delinquent behavior at some point, but more than 90 percent of delinquent acts go unreported.
- Lower-class youths are involved in more frequent and more serious offenses than are middle-class youths, and long-lasting serious youth crime is primarily found among the lower classes.
- Nonwhites commit more frequent and more serious offenses than do whites.
- Males commit more frequent and more serious offenses than do females.

- Urban youths commit more frequent and more serious offenses than do suburban or rural youths.
- The dimensions of delinquency that can affect delinquency across the life course have been examined, and the most significant of these dimensions are age of onset, escalation of offenses, specialization of offenders, specialization of offenders, and tendency toward chronic offending that continues into adulthood.
- Young people who begin offending early tend to have long delinquent careers.
- Evidence exists that at least some youthful offenders progress to increasingly serious forms of delinquency.
- A small group of youthful offenders, primarily lower-class minority males, commit half or more of all serious offenses in urban areas.
- Some youthful offenders go on to become career offenders.
- The easy availability of handguns has contributed to a growing trend in youth violence in this country.

KEY TERMS

age of onset, p. 41

chronic youthful offender, p. 43

clearance by arrest, p. 28

cohort, p. 27

cohort studies, p. 27

crime index, p. 28

desistance, p. 41

escalation of offenses, p. 41

hidden delinquency, p. 32

incidence of delinquency, p. 27

juvenile court statistics, p. 27

National Crime Victimization Survey (NCVS), p. 34

Positive Youth Development (PYD), p. 39

prevalence of delinquency, p. 27

reliability, p. 28

self-report study, p. 31

specialization, p. 42

Uniform Crime Reporting (UCR) Program, p. 27

validity, p. 28

JUVENILE DELINQUENCY VIDEOS

The Hearing Process

The Hearing Process video is about two brothers, both with prior records, within the beginning steps of the juvenile justice system. What are the boys being charged with by the court? Both boys display different needs; how do the recommendations of the attorney and the judge reflect these differences? The judge discusses her faith in the juvenile justice system. Do the sentences given by the judge accommodate the needs of each youth? Why or why not?

REVIEW QUESTIONS

1. What do the data from the FBI publication *Crime in the United States* indicate about delinquency in U.S. society?
2. What do official juvenile court statistics reveal about juvenile delinquency in the United States?
3. Are self-reports and official statistics consistent in their findings about delinquency?
4. What do victimization surveys contribute to our understanding of the extent of youth crime in U.S. society?
5. What is a cohort study? Why are cohort studies important in understanding delinquency behavior?
6. What is the relationship between life-course criminology and the dimensions of delinquent behavior?

DISCUSSION QUESTIONS

1. Do you think improved decisions and investigation procedures have impacted the public's perception of juvenile crime rates and severity?
2. Do you think the media's wider scope of inquiry and faster communication capabilities have impacted the public's perception of juvenile crime rates and severity?
3. What factors in society have contributed to the seemingly greater willingness of youths to use guns to resolve conflicts and their apparently reduced concern for the consequences of doing so?
4. Do you think respondents are more or less truthful on self-report studies? Explain your position.
5. The youthful chronic offender is a concern to the public and its policy makers. What do you think can be done to reduce the numbers of chronic offenders, who commit a disproportionate number of serious and violent delinquent acts?
6. Why are the dimensions of delinquent behavior important in understanding delinquency in U.S. society?
7. What factors make the experience of being victimized increase the likelihood of becoming an offender?

GROUP EXERCISES

1. Appoint two teams to research the *Uniform Crime Reports* and *CIUS* juvenile crime data for the past 25 years. Have one team report the data for your state and the other report the data for the nation. Have the class discuss factors that might explain any variation between state and national trends.
2. Designate two teams. Have Team 1 research juvenile arrest, conviction, and incarceration data for your state's five lowest-risk, highest-income communities, and have Team 2 research the same data for the five highest-risk, lowest-income communities. Ask the teams to make a joint presentation; then have the class discuss the findings.
3. Assign three students to report on the data and resources available at the Office of Juvenile Justice and Delinquency Prevention website at http://www.ojjdp.ncjrs.org.
4. Have students collect clippings from newspapers and articles from the Web regarding juvenile justice issues. A useful website for juvenile justice–specific events is http://www.usatoday.com.

NOTES

1. Rafael A. Olmeda, "Burn Survivor Michael Brewer's Family Satisfied with Verdict," *Boston Herald*, June 21, 2012, http://news.bostonherald.com/news/national/south/view/20120621burn_survivor_michael_brewers_family_satisfied_with_verdict (accessed July 2, 2012).

2. "Police: Juveniles Laughed after Setting 15-Year-Old on Fire," CNN.com/crime, October 14, 2009, http://edition.cnn.com/2009/CRIME/10/13/florida.teen.burned/index.html (accessed November 26, 2010).

3. Kealan Oliver, "Text Message Led to Brutal Beating of Teenage Girl, Say Cops," CBS Crimesider, http://www.cbsnews.com/8301-504083_162-20000777-504083.html?tag=contentMain;contentBody (accessed November 26, 2010).

4. "Family Marks Anniversary of Ratley Beating," Miami CBS Local Media, March 17, 2011, http://miami.cbslocal.com/2011/03/17/family-marks-anniversary-of-ratley-beating (accessed September 7, 2011).

5. Donald J. Shoemaker, *Theories of Delinquency: An Examination of Explanations of Delinquent Behavior*, 6th ed. (New York: Oxford University Press, 2009.

6. Federal Bureau of Investigation, *Crime in the United States 2010* (Washington, D.C.: FBI, 2011), http://www.fbi.gov/ucr/10cius/index.html.

7. Charles Puzzanchera and Melissa Sickmund, *Juvenile Court Statistics 2009* (Pittsburgh: National Center for Juvenile Justice, 2012).

8. Ibid.

9. Stephen A. Cernkovich, Peggy C. Giordano, and Meredith D. Pugh, "Chronic Offenders: The Missing Cases in Self-Report Delinquency," *Journal of Criminal Law and Criminology* 76 (1985), pp. 705–32.

10. Michael J. Hindelang, Travis Hirschi, and Joseph G. Weis, *Measuring Delinquency* (Beverly Hills, Calif.: Sage, 1981), p. 22.

11. Ibid.

12. Ibid., p. 126. Subsequent research has supported this finding.

13. Ibid., p. 126. For the reliability of self-report studies, see also David H. Huizinga and Delbert S. Elliot, *A Longitudinal Study of Drug Use and Delinquency in a National Sample of Youth: An Assessment of Causal Order: A Report of the National Youth Survey* (Boulder, Colo.: Behavioral Research Institute, 1981); and Beatrice A. Rouse, Nicholas J. Kozel, and Louise G. Richards, eds., *Self-Report Methods of Estimating Drug Use: Meeting Current Challenges to Validity*, NIDA Research Monograph 57 (Rockville, Md.: National Institute on Drug Abuse, 1985).

14. David H. Huizinga and Delbert S. Elliott, "Juvenile Offenders: Prevalence, Offender Incidence, and Arrest Rates by Race," *Crime and Delinquency* 33 (April 1987), pp. 206–23.

15. Franklyn W. Dunford and Delbert S. Elliott, "Identifying Career Offenders Using Self-Reported Data," *Journal of Research in Crime and Delinquency* 21 (February 1984), pp. 57–82.

16. David H. Huizinga, Rolf Loeber, and Terence P. Thornberry, *Urban Delinquency and Substance Abuse: Initial Findings* (Washington, D.C.: U.S. Department of Justice, Office of Juvenile Justice and Delinquency Prevention, 1994).

17. Katharine Browning, Terence P. Thornberry, and Pamela K. Porter, *Highlights of Findings from the Rochester Youth Development Study*, OJJDP Fact Sheet (Washington, D.C.: Office of Justice and Juvenile and Delinquency Prevention, 1999).

18. David H. Huizinga et al., *Urban Delinquency and Substance Abuse*.

19. David S. Kirk, "Examining the Divergence across Self-Report and Official Data Sources on Inferences about the Adolescent Life-Course of Crime," *Journal of Quantitative Criminology* 22 (2006), pp. 107–29.

20. Andre B. Rosay, Stacy Skroban Najaska, and Denise C. Herz, "Differences in the Validity of Self-Reported Drug Use across Five Factors: Gender, Race, Age, Type of Drug, and Offense Seriousness," *Journal of Quantitative Criminology* 23 (2007), pp. 41–58.

21. Bureau of Justice Statistics, *Criminal Victimization, 2010* (Washington, D.C.: Bureau of Justice Statistics, 2011).

22. Ibid.

23. Ibid.

24. Ibid.

25. Ibid.

26. David Farrington, Darrick Jolliffe, J. David Hawkins, Richard F. Catalano, Karl G. Hill, and Rick Kosterman, "Why Are Boys More Likely to Be Referred to Juvenile Court? Gender Differences in Official and Self-Reported Delinquency," *Victims and Offenders* 5 (2010), pp. 25–44.

27. David P. Farrington, Rolf Loeber, Magda Stouthamer-Loeber, Welmoet B. Van Kammen, and Laura Schmidt, "Self-Reported Delinquency and a Combined Delinquency Seriousness Scale Based on Boys, Mothers, and Teachers: Concurrent and Predictive Validity for African Americans and Caucasians," *Criminology* 34 (November 1996), pp. 493–517.

28. Kathleen Mullan Harris, *National Longitudinal Study of Adolescent Health* (Chapel Hill: University of North Carolina, 2011).

29. Alex R. Piquero and Robert W. Brame, "Assessing the Race-Crime and Ethnicity-Crime Relationship in a Sample of Serious Adolescent Delinquents," *Crime and Delinquency* 20 (2008), pp. 1–33.

30. Harris, *National Longitudinal Study of Adolescent Health*.

31. Joanne M. Kaufman, "Explaining the Race/Ethnicity-Violence Relationship: Neighborhood Context and Psychological Processes," *Justice Quarterly* 22 (June 2005), pp. 224–51.

32. Michael Rocques and Raymond Paternoster, "Understanding the Antecedents of the 'School-to-Jail' Link: The Relationship between Race and School Discipline," *Journal of Criminal Law and Criminology* 101, no. 2 (2011), pp. 633–55.

33. Michael O'Hear, *Life Sentences Blog*, http://www .lifesentencesblog.com/?p=4043 (accessed June 14, 2011).

34. Rocques and Paternoster, "Understanding the Antecedents of the 'School-To-Jail' Link.

35. Ruth D. Peterson, "The Central Place of Race in Crime and Justice—The American Society of Criminology 2011 Sutherland Address," *Criminology* 50 (2012), pp. 303–27. See also Ruth D. Peterson and Lauren J. Krivo, *Divergent Social Worlds: Neighborhood Crime and the Racial-Spatial Divide* (New York: Russell Sage Foundation, 2010).

36. Charles Tittle, Wayne Villemez, and Douglas Smith, "The Myth of Social Class and Criminality: An Empirical Assessment of the Empirical Evidence," *American Sociological Review* 43 (1978), pp. 643–56.

37. Suzanne S. Ageton and Delbert S. Elliott, *The Incidence of Delinquent Behavior in a National Probability Sample of Adolescents* (Boulder, Colo.: Behavioral Research Institute, 1978).

38. Delbert Elliott and David Huizinga, "Social Class and Delinquent Behavior in a National Youth Panel," *Criminology* 21 (May 1983), pp. 149–77. For a discussion about whether different definitions of class are likely to produce different results on social class and delinquency, see Margaret Farnworth, Terence P. Thornberry, Alan J. Lizotte, and Marvin D. Krohn, *Social Background and the Early Onset of Delinquency: Exploring the Utility of Various Indicators of Social Class Background* (Albany, N.Y.: Rochester Youth Development Study, June 1990).

39. Gregory M. Zimmerman and Bob Edward Vasquez, "Decomposing the Peer Effect on Adolescent Substance Use: Mediation, Nonlinearity, and Differential Nonlinearity," *Criminology* 49 (November 2011), p. 1236.

40. Ibid.

41. Travis Hirschi, *Causes of Delinquency* (Berkeley: University of California Press, 1960), p. 141.

42. Peggy C. Giordano, Robert A. Lonardo, Wendy D. Manning, and Monica A. Llongmore, "Adolescent Romance and Delinquency: A Further Exploration of Hirschi's 'Cold and Brittle' Relationships Hypothesis," *Criminology* 48 (November 2010), pp. 919–46.

43. Jeffrey A. Butts, *Beyond the Tunnel Problem: Addressing Cross-Cutting Issues That Impact Vulnerable Youth* (Chicago: University of Chicago, Chapin Hall Center for Children, 2008).

44. White House Task Force for Disadvantaged Youth, *Final Report*, October 2003, p. 11.

45. Melvin Delgado, *New Frontiers for Youth Development in the Twenty-First Century* (New York: Columbia University Press, 2002), p. 164. Reprinted with permission of the publisher.

46. Howard N. Snyder and Melissa Sickmund, *Juvenile Justice and Victims: 2006 National Report* (Washington, D.C.: U.S. Department of Justice Programs, Office of Juvenile Justice and Delinquency Prevention, 2006).

47. For a listing of some of this longitudinal research, see David P. Farrington, *Integrated Developmental Life-Course Theories of Offending: Advances in Criminological Theory* (New Brunswick and London: Transaction Publishers, 2005), pp. 3–4.

48. Lila Kazemian and David P. Farrington, "Comparing the Validity of Prospective, Retrospective, and Official Onset for Different Offending Categories," *Journal of Quantitative Criminology* 21 (June 2005), pp. 224–51.

49. Kevin W. Alltucker, Michael Bullis, Daniel Close, and Paul Yovanoff, "Different Pathways to Juvenile Delinquency: Characteristics of Early and Late Starters in a Sample of Previously Incarcerated Youth," *Journal of Child and Family Studies* 15 (August 2006), pp. 479–92.

50. R. Loeber, D. P. Farrington, and D. Peterchuk, *Child Delinquency: Early Intervention and Prevention*, Child Development Bulletin Series (Washington, D.C.: Office of Juvenile Justice and Delinquency Prevention, 2003).

51. T. Moffitt, A. Caspi, M. Rutter, and P. A. Silva, *Sex Differences in Antisocial Behavior* (Cambridge, England: Cambridge University Press, 2001), p. 83.

52. Rolf Loeber, Magda Stouthamer-Loeber, Welmoet Van Kammen, and David P. Farrington, "Initiation, Escalation and Desistance in Juvenile Offending and Their Correlates," *Journal of Criminal Law and Criminology* 82 (1991), pp. 36–82.

53. Rolf Loeber, Phen Wung, Kate Keenan, Bruce Giroux, Magda Stouthamer-Loeber, and Welmoet B. Van Kammen, "Developmental Pathways in Disruptive Child Behavior," *Development and Psychopathology* 5 (Winter–Spring, 1993), pp. 103–33.

54. See Barbara Tatem Kelley, Rolf Loeber, Kate Keenan, and Mary DeLamatre, *Developmental Pathways in Boys' Disruptive and Delinquent Behavior* (Washington, D.C.: Office of Juvenile Justice and Delinquency Prevention, 1997).

55. Alex R. Piquero, Leah E. Daigle, Chris Gibson, Nicole Leeper Piquero, and Stephen G. Tibbetts, "Are Life-Course-Persistent Offenders at Risk for Adverse Health Outcomes?" *Journal of Research in Crime and Delinquency* 44 (May 2007), pp. 186–207.

56. Paul Mazerolle, Robert Brame, Ray Paternoster, Alex Piquero, and Charles Dean, "Onset Age, Persistence, and Offending Versatility: Comparisons across Gender," *Criminology* 38 (November 2000), pp. 1143–172.

57. Glenn Deanne, David P. Armstrong, and Richard B. Felson, "An Examination of Offense Specialization Using Marginal Logit Models," *Criminology* 43 (November 2005), pp. 955–88.

58. D. Wayne Osgood and Christopher J. Schreck, "A New Method of Studying the Extent, Stability, and Predictors of Individual Specialization in Violence," *Criminology* 45 (2007), pp. 273–312.

59. For an investigation of gang involvement in crack cocaine sales, see Malcolm W. Klein, Cheryl L. Maxson, and Lea C. Cunningham, "'Crack,' Street Gangs, and Violence," *Criminology* 29 (1991), pp. 623–50.

60. Alfred Blumstein, David P. Farrington, and Soumyo Moitra, "Delinquency Careers, Innocents, Desisters, and Persisters," in *Crime and Justice: An Annual Review*, 6th ed., edited by Michael Tonry and Norval Morris (Chicago: University of Chicago Press, 1985), pp. 187–220.

61. Lila Kazemian and David P. Farrington, "Exploring Residual Career Length and Residual Number of Offenses for Two

Generations of Repeat Offenders," *Journal of Research in Crime and Delinquency* 47 (February 2006), pp. 89–113.

62. Nadine Lanctot, Stephen A. Cernkovich, and Peggy C. Giordano, "Delinquent Behavior, Official Delinquency, and Gender: Consequences for Adulthood Functioning and Well-Being," *Criminology* 45 (2007), pp. 191–222. See also Michael Massoglia, "Desistance or Displacement? The Changing Patterns of Offending from Adolescence to Young Adulthood," *Journal of Quantitative Criminology* 22 (2006), pp. 215–29.

63. Michael Gottfredson and Travis Hirschi, *A General Theory of Crime* (Palo Alto, Calif.: Stanford University Press, 1990), p. 107.

64. Daniel S. Nagin and Raymond Paternoster, "On the Relationship of the Past to Future Delinquency," *Criminology* 29 (May 1991), p. 165.

65. Robert J. Sampson and John H. Laub, *Crime in the Making: Pathways and Turning Points through Life* (Cambridge, Mass.: Harvard University Press, 1993). For further support of life-course theory, see Ronald L. Simons, Christine Johnson, Rand D. Conger, and Glen Elder, Jr., "A Test of Latent Trait versus Life-Course Perspectives on the Stability of Adolescent Antisocial Behavior," *Criminology* 36 (May 1998), pp. 217–43.

66. John H. Laub and Robert J. Sampson, "Turning Points in the Life Course: Why Change Matters to the Study of Crime," *Criminology* 31 (August 1993), pp. 301–20.

67. Brian Francis, Keith Soohill, and Alex R. Piquero, "Estimation Issues and Generational Changes in Modeling Criminal Career Length," *Crime and Delinquency* 53 (January 2007), pp. 84–107. See also Michael E. Ezell, "Examining the Overall and Offense-Specific Criminal Career Lengths of a Sample of Serious Offenders," *Crime and Delinquency* 53 (January 2007), pp. 3–37; Rudy Haapanen, Lee Britton,

and Tim Croisdale, "Persistent Criminality and Career Length," *Crime and Delinquency* 53 (January 2007), pp. 133–55; and Lili Kazemian and Marc Le Blanc, "Differential Cost Avoidance and Successful Criminal Careers: Random or Rational?" *Crime and Delinquency* 53 (January 2007), pp. 38–63.

68. A. Piquero, R. Brame, and D. Lynam, "Studying Criminal Career Length through Early Adulthood among Serious Offenders," *Crime and Delinquency* 50 (2004), pp. 412–35.

69. Ezell, "Examining the Overall and Offense-Specific Criminal Career Lengths."

70. For more discussion on these issues, see David P. Farrington, "Introduction to Integrated Developmental and Life-Course Theories of Offending," in *Integrated Developmental Life-Course Theories of Offending*, pp. 1–14.

71. Alan J. Lizotte, Marvin D. Krohn, James C. Howell, Kimberly Tobin, and Gregory J. Howard, "Factors Influencing Gun Carrying among Young Urban Males over the Adolescent–Young Adult Life Course," *Criminology* 38 (2000), pp. 811–34; Philip J. Cook and Jens Ludwig, "Does Gun Prevalence Affect Teen Gun Carrying after All?" *Criminology* 42 (2004), pp. 27–54; and Anthony A. Braga, "Serious Youth Gun Offenders and the Epidemic of Youth Violence in Boston," *Journal of Quantitative Criminology* 19 (March 2003), pp. 33–54.

72. Ibid.

73. David M. Kennedy, Anthony A. Braga, and Anne M. Piehl, *Reducing Gun Violence: The Boston Gun Project's Operation Ceasefire* (Washington, D.C.: National Institute of Justice, 2001).

74. Office of Juvenile Justice and Delinquency Prevention, *Partnerships to Reduce Youth Gun Violence Programs*, "http://www.ojjdp.gov/pubs/96kit/juvgunvi.htm (accessed December 23, 2012).

Chapter Objectives

After reading this chapter, you should be able to:

1. Describe the theoretical constructs of the classical school of criminology.

2. Describe the concept of rationality of crime as well as its limitations.

3. Summarize how different forms of positivism explain delinquency.

4. Explain how sociobiology links delinquency to certain biological and environmental factors.

5. Summarize various psychological theories of delinquency.

6. Compare the important developmental studies of delinquency.

7. Describe the different explanations for desistance from crime.

America's best hope for reducing crime is to reduce juvenile delinquency and youth crime.

—President's Commission on Law Enforcement and Administration of Justice, 1967

Introduction

A few years ago, researchers at Shippensburg University in Pennsylvania released results of a study showing that unpopular first names are frequently associated with juvenile delinquency for children of all races.[1] The researchers concluded that unpopular names are probably not the direct cause of crime but are instead correlated with socioeconomic factors that increase the tendency toward juvenile delinquency, such as a disadvantaged home environment, low income, place of residence, and acquisition of cultural values supportive of delinquency. At the same time, it is possible to imagine that some people are unconsciously influenced by the need to live up to their name. The study's authors reviewed other literature that showed that job applicants with certain first names were more likely to receive calls back from potential employers, even when their skills and other qualifying attributes were similar to those of other job candidates. The authors suggested that juveniles with unpopular names may be treated differently by their peers, making it more difficult for them to form positive relationships and that they may turn to crime or delinquency when their names result in a negative employment bias. Finally, as noted by the study authors, their findings have "potential implications for identifying … who may engage in disruptive behavior or relapse into criminal behavior."[2]

In this chapter we offer some possible explanations for delinquent behavior. In contrast to the unconscious influence exerted by unpopular first names, described in this chapter's opening story, some authors suggest that much delinquency is caused not by factors beyond the offender's control but by a conscious thought process that considers the costs and benefits of particular behavior and with some degree of planning and foresight goes on to reason whether the behavior is desirable or not.[3]

On the other hand, if something as simple as a first name can impact people's behavior, then they might not be able to make fully conscious choices. This kind of deterministic view—that delinquents cannot stop themselves from committing socially unacceptable behavior because of some overpowering influences—builds on a perspective known as **positivism**, a major theoretical position in criminology.

A third explanation discussed in this chapter highlights the significance of developmental theories. A developmental approach suggests that while some young people have the opportunity to learn how to act legally and morally, others do not. In such cases, the effects of life circumstances and a lack of moral development can place adolescents on a trajectory with tragic consequences.

positivism
The view that just as laws operate in the medical, biological, and physical sciences, laws govern human behavior and these laws can be understood and used.

social contract
An unstated or explicit agreement between a people and their government as to the rights and obligations of each.

▲ High school students in Mission Viejo, California, fill out applications at a community college recruiting fair. Rational choice approaches to explaining delinquency claim that juvenile offenders are active, rational decision makers who respond to the incentives and deterrents they encounter.

■ **What implications might rational choice theory have for delinquency prevention and control?**

Classical School and Delinquency

The association between criminal behavior and the rationality of crime has roots in the eighteenth-century classical school of criminology. This school's founders were Charles de Secondat, Baron de Montesquieu; Cesare Bonesana, Marquis of Beccaria; and Jeremy Bentham. These thinkers viewed humans as rational creatures who are willing to surrender enough liberty to the state so that society can establish rules and sanctions for the preservation of the social order[4]:

- *Montesquieu.* In Baron Charles-Louis Montesquieu's 1747 book, *On the Spirit of the Laws,* he argued that "the severity of punishment is fitter for despotic governments whose principle is terror, than for a monarchy or a republic whose strength is honor and virtue." Montesquieu added that under a moderate government "the love of one's country, shame and the fear of blame, are restraining motives, capable of preventing a great multitude of crimes."[5] Montesquieu added that under a moderate and lenient government, "the greatest punishment of a bad action is conviction."[6]

- *Beccaria.* In 1764, Cesare Bonesana, Marquis of Beccaria (formally known as Cesare Beccaria), published *On Crimes and Punishments.* Beccaria based the legitimacy of criminal sanctions on the **social contract**. Beccaria saw punishment as a necessary evil and suggested that "it should be public, immediate, and necessary; the least possible in the case given; proportioned to the crime; and determined by the laws."[7] He then defined the purpose and consequences of punishment as being "to deter persons from the commission of crime and not to provide social revenge. Not severity, but certainty and swiftness in punishment best secure this result."[8]

• *Bentham.* In 1780, the Englishman Jeremy Bentham published *An Introduction to the Principles of Morals and Legislation*, which further developed the philosophy of the classical school. Believing that a rational person would do what was necessary to achieve the most pleasure and the least pain, Bentham contended that punishment would deter criminal behavior, provided it was made appropriate to the crime. He stated that punishment has four objectives: (1) to prevent all offenses if possible; (2) to persuade a person who has decided to offend to commit a less rather than a more serious offense; (3) "to dispose [a person who has resolved on a particular offense] to do no more mischief than is necessary to his purpose"; and (4) to prevent crime at as cheap a cost to society as possible.[9]

See Figure 3–1 for an overview of the founders of the classical school and their principles. Figure 3–2 outlines the basic theoretical constructs of the classical school of criminology.

According to the principles of the classical school, juveniles who commit serious crimes or continue to break the law are presumed to deserve punishment rather than treatment because they possess free will and know what they are doing. Proponents of the classical school view delinquency as purposeful activity resulting from rational decisions in which offenders weigh the pros and cons and perform the acts that promise the greatest potential gains.[10]

Rationality of Crime

Library Extra 3–1
Rational Choice Theory

In the 1970s and 1980s, workers in a variety of academic disciplines, including the sociology of deviance, criminology, economics, and cognitive psychology, began to view crime as the outcome of rational choices and decisions. The ecological tradition in criminology and the economic theory of markets, especially, have applied the notion of rational choice to crime. Ecological researchers have inferred from the distribution of particular crimes that offenders make rational choices. For example, findings from several studies have revealed that homes on the borderline of affluent districts are at most risk of burglary.[11]

Economic analysis of criminal behavior argues that criminals, like noncriminals, are active, rational decision makers who respond to incentives and deterrents. In economic models of criminal decision making, crime is assumed to involve rational calculation and is viewed essentially as an economic transaction or a question of occupational choice.[12]

Rational Choice Theory

Rational choice theory, borrowed primarily from the utility model in economics, is one of the hottest topics today in criminology, sociology, political science, and law.[13] It is based on the assumption that the delinquent or the criminal chooses to violate the law and has free will. Rational choice theory in its pure form can be seen, at least in part, as an extension

---

TIMELINE

1747	**1764**	**1780**
Charles de Secondat, Baron de Montesquieu argued against severe punishments for crime in his book, *On the Spirit of the Laws.*	**Cesare Bonesana, Marquis of Beccaria** developed notion of the social contract, and suggested that the purpose of punishment should be "to deter persons from the commission of crime and not to provide social revenge."	**Jeremy Bentham** contended that punishment would deter criminal behavior, provided it was made appropriate to the crime.

FIGURE 3–1
Founders of the Classical School

of the deterrence doctrine found in the classical school, which includes incentives as well as disincentives and focuses on individuals' rational calculations of payoffs and costs before delinquent and criminal acts are committed. [14]

In a contribution to rational choice theory, some years ago Raymond Paternoster presented what he called a "deterrence/ rational choice model" to examine a youth's decision to participate in, continue with, or desist from delinquent acts. Rational choice, according to Paternoster, recognizes that there are "choice-structuring" variables and that choices do not require complete information or rational analytic methods.[15] Similarly, in 2011 Carnegie Mellon University professor Shamena Aniwar and University of Maryland professor Thomas Loughran found, in their test of a learning theory of deterrence among serious juvenile offenders, that individuals will tend to increase the accuracy of their risk perceptions over time in response to cues they receive during their offending experiences.[16]

Recently, Jeffrey Fagan and Alex R. Piquero showed that both legal socialization and rational choice factors influence patterns of criminal offending over time. When punishment risks and costs increase, crime rates are lower over time. This study also shows that both developmental maturity and mental health moderate the effects of perceived crime risks and costs on criminal offending.[17]

The Routine Activities Approach

Another approach to the rationality of crime is the **routine activities approach**. This approach links variations in crime rates to changes in the routine activity structure of U.S. society, and to a corresponding increase in target suitability and a decrease in the presence of "guardians" such as neighbors, friends, and family. For example, the decline of the presence of daytime adult caretakers in homes and neighborhoods, which is partly the result of a trend toward increased female participation in the labor force, has left homes and neighborhoods increasingly vulnerable to criminal activity. Some of the most important studies contributing to the routine activities literature include the following theorists and their findings:

- Lawrence E. Cohen and Marcus Felson, guided by ecological concepts and the presumed rationality of offenders, developed a routine activities approach for analyzing crime rate trends and cycles. They believed that the volume and distribution of predatory crime are related to the interaction of three variables relating to the routine activities of life in the United States: (1) the availability of suitable targets, (2) the absence of capable guardians, and (3) the presence of motivated offenders.[18]

- Wayne Osgood and Amy Anderson were able to link the routine activities perspective to key themes of social disorganization theory. In their analysis of 4,358 eighth-grade students from thirty-six schools in ten cities, they found that time spent in unstructured informal socializing with peers explains a large share of variations in rates of delinquency among adolescents who attend different schools.[19]

- A 2010 study by Katherine Novak and Lizabeth Crawford examined the extent to which gender differences in delinquency can be explained by gender differences in participation in various routine activity patterns. While differential participation in routine activities by gender failed to explain males' high levels of deviance relative to females, participation in religious and community activities during the sophomore year in high school seemed to moderate the effect of gender on subsequent deviant behavior.[20]

Table 3–1 provides an explanation of rational choice and routine activities theories or approaches.

Theoretical Constructs of the Classical School of Criminology

- Human beings are seen as rational creatures who, being free to choose their actions, could be held responsible for their behavior. This doctrine of **free will** was substituted for what had been previously the widely accepted concept of theological determinism, which saw humans as predestined to certain actions.

- Punishment is justified because of its practical usefulness, or utility. No longer was punishment acceptable for purposes of vengeful retaliation or as expiation on the basis of superstitious theories of guilt and repayment. According to **utilitarianism**, the aim of punishment is the protection of society, and the dominant theme is deterrence.

- The classical school sees the human being as a creature governed by a **felicific calculus**—an orientation toward obtaining a favorable balance of pleasure and pain.

- There should be a rational scale of punishment painful enough to deter the criminal from further offenses and to prevent others from following his or her negative example.

- Sanctions should be proclaimed in advance of their use; these sanctions should be proportionate to the offense and should outweigh the rewards of crime.

- Equal justice should be available to everyone.

- Individuals should be judged by the law solely for their acts, not for their beliefs.

FIGURE 3–2
Theoretical Constructs of the Classical School of Criminology

free will
The ability to make rational choices among possible actions and to select one over the others.

utilitarianism
A doctrine that holds that what is useful is good and that the aim of social or political action should be the greatest good for the greatest number.

felicific calculus
A method for determining the sum total of pleasure and pain produced by an act; also the assumption that human beings strive to obtain a favorable balance of pleasure and pain.

routine activities approach
The contention that crime rate trends and cycles are related to the nature of everyday patterns of social interaction that characterize the society in which they occur.

TABLE 3–1
Rational Choice and Routine Activities Approaches

Perspective	Theorist(s)	Principle(s)
Rational choice	Paternoster	Rational choice does not require complete information for behavior to occur.
Rational choice	Aniwar and Loughran	Individuals will update their risk perceptions over time according to the feedback they receive during offending experiences.
Rational choice	Fagan and Piquero	They found that when punishment risks and costs increase, crime rates are lower over time.
Routine activities	Cohen and Felson	The availability of targets, absence of capable guardians, and presence of motivated offenders reflect the routine activities of life and contribute to the rise of predatory crime.
Routine activities	Osgood and Anderson	Time spent in unstructured activities with peers explains a large share of the variations in rates of delinquency among adolescents, even among those who attend different schools.
Routine activities	Novak and Crawford	Participation in religious and community activities moderated girls subsequent deviant behavior.

Rational Choice and Delinquency

Some youthful offenders clearly engage in delinquent behavior because of what they see as the low risk of such behavior. Hence, much delinquency can be interpreted as a form of problem-solving behavior in response to the pressures of adolescence. Finding themselves struggling with issues of perceived control, seeking positive self-evaluation, and facing the negative impact of others who punish, sanction, or reject them, delinquents solve such problems by deriving short-term pleasures from delinquent involvements.[21] Conversely, offenders also may decide on rational grounds that the risks of continued delinquent behavior are not justified by the rewards. Even more to the point, most persistent offenders appear to desist from crime as they reach their late teens or early twenties, claiming that continued criminality is incompatible with the demands of holding a full-time job or settling down to marriage and a family. Desistance from crime, or maturing out of crime, is a process of deciding that the benefits of crime are less than the advantages of ceasing to commit crime.[22]

Yet important issues arise when assuming too much rationality in delinquent behavior. Rational choice theory is based on the notion that delinquent behavior is planned—at least to some degree. Planning has to do both with (1) formulating a scheme or a procedure for doing something before doing it or having an intention of acting and (2) assessing the possible alternative courses of actions available, choosing a particular course, and constructing a complex set of acts to achieve the intended results. But many studies of delinquency have reported that most delinquent behavior is not planned; spur-of-the-moment decision making most frequently characterizes juvenile wrongdoing.[23]

The concept of rationality also assumes that individuals have free will and are not controlled by their emotions, but many youngsters do not appear to have such control. Youths who are mentally ill or who engage in obsessive-compulsive acts, such as compulsive arsonists, kleptomaniacs, or sex offenders, seem to be held in bondage by their emotions. Furthermore, in examining the actual process of rational choice, it is apparent that there are degrees of freedom for all juveniles and that juveniles' rationality is contextually oriented. The notion of degrees of freedom suggests, then, that delinquents "are neither wholly free nor completely constrained but fall somewhere between."[24] Because the ability to make rational decisions and to act on them depends to a considerable degree on the social situation, delinquents do have some control over their actions in some situations, but in others they may have little or no control.

Emory University professor Robert Agnew's examination of hard and soft **determinism** led him to conclude that freedom of choice varies from one individual to another. It is dependent, he said, on factors—such as one's biological, psychological, or social nature—that exist prior to choices that arise. For example, one individual may be forced to choose between two different alternatives because of psychological limits, but another may have six different alternatives available to him or to her because that person is less limited in his or her perceptions. The latter, Agnew says, has greater freedom of choice.[25]

—determinism
A philosophical position that suggests that individuals are driven into delinquent or criminal behavior by biological or psychological traits that are beyond their control.

Positivism and Delinquency

This section examines perspectives such as biological and psychological positivism to see how they might enhance our understanding of why delinquent behavior occurs. Instead of viewing delinquency as a logical choice from among an available set of alternative behaviors, as rational choice theorists do, positivists argue that the social world operates according to laws or rules like the physical world. Hence, according to positivism, delinquents are affected by biological or psychological factors that (1) impair or alter their decision-making abilities and (2) can be identified through the use of social scientific techniques.

Positivism became the dominant philosophical perspective of juvenile justice about the same time that the juvenile court was established at the end of the nineteenth century. During the **Progressive era** (the period from about 1890 to 1920), the wave of optimism that swept through U.S. society led to the acceptance of positivism, or a social scientific approach, to social problems. The doctrines of the emerging social sciences led reformers to believe that social problems could be solved through the application of positivistic principles. The initial step was to gather all the facts of the case; equipped with these data, reformers then expected to analyze the issues in scientific fashion and discover appropriate solutions.[26]

Armed with a positivistic approach, social reformers of the early twentieth century set out to deal with the problem of delinquency, confident that they knew how to find its cause. Some progressives looked first to environmental factors, pinpointing poverty as a major cause of delinquency. Other positivists were attracted to the doctrine of eugenics, and believed that certain biological features drove youthful offenders to delinquency. But eventually the psychological origins of delinquency came to be more widely accepted than either the environmental or biological perspectives. The positivist approach to youth crime is based on three basic assumptions, as Figure 3–3 shows.[27]

Biological, sociological, and psychological positivism are the three types of positivism that have been used to explain delinquency. Each is reviewed in the following sections.

Voices of Delinquency 3–1
Read "The Thinker." This is the story of a fifteen-year-old who, with his brother, committed a vicious murder. How much rationality do you believe affected his brief life of crime? To what extent did his life of abuse, family disruption, and peers affect his rational choice?

Video 3–1 Positivism

progressive era
The period from around 1890 to 1920, when a wave of optimism swept through American society and led to the acceptance of positivism.

biological positivism
The belief that juveniles' biological characteristics and limitations drive them to delinquent behavior.

Early Forms of Biological Positivism

The belief in a biological explanation for criminality has a long history. For example, the study of physiognomy, which attempts to discern personal inner qualities through outward physical appearance, was developed by the ancient Greeks. Indeed, a physiognomist of that period charged that Socrates' face reflected a brutal nature.[28]

The attention given to **biological positivism** in the United States may be divided into two periods. The first period was characterized by (1) the nature–nurture debate during the latter part of the nineteenth century and the early twentieth century and (2) the influence of Italian criminologist Cesare Lombroso's late-nineteenth-century theory of physical anomalies, genealogical studies, and related theories of human somatotypes (body types), which represent early approaches that related crime and delinquency to biological factors.

🛡 Three Assumptions of the Positivist Approach

- The character and personal backgrounds of individuals explain delinquent behavior. Positivism, relegating the law and its administration to a secondary role, looks for the cause of deviancy in the actor.

- The existence of determinism is a critical assumption of positivism. Delinquency, like any other phenomenon, is seen as determined by prior causes—it does not just happen. Because of this deterministic position, positivism rejects the view that the individual exercises freedom, possesses reason, and is capable of choice.

- The delinquent is fundamentally different from the nondelinquent, so the task is to identify the factors that have made the delinquent a different kind of person. In attempting to explain this difference, positivism concluded that wayward youths are driven into crime by something in their physical makeup, by aberrant psychological impulses, or by the meanness and harshness of their social environment.

FIGURE 3–3
Three Assumptions of the Positivist Approach

Source: Adapted from Donald C. Gibbons, "Differential Treatment of Delinquents and Interpersonal Maturity Level: A Critique," *Social Services Review* 44 (1970), pp. 22–33.

born criminal
An individual who is atavistic, who reverts to an earlier evolutionary level and is unable to conform his or her behavior to the requirements of modern society; thus, an individual who is innately criminal.

Frequently regarded as the founder of biological positivism, Lombroso is best known for his theory of the atavistic criminal. According to Lombroso, the **born criminal** was atavistic; that is, he is someone who reverts to an earlier evolutionary form or level. Atavistic individuals, according to Lombroso, displayed the primitive characteristics of men and women in earlier evolutionary periods. Such characteristics, Lombroso said, would periodically reappear in certain individuals, leading them to crime because of the primitive impulses that they were also likely to possess.[29]

Around the same time, prominent American psychologist and eugenicist Henry Goddard found that at least half of all juvenile delinquents he studied were mentally defective. His findings sparked intense debate for more than a decade,[30] but conflicted with those of American criminologist Edwin Sutherland who soon discouraged future investigations of the correlation between intelligence and delinquency.[31] Sutherland, in evaluating IQ studies of delinquents and criminals, concluded that the lower IQs of offenders were related more to testing methods and scoring than to the offenders' actual mental abilities.[32]

Finally, German medical researcher Ernst Kretschmer advanced the idea that there are two body types: the schizothyme and the cyclothyme. Schizothymes were said to be strong and muscular and, according to Kretschmer, they were more likely to be delinquent than were cyclothymes, who were soft-skinned and lacked muscle.[33]

Other famous social researchers of the early 1900s, such as Americans William Sheldon,[34] Sheldon Glueck and Eleanor Glueck,[35] and Juan B. Cortes and Florence M. Gatti, also supported body-type theory. Cortes and Gatti even drew on body-type theory to develop an extensive biopsychosocial theory of delinquency.[36]

sociobiology
An expression of biological positivism that stresses the interaction between biological factors within an individual and the influence of the person's particular environment; also the systematic study of the biological basis of all social behavior.

Library Extra 3–2
DNA and Behavior: Is Our Fate in Our Genes?

Contemporary Biological Positivism: Sociobiology

Central to the second period of biological positivism was **sociobiology**, which stresses the interaction between the biological factors within an individual and the influence of the particular environment. Supporters of this form of biological positivism claim that what produces delinquent behavior, like other behaviors, is a combination of genetic traits and social conditions.[37]

Sociological research has examined the influence of environment and genetics through twin and adoption studies and has also addressed intelligence; neuropsychological factors, including brain functioning and temperament as well as learning disabilities; and biochemical factors in delinquency. Let's look at each of these areas of investigation.

Twin and Adoption Studies

The role of genetic influences on behavior has been suggested by numerous twin and adoption studies.[38] These studies were supported early on by research done in Denmark and other European countries, but more recently they have found support among researchers in the United States.

Twin Studies

The comparison of identical twins (monozygotic [MZ]) with same-sex nonidentical, or fraternal, twins (dizygotic [DZ]) provides the most comprehensive data for exploring genetic influences on human variation. Identical twins develop from a single fertilized egg that divides into two embryos; hence, their genes are the same. Fraternal twins develop from two separate eggs that were both fertilized during the act of conception, so about half their genes are the same.[39]

A number of twin studies have found support for genetic contributions to criminal behavior. In one such early study, whose results were published in 1955, Scandinavian social scientist Karl O. Christiansen and University of Southern California professor S. A. Mednick reported on a sample of 3,586 twin pairs from Denmark who were followed between the years 1870 and 1920. The subset used by these researchers included almost all the twins born between 1881 and 1910 in a certain region of Denmark. An examination of criminal justice statistics for the period turned up 926 offenses involving the 7,172 twins, coming

▲ The infamous Kray twins, English gangsters Ronald and Reginald Kray, committed many crimes during the 1960s throughout the United Kingdom. They are shown with Francis Shae, at her wedding to Reggie. Genealogical studies seem to say that a predilection for various types of behavior, including delinquency, might have at least a partial genetic basis.

■ **What implications might such theories have for controlling delinquency?**

from 799 twin pairs. Although the concordance rates (i.e., frequency of both twins showing the same trait) in this study were lower than in earlier surveys, they were still significant and indicated a genetic contribution to criminal behavior.[40]

Almost twenty years later, Thomas Bouchard, Jr., director of the Minnesota Center for Twin and Adoption Research at the University of Minnesota, examined three large data sets to assess the heritability of five basic personality traits: extroversion, neuroticism, agreeableness, conscientiousness, and openness.[41] Bouchard concluded, "The similarity we see in the personality between biological relatives is almost entirely genetic in origin."[42]

In 2003, a study of 3,853 twin pairs undertaken by Dutch researcher M. J. H. Rietveld and colleagues found that shared environment, which is usually conceived of as the family environment, had little effect on a child's level of overactivity.[43] This study of twins, drawn from the Netherlands Twin Registry, suggests that attention problems are due more to genetic factors than to environmental influences. The study adds weight to the literature supporting a significant role for genetic factors as determinants of human behavior.[44]

In 2009, an analysis of data taken from the Minnesota Twin Family Study of twins raised apart from each other found that identical (MZ) twin children have similar brain wave patterns, become more similar in terms of abilities (arithmetic scores and vocabularies), and tend to die at about the same age. Fraternal twins become less similar in terms of abilities as they age, do not show as much similarity in brain wave patterns, and they are likely to die at different ages.[45]

Adoption Studies

The largest systematic adoption study of criminality examined all nonfamilial adoptions in Denmark from 1924 to 1947, a sample that included 14,427 male and female adoptees and their biological and adoptive parents. In that study, Danish researcher Karl O. Christiansen concluded that criminality of the biological parents is more important than that of the adoptive parents in predicting a child's propensity to offend, a finding that suggests genetic transmission of some factor or factors associated with crime.[46]

In sum, the evidence from these and other studies of twins and adoptees is impressive. However, the twin method does have a number of weaknesses. The differences in MZ and DZ twin similarities tell us about genetic involvement only to the extent that the MZ–DZ difference is not related to environmental differences; also, the small number of twin pairs makes adequate statistical comparisons difficult. Further, it is not always easy to determine if twins are monozygotic or dizygotic. Finally, official definitions of crime and delinquency, with all their limitations, are exclusively used.[47]

Intelligence

With the growing acceptance of sociobiology in the 1960s and 1970s, researchers again turned their attention to intelligence as a possible factor in delinquent behavior. A number of studies have been done, including one by sociologist Robert A. Gordon, who compared delinquency prevalence rates and delinquency incidence rates, and concluded that minority juvenile males had higher arrest rates and court appearance rates than white males or females regardless of any specific geographic location, rural or urban. Gordon proposed that differences in IQ might provide the strongest explanation of these persistent differences in unlawful behavior.[48] In another paper, Gordon stated that "[lower] IQ was always more successful in accounting for the black–white differences [in crime] than income, education, or occupational status."[49]

Travis Hirschi and Michael Hindelang reexamined three research studies—including earlier data gathered by Hirschi from California, Marvin Wolfgang and associates' Philadelphia data, and Joseph Weis's data from the state of Washington—and found that "the weight of evidence is that IQ is more important than race and social class" in predicting delinquency.[50] These researchers also rejected the contention that IQ tests are race and class biased, and said that such tests did not favor middle-class whites youth over minorities. They concluded that low IQ, independent of race and ethnicity, affects school performance, resulting in an increased likelihood of delinquent behavior.[51]

In 2011 Tom Kennedy, Kent Burnett, and William Edmonds examined a population of juvenile offenders in order to identify which were more likely to be incarcerated for violent versus nonviolent offenses. They found that lower verbal intelligence, specifically reading ability as measured by school achievement tests, correlates strongly with offender status and can be used to correctly classify violent offenders.[52]

A recent study by Roos Koolhof, Rolf Loeber, Evelyn Wei, Dustin Pardini, and Annematt Collot D'Escury found that seriously delinquent boys are generally impulsive, but the higher IQ serious delinquents seem to have better cognitive control systems. This study concluded that interventions aimed at boys with low IQs should focus on the remediation of behavioral impulsivity as well as cognitive impulsivity.[53]

Researchers today understand that whatever the correlation between IQ and delinquency may be, the association is further strengthened by environmental factors, such as the home environment, school performance, and peers.[54]

Neuropsychological Factors

Some neuropsychological factors appear to be more directly related to delinquent behavior than others, and some have received wider attention than others in various studies:

- The classic study by German-British psychologist Hans Eysenck on the **autonomic nervous system** has its origins in earlier attempts to understand the relationship between constitutional factors and delinquency. But Eysenck's sociobiological theory goes one step further by noting the interactions of both biological and environmental factors. Eysenck contended that some children are more difficult to condition morally than others because of the inherited sensitivity of their autonomic nervous system. He argued that individuals range from those in whom it is easy to excite conditioned reflexes and whose reflexes are difficult to inhibit, to those whose reflexes are difficult to condition and easy to extinguish. Yet the moral conditioning of the child, Eysenck said, also depends on the quality of the socialization the child receives within the family.[55]

- Ronald Simons and colleagues' study used longitudinal data from a sample of several hundred African American males and examined the manner in which variants in three genes—the 5 serotonin transporter gene (5-HTT), the dopamine receptor gene (DRD4), and the monoamine oxidase gene (MAOA)—modulate the effects of community and family adversity on adoption of the street code and aggression. They found that variants in any of these three genes made offenders more susceptible to the adoption of the street code and patterns of behavioral aggression.[56]

Brain Functioning and Temperament

A child's temperament is hard to define but can more easily be identified by the behaviors associated with it. Activity and emotionality are two of these behaviors. The term *activity* in this context refers to gross motor movements, such as moving the arms and legs, crawling, or walking.

It has been a standard finding that youth involved with juvenile court often suffer from mental health difficulties and disorders, and these mental health disorder have been a serious factor leading to the juvenile's delinquent behaviors and activities. Patricia Stoddard-Dare and colleagues' study investigated which specific mental health disorders predicted detention for serious or violent crimes, and they found that youth with attention deficit/hyperactivity disorder and conduct disorder diagnoses were significantly less likely to commit personal crimes and experience subsequent detention; in contrast, youth with bipolar diagnoses were significantly more likely.[57]

Children who exhibit an inordinate amount of movement compared with peers are sometimes labeled "hyperactive" or are said to have **attention deficit/hyperactivity disorder (ADHD)**. **Emotionality** ranges from very little reaction to intense emotional reactions that are out of control.

Library Extra 3–3
Problem Behaviors in Maltreated Children and Youth: Influential Child, Peer, and Caregiver Characteristics

autonomic nervous system
The system of nerves that govern reflexes, glands, the iris of the eye, and activities of interior organs that are not subject to voluntary control.

Library Extra 3–4
OJJDP Research Overview: *Juvenile Firesetting*

Attention Deficit/Hyperactivity Disorder (ADHD)
A cognitive disorder of childhood that can include inattention, distractibility, excessive activity, restlessness, noisiness, and impulsiveness.

emotionality
An aspect of temperament. It can range from a near absence of emotional response to intense, out-of-control emotional reactions.

▲ Two toddlers having a fight. Some research suggests that temperament, including tendencies toward aggression, has a biological basis.
■ **What implications might such theories have for controlling or preventing delinquency?**

FIGURE 3–4
Attention Deficit/Hyperactivity
Disorder—Impulsive Type

Attention Deficit-Hyperactivity Disorder—Impulsive Type

- Lacks attention to details or makes careless mistakes
- Fails to sustain attention
- Does not seem to listen
- Has difficulty following through on instructions
- Lacks organizational skills
- Does not care for tasks that require continuous mental effort
- Misplaces things
- Can be easily distracted
- Tends to be forgetful

AD/HD Predominantly Hyperactive—Impulsive Type: (AD/HD-HI)

- Squirms in chair or fidgets with hands or feet
- Has a problem remaining seated
- Climbs or runs about excessively
- Finds it difficult to quietly engage in activities
- Is hyperactive in his or her movements
- Talks excessively
- Has difficulty not blurting out answers before questions are completed
- Struggles to take turns or wait on others
- Frequently interrupts or intrudes upon the rights of others

The hyperactive child remains a temperamental mystery. This child's three behaviors are inattention (the child is easily distracted and does not want to listen), impulsivity (he or she shifts quickly from one activity to another), and excessive motor activity (he or she cannot sit still, runs about, is talkative and noisy). Educators note that children with ADHD have difficulty staying on task, sustaining academic achievement in the school setting, remaining cognitively organized, and maintaining control over their behavior.[58]

ADHD is the most common neurobehavioral disorder affecting children, with the condition impacting between 5 and 10 percent of the children in the United States.[59] One study showed that two-thirds of children with ADHD have at least one other condition, such as depression, anxiety, or learning disabilities.[60] There is also evidence that children with ADHD have other problem behaviors, in addition to those in school, and that these problem behaviors increase the likelihood that such youngsters will become involved in delinquent acts and perhaps even go on to adult crime.[61] Figure 3–4 provides additional information about ADHD.

Learning Disabilities

Some evidence points to a link between **learning disabilities (LDs)** and involvement in delinquency. LDs can affect people's "ability . . . either [to] interpret what they see and hear or to link information from different parts of the brain. These limitations can show up in many ways—as specific difficulties with spoken and written language, coordination, self-control, or attention. Such difficulties extend to schoolwork and can impede learning to read or write or to do math."[62]

An LD can be a lifelong condition that affects many parts of an individual's life: school or work, family life, daily routines, and even friendships and play. Some people have many overlapping LDs, while others may have a single isolated learning problem that has little impact on other areas of their lives. LDs can be divided into three broad categories:

1. Developmental speech and language disorders
2. Academic skills disorders

learning disability (LD)
A disorder in one or more of the basic psychological processes involved in understanding or using spoken or written language.

▲ Fighting is characteristic of children who have ADHD.

■ **What is likely to happen to such children as they grow up?**

3. Other (a catchall category including certain coordination disorders and learning handicaps not covered by the other classifications).[63]

The most common types of LDs are dyslexia, aphasia, and hyperkinesis. Dyslexia is expressed in reading problems, particularly the inability to interpret written symbols. Aphasia consists of speech difficulties, often resulting from both auditory and visual deficiencies. Hyperkinesis, frequently equated with hyperactivity, is excessive muscular movement.[64] The dominant explanations for the cause of an LD lie in organic or neurological disorders, including birth injury or anything contributing to premature birth, infant or childhood disease, head injury, or lack of proper health care or nutrition.[65]

A recent study examined the link between learning disabilities and delinquency. Social worker Karen Matta Oshima and colleagues, using empirical data from a Midwestern state, found that youths with disabilities had higher rates of juvenile court petitions than similar low-income peers.[66]

Although the link between LDs and delinquency is complex, the fact is that youngsters with LDs frequently do fail in school, and officials of the justice system seem to be influenced by this evidence of school failure in wanting to process them through the juvenile justice system.

Biochemical Factors

orthomolecular imbalance
A chemical imbalance in the body, resulting from poor nutrition, allergies, and exposure to lead and certain other substances, which is said to lead to delinquency.

Research has shown that some delinquent behavior can be attributed to an **orthomolecular imbalance** in the body or to brain toxicity. (The term *orthomolecular* refers to "chemical balance in the body.") Biochemists suggest that when normal functioning is affected by diet, pollutants, and/or genetic deficiencies such as allergies, abnormal deficits or excesses in molecular brain concentrations of certain substances can lead to various mental and behavioral problems, including delinquency.[67]

A 2011 study, for example, examined propensity for violence and identified early health risk factors that influence negative behavioral outcomes. They were found to include prenatal and postnatal nutrition, tobacco use during pregnancy, maternal depression, birth complications, traumatic brain injury, lead exposure, and child abuse. The framework developed by this emphasized the pre-perinatal and postnatal periods, when a child's development is crucial and the opportunity for behavioral and environmental modification is high.[68]

In sum, there is some support for the idea that chemical imbalances in the body, resulting from faulty nutrition, allergies, and lead, are related to delinquent behavior. At best, however, the link is very weak. Although faulty diet and vitamin deficiencies may affect how a juvenile feels, it does not necessarily follow that the adolescent will become involved in delinquent behavior.

Psychological Positivism

Library Extra 3–5
Greater Boston Physicians for Social Responsibility: *In Harm's Way: Toxic Threats to Child Development*

Some theories claim that juveniles commit delinquent acts because they have some underlying emotional problems or disturbances. According to these theories, juveniles may not have received adequate nurturing at home, and with that emotional deprivation, they find it difficult to function in social contexts, such as school, sports, or community activities. They may also feel depressed, angry, or alienated, and this can influence their becoming involved in drugs and alcohol, property crimes, or even violent crimes. Psychologists view these emotional behaviors, which exist across gender, race/ethnicity, and class, as ultimately more important than social factors in explaining delinquency. Thus, psychological positivism differs from both classical and contemporary biological positivism because its focus is more on the emotional makeup of the personality than on the biological nature of the individual. At first, psychoanalytic (Freudian) theory was widely used with delinquents, but more recently other behavioral and humanistic schools of psychology have been applied to the problem of youth crime.

Psychoanalytic Explanations

psychoanalytic theory
A theory based on Sigmund Freud's insights, which have helped to shape the handling of juvenile delinquents. They include these axioms: (1) The personality is made up of three components—id, ego, and superego; (2) a normal child passes through three psychosexual stages of development—oral, anal, and phallic; and (3) a person's personality traits are developed in early childhood.

Sigmund Freud, the most famous psychologist of the twentieth century, developed his now-famous **psychoanalytic theory**, which contributed three insights that shaped the handling

Exhibit 3–1
Signature Brains

Developmentally minded researchers are now beginning to map out violence-prone paths that lead to delinquency in the hopes of creating new and better family and school interventions. In one example of the kind of research that is occurring, some researchers have found evidence indicating that a gene variant inherited by some people influences brain development in ways that foster impulsive violence—but only in combination with environmental hardships. Other new studies explore how family and peer interactions build on a child's psychological and biological makeup to promote delinquency. Separate work examines ways to significantly counteract the adverse effect of bullying and other types of coercion in schools.

Among the researchers working in these new areas, one of them, German neuroscientist Andreas Meyer-Lindenberg, says that he knows what a genetic risk for impulsive violence looks like in the brain from his study of brain scans. Ironically, Meyer-Lindenberg and his former colleagues at the National Institute of Mental Health in Bethesda, Maryland, developed such a portrait of brain-based violence by inducing aggression in the brains of generally placid people free of emotional problems, brain disorders, substance abuse, and arrest records.

Meyer-Lindenberg undertook the study of 142 white adults who had inherited one of two common versions of a gene that triggers production of an enzyme called monoamine oxidase A (MAOA). That enzyme controls the supply of an important brain chemical, serotonin. One of the gene variants yields weak MAOA activity in the brain, resulting in elevated concentrations of serotonin. Too much of that chemical messenger upsets the regulations of emotions and impulses. The other gene variant sparks intense MAOA activity, leading to serotonin concentrations at the low end of the normal range.

Significant among Meyer-Lindenberg's findings was that people born with a common variation of the gene that triggers MAOA production had smaller brain regions that manage fear and anger. This suggests they have less ability to control such feelings. Brain regions associated with fear were smaller, yet more active, in the people with the version of the gene that makes less of the enzyme. Among individuals in the study, males displayed less ability to inhibit impulsive reactions than did females.

"This is a first step in a revolution in the field," says Meyer-Lindenberg. "We are trying to get a handle on brain mechanisms for complex social phenomena." Meyer-Lindenberg says that it appears likely that having the gene variant affects brain development and helps account for neural mechanisms that may make some people more prone to impulsive violence, as distinct from premeditated violence. He concluded that behavior affected by the gene is probably caused by the interplay of social and environmental factors, as well as by other genetic differences.

In other studies similar to those cited here, research teams have reported that children who endure severe physical or emotional abuse and also possess the weak-MAOA gene variant commit violent and delinquent acts later in life far more often than do abused kids who carry the strong-MAOA gene variant.

Source: Jeffrey Tannenbaum, "Gene Variant Suggests a Reason for Impulsive Violence," *Bloomberg News*, March 21, 2006, http://archive.sltrib.com/printfriendly.php?id=3623319&itype=ngpsid; and Bruce Bower, "Violent Developments: Disruptive Kids Grow into Their Behavior," *Science News*, May 27, 2006.

of juvenile delinquents throughout much of the last century: (1) Children who have not yet learned to control the primitive drive of the id (raw instincts and primitive drives) have difficulty distinguishing socially acceptable behavior from socially unacceptable behavior.[69] (2) Children must learn to control their sexual and aggressive drives, which create inner tensions that a child must resolve in socially acceptable ways.[70] (3) What a child has experienced emotionally by the age of five affects that child for the rest of his or her life. Emotional traumas experienced in childhood, including an unconscious sense of guilt, are likely to cause lifelong psychological problems.[71]

Other psychologists have taken the insights of psychoanalysis and applied them to delinquency, including:

- Pioneer psychiatrist William Healy, who focused on mental conflicts that originated in unsatisfactory family relationships.[72]

- Viennese-born psychoanalyst August Aichhorn, who thought that delinquents had considerable hatred toward their parents because of the conflictual nature of family relationships, and believed that adolescents transfer their hatred to other authority figures.[73]

- Austrian-born psychiatrist Kate Friedlander, who focused on the development of antisocial characteristics in the personality, such as selfishness, impulsiveness, and irresponsibility, which she defined as the results of disturbed ego development in early childhood.[74]

Sensation Seeking and Delinquency

Sensation seeking is a much different approach to psychological positivism. Derived from optimal arousal theory, sensation seeking can be defined as "an individual's need for varied,

Library Extra 3–6
The Juvenile Psychopath: Fads, Fictions, and Facts

novel and complex sensations and experiences and the willingness to take physical and social risks for the sake of such experiences."[75] Ideas about sensation seeking assume that organisms are driven or motivated to obtain an optimal level of arousal.[76] Could this desire for excitement be a factor in delinquency?

Several observers have noted that delinquency is an enjoyable activity.[77] In 2004 research, R. N. Robbins examined relationships between impulsive sensation seeking and future orientation. He found that individuals with more positive future orientation were less likely to use marijuana, hard drugs, and alcohol during sex, and had fewer alcohol problems than those with a less positive outlook. In contrast, higher impulsive adolescents had more alcohol problems, alcohol use, condom use, and cigarette smoking.[78] In another 2004 article, M. D. Slater and colleagues examined the relationship between violent media and aggressiveness. Their findings indicated that this relationship is more robust among sensation-seeking students who are victimized by their peers.[79]

In his controversial book *Seductions of Crime,* UCLA sociologist Jack Katz conjectured that when individuals commit a crime, they become involved in "an emotional process" involving "seductions and compulsions that have special dynamics," and that it is this "magical" and "transformative" experience that makes crime "sensible," even "sensually compelling." For example, Katz stated that for many adolescents, shoplifting and vandalism offer "the attractions of a thrilling melodrama," because "quite apart from what is taken, they may regard 'getting away with it' as a thrilling demonstration of personal competence, especially if it is accomplished under the eyes of adults."[80]

Katz argued that instead of approaching criminal or delinquent behavior from the traditional focus on background factors, we need to give more consideration to the foreground or situational factors that directly precipitate antisocial acts and reflect crimes' sensuality. According to Katz, offenders' immediate social environment and experiences encourage them to construct crimes as sensually compelling.[81]

Reinforcement Theory

James Q. Wilson and Richard Herrnstein's *Crime and Human Nature* combined biosocial factors and psychological research with rational choice theory to redevelop reinforcement theory.[82] Wilson and Herrnstein considered potential causes of crime and of noncrime within the context of **reinforcement theory**, the theory that behavior is governed by its consequent rewards and punishments, as reflected in the history of the individual.

reinforcement theory
A perspective that holds that behavior is governed by its consequences, especially rewards and punishments that follow from it.

The rewards of crime, according to Wilson and Herrnstein, are found in the form of material gain, revenge against an enemy, peer approval, and sexual gratification. The consequences of crime include pangs of conscience, disapproval of peers, revenge by the victim, and, most important, possibility of punishment. The rewards of crime tend to be more immediate, whereas the rewards of noncrime generally are realized in the future. Wilson and Herrnstein showed how gender, age, intelligence, families, schools, communities, labor markets, mass media, and drugs, as well as variations across time, culture, and race, greatly influence the propensity to become involved in criminal behavior, especially violent offenses.[83]

In 2011 Jennifer Stevens and colleagues, in research that is part of the developmental models that explain different types of delinquency at different phases in the life course, found from their examination of data of eight hundred delinquents incarcerated in a Midwestern state that youths may begin their involvement in delinquency in pursuit of intrinsic gratification but continue that involvement because of the external gratification that they receive from their peers.[84]

Personality and Crime

trait-based personality model
A theory that attributes delinquent behavior to an individual's basic inborn characteristics.

A **trait-based personality model** offers another set of perspectives on the sources of criminal behavior.[85] Traits are essential personal characteristics of individuals that are relevant to a wide variety of behavioral domains, including delinquency and criminality.[86] A number of researchers have made contributions in this area, including:

- Sheldon Glueck and Eleanor Glueck's classic study *Unraveling Juvenile Delinquency* examined a sample of five hundred juvenile offenders and five hundred nonoffenders in an effort to discover significant distinctions in the personality traits of the two groups. They found that the delinquents were more defiant, ambivalent about authority, extroverted, fearful of failure, resentful, hostile, suspicious, and defensive than the nondelinquents.[87]

- Joshua D. Miller and Donald Lynam conducted a meta-analysis of the basic models of personality and identified certain traits that are characteristic of antisocial personalities: hostility, self-centeredness, spitefulness, jealousy, and indifference to others. Antisocial individuals also typically lack ambition, perseverance, and motivation; hold nontraditional and unconventional values and beliefs (e.g., are low in conscientiousness); and have difficulty controlling their impulses.[88]

- Rolf Loeber and Jeffrey Burke's 2011 article summarizes the empirical studies showing pathways in the development of delinquent behavior. One of its significant contributions is that it identifies pathways between different diagnoses of disruptive behavior disorders, including oppositional defiant disorder (ODD), conduct disorder (CD), and antisocial personality disorder (APD).[89]

The Psychopath

Hard-core juvenile delinquents are sometimes diagnosed as **psychopaths** (also called *sociopaths*). According to the DSM-IV, these individuals are usually diagnosed with a conduct disorder. The claim is made that the psychopath or sociopath is the unwanted, rejected child who grows up but remains an undomesticated "child" and never develops trust in or loyalty to other adults. Hervey Cleckley gave an early description of this type of personality, listing 16 characteristics he had noted in his practice.[90] More recently, criminal psychologist Robert D. Hare and colleagues developed a new psychopathy checklist for those with antisocial personality with a conduct disorder. Among the most significant items on the list are the following:

1. Conning and manipulativeness
2. Lack of remorse or guilt
3. Callousness and lack of empathy
4. Lack of realistic long-term goals
5. Impulsivity
6. Failure to accept responsibility for one's actions.[91]

Psychologist Linda Mealey argued that there are two kinds of sociopaths: primary sociopaths and secondary sociopaths. *Primary sociopaths* are said to have inherited traits that predispose them to illegal behavior. *Secondary sociopaths*, in contrast, are constitutionally normal but are influenced by environmental factors such as poor parenting. Thus, Mealey argued that one type of sociopathic behavior has a genetic basis and the other is environmentally induced.[92]

Some interest has been expressed in measuring the relationship between psychopathy and violent behavior in juveniles. At least four instruments have been designed to assess psychopathic features among juveniles: the Psychopathy Checklist, Youth Version (PCL:YV); two versions of the Antisocial Processes Screening Device (APSD); and a Psychopathy Content scale on the Millon Adolescent Clinical Inventory (MACI). In a recent study, Daniel C. Murrie and colleagues found that the PCL:YV scores were significantly correlated with the severity of prior violence, violent offense history, and institutional violence.[93] About the same time, Raymond R. Corrado and colleagues' study also revealed that the PCL:YV significantly predicted violent and general recidivism among male adolescent offenders.[94]

In 2012 Jason Netland and Michael Miner examined psychopathic traits in adolescent males who offend against children as well as those who offend against peers. They found that most psychopathy traits and antisocial behavior are similar in all sexual offenders, while maternal dysfunction and narcissistic traits distinguish sexual offenders from delinquents involved in nonsex crimes.[95]

psychopath
An individual with a personality disorder, or a hard-core juvenile delinquent/adult criminal; also called a *sociopath*.

Web Extra 3–1
Society for Research in Psychopathology

Voices of Delinquency 3–2
Read "Forgotten Children." This is an account of an offender who has been diagnosed as having a conduct disorder or psychopathic tendencies. How does the subject explain why he became a violent person? From your reading of this story, do you believe that he is psychopathic?

Cognitive Theory

Another psychological approach that has been applied to delinquent behavior is **cognitive theory**, which is indebted to the mid-twentieth-century Swiss psychologist Jean Piaget who proposed that children's reasoning processes develop in an orderly fashion. He asserted that children build cognitive abilities through self-motivated action in the world, and he proposed that children develop through four main periods: (1) the sensorimotor period (ages 0 to 2), (2) the preoperational period (ages 2 to 7), (3) the concrete operational period (ages 7 to 11), and (4) the formal operational period (ages 11 to adulthood). This final period is when children make the transition to adulthood and begin to effectively use abstract and logical thinking.[96]

Lawrence Kohlberg later adapted cognitive theory to moral development in children's decision making, using three levels and six stages. He interviewed seventy-two white boys in Chicago about the "dilemma of Heinz," asking the boys whether a fictional and financially strapped person named Heinz did right or wrong in stealing a drug for his dying wife. Kohlberg found that young children assumed they had no choice but to obey the rules handed down by authorities. Accordingly, Heinz was wrong to steal the drug, a child will typically say in stage 1, "because it is bad to steal" or "because it is against the law to steal." However, most children later become aware of dilemmas involved with making moral decisions from a position of self-interest (stage 2). Improving individual relationships becomes the main concern in stage 3, whereas by stage 6, a person works for a moral society—for justice—to the point of disobeying unjust laws.[97]

Kohlberg later extended his studies to a population of criminals and found that they were significantly lower in moral judgment than noncriminals. The majority of criminals fell into stages 1 and 2, whereas the majority of nonoffenders could be placed in stages 3 and 4.[98] In later studies of delinquents, Kohlberg found that they were "stuck" in a state of moral immaturity and usually could be placed in any of the first three stages. Many hard-core delinquents, he further found, would be placed at the punishment stage (stage 1), because they only believe something is right or wrong because it hurts if you do what society thinks is wrong.[99]

Aaron T. Beck, who became a spokesperson for cognitive theory, found that offenders' sense of personal vulnerability is seen in their hypersensitivity to specific kinds of social confrontations, including domination or disparagement. These individuals react by fighting back or by attacking a weaker adversary. Whether juveniles or adults, violent offenders see themselves as victims and others as victimizers. Offenders' thinking is shaped by such rigid beliefs as "authorities are controlling and punitive," "spouses are deceitful, rejecting, and manipulative," "outsiders are self-serving, hostile, and treacherous," and "nobody can be trusted."[100]

In sum, several psychological theories have been used to understand delinquency and crime. A literature review categorizes them into five areas: (1) learning theories, (2) intelligence theories, (3) personality theories, (4) theories of psychopathy, and (5) cognitive and social development theories.[101] An overview of psychological theories would conclude that most delinquents have psychological traits within the normal adolescent range, but that some delinquents have acute emotional deficits. Table 3–2 summarizes the biological, sociobiological, and psychological theories of delinquency.

Developmental Theories of Delinquency

This section presents information about three well-known longitudinal studies (or studies over time) of offenders and offending: (1) the Dunedin (New Zealand) Multidisciplinary Health and Development Study undertaken by Terrie E. Moffitt and colleagues, (2) the Montreal Longitudinal Experimental Study conducted by Richard E. Tremblay and colleagues, and (3) the Cambridge Study in Delinquent Development led by David P. Farrington. A fourth longitudinal study, published by Stacy Tzoumakis in 2012, analyzed female offending, but is not discussed here.[102]

The Dunedin Longitudinal Study

Terrie E. Moffitt, Donald R. Lynam, and Phil A. Silva, in their examination of the neuropsychological status of a thousand New Zealanders born in 1972 found that poor neuropsychological scores "were associated with early onset of delinquency [but were] unrelated

TABLE 3–2
Summary of Biological, Sociobiological, and Psychological Theories of Delinquency

Theory	Classic Studies	Causes of Crime Identified	Supporting Research
Atavistic (or born) criminal	Lombroso	The atavistic criminal is a reversion to an earlier evolutionary form.	Weak
Genealogical studies	Dugdale, Goddard	Criminal tendencies are inherited.	Weak
Body type	Sheldon, Glueck and Glueck, Cortes and Gatti	Mesomorphic body type correlates with criminality.	Weak
Genetic factors	Christiansen and Mednick	Twin and adoption studies show a genetic influence on criminal tendencies.	Moderately strong
Intelligence	Hirschi and Hindelang	IQ is a meaningful factor in criminal behavior when combined with environmental factors.	Moderately strong
Autonomic nervous system	Eysenck	Insensitivity of the autonomic nervous system, as well as faulty conditioning by parents, may cause delinquent behavior.	Weak
Psychoanalytic theory	Freud	Unconscious motivations resulting from early childhood experiences lead to criminality.	Weak
Psychopathic or sociopathic personality	Cleckley	Inner emptiness as well as biological limitations causes criminal tendencies.	Moderately strong
Reinforcement theory	Wilson and Herrnstein	Several key constitutional and psychological factors cause crime.	Weak
Cognitive theory	Piaget, Kohlberg, and Beck	Lack of reasoning and moral development result in delinquent behavior.	Moderately strong

to delinquency that began in adolescence."[103] The term *neuropsychological* refers to the relationship between the nervous system, especially the brain, and mental skills such as perception, memory, and language. Moffitt's developmental theory views the emergence of delinquency as proceeding along two developmental paths:

1. Children develop a lifelong tendency toward delinquency and crime at an age as early as three years, according to one path.[104] These "life-course-persistent" (LCP) offenders, according to Moffitt, are likely to continue to engage in illegal activity throughout their lives, regardless of the social conditions and personal situations they experience.[105]

2. Moffitt also identified a path wherein the delinquents start offending during their adolescent years and then begin to desist from delinquent behavior around their eighteenth birthday. Moffitt refers to these youthful offenders as "adolescent-limited" (AL) delinquents, and it is this limited form of delinquency that characterizes most children who become involved in illegal activity.

Moffitt's Dunedin study is continuing today, and she is also following the development of 1,100 British twins born between 1994 and 1995 through the Environmental-Risk Longitudinal Twin Study.

Montreal Longitudinal Experimental Study

The Montreal Longitudinal Experimental Study (MLES) began in 1984. The principal investigator was Richard E. Tremblay, and it focused on aggressive seven- to nine-year-old children. Its original aim was to study the development of antisocial behavior from kindergarten to high school with a major focus on the role of parent–child interactions. The study initially assessed all kindergarten boys in fifty-three schools located in poor socioeconomic areas in Montreal in an effort to identify the most disruptive boys. Mother and teacher ratings and self-reported delinquency were the main instruments used to assess behavioral problems under the MLES. The study produced the following key findings:

- Higher levels of disruptive behavior during kindergarten effectively predicted higher levels of delinquency before entry into high school.
- Physical aggression during kindergarten is the best behavioral predictor of later delinquency.
- No significant group of boys started to show chronic problems of physical aggression, opposition, or hyperactivity after their kindergarten year.
- Hyperactivity and anxiety significantly predicted the age of onset of smoking cigarettes, drinking to excess, and using drugs up to fifteen years of age. Boys who had a high score on hyperactivity and a low score on anxiety were more likely to use substances at an early age.
- Boys exhibiting high levels of aggression and fighting between five and twelve years of age had generally lower heart rates at eleven and twelve years of age than other boys, controlling for pubertal status, body size, and level of family diversity.

Cambridge Study in Delinquent Development

This Cambridge Study in Delinquent Development, undertaken by principle investigator David P. Farrington at the Institute of Criminology at the University of Cambridge, England, was a forty-year longitudinal survey that followed the development of antisocial behavior in 411 South London boys, most of whom were born in 1953.[106] The study aimed to measure as many factors as possible that might contribute to the development of delinquency. Participants in the study were periodically interviewed from ages 8 to 46 years (i.e., between 1961 and 2001). They were also periodically tested in their schools, in their homes, and at the researchers' offices.[107] Teachers, parents, and significant others in the children's lives were interviewed as well. The study's chief findings were as follows:

- The prevalence of offending increased up to age 17 years and then decreased.
- The peak age of increase in the prevalence of offending was age 14.
- Persistence in offending was seen in the significant continuity of offending that took place from one age range to another.
- Most juvenile and young adult offenses resulting in convictions were committed with others, but the incidence of co-offending declined steadily with age.
- The most important risk factors of later offending were (1) antisocial behavior during childhood, including troublesomeness, dishonesty, and aggressiveness; (2) hyperactivity-impulsivity; (3) low intelligence; (4) poor school achievement; (5) family criminality; (6) family poverty; and (7) poor parenting.[108]

See Table 3–3 for a summary of the developmental studies discussed here.

Prevention of Delinquency

Delinquency prevention has a sad history, and the highway of delinquency prevention is paved with punctured panaceas.[109] A member of the House's Subcommittee on Human Resources of the Committee on Education and Labor put it this way: "The public is looking for an inexpensive panacea. . . . These periodic panaceas for delinquents come along every 2 to 3 years in my experience. The harm they do is to divert the attention of the public from any

TABLE 3–3
Comparison of Developmental Studies

	The Dunedin Multidisciplinary Health and Development Study	Montreal Longitudinal Experimental Study	Cambridge Study in Delinquent Development
Principal investigator	Terrie Moffitt	Richard E. Tremblay	David P. Farrington
Sample	Followed 1,000 males and females from ages 3 to 29	Followed Montreal children from birth	Males born between 1951 and 1954
Delinquent population	Two groups of offenders were identified: adolescence-limited (AL), and life-course-persistent (LCP) offenders.	Potential for delinquency could be identified as early as kindergarten.	About one-third of the cohort was delinquent.
Gender	The persistent path is extremely rare with females.	Only boys in study	Only boys in study
Race	N/A	N/A	N/A
Chronic offenders	N/A	N/A	6%; 23 boys of the 396 had six or more convictions.
Patterns of delinquent behavior	AL may be as high as LCP during adolescence, but LCPs continue into adult behavior.	Higher levels of disruptive behavior during kindergarten predicts higher levels of delinquency before high school.	Early discrimination and treatment of persistent delinquency can help prevent adult criminality.

People In the Know
Interview with Terrie E. Moffitt

Question: What do you feel are the best features of development theory as you and your colleagues have developed it?

Moffitt: We proposed that people who engage in delinquent and offending behavior should be viewed as falling into two main patterns, life-course-persistent and adolescence-limited. I think one of the main advantages of this two-group approach is that it accounts for the known "big facts" about antisocial behavior's relations with age, sex, and social class. The two-group approach also explains why some correlates of antisocial behavior appear, disappear, and reappear across the life course. For example, low social class, reading difficulties, and genetic risk are all strong correlates of antisocial behavior during childhood and adulthood, but not during adolescence. Conversely, peer influences on antisocial behavior are strong during adolescence, but not during childhood and adulthood. If two different kinds of people take part in antisocial behavior at different developmental stages, that would explain these curious "disappearing" findings. Finally, the two-group approach focuses attention on different intervention plans needed to prevent early-onset versus late-onset delinquency.

Question: Do you see any areas that need to be expanded or reformulated?

Moffitt: One aspect that clearly needs to be expanded is the number of offender groups. The original theory proposed only two, life-course-persistent and adolescence-limited.

But subsequently researchers have tested for the correct number of groups needed to account for the delinquent activity in representative samples. From this work a third group of offenders has emerged: the "low-level chronics." In my own longitudinal study this group was highly aggressive in childhood, but then was only minimally involved in delinquency during adolescence. As adults, the group emerged as steady low-level chronic offenders. They are very unusual males, because they are socially isolated, have many fears and phobias, lack friendships or female partners, and have low intelligence and low-status jobs, or no jobs. David Farrington's London longitudinal study finds the same low-level chronic offenders who are poorly functioning social isolates. We need to know more about them.

Question: How did you come to be involved in the formulation of this theory?

Moffitt: I was taught an important lesson by the birth cohort of a thousand young New Zealanders we followed as they grew up. In the 1980s, when the cohort were children, my students and I found there were not many antisocial study members, but their antisocial behavior had many strong correlates, such as difficult temperament, harsh parenting, and low IQ. We published lots of papers about this. When we recontacted the cohort in the 1990s at age 15 to collect more data from them, we found many more study members had taken up antisocial behavior. We were pleased about that because we now had more

(Continued)

delinquents to study. However, we found that all the former correlates of antisocial behavior had suddenly dropped to nonsignificance. What a surprise! Because we had nothing to publish, we had to find an explanation for these disappearing findings! This motivated me to brainstorm about why more participants in delinquency would be associated with disappearing correlates of delinquency. While thinking about this puzzle, I remembered my own experience of school. In my primary school, there were some really bad kids that my good-student friends and I were afraid of, but by junior high school, many of us began to hang out with those bad kids and got into a fair amount of serious trouble ourselves. After high school, my good-student friends and I moved on to be more successful. I wondered if this small-town story applied to young people more widely, and apparently it does.

Question: Have you been encouraged or discouraged by the response that the theory has received?

Moffitt: I am delighted that so many people have found this simple two-group theory worthy of their attention, and I am even overwhelmed by this. This taxonomy of childhood versus adolescent onset antisocial behavior is codified in the American Psychiatric Association's guidelines for diagnosing conduct disorders, and has been invoked in the National Institute of Mental Health's Factsheet on Child and Adolescent Violence and the

Surgeon General's Report on Youth Violence. The original paper that proposed the two prototypes and their different etiologies appeared about ten years ago, and in the seven years since it has been cited by readers more than six hundred times in their own papers, which is a high compliment. Several research teams in nine countries have tested hypotheses put forward from the theory. Most of the research teams have reported findings that are consistent with the theory, but some have pointed to important issues that need to be resolved. For example, a Baltimore study found that the theory fit young African American men better than young white men, but a California study found the theory did not fit African American men at all. Obviously, this needs more work! It is exciting that the theory is stimulating so much research activity and debate, and I'm pleased that it can make this contribution. Most criminologists now think about human development, and this is quite gratifying to me.

Source: Reprinted with permission from Terrie E. Moffitt. Terrie E. Moffitt is the Knut Schmidt Nielsen Professor of Psychology and Neuroscience at Duke University in Durham, North Carolina. She does life-span longitudinal research with large samples in field settings. Her research topics include (1) natural history of antisocial behavior from childhood to adulthood; (2) etiology of conduct disorder, juvenile delinquency, and antisocial personality disorder; (3) interactionist approaches to psychopathology; (4) longitudinal research methodology; (5) neuropsychological assessment; and (6) neurobehavioral disorders. This interview took place in February 2002.

long-term comprehensive program of helping youth, working to strengthen school systems, communities, job opportunities, housing and recreational programs."[110]

Prevention panaceas have ranged from biological and psychological interventions to group therapy, gang intervention, recreational activities, job training and employment, community organizations, and even structured reorganization of the entire society. The most widely known models of delinquency prevention are the Chicago Area Project; the Cambridge-Somerville Youth Study in Massachusetts; the New York City Youth Board; the Mobilization for Youth Project in New York City; Boston's Midcity Project; and Walter C. Reckless and Simon Dinitz's self-concept studies in Columbus, Ohio. Each is described briefly in what follows.

- *Cambridge-Somerville Youth Study.* One of the best known of the prevention programs identified those youths who were headed for trouble with the law. It took place in Cambridge and Somerville, Massachusetts, from November 1937 to December 31, 1945. This individual approach to delinquency prevention presumed that psychological disturbances led to delinquent behavior, so it focused on efforts made through a counseling relationship to alter the psychological states of respondents as well as their ability to function in school and at home. In a 30-year follow-up, Temple University professor Joan McCord found that "none of the measures confirmed hopes that treatment had improved the lives of those in the treatment group."[111]

- *New York City Youth Board.* Another study also presumed that psychological disturbances led to delinquent behavior and provided psychiatric and social work services to identify predelinquents through the New York City Youth Board. The study was conducted from 1952 to 1953, when researchers used the Glueck social prediction table to examine 223 boys in two public schools located in high-delinquency areas in the New York City school system. This prediction table was made up of five family-related factors: discipline of boy by father, supervision of boy by mother, affection of father for boy, affection of mother for boy, and family cohesiveness. The evaluation at the conclusion of the study (like that of the Cambridge-Somerville Youth Study) revealed disappointing results. The Glueck social prediction table did not accurately predict delinquency, nor did the psychiatric and social work services appear to have any positive effect on those youths identified as predelinquent.[112]

- *Mobilization for Youth Project.* In 1961, one of the most ambitious attempts to prevent and control juvenile delinquency took place in a sixty-seven-block area of Manhattan's Lower East Side in New York City. This endeavor—New York's Mobilization for Youth (MFY) Project—built on Richard A. Cloward and Lloyd E. Ohlin's delinquency and opportunity theory and sought to reduce the gap between the social and economic aspirations of youths and their opportunities to achieve these goals through legitimate means. This approach to delinquency prevention became the major strategy for the new federal delinquency initiatives endorsed by the President's Committee on Juvenile Delinquency and Youth Crime as well as the prototype project for many of the federally funded "war on poverty" programs during the 1960s. Supporters claimed that the MFY project was on the right track but was not taken far enough; detractors countered that the danger in trying to do too much was to end up doing too little.[113]

- *Boston's Midcity Project.* The Midcity Project began in inner-city Boston in 1954 largely as a result of widely publicized gang violence. Detached gang workers served as intermediaries between gang members and employers, school officials, and the police. An evaluation of this program by youth-gang authority Walter B. Miller found that there was no significant measurable inhibition of law-abiding behavior.[114] The project did lead to the development of the detached gang worker projects, which was based on the belief that delinquency stems from the influence of peers and from weak attachments between youths and conforming members of society.

- *Self-Concept and the Prevention of Delinquency.* Walter C. Reckless and Simon Dinitz used role development and educational strategies in order to improve the self-concept of students who were veering toward delinquency (see Chapter 5). In the late 1950s and early 1960s, the Columbus, Ohio, school system permitted Reckless and Dinitz to set up pilot projects in elementary schools in high-delinquency areas, with the purpose of improving the self-concept of male students who had been identified as prone to delinquency. In all, 1,762 boys were examined at four consecutive yearly periods—at the end of the seventh, eighth, ninth, and tenth grades—but the researchers found that in none of the outcome variables were the experimental subjects significantly different from the controls.[115]

Fortunately, as future chapters will reveal, the present history of delinquency prevention is much more encouraging than efforts in this early period.

The Importance of Theory

The last chapter pointed out that theory and research are intertwined and that they need to be the foundation for policy recommendations to deal with juvenile delinquency in the United States. Researchers have spent considerable time and effort trying to understand the causes and correlates of delinquency.[116] The question is: What is the value of studying theories of delinquent behavior? Perhaps the answer to this question can be found in the *Voices of Delinquency* that supplements this text.

With nearly every story, questions can be raised: How did this person's family background influence the course of his or her behavior? How did success or failure in school influence subsequent behaviors? How was he or she affected by the environment? Why did he or she become involved in a youth gang? Why did this person become a drug user? What influenced this person to stop taking drugs or becoming involved in other illegal behaviors?

More specifically, the student can make these inquiries: Which delinquency theory found in Chapters 3 through 6 of this text seems to apply closely to the choices that this person made? If more than one theory is required to explain behavior, what theories would you use? If none of the theories found in these chapters seems to apply to a particular story, what theoretical constructs are needed to understand this behavior?

Delinquency theory, it will be found, is helpful in understanding why youngsters do what they do. With this understanding comes the ability to provide guidance and direction for those who work with delinquent youths. With this understanding, parents can also have insight regarding how to provide nurturance and acceptance to their children. Finally, with this understanding, researchers are able to design studies that will further the knowledge of delinquent behavior.

Delinquency across the Life Course: Desistance from Crime

desistance
The termination of a delinquent career or behavior.

An important consideration of life-course criminology is the matter of **desistance** from crime. One of the problems of establishing desistance is the difficulty of distinguishing between a gap in a delinquent career and true termination. There are bound to be crime-free intervals in the course of delinquent careers. To explain changes in offending over time, or desistance, theorists have proposed several explanations, which we'll consider by category:

- *Maturation and aging account for desistance.* The maturation process appears to be involved in desistance, as youths or adults become aware either of the desirability of pursuing a conventional lifestyle or of the undesirability of continuing with unlawful activities. James Q. Wilson and Richard Herrnstein contended that the relatively minor gains from crime lose their power to reinforce deviant behavior as juveniles mature and develop increasing ties to conventional society.[117]

- *Developmental accounts of desistance.* One developmental explanation of desistance is that identity changes account for reduction or cessation of crime. Edward Mulvey and John LaRosa, focusing on the period from ages 17 to 20 years—the period they call the time of "natural" recovery—found that desistance was linked to a cognitive process taking place in the late teens when delinquents realized that they were "going nowhere" and that they had better make changes in their lives if they were going to be successful as adults.[118]

- *Rational choice accounts for desistance.* The main idea of the rational choice framework is that the decision to give up or continue with crime is based on a person's conscious reappraisal of the costs and benefits of criminal activity. Proponents of this theory saw persisters and desisters as "reasoned decision makers."[119] David Farrington also noted that the severity of the adult penal system appeared to be a deterrent with the population he studied.[120]

- *Life-course perspective accounts for desistance.* The major objective of the life-course perspective, whose framework was discussed in Chapters 1 and 2, is to link social history and social structure. In 2003, Laub and Sampson published *Shared Beginnings, Divergent Lives,* which promises to be a classic study of life-course and developmental criminology. They argued that the data from the Gluecks' original study support the notion that explanations of desistance from crime and of persistence in crime are two sides of the same coin. From their analysis of offender narratives and life histories, Laub and Sampson perceived desistance as a process rather than an event—a process that operates simultaneously at different levels (individual, situational, and community) and across different contextual environments (especially family, work, and military service). They concluded that "offenders desist as a result of individual actions (choice) in conjunction with situational contexts and structural influences linked to key institutions that help sustain desistance."[121]

A central element in the desistance process, according to Laub and Sampson, is any change that "knifes off" individual offenders from their environment and at the same time offers them a new script for the future. The major turning points implicated in this study's desistance process included marriage/spouse, employment, reform school, the military, and neighborhood change. All of these turning points involve, to varying degrees, the following: "(1) New situations that knife off the past from the present. (2) New situations that provide both supervision and monitoring as well as new opportunities of social support and growth.

(3) New situations that change and structure routine activities. (4) New situations that provide the opportunity for identity transformation."[122] In sum, offenders "choose to desist in response to structurally induced turning points that serve as the catalyst for sustaining long-term behavior change."[123]

The Case

The Life Course of Amy Watters, Age 9

When Amy turned nine years old, her father held a birthday party for her that included a number of invited guests from among Amy's school friends. The party was organized around a picnic table in the backyard of Amy's home. One of the guests, Cassandra—a girl of about the same age as Amy—gave Amy a first-grade reader as a birthday gift. It was never clear whether "Cassie," as the girl was known to Amy, meant to give that particular book, or whether she had somehow confused the book with another. When Amy opened the present, however, she thought that it was meant as an insult. "How," she thought, "could anyone give me such a childish present." Was Cassie trying to say that Amy was like a first-grader? Feeling embarrassed in front of her friends, Amy flew into a rage immediately upon opening the present and attacked Cassie, grabbing her hair and dragging her to the ground. Her father had to pull a screaming Amy off of Cassie, as the two rolled in the backyard grass.

This chapter says, "The concept of rationality ... assumes that individuals have free will and are not controlled by their emotions, but many youngsters do not appear to have such control." Why might Amy be lacking in self-control? What experiences can help build self-control among adolescents?

Follow the continuing Amy Watters saga in the next chapter.

Learn more on the Web:
* Family Structure and Parental Behavior: Identifying the Sources of Adolescent Self-Control: http://wcr.sonoma.edu/v09n2/phythian.pdf

CHAPTER SUMMARY

This chapter examines individual-level explanations for delinquency, including personal decision making and the behavioral impact of rational choices made by young people. This chapter also points out the following:

* To justify punishing juveniles, theorists have turned to classical school principles or to the principles of rational choice theory, which build on classical thought. Both perspectives assert that individuals have free will and should be held responsible for their behavior.

* Policy makers in growing numbers are concluding that increasing the "cost" of crime to the perpetrator is the best way to reduce serious youth crime in the United States.

* Biological positivism and psychological positivism point to biological and psychological factors within the individual as the most significant determinants of delinquency.

* Biological and psychological factors may be very elusive, such as a difficult-to-condition autonomic nervous system or the level of MAOA in the brain, or they may be more easily discerned, such as inappropriate interpersonal relationships.

* Both early biological and psychological positivism theories have developed into more refined explanations of delinquent behavior. Early biological positivism has largely been replaced

by sociobiology, and psychoanalysis has been replaced by developmental models that give greater weight to the interactions between the individual and the environment.

* Children who have attention deficit/hyperactivity disorder (ADHD) and learning disorders (LDs) tend to have problems in school; in turn, they tend to become involved with peers who demonstrate higher rates of delinquency.

* According to developmental perspectives, human behavior progresses along certain paths, with outcomes that are relatively predictable.

* Terrie Moffitt identified life-course-persistent (LCP) and adolescent-limited (AL) paths, in which young people either engage in persistent crime violation or temporarily experiment with delinquency.

* Richard Tremblay and colleagues' Montreal Longitudinal Experimental Study found that antisocial behavior was at its peak during the kindergarten years and that physical aggression during the kindergarten years is the best behavior predictor of later delinquency.

* In the Cambridge Study in Delinquent Development, David P. Farrington found that the types of acts that lead to convictions tend to be components of a larger pattern of antisocial behavior.

KEY TERMS

attention deficit/hyperactivity disorder (ADHD), p. 60
autonomic nervous system, p. 60
biological positivism, p. 57
born criminal, p. 58
cognitive theory, p. 66
desistance, p. 72
determinism, p. 57

emotionality, p. 60
felicific calculus, p. 55
free will, p. 55
learning disability (LD), p. 61
orthomolecular imbalance, p. 62
positivism, p. 53
Progressive era, p. 57
psychoanalytic theory, p. 62

psychopath, p. 65
reinforcement theory, p. 64
routine activities approach, p. 55
social contract, p. 53
sociobiology, p. 58
trait-based personality model, p. 64
utilitarianism, p. 55

JUVENILE DELINQUENCY VIDEOS

Mental Illness

Mental Illness focuses on the complicated issues the juvenile court system handles when dealing with juveniles who have mental illnesses. In the video a situation arises where an institutionalized offender engages in the abnormal behavior of self-mutilation and extreme anger. The individual injures himself repeatedly and has a long history of violent outbursts, often victimizing himself as well as others. How does the facility handle the situation? The individual has difficulty following orders; what does the institution do to assist the youth? Based on the readings, how do the juvenile court systems assess and handle youths who suffer from mental illnesses? Discuss what treatments juvenile institutions may use to deal with these children.

REVIEW QUESTIONS

1. How do you explain the main contentions of the classical school?
2. How do you define positivism? Who were the early biological positivists?
3. How would you describe the psychopath? Why are psychopaths so difficult to treat?
4. What is sociobiology? What areas of sociobiology have findings related to delinquency?
5. What is psychological positivism? What has this position contributed to our understanding delinquency?
6. What developmental studies were discussed in this chapter?

DISCUSSION QUESTIONS

1. Does determinism negate the concepts of free will and choice? From your own experience, do you recall ever being so compelled to take some action that you could not avoid participation through the simple expedient of making a responsible choice? If so, what happened?
2. Does punishment deter delinquency or simply provoke escalation of delinquency as a retaliatory response?
3. Rational choice theory posits that crime and delinquency are the results of rational choices that people make. With this in mind, how might an increase in penalties associated with shoplifting impact the incidence of shoplifting in stores in your area? To what extent do you believe that increased punishments would reduce the number of offenses? What does that say about the rationality of crime?
4. Researchers seem to expend extraordinary effort seeking reliable means to predict delinquency and/or criminality. Do you think this indicates an unreasonable disregard for the roles of free will and personal choice in behavioral decisions? Explain your position.
5. A cynic might dismiss the causation research cited here as a waste of time, suggesting instead that human behavioral choices are simply elective decisions to behave one way or another. How would you respond?

GROUP EXERCISES

1. Have the class debate this question: Does the inability of the juvenile justice system to impose genuinely punitive responses to delinquency and criminality make a mockery of the concept of justice and, in fact, encourage continued delinquency/criminality?
2. Divide the class into two teams: the "naturists" and the "nurturists." Hold a debate on these two causational concepts.
3. Have students research the rates of learning disabilities (LDs) identified within the population of your state's prison system; then have them discuss their findings, specifically addressing whether they believe having an LD is a major causative contributor to criminality.

NOTES

1. David E. Kalist and Daniel Y. Lee, "First Names and Crime: Does Unpopularity Spell Trouble?" *Social Science Quarterly* 90, no. 1 (2009), pp. 39–49.
2. Ibid., p. 40.
3. Ronald V. Clarke and Derek B. Cornish, "Modeling Offenders' Decisions: A Framework for Research and Policy," in *Crime and Justice*, 6th ed., edited by Michael Tonry and Norval Morris (Chicago: University of Chicago Press, 1985), pp. 147–85.
4. C.-L. Montesquieu, *On the Spirit of the Laws*, translated by Thomas Nugent, edited by David W. Carithers (Berkeley: University of California Press, 1977), originally published as *L'Esprit des Lois* (1747); Cesare Bonesana Beccaria, *On Crimes and Punishments*, translated by H. Paolucci (1764; reprint ed., Indianapolis: Bobbs-Merrill, 1963); Jeremy Bentham, *An Introduction to the Principles of Morals and Legislation* (1823; reprint ed., New York: Hafner Publishing, 1948).
5. Montesquieu, *On the Spirit of the Laws*, p. 158.
6. Ibid.
7. Bentham, *An Introduction to the Principles of Morals and Legislation*.
8. Beccaria, *On Crimes and Punishments*.
9. Bentham, *An Introduction to the Principles of Morals and Legislation*.
10. Edward Cimler and Lee Roy Bearch, "Factors Involved in Juvenile Decisions about Crime," *Criminal Justice and Behavior* 8 (September 1981), pp. 275–86.
11. A. Tseloni, K. Wittebrood, and G. Farrell, "Burglary Victimization in England and Wales." *Brutish Journal of Criminology* 44 (2004), pp. 66–91.
12. Clarke and Cornish, "Modeling Offenders' Decisions."
13. Derek B. Cornish and Ronald V. Clarke, eds., *The Reasoning Criminal: Rational Choice Perspectives on Offending* (New York: Springer, 1986); Raymond Paternoster, "Absolute and Restrictive Deterrence in a Panel of Youth: Explaining the Onset, Persistence/Desistance, and Frequency of Delinquent Offending," *Social Problems* 36 (1989), pp. 289–309; Marcus Felson, *Crime and Everyday Life: Insight and Implications for Society* (Thousand Oaks, Calif.: Pine Forge Press, 1994).
14. Jeffrey Fagan and Alex R. Piquero, "Rational Choice and Developmental Influences on Recidivism among Adolescent Felony Offenders," *Journal of Empirical Legal Studies* 4 (2007), pp. 715–48.
15. Paternoster, "Absolute and Restrictive Deterrence in a Panel of Youth" and "Decisions to Participate in and Desist from Four Types of Common Delinquency: Deterrence and the Rational Choice Perspective," *Law and Society Review* 23 (1989), pp. 7–40.
16. Shamena Aniwar and Thomas Loughran, "Testing a Bayesian Learning Theory of Deterrence among Serious Juvenile Offenders," *Criminology* 49 (2011), pp. 667–98.
17. Fagan and Piquero, "Rational Choice and Developmental Influences."
18. Lawrence E. Cohen and Marcus Felson, "Social Change and Crime Rate Trends: A Routine Activity Approach," *American Sociological Review* (August 1979), pp. 588–609.
19. Wayne Osgood and Amy Anderson, "Unstructured Socializing and Rates of Delinquency," *Criminology* 42 (2004), pp. 519–49.
20. Katherine Novak and Lizabeth Crawford, "Routine Activities as Determinants of Gender Differences in Delinquency," *Journal of Criminal Justice* 38 (2010), pp. 913–20.
21. Timothy Brezina, "Delinquent Problem-Solving: An Interpretive Framework," *Journal of Research in Crime and Delinquency* (2000), pp. 3–30.
22. See the desistance studies at the end of this chapter.
23. Marvin E. Wolfgang, Terence P. Thornberry, and Robert M. Figlio, *From Boy to Man: From Delinquency to Crime* (Chicago: University of Chicago Press, 1987). See also James F. Short, Jr., and Fred L. Strodtbeck, *Group Process and Gang Delinquency* (Chicago: University of Chicago Press, 1965), pp. 248–65; and Charles W. Thomas and Donna M. Bishop, "The Effect of Formal and Informal Sanctions on Delinquency: A Longitudinal Comparison of Labeling and Deterrence Theories," *Journal of Criminal Law and Criminology* 75 (1984), p. 1244.
24. David Matza, *Delinquency and Drift* (New York: Wiley, 1964), p. 27. See also Silvan S. Tomkins, *Affect, Imagery, Consciousness: The Positive Affects* (New York: Springer, 1962), pp. 108–09.
25. Robert Agnew, "Determinism, Indeterminism, and Crime: An Empirical Exploration," *Criminology* 33 (1995), pp. 83–109.
26. This section on the Progressive era and the influence of positivism is based on David J. Rothman, *Conscience and Convenience: The Asylum and Its Alternatives in Progressive America* (Boston: Little, Brown, 1980). See p. 32.
27. Ibid. See pp. 43–60.
28. James Q. Wilson and Richard J. Herrnstein, *Crime and Human Nature* (New York: Simon and Schuster, 1985).
29. Ian Taylor, Paul Walton, and Jock Young, *The New Criminology: For a Social Theory of Deviance* (New York: Harper and Row, 1973).
30. Ibid.
31. John Slawson, *The Delinquent Boys* (Boston: Budget Press, 1926).
32. Edwin Sutherland, "Mental Deficiency and Crime," in *Social Attitudes*, edited by Kimball Young (New York: Henry Holt, 1931), pp. 357–75.
33. William Sheldon, *Varieties of Delinquent Youth* (New York: Harper and Row, 1949).
34. Ibid.
35. Sheldon Glueck and Eleanor Glueck, *Physique and Delinquency* (New York: Harper and Row, 1956), p. 9.
36. Juan B. Cortes with Florence M. Gatti, *Delinquency and Crime: A Biopsychosocial Approach: Empirical, Theoretical, and Practical Aspects of Criminal Behavior* (New York: Seminar Press, 1972); Saleem A. Shahn and Loren H. Roth, "Biological and Psychophysiological Factors

in Criminality," in *Handbook of Criminology*, edited by Daniel Glaser (Chicago: Rand McNally, 1974), pp. 101–73.

37. Shahn and Roth, "Biological and Psychophysiological Factors in Criminality."

38. Karl O. Christiansen, "A Preliminary Study of Criminality among Twins," in *Biosocial Bases of Criminal Behavior*, edited by S. A. Mednick and K. O. Christiansen (New York: Gardner, 1977), pp. 89–108; D. R. Cloninger et al., "Predisposition to Petty Criminality: II. Cross-Fostering Analysis of Gene–Environment Interaction," *Archives of General Psychiatry* 39 (November 1982), pp. 1242–47; R. Crowe, "An Adoptive Study of Psychopathy: Preliminary Results from Arrest Records and Psychiatric Hospital Records," in *Genetic Research in Psychiatry*, edited by R. Fieve et al. (Baltimore: Johns Hopkins University Press, 1975); William F. Gabrielli and Sarnoff A. Mednick, "Urban Environment, Genetics, and Crime," *Criminology* 22 (November 1984), pp. 645–52; S. Sigvardsson et al., "Predisposition to Petty Criminality in Swedish Adoptees: III. Sex Differences and Validation of Male Typology," *Archives of General Psychiatry* 39 (November 1982), pp. 1248–53.

39. Donald J. Shoemaker, *Theories of Delinquency: An Examination of Explanations of Delinquent Behavior*, 6th ed. (New York: Oxford University Press, 2009)).

40. Christiansen, "A Preliminary Study of Criminality among Twins."

41. Thomas Bouchard, Jr., "Genes, Environment, and Personality," *Science* 264 (1994), pp. 1700–01.

42. Ibid., p. 1701.

43. M. J. H. Rietveld, J. J. Hudziak, M. Bartels, C. E. M. van Beijsterveldt, and D. I. Boomsma, "Heritability of Attention Problems in Children: Cross-Sectional Results from a Study of Twins, Age 3 to 12," *Neuropsychiatric Genetics* 1176 (2003), pp. 102–13.

44. The discussion on recent studies of twins is based on John Paul Wright and Kevin M. Beaver, "Do Parents Matter in Creating Self-Control in Their Children? A Genetically Informed Test of Gottfredson and Hirschi's Theory of Low Self-Control," *Criminology* 43 (November 2005), pp. 1169–1202.

45. Minnesota Twin Family Study, http://www.psych.umn.edu/psylabs/mtfs/specialhtm (accessed April 16, 2009).

46. Christiansen, "A Preliminary Study of Criminality among Twins."

47. Edwin H. Sutherland and Donald R. Cressey, *Criminology*, 10th ed. (New York: Lippincott, 1978).

48. Robert A. Gordon, "Prevalence: The Rare Datum in Delinquency Measurement and Its Implications for the Theory of Delinquency," in *The Juvenile Justice System*, edited by Malcolm Klein (Beverly Hills, Calif.: Sage, 1976), pp. 201–84.

49. Robert A. Gordon, "IQ—Commensurability of Black–White Differences in Crime and Delinquency," paper presented at the annual meeting of the American Psychological Association, Washington, DC, August 1986, p. 1.

50. Travis Hirschi and Michael Hindelang, "Intelligence and Delinquency: A Revisionist Review," *American Sociological Review* 42 (1977), pp. 471–86.

51. Ibid.

52. Tom Kennedy, Kent Burnett, and William Edmonds, "Intellectual, Behavioral, and Personality Correlates of Violent vs. Non-Violent Juvenile Offenders," *Aggressive Behavior* 37 (2011), pp. 315–25.

53. Roos Koolhof, Rolf Loeber, Evelyn Wei, Dustin Pardini, and Annematt Collot d'Escury," Inhibition deficits of Serious Delinquent Boys of Low Intelligence," *Criminal Behavior & Mental Health* 17 (2007), pp. 274–92.

54. For a study that supported the school performance model over the IQ/LD connection, see David A. Ward and Charles R. Tittle, "IQ and Delinquency: A Test of Two Competing Explanations," *Journal of Quantitative Criminology* 10 (1994), pp. 189–200.

55. Hans Eysenck, "The Technology of Consent," *New Scientist* 26 (June 1969), p. 689. For two papers that tested Eysenck's contributions, see Coleta van Dam, Eric E. J. De Bruyn, and Jan M. A. A. Janssens, "Personality, Delinquency, and Criminal Recidivism," *Adolescence* 42 (Winter 2007), pp. 763–776; and Penelope A. Hasking, "Reinforcement, Sensitivity, Coping, and Delinquent Behaviour in Adolescents," *Journal of Adolescence* 30 (2007), pp. 739–49.

56. Ronald Simons, Kit Man Lei, Eric Steward, Steven Beach, R. Gene, H. Brody, Robert Philbert, and Frederick Gibbons, "Social Adversity, Genetic Variation, Street Code, and Aggression: A Genetically Informed Model of Violent Behavior," *Youth Violence & Juvenile Justice* 10 (2012), pp. 3–24.

57. Patricia Stoddard-Dare, Christopher Mallet, and Craig Boitel, "Association between Mental Health Disorders and Juveniles' Detention for a Personal Crime," *Child & Adolescent Mental Health* 16 (2011), pp. 208–13.

58. For additional information on reading disability in delinquent youths, see John Shelley-Tremblay, Natalie O'Brien, and Jennifer Langhinrichsen-Rohling, "Reading Disability in Adjudicated Youth: Prevalence Rates, Current Models, Traditional and Innovative Treatments," *Aggression and Violent Behavior* 12 (2007), pp. 376–92.

59. Attention Deficit Disorder (ADD), http://www.dg58.dupage.kl2il.usx/counselors/add.htm (accessed July 15, 2004).

60. MTA Cooperative Group, "A 14-Month Randomized Clinical Trial of Treatment Strategies for Attention Deficit Hyperactivity Disorder," *Archives of General Psychiatry* 56 (1999), pp. 1088–96.

61. Karen Stern, *A Treatment Study of Children with Attention Deficit Hyperactivity Disorder*, OJJDP Fact Sheet No. 20 (Washington, D.C.: Office of Justice and Juvenile and Delinquency Prevention, May 2001).

62. Sharyn Neuwirth, *Learning Disabilities* (Washington, D.C.: National Institute of Mental Health, 1993), p. 3.

63. Ibid.

64. Donald Shoemaker, *Theories of Delinquency*, 6th ed. (New York: Oxford University Press, 2009).

65. Shahn and Roth, "Biological and Psychophysiological Factors in Delinquency."

66. Karen Matta Oshima, Jin Huang, Melissa Jonson-Reid, and Brett Drake, "Children with Disabilities in Poor Households: Association with Juvenile and Adult Offending," *Social Work Research* 34 (2010), pp. 102–13.

67. See Jianghong Liu, "Early Health Risk Factors for Violence, Conceptualization, Evidence, and Implications," *Aggression and Violent Behavior* 16 (2011), pp. 63–73.

68. Ibid.

69. Sigmund Freud, *An Outline of Psychoanalysis*, translated by James Strachey (1940; reprint ed., New York: W. W. Norton, 1963).

70. Ibid.

71. Ibid.

72. William Healy, *Twenty-Five Years of Child Guidance: Studies from the Institute of Juvenile Research, Series C*, no. 256 (Chicago: Illinois Department of Public Welfare, 1934).

73. August Aichhorn, *Wayward Youth* (New York: Viking Press, 1963).

74. Kate Friedlander, *The Psychoanalytic Approach to Juvenile Delinquency* (London: Routledge, 1947).

75. Marvin Zuckerman, *Sensation Seeking beyond the Optimal Level of Arousal* (Hillsdale, N.J.: Lawrence Erlbaum, 1979), p. 10.

76. Ibid.

77. Frederick Thrasher, *The Gang* (Chicago: University of Chicago Press, 1936); Henry D. McKay, "The Neighborhood and Child Conduct," *Annals of the American Academy of Political and Social Science* 261 (1949), pp. 32–41; P. Tappan, *Juvenile Delinquency* (New York: McGraw-Hill, 1949); A. Cohen, "The Delinquent Subculture," in *The Sociology of Crime and Delinquency*, 2d ed., edited by M. Wolfgang, L. Savitz and N. Johnston (New York: Wiley, 1970), pp. 127–40; J. J. Tobias, "The Affluent Suburban Male Delinquent," *Crime and Delinquency* 16 (1970), pp. 273–79; and M. J. Hindelang, "The Relationship of Self-Reported Delinquency to Scales of the CPI and MMPI," *Journal of Criminal Law, Criminology and Police Science* 63 (1972), pp. 75–81.

78. R. N. Robbins, "Relationships between Future Orientations, Impulsive Sensation Seeking, and Risk Behavior among Adjudicated Adolescents," *Journal of Adolescent Research* 19 (2004), pp. 428–55.

79. M. D. Slater, K. L. Henry, and R. C. Swaim, "Vulnerable Teens, Vulnerable Times: How Sensation Seeking, Alienation, and Victimization Moderate the Violent Media Content-Aggressiveness Relation," *Communication Research* 3 (2004), pp. 642–68.

80. Jack Katz, *Seductions of Crime: Moral and Sensual Attractions in Doing Evil* (New York: Basic Books, 1988).

81. Bill McCarthy, "Not Just 'For the Thrill of It': An Instrumentalist Elaboration of Katz's Explanation of Sneaky Thrill Property Crimes," *Criminology* 33 (November 1995). For other studies that have identified the importance of sensual experiences, see S. Lyng, "Edgework: A Social Psychological Analysis of Voluntary Risk Taking," *American Journal of Sociology* 95 (1990), pp. 851–56; and William J. Miller, "Edgework: A Model for Understanding Juvenile Delinquency," paper presented at the annual meeting of the Academy of Criminal Justice Sciences, Albuquerque, NM, March 1998.

82. Wilson and Herrnstein, *Crime and Human Nature*.

83. Ibid.

84. Jennifer Stevens, David May, Nancy Rice, and Roger Jarjoura, "Nonsocial Versus Social Reinforcers: Contrasting Theoretical Perspectives on Repetitive Serious Delinquency and Drug Use," *Youth Violence & Juvenile Justice* 9 (2011), pp. 295–312.

85. Avshalom Caspi, Terrie E. Moffitt, Phil A. Silva, Magda Stouthamer-Loeber, Robert F. Krueger, and Pamela S. Schmutte, "Are Some People Crime-Prone? Replications of the Personality–Crime Relationships across Countries, Genders, Races, and Methods," *Criminology* 32 (1994), pp. 175–82. See also Douglas T. Kenrick and David C. Funder, "Profiting from Controversy: Lessons from the Person–Situation Debate," *American Psychologist* 43 (1988), pp. 23–34.

86. Caspi et al., "Are Some People Crime-Prone?"

87. Sheldon Glueck and Eleanor Glueck, *Unraveling Juvenile Delinquency* (Cambridge, Mass.: Harvard University Press for the Commonwealth Fund, 1950).

88. Joshua D. Miller and Donald Lynam, "Structural Models of Personality and Their Relation to Antisocial Behavior: A Meta-Analytic Review," *Criminology* 39 (2001), pp. 765–98.

89. Rolf Loeber and Jeffrey Burke, "Developmental Pathways in Juvenile Externalizing and Internalizing Problems," *Journal of Research on Adolescence* 21 (2011), pp. 34–46.

90. See Hervey Cleckley, *The Mask of Sanity*, 3d ed. (St. Louis, Mo.: Mosby, 1955), pp. 382–417.

91. See R. Hare, "Psychopathy: A Clinical Construct Whose Time Has Come," *Criminal Justice and Behavior* 23 (1996), pp 25–54.

92. Linda Mealey, "The Sociobiology of Sociopathy: An Integrated Evolutionary Model," *Behavioral and Brain Sciences* 18 (1995), pp. 523–40.

93. Daniel C. Murrie, Dewey G. Cornell, Sebastian Kaplan, David McConville, and Andrea Levy-Elkon, "Psychopathy Scores and Violence among Juvenile Offenders: A Multi-Measure Study," *Behavioral Sciences and the Law* 22 (2004), pp. 49–67.

94. Raymond R. Corrado, Gina M. Vincent, Stephen D. Hart, and Irwin M. Cohen, "Predictive Validity of the Psychopathy Checklist: Youth Version for General and Violent Recidivism," *Behavioral Sciences and the Law* 22 (2004), pp. 5–22.

95. Jason Netland and Michael Miner, "Psychopathy Traits and Parental Dysfunction in Sexual Offending and General Delinquent Adolescent Males" *Journal of Sexual Aggression* 18 (2012), pp. 4–22.

96. Jean Piaget, *The Mechanisms of Perception* (New York: Basic Books, 1969).

97. Catherine Walsh, "Reconstructing Larry: Assessing the Legacy of Lawrence Kohlberg," *Ed Magazine*, October 1, 2000, p. 2, http://www.gse.harvard.edu/news/features/larry10012000_page2.html.

98. See Thomas O'Connor, "Moral Development and Theories of Crime," http://www.drtomoconnor.com/1060/1060lect04.htm (accessed October 19, 2012).

99. Ibid.

100. Aaron T. Beck, *Prisoners of Hate: The Cognitive Basis of Anger, Hostility, and Violence* (New York: HarperCollins Publishers, 1999).

101. Megan Moore, "Psychological Theories of Crime and Delinquency," *Journal of Human Behavior in the Social Environment* 21 (2011), pp. 226–39.

102. Stacy Tzoumakis, Patrick Lussier, and Raymond Corrado, "Female Juvenile Delinquency, Motherhood, and the Intergenerational Transmission of Aggression and Antisocial Behavior," *Behavioral Sciences & the Law* (2012), pp. 211–37.

103. Terrie E. Moffitt, Donald R. Lynam, and Phil A. Silva, "Neuropsychological Tests Predicting Persistent Male Delinquency," *Criminology* 32 (May 1994), p. 277.

104. Terrie E. Moffitt, "Adolescent-Limited and Life-Course-Persistent Antisocial Behavior: A Developmental Taxonomy," *Psychological Review* 100 (1993), pp. 674–701.

105. Terrie E. Moffitt, "The Neuropsychology of Conduct Disorder," *Development and Psychopathology* 5 (1993), pp. 135–51; and Terrie E. Moffitt, Avshalom Caspi, N. Dickson, Phil A. Silva, and W. Stanton, "Childhood-Onset versus Adolescent-Onset Antisocial Conduct Problems in Males: Natural History from Ages 3 to 18," *Development and Psychopathology* 8 (1996), pp. 399–424.

106. Richard E. Tremblay, Frank Vitaro, and Daniel Nagin, et al., "The Montreal Longitudinal and Experimental Study: Rediscovering the Power of Description," in *Taking Stock of Delinquency: An Overview of Findings from Contemporary Longitudinal Studies*, edited by Terence P. Thornberry and Marvin D. Krohn (New York: Kluwer Academic Publishers, 2003), pp. 205–254.

107. David P. Farrington, "Key Results from the First Forty Years of the Cambridge Study in Delinquent Development," revised November 2001, http://www.bgsu.edu/downloads/cas/file39372.pdf. (accessed June 22, 2012).

108. Ibid.

109. James O. Finckenauer, *Scared Straight! and the Panacea Phenomenon* (Englewood Cliffs, N.J.: Prentice-Hall, 1982).

110. U.S. Congress, House, Subcommittee on Human Resources of the Committee on Education and Labor, Hearings, Oversight on Scared Straight! 96th Cong. 1st Sess. (June 4, 1979), p. 305.

111. Joan McCord, "A Thirty-Year Follow-Up of Treatment Efforts," *American Psychologist* 33 (1978), p. 284. See also Joan McCord, "Crime in Moral and Social Contexts—The American Society of Criminology, 1989 Presidential Address," *Criminology* 28 (1990), pp. 1–25.

112. Richard J. Lundman, *Prevention and Control of Juvenile Delinquency* (New York: Oxford University Press, 1984).

113. Ibid.

114. Walter B. Miller, "The Impact of a Total Community Delinquency Control Project," *Social Problems* 10 (Fall 1962), pp. 168–191.

115. Walter C. Reckless and Simon Dinitz, *The Prevention of Juvenile Delinquency: An Experiment* (Columbus: Ohio State University Press, 1972).

116. Richard E. Tremblay, Frank Vitaro, Daniel Nagin, et al., "The Montreal Longitudinal and Experimental Study: Rediscovering the Power of Description," in Taking Stock of Delinquency: An Overview of Findings from Contemporary Longitudinal Studies, edited by Terence P. Thornberry and Marvin D. Krohn (New York: Kluwer Academic/Plenum Publishers, 2003), pp. 205–254.

117. James Q. Wilson and Richard J. Herrnstein, "Crime and Human Nature," *Criminology* 23, no. 2 (May 1985), pp. 381–88.

118. Edward P. Mulvey and John F. LaRosa, Jr., "Delinquency Cessation and Adolescent Development: Preliminary Data," *American Journal of Orthopsychiatry* 56, no. 2 (1986), pp. 212–24.

119. David Farrington, "Age and Crime." In *Crime and Justice*, ed. by Michael Tonry, pp. 189-250, Volume 7 (Chicago: University of Chicago Press, 1986). This chapter's section on desistance and crime is adapted in part from Robert J. Sampson and John H. Laub, "Understanding Desistance from Crime," in *Crime and Justice*, Vol. 28, edited by Michael Tonry (Chicago: University of Chicago Press, 2001), pp. 1–69.

120. Farrington, "Age and Crime."

121. Robert J. Sampson and John H. Laub, "A General Age-Graded Theory of Crime: Lessons Learned and the Future of Life-Course Criminology," in *Integrated Developmental and Life Course Theories of Offending: Advances in Criminological Theory*, edited by David P. Farrington (New Brunswick, NJ: Transaction Publishers, 2005), pp. 165–81.

122. Ibid. For another study that found incarceration to be negatively associated with marriage and employment, see Beth M. Huebner, "The Effect of Incarceration on Marriage and Work over the Life Course," *Justice Quarterly* 22 (September 2005), pp. 281–303.

123. Ibid., p. 11.

4 Social Structural Causes of Delinquency

Chapter Objectives

After reading this chapter, you should be able to:

1. Describe the social disorganization theory of delinquency.
2. Explain the cultural deviance theories of delinquency.
3. Compare different strain theories.
4. Describe different structural explanations of delinquency across the life course.
5. Describe the structure and early findings of the Project on Human Development in Chicago Neighborhoods.

> When we speak of a delinquent subculture, we speak of a way of life that has somehow become traditional among certain groups in American society.
>
> —Albert K. Cohen, *Delinquent Boys*

Introduction

In 2012, New York City police arrested a twelve-year-old girl from Queens and charged her with selling marijuana and crack cocaine. Her arrest came as part of a city-wide sweep of drug dealers. Rahiem Newkirk, a youth program coordinator with the city, told television reporters that he knew the girl personally. "She's actually a pretty nice young lady," he said. "I'm actually really, really, really surprised to hear that she's involved in this activity."[1]

Neighborhood residents, however, told a different story, saying that gangs run everything in their neighborhood, and that children as young as seven and eight years old routinely sell drugs and run guns for their older brothers and sisters.

This chapter looks closely at features of the social environment, also known as the **social structure**, that influence young people, causing some of them to commit delinquent acts. Along with Chapters 5 and 6, it provides a variety of sociological explanations for delinquency.

The term *social structure* can have a variety of meanings. As used by sociologists, it can refer to patterns of group relationships, to relatively enduring forms of individual behavior within social systems, or to social institutions and norms embedded in social systems in such a way that they shape the behavior of actors within those systems. Social structure leads to delinquency by way of factors such as child poverty, racial disparity, disorganized communities, and rising levels of unemployment.

Many of the social structural elements that we'll examine in this chapter would likely be found in the life of the twelve-year-old girl whose story opened this chapter. She appears to have come from a socially disorganized and impoverished community. She was likely part of a peer culture that has little stake in conventional values. Indeed, the pressure she must have felt to earn money, combined with her lack of ability to acquire it legitimately, could have led her into the illegal drug trade.

According to social structural theorists, individual-level explanations, like those offered by psychologists, fail to grasp the more significant underlying social and cultural conditions that give rise to delinquent behavior. Sociocultural theorists believe that the overall crime picture reflects social conditions that give rise to collective solutions. They urge that social reform, not individual counseling, be given the highest priority in efforts to reduce crime and delinquency.

The causes of delinquency, as suggested by social structural theorists, include the social and cultural environment in which adolescents grow up and/or the subcultural groups in which they become involved. Elijah Anderson's has written an influential book that traces the relationship between the structural breakdown of the community and crime (see Exhibit 4–1).

social structure
The relatively stable formal and informal arrangements that characterize a society, including its economic arrangements, social institutions, and values and norms.

Exhibit 4–1
Elijah Anderson and the Code of the Street

Elijah Anderson's *Code of the Streets*, which grew out of the ethnographic work Anderson did in two urban communities in Philadelphia, focused on the theme of interpersonal violence in the lives of inner-city youths. In questioning why so many inner-city adolescents are involved in violence and aggression, he concluded that in the economically deprived and drug-ridden communities in which they live, a "code of the streets" has replaced or at least weakened the rule of civil law.

A set of informal rules, or prescriptions for behavior, focuses on a search for respect. What is understood as respect is the "props" (or proper due). In this street culture, according to Anderson, respect is difficult to win and can be easily lost and requires constant vigilance. Respect is a form of social capital that is particularly valuable when other forms of capital are unavailable or have been lost.

The concept of "manhood" expresses respect and identity in the lives of these inner-city youths. This concept of manhood requires a certain ruthlessness and the ability to take care of oneself. It also requires having a sense of control, of being in charge, and of showing nerve. One's manhood must be communicated through words, gestures, and actions. Youths make it clear that everyone understands that if you mess with them, there will be "street justice or severe consequences because they are man enough to make you pay."

References: Elijah Anderson, *Code of the Streets: Decency, Violence, and the Moral Life of the Inner City*; "The Code of the Street and African-American Adolescent Violence," *Research in Brief*, February 2009, http://www.ojp.usdoj.gov/nij; Karen F. Parker and Amy Reckdenwald, "Concentrated Disadvantage, Traditional Male Role Models, and African-American Juvenile Violence," *Criminology* 46 (2008), pp. 711–735; Nikki Jones, "Working 'the Code': On Girls, Gender, and Inner-City Violence," *Australian and New Zealand Journal of Criminology*, 41 (2008), pp. 63–83.

Social structural theorists typically use official statistics as proof of their claim that forces such as social disorganization, cultural deviance, status frustration, and social mobility are so powerful that they induce lower-class youths to become involved in delinquent behavior. This chapter will examine several of these perspectives.

Video 4–1 Introduction to Social Disorganization

Social Disorganization Theory

Social disorganization can be defined as "the inability of a community structure to realize the common values of its residents and maintain effective social control."[2] **Social disorganization theory** suggests that macrosocial forces (e.g., large-scale effects such as migration, segregation, structural transformation of the economy, housing discrimination) interact with community-level factors (e.g., local-level poverty, family disruption, residential turnover) to impede effective social organization. This sociological viewpoint focuses attention on the structural characteristics and mediating processes of community social organization that help explain crime while also recognizing the larger historical, political, and social forces that contribute to shaping local communities.[3]

The intellectual antecedents of social disorganization theory can be traced to the work of French sociologist Emile Durkheim. In Durkheim's view, *anomie*, or normlessness, resulted from society's failure to provide adequate regulation of its members' attitudes and behaviors. Loss of regulation was particularly likely when society and its members experienced rapid change and laws did not keep pace.[4]

social disorganization theory
An approach that posits that juvenile delinquency results when social control among the traditional primary groups, such as the family and the neighborhood, breaks down because of social disarray within the community.

Shaw and McKay

Social disorganization theory was developed by Clifford R. Shaw and Henry D. McKay during the first half of the twentieth century. Shaw and McKay, whose work helped found the Chicago School of Sociology, focused specifically on the social characteristics of the community as a cause of delinquency.[5] Their pioneering investigations established that delinquency varied in inverse proportion to the distance from the center of the city, that it varied inversely with socioeconomic status, and that delinquency rates in a residential area persisted regardless of changes in racial and ethnic composition of the area.[6]

Social Disorganization and the Community

Shaw and McKay viewed juvenile delinquency as resulting from the breakdown of social control among the traditional primary groups, such as the family and the neighborhood,

◀ A former Hispanic gang member in a wheelchair counsels teens at a Los Angeles school.
■ **How might the social environment of a community contribute to delinquency?**

because of the social disorganization of the community. Rapid industrialization, urbanization, and immigration processes contributed to the disorganization of the community. Delinquent behavior, then, became an alternative mode of socialization through which youths who were part of disorganized communities were attracted to deviant lifestyles.[7] The delinquent values and traditions, replacing traditional ones, were passed from one generation to the next.

Shaw and McKay turned to the concept of ecology to show this relationship between social disorganization and delinquency. Park and Burgess had earlier used the idea of social ecology, which examines the spacing and interdependence of people and institutions, in explaining the growth of cities. Burgess, for example, suggested that cities do not merely grow at their edges but rather have a tendency to expand radially from their centers in patterns of concentric circles, each moving gradually outward.[8] Figure 4–1 is a diagram of the growth zones as Burgess envisioned them.

In 1929, Shaw reported that marked variations in rates of school truancy, juvenile delinquency, and adult criminality existed within different areas in Chicago. These rates varied inversely with the distance from the center of the city; that is, the nearer a given locality was to the center of the city, the higher its rates of delinquency and crime.[9] In 1942, Shaw and McKay published their classic work *Juvenile Delinquency and Urban Areas*, which further developed these ecological insights.[10] They discovered that over a thirty-three-year period, the vast majority of delinquent boys came either from areas adjacent to the central business and industrial districts of the city, or from neighborhoods along two forks of the Chicago River.

Then, applying Burgess's concentric zone hypothesis of urban growth, they constructed a series of concentric circles, like the circles on a target, with the bull's-eye in the central city. Measuring delinquency rates by zones and by areas within the zones, they found that the highest rates of delinquency were in Zone I (the central city), the next highest were in Zone II (next to the central city), and so forth, in progressive steps outward to the lowest rates in Zone VI. Significantly, although the delinquency rates changed from one time period to the next, the relationships among the different zones remained constant, even though in

FIGURE 4–1
Concentric Zones in Chicago

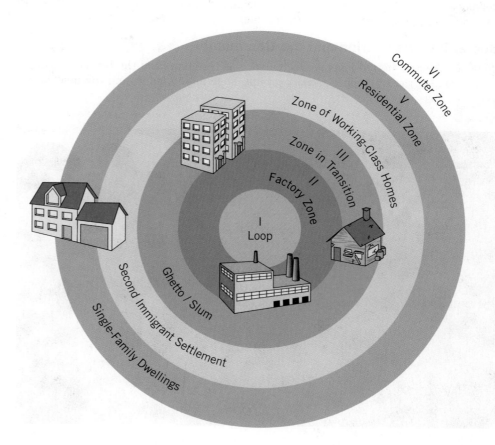

some neighborhoods the ethnic compositions of the population totally changed. During the first decade of the twentieth century, for example, the largest portion of the population in the crime-prone areas was German or Irish, but 30 years later it was Polish and Italian.[11]

Opportunity Structure and Delinquency

Shaw and McKay eventually refocused their analysis from the influence of social disorganization of the community to the importance of economics on high rates of delinquency. They found that the economic and occupational structures of the larger society were more influential in the rise of delinquent behavior than was the social life of the local community. They concluded that the reason members of lower-class groups remained in the inner-city community was less a reflection of their newness of arrival and their lack of acculturation to American institutions than a function of their class position in society.[12]

The consequences of this **differential opportunity structure** led to a conflict of values in local communities: Some residents embraced illegitimate standards of behavior, whereas others maintained allegiance to conventional values. Delinquent groups were characterized by their own distinctive standards, and Shaw and McKay became increasingly involved in examining the process through which delinquents came to learn and to pass on these standards.[13]

Cultural Transmission Theory

Shaw and McKay also elaborated on social disorganization theory by arguing that delinquent behavior became an alternative mode of socialization through which youths who were part of disorganized communities were attracted to deviant lifestyles.[14] This line of thought became known as the cultural deviance component of social disorganization theory.

Shaw and McKay further contended that the delinquent values and traditions that replaced traditional social standards were not the property of any one ethnic or racial group but were culturally transmitted from one generation to the next.[15] As evidence in support of this **cultural transmission theory**, these researchers found that certain inner-city areas continued to have the highest delinquency rates in Chicago despite shifts in population of nearly all of these areas.

Shaw and McKay assumed that juvenile and adult gangs in these areas accounted for the transmission of this tradition of delinquency. Figure 4–2 diagrams the theoretical constructs of Shaw and McKay's social disorganization theory.

Evaluation of Shaw and McKay's Disorganization Theory

Social disorganization theory lost much of its vitality as a prominent criminological perspective in the late 1960s and 1970s. That's because theory and research in that period focused primarily on individual characteristics, rather than on group and community characteristics.[16] Despite criticisms of social disorganization theory, it experienced "a quiet, but significant revival" in the 1980s and later.[17] As the reemergence of interest in social disorganization theory shows, the works of Shaw and McKay and social ecology have had an enduring impact on the study of delinquency in the United States. In particular:

- Shaw and McKay's studies addressed the problem of crime in terms of multiple levels of analysis. They shifted attention away from individual characteristics of delinquents and nondelinquents and toward group traditions in delinquency and the influence of the larger community.

- Shaw and McKay's social disorganization theory contributed to a rediscovery of the importance of the community in studies of delinquency. This rediscovery led to the conclusion that an adequate understanding of the causes of illegal behavior requires an examination of the social structure, the individual, and other social contexts (such as primary groups) that mediate between the individual and that structure.[18]

Voices of Delinquency 4–1
Read "I Grew Up in New Orleans." How did the influence of his environment affect this youth? What aspects of Shaw and McKay's theory of social disorganization are found in the life of this youth?

differential opportunity structure
The differences in economic and occupational opportunities open to members of different socioeconomic classes.

cultural transmission theory
An approach that holds that areas of concentrated crime maintain their high rates over a long period, even when the composition of the population changes rapidly, because delinquent "values" become cultural norms and are passed from one generation to the next.

Socially Disorganized Neighborhood → Failure of Informal Social Controls → Increased Gang Activity → Cultural Transmission of Delinquent Traditions → Increased Delinquent Activity

FIGURE 4–2
Shaw and McKay's Social Disorganization Theory

▲ According to sociologist Albert Cohen, the destruction of property is a consequence of reaction formation, in which lower-class youths respond to the strain of being held to the standards of middle-class culture.

■ **What about middle-class youths who commit such acts? Does Cohen's theory hold true for them, or can their acts be attributed to other factors?**

Web Extra 4–1
Project on Human Development in Chicago Neighborhoods (PHDCN)

✎ **cultural deviance theory**
A theory wherein delinquent behavior is viewed as an expression of conformity to cultural values and norms that are in opposition to those of the larger U.S. society.

- Shaw and McKay's theory influenced research on how people and institutions adapt to their environment.[19] It saw the delinquent gang as a normal response to slum conditions and the social deprivations of local environments.

Recent examination of the social disorganization perspective has opened up exciting new avenues of research inquiry that have gone beyond Shaw and McKay's original work.[20] For example, Shaw and McKay's work has been updated by the ideas inherent in social ecology. The main contention of this position is that living in deteriorated social environments, in which poverty, drugs, violence, and alienation exist, leads to high delinquency rates. Later in this chapter, the Project on Human Development in Chicago Neighborhoods and the concept of collective efficacy are discussed as promising approaches to revitalizing deteriorating communities.[21]

In a final test of the social disorganization perspective, one 2009 study questioned whether neighborhood social processes operate in a similar way across all types of disadvantaged neighborhoods. This test of social disorganization theory in high-risk urban neighborhoods used data from forty-four impoverished Denver neighborhoods and found that, for this high-risk sample, the most consistent predictor of rates of problem behavior is juveniles' perceptions of limited opportunities for the future.[22]

Cultural Deviance Theory and Delinquency

Social disorganization theory focused on the structural breakup of urban communities, but the next theory, **cultural deviance theory**, focuses instead on the delinquent values that are found in some lower-class cultures. Both perspectives, however, can be termed "cultural transmission theories" because the disorganization of the environment seen in social disorganization theory leads to cultural deviance.

Central to cultural deviance theory is the belief that delinquent and criminal behaviors are expressions of conformity to cultural values and norms that are in opposition to those of the larger society. According to sociologist Ruth Rosner Kornhauser, the necessary and sufficient cause of delinquency in cultural deviance models "is socialization to subcultural values condoning as right conduct what the controlling legal system defines as crime."[23]

Miller's Lower-Class Culture and Delinquent Values

Walter B. Miller's theory of lower-class culture and delinquent values provides a cultural deviance approach that is useful in explaining delinquent behavior. In Miller's version of cultural deviance theory, the motivation to become involved in delinquent behavior is endemic to lower-class culture:

> The cultural system which exerts the most direct influence on [delinquent] behavior is that of the lower-class community itself—a long-established, distinctively patterned tradition with an integrity of its own—rather than a so-called "delinquent subculture" which has arisen through conflict with middle-class culture and is oriented to the deliberate violation of middle-class norms.[24]

focal concerns
The values or focal concerns (trouble, toughness, smartness, excitement, fate, and autonomy) of lower-class youths that differ from those of middle-class youths.

Focal Concerns of Lower-Class Culture

Miller argued that a set of **focal concerns** characterizes lower-class culture. These concerns—trouble, toughness, smartness, excitement, fate, and autonomy—command widespread attention and a high degree of emotional involvement.[25] Miller described each as follows:

- *Trouble.* Miller contended that staying out of trouble represents a major challenge for lower-class citizens, and that personal status is often determined by how often an individual gets into "trouble" with the law. The more "trouble" in a person's life, the more he is looked up to by others.

- *Toughness.* Physical prowess, as demonstrated by strength and endurance, is valued in lower-class culture. In the eyes of lower-class boys, the tough guy who is hard, fearless, and undemonstrative, as well as a good fighter, is the ideal man.

- *Smartness.* The capacity to outsmart, outfox, outwit, con, dupe, and "take" others is valued in lower-class culture. In addition, a man also must be able to avoid being outwitted, duped, or "taken" himself. Smartness is also required as a way to acquire material goods and achieve personal status without physical effort.

- *Excitement.* The search for excitement, or thrill-seeking, is another of the focal concerns of lower-class life.

- *Fate.* Lower-class individuals, according to Miller, often feel that their lives are subject to a set of forces over which they have little control. They accept the concept of destiny and may sense that their lives are guided by strong spiritual forces.

- *Autonomy.* The desire for personal independence is an important concern, partly because the lower-class individual feels controlled by others so much of the time.

Central to Miller's thesis is the belief that persons of lower socioeconomic status share a distinctive culture of their own and that the focal concerns, or values, of that culture make lower-class boys more likely to become involved in delinquent behavior. Those boys, said Miller, want to demonstrate that they are tough and are able to outwit others. They also look at the pursuit of crime as a thrill, yet they are likely to believe that if an individual is going to get caught, there is nothing he or she can do about it. Crime, then, permits lower-class youths to show personal independence from the controls placed on them and also provides an avenue through which youths hope to gain material goods and personal status with a minimum of physical effort. See Figure 4–3 for the theoretical constructs of Miller's theory.

Evaluation of Miller's Theory

Miller's theory appears most plausible when applied to the behavior of lower-class gang members. As a number of researchers have noted, gangs appear to have their own values and norms, distinct from the values and norms of the larger culture. In keeping with this perspective, Marvin E. Wolfgang and Franco Ferracuti, contemporaries of Miller, argued

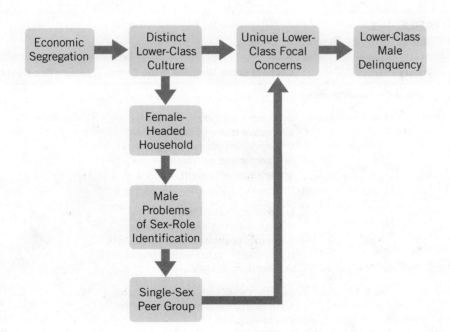

FIGURE 4–3
Miller's Theory of Lower-Class Culture

that a subculture of violence among young males in the lower social classes legitimates the use of violence.[26]

Miller's contention that the lower classes have distinctive values has been widely criticized, however. Some critics argue that the evidence shows that lower-class youths hold the same values as those of the larger culture. For example, Richard A. Cloward and Lloyd E. Ohlin (discussed later in this chapter), as well as criminologist Albert K. Cohen, claimed that lower-class youths internalize middle-class values and that their delinquent acts reflect middle-class values.[27] See Table 4–1 for an overview of cultural deviance theories.

Voices of Delinquency 4–2
Read "The Life and Times of Herron Lewiel, Jr."
When Herron was growing up in Chicago, did he adhere to a set of lower-class values? What role did the gang play in accepting these values or norms?

Strain Theory and Delinquency

strain theory
A theory that proposes that the pressure the social structure exerts on youths who cannot attain cultural success goals will push them to engage in nonconforming behavior.

Strain theory proposes that delinquency results from the frustrations individuals feel when they are unable to achieve the goals they desire. One of the most important strain theorists is Robert K. Merton.

Merton's Theory of Anomie

Robert K. Merton, who was one of the most influential sociologists of the twentieth century, made an important contribution to our understanding of how deviant behavior is produced by different social structures. In his now-classic work, *Social Theory and Social Structure*, Merton wrote:

> Socially deviant behavior is just as much a product of social structure as conformist behavior.... Our primary aim is to discover how some social structures exert a definite pressure upon certain persons in the society to engage in nonconforming rather than conforming behavior.[28]

culturally defined goals
In Merton's strain theory, the set of purposes and interests a culture defines as legitimate objectives for individuals.

institutionalized means
In Merton's theory, culturally sanctioned methods of attaining individual goals.

Merton placed emphasis on two elements of social and cultural systems: **culturally defined goals** and **institutionalized means**. Culturally defined goals, purposes, and interests are "held out as legitimate objectives for all or for diversely located members of the society."[29] These are the goals that people feel are worth striving for. A second important aspect, socially approved institutionalized means, "defines, regulates, and controls the acceptable means of reaching out for these goals."[30] Although a specific goal may be attained by a variety of means, the wider culture does not approve of all of these means. Hence, Merton referred to the acceptable method as institutionalized means. Merton contended that the two elements,

TABLE 4–1
Cultural Deviance Theories of Crime

Theory	Cause of Crime Identified in the Theory	Supporting Research
Cultural Deviance Theories		
Shaw and McKay	Delinquent behavior becomes an alternative mode of socialization through which youths who are part of disorganized communities are attracted to delinquent values and traditions.	Moderate
Miller	Lower-class culture has a distinctive culture of its own, and its focal concerns, or values, make lower-class boys more likely to become involved in delinquent behavior.	Weak
Wolfgang and Ferracuti	Subcultures of violence exist among lower-class males and legitimize the use of violence.	Weak

or goals and means, must be reasonably well integrated if a culture is to be stable and run smoothly. If individuals believe that a particular goal is important, they should have a legitimate means to attain it; but when a culture lacks such integration, then a state of normlessness, or *anomie*, occurs. Merton further asserted that contemporary U.S. culture seemed to "approximate the polar type in which great emphasis upon certain success goals occurs without equivalent emphasis upon institutional means."[31] For example, most members of the lower social classes are asked to orient their behavior toward the prospect of accumulating wealth, but they are largely denied the means to do so legitimately. The clash between cultural ideals and the possibilities held out by social structure creates a condition of *anomie*, or intense pressure for deviance. Such pressure can also be described as tension or *strain*.

Merton developed a typology of the modes of adaptation that individuals may use when confronted with *anomie*. Table 4–2 lists five types of individual adaptation: conformity, innovation, ritualism, retreatism, and rebellion. A plus sign (+) signifies acceptance, a minus sign (–) signifies rejection, and a plus/minus sign (±) signifies a rejection of the prevailing values and a substitution of new ones. Merton's theory uses these modes of adaptation to explain how deviant behavior in general is produced by the social structure, and it can also be applied to juvenile law-breaking.[32] The five types of adaptation are described more fully in the following subsections.

Conformity

If a society is well integrated and *anomie* is absent, conformity both to cultural goals and to institutionalized means will be the most common form of adaptation assumed by most people. Conforming juveniles accept the cultural goals of society as well as the institutionalized means of attaining them; they work hard in legitimate ways to become successful.

Innovation

When adolescents accept cultural goals but reject the institutionalized means of attaining them, they may pursue other paths that frequently are not legitimate in terms of cultural values. Such nonlegitimate innovative behavior is often what we call criminal behavior.

Ritualism

Although they may have abandoned the attempt to achieve approved cultural goals, some juveniles will continue to participate in acceptable means for attaining them. Ritualism consists of "individually seeking a private escape from the dangers and frustrations ... inherent in the competition for major cultural goals by abandoning these goals and clinging all the more closely to the safe routines and institutional norms."[33]

Retreatism

Some people reject both culturally approved goals and means and retreat from society. Homeless people, survivalists, drug addicts, and some people with mental illnesses could be classified as retreatists.

TABLE 4–2
Merton's Theory of Anomie

Modes of Adaptation	Cultural Goal	Institutionalized Means
Conformity	+	+
Innovation	+	–
Ritualism	–	+
Retreatism	–	–
Rebellion	±	±

Source: This material appears in Robert K. Merton, "Social Structure and Anomie," *American Sociological Review* 3 (1938), p. 676.

FIGURE 4-4
Merton's Strain Theory

Library Extra 4-1
National Institute of Justice: *National Evaluation of the "I Have a Dream" Program*

blocked opportunity
The limited or nonexistent chance of success; according to strain theory, a key factor in delinquency.

Rebellion

Rebellion consists of rejecting the goals and values of one's culture and substituting a new set of goals and values for them. Anarchists and revolutionaries are the epitome of rebels in American society, although anyone who adopts a dramatically alternative lifestyle can also fit into this category.

Merton argued that his theory of anomie was "designed to account for some, but not all, forms of deviant behavior customarily described as criminal or delinquent."[34] Thus, instead of attempting to explain all the behaviors prohibited by criminal law, Merton focused attention on the pressure or strain resulting from the discrepancy between culturally induced goals and the opportunities inherent in the social structure.[35] See Figure 4-4 for an overview of the theoretical constructs of Merton's theory.

Institutional Anomie Theory

Twenty years ago, Steven Messner and Richard Rosenfeld authored a book named *Crime and the American Dream*. In it, they developed a theory of institutional anomie. They agreed with Merton that the success goal is widespread in society, and described the "American dream," which they viewed as both a goal and a process. As a goal, they said, the American dream involves accumulating materialistic goods and wealth. As a process, Americans are socialized to believe that this goal is attainable and are taught that they can achieve it. The desire to attain the American dream generates pressures toward delinquency.[36]

According to Messner and Rosenfeld, American society is unique in that anomic conditions have been permitted to develop to such a high degree; and this, in turn, is what feeds high delinquency rates.[37] In a testing of cross-national data sets, University of Nebraska criminologist Jukka Savolainen found support for institutional anomie theory in a study in 2000. Savolainen's study indicated that the demonstrable effects of economic inequality on the level of lethal violence are largely limited to nations characterized by weak social welfare systems.[38]

Evaluation of Merton's Theory

Merton's revision of anomie theory has been called "the most influential single formulation in the sociology of deviance ... and possibly the most frequently quoted single paper in modern sociology."[39] One of the main emphases of Merton's theory—an emphasis that has been largely ignored—is that it is "a theory of societal *anomie*, not of individually felt strain."[40] The theory's influence on the later theoretical contributions of well-known delinquency theorists Richard A. Cloward and Lloyd E. Ohlin as well as Albert K. Cohen demonstrates its importance to delinquency theory.[41]

Strain Theory and the Individual Level of Analysis

Strain theory, especially in the form of *anomie*, dominated criminology in the 1960s before labeling theory gained acceptance in the late 1960s and early 1970s. A major reason for the widespread acceptance of strain theory was that its central thesis of **blocked opportunity** resonated with Americans' growing concern over equal opportunity, and with the fear that social injustice had deep cultural roots.[42]

Strain theory met increased criticism in the late 1970s, when people began to argue that the theory had found little empirical support and ought to be abandoned as an explanation for crime.[43] In the 1980s, Thomas J. Bernard successfully defended the conceptual underpinnings of strain theory, but recognized that it had not been tested adequately.[44]

Developed in the 1980s, Robert Agnew's revised strain theory of delinquency points to another source of frustration and strain: the blockage of pain–avoidance behavior.[45] Agnew argued that when juveniles are compelled to remain in painful or aversive environments, such as dysfunctional families or schools in which they have little interest, the ensuing frustration is likely to lead to escape attempts or anger-based delinquent behavior. His examination of data from the Youth in Transition survey revealed that a juvenile's location in aversive environments in the school and family "has a direct effect on delinquency and an indirect effect through anger."[46] Fundamental to Agnew's findings was his use of an autonomy scale, through which he was able to accurately predict the delinquency of boys two years following testing. The questionnaire he used included questions such as "One of my goals in life is to be free of the control of others." Boys who were most driven to achieve autonomy were most likely to turn to delinquency, regardless of their socioeconomic status or the presence or absence of social controls at home or at school.[47]

General Strain Theory

Agnew also developed a general strain theory of crime and delinquency that distinguishes three different sources of strain: (1) "failure to achieve positively valued goals," (2) "the removal of positively valued stimuli from the individual," and (3) the presentation of negative stimuli."[48] Anger and frustration are negative emotions resulting from such strain, and juveniles may cope with these strains through delinquent behaviors. Delinquency may be a way of escaping from or reducing strain (e.g., theft to achieve monetary goals). Certain strains are seen as more likely to lead to delinquency than others: (1) those high in magnitude, (2) those viewed as unjust, (3) those associated with lower self-control, and (4) those creating some pressure or incentive to engage in crime.[49] Agnew's general strain theory then presents guidelines, or a strategy, for measuring strain and explores under what conditions strain is likely to result in "nondelinquent and delinquent coping."[50]

John Rodriguez and Scott Belshaw's 2010 study on general strain theory examined how general strain theory may aid in explaining racial differences in offending. The study compared measures of general strain theory and white juvenile delinquency to that of Latino juvenile delinquency, and found that even though Latino youth suffer from strain and might handle strain differently, they are less likely to commit delinquent acts due to strain. In contrast, the study found that white youths have a greater propensity to commit more serious acts of delinquency because of strain than do Latino youths.[51]

Wen-Hsu Lin and colleagues' 2011 study used general strain theory to evaluate how violent victimization, vicarious violent victimization (which occurs when witnessing the violent victimization of others), and dual violent victimization (which occurs when a person is the victim of a violent crime *and* also witnesses the violent victimization of others) affect juvenile violent/property crime and drug use. They found that all three types of violent victimization have significant and positive direct effects on violent/property crime and drug use.[52]

In sum, after a period of neglect, individual-level strain theory has experienced a revival, primarily through the work of Robert Agnew, especially in the form of his general strain theory.[53]

Library Extra 4–2
"Robert Agnew's Strain Theory Approach"

Voices of Delinquency 4–3
Read "A Sad Story." What strain was present in this youth's life? How did he cope with this strain?

Cohen's Theory of Delinquent Subcultures

In 1955 the famous sociologist Albert K. Cohen published his well-received book, *Delinquent Boys: The Culture of the Gang*. In it Cohen suggested that lower-class youth are fully internalizing the goals of middle-class culture but that they experience **status frustration**, or strain, because they are unable to attain them. Consequently, strain explains their membership in delinquent gangs and their nonutilitarian, malicious, and negativistic behavior.[54]

status frustration
The stress that individuals experience when they cannot attain their goals because of their socioeconomic class.

Delinquent Subculture

The social structure in American society, Cohen claimed, has an immense hold on citizens— even twelve- and thirteen-year-old children know the realities of socioeconomic status.[55] The American class system, said Cohen, determines the middle-class values and norms children are expected to aspire to and to achieve:

> These norms are, in effect, a tempered version of the Protestant ethic which has played such an important part in the shaping of American character and American society. In brief summary, this middle-class ethic prescribes an obligation to strive, by dint of rational, ascetic, self-disciplined, and independent activity, to achieve in worldly affairs. A not irrebuttable but common corollary is the presumption that "success" is itself a sign of the exercise of these moral qualities.[56]

Status at school is especially measured by these middle-class standards. The first job of the teacher is to instill American values and to foster the development of middle-class personalities among his or her students. Second, the teacher is likely to be a middle-class person who values ambition and achievement, and is quick to recognize and reward these virtues in others. Third, Cohen pointed out, the educational system itself favors "quiet, co-operative, 'well-behaved' pupils" who make the teacher's job easier, and it greets with disapproval the "lusty, irrepressible, boisterous youngsters who are destructive of order, routine, and predictability in the classroom."[57]

As mentioned previously, a pivotal assumption in Cohen's theory is that lower-class males internalize middle-class norms and values but then find themselves unable to attain middle-class goals. Status frustration then occurs, and the mechanism of **reaction formation** is used to address it. On the one hand, according to Cohen, the delinquent claims that the middle-class standards do not matter; but on the other hand, he or she reacts by directing irrational, malicious, unaccountable hostility toward the norms of the respectable middle-class society.[58]

Cohen defined nine norms that he said make up the middle-class measuring rod:

1. Ambition
2. Individual responsibility
3. Achievement
4. Temperance
5. Rationality
6. Courtesy and likeability
7. Lowered physical aggression
8. Educational recreation
9. Respect for property.[59]

Failing to achieve many of these goals, the delinquent subculture offers lower-class males the status they cannot achieve in the larger culture, but the status offered by the delinquent subculture is status only in the eyes of fellow delinquents.[60]

Cohen added that the delinquent subculture is nonutilitarian: Delinquents commit crimes "for the hell of it," without intending to gain or profit from their crimes. Cohen also claimed that malice is evident in the crimes fostered by delinquent subculture, that delinquents often display joy in the discomfort of others, and delight in the defiance of taboos. Further, the delinquent's conduct is right by the standards of delinquent subculture precisely because it is wrong by the norms of the larger culture.[61] Moreover, the delinquent subculture demonstrates versatility in its delinquent behaviors; members of this subculture do not specialize in any particular form of crime or deviance, as do many adult criminal gangs and "solitary" delinquents. The delinquent subculture is characterized by "short-run hedonism." Its members have little interest in planning activities, setting long-term goals, budgeting time, or gaining knowledge and skills that require practice, deliberation, and study. Instead, gang members literally hang around the corner waiting for something to turn up. A further characteristic of delinquent subculture is its emphasis on group autonomy, which makes gang members intolerant of any restraint except the informal pressures of the gang itself.[62] See Figure 4–5 for an outline of the theoretical constructs of Cohen's theory.

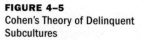

reaction formation
The psychological strategy for dealing with frustration by becoming hostile toward an unattainable object.

Voices of Delinquency 4–4
Read "My Experiences as a Juvenile Delinquent." How did this middle-class youngster ever end up the way he did? How many of Cohen's norms did he rebel against? What turned him around?

FIGURE 4–5
Cohen's Theory of Delinquent Subcultures

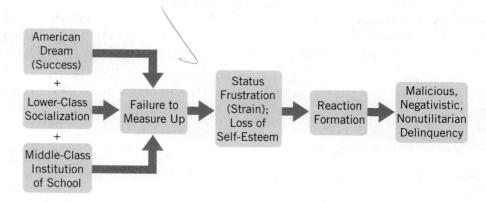

People In the Know
Interview with Albert K. Cohen

Question: Let's begin with the thesis that you expressed in *Delinquent Boys* thirty years ago. Would you express it any differently today?

Cohen: I don't know what form it would take, except that it would be different. It has been subject to a lot of criticisms, and I have developed some of my own reservations about it, which have not necessarily been embodied in the public criticism in the literature. It obviously would have to be rethought. But I think in certain respects my own thinking has not been altered—the notion that most delinquent activity, like most human activity, consists of actions that people do more or less together, or that are at least oriented to other people, is still true. The motivation to engage in those activities always is to some extent the function of a person's relationships to other people, and one's participation in those activities is in some sense instrumental to the promotion of satisfying relationships with others. This, I think, is the fundamental premise of the whole book; it's a basic premise, I think, to the whole idea of sociology. What has bothered me most in the years since the publication of that book is not so much the declining influence or acceptance of some of the ideas specific to that particular interpretation of delinquency, but rather the decline of this general perspective on human conduct as applied to delinquency. I think it is a safe generalization that, in the past fifteen years or so, the literature is coming to focus more and more on the nature, the character, and the individual circumstances of persons. Thus, rather than seeing the delinquent act as something that occurs in an interactive situation and is the product of an interaction, the delinquent's actions are interpreted through that person's personality and background. Delinquency needs to be perceived and treated as events performed in the company of others or oriented to others, guided somehow by the norms, expectations, and beliefs that are derived from and are sustained by one's communication with other people. The delinquent act is an event in a matrix of interaction, and in that matrix there are a number of people. One of the persons will be the person to whom the act will be accredited. Amongst all the people there is one person whom we point the finger at and we say, "That's the person who did it!" But if you are trying to explain the action or the event, you don't explain it by saying, "This person did it," and then look at that person and try to find out what's special about that person, because the event was a product of the whole context in which it was embedded. What was going on at the time will include all the contributions by all the participants. I think there is a very fundamental kind of linkage between the sociological and the psychological level. But having answered the psychological question, you are still left with the sociological question. I think *Delinquent Boys* was in a way quintessentially sociological. That doesn't make it superior to Hirschi or other studies of delinquency. The sociological question is not any more legitimate than the psychological question. But this book was addressed to the sociological question. By this I mean, it looked at certain kinds of events, in this case delinquency. It located these events in a certain space, and that space was within the social system. It raised such questions as: What's going on in this society? Where does it happen? On what scale? And why?

Source: Albert K. Cohen, professor emeritus of sociology at the University of Connecticut, is the author of the classic study *Delinquent Boys: The Culture of the Gang*. He is also the author of *Deviance and Control* and edited the *Sutherland Papers* and *Prison Violence*. This interview took place in November 1983.

Evaluation of Cohen's Theory

Cohen's *Delinquent Boys* made a seminal contribution to the delinquency literature. Cohen's theory is important because it views delinquency as a process of interaction between delinquent youths and others, rather than as the abrupt and sudden product of strain or anomie, as proposed by Merton's theory. Cohen contended that delinquency arises during a continuous interaction process whereby changes in one's self result from the activities of others.[63] One of the most serious criticisms leveled at Cohen's theory was offered by Travis Hirschi, who questioned the feasibility of using status frustration as the motivational energy to account for delinquency because most delinquent boys eventually become law-abiding citizens, even though their lower-class status does not change.[64] Also, Cohen does not offer any empirical evidence to support his theory, and the vagueness of such concepts as reaction formation and lower-class internalization of middle-class values makes it difficult to test his theory.

Nevertheless, both Cohen's theory and the critiques and controversies surrounding it have done much to spark the further development of delinquency theory, and much of the research

▲ Members of the Pico Norte 19th Street gang in El Paso, Texas, flash hand signs and tattoos.
■ **How might Cohen's notion of status frustration explain youth gang membership and delinquency?**

Video 4–2 Cloward and Ohlin

into delinquency causation has built on Cohen's findings. See the People In the Know interview with Albert K. Cohen in this chapter, as well as Table 4–3 for further insights.

Cloward and Ohlin's Opportunity Theory

Sociologists Richard A. Cloward and Lloyd E. Ohlin sought to integrate the theoretical contributions of Merton and Cohen with the ideas of Edwin H. Sutherland (see Chapter 5). Although Merton argued that lower-class youths strive for monetary success and Cohen contended that they strive for status, Cloward and Ohlin conceptualized success and status as separate strivings that can operate independently of each other. In their **opportunity theory**, Cloward and Ohlin portrayed delinquents who seek an increase in status as striving for membership in the middle class, whereas other delinquent youths try to improve their economic position without changing their class position.

opportunity theory
A perspective that holds that gang members turn to delinquency because of a sense of injustice about the lack of legitimate opportunities open to them.

Cloward and Ohlin argued that the most serious delinquents are those who experience the greatest conflict with middle-class values, since they "are looked down upon both for what they do want (i.e., the middle-class style of life) and for what they do not want (i.e., 'crass materialism')."[65] Cloward and Ohlin use Merton's theory to explain the delinquency that youths commit. They assume that these youths have no legitimate opportunities to improve their economic position and therefore that they will become involved in one of three specialized gang subcultures: "criminal," "conflict," or "retreatist."[66] Each is characterized by its own set of values and behaviors, or subcultures, as we discuss next.

Criminal Subculture

The criminal subculture is primarily based on criminal values. Within this subculture, illegal acts such as extortion, fraud, and theft are accepted as means to achieve economic success. This subculture provides the socialization by which new members learn to admire and respect older criminals and to adopt their lifestyles and behaviors. As new members master the techniques and acquire the values of the criminal world through criminal episodes, they become hostile toward and distrustful of representatives of the larger society, whom they regard as "suckers" to be exploited whenever possible.[67]

Conflict Subculture

Violence is the key ingredient in the conflict subculture, whose members pursue status (or "rep") through force or threats of force. Warrior youth gangs exemplify this subculture. The "gangster bopper," the basic role model, fights to win respect from other gangs and to demand deference from the adult world. Because of the role he plays in his subculture, he is expected to show great courage in the face of personal danger and always to defend his personal integrity and the honor of the gang.[68]

TABLE 4–3
Summary of Strain Theories of Delinquency

Strain Theories	Features	Supporting Research
Merton	Social structure exerts pressure on individuals who cannot attain the cultural goal of success, leading them to engage in nonconforming behavior.	Moderate
Agnew	Blocked pain-avoidance behavior promotes crime	Moderate
Cohen	Lower-class boys are unable to attain the goals of middle-class culture, and hence become involved in nonutilitarian, malicious, and negative behavior.	Weak

A reputation for toughness—the primary goal of fighting gangs—ensures respect from peers and fear from adults, and provides a means of gaining access to scarce resources that provide pleasure and opportunity in underprivileged areas. Relationships with the adult world are typically weak, because gang members are unable to find appropriate adult role models who offer approved opportunities leading to adult success.[69]

Retreatist Subculture

The consumption of drugs is the basic activity of the retreatist subculture. Feeling shut out from conventional roles in the family or occupational world, members of this subculture withdraw into an arena where the ultimate goal is the "kick," which may mean alcohol, marijuana, hard drugs, sexual experiences, exciting music, or any combination of these. Whatever is chosen, retreatists are seeking an intense awareness of living and a sense of pleasure that is "out of this world."[70] The retreatist subculture generates a new order of goals and criteria for achievement, but instead of attempting to impose their system of values on the rest of the world, retreatists are content merely to strive for status and deference within their own subculture.

Cloward and Ohlin noted that although the three subcultures exhibit essentially different orientations, the lines between them may become blurred. For example, a subculture primarily involved with conflict may on occasion become involved in systematic theft, or members of a criminal subculture may sometimes become involved in conflict with a rival gang.[71] Table 4–4 and Figure 4–6 outline the main theoretical constructs of Cloward and Ohlin's theory.

Voices of Delinquency 4–5
Read "I Want What Other Kids Want." How much did economic deprivation affect this youth? Is it hard to believe that this person later graduated from college and is now working with troubled youths?

TABLE 4–4
Opportunity Theory

Opportunity Theory	Features	Supporting Research
Cloward and Ohlin	Lower-class boys seek out illegitimate means to attain middle-class success goals, usually through one of three specialized gang contexts, if they are unable to attain them through legitimate means.	Moderate

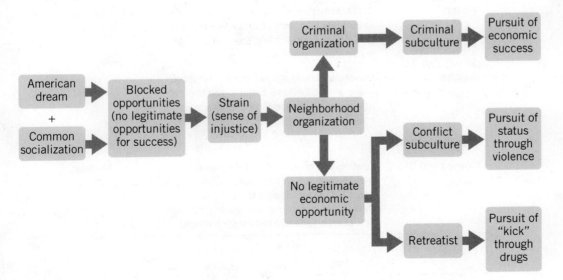

FIGURE 4–6
Cloward and Ohlin's Opportunity Theory

Evaluation of Cloward and Ohlin's Theory

Cloward and Ohlin's opportunity theory is important because of the impact it has had on the development of public policy and other criminological theories.[72] However, the findings of several studies sharply disagree with the assumptions of Cloward and Ohlin's opportunity theory.[73] In 1978, Ruth Kornhauser, having reviewed the empirical research on the aspirations and expectations of delinquents, said that research showed that delinquency was consistently associated with both low expectations and low aspirations—hence, delinquents might not expect to get much, but they did not want much either.[74]

In summary, strain theory explains that juveniles are "pushed" into delinquency as a result of a lack of access to legitimate opportunities for the attainment of success goals that are held out by the wider society. Delinquency arises when those who are denied legitimate opportunities turn to innovative (and illegal) means of reaching desired goals or of striking back at an unfair system.[75] The role of blocked opportunity, whether found in the writings of Merton, or Cloward and Ohlin, has received considerable attention in the sociological analysis of male delinquency. Table 4–5 compares social structural theories of delinquency.

TABLE 4–5
Summary of Social Structural Theories of Crime

Theory	Cause of Crime Identified in the Theory	Supporting Research
Cultural Deviance Theories		
Shaw and McKay	Delinquent behavior becomes an alternative mode of socialization through which youths who are part of disorganized communities are attracted to delinquent values and traditions.	Moderate
Miller	Lower-class culture has a distinctive culture of its own, and its focal concerns, or values, make lower-class boys more likely to become involved in delinquent behavior.	Weak
Wolfgang and Ferracuti	Subcultures of violence exist among lower-class males and legitimize the use of violence.	Weak
Strain Theories		
Merton	Social structure exerts pressure on individuals who cannot attain the cultural goal of success, leading them to engage in nonconforming behavior.	Moderate
Cohen	Lower-class boys are unable to attain the goals of middle-class culture, and therefore they become involved in nonutilitarian, malicious, and negative behavior.	Weak
Opportunity Theory		
Cloward and Ohlin	Lower-class boys seek out illegitimate means to attain middle-class success goals if they are unable to attain them through legitimate means, usually through one of three specialized gang contexts.	Moderate

Prevention of Delinquency

In Chapter 3, our discussion of the development of delinquency prevention strategies in the United States provided an overview of the ineffective prevention strategies of the past. In this chapter, we want to examine another past prevention effort, the Chicago Area Projects. In Chapter 5, we then will examine a number of contemporary prevention efforts that are receiving positive accolades.

The Chicago Area Projects

Clifford Shaw and Henry McKay began the Chicago Area Projects (CAP) in 1934. They were committed to creating community consciousness directed at solving social problems on the local level. The first projects were initiated in three areas: South Chicago, the Near West Side, and the Near North Side. Each project area had a committee that operated as an independent unit under the guidance of a board of directors chosen by local community residents. Twenty such projects have functioned in Chicago, and others have formed throughout the state. In addition, other groups in Illinois have taken the projects as the model for their own delinquency control programs.

The projects have three basic goals: First, they provide a forum for local residents to become acquainted with new scientific perspectives on child rearing, child welfare, and juvenile delinquency. Second, they initiate new channels of communication between local residents and the institutional representatives of the larger community, those influencing the life chances of local youth. Third, they bring adults into contact with local youths, especially those having difficulties with the law.

The philosophy of CAP is based on the belief that instead of turning over youth so quickly to the justice system, the community should deal with its own problems and intervene on behalf of its youth. Citizens of the community show up in juvenile court to speak on behalf of the youths; they organize social and recreational programs so that youths can participate in constructive activities. The leaders of the local groups, often individuals who were once in CAP programs, know how to relate to and deal with youths who are having problems at school or with the law.

More than fifty years ago, community organizer Saul Alinsky said, "It's impossible to overemphasize the enormous importance of people doing things for themselves." What is ultimately significant about CAP is that this do-it-yourself philosophy was its basic approach to delinquency prevention. CAP advocated grassroots leadership, neighborhood revitalization, the community's role in policing itself, and the importance of community dispute resolution. These same emphases were incorporated into most community crime prevention strategies in the late 1990s and early 2000s.[76] Similarly, community policing, and most of the more effective efforts to prevent and control youth gangs, are based on this grassroots community orientation model.

Delinquency across the Life Course: Explanations of Delinquency

Social structure explanations of delinquency relate delinquent behavior to the structural and cultural characteristics of youths in the United States. As we have seen, social structure theorists suggest that a youth may become delinquent because he or she lives in a disorganized community, because he or she is unable to achieve middle-class standards, because he or she becomes part of a delinquent subculture due to status frustration, or because the social class to which he or she belongs has values held by deviant subculture.

Structural explanations remind us that some adolescents are seriously impacted by their low socioeconomic status. Some are influenced by living in deteriorated neighborhoods, others by rapid social change, still more by racial disparity and discrimination. Adolescents are further influenced by disrupted social relations in their families, schools, and among peers. The scarcity of employment in local communities provides another structural cause that produces delinquency. Because many of these factors are closely correlated with socioeconomic status, structural theories of delinquency are ultimately influenced by the significant variables of socioeconomic position and social class in the explanation of delinquent behavior.

Three important structural explanations of delinquency across the life course point to the consequences of the reduced social capital that lower-class children have, the importance of disorganized communities in affecting the decisions of lower-class children, and the relationship between human agency and structure in the process of desistance from crime. We will discuss each concept in turn.

Reduced Social Capital

social capital
The resources that reside in the social structure itself—norms, social networks, and interpersonal relationships that contribute to a child's growth.

Social capital theory, developed by James S. Coleman in the late 1980s, suggests that one of the reasons lower-class individuals have higher rates of crime and delinquency is that they lack social capital. Coleman defines **social capital** as "the resources that reside in the social structure itself—norms, social networks and interpersonal relationships that contribute to a child's growth."[77] In a subsequent paper, he adds that "just as physical capital is created by making changes in materials so as to form tools and facilitate production, human capital is created by changing persons so as to give them skills and capabilities that make them able to act in new ways."[78] Coleman goes on to suggest how high levels of social capital can be found in effective, functioning, intact nuclear and extended families, as well as in well-integrated neighborhoods and communities.[79]

Some researchers have contrasted the idea of positive social capital with criminal capital. Bill McCarthy and John Hagan, for example, in combining insights from Coleman's work on social capital, Sutherland's theory of differential association, and M. Granovetter's research on embeddedness, suggest that "embeddedness in networks of deviant associations provides access to tutelage relationships that facilitate the acquisition of criminal skills and attitudes, assets that we call 'criminal capital.'"[80] In testing their hypothesis with a sample of homeless youth who were involved in drug selling, theft, and prostitution, the researchers found support for the concept of embeddedness.[81]

Hagan and McCarthy's prize-winning 1997 book, *Mean Streets: Youth Crime and Homelessness*, addressed the issue of the lack of social capital in the lives of homeless youths. Using survey and interview data gathered in Toronto and Vancouver, Canada, they documented the family and school histories, living conditions, and criminal experiences of street youth. The homeless population they studied was about two-thirds male and one-third female, and the males were a little older than the females (18.1 versus 17.1 years old). Between a quarter and a third came from families that experienced frequent unemployment. Less than a third of these youths lived with both biological parents at the time they left home. Most (87 percent) had experienced physical abuse and neglect. Also common was parental use of alcohol and drugs.[82] One youth told why he left home at sixteen:

> My parents threw me out.... They're drug addicts. Hash, weed, coke, crack—everything. I didn't want to leave but they just threw me out. I had a huge fight with my dad. We'd fight cause I go, "quit drugs," and he would go "no." ... I'd go, "quit drinking." He'd say, "no." So we just argued about that most of the time. And one day he goes, "I think it's about time you leave, get on your own." So I just left.[83]

Thus, lower-class youngsters often lack access to social capital—to the norms, networks, and supportive relationships they need if they are to realize their potential. They may be forced to struggle to meet their basic survival needs. Economic deprivation is first felt at home, and it is this deprivation that drives many youths to the streets.[84] Not surprisingly, the father frequently leaves, and the mother is out of the home much of the time simply trying to make ends meet. In a study that further supports the lack of social capital as a cause of delinquency, G. Roger Jarjoura, Ruth A. Triplett, and Gregory P. Brinker, using fourteen years of longitudinal data for a national sample of younger adolescents, found that the exposure to poverty and the timing of such exposure are related to an increased likelihood of delinquent involvement.[85]

Lower-class youngsters further encounter the difficulty of coping in constructive ways when they are not able to meet the success goals of society, an inability that usually becomes evident at school. Both lower- and middle-class youths may respond to lack of success with disruptive behavior, truancy, and crime. The inability to find a job or to compete in the marketplace further encourages these adolescents to pursue illegitimate means.[86] Robert Gillespie's survey of fifty-seven studies shows considerable support for a relationship between unemployment and property crime. He found the relationship most evident in studies that use such variables as class, crime, and delinquency in a methodologically sophisticated manner.[87] Stephen W. Baron and Timothy F. Hartnagel's study of two hundred homeless male street youths found that lengthy unemployment and lack of income, as well as anger, increase youths' criminal activities.[88] However, Steven F. Messner and his colleagues, using national data gathered between 1967 through 1998, found that child poverty is positively related to arrest rates, but that rising unemployment results in less delinquency.[89]

Disorganized Communities

Lower-class children must deal with the impact of disorganized communities in which they live on their personal attitudes and worldview. To adapt to a disorganized community, adolescents may learn to accept cultural patterns that are conducive to delinquent behavior. For youths who experience economic deprivation at home, the streets offer the promise of attaining goods and services that their parents can't afford. In these disorganized communities, youth gangs typically are well established; in many communities youngsters may feel required to join a gang for safety. Disorganized communities also offer illegal drugs, frequent contact with adult criminals, and ongoing exposure to violence, and many disorganized communities are comprised of ethnic minorities. Mary E. Pattillo's study of an African American middle-class neighborhood in Chicago, for example, found that the neighborhood was closer to high-poverty and high-crime areas than were white middle-class neighborhoods and, as a result, had more problems with gang members and drug dealers.[90]

Thomas J. Bernard's article, "Angry Aggression among the 'Truly Disadvantaged,'" explained the high levels of anger and aggression among members of the underclass.[91] Bernard theorized that three social factors—urban environment, low social position, and racial and ethnic discrimination—increase the likelihood that the "truly disadvantaged" will react with frequent or intense physiological arousal. In Bernard's model, social isolation (a fourth social factor) concentrates the effects of the first three factors through multiple feedback loops, and the end result, according to Bernard's theory, is a "peak" of angry aggression.[92]

Thus, research evidence appears to support a relationship between social class, disorganization of the local community, and delinquency.[93] The type of informal community controls found in the Chicago Area Projects during the 1930s and 1940s perhaps offers one of the most hopeful means to reduce the rates of delinquency in high-crime areas. In their innovative work on neighborhoods and crime, Robert J. Sampson and colleagues developed the notion of "collective efficacy" (discussed in greater detail later in this chapter), which relates to informal social control and cohesion, or mutual trust, found among neighborhoods that effectively control youth crime.[94] This collective efficacy characterized the most effective of the Chicago Area Projects' communities and is found in present-day low-crime urban communities. The task of policy makers is to provide the structure or framework from which neighborhood solidarity and grassroots community organization can arise.

Final Thoughts on Social Structural Explanations: Human Agency

There has been intense interest among sociological theorists in the relationship between human agency and structure. British sociologist Margaret Archer contended that "the problem of structure and agency has rightly come to be seen as the basic issue in modern social theory."[95]

The theories presented in this chapter focus on structural features and cultural values inherent in our society without much concern for how individuals choose to respond to the influence of the sociocultural context and to economic factors. Consequently, these theories leave two basic questions unanswered: (1) What explains the fact that many youths in the same cultural setting do not become delinquent and (2) why do many culturally deprived youths who do become delinquent desist from delinquent behavior at the end of their teenage years, even when their social and economic situations remain the same?

John H. Laub and Robert J. Sampson, in their follow-up of the delinquent boys from the Gluecks' sample (see Chapter 1) to the age of 70 years, emphasized the importance of human agency in the desistance process. They viewed the men who desisted as "acting players," or as those who accepted responsibility for what they had done. Laub and Sampson concluded that desistance takes place "as a result of individual actions (choice) in conjunction with situational contexts and structural influences linked to important institutions that help sustain desistance."[96]

In the Laub and Sampson study, work and employment, as well as the structured role stability that came from marriage and family, provided the desisters with a social context in which they could choose to forge a new identity and from which they could receive support and encouragement. Offenders who persisted were those whose lives were characterized by a failure to maintain regular employment, by a tendency to abuse alcohol, and by an inability to receive the support of marriage and family. Persisters seemed to be unable to rise above the lower-class background of their childhood and, in fact, continued much of the defiance that they had expressed in their younger years. Not surprisingly, their lives were characterized by ongoing contact with the criminal justice system and imprisonment.[97] See Figure 4–7.

Delinquency and Social Policy: PHDCN and LAFANS

The Project on Human Development in Chicago Neighborhoods (PHDCN) is an interdisciplinary study of how families, schools, and neighborhoods affect child and adolescent development.[98] It was launched in the mid-1990s with major support from the National Institute of Justice and the John D. and Catherine T. MacArthur Foundation. PHDCN was led by Felton Earls, M.D., at the Harvard University School of Public Health and Medical School. Project directors represent a variety of disciplines and major universities.[99]

FIGURE 4–7
Three Structural Explanations of
Delinquency across the Life Course

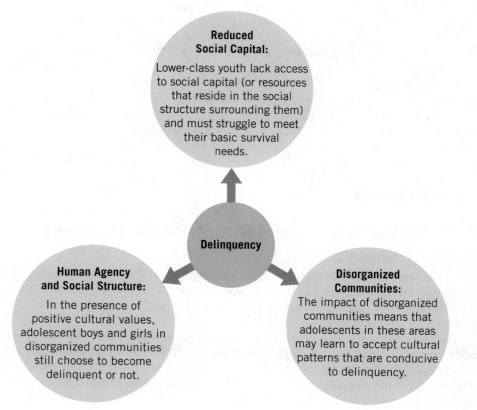

Reduced Social Capital:
Lower-class youth lack access to social capital (or resources that reside in the social structure surrounding them) and must struggle to meet their basic survival needs.

Delinquency

Human Agency and Social Structure:
In the presence of positive cultural values, adolescent boys and girls in disorganized communities still choose to become delinquent or not.

Disorganized Communities:
The impact of disorganized communities means that adolescents in these areas may learn to accept cultural patterns that are conducive to delinquency.

The project, whose data continue to be made available through the University of Michigan's Inter-university Consortium for Political and Social Research (ICPSR), is remarkable in both its scope and design. It combined (1) a longitudinal study of youths, with repeated interviews of more than six thousand youths and their caregivers, along with (2) a neighborhood study that included a survey of almost nine thousand neighborhood residents and systematic observation of levels of social and physical disorder in eighty neighborhoods. Data collection was conducted based on four separate components that focused on a variety of individual and community characteristics[100]:

1. *Community survey.* The dynamic structure of the local community, neighborhood organizational and political structures, cultural values, informal and formal social controls, and social cohesion were measured.

2. *Systematic social observation.* A standardized approach for directly observing the physical, social, and economic characteristics of neighborhoods, one block at a time, was applied to 80 of 343 neighborhoods (i.e., over twenty-three thousand blocks) in the study. These observations were coded to assess neighborhood characteristics such as land use, housing, litter, graffiti, and social interactions.

3. *Longitudinal cohort study.* An accelerated longitudinal design with seven cohorts was separated by three-year intervals. These randomly selected cohorts of children, adolescents, and young adults and their primary caregivers were followed over a period of seven years to study changes in their personal characteristics and circumstances.

4. *Infant assessment unit.* As part of the longitudinal cohort study, 412 infants from the birth cohort and their primary caregivers were studied during wave 1 (1994–1997) to examine the effects of prenatal and postnatal conditions on their growth and health, cognitive abilities, and motor skills.

Early Findings from the PHDCN Study

Findings from the PHDCN's neighborhood study received widespread attention in both the professional and general media. For example, in a widely cited article published in *Science* in 1997 and summarized in a National Institute of Justice *Research Review*, Robert J. Sampson, Stephen Raudenbush, and Felton Earls found that neighborhood social processes had a significant impact on homicide and violence in the community. In particular, homicide and violent victimization rates were found to be lower in neighborhoods where residents shared values, had common expectations that neighbors would intervene in problem behavior, and trusted each other. The researchers called this combination of shared values, trust, and expectations for social intervention "collective efficacy" to control crime and deviance. The level of collective efficacy, in turn, was strongly influenced by neighborhood conditions such as the extent of poverty and the lack of residential stability. Collective efficacy thus seems to be a mediating link between neighborhood conditions and crime and violence. Equally important, among neighborhoods with similar conditions, those with greater collective efficacy experienced less violence.[101]

Robert J. Sampson, a Harvard University professor, and colleagues developed the concept of collective efficacy as characteristics of a community that they felt would work together to prevent and control crime. Sampson and colleagues contended that the most important influence on a neighborhood's crime is neighbors' willingness to act, when necessary or needed, for one another's benefit, especially for the benefit of one another's children. Several studies have found that collective efficacy does function to mediate much of the effect of such community structural variables as high prevalence of poverty, unemployment, single-parent families, and racial/ethnic heterogeneity.[102]

PHDCN is perhaps the largest interdisciplinary study of the complex influences exerted on human development ever undertaken. The National Institute of Justice has so far spent over $18 million on the project, and the MacArthur foundation has spent another $23.6 million. Jeremy Travis, director of the National Institute of Justice from 1994 to 2000, noted, "It is far and away the most important research insight in the last decade. I think it will shape policy for the next generation."[103]

In 2011, PHDCN entered a new phase as part of the Mixed-Income Project, a longitudinal study of families and neighborhoods funded by the John D. and Catherine T. MacArthur Foundation. The aim of the Mixed-Income Project is to produce a view of the individual and aggregate dynamics of mixed-income housing, including residential mobility, housing change, job loss, and key aspects of physical and mental well-being that occurred during the great recession that began in 2008.[104]

In 2012, Robert J. Sampson, who continues to direct data gathering under the project, published *Great American City: Chicago and the Enduring Neighborhood Effect*. Sampson concluded that, even in today's complex and highly technological world, "communities still matter because life is decisively shaped by where you live."[105]

The Los Angeles Family and Neighborhood Survey (LAFANS), which builds on key PHDCN findings, is an ongoing project, begun in 2000, that seeks to answer the question of "What makes a neighborhood a positive place to live?"[106] The survey gathered data on three thousand families in sixty-five Los Angeles neighborhoods in two waves: one between 2000 and 2001, and another between 2006 and 2008. LAFANS, which is being conducted by the RAND Corporation and the UCLA School of Public Health, has resulted in numerous publications, including at least one that shows that members of racial/ethnic groups "appear to exhibit negative health risk behaviors when they reside in areas that are disproportionately populated with their co-ethnic peers."[107]

THE CASE

The Life Course of Amy Watters, Age 9

Amy was in the middle of her third year in school and earning good grades. In fact, she took pride in her accomplishments, having been named to the honor roll before Christmas break, and receiving praise from her teacher who wrote on her mid-year report card that "Amy is a bright student, who shows lots of promise."

It came as a shock, therefore, when Amy went window shopping with her father in an expensive store—one where she had never been before—and the clerk standing by a rack of brightly colored silk scarves looked askance at her and her father, and muttered what sounded like an insult under her breath. Amy heard something like, "Why do all these poor people want to waste my time?"

Her father, who heard the clerk, too, grabbed Amy by the hand and quickly led her out of the store. It was the first time in Amy's life that she felt different, and somehow unworthy.

This chapter says that the social structure of a society influences the behavior that occurs in that society because of the way in which it structures opportunities. How might Amy's life opportunities be limited by her socioeconomic status? Can achievement in school help her overcome those limitations?

Learn More on the Web:

- The Anomie Tradition: Explaining Rates of Deviant Behavior: http://deviance.socprobs.net/Unit_3/Theory/Anomie.htm

Follow the continuing Amy Watters saga in the next chapter.

CHAPTER SUMMARY

This chapter describes social structural theories of delinquency. The term *social structure* refers to the relatively stable formal and informal arrangements that characterize a society—including its economic arrangements and social institutions as well as its values and norms. Social structural theories propose that the structured arrangements within society can lead to delinquency, whereas structural and cultural disorder may result in high rates of crime and unsafe and disruptive living conditions. Among the best-known social structural approaches are the following:

- Clifford R. Shaw and Henry D. McKay, members of the Chicago School of Sociology, demonstrated the importance of social ecology, specifically the locations where young people live. The closer they live to the inner city, the researchers said, the more likely young people are to become involved in delinquency.

- Explanations for delinquency in inner-city areas go beyond social disorganization, however. It is well known, for example, that cultural traditions characteristic of the inner city pass criminogenic norms and values from one generation to the next.

- Walter B. Miller contends that lower-class youths do not aspire to middle-class values because they have their own lower-class values, or focal concerns, which encourage involvement in delinquent behavior.
- Robert K. Merton's anomie theory says that the social structure of a society influences the behavior that occurs in that society because of the way in which it structures opportunities. Merton notes that young people who are caught up in anomie, or normlessness, feel the strain that such conditions produce and are more likely to become deviant or delinquent than those who are not.
- Albert K. Cohen's theory of reaction formation contends that lower-class youths aspire to middle-class values but that their inability to attain those values causes them to invert the values and become involved in negativistic, malicious, and nonutilitarian behaviors.
- Richard A. Cloward and Lloyd E. Ohlin argue that youthful lower-class gang members aspire to middle-class values but become involved in illegitimate pursuits because they are unable to attain their goals legitimately.

All of the theories discussed in this chapter see delinquency as a response to inequalities built into the very structure of society.

KEY TERMS

blocked opportunity, p. 88
cultural deviance theory, p. 84
cultural transmission theory, p. 83
culturally defined goals, p. 86
differential opportunity structure, p. 83

focal concerns, p. 84
institutionalized means, p. 86
opportunity theory, p. 92
reaction formation, p. 90
social capital, p. 96

social disorganization theory, p. 81
social structure, p. 80
status frustration, p. 89
strain theory, p. 86

JUVENILE DELINQUENCY VIDEOS

Differential Association

Differential Association discusses the criminological theory of differential association for the causation of crime. The video explains that Edwin Sutherland's work of differential association argues that crime is a learned behavior from peers. An individual becomes delinquent through an excess of exposure to behavior that violates the law. Explain the theory of differential association. How would differential association explain the criminal behavior of a juvenile? From the readings in this chapter and this video, do you believe that differential association can be used in all situations to explain the causation of crime? Why or why not?

REVIEW QUESTIONS

1. According to Shaw and McKay, what are the relationships among ecology, social disorganization, and transmission of deviant culture?
2. What are Miller's focal concerns, or values, of lower-class delinquency?
3. What is strain theory?
4. What has Merton contributed to strain theory?
5. What does Cohen contribute to strain theory?
6. What contribution do Cloward and Ohlin make to strain theory and delinquency?

DISCUSSION QUESTIONS

1. Which of the theories in this chapter impressed you as being most logical? Why?
2. Are succeeding generations of researchers using Shaw and McKay's impressive body of work as starting points for inquiries that further advance our body of knowledge, or is present-day research simply a slick repackaging of past successful efforts?
3. Do you believe that lower-class youngsters aspire to middle-class values, or do they have their own values?
4. What structural explanations of delinquency are most likely to explain middle-class delinquency?
5. Are Miller's focal concerns of the lower-class thesis valid? Should any of the concerns he includes be removed from the list? Are there other concerns you think should be added?
6. Do you think status frustration, which is described as being derived from an inability to attain desired goals, is unique to adolescents? Might it also explain adult criminal behavior?

GROUP EXERCISES

1. Have the class discuss/debate the merits and main criticisms of social disorganization theory.
2. Have the class debate/discuss the merits of Cohen's theory of delinquent subcultures.
3. Have the class debate/discuss the merits of Cloward and Ohlin's opportunity theory.

4. Have the students read Baron and Hartnagel's article, "Attributions, Affect, and Crime: Street Youths' Reactions to Unemployment," accessed at http://www.blackwell-synergy.com/doc/abs/10,111/j.1745-9125,1997.tb01223.x; then have them discuss the material in class.

NOTES

1. "Young Girl Arrested; Accused of Selling Drugs," WABC, August 20, 2010, http://abclocal.go.com/wabc/story?section=news/local&id=7619344 (accessed October 23, 2012).
2. Robert J. Sampson and W. B. Groves, "Community Structure and Crime: Testing Social-Disorganization Theory," *American Journal of Sociology* 94 (1989), pp. 774–802.
3. Robert J. Sampson and William Julius Wilson, "Toward a Theory of Race, Crime, and Urban Equality," in *Crime and Inequality,* edited by John Hagan and Ruth D. Peterson (Stanford, Calif.: Stanford University Press, 1995), pp. 37–54.
4. See Emile Durkheim, *Suicide,* translated by John A. Spaulding and George Simpson (New York: Free Press of Glencoe, 1893).
5. There is a cultural deviance component to Shaw and McKay's perspective, but Ruth Rosner Kornhauser claims it is an unnecessary aspect of their social disorganization theory. See Ruth Rosner Kornhauser, *Social Sources of Delinquency: An Appraisal of Analytic Models* (Chicago: University of Chicago Press, 1978), p. 79.
6. Albert J. Reiss, Jr., "Settling the Frontiers of a Pioneer in American Criminology: Henry McKay," in *Delinquency, Crime and Society,* edited by James F. Short, Jr. (Chicago: University of Chicago Press, 1976), pp. 64–86.
7. Harold Finestone, *Victims of Change: Juvenile Delinquents in American Society* (Westport, Conn.: Greenwood Press, 1976).
8. George B. Vold and Thomas J. Bernard, *Theoretical Criminology,* 3d ed. (New York: Oxford University Press, 1986).
9. Clifford R. Shaw, *Delinquency Areas* (Chicago: University of Chicago Press, 1929).
10. Clifford R. Shaw and Henry D. McKay, *Juvenile Delinquency and Urban Areas* (Chicago: University of Chicago Press, 1941).
11. Ysabel Rennie, *The Search for Criminal Man* (Lexington, Mass.: Lexington Books, 1978).
12. Finestone, *Victims of Change.*
13. Ibid.
14. Ibid.
15. Shaw and McKay, *Juvenile Delinquency and Urban Areas.*
16. Rodney Stark, "Deviant Places: A Theory of the Ecology of Crime," *Criminology* 25 (1987), pp. 893–909.
17. Robert J. Bursik, Jr., "Ecological Stability and the Dynamics of Delinquency," in *Communities and Crime,* edited by

Albert J. Reiss and Michael Tonry (Chicago: University of Chicago Press, 1986), p. 36.
18. Robert J. Bursik, Jr., "Social Disorganization and Theories of Crime and Delinquency: Problems and Prospects," *Criminology* 26 (November 1988), pp. 519–51. See also Justice W. Patchin, Beth M. Huebner, John D. McCluskey, Sean P. Varano, and Timothy S. Bynum, "Exposure to Community Violence and Childhood Delinquency," *Crime and Delinquency* 52 (April 2006), pp. 307–32; and Amie L. Nielsen, Matthew T. Lee, and Ramiro Martinez, Jr., "Integrating Race, Place and Motive in Social Disorganization Theory: Lessons from a Comparison of Black and Latino Homicide Types in Two Immigrant Destination Cities," *Criminology* 43 (August 2005), pp. 837–71.
19. Bursik, "Social Disorganization"; James M. Byrne and Robert J. Sampson, eds., *The Social Ecology of Crime* (New York: Springer-Verlag, 1986); Reiss and Tonry, eds., *Communities and Crime;* and Stark, "Deviant Places."
20. Bursik, "Social Disorganization." See also Charis E. Kubrin and Eric A. Stewart, "Predicting Who Reoffends: The Neglected Role of Neighborhood Context in Recidivism Studies," *Criminology* 44 (February 1, 2006), p. 165; and Barbara D. Warner, "The Role of Attenuated Culture in Social Disorganization Theory," *Criminology* 41 (2006), pp. 73–98.
21. Bursik, "Social Disorganization"; and Stacy DeCoster, Karen Heimer, and Stacy Wittrock, "Neighborhood Disadvantage, Social Capital, Street Context, and Youth Violence," *Sociological Quarterly* 47 (2006), pp. 723–53. For the relationship between social disorganization and drug trafficking, see Ramino Martinez, Jr., Richard Rosenfeld, and Dennis Mares, "Social Disorganization, Drug Market Activity, and Neighborhood Violent Crime," *Urban Affairs Review* 43 (July 2008), pp. 846–74.
22. Beverly Kingston, David Huizinga, and Delbert Elliott, "A Test of Social Disorganization Theory in High-Risk Urban Neighborhoods," *Youth and Society* 41 (2009), pp. 53–79.
23. Kornhauser, *Social Sources of Delinquency,* p. 25. For a review of the decline of cultural deviance theory, see J. Mitchell Miller, Albert K. Cohen, and Kevin M. Bryant, "On the Demise and Morrow of Subculture Theories of Crime and Delinquency," *Journal of Crime and Justice* 20 (1997), pp. 167–78.
24. Walter B. Miller, "Lower-Class Culture as a Generation Milieu of Gang Delinquency," *Journal of Social Issues* 14 (1958), pp. 9–10.

25. Ibid.

26. Marvin E. Wolfgang and Franco Ferracuti, *The Subculture of Violence* (London: Tavistock, 1957). For a study that challenges the black subculture of violence thesis, see Liqun Cao, Anthony Adams, and Vickie J. Jensen, "A Test of the Black Subculture of Violence Thesis: A Research Note," *Criminology* 35 (May 1997), pp. 367–79.

27. Richard A. Cloward and Lloyd E. Ohlin, *Delinquency and Opportunity: A Theory of Delinquent Boys: The Culture of the Gang* (Glencoe, Ill.: Free Press, 1955).

28. This section's analysis of social structure and anomie is based on Robert K. Merton, *Social Theory and Social Structure,* 2d ed. (New York: Free Press, 1957), pp. 131–32.

29. Ibid., p. 131.

30. Ibid.

31. Morton Deutsch and Robert M. Krauss, *Theories in Social Psychology* (New York: Basic Books, 1965), p. 198.

32. Merton, *Social Theory and Social Structure.*

33. Merton, *Social Theory and Social Structure,* p. 151.

34. Ibid.

35. For Merton's more recent thoughts about the emergence and present status of strain theory, see Robert K. Merton, "Opportunity Structure: The Emergence, Diffusion, and Differentiation of a Sociological Concept, 1930s–1950s," in *The Legacy of Anomie Theory: Advances in Criminological Theory,* Vol. 6, edited by Freda Adler and William S. Laufer (New Brunswick, N.J.: Transaction Publishers, 1995), pp. 3–78.

36. Steven F. Messner and Richard Rosenfeld, *Crime and the American Dream* (Belmont, Calif.: Wadsworth Publishing Company, 1994).

37. Ibid.

38. Jukka Savolainen, "Inequality, Welfare State, and Homicide: Further Support for the Institutional Anomie Theory," *Criminology* 38 (November 2000), pp. 617–63.

39. Marshall B. Clinard, "The Theoretical Implications of Anomie and Deviant Behavior," in *Anomie and Deviant Behavior,* edited by Marshall B. Clinard (New York: Free Press, 1964), p. 10.

40. Velmer S. Burton, Jr., and Francis T. Cullen, "The Empirical Status of Strain Theory," *Journal of Crime and Justice* 15 (1992), p. 5.

41. Cloward and Ohlin, *Delinquency and Opportunity*; and Albert K. Cohen, *Delinquent Boys: The Culture of the Gang* (Glencoe, Ill.: Free Press, 1955).

42. Burton and Cullen, "The Empirical Status of Strain Theory," pp. 2–3.

43. Travis Hirschi, *Causes of Delinquency* (Berkeley: University of California Press, 1969); and Kornhauser, *Social Sources of Delinquency.*

44. Thomas J. Bernard, "Control Criticisms of Strain Theory: An Assessment of Theoretical and Empirical Adequacy," *Journal of Research in Crime and Delinquency* 21 (1984), pp. 353–72; and Thomas J. Bernard, "Testing Structural Strain Theories," *Journal of Research in Crime and Delinquency* 24 (1987), pp. 262–80.

45. Robert Agnew, "A Revised Strain Theory of Delinquency," *Social Forces* 64 (1985), pp. 151–67.

46. Ibid., p. 151.

47. Terence P. Thornberry, *Developmental Theories of Crime and Delinquency* (New Brunswick, N.J.: Transaction Publishers, 2004), p. 32.

48. Robert Agnew, "The Contribution of 'Mainstream' Theories of the Explanation of Female Delinquency," in *The Delinquent Girl,* edited by Margaret A. Zahn (Philadelphia: Temple University Press, 2009), p. 8.

49. Ibid., pp. 7–29.

50. Robert Agnew, "Foundations for a General Theory of Crime and Delinquency," *Criminology* 30 (February 1992), pp. 47–87. See also Robert Agnew, "Building on the Foundation for a General Strain Theory," paper presented at the Annual Meeting of the American Society of Criminology in Washington, DC, November 1998; and John P. Hoffman and Alan S. Miller, "A Latent Variable Analysis of General Strain Theory," *Journal of Quantitative Criminology* 14 (1998), pp. 83–110.

51. John Rodriguez and Scott Belshaw, "General Strain Theory: A Comparative Analysis of Latino & White Youths," *Southwest Journal of Criminal Justice* 7 (2010), pp. 138–58.

52. Wen- Hsu Lin, John Cochran, and Thomas Mieczkowski, "Direct and Vicarious Violent Victimization and Juvenile Delinquency: An Application of General Strain Theory," *Sociological Inquiry* 8 (2011), pp. 195–222.

53. Agnew, "Foundations for a General Theory of Crime and Delinquency." See also Agnew, "Building on the Foundation for a General Strain Theory," and Hoffman and Miller, "A Latent Variable Analysis of General Strain Theory"; Stephen W. Baron, "Street Youth, Unemployment, and Crime: Is It That Simple? Using General Strain Theory to Untangle the Relationship," *Canadian Journal of Criminology and Criminal Justice* 50 (2008), pp. 399–434; Deanna M. Penez, Wesley G. Jennings, and Angela R. Gover, "Specifying General Strain Theory: An Ethnically Relevant Approach," *Deviant Behavior* 29 (2008), pp. 544–78; and Byongoof Moon, David Blurton, and John D. McCluskey, "General Strain Theory and Delinquency: Focusing on the Influences of Key Strain Characteristics on Delinquency," *Crime and Delinquency* 54 (2008), pp. 582–613.

54. Cohen, *Delinquent Boys.*

55. Ibid.

56. Ibid., p. 87.

57. Ibid., pp. 113–14.

58. Ibid.

59. Ibid.

60. Ibid.

61. Ibid.

62. Ibid.

63. Albert K. Cohen, "The Sociology of the Deviant Act: Anomie Theory and Beyond," *American Sociological Review* 30 (1965), pp. 5–14.

64. Hirschi, *Causes of Delinquency.*

65. Vold and Bernard, *Theoretical Criminology,* p. 197.

66. Cloward and Ohlin, *Delinquency and Opportunity,* p. 97.

67. Ibid.

68. Ibid.

69. Ibid.

70. Ibid., p. 25.

71. Ibid.

72. Delbert S. Elliott and Harwin L. Voss, *Delinquency and Dropout* (Lexington, Mass.: Lexington Books, 1974).

73. Gwynn Nettler, *Explaining Crime*, 3d ed. (New York: McGraw-Hill, 1984).

74. Kornhauser, *Social Sources of Delinquency*.

75. Merton, "Social Structure and Anomie," and Cloward and Ohlin, *Delinquency and Opportunity*.

76. The following description of CAP is largely derived from Harold Finestone, *Victims of Change*, pp. 125–30. For more recent evaluations of CAP, see Steven Schlossman and Michael Sedlak, "The Chicago Area Projects Revisited," *Crime and Delinquency* 26 (July 1983), 398–460; and Steven Schlossman, Gail Zellman, and Richard Shavelson, *Delinquency Prevention in South Chicago: A Fifty-Year Assessment of the Chicago Area Project* (Santa Monica, Calif.: Rand, 1984).

77. James S. Coleman, "Social Capital in the Development of Human Capital: The Ambiguous Position of Private Schools," paper presented to the annual conference of the National Association of Independent Schools in New York, February 25–26, 1988, pp. 1–5.

78. James Coleman, *Foundations of Social Theory* (Cambridge: Harvard University Press, 1990), p. 304.

79. Coleman, "Social Capital in the Development of Human Capital.

80. Bill McCarthy and John Hagan, "Getting in Street Crimes: The Structure and Process of Criminal Embeddedness," *Social Science Research* 24 (1995), p. 65.

81. Ibid.

82. John Hagan and Bill McCarthy, *Mean Streets: Youth Crime and Homelessness* (Cambridge, UK: Cambridge University Press, 1997), pp. 23–25. See also Patrick T. Sharkey, "Navigating Dangerous Streets: The Sources and Consequences of Street Efficacy," *American Sociological Review* 71 (October 2006), pp. 826–46, and David J. Harding, "Violence, Older Peers, and the Socialization of Adolescent Boys in Disadvantaged Neighborhoods," *American Sociological Review* 74 (June 2009), pp. 443–84.

83. Hagan and McCarthy, *Mean Streets*, p. 25.

84. For articles that examine children's poverty, see Greg J. Duncan, "Has Children's Poverty Become More Persistent?" *American Sociological Review* 56 (August 1991), pp. 538–50; and David J. Eggebeen and Daniel T. Lichter, "Race, Family Structure, and Changing Poverty among American Children," *American Sociological Review* 56 (December 1991), pp. 801–17.

85. G. Roger Jarjoura, Ruth A. Triplett, and Gregory P. Brinker, "Growing Up Poor: Examining the Link between Persistent Poverty and Delinquency," *Journal of Quantitative Criminology* 18 (June 2002), pp. 159–87.

86. Stephen W. Baron, "Street Youth, Unemployment and Crime: Is It That Simple? Using General Strain Theory to Untangle the Relationship," *Canadian Journal of Criminology and Criminal Justice* 50 (2008), pp. 399–434; Stephen W. Baron, "Street Youth, Gender, Financial Strain, and Crime: Exploring Broidy and Agnew's Extension to General Strain Theory," *Deviant Behavior* 28 (2007), pp. 273–302.

87. Robert Gillespie, "Economic Factors in Crime and Delinquency: A Critical Review of the Empirical Evidence," Hearings, Subcommittee on Crime of the Committee of the Judiciary, House of Representatives, 95th Congress, Serial 47 (Washington, D.C.: U.S. Government Printing Office, 1978), pp. 601–25.

88. Stephen W. Baron and Timothy F. Hartnagel, "Attributions, Affect, and Crime: Street Youths' Reactions to Unemployment," *Criminology* 35 (August 1997), pp. 409–34. However, another study challenges this relationship between employment and reduced rates of delinquency; see Matthew Ploeger, "Youth Employment and Delinquency: Reconsidering a Problematic Relationship," *Criminology* 35 (November 1997), pp. 659–75.

89. Steven F. Messner, Lawrence E. Raffalovich, and Richard McMillan, "Economic Deprivation and Changes in Homicide Arrest Rates for White and Black Youths, 1967–1998: A National Time-Series Analysis," *Criminology* 39 (August 2001), pp. 591–613.

90. Mary E. Pattillo, "Sweet Mothers and Gangbangers: Managing Crime in a Black Middle-Class Neighborhood," *Social Forces* (March 1998), pp. 747–74.

91. Thomas J. Bernard, "Angry Aggression among the 'Truly Disadvantaged,'" *Criminology* 28 (1990), pp. 73–96. See also William Julius Wilson, *The Truly Disadvantaged* (Chicago: University of Chicago Press, 1987).

92. Bernard, "Angry Aggression."

93. Ramiro Martinez, Jr., Richard Rosenfeld, and Dennis Mares, "Social Disorganization, Drug Market Activity, and Neighborhood Violent Crime," *Urban Affairs Review* 43 (2008), pp. 846–74.

94. Robert J. Sampson, Jeffrey D. Morenoff, and Felton Earls, "Beyond Social Capital: Spatial Dynamics of Collective Efficacy for Children," *American Sociological Review* 64 (1999), pp. 633–60.

95. Margaret S. Archer, *Culture and Agency: The Place of Culture in Social Theory* (Cambridge, England: Cambridge University Press, 1988), p. ix.

96. John H. Laub and Robert J. Sampson, *Shared Beginnings, Divergent Lives: Delinquent Boys to Age 70* (Cambridge, Mass.: Harvard University Press, 2003), p. 145.

97. Ibid. See Chapters 6 and 7.

98. Inter-university Consortium for Political and Social Science, "Project on Human Development in Chicago Neighborhoods," http://www.icpsr.umich.edu/icpsrweb/PHDCN/about.jsp (accessed June 24, 2012).

99. Akiva Liberman, *Adolescents, Neighborhoods and Violence: Recent Findings from the Project on Human Development in Chicago Neighborhoods* (Washington, D.C.: National Institute of Justice, 2007), pp. 4–5, from which some of the wording in this section is taken.

100. From http://www.icpsr.umich.edu/PHDCN. For more information on collective efficacy, see Robert J. Sampson, "The Embeddedness of Child and Adolescent Development: A Community-Level Perspective on Urban Violence," in *Childhood Violence in the Inner City*, pp. 31–77 edited by Joan McCord (New York: Cambridge, 1997); Robert J. Sampson, Jeffrey Morenoff, and Felton Earls, "Beyond Social Capital: Spatial Dynamics of Collective Efficacy for Children,"

American Sociological Review 64 (1999); and Robert J. Sampson, Stephen W. Raudenbush, and Felton Earls, "Neighborhoods and Violent Crime: A Multilevel Study of Collective Efficacy," *Science* 277 (1997), pp. 918–24.

101. http://www.icpsr.umich.edu/PHDCN.

102. Sampson et al., "Beyond Social Capital"; and Robert J. Sampson et al., "Neighborhoods and Violent Crime."

103. Ibid.

104. Adapted from Robert J. Sampson, "Chicago Project (PHDCN)," http://scholar.harvard.edu/sampson/content/chicago-project-phdcn-0 (accessed June 24, 2012).

105. Robert J. Sampson, *Great American City: Chicago and the Enduring Neighborhood Effect* (Chicago, Ill.: University of Chicago Press, 2012).

106. RAND Corporation, "L.A. FANS: The Los Angeles Family and Neighborhood Survey," http://lasurvey.rand.org (accessed June 24, 2012).

107. Reanne Frank and Eileen Bjornstrom, "A Tale of Two Cities: Residential Context and Risky Behavior among Adolescents in Los Angeles and Chicago," *Health and Place* 17, no. 1 (January 2011), pp. 67–77.

CHAPTER

5 Social Process Theories of Delinquency

Chapter Objectives

After reading this chapter, you should be able to:

1. **Summarize the propositions of differential association theory.**
2. **Summarize the concepts of drift theory.**
3. **Summarize the concepts of control theories of delinquency.**
4. **Summarize various integrated theories of delinquency.**
5. **Explain how various ongoing processes affect delinquency across the life course.**

The theory I advocate sees in the delinquent a person relatively free of the intimate attachments, the aspirations, and the moral beliefs that bind people to a life within the law.

—Travis Hirschi, *Causes of Delinquency*

Introduction

Dale Vincent Bogle, first imprisoned before age 20, went on to father nine children and quickly became a negative role model, steering most of them into lives of crime.

"Rooster," as he was called, grew up in Texas and as a young man moved to Oregon in 1961. Starting a family, he regularly beat his wife and taught his boys to shoplift at an early age. Bogle boys broke into liquor stores and stole tractor-trailer trucks, while Bogle girls turned to petty crimes to support drug habits.

The family patriarch died in 1998, and today twenty-eight members of the Bogle clan, including Rooster's brothers and their families and Rooster's grandchildren, have served time. However, one of Rooster's daughters, who has never been arrested or abused drugs, has devoted her life to felons, helping to run halfway houses for newly released inmates.

Rooster may have been unusually prolific, but his legacy is not unusual. The U.S. Justice Department reports that 47 percent of inmates in state prisons have a parent or other close relative who has been incarcerated. Similarly, half of all juveniles in custody today have one parent or close relative with a criminal record.

Recognizing that parents "train" their children for a life of crime, Oregon correctional officials plan to identify families of offenders and set them on the right path with alcohol and drug counseling, anger management, and mental health guidance.

Experts do not entirely agree on why so many offspring of felons pursue a life of crime. While some cite poor role models and dysfunctional homes, others say it could also have to do with poverty, poor schooling, lack of opportunities, and even the parents' DNA.[1]

The various **social process theories** of delinquency, which provide the focus of this chapter, examine the interaction between individuals and their environments for clues to the root causes of delinquency. Most youngsters are influenced by the family, the school experience, and their peers, all of which are discussed in the next section on delinquency and environment. It is the process of socialization occurring within these social institutions that, along with social structure, provides the forces that insulate youths from or influence them to commit delinquent acts.

Several theories focusing on social process have been widely used to explain juvenile delinquency. Differential association, drift, and social control theories, for example, became popular in the 1960s because they provided a theoretical mechanism for understanding aspects of the social environment as a determinant of individual behavior. Differential association theory examines how delinquents learn crime from others, drift theory proposes that any examination of the process of becoming deviant must take seriously both the internal components of the individual and the influence of the external environment, and social control theory provides an explanation for why some young people violate the law while others resist pressures to become delinquent. In addition to discussing these three social process perspectives, this chapter also describes and evaluates three integrated theories and considers process theories within a life-course perspective.

social process theory
A theoretical approach to delinquency that examines the interactions between individuals and their environments, especially those that might influence them to become involved in delinquent behavior.

Differential Association Theory

Edwin H. Sutherland's formulation of **differential association theory** proposed that delinquents learn crime from others. His basic premise was that delinquency, like any other form of behavior, is a product of social interaction. In developing the theory of differential association, Sutherland contended that individuals are constantly being changed as they take on the expectations and points of view of the people with whom they interact in intimate small groups.[2] Sutherland began with the notion that criminal behavior is to be expected of individuals who have internalized a preponderance of definitions that are favorable to law violations.[3] In 1939, he first developed the theory in his text *Principles of Criminology*, and he continued to revise it until its final form appeared in 1945. Exhibit 5–1 provides a look at the development of Sutherland's theory of differential association.

differential association theory
The view that delinquency is learned from others and that delinquent behavior is to be expected of individuals who have internalized a preponderance of definitions that are favorable to law violations.

Video 5–1 Differential Association

Library Extra 5–1
NIJ-sponsored research publication: *Trajectories of Violent Offending and Risk Status in Adolescence and Early Adulthood*

Exhibit 5–1
Edwin H. Sutherland's Background

Edwin H. Sutherland had much in common with Clifford R. Shaw and Henry D. McKay (see Chapter 4). All were born before the turn of the twentieth century and hailed from small Midwestern towns. They all did their graduate work at the University of Chicago during the early decades of the twentieth century; they also knew one another personally and frequently responded to each other's work.

McKay and Sutherland were very good friends. They corresponded regularly and got together each year during the summer. Their friendship was not surprising because the two men were so alike in ancestry, geography, demeanor, and character. It was McKay who first identified the theory of differential association in the second edition of Sutherland's 1934 criminology textbook.

In a conversation with Sutherland in 1935, McKay referred to the "Sutherland theory." Sutherland sheepishly inquired what the "Sutherland theory" was, and McKay responded that he should read pages 51–52 of his own criminology text. Sutherland quickly located the pages and was surprised to find this statement: "The conflict of cultures is the fundamental principle in explanations of crime." In helping Sutherland discover his own theory in his own book, McKay actually stimulated the evolution of differential association theory.

Source: Derived from Jon Snodgrass, *The American Criminological Tradition: Portraits of the Men and Ideology in a Discipline,* Ph.D. dissertation, University of Pennsylvania, 1972.

Propositions of Differential Association Theory

Sutherland's theory of differential association is outlined in seven propositions:

1. Criminal behavior, like other behavior, is learned from others; that is, delinquent behavior is not an inherited trait but rather an acquired one.

2. Criminal behavior is learned through a youth's active involvement with others in a process of communication, a process that includes both verbal and nonverbal communication.

3. The principal learning of criminal behavior occurs within intimate personal groups. The meanings that are derived from these intimate relationships are far more influential for adolescents than is any other form of communication, such as movies and newspapers.

4. When criminal behavior is learned, the learning includes techniques of committing the crime, which are sometimes very simple, and the specific direction of motives, drives, rationalizations, and attitudes. For example, a youth may learn how to hot-wire a car from a delinquent companion with whom he is involved; he also acquires from the other boy the attitudes or mind-set that will enable him to set aside the moral bounds of the law.

5. The specific direction of motives and drives is learned from definitions of legal codes as favorable or unfavorable. Adolescents come in contact both with people who define the legal codes as rules to be observed and with those whose definitions of reality favor the violation of the legal codes. This creates culture conflict; the next proposition explains how this conflict is resolved.

6. Differential associations may vary in frequency, duration, priority, and intensity. The impact that delinquent peers or groups have on a young person depends on the frequency of the social contacts, the time period over which the contacts take place, the age at which a person experiences these contacts, and the intensity of these social interactions.

7. Although criminal behavior is an expression of general needs and values, it is not explained by those general needs and values, because noncriminal behavior is an expression of the same needs and values. The motives for delinquent behavior are different from those for conventional behavior because they are based on an excess of delinquent definitions learned from others.[4]

The seven propositions of differential association theory build on three interrelated concepts—normative (culture) conflict, differential association, and differential social organization. These concepts operate at two levels of explanation: (1) the society or group level and (2) the individual level.[5]

Sutherland assumed that delinquents must be taught antisocial behavior. Those who do not engage in socially unacceptable behavior have been socialized or enculturated into conventional values, but those who become involved in delinquent behavior do so because they have been taught other values. Sutherland developed a quantitative metaphor, in which conventional and criminal value systems are composed of elementary units called "definitions." A person becomes delinquent, according to Sutherland, because he or she encounters (and assimilates) more definitions of criminality than of conformity. Each unit of Sutherland's "definitions" can be weighted by the modalities of frequency, priority, duration, and intensity of contact; delinquency or criminality is determined by the algebraic sum of these weighted units.[6] Figure 5–1 depicts Sutherland's explanation of differential association.

Evaluation of Differential Association Theory

Sutherland's differential association theory represented a watershed moment in criminology. Criminology was under heavy criticism in academic circles before Sutherland's theory was developed, because it lacked a general theoretical perspective that could be used to integrate findings and guide research.[7] In addition to providing this theoretical perspective, differential association theory has the following strengths:

- It is difficult to reject the argument that juveniles learn crime from others. Needless to say, juveniles learn their basic values, norms, skills, and self-perceptions from others. Accordingly, the idea that they also learn criminal behavior patterns from significant others seems irrefutable.

- The proposition that youngsters learn from people whose definitions are favorable to law violations appears to fit our understanding of juveniles and of their extreme vulnerability to the influence of the group. One recent study found that association with delinquent peers is the greatest predictor of delinquent behavior, regardless of race.[8] Another recent study examined the role of best friends' delinquency and perceived friendship quality in the development of delinquency and found that this study is more in support of differential association theory than social control theory.[9]

- The theory does not reduce delinquency to psychological and biological models, which postulate that personal inadequacies cannot be penetrated by outside influence. Instead, Sutherland saw individuals as changeable and as subject to the opinions and values of others. The chief task in delinquency prevention, then, is to strive for change in the small groups in which adolescents are involved rather than attempting to change an entire society.

Differential association theory has had an enduring impact on the study of juvenile delinquency, as is apparent in the ongoing attempts to revise the theory. One such revision, Daniel Glaser's modification of differential association theory, which is called **differential identification theory**, applied the interactionist concept of the self: "A person pursues criminal behavior to the extent that he identifies himself with real or imaginary persons

Voices of Delinquency 5–1
Read "The Athlete." How did peers influence her drug use? Did she, as Sutherland proposed, learn crime from others? What social process did this learning involve?

differential identification theory
A modification of differential association theory that applies the interactionist concept of the self, allows for choice, and stresses the importance of motives.

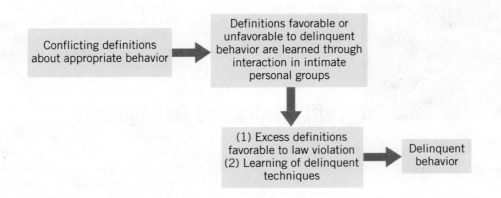

FIGURE 5–1
The Development of Sutherland's Differential Association Theory

from whose perspective his criminal behavior seems acceptable."[10] Robert J. Burgess, Jr., and Ronald L. Akers's differential reinforcement theory proposed a step-by-step restatement of differential association according to such ideas as reinforcement and punishment (operant conditioning). This reformulation, now known as *social learning theory*, contended that criminal or delinquent behavior is learned primarily "in those groups which comprise the individual's major source of reinforcements."[11] Marvin D. Krohn's network approach to delinquent behavior incorporates some of the elements of differential association theory. Krohn's term *network analysis* refers to sets of groups or organizations linked by the web of social relationships. Krohn suggested that the most important concept in accounting for delinquency is *multiplexity* (the tendency for social ties of different kinds to occur together)—if members of a social network participate jointly in a number of activities, they are likely to influence the behavior of actors within the network.[12]

Three of the most serious criticisms of differential association theory are as follows:

1. The terminology of differential association theory is so vague that it is nearly impossible to test the theory empirically.[13] For example, how can an "excess of definitions of criminality" be measured statistically?[14] How can "frequency," "duration," "priority," and "intensity" be studied? How can the "learning process" be more clearly specified? What defines an "intimate personal group"? Exactly what techniques, motives, and rationalizations do youngsters learn from others?

2. Differential association theory has been accused of failing to deal with several critical questions relating to the process of learning crime from others. For example, why is it that one youth succumbs to delinquency but another does not? Why do youths who are exposed to delinquent definitions still engage in conforming behavior most of the time? How did the first "teacher" learn delinquent techniques and definitions to pass on? Why do most youths desist from delinquent behavior at the age of 17 or 18 years? Why do youths frequently continue delinquent behavior even after the removal of the antisocial stimuli (delinquent peers)? Finally, what is the effect of punishment on delinquents?

3. Critics point out that differential association theory has no room for human purpose and meaning, because it ultimately reduces the individual to an object that merely reacts to the bombardment of external forces and cannot reject the material being presented.[15] According to the theory, then, the delinquent is a passive vessel into which various definitions are poured, and the resultant mixture is something over which the youth has no control.[16]

▲ In the movie *Mean Girls*, this wannabe is hoping for acceptance from the Queen Bees.

■ **How might the concept of differential association explain the interaction depicted here?**

On balance, although differential association theory has been subjected to sharp attacks over the years, it remains one of the best-known and most enduring theories of delinquent behavior. Twenty-five years ago, University of Washington sociologist Ross L. Matsueda offered a favorable analysis of differential association theory, proposing that research be done to specify "the concrete elements of the theory's abstract principles" and especially to identify "the content of definitions favorable to crime."[17] Contemporary researchers continue to work along the lines laid out by Matsueda.

Drift Theory and Delinquency

In his now-classic 1964 work, *Delinquency and Drift*, University of California at Berkeley sociologist David Matza noted that the process of becoming a delinquent begins when a juvenile neutralizes himself or herself from the moral bounds of the law and "drifts" into delinquency. Drift, said Matza, means that "the delinquent transiently exists in limbo between convention and crime, responding in turn to the demands of each, flirting now with one, now the other, but postponing commitment, evading decision. Thus he drifts between criminal and conventional action."[18]

Matza's concepts of drift and differential association have many assumptions in common, but Matza's **drift theory** places far greater importance than differential association theory on the exercise of juveniles' choices and on the sense of injustice that juveniles feel about the discriminatory treatment they have received as a result of their being nonconformists.

Having established that the delinquent is one who drifts back and forth between convention and deviancy, Matza then examined the process by which legal norms are neutralized. But fundamental to his analysis was the contention that delinquent youths remain integrated into the wider society and that a violation of legal norms does not mean surrendering allegiance to them.[19]

Delinquency, for Matza, becomes permissible when responsibility is neutralized. **Neutralization theory** provides a means of understanding how delinquents insulate themselves from responsibility for wrongdoing. There are five techniques of neutralization, or justifications, of delinquent behavior that precede delinquent behavior and that make such behavior possible by defining it as acceptable[20]:

1. Denial of responsibility ("I didn't mean it.")
2. Denial of injury ("I didn't hurt anyone.")
3. Denial of the victim ("They had it coming to them.")
4. Condemnation of the condemners ("Everyone is picking on me.")
5. Appeal to higher loyalties ("I didn't do it for myself.").[21]

Matza claimed that subcultural delinquents are filled with a sense of injustice because they depend on a kind of memory file that collects examples of inconsistencies. The male delinquent adheres to the virtues of his subculture, and these virtues stress the "traditional precepts of manliness, celebrating as they do the heroic themes of honor, valor, and loyalty."[22]

The missing element that provides "the thrust or impetus by which the delinquent act is realized is *will*."[23] The will is activated both on mundane occasions and in extraordinary situations.[24] But the delinquent is not likely to have the will to repeat an old offense if he or she has failed in the past: "Few persons—clowns and fools are among them—like to engage in activities they do badly."[25] Desperation, reasoned Matza, also can activate one's will to commit infractions, and he saw desperation intertwined with the mood of fatalism—because the delinquent feels pushed around, he or she needs to make something happen to restore his or her sense of power and control. Crime then enables the delinquent to see himself or herself as cause rather than as effect.[26] Matza developed drift theory to account for the majority of adolescents who, from time to time, engage in delinquent behavior (see Figure 5–2). See the *People In the Know* interview with David Matza for more about his thinking.

A recent study by British criminologist Gemma Shears investigated whether life goals and attitudes differ among young offenders, those evaluated at risk of turning to offending behavior, and nonoffenders. Shears' study found that there were differences between the three groups in terms of the life goals to which the members ascribed. Delinquent young people attached more importance to delinquency, freedom, autonomy, and goals associated with achieving a social image, whereas nonoffenders attached more important to interpersonal and educational goals. In other words, Shears' study reported that delinquents and nondelinquents do have significantly different life goals and attitudes.[27]

▲ A teenager argues with his mother.

■ **What parental role might drift theory posit in the prevention of delinquency?**

drift theory
The theoretical perspective that juveniles neutralize the moral hold of society and drift into delinquent behavior.

neutralization theory
A theory examining how youngsters attempt to justify or rationalize their responsibility for delinquent acts.

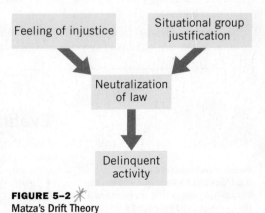

FIGURE 5–2
Matza's Drift Theory

People In the Know
Interview with David Matza

Question: Has your thinking changed concerning the process of becoming a delinquent since you wrote *Delinquency and Drift*?

Matza: Not too much, but some. I would now place more emphasis on racial oppression and the class correlates of racial oppression. The underlying social and political basis for the sense of injustice is left too implicit in *Delinquency and Drift*. Partly that was because the usual theories in the early sixties were based on class injustice and such theories were not very firmly based in fact, as I tried to point out in sections of the book and in *Becoming Deviant*. In my opinion, the thesis of racial injustice is based much more securely in the known facts of American history and social structure and very accurately reflected in the composition of prison and juvenile correctional populations.

Question: Are you as convinced that most subcultural delinquents adhere to societal norms as you were when you wrote *Delinquency and Drift*?

Matza: I am not as convinced, yet I still believe that even in rebellion against a morality whose application is unjust, a belief in the truth of an uncorrupted morality is asserted. When Frederick Douglass asserted that to be free, the slave was compelled to break most, if not all, of the rules of the oppressor, he was not by that statement breaking with the idea of society or with the belief in morality. Increasingly, I have come to think that what we call juvenile delinquency is, in part, the behavior of the youthful section of what traditionally has been termed the dangerous classes. The nineteenth-century ideas of the dangerous classes are today lodged in the writings of Edward Banfield. Without understanding the oppressive context of social life among oppressed populations, the dangerous behavior of youth is likely to be misconceived as deriving from biological factors, a tendency which is once again rampant in criminology and sociology thanks to ideologues like Banfield and his followers.

Question: Commitment to delinquency is one concept in your publications which has been widely debated. What is your reaction to this concept today?

Matza: I still do not think that very many youngsters are committed to delinquency. I am not sure how fruitful the debate is since "commitment" is a very slippery term. Commitment to an institution is a much firmer basis for subsequent juvenile delinquency than anything so intangible as an attitudinal commitment.

Question: In a 1971 interview, you indicated that *Delinquency and Drift* is a "confused jumbling of conservative, liberal, and radical views" and that "*Becoming Deviant* is sort of liberal and radical, maybe a little conservative too." What did you mean by these comments?

Matza: I meant to imply that I was quite disappointed if not angry at the way criminal justice systems were already beginning to twist much of the writings of the sixties toward their punitive and correctional ends. I guess I thought and still think that if my writing was unclear enough to appeal to conservatives, I must have been pretty confused. I was being critical of myself and perhaps others of similar perspective for having presented material so easily absorbed by an establishment which, between 1970 and 1984, abandoned and then turned against improving or at least reforming the penal system. I also meant that I was not very happy about my work, that a deeper formulation of the phenomenon would eliminate some of the philosophical ambiguity.

Question: Interest and research in the attributes, motivations, and socialization of youthful offenders have largely waned today. Instead, theorists are discussing the neoclassical revival; biosociological focus; radical, or critical, criminology; and the labeling perspective. What is your reaction to this current emphasis? Does this take us further away from the real delinquent?

Matza: I think the emphasis is intellectually and scientifically repressive, taking us very far from the actual person caught breaking the rules. My reaction is to continue being critical of such tendencies in my classroom teaching and perhaps awaiting the opportunity to propose more realistic theories of practice when the population finally realizes the conservative fringe has led absolutely nowhere with regard to the problems of poverty, injustice, and crime. Even talking about crime to students over the past fifteen years has been difficult. Under the conservative mentality the study of crime is not really possible, not in any deep scientific or intellectual sense.

Question: What other thoughts about the prevention and control of delinquency in American society would you like to add?

Matza: Delinquency cannot be controlled when government is hostile to poor and working people. Delinquency can only be prevented by a just and peaceful social order.

Source: David Matza is professor emeritus of sociology at the University of California, Berkeley. He is the author of *Delinquency and Drift* and *Becoming Deviant* and coauthor of the article "Techniques of Neutralization." This interview took place in April 1984 and is used with permission.

Evaluation of Drift Theory

Drift theory has been largely ignored in recent years, which is unfortunate because it has several strengths:

Voices of Delinquency 5–2
Read "She's Just a Party Animal." This is the story of a girl who did not see herself as a delinquent but who committed delinquent acts from time to time. Is her life, in any way, an expression of Matza's drift theory?

- Drift theory builds on the assumption that delinquent behavior is a learning process that takes place in interactions with others. The theory examines how group influence can encourage youth to release themselves from a shared sense of conventional morality.

- Drift theory can help account for the fact that the majority of adolescents commit occasional acts of delinquency, but then go on to become law-abiding adults. Matza's explanation for the fact that delinquency declines as adolescents approach adulthood is that many teenage delinquents were not committed to delinquent norms in the first place.

- Drift theory helps us understand the situational aspects of delinquent behavior. Matza viewed the delinquent as a youth who is pressured to engage in delinquent behavior by a specific situational context and by the norms of that context. Matza rightly contended that youths are influenced by group processes to commit behaviors that they might not otherwise commit.

- In *Delinquency and Drift*, Matza challenged the notion that delinquents are "constrained" (compelled) to engage in delinquency, contending that hard determinism predicts far too much delinquency and that a **soft determinism** much more accurately explains delinquent behavior.[28] This argument for soft determinism, first found in drift theory, is similar to later versions of soft determinism or indeterminism found in control theory,[29] rational choice theory,[30] social learning theory,[31] and conflict theory.[32]

soft determinism
The view that delinquents are neither wholly free nor wholly constrained in their choice of actions.

Drift theory holds that the attitudes of delinquents and nondelinquents toward unlawful behaviors are basically the same. There are mixed findings in the literature concerning this belief.[33]

Finally, Northwestern University sociologist John Hagan integrated drift theory with social control theory and a life-course conceptualization to study cultural stratification (i.e., social class), finding that "adolescents adrift from parental and educational control are more likely than those with more controls to develop mild or more seriously deviant subcultural preferences [and that] among males with working-class origins, identification with the subculture of delinquency has a negative effect on trajectories of early adult status attainment."[34]

In sum, even though Matza's drift theory has received less attention than neutralization theory in recent years, it is still one of the most useful explanations of the dynamics of why individuals become involved in delinquent behavior.

Video 5–2 Sykes and Matza

Control Theory and Delinquent Behavior

Differential association and drift theories are both learning theories of crime, but **control theory** is focused more on an internal mechanism that helps youngsters avoid delinquent behavior. The core ideas of control theory have a long history, going back at least to the nineteenth century. Control theorists agree on one especially significant point: Human beings must be held in check, or somehow controlled, if delinquent tendencies are to be repressed. Control theorists also generally agree that delinquency is the result of a deficiency in something, and that juveniles commit delinquency because some controlling force is absent or defective.[35]

Early versions of control theory include Albert J. Reiss, Jr.'s theory of personal and social controls and F. Ivan Nye's family-focused theory of social control. Reiss described how the weak egos of delinquents lack the personal controls to produce conforming behavior.[36] Nye added that the problem for the theorist was not to find an explanation for delinquent behavior; rather, it was to explain why delinquent behavior is not more common.[37] Walter C. Reckless's containment theory and Travis Hirschi's social control theory are the most developed examples of control theory, and we'll examine them next.

control theory
Any of several theoretical approaches that maintain that human beings must be held in check, or somehow be controlled, if delinquent tendencies are to be repressed.

Containment Theory

Ohio State University sociologist Walter C. Reckless developed **containment theory** in the 1950s and 1960s to explain crime and delinquency. Containment theory, which can explain both conforming behavior and deviancy, has two reinforcing elements: an inner control system and an outer control system. The assumption is that strong inner containment and reinforcing external containment provide insulation against deviant behavior.[38]

containment theory
A theoretical perspective that strong inner containment and reinforcing external containment provide insulation against delinquent and criminal behavior.

Elements of Containment Theory

Reckless defined the ingredients of inner containment as self-control, positive self-concept, well-developed superego, ego strength, high frustration tolerance, high resistance to diversions, high sense of responsibility, ability to find substitute satisfactions, goal orientations, and tension-reducing rationalizations.

Outer containment, or external regulators, represents the structural buffers in the person's immediate social world or environment that are able to hold him or her within bounds. External controls consist of such items as the presentation of a consistent moral front to the potential deviant; institutional reinforcement of his or her norms, goals, and expectations; effective supervision and discipline; provision for a reasonable scope of activity, including limits and responsibilities; and opportunity for acceptance, identity, and belongingness.

Internal pushes toward crime or deviance consist of the drives, motives, frustrations, restlessness, disappointments, rebellion, hostility, and feelings of inferiority that encourage a person to become involved in socially unacceptable behavior. Environmental pressures are those associated with poverty or deprivation, conflict and discord, external restraint, minority group status, and limited access to success in an opportunity structure. Finally, the environment is full of pulls toward crime and deviance, including things such as distractions, attractions, temptations, patterns of deviancy, peers, the media, and criminogenic advertising and propaganda in society.

Library Extra 5–3
OJJDP publication: *Causes and Correlates: Findings and Implications*

Relationship of Containment and Delinquency

If a person has weak outer containment, the external pressures and pulls need to be handled by the inner control system if he or she is to obey the law. But if a person's outer buffer is relatively strong and effective, his or her inner defense does not have to play such a critical role. Similarly, if the youth's inner controls are not equal to the ordinary pushes, an effective outer defense may help to hold him or her within socially acceptable behavior. But, if the inner defenses are in good working order, the outer structure does not have to come to the rescue. Juveniles who have both strong external and internal containment, then, are much less likely to become delinquent than those who have only either strong external containment or strong internal containment. Youths who have both weak external and internal controls are the most prone to delinquent behavior, although weak internal controls appear to result in delinquent behavior more often than do weak external controls.

Library Extra 5–4
Testimony of John Wilson, Acting Administrator of the Office of Juvenile Justice and Delinquency Prevention, before the U.S. House of Representatives, Committee on the Judiciary, on October 2, 2000

Self-Concept as Insulation against Delinquency

Reckless worked with Simon Dinitz at the Ohio State University in the middle of the twentieth century. The pair concluded from their research that one of the preconditions of law-abiding conduct is a good self-concept. This insulation against delinquency may be viewed as an ongoing process reflecting internalization of nondelinquent values and conformity to the expectations of significant others—parents, teachers, and peers. Thus, a good self-concept, the product of favorable socialization, steers youths away from delinquency by acting as an inner buffer or containment against delinquency.

Several studies have found that a positive self-concept does help insulate adolescents from delinquent behavior.[39] Other studies have found little relationship between positive self-esteem and reduced rates of delinquency.[40] Still other researchers have argued that people behave in a fashion designed to maximize their self-esteem, so youngsters adopt deviant reference groups for the purpose of enhancing self-esteem.[41] Delinquent behavior then becomes a coping strategy to defend against negative self-evaluation.[42]

In a recent dual study in the United States and Turkey, Joanne Roberts and colleagues examined whether family rituals and self-esteem might contribute to social control and, as a result, reduce deviant behavior. The Turkish study also assessed the impact of religiosity on social control, while the U.S. Study assessed the impact of participation in conforming activities. Based on Reckless's containment theory, it was proposed that the inner containment concepts of self-esteem and religiosity, and the outer containment concepts of family rituals and participation in conforming activities, would reduce the number of delinquent behaviors committed by respondents. They found, however, that among the things studied, only participation in conforming activities for U.S. college students reduced the frequency of delinquent behavior.[43]

The major flaw of inner containment, or self-concept, theory is the difficulty of defining self-concept in such a way that researchers can be certain they are accurately measuring the key variables of this concept.[44] Michael Schwartz and Sandra S. Tangri proposed that a poor self-concept might have other outcomes besides vulnerability to delinquency. They further disputed the adequacy of Reckless and Dinitz's measures of self-concept and questioned the effects of labeling on the subsequent behavior of both "good" and "bad" boys.[45]

Social Control Theory

Travis Hirschi, an American criminologist, is the theorist most closely identified with **social control theory**, or bonding theory. In his book *Causes of Delinquency*, Hirschi linked delinquent behavior to the quality of the bond an individual has with society, stating that "delinquent acts result when an individual's bond to society is weak or broken."[46] In Hirschi's words, "We are all animals and thus all naturally capable of committing criminal acts."[47] He argued that humans' basic impulses motivate them to become involved in crime and delinquency unless there is reason for them to refrain from such behavior. Instead of the standard question "Why do they do it?" Hirschi asserted that the most important question becomes "Why don't they do it?"[48]

Hirschi theorized that individuals who are most tightly bonded to positive social groups such as the family, the school, and successful peers are less likely to commit delinquent acts.[49] **Commitment to the social bond**, according to Hirschi, is made up of four main elements: attachment, commitment, involvement, and beliefs.

Attachment

An individual's attachment to conventional others is the first element of the social bond. Sensitivity toward others, argued Hirschi, relates to the ability to internalize norms and to develop a conscience.[50] Attachment to others also includes the ties of affection and respect children have to parents, teachers, and friends. The stronger his or her attachment is to others, the more likely it is that an individual will take this into consideration when or if he or she is tempted to commit a delinquent act.[51] Attachment to parents is the most important variable insulating a child against delinquent behavior, and even if a family is broken by divorce, the child needs to maintain attachment to one or both parents in order to be insulated from delinquent influences. "If the child is alienated from the parent," Hirschi asserted, "he will not develop an adequate conscience or superego."[52]

Commitment

The second element of the social bond is commitment to conventional activities and values. An individual is committed to the degree that he or she is willing to invest time, energy, and his or her sense of self in attaining conventional goals such as education, property, or reputation. When a committed individual considers the cost of delinquent behavior, he or she uses common sense and concludes that the risk of losing the investment already made in conventional behavior is unacceptable.[53] Hirschi contended that if juveniles are committed to conventional values and activities, they develop a stake in conformity and will refrain from delinquent behavior.

Involvement

Involvement also protects an individual from delinquent behavior. Because any individual's time and energy are limited, involvement in conventional activities leaves no time for delinquent behavior: "The person involved in conventional activities is tied to appointments, deadlines, working hours, plans, and the like," reasoned Hirschi, "so the opportunity to commit deviant acts rarely arises. To the extent that he is engrossed in conventional activities, he cannot even think about deviant acts, let alone act out his inclinations."[54]

social control theory
A perspective that delinquent acts result when a juvenile's bond to society is weak or broken.

commitment to the social bond
The attachment that a juvenile has to conventional institutions and activities.

▲ A father helps his children with schoolwork. According to social control theorists, a child's attachment to and respect for his or her parents are the most important variables in preventing delinquency.

■ **What might rank third? Fourth?**

Beliefs

The fourth element of the social bond is beliefs. Delinquency results from the absence of effective beliefs that forbid socially unacceptable behavior.[55] Such beliefs, for example, include respect for the law and for the social norms of society. This respect for the values of the law and legal system develops through intimate relations with other people, especially parents. Hirschi portrayed a causal chain "from attachment to parents, through concern for the approval of persons in positions of authority, to belief that the rules of society are binding on one's conduct."[56] (See the *People In the Know* interview with Travis Hirschi).

Empirical Validation of the Theory

Hirschi tested his theory by administering a self-report survey to 4,077 junior high and high school students in Contra Costa County, California. He used school-based files and police records to analyze the data he received from the questionnaires about basic elements of the social bond.

Hirschi analyzed attachment of respondents in his sample to parents, to the school, and to peers. The greater the attachment to parents, he found, the less likely the child was to become involved in delinquent behavior. More than communication with parents, however, the quality or the intimacy of the communication was the critical factor. The more love and respect found in the relationship with parents, the more likely it was that the child would recall the parents when and if a situation of potential delinquency arose.[57]

People In the Know
Interview with Travis Hirschi

Question: If you were to rewrite *Causes of Delinquency*, would you reformulate control theory in any way?

Hirschi: Control theory as I stated it can't really be understood unless one takes into account the fact that it was attached to a particular method of research. When I was working on the theory, I knew that my data were going to be survey data; therefore, I knew I was going to have mainly the perceptions, attitudes, and values of individuals as reported by them. So I knew the theory had to be stated from the perspective of individuals committing or not committing delinquent acts. Had I data on other people, or on the structure of the community, I would have stated the theory in a quite different way. There are lots of control theories, but the major differences among them stem from differences in the vantage point of the theorists, not from differences in their understanding of the theory. For example, I was aware at the time I wrote my theory that it was well within the social disorganization tradition. I knew that, but you have to remember the status of social disorganization as a concept in the middle 1960s when I was writing. I felt I was swimming against the current in stating a social control theory at the individual level. Had I tried to sell social disorganization at the same time, I would have been in deep trouble. So I shied away from that tradition. As a result, I did not give social disorganization its due. I went back to Durkheim and Hobbes and ignored an entire American tradition that was directly relevant to what I was saying. But I was aware of it and took comfort in it. I said the same things the social disorganization people had said, but since they had fallen into disfavor I had to disassociate myself from them. Further, as Ruth Kornhauser so acutely points out, social disorganization theories had been associated with the cultural tradition. That was the tradition I was working hardest against; so in that

sense, I would have compromised my own position or I would have introduced a lot of debate I didn't want to get into had I dealt explicitly with social disorganization theory. Now, with people like Kornhauser on my side, and social disorganization back in vogue, I would emphasize my roots in this illustrious tradition.

Question: Can control theory be expanded? What would be the main propositions and underpinnings of this expanded control theory?

Hirschi: Jack Gibbs mentioned the other day that, traditionally, the problem with social control as a concept is that it tends to expand until it becomes synonymous with sociology, and then it dies. It dies because then there is nothing unique or distinct about it. This danger is present even when the concept is limited initially to delinquency. I enjoy papers that apply my theory to areas other than delinquency, such as Watergate and white-collar crime, but I recognize the risk. Because of it, generality is not something I would move toward. Instead, I would try to focus on the theory's image of criminality and ask how far that might take us. I think I've generally worked with a too restrictive image of delinquency. I did this because I thought the field had made a mistake by bringing things into delinquency that were not delinquency. If, for example, smoking and drinking are part of delinquency, they cannot be causes of delinquency. I thought that was a mistake because I wanted to use those kinds of behaviors as independent variables. I now believe that smoking and drinking are delinquency.

Source: Travis Hirschi is professor emeritus of sociology at the University of Arizona. He is the author of *Causes of Delinquency* and most recently is coauthor of *A General Theory of Crime*. This interview took place in 1984.

Hirschi also found that in terms of attachment to the school, students with little academic competence and those who performed poorly academically were more likely to become involved in delinquent behavior. Significantly, he found that students with weak affectional ties to parents tended to have little concern for the opinions of teachers and to dislike school.[58]

The attachment to peers, Hirschi added, did not imply lack of attachment to parents. The respondents who were most closely attached to and respectful of their friends were least likely to have committed delinquent acts. Somewhat surprisingly, delinquents were less dependent on peers than nondelinquents. Hirschi theorized from his data "that the boy's stake in conformity affects his choice of friends rather than the other way around."[59]

In terms of commitment, Hirschi found that if a boy claimed the *right* to smoke, drink, date, and drive a car, he was more likely to become involved in delinquency. The automobile, like the cigarette and bottle of beer, indicated that the boy had put away childish things. Also, the more a boy was committed to academic achievement, the less likely he was to become involved in delinquent acts. Hirschi further reported that the higher the occupational expectations of boys, the less likely it was that they would become involved in delinquent behavior.[60]

Hirschi found that the more a boy was involved in school and leisure activities, the less likely he was to become involved in delinquency. In other words, the more that boys in the sample felt that they had nothing to do, the more likely they were to become involved in delinquent acts. Hirschi theorized that lack of involvement in and commitment to school releases a young person from a primary source of time-structuring positive activities.[61]

Moreover, he found that the less boys believed they should obey the law, the less likely they were to obey it. He added that delinquents were relatively free of concern for the morality of their actions, so they were relatively amoral and differed significantly in values from nondelinquents. Additionally, the data in this study failed to show much difference between lower- and middle-class young people in terms of values. Figure 5–3 depicts the main constructs of Hirschi's theory.

Evaluation of Social Control Theory

Social control theory has received wide support.[62] It has several strengths:

- It is amenable to empirical examination. Unlike other theorists discussed in this section, Hirschi was able to test his theory using a group of adolescents. The basic theoretical constructs of control theory—concepts such as attachment to parents, involvement in school, and commitment to conventional activities—are clearly defined and measurable.

- It has provided valuable insights into delinquent behavior. For example, the importance of the intrafamily relationship has been substantiated by tests of the theory. The relationship between the school and delinquency is another important area that social control theory addresses. Especially valid, according to tests of the theory, is the proposition that attachments and commitments to societal institutions (the social bond) are associated with low rates of delinquency.

- Researchers are increasingly using social control theory to develop integrated explanations of delinquent behavior.

In sum, although social control theory cannot explain all acts of delinquency, it has more empirical support today than any other explanation of delinquency. However, even if Hirschi's theory adequately explains delinquency in juveniles who are involved only in relatively trivial offenses, the question can be raised as to whether its findings apply as well to serious delinquency. Social control theory also fails to describe the chain of events that weaken the social bond.[63] A 2012 study found a reciprocal relationship between parenting and delinquency; that is, while a parental attachment has an effect on delinquency, an adolescent's delinquency also impacts parental attachment.[64]

Voices of Delinquency 5–3
Read "My Father Was an Alcoholic." The writer of this story is on death row. Did this person's lack of social control, or bonding, contribute to his delinquencies as a juvenile and crimes as an adult? In your opinion, why did he turn out the way he did? If you, as one of the authors did, had a chance to work with him as a juvenile, what would your interventions have been?

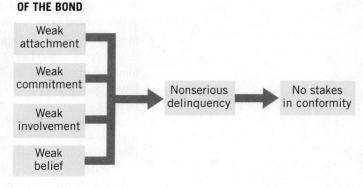

FIGURE 5–3
Hirschi's Social Control Theory

TABLE 5–1
Summary of Social Process Theories of Delinquency

Theory	Proponents	Cause of Delinquency Identified in the Theory	Supporting Research
Differential association	Edwin Sutherland	Criminal behavior is to be expected in individuals who have internalized a preponderance of definitions favorable to law violations.	Moderate
Drift	David Matza	Juveniles neutralize themselves from the moral bounds of the law and drift into delinquent behavior.	Moderate
Containment	Walter Reckless	Strong inner containment and reinforcing external containment provide insulation against criminal behavior.	Moderate
Social control	Travis Hirschi	Criminal acts result when an individual's bond to society is weak or broken.	Strong

As important as this theory is, greater attention must be given to the operational definitions of the elements of the social bond before the theoretical merits of social control theory can be fully ascertained.[65] Social process theories, including Hirschi's theory of social control, are summarized in Table 5–1.

Contextual Analysis: Integrated Theories of Delinquency

The theoretical development of integrated explanations for delinquency has been one of the most highly praised concepts in criminology.[66] Theory integration generally implies the combination of two or more contexts, including existing theories, levels of theory, social contexts, or individual contexts, on the basis of their perceived commonalities. Attempts to combine theoretical explanations of delinquency into a coherent sequence of connecting events and outcomes give rise to several issues and concerns:

- Because the specific form of delinquent behavior to be explained may vary from one theory to another, variations will likely be present in the power and utility of any integrated theory.[67]

- The question of which theoretical explanations to use as a representation of the various perspectives used in the model becomes an issue. Differential association theory illustrates this second issue. It is divided into seven propositions and even further subcategories. The question becomes: Which proposition(s) should be used as representative of differential association theory?[68]

- In regard to synthesis efforts, an issue sometimes arises as to the generalizability of the theory to all segments of the population. For example, most theories of delinquency focus on lower-class adolescent males, but these theories may or may not apply to lower-class adolescent females or to middle- or upper-class adolescent males and females.[69]

- Another concern is the fact that included theories may have different basic assumptions with respect to motivations, attitudes, and specific factors contributing to delinquency. Interdisciplinary theories, especially, offer opposing views on the feelings and attitudes of delinquents, and it is not uncommon for structural or process sociological theories to have widely divergent views both on delinquents' attitudes and motivations and on the effects of stimuli.[70]

Despite these daunting challenges, several integrated theories for delinquent behavior have been developed.[71] Three of the most important are Michael R. Gottfredson and Hirschi's *general theory of crime*, Delbert S. Elliott's *integrated social process theory*, and Terence P. Thornberry's *interactional theory*[72]

Gottfredson and Hirschi's General Theory of Crime

In their 1990 publication, *A General Theory of Crime*,[73] American criminologists Gottfredson and Hirschi defined lack of self-control as the common factor underlying problem behaviors:

> People who lack self-control will tend to be impulsive, insensitive, physical (as opposed to mental), risk-taking, short-sighted, and non-verbal, and they will tend, therefore, to engage in criminal and analogous acts [which include smoking, drinking, using drugs, gambling, having children out of wedlock, and engaging in illicit sex]. Since these traits can be identified prior to the age of responsibility for crime, since there is [a] considerable tendency for these traits to come together in the same people, and since the traits tend to persist through life, it seems reasonable to consider them as comprising a stable construct useful in the explanation of crime.[74]

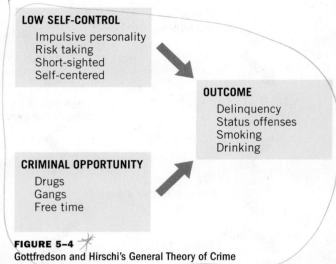

LOW SELF-CONTROL
Impulsive personality
Risk taking
Short-sighted
Self-centered

OUTCOME
Delinquency
Status offenses
Smoking
Drinking

CRIMINAL OPPORTUNITY
Drugs
Gangs
Free time

FIGURE 5–4
Gottfredson and Hirschi's General Theory of Crime

Video 5–3 Self-Control Theory

Thus, self-control is the degree to which an individual is "vulnerable to the temptations of the moment."[75] The other pivotal construct in this theory of crime is crime opportunity, which is a function of the structural or situational circumstances encountered by the individual. In combination, these two constructs are intended to capture the simultaneous influence of external and internal restraints on behavior[76] (see Figure 5–4).

More than two dozen studies have been conducted on the general theory of crime, and the vast majority have been largely favorable.[77] Self-control has been found to be related to self-reported crime among college students, juveniles, and adults; it tends to predict future criminal convictions and self-reported delinquency; and it is related to social consequences other than crime.

Gottfredson and Hirschi's theory of self-control is part of a trend that pushes the causes of crime and delinquency further back in the life course into the family. In some respects, it is a return to the emphasis found in the works of the Gluecks (see Chapter 3) and also resembles the important themes in Wilson and Herrnstein's reinforcement theory. This emphasis on early childhood socialization as the cause of crime, of course, departs from the emphasis on more proximate causes of crime found in rational choice theory and in most sociological theories.[78] Gottfredson and Hirschi's focus on a unidimensional trait also departs from the movement toward multidimensional and integrated theories of crime.[79]

Criticisms of the general theory of crime have focused largely on its lack of conceptual clarity.[80] It is argued that key elements of the theory remain to be tested,[81] that the theory does not have the power to explain all forms of delinquency and crime,[82] and that "questions remain regarding the ubiquity of self-concept."[83] Nevertheless, in spite of these criticisms, the general theory of crime will likely continue to spark continued interest and research.

▲ A group of Drug Free Youth gather at the organization's annual youth summit in Miami, Florida.

■ **How does the social development model explain positive achievement? How does it explain delinquency?**

Elliott and Colleagues' Integrated Social Process Theory

Delbert Elliott and colleagues offer "an explanatory model that expands and synthesizes traditional strain, social control, and social learning perspectives into a single paradigm

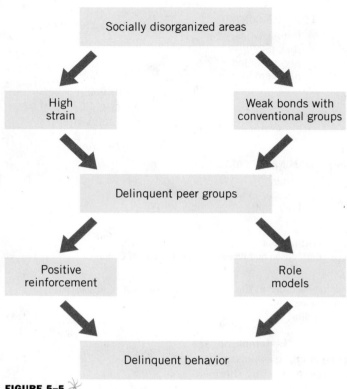

Socially disorganized areas

High strain

Weak bonds with conventional groups

Delinquent peer groups

Positive reinforcement

Role models

Delinquent behavior

FIGURE 5–5
Elliott's Integrated Social Process Theory

that accounts for delinquent behavior and drug use."[84] They argued that all three theories are flawed in explaining delinquent behavior: Strain theory is able to account for some initial delinquent acts but does not adequately explain why some juveniles enter into delinquent careers, whereas others avoid them; control theory is unable to explain prolonged involvement in delinquent behavior in light of there being no reward for this behavior; and social learning theories portray delinquents as passive and susceptible to influence when they are confronted with delinquency-producing reinforcements.

Integrating the strongest features of these theories into a single theoretical model, Elliott and colleagues contended that the experience of living in socially disorganized areas leads youths to develop weak bonds with conventional groups, activities, and norms. High levels of strain, as well as weak bonds with conventional groups, lead some youths to seek out delinquent peer groups, and these antisocial peer groups provide both positive reinforcement for delinquent behavior and role models for this behavior. Consequently, Elliott and colleagues theorized, there is a high probability of involvement in delinquent behavior when bonding to delinquent groups is combined with weak bonding to conventional groups[85] (see Figure 5–5).

This theory represents a pure type of integrated theory. It can be argued that both general theory and interactional theory are not fully integrated theories but are rather elaborations of established theories. In contrast, there is no question that integrated social process theory is an integrated theory.

Examinations of this theory have generally been positive, yet some doubt has been raised about its application to various types of delinquent behaviors. Questions have even been raised about its power and utility with different types of drug activity. For example, integrated social process theory explained 59 percent of the variation in marijuana use but only 29 to 34 percent of the distribution of hard drug use.[86]

Thornberry's Interactional Theory

In Thornberry's interactional theory of delinquency, the initial impetus toward delinquency comes from a weakening of the person's bond to conventional society, represented by attachment to parents, commitment to school, and belief in conventional values. Associations with delinquent peers and delinquent values make up the social setting in which delinquency, especially prolonged serious delinquency, is learned and reinforced. These two variables, along with delinquent behavior itself, form a mutually reinforcing causal loop that leads toward increasing delinquency involvement over time.[87]

Moreover, this interactive process develops over the person's life cycle. During early adolescence, the family is the most influential factor in bonding the youngster to conventional society and reducing delinquency. But as the youth matures and moves through middle adolescence, the world of friends, school, and youth culture becomes the dominant influence over his or her behavior. Finally, as the person enters adulthood, commitments to conventional activities and to family, especially, offer new avenues to reshape the person's bond to society and involvement with delinquent behavior.[88]

Finally, interactional theory holds that these process variables are systematically related to the youngster's position in the social structure. Class, minority group status, and social disorganization of the community all affect the initial values of the interactive variables as well as the behavioral trajectories. It is argued that youths from the most socially disadvantaged backgrounds begin the process least bonded to conventional society and most exposed to the world of delinquency. The nature of the process increases the chances that they will continue on to a career of serious criminal involvement; on the other hand, youths

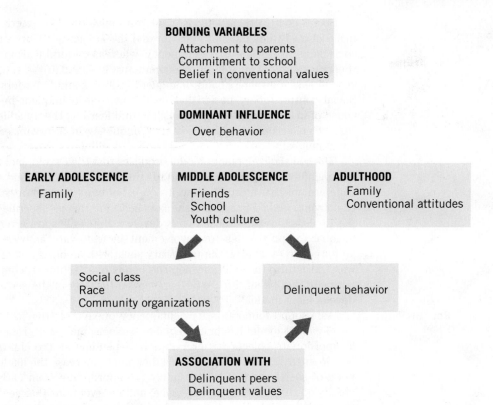

FIGURE 5–6
Thornberry's Interactional Theory

from middle-class families enter a trajectory that is oriented toward conformity and away from delinquency (see Figure 5–6).

Thornberry's theory essentially views delinquency as the result of events occurring in a developmental fashion. Delinquency is not viewed as the end product; instead, it leads to the formation of delinquent values, which then contribute to disconnections in social bonds, more attachments to antisocial peers, and additional involvement in delinquent behavior. As found in other developmental theories, some variables affect unlawful behavior at certain ages and other factors at other ages.[89]

Interactional theory has several positive features that should ensure its continued examination. It seems to make sense of much of the literature on explanations of delinquent behavior; in addition, studies that use an interactional framework not only are more commonly used among delinquency researchers but also are being increasingly used in interdisciplinary research. Furthermore, interactional approaches are consistent with the social settings in which individuals live and interact with others.[90]

Interactional theory also has several shortcomings. Most significantly, interactional theory fails to address the presence of middle-class delinquency and basically ignores racial and gender issues. Its viewpoint that delinquency will persist throughout adolescence and into adulthood (with which Gottfredson and Hirschi would agree) leaves little room for short-term discontinuation or permanent termination of illegal behavior patterns.[91]

Prevention of Delinquency

In terms of developing a new strategy, J. David Hawkins and Joseph G. Weis's **social development model** offers an integrated approach to delinquency prevention that could have long-range consequences for dealing with youth crime in American society.[92]

The social development model is based on the integration of social control theory and cultural learning theory. According to social control theory, the weakening, absence, or breakdown of social controls leads to delinquency[93]; cultural learning, or cultural deviance, theory emphasizes the role of peers and the community in the rise of delinquency, so in disorganized communities, youths are at greater risk of delinquency.[94]

social development model
A perspective based on the integration of social control and cultural learning theories that proposes that the development of attachments to parents will lead to attachments to school and a commitment to education as well as a belief in and commitment to conventional behavior and the law.

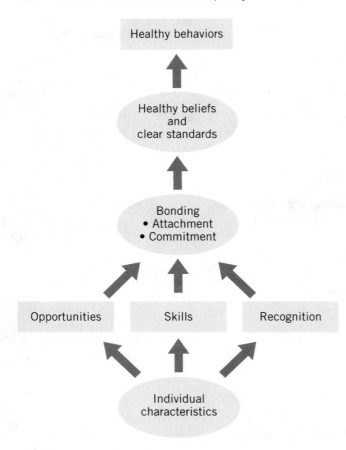

FIGURE 5–7
Hawkins and Weis's Social Development Model

Source: James C. Howell, ed., *Guide for Implementing the Comprehensive Strategy for Serious, Violent, and Chronic Juvenile Offenders* (Washington, D.C.: Office of Juvenile Justice and Delinquency Prevention, 1995), p. 23.

Social control theory focuses on the individual characteristics that lead to delinquent behavior and the impact of the major socializing institutions on delinquency, whereas cultural learning theory examines the role of the community context in the process of learning criminal and delinquent attitudes and behaviors. Social control theory posits that youths become delinquent because of inadequate social controls; cultural learning theory adds that juveniles become socialized to delinquency in disorganized communities.

The social development model proposes that the development of attachments to parents will lead to attachments to school and a commitment to education, as well as a belief in and commitment to conventional behavior and the law. Learning theory describes the process by which these bonds develop: If juveniles are given adequate opportunities for involvement in legitimate activities and are able to acquire the necessary skills with a consistent reward structure, they will develop the bonds of attachment, commitment, and belief. Figure 5–7 presents a diagram of the social development model.

As a sound foundation for delinquency prevention, the social development model has linked families, schools, and peer groups as appropriate objects for intervention, depending on the child's developmental stage. Interventions that aim to increase the likelihood of social bonding to the family are appropriate from early childhood through early adolescence, and interventions that seek to increase the likelihood of social bonding to school are appropriate throughout the years of school attendance and are especially important as juveniles approach and enter adolescence.[95] Thus, the social development model offers communities an empirically grounded basis for designing, implementing, and assessing delinquency prevention programs.

Delinquency across the Life Course: Social Process

The theories in this chapter focus on social process. Delinquency, like other social processes, starts at a particular point and either continues or ceases. Crime continuation or desistance involves several ongoing processes: lack of competence in adolescence, cumulative disadvantage, and turning points and/or establishment of a new identity.

Lack of Competence in Adolescence

John Claussen's classic study of children of the Great Depression followed the study members of the Berkeley longitudinal studies for nearly fifty years, from childhood through the later years of the participants' lives. Claussen found that competence and social influence at the end of adolescence gave shape to the evolving life course.[96] Claussen defined what he called "planful competence" as comprising the dimensions of self-confidence, dependability, and intellectual investment. He found that a youth who demonstrated planful competence was "equipped with an ability to evaluate accurately personal efforts as well as the intentions and responses of others, with an informed knowledge of self, others, and options, and with the self-discipline to pursue chosen goals."[97]

Early competence in study participants, according to Claussen, meant fewer crises in every decade up to their fifties. Highly competent men were more likely to find the right job and to remain in this rewarding line of work, and highly competent women were more likely to find the right husband and to feel rewarded in family life. Choice and selection were both involved: A choice of attractive options and an ability to be selective permitted the most competent to take advantage of their opportunities. In contrast, Claussen concluded that adolescents who lacked planful competence had different trajectories or pathways and made choices that led to job difficulties, marital breakup, and personal difficulties with the law and with figures of authority.[98]

Cumulative Disadvantage

Most juvenile delinquents' lives are not characterized by the kind of planful competence that leads to one successful experience after another throughout the life course. Instead, delinquent youths deal with personal deficits that lead to a series of cumulative disadvantages. For example, Thornberry and colleagues' examination of the Rochester data revealed that individuals who begin antisocial behavior early have individual deficits (e.g., negative temperamental qualities) that both contribute to and are adversely affected by parental deficits (e.g., explosive physical disciplinary styles and low affective ties).

▲ A young man accepts a job from an employer.

■ **How does the social development model explain positive achievement? How does it explain delinquency?**

Over time, these researchers contended, these parents and children develop a coercive interaction, the result being children who express persistent patterns of oppositional and aggressive behavior.[99]

The disorders in these adolescents' lives make delinquent behavior, drug use, and gang involvement more attractive. Involvement in various forms of delinquency then makes these young people more likely to drop out of school; to become pregnant or impregnate someone else; to be unemployed into their adult years; and to be arrested, convicted, and sentenced in the juvenile and later the adult system. Thus, distracted from conventional pathways, they become more involved in antisocial behaviors, which can continue from adolescence into adulthood.[100]

What this concept of cumulative disadvantage suggests is that each negative event in an offender's life tends to limit the positive options available to the individual and becomes a disadvantage in living a crime-free life. Incarceration, especially, leads to cumulative disadvantage in other areas. Thus, arrest and incarceration may spark failure in school, unemployment, and weak community bonds, which in turn increase adult crime.[101]

Web Extra 5–1
Juvenile Justice Evaluation Center website, section titled "Serious, Violent, and/or Habitual Offenders"

Turning Points

As discussed in Chapter 2, Robert J. Sampson and John H. Laub explored the concept of a "turning point" in *Crime in the Making: Pathways and Turning Points through Life*[102] and further developed the idea in *Shared Beginnings, Divergent Lives*.[103] Sampson and Laub's social control explanation emphasizes the gradual buildup of investments that accrue in the presence of social bonds of attachment. They found five turning points in the desistance process: marriage/spouses, employment, reform school, the military, and neighborhood change. These are "structurally induced turning points that serve as the catalyst for sustaining long-term behavioral change."[104]

Web Extra 5–2
National Youth Violence Prevention Resource Center website

Another view of the turning point emerges in the research that Shadd Maruna conducted on English ex-offenders. Maruna contended that ex-offenders desist from crime when they develop a coherent and prosocial identity for themselves. Accordingly, they need a coherent and credible self-story to explain to themselves and to others how their past could have led to their new identity. Maruna referred to this self-story as a "redemptive script" and described how interviewees used such scripts to link their past lives to positive outcomes.[105]

Peggy C. Giordano and colleagues developed a theory of cognitive transformation to explain desistance in their follow-up of a sample of serious adolescent female delinquents. These researchers found that four types of cognitive transformation take place as an integral part of the desistance process: (1) There is a shift in the actor's openness to change; (2) the individual is exposed to a hook or set of hooks for change; (3) the individual begins to envision and fashion an appealing and conventional "replacement self"; and (4) a transformation takes place in the way the actor views the former deviant behavior or lifestyle.

These various cognitive transformations or shifts not only influence receptivity to one or more hooks of change but also inspire and direct behavior.[106]

In sum, desistance requires that a combination of positive attitudes, prosocial behaviors, and reinforcing transitions in marriage, family, and employment replace the negative patterns found in delinquency, criminality, and drug involvement. These processes not only require human agency but also are gradual, perhaps even unknown to the offender at the time.

Social Process Theories and Social Policy

Each of the social process theories discussed in this chapter can influence those who make social policy. Differential association theory suggests that delinquents learn from their association with small groups, so the more they are exposed to prosocial groups, the more likely it is that they will be deterred from delinquent behavior. Several treatment technologies, such as Positive Youth Development (PYD), suggest that some delinquent youths are influenced by positive group norms. The task, then, is to generate opportunities for delinquency-prone youths to be exposed to more positive definitions of the social order.

Social control theory suggests that the more attached youths are by social bonds, the more likely it is that they will refrain from delinquent behavior. Thus, attachment to the family, positive experiences in school, and exposure to prosocial groups in the community become important components in the design of delinquency prevention and control programs. Containment theory also proposes that positive experiences in the home, the school, and the community will lead to a good self-concept, thereby insulating youths from delinquent behavior.

Both drift theory and labeling theory suggest that a key element in the process of becoming delinquent is the reaction of society to unacceptable behavior. Delinquency in America is widespread throughout the social order, and the danger is that identifying and tagging individuals who have come to the attention of the justice system will increase their chances of continuing delinquent behavior or, even worse, that their official contacts with the system may encourage them to choose a delinquent career. Accordingly, policy makers would be wise to discourage the labeling of youths, both in the school system and in the justice system.

The Case

The Life Course of Amy Watters, Age 10

If you could ask Amy what the most significant event that took place in the tenth year of her life had been, she would likely say that it was the day that the police called and said that her father, Simon, was in jail. He'd been arrested for driving while under the influence of an intoxicating substance (marijuana). Amy was frantic when she received the call because there was no adult in the house to whom she could turn for help. About an hour later, her father called from jail and asked Amy to phone Uncle Fred, who lived only a few miles away, for help. Fred would post bail, her dad said, and he could get out of jail. Sure enough, Uncle Fred came through, and Amy's dad came home later that same evening.

Research suggests that delinquency is more likely to occur in those families in which parental self-control is low. One study, in particular (see the first link below), seemed to demonstrate a significant link between parental low self-control and child low self-control. Moreover, that link was shown to be correlated with a greater incidence of delinquency among children raised in families exhibiting low parental self-control. Does the incident described in this box mean that Amy's father suffered from low self-control? If so, what might the consequences be for Amy?

Learn More on the Web:

- Parental Criminality and Low Self-Control: An Examination of Delinquency: http://www .informaworld.com/smpp/content~content=a912500787~db=all~jumptype=rss
- A Life-Course Perspective on Stress, Delinquency, and Young Adult Crime: http://www .springerlink.com/content/b73t8834mq68jm47

Follow the continuing Amy Watters saga in the next chapter.

SUMMARY

Each of the social process theories discussed in this chapter contributes to our understanding of how adolescents become delinquent. Among the perspectives discussed are the following:

- Differential association theory suggests that individuals learn from their association with small groups; if they are involved in antisocial groups, they are more likely to accept and internalize antisocial conduct norms and behavioral definitions.
- Social control approaches, including bonding theory, maintain that the more strongly adolescents are attached by positive social bonds, the more likely it is that they will refrain from delinquent behavior.
- Containment theory states that positive experiences in the home, the school, and the community will lead to the development of a positive self-concept, thereby insulating individuals from delinquency.
- Process theories, such as those discussed in this chapter, are also helpful in understanding the continuation of, or desistance from, delinquency across the life course. Bonding with significant others, drifting in and out of delinquent behavior, and developing a self-concept are key ideas in these theories.
- Theories of delinquency and drift, as well as other social control theories, emphasize the decision-making process at the individual level.
- Gottfredson and Hirschi's general theory of crime defines the lack of self-control as the common element underlying problem behaviors.

- Theory integration usually implies the combination of two or more existing theories on the basis of their perceived commonalities.
- Elliott and colleagues' integrated social process theory contends that the experience of living in socially disorganized areas leads young people to develop weak social bonds with conventional groups, activities, and norms. High levels of strain, as well as weak bonds, lead some youths to seek out delinquent peer groups.
- Thornberry's interactional theory suggests that delinquency leads to the formation of delinquent values, which then contribute to the disintegration of conventional bonds and greater attachment to antisocial peers.
- Hawkins and Weis's social development model proposes that that the development of attachments to parents will lead to further attachments to school and a commitment to education, as well as a belief in and commitment to conventional behavior and values.
- Criticisms of social process theories center on their level of analysis—which is the individual delinquent and the personal decision-making process. Critics point out that these theories fail to place sufficient emphasis on the impact of larger political and economic systems on adolescents and their development.

KEY TERMS

commitment to the social bond, p. 115
containment theory, p. 113
control theory, p. 113
differential association theory, p. 107

differential identification theory, p. 109
drift theory, p. 111
neutralization theory, p. 111
social control theory, p. 115

social development model, p. 121
social process theory, p. 107
soft determinism, p. 113

JUVENILE DELINQUENCY VIDEOS

Introduction to Social Control Theory

Introduction to Social Control Theory describes the philosophy behind social control theory, which explains trends of criminal behavior. Social control theory states that individuals are restrained by social norms and values that prevent the naturally occurring deviant behavior that exists out of human self-interest.

How would social control theory explain crime trends? Why would females be less involved in crime than males? From the readings in this chapter as well as this video, do you believe that social control theory can be used in all situations to explain criminal behavior? Why or why not?

REVIEW QUESTIONS

1. Why is differential association theory called a "learning" theory?
2. Self-concept, according to containment theory, is vitally important in affecting behavior. Do you agree?
3. Matza and Hirschi proposed different interpretations of the degree to which delinquents identify with the norms and values of society. What is the position of each theorist? Which position do you find more credible?

4. Which one of the three integrated theories makes the most sense to you? What are the advantages of an integrated theory? What are its disadvantages?
5. Does Matza's drift theory seem to be present in the lives of delinquents? What forces seem to set in motion the drift toward delinquency?

DISCUSSION QUESTIONS

1. Does differential association theory support the "nature" argument of crime causation? Explain your response.
2. Does cultural stratification naturally occur between generations? If so, how might it contribute to delinquency?
3. How does containment theory relate to the concept of peer pressure?

4. What do you think might account for youths reporting both the development of strong bonds to delinquent peers and the acceptance of the values of conventional society?

GROUP EXERCISES

1. Have students recount experiences when they were presented with opportunities to learn delinquent behavior (e.g., smoking and shoplifting), and ask them to explain what motivated them to take the course of action they ultimately took.
2. Have the class debate/discuss the merits and criticisms of each of the theories in this chapter. Have the students attempt to develop a workable definition of the term *self-concept*.
3. Have the class debate/discuss the merits and concerns of integrated theory.

4. Have the students read Mears and Field's article "A Closer Look at the Age, Peers, and Delinquency Relationship," accessible at http://wcr.sonoma.edu/v4nl/mears.html; have them discuss the authors' use of interactional theory in their research.
5. Take an anonymous poll of the class that asks these questions about their elementary and secondary school years: (1) Were you highly involved, moderately involved, or little involved in conventional activities? (2) Did you have a close, ambivalent, or distant relationship with your parents? (3) Did you become involved in delinquent behavior? Total the responses, and discuss the results with the class.

NOTES

1. Fox Butterfield, "Father Steals Best: Crime in an American Family," *New York Times*, August 21, 2002; Charles Laurence, "Liars, Cheats and Thieves All: Pa Would Have Been So Proud," *Daily Telegraph*, August 25, 2002; John Ritter, "A Town Wonders: Does Crime Run in Families?" *USA Today*, September 4, 2002.
2. For this symbolic interactionist perspective, see Charles H. Cooley, *Human Nature and the Social Order* (1902; reprint ed., New York: Schocken Books, 1964); George H. Mead, *Mind, Self and Society* (Chicago: University of Chicago Press, 1934).
3. Edwin H. Sutherland, "A Statement of the Theory," in *The Sutherland Papers*, edited by Albert Cohen, Alfred Lindesmith, and Karl Schuessler (Bloomington: Indiana University Press, 1956), pp. 7–29.
4. Edwin H. Sutherland, *Principles of Criminology* (Philadelphia: J. B. Lippincott, 1947).
5. Ross L. Matsueda, "The Current State of Differential Association Theory," *Crime and Delinquency* 34 (July 1988), pp. 277–306.
6. Harold Finestone, *Victims of Change: Juvenile Delinquents in American Society* (Westport, Conn.: Greenwood Press, 1976).
7. Matsueda, "The Current State."
8. Tracy Wharton Church II and Julie Taylor, "An Examination of Differential Association and Social Control Theory: Family Systems and Delinquency," *Youth Violence & Juvenile Justice* 7 (2009), pp. 3–15.
9. M. H. Selfhout, S. J. Branje, and W. H. Meeus, "The Development of Delinquency and Perceived Friendship Quality in Adolescent Best Friendship Dyads," *Journal of Abnormal Child Psychology* 36 (2008), pp. 471–85.
10. Daniel Glaser, "Differential Association and Criminological Prediction," *Social Problems* 8 (1960), p. 6.
11. Robert J. Burgess, Jr., and Ronald L. Akers, "A Differential Association–Reinforcement Theory of Criminal Behavior," *Social Problems* 14 (1966), p. 128. See also Ronald L. Akers, *Deviant Behavior: A Social Learning Approach*, 3rd ed. (Belmont, Calif.: Wadsworth, 1985), p. 41.
12. Marvin D. Krohn et al., "Social Learning Theory and Adolescent Cigarette Smoking: A Longitudinal Study," *Social Problems* 32 no. 5 (June 1985), pp. 455–74.
13. For those who see little value in a theory, such as differential association, that cannot be tested, see Jack P. Gibbs, "The State of Criminology Theory," *Criminology* 25 (1987), pp. 821–40; Sheldon Glueck, "Theory and Fact in Criminology," *British Journal of Criminology* 7 (1956), pp. 92–109; and Travis Hirschi, *Causes of Delinquency* (Berkeley: University of California Press, 1969). For a defense of the testability of differential association theory, see James D. Orcutt, "Differential Association and Marijuana Use: A Closer Look at Sutherland (with a Little Help from Becker)," *Criminology* 25 (1987), pp. 341–58.
14. Ronald L. Akers, "Is Differential Association/Social Learning Cultural Deviance Theory?" *Criminology* 34 (1996), pp. 229–47.
15. Steven Box, *Deviance, Reality and Society* (New York: Holt, Rinehart and Winston, 1971).
16. C. R. Jeffery, "An Integrated Theory of Crime and Criminal Behavior," *Journal of Criminal Law, Criminology and Police Science* 49 (1959), pp. 533–52.
17. Matsueda, "The Current State," p. 295.
18. David Matza, *Delinquency and Drift* (New York: Wiley, 1964), p. 28.

19. Ibid.

20. Gresham M. Sykes and David Matza, "Techniques of Neutralization: A Theory of Delinquency," *American Sociological Review* 22 (December 1957), pp. 644–70.

21. Ibid.

22. Matza, *Delinquency and Drift*, p. 156.

23. Ibid.

24. Ibid.

25. Ibid., p. 185.

26. Ibid.

27. Gemma Shears, "What Do We Think? Investigating the Attitudes and Life Goals of Young Offenders," *International Journal of Police Science & Management* 6 (2004), pp. 126–35.

28. Matza, *Delinquency and Drift*. See also Robert Agnew, "Determinism, Interdeterminism, and Crime: An Empirical Exploration," *Criminology* 33 (February 1995), p. 83.

29. Travis Hirschi, "On the Compatibility of Rational Choice and Social Control Theories of Crime," in *The Reasoning Criminal,* edited by Derek B. Cornish and Ronald V. Clarke (New York: Springer-Verlag, 1986), pp. 105–18; Michael R. Gottfredson and Travis Hirschi, eds., *Positive Criminology* (Newbury Park, Calif.: Sage, 1987); and Michael R. Gottfredson and Travis Hirschi, *A General Theory of Crime* (Palo Alto, Calif.: Stanford University Press, 1990).

30. See John S. Goldkamp, "Rational Choice and Determinism," in *Positive Criminology,* (Thousand Oaks, Calif.: Sage, 1987), pp. 125–137.

31. Ronald L. Akers, "Rational Choice, Deterrence, and Social Learning in Criminology: The Path Not Taken," *Journal of Criminal Law and Criminology* 81 (1990), pp. 653–76.

32. Ian Taylor, Paul Walton, and Jock Young, *The New Criminology* (New York: Harper and Row, 1973).

33. Robert Regoli and Eric Poole, "The Commitment of Delinquents to Their Misdeeds: A Reexamination," *Journal of Criminal Justice* 6 (1978), pp. 261–69; Michael J. Hindelang, "The Commitment of Delinquents to Their Misdeeds: Do Delinquents Drift?" *Social Problems* 17 (1970), pp. 50–59; and Michael J. Hindelang, "Moral Evaluation of Illegal Behaviors," *Social Problems* 21 (1974), pp. 370–85.

34. John Hagan, "Destiny and Drift: Subcultural Preferences, Status Attainments, and the Risks and Rewards of Youth," *American Sociological Review* 56 (1991), p. 567.

35. Donald J. Shoemaker, *Theories of Delinquency: An Examination of Explanations of Delinquent Behavior*, 6th ed. (New York: Oxford University Press, 2009).

36. Albert J. Reiss Jr., "Delinquency as the Failure of Personal and Social Controls," *American Sociological Review* 16 (1951), pp. 196–207.

37. F. Ivan Nye, *Family Relationships and Delinquent Behavior* (New York: John Wiley, 1958).

38. The principles of containment theory draw on Walter C. Reckless, "A New Theory of Delinquency and Crime," *Federal Probation* 24 (December 1961), pp. 42–46.

39. E. D. Lively, Simon Dinitz, and Walter C. Reckless, "Self-Concept as a Prediction of Juvenile Delinquency," *American Journal of Orthopsychiatry* 32 (1962), pp. 159–68; Gary F. Jensen, "Inner Containment and Delinquency," *Criminology*

64 (1973), pp. 464–70; and Franco Ferracuti, Simon Dinitz, and E. Acosta de Brenes, *Delinquents and Nondelinquents in the Puerto Rican Slum Culture* (Columbus: Ohio State University Press, 1975).

40. Timothy J. Owens, "Two Dimensions of Self-Esteem: Reciprocal Effects of Positive Self-Worth and Self-Deprecations on Adolescent Problems," *American Sociological Review* 59 (1994), pp. 391, 405; L. Edward Wells and Joseph H. Rankin, "Self-Concept as a Mediating Factor in Delinquency," *Social Psychology Quarterly* 46 (1983), p. 19; John D. McCarthy and Dean R. Hoge, "The Dynamics of Self-Esteem and Delinquency," *American Journal of Sociology* 90 (1984), p. 396; and W. E. Thompson and R. A. Dodder, "Juvenile Delinquency Explained? A Test of Containment Theory," *Youth and Society* 15 (December 1983), pp. 171–94.

41. Florence R. Rosenberg and Morris Rosenberg, "Self-Esteem and Delinquency," *Journal of Youth and Adolescence* 7 (1978), p. 280.

42. H. B. Kaplan, *Deviant Behavior in Defense of Self* (New York: Academic Press, 1980); and Rosenberg and Rosenberg, "Self-Esteem and Delinquency." See also Morris Rosenberg, Carmi Schooler, and Carrie Schoenbach, "Self-Esteem and Adolescent Problems," *American Sociological Review* 54 (1989), pp. 1004–18.

43. Joanne Roberts, Ismail Dincer Gunes, and Rudy Ray Seward, "The Impact of Self Esteem, Family Rituals, Religiosity, and Participation in Conforming Activities upon Delinquency: A Comparison of Young Adults in Turkey and the United States," *Journal of Comparative Family Studies* 42 (2011), pp. 59–76.

44. Simon Dinitz and Betty A. Pfau-Vicent, "Self-Concept and Juvenile Delinquency: An Update," *Youth Society* 14 (December 1982), pp. 133–58.

45. Michael Schwartz and Sandra S. Tangri, "A Note on 'Self-Concept as an Insulator against Delinquency,'" *American Sociological Review* 30 (1965), pp. 922–26.

46. Hirschi, *Causes of Delinquency*, p. 16.

47. Ibid., p. 31.

48. Ibid., p. 34.

49. Ibid.

50. Ibid.

51. Ibid.

52. Ibid., p. 86.

53. Ibid.

54. Ibid., p. 22.

55. Ibid.

56. Ibid., p. 200.

57. Ibid.

58. Ibid.

59. Ibid., p. 135.

60. Ibid.

61. Ibid.

62. Barbara J. Costello and Paul R. Vowell, "Testing Control Theory and Differential Association: A Reanalysis of the Richmond Youth Project Data," *Criminology* 37 (November 1999), pp. 479–514; and Charles R. Tittle, *Control Balance: Toward a General Theory of Deviance* (Boulder, Colo.: Westview, 1995). For a recent attempt to test Tittle's control

balance theory, see Alex R. Piquero and Matthew Hickman, "An Empirical Test of Tittle's Control Balance Theory," *Criminology* 37 (May 1999), pp. 319–41. See also Steven A. Cernkovich, "Evaluating Two Models of Delinquency Causation: Structural Theory and Control Theory," *Criminology* 25 (1987), pp. 335–52; Raymond A. Eve, "A Study of the Efficacy and Interactions of Several Theories for Explaining Rebelliousness among High School Students," *Journal of Criminal Law and Criminology* 69 (1978), pp. 115–25; Marvin D. Krohn and James L. Massey, "Social Control and Delinquent Behavior: An Examination of the Elements of the Social Bond," *Sociological Quarterly* 21 (August 1980), p. 542; Elliott et al., *Explaining Delinquency and Drug Use*; Joseph H. Rankin, "Investigating the Interrelations among Social Control Variables and Conformity," *Journal of Criminal Law and Criminology* 67 (1977), pp. 470–80; Robert Agnew, "Social Control Theory and Delinquency: A Longitudinal Test," *Criminology* 23 (1985), pp. 47–61; Randy L. LaGrange and Helene Raskin White, "Age Differences in Delinquency: A Test of Theory," *Criminology* 23 (1985), pp. 19–45; Kimberly Kempf Leonard and Scott H. Decker, "Theory of Social Control: Does It Apply to the Very Young?" *Journal of Criminal Justice* 22 (1994), pp. 89–105; Robert L. Gardner and Donald J. Shoemaker, "Social Bonding and Delinquency: A Comparative Analysis," *Sociological Quarterly* 39 (1989), pp. 481–500; and Eric A. Stewart, "School Social Bonds, Social Climate, and School Misbehavior: A Multilevel Analysis," *Justice Quarterly* 20 (September 2003), pp. 575–604.

63. Shoemaker, *Theories of Delinquency*.
64. Martha Gault-Sherman, "It's a Two-Way Street: The Bidirectional Relationships between Parenting and Delinquency," *Journal of Youth & Adolescence* 41 (2012), pp. 121–45.
65. Leonard and Decker, "Theory of Social Control."
66. Among the growing number of works citing the advantages of integrated theory are Richard Johnson, *Juvenile Delinquency and Its Origins: An Integrated Theoretical Approach* (New York: Cambridge University Press, 1979); J. David Hawkins and Joseph G. Weis, *Journal of Primary Prevention 6 (Winter 1995)*, pp. 77-78; Steven Messner, Marvin Krohn, and Allen Liska, eds., *Theoretical Integration in the Study of Deviance and Crime: Problems and Prospects* (Albany: State University of New York at Albany Press, 1989); and John Hagan and Bill McCarthy, *Mean Streets: Youth Crime and Homelessness* (New York: Cambridge University Press, 1997).
67. Shoemaker, *Theories of Delinquency*.
68. Ibid.
69. Ibid.
70. Ibid.
71. For other integrated theories, see James Q. Wilson and Richard J. Herrnstein, *Crime and Human Nature* (New York: Simon and Schuster, 1985), which is discussed in Chapter 3; Robert J. Sampson and John H. Laub, *Crime in the Making: Pathways and Turning Points through Life* (Cambridge, Mass.: Harvard University Press, 1993), which is discussed in Chapter 2; and Colvin and Pauly, "A Critique of

Criminology: Toward an Integrated Structural–Marxist Theory of Delinquency Production," *American Journal of Sociology* 89 (November 1983), pp. 513–51, which is discussed in Chapter 6; John Hagan, A. R. Gillis, and John Simpson, "The Class Structure of Gender and Delinquency: Toward a Power-Control Theory of Common Delinquent Behavior," *American Journal of Sociology* 90 (1985), pp. 1151–78.
72. Michael R. Gottfredson and Travis Hirschi, *A General Theory of Crime* (Palo Alto, Calif.: Stanford University Press, 1990); Elliott et al., *Explaining Delinquency and Drug Use*; Delbert S. Elliott, Suzanne S. Ageton, and Rachelle J. Canter, "An Integrated Theoretical Perspective on Delinquent Behavior," *Journal of Research in Crime and Delinquency* 16 (1979), pp. 3–27; Terence P. Thornberry, "Toward an Interactional Theory of Delinquency," *Criminology* 25 (1987), pp. 862–91; Terence P. Thornberry, Alan J. Lizotte, Marvin D. Krohn, Margaret Farnworth, and Sung Joon Jang, "Testing Interactional Theory: An Examination of Reciprocal Causal Relationships among Family, School, and Delinquency," *Journal of Criminal Law and Criminology* 82 (1991), pp. 3–35; and J. David Hawkins and Joseph G. Weis, "The Social Development Model: An Integrated Approach to Delinquency Prevention," *Journal of Primary Prevention* 6 (Winter 1985), pp. 73–97.
73. Gottfredson and Hirschi, *A General Theory of Crime*.
74. Ibid., pp. 90–91.
75. Ibid., p. 87.
76. Ibid.
77. For a review of these studies, see T. David Evans, Francis T. Cullen, Velmer S. Burton, Jr., R. Gregory Dunaway, and Michael L. Benson, "The Social Consequences of Self-Control: Testing the General Theory of Crime," *Criminology* 35 (1997), pp. 476–77. See also Ryan Charles Meldrum, "Beyond Parenting: An Examination of the Etiology of Self-Control," *Journal of Criminal Justice* 36 (2008), pp. 244–51; Alexander T. Vazsonyi and Rudi Klanjsek, "A Test of Self-Control Theory across Different Socioeconomic Strata," *Justice Quarterly* 25 (March 2008), pp. 101–31; and Stacey Nofziger, "The 'Cause' of Low Self-Control: The Influence of Maternal Self-Control," *Journal of Research in Crime and Delinquency* 45 (2008), pp. 191–224.
78. Harold G. Grasmick, Charles R. Tittle, Robert J. Bursik, Jr., and Bruce J. Arneklev, "Testing the Core Empirical Implications of Gottfredson and Hirschi's General Theory of Crime," *Journal of Research in Crime and Delinquency* 30 (February 1993), pp. 47–54.
79. See Ronald L. Akers, "Self-Control as a General Theory of Crime," *Journal of Quantitative Criminology* 7 (1991), pp. 201–11.
80. Shoemaker, *Theories of Delinquency*.
81. Dennis M. Giever, Dana C. Lynskey, and Danette S. Monnet, "Gottfredson and Hirschi's General Theory of Crime and Youth Gangs: An Empirical Test on a Sample of Middle-School Students," unpublished paper sent to the authors, 1998. See also Meldrum, "Beyond Parenting"; Vazsonyi and Klanjsek, "A Test of Self-Control Theory"; and Nofziger, "The 'Cause' of Low Self-Control."

82. Callie Harbin Burt, Ronald L. Simons, and Leslie G. Simons, "A Longitudinal Test of the Effects of Parenting and the Stability of Self-Control: Negative Evidence for the General Theory of Crime," *Criminology* 44 (2006), pp. 353–96.
83. Ibid, p. 353.
84. Delbert S. Elliott, Suzanne S. Ageton, and Rachelle J. Canter, "An Integrated Theoretical Perspective on Delinquent Behavior," *Journal of Research in Crime and Delinquency* 16 (1979), pp. 3–27.
85. Ibid.
86. Cynthia Jacob Chien, "Testing the Effect of the Key Theoretical Variable of Theories of Strain, Social Control and Social Learning on Types of Delinquency," paper presented at the annual meeting of the American Society of Criminology, Baltimore, MD, November 1990.
87. Thornberry, "Toward an Interactional Theory of Delinquency."
88. Ibid.
89. Shoemaker, *Theories of Delinquency*.
90. Ibid.
91. Ibid.
92. Hawkins and Weis, "The Social Development Model."
93. Hirschi, *Causes of Delinquency*.
94. Clifford R. Shaw, *Delinquent Areas* (Chicago: University of Chicago Press, 1929); and Clifford Shaw and Henry D. McKay, *Juvenile Delinquency in Urban Areas* (Chicago: University of Chicago Press, 1942).
95. J. David Hawkins., *Typology of Cause-Focused Strategies of Delinquency Prevention* (Washington, D.C.: Office of Juvenile Justice and Delinquency Prevention, 1980.
96. John A. Claussen, *American Lives: Looking Back at the Children of the Great Depression* (New York: Free Press, 1993).
97. Ibid., p. viii.
98. Ibid.
99. Marvin D. Krohn, Terence P. Thornberry, Craig Rivera, and Marc Le Blanc, "Later Delinquency Careers," in *Child Development,* edited by Rolf Loeber and David P. Farrington (Thousand Oaks, Calif.: Sage, 2001), pp. 67–93.
100. Terence P. Thornberry, Marvin D. Krohn, Alan J. Lizotte, Carolyn A. Smith, and Kimberly Tobin, *Gangs and Delinquency in Developmental Perspective* (Cambridge, England: Cambridge University Press, 2003).
101. John H. Laub and Robert J. Sampson, *Shared Beginnings, Divergent Lives: Delinquent Boys to Age 70* (Cambridge, Mass.: Harvard University Press, 2003). See also Robert J. Sampson and John H. Laub, "A Life-Course Theory of Cumulative Disadvantage and the Stability of Delinquency," in *Developmental Theories of Crime and Delinquency,* edited by Terence P. Thornberry (New Brunswick, N.J.: Transaction Publishers, 1997), pp. 133–61.
102. Robert J. Sampson and John H. Laub, *Crime in the Making: Pathways and Turning Points through Life* (Cambridge, Mass.: Harvard University Press, 1993).
103. Laub and Sampson, *Shared Beginnings, Divergent Lives;* see especially Chaps. 3 and 6.
104. Ibid., p. 149.
105. Shadd Maruna, *Making Good: How Ex-Convicts Reform and Rebuild Their Lives* (Washington, D.C.: American Psychological Association, 2001).
106. Peggy C. Giordano, Stephen A. Cernkovich, and Jennifer L. Rudolph, "Gender, Crime, and Delinquency: Toward a Theory of Cognitive Transformation," *American Journal of Sociology* 107 (January 2002), pp. 990–1064.

Chapter Objectives

After reading this chapter, you should be able to:

1. **Explain the significance of labeling as a cause of future behavior.**
2. **Summarize the symbolic interaction theory of delinquency.**
3. **Explain the conflict theory of delinquency.**
4. **Describe restorative justice and peacemaking.**

We worry about what a child will become tomorrow, yet we forget that he is someone today.

—Stacia Tauscher, National Center for Juvenile Justice, Annual Report, 2003

Introduction

A recent study that tracked twenty thousand children in grades seven through twelve found that 15 percent believed that they were likely to die before they reached age 35. The study concluded that "teenagers who engage in risky behavior may do so because they believe they're going to die young anyway."[1] Such fatalistic children, researchers found, were more likely to attempt suicide, get into serious physical altercations, and engage in recreational drug use. Pessimistic attitudes were found to be more common among black, low-income, and Native American teens—perhaps reinforcing a cycle of desperation, and imposing negative definitions of self onto a group of children already facing serious challenges. The study seemed to contradict traditional notions that young people engage in risk-taking behavior because they feel invincible due to their age.

This chapter discusses labeling theory, symbolic interactionist theory, and conflict theory. Labeling theory describes the creation and enforcement of society's rules and explains the important role those rules play in determining the nature and extent of delinquency. Symbolic interactionist theory considers the process by which deviant or delinquent behavior is influenced by reference groups and peers, and conflict theory sees delinquency as a by-product of the conflict that results when groups or classes with differing interests interact with one another.

These three perspectives are termed **social interactionist theories** of delinquency because they derive their explanatory power from the give-and-take that continuously occurs between social groups and between individuals and society.

social interactionist theory
A theoretical perspective that derives its explanatory power from the give-and-take that continuously occurs between social groups and between individuals and society.

Labeling Theory

During the 1960s and 1970s, the labeling perspective was one of the most influential approaches to understanding crime and delinquency.[2] **Labeling theory** or the labeling perspective, sometimes called the interactional theory of deviance or the social reaction perspective, is based on the premise that society creates deviants by labeling those who are apprehended as different from other individuals when in reality they are different only because they have been tagged with a deviant label. Accordingly, labeling theorists focus on the processes by which individuals become involved in deviant behavior and stress the part played by social audiences and their responses to the norm violations of individuals.

labeling theory
The view that society creates the delinquent by labeling those who are apprehended as different from other youths when in reality they are different primarily because they have been tagged with a deviant label.

The view that formal and informal social reactions to criminality can influence criminals' subsequent attitudes and behaviors has been recognized for some time. Frank Tannenbaum, Edwin M. Lemert, and Howard Becker, three of the chief proponents of the labeling perspective, focus on the process by which formal social control agents change the self-concept of individuals through these agents' reactions to their behavior. Recent work in labeling theory is also discussed in this section.

Frank Tannenbaum: Dramatization of Evil

In 1938, Austrian-American sociologist Frank Tannenbaum developed the earliest formulation of labeling theory in his book *Crime and the Community*. Tannenbaum examined the process whereby a juvenile came to the attention of the authorities and was labeled as different from other juveniles, and he theorized that this process produced a change in both how those individuals were then handled by the justice system and how they came to view themselves:

> The process of making the criminal, therefore, is a process of tagging, defining, identifying, segregating, describing, emphasizing, making conscious and self-conscious; it becomes a way of stimulating, suggesting, emphasizing, and evoking the very traits that are complained of.[3]

▲ A young woman mentors a girls' softball team.

■ **How can mentoring programs help young people avoid the potential negative consequences of labeling?**

Video 6–1 Edwin Lemert

Tannenbaum called this process the "dramatization of evil," writing that the process of tagging a juvenile resulted in the youth becoming involved with other delinquents and that these associations represented an attempt to escape the society that was responsible for the negative labeling. The delinquent then became involved in a deviant career, and regardless of the efforts of individuals in the community and the justice system to change his or her "evil" behavior, the negative behavior became increasingly hardened and resistant to positive values. Tannenbaum proposed that the less the evil is dramatized, the less likely youths are to become involved in deviant careers.[4]

Edwin Lemert: Primary and Secondary Deviation

The social reaction theory developed by American sociologist Edwin M. Lemert in the midtwentieth century provided a distinct alternative to the social disorganization theory of Shaw and McKay, the differential association notion of Edwin H. Sutherland, and the social structural approach of Merton. Lemert focused attention on the interaction between social control agents and rule violators as well as on how certain behaviors came to be labeled criminal, delinquent, or deviant.[5]

Lemert's concept of primary and secondary deviation is regarded as one of the most important theoretical constructs of the labeling perspective. According to Lemert, **primary deviation** consists of the individual's behavior, and **secondary deviation** is society's response to that behavior. The social reaction to the deviant, Lemert charged, could be interpreted as forcing a change in status or role; that is, society's reaction to the deviant person resulted in a transformation in the individual's identity.[6] The social reaction to the deviant person, whether a disapproving glance or a full-blown stigmatization, is critical in understanding the progressive commitment of a person to a deviant mode of life.

Lemert describe the **process of becoming deviant** as follows:

> The sequence of interaction leading to secondary deviation is roughly as follows: (1) primary deviation; (2) social penalties; (3) further primary deviation; (4) stronger penalties and rejection; (5) further deviation, perhaps with hostilities and resentment beginning to focus upon those doing the penalizing; (6) crisis reached in the tolerance quotient, expressed in formal action by the community stigmatizing of the deviant; (7) strengthening of the deviant conduct as a reaction to the stigmatizing and penalties; (8) ultimate acceptance of deviant social status and efforts at adjustment on the basis of the associated role.[7]

The social reaction to deviance is expressed in this process of interaction. *Social reaction* is a general term that summarizes both the moral indignation of others toward deviance and the action directed toward its control. This concept also encompasses a social organizational perspective; as an organizational response, the concept of social reaction refers to the capacity of control agents to impose such constraints on the behavior of the deviant person as are reflected in terms such as *treat, correct,* and *punish.*[8]

Howard Becker: Deviant Careers

Howard Becker, another major labeling theorist, writing a bit later than Lemert, conceptualized the relationship between the rules of society and the process of being labeled as an outsider in these words:

> Social groups create deviance by making the rules whose infraction constitutes deviance, and by applying those rules to particular people and labeling them as outsiders. From this point of view, deviance is not a quality of the act the person commits, but rather a consequence of the application by others of rules and sanctions to an "offender." The deviant is one to whom that label has successfully been applied; deviant behavior is behavior that people so label.[9]

Becker argued that once a person is caught and labeled, that person becomes an outsider and gains a new social status, with consequences for both the person's self-image and his or her public identity. The individual is now regarded as a different kind of person.[10] Although the sequence of events that leads to the imposition of the label of "deviant" is

primary deviation
According to labeling theory, the initial act of deviance that causes a person to be labeled a deviant.

secondary deviation
According to labeling theory, deviance that is a consequence of societal reaction to an initial delinquent act.

process of becoming deviant
In labeling theory, the concept that the process of acquiring a delinquent identity takes place in a number of steps.

presented from the perspective of social interaction, the analytical framework shifts to that of social structure once the label is imposed. In other words, before a person is labeled, he or she participates in a process of social interaction, but once labeling has occurred, the individual is assigned a status within a social structure.[11]

Web Extra 6–1
Labeling theory from About.com

Juvenile Justice Process and Labeling

There is a long history of arguments that the labeling found in the formal processing of youths through the juvenile justice system is what influences the secondary response of continued delinquent acts. Tufts University economist Edwin Schur contended that most delinquent acts are insignificant and benign and that punishment is not needed. But when youths are arrested and brought before the juvenile court, they are stereotyped as different. Having acquired this label, they receive greater attention from authorities, and they are likely to be processed more deeply in the justice system because of this increased attention. Delinquency laws are actually counterproductive, Schur suggested, because they produce more delinquency than they deter. In 1973, Schur went so far as to argue for a policy of **radical nonintervention**, which simply means to "leave the kids alone whenever possible."[12]

More recently, several studies have suggested that under certain circumstances, "official punishment appears to increase the likelihood of subsequent deviance as suggested by labeling theory."[13] Francis Polymaria, Francis T. Cullen and Joanne C. Gersten found that the formal reaction to delinquency affects the likelihood of subsequent delinquent behavior but that these effects are related to the types of reactions and the types of deviance.[14] About ten years ago, Anthony Matarazzo, Peter J. Carrington, and Robert D. Hiscott investigated the relationship between prior and current youth court dispositions and found support for labeling theory. Their findings indicated that prior juvenile court dispositions exerted a significant impact on current disposition, even with the control of relevant variables.[15] See Figure 6–1 for an overview of the general assumptions of labeling theory.

Voices of Delinquency 6–1
Read "I Have Come a Long Way." How big a factor is labeling in whether this youth becomes a delinquent or not? If he had been labeled, how would his life have turned out differently?

radical nonintervention
A policy toward delinquents that advises authorities to "leave the kids alone whenever possible."

New Developments in Labeling Theory

The early versions of labeling theory came under serious attack for theoretical flaws and lack of support.[16] Critics of this perspective charged that "labeling theorists had grossly exaggerated the role of labeling by suggesting that it is the only factor responsible for persistent deviance and by implying that it always increases the likelihood of subsequent rule breaking."[17] Assailed by these and other criticisms, the theory was under serious challenge by 1980 and, as University of Maryland criminologist Raymond Paternoster and Aalborg University professor Leeann Iovanni observed, was "pronounced dead by 1985."[18] However, the labeling perspective later enjoyed a resurgence because of its more sophisticated application.[19]

Recent Applications of Labeling Theory

Criminologists Ruth Ann Triplett and G. Roger Jarjoura developed "new avenues for exploring the effects of labeling."[20] They separated labeling into formal and informal labeling: Formal labels, the emphasis of early labeling theorists, are the reactions by official agents of the justice system to illegal behaviors; in contrast, an informal label is "an attempt to characterize a person as a given 'type' ... by persons who are not acting as official social control agents, and in social situations that are not formal social control 'ceremonies.'"[21] In other words, informal labels are those given by parents, neighbors, and friends. For example, Australian criminologist John Braithwaite examined shaming in the family, and found that families purposefully used shaming, or what Braithwaite termed "reintegrative shaming," to bring an offender back into line with their beliefs.[22]

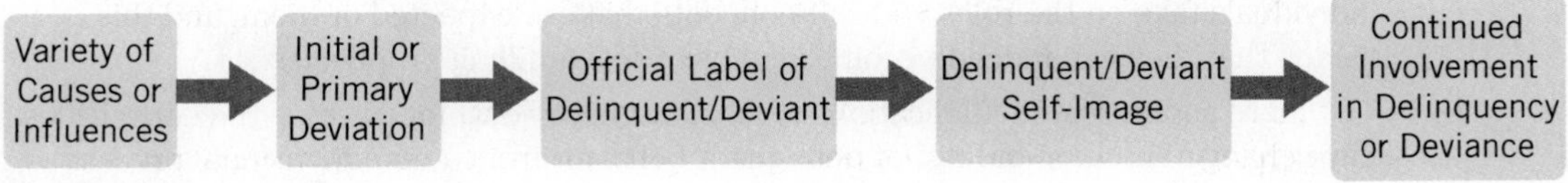

Variety of Causes or Influences → Initial or Primary Deviation → Official Label of Delinquent/Deviant → Delinquent/Deviant Self-Image → Continued Involvement in Delinquency or Deviance

FIGURE 6–1
General Assumptions of Labeling Theory

Triplett and Jarjoura also divided labels into subjective and objective labels. An audience's reaction to an actor is an objective label, whereas the actor's interpretation of that reaction is a subjective label. Although the importance of subjective labels has always been emphasized in symbolic interactionism, which is one of the important roots of labeling theory, it has remained largely unexplored in labeling theory and research.[23] Triplett, using the four waves of Elliott's National Youth Survey, concluded that the informal labels of significant others (parents) affect delinquent behavior both directly and indirectly for whites but that informal or subjective labels of significant others have no consistent direct or indirect effect on delinquent behavior for nonwhites.[24]

Moreover, Triplett and Jarjoura separated labels into exclusive and inclusive social reactions. J. D. Orcutt referred to these two types of reactions in his research on small-group reactions to deviance:

> Inclusive reactions [are] those attempts at social control which are premised on the assumption that the rule-breaker is and will continue to be an ordinary member of the community.... This form of social reaction attempts to control rule-infractions by bringing the present or future behavior of the rule-breaker into conformity with the rules without excluding him from it. Exclusive reactions are those attempts at social control which operate to reject the rule-breaker from the group and revoke his privileges and status as an ordinary member.[25]

Robert J. Sampson and John H. Laub claimed that labeling is one factor leading to "cumulative disadvantage" in future life chances (see Chapter 4), which increases the likelihood of a person's involvement in criminal acts during adulthood. This life-course approach views public labeling as a transitional event pushing young people on a trajectory of structural disadvantage and involvement in deviance and crime.[26] University of Iceland sociologist Jon Gunnar Bernburg and American criminologist Marvin D. Krohn, in their analysis of data from the Rochester Youth Development Study, found support for the thesis that official intervention by the justice system decreases the odds that those labeled will graduate from high school. Because educational attainment has a direct effect on employment, they believed that official intervention during adolescence can increase the likelihood of involvement in crime in early adulthood by helping to block the life chances afforded by education and gainful employment.[27]

Bernburg and colleagues' longitudinal test of labeling theory found further support for the belief that official intervention leads to continued criminality. Their research, derived from the Rochester Youth Development Study, revealed that juvenile justice intervention affects subsequent involvement in serious delinquency or with delinquent peers and street gangs. In many cases, according to this study, the formal labeling did increase the involvement both with delinquent others and in subsequent deviance.[28]

Evaluation of Labeling Theory

The labeling perspective has received mixed reviews, but it does have several strengths:

- Labeling theory provides an explanation for why youths who become involved in the juvenile justice process frequently continue delinquent acts until the end of their adolescent years.

- Labeling theory emphasizes the importance of rule making and social power in the creation of deviance.

- Consideration of the broader contexts of the labeling process lifts the focus of delinquency involvement away from the individual, and places the emphasis on the interactions of an actor and his or her social context.

- As part of a larger symbolic interactionist perspective, labeling theory points out that individuals take on the roles and self-concepts that are expected of them; and this means that they can indeed become victims of self-fulfilling prophecies.

- The more sophisticated applications of labeling theory developed since the early 1990s have changed understandings of delinquent behavior from a unidimensional process involving individual choice to a more complex process of social interaction—including both direct and indirect effects of labeling.

The labeling perspective has been criticized, however, because it fails to answer several critical questions: Are the conceptions that we hold of one another (as conformist or deviant) actually correct? Whose label really counts? When is personal identity changed by the labeling process, and by whose stigmatizing effort is it altered? Does a bad name cause bad action? Is the social response to crime generated more by the fact of the crime or by the legally irrelevant social characteristics of the offender? If official labels are so important, why do so many youths mature out of delinquency during their later adolescent years?[29] See Table 6–1 for an evaluation of labeling theory.

In sum, delinquency is clearly related to factors other than official labels, and it is extremely questionable to ascribe too much significance to the influence of the labeling process on adolescents' subsequent identities and behaviors.[30] Nevertheless, resurgence of interest in labeling theory during the past twenty years proves that it may have something to offer criminologists.

Symbolic Interactionist Theory

The **symbolic interactionist theory** of delinquency was developed by American sociologists Ross L. Matsueda and Karen Heimer.[31] This theory sees the social order as a dynamic process that is the ever-evolving product of an ongoing system of social interaction and communication.[32] It proposes to explain delinquent behavior in terms of self-development mediated by language—which is the central medium through which symbolic interaction occurs.[33] Of crucial importance is the process by which shared meanings, behavioral expectations, and reflected appraisals (i.e., our understandings of how other people see us) are built up through interaction and applied to behavior.[34] This interactionist perspective, according to Heimer, also has the "potential for illuminating the dynamic relationship among gender inequality, racial inequality, and law violation."[35]

Video 6–2 Closing Statement about Labeling

symbolic interactionist theory
A perspective in social psychology that analyzes the process of interaction among human beings at the symbolic level and that has influenced the development of several social process theories of delinquent behavior.

TABLE 6–1
An Evaluation of Labeling Theory

Proponents	Theory	Outcome of Labeling	Strengths	Criticisms
Tannenbaum	Processed youths were labeled and viewed as different.	Deviant career and dramatization of evil.	Introduced the labeling concept.	Did not consider secondary deviation of youths.
Lemert	Concept of primary and secondary deviation.	Transformation in the individual's identity.	Identified the process of becoming deviant.	Did not consider secondary deviation of youths.
Becker	Conceptualized relationship between rules of society and process of becoming an outsider.	Individual becomes an outsider.	Outsiders are given a new status.	Did not consider secondary deviation of youths.
Schur	Labeled youths are processed more deeply in the justice system.	Official punishment increases the likelihood of deviancy.	Support in the literature.	Did not consider secondary deviation of youths.
Triplett and Jarjoura	Developed formal and informal labeling and exclusive and inclusive labeling.	Examined more fully the effects of labeling.	Expanded the effects of labeling.	Did not consider secondary deviation of youths.

The intellectual roots of symbolic interactionism lie in the tradition of Scottish moral philosophers (e.g., David Hume and Adam Smith), and in the tradition of American pragmatists (e.g., Charles H. Cooley, John Dewey, William James, and George Herbert Mead). By the midtwentieth century, symbolic interactionism had achieved a dominant position among sociological theories through the scholars who collectively became known as the Chicago School of Sociology. For symbolic interactionism, individuals, groups, social systems, and situations constitute an ongoing social process, mutually influencing one another and merging imperceptibly in the web of daily interactions. The work of Mead was especially influential in the development of this theoretical tradition. Mead's emphasis on the social act is the basis of most versions of contemporary symbolic interactionism.[36]

Role Taking and Delinquency

Matsueda and Heimer also built on the social act as the basic unit of analysis. They began with the immediate situation of delinquent behavior, which is made up of social interaction between two or more individuals.[37] The situation can influence delinquency in two ways: First, the specific situation that juveniles encounter may present opportunities for delinquent behavior; second, and more importantly, the immediate situation influences delinquent behavior through its effects on the content and direction of social interaction.[38]

In analyzing social interaction, symbolic interactionists define the unit of analysis as the transaction that takes place in interaction between two or more individuals.[39] The important mechanism by which interactants influence each other is role taking, which Mead viewed as the key to social control.[40] According to Matsueda, role taking consists of the following:

> [It is] projecting oneself into the role of other persons and appraising, from their standpoint, the situation, oneself in the situation, and possible lines of action. With regard to delinquency, individuals confronted with delinquent behavior as a possible line of action take each other's roles through verbal and nonverbal communication, fitting their lines of action together into joint delinquent behavior.[41]

Library Extra 6–1
OJJDP publication: *Report of the Comprehensive Strategy Task Force on Serious, Violent and Chronic Juvenile Offenders—Part 1*

The transaction is built up through this process of reciprocal role taking, in which one person initiates a lawful or unlawful action and a second takes the role of the other and responds. The first person then reacts to the response, which continues until a jointly developed goal is reached, a new goal is substituted, or the transaction is ended. Through such reciprocal role taking, individual lines of action are coordinated, and concerted action is taken toward achieving the goal. This means that the initiated delinquent act of one juvenile might elicit a negative response from another juvenile, perhaps contributing to the group's searching for another, more suitable alternative. Matsueda suggested, "Whether or not a goal is achieved using unlawful means is determined by each individual's contribution to the direction of the transaction; those contributions, in turn, are determined by the individual's prior life experience or biography."[42]

Matsueda concluded that this discussion of role taking implies four features of a theory of the self and delinquent behavior. First, the self is formed by how an individual perceives that others view him or her and thus is rooted in symbolic interaction. Second, the self is an object that "arises partly endogenously within situations, and partly exogenously from prior situational self being carried over from previous experience." Third, the self as an object becomes a process that has been determined by the self at a previous point in time and by prior resolutions of problematic situations. Fourth, delinquent behavior takes place partly because habits are formed and partly because the stable perception of oneself is shaped by the standpoint of others.[43]

▲ Students having lunch the the Fabius-Pompey Middle School-High School cafeteria in Fabius, NY.

■ **How do mode of dress, hairstyle, and so on signify a person's understanding of who he or she is? How do such understandings relate to social roles?**

Using classic symbolic interactionist theory, Matsueda talked about the self as a consistent "me" that is relatively stable across situations. This self, which is called "a looking-glass self" by Charles H. Cooley[44] or the "self as an object" by Mead,[45] is a process that consists of three components: how others actually see us (others' actual appraisals), how we perceive the way others see us (reflected appraisals), and how we see ourselves (self-appraisals).[46] A person's self, then, is made up in part of a "reflected appraisal" of how significant others appraise or evaluate him or her.[47]

Matsueda used a sample from the National Youth Survey to test his theory. His findings supported a symbolic interactionist conceptualization of reflected appraisals and delinquency in a number of ways. Juveniles' reflected appraisals of themselves from the standpoint of parents, friends, and teachers "coalesced into a consensual self, rather than remaining compartmentalized as distinct selves."[48] This remained true whether the reflected appraisals were found in rule violators or socialized youths. In agreement with labeling theory, parental labels of youths as rule violators were more likely among nonwhites, urban dwellers, and delinquents. Delinquent youths' "appraisals of themselves are also strongly influenced by their parents' independent appraisals of them."[49] Moreover, prior delinquent behavior, both directly and indirectly, reflected appraisals of self. In addition, reflected appraisals as a rule violator exerted a large effect on delinquent behavior and mediated much of the effect of parental appraisals as a rule violator on delinquent behavior. Finally, age, race, and urban residence exerted significant effects on delinquency, most of which worked indirectly through prior delinquency and in part through the rule violator's reflected appraisal.[50]

Interactionist Perspectives on Gender, Race, and Delinquency

Heimer argued that "structural conflict gives rise to gender and race differences in motivations to break the law."[51] (See the *People In the Know* interview with Karen Heimer in this chapter.) From the interactionist perspective, then, racial and gender inequalities are consequential for law violation because they restrict the positions of minorities and females and therefore constrain communication networks and the power needed to influence others.[52] She goes on to say:

> Hence, these forms of structural inequality influence definitions of situations because they partially determine the significant others and reference groups considered in the role-taking process. Through shaping definitions of situations, gender and racial inequality contribute to the patterning of crime and delinquency. Thus, consistent with the tradition of differential association in criminology, an interactionist theory of delinquency argues that there will be differences across groups in definitions of situations and the law to the extent that communication networks vary.[53]

People In the Know
Interview with Karen Heimer

Question: What do you feel are the best features of symbolic interactionist theory?

Heimer: One of the strengths of symbolic interactionist approaches is that they locate the individual within the social situation. These approaches share an emphasis on the general idea that people come to know the world around them and themselves through taking the perspectives of others. Consistent with some other interactionist theories of crime, differential social control theory focuses on how the role-taking process can lead to delinquency or crime. More specifically, differential social control posits that the following five key elements of interactions are consequential for law violation: (1) identities or reflected appraisals of self; (2) anticipated reactions to law violation from significant others (including family and peers); (3) definitions of the law and morality; (4) influence of delinquent peers; and (5) habitual or scripted responses to opportunities to break the law. All of these influence law violation through role taking in situations. I think that an important strength of differential social control theory, therefore, is the specification of the mechanisms through which situations affect delinquency and crime. We have attempted to elaborate the theory to show how the link between changes over the life course and offending might be better understood, how gender differences in delinquency emerge, and how delinquency and depression are linked.

Question: Do you see any areas that need to be expanded or reformulated?

Heimer: There are several areas of the theory that need further refinement and elaboration. For example, there likely are dimensions of role taking in situations other than those we have

(Continued)

identified that are important for crime and delinquency. I hope that future research will uncover some of these. In addition, I would like to see research on the theory attempt to further elaborate the ways in which social structural circumstances constrain or facilitate interactions that lead to law violations. In our published work to date, we have shown how disadvantaged social circumstances increase the chances that individuals will associate with delinquent youths and criminal adults, and thereby become more likely to see themselves as deviant, perceive that others would not strongly disapprove of law violations, and adopt delinquent attitudes and beliefs. But the ways in which social structures can influence role taking are certainly more complex and diverse. I would like to see this part of the theory elaborated more fully in future work. Finally, I think that our recent work on an interactionist view of the connections between delinquency and depression opens the door to exploring how a variety of "deviant" outcomes might be linked via similar role-taking mechanisms.

Question: How did you come to be involved in the formulation of the theory?

Heimer: My early education in graduate school was in sociological social psychology. When I began my graduate work in sociology, I took a course on sociological social psychology in which

I learned about the richness of theory and research on symbolic interactionism. So my interest in working on a symbolic interactionist approach to crime and delinquency can be traced to my early intellectual history.

Question: Have you been encouraged or discouraged by the response that the theory has received?

Heimer: I am very pleased that the differential social control perspective has come to gain recognition within criminology. I hope that future work will chart new territory by elaborating and extending the theory, especially along the lines of the areas that I mention above. I think that the theory has much promise for integrating a variety of theoretical approaches to crime and delinquency, as we argued in our 1994 paper. I also think that attention to the ways that social interactions lead to law violation is essential for understanding law violation more fully. For these reasons, I think that the theory offers a fruitful avenue for future work.

Source: Karen Heimer is professor of sociology at the University of Iowa. She is interested in developing and testing theories of juvenile delinquency and violence, with an emphasis on gender and racial disparities. This interview took place in February 2002 and is reprinted with permission.

Evaluation of Symbolic Interactionist Theory

The symbolic interactionist theory of delinquency has several strengths:

- It builds on symbolic interactionist theory, a great tradition in American sociology. This tradition has identified the locus of social control in the process of taking the role of the other and of linking with the broader social organization through role commitments, generalized others, and reference groups.[54]

- It builds on and adds to the insights of labeling theory. At a time in which labeling is being reformulated and is emerging in a more sophisticated form, the insights that Matsueda, Heimer, and their colleagues provide in relating symbolic interactionism and delinquency promise to further enrich labeling's contributions to our understanding of delinquency.

- The symbolic interactionist theory of delinquent behavior is insightful regarding how both law-abiding and delinquent youths form their conceptions of themselves and how these perceptions influence their decision making.

- This theory contributes helpful insights about the influence of delinquent peers and the group context on youths' self-appraisals.

See Table 6–2 for a summary of symbolic interactionist theory.

An evaluation of symbolic interactionist theory, of course, is limited by the fact that it has been tested by Matsueda, Heimer, and colleagues in only a few settings. At this point, it is uncertain how much delinquency it explains, even among group delinquents, and many of the criticisms aimed at labeling theory also apply to this theory. Nevertheless, symbolic interactionist theory is still a promising attempt to explain delinquent behavior.

Library Extra 6–2

OJJDP publication: *Report of the Comprehensive Strategy Task Force on Serious, Violent and Chronic Juvenile Offenders—Part 2*

Conflict Theory

conflict theory

A perspective that holds that delinquency can be explained by socioeconomic class, by power and authority relationships, and by group and cultural differences.

Conflict theory sees social control as the end result of the differential distribution of economic and political power in any society, and conflict theorists view laws as tools created by the powerful for their own benefit.[55] The development of the conflict model is indebted

TABLE 6–2
Summary of Symbolic Interactionist Theory

Proponents	Definition of Symbolic Interaction	Role Taking and Delinquency	Gender and Race	Strengths	Criticisms
Heimer and Matsueda	Dynamic process that is the ever-evolving product of an ongoing system of social interaction and communication.	One person initiates an unlawful action and a second takes the role of the other and responds.	Structural conflict gives rise to gender and racial differences in motivations to break the law.	Builds on and adds to the strengths of labeling theory.	Has been tested in only a few settings.

to the concept of "dialectics." This concept, like that of order, can be traced back to the philosophers of ancient Greece. In antiquity the term *dialectics* referred to the art of conducting a dispute or bringing out the truth by disclosing and resolving contradictions in the arguments of opponents.[56]

Georg F. Hegel used this concept of dialectical thinking to explain human progress and social change. A prevailing idea, or "thesis," according to Hegel, would eventually be challenged by an opposing idea, or "antithesis." The resultant conflict usually would result in the merging of the two, or "synthesis." The synthesis gradually would be accepted as the thesis but then would be challenged by a new antithesis, and so it would go throughout history.[57] Karl Marx, rather than applying the method to ideas as Hegel did, applied the concept to the material world. Marx's theory became one of dialectical materialism; he contended that the conflict was one of competing economic systems, in which the weak must ward off exploitation by the strong or powerful in society.[58]

Georg Simmel, a twentieth-century conflict theorist, argued that unity and discord are inextricably intertwined and together act as an integrative force in society. Simmel added that "there probably exists no social unity in which convergent and divergent currents among its members are not inseparably interwoven."[59] Simmel's notion of dialectics thus acknowledged the existence of tendencies for order and disorder.

More recently, Ralf Dahrendorf contended that functionalists misrepresented reality by being overconcerned with order and consensus, arguing that functionalists present a description of a utopian society—a society that never has existed and probably never will. Dahrendorf proposed that social researchers would be wise to opt for the conflict model because of its more realistic view that society is held together by constraint rather than consensus, not by universal agreement but by the coercion of some people by others.[60]

Richard Quinney has argued that criminal law is a social control instrument of the state "organized to serve the interests of the dominant economic class, the capitalist ruling class."[61] William Bonger earlier made this same point: "In every society which is divided into a ruling class and a class ruled, penal law has been principally constituted according to the will of the former."[62] (See the *People In the Know* interview with Quinney in this chapter.)

A more humane social order is the vision of some radical criminologists.[63] The goals of this ideal society are reduced inequality, reduced reliance on formal institutions of justice, and reduced materialism, and the social relations of this social order are committed to developing self-reliance, self-realization, and mutual aid.[64] This peaceful society can be attained by using compromise and negotiation on a community level to defuse violent social structures. Communities must organize themselves in such a way as to prevent crime and to help victims without punishing offenders when crime does occur.[65] See Exhibit 6–1 for further discussion of criminology and peacemaking.

Voices of Delinquency 6–2
Read "Wrong Place at the Wrong Time." Do you see elements of symbolic interactionist theory in the delinquent and adult crimes of the writer of this story? How did she take on roles during the years she talks about?

Video 6–3 Basic Principles of Conflict Theory

Exhibit 6–1
Peacemaking and Criminology

There are various approaches to peacemaking criminology including humanist, religious, feminist, and critical traditions. These approaches to peacemaking criminology, however, do have a number of commonalities:

- One commonality consists of the themes of connectedness, caring, and mindfulness.
- Another commonality within peacemaking criminology, regardless of the specific approach or tradition undertaken, is that it provides an alternative to the "war on crime" model within criminal justice.
- A third commonality within peacemaking pertains to the notion of personal and social transformation. As H. E. Pepinsky views it, "peacemaking is the art and science of weaving and reweaving oneself with others into a social fabric of mutual, love, respect, and concern." Or as R. M. Bohm expressed it, "Emphasis is placed on the transformation of human beings, on an inner rebirth or spiritual rejuvenation (inner peace) that enables individuals to experience empathy with those less fortunate and respond to other people's needs."

- A final commonality within peacemaking criminology can be seen in its critique of theories and policies within mainstream criminology.

Thus, peacemaking criminologists tend to study varying types of crime (from street to white collar to political in terms of their diverse kinds of social harms (interpersonal to social structural to international). To reduce these crimes/social harms, peacemaking criminologists propose peacemaking alternatives (from group to organization to national to international) while also attempting to transform the present criminal justice system through greater humanization of court processing, police work, and corrections.

Source: John F. Wozniak, "Introduction to the Relevance of Richard Quinney's Writings on Peacemaking Criminology: Toward Personal and Social Transformation," in *Transformative Justice: Critical and Peacemaking Themes Influenced by Richard Quinney,* edited by John F. Wozniak, Michael E. Braswell, Ronald E. Vogel, and Kristie R. Blevins (Lanham, Md.: Lexington Books, 2008), pp. 167–89; H. E. Pepinsky, "Peacemaking: Primer," in *Social Justice/Criminal Justice: The Maturation of Critical theory in Law, Crime, and Deviance,* edited by B. A. Arrigo (Belmont, Calif.: Wadsworth, 1999), p. 59; and R. M. Bohm, *A Primer on Crime and Delinquency Theory,* 2d ed. (Belmont, Calif.: Wadsworth, 2001), p. 121.

Dimensions of Conflict Criminology

A great deal of variation exists among the ideas of conflict criminologists. Some theories emphasize the importance of socioeconomic class, some focus primarily on power and authority relationships, and others emphasize group and cultural conflict.

Socioeconomic Class and Radical Criminology

radical criminology
A perspective that holds that the causes of crime are rooted in social conditions that empower the wealthy and the politically well organized but disenfranchise the less fortunate.

Even though Marx wrote very little on the subject of crime as the term is used today, he inspired a new school of criminology that emerged in the early 1970s. This school is variously described as Marxist, critical, socialist, left-wing, new, or **radical criminology**. Marx was concerned both with deriving a theory of how societies change over time and with discovering how to go about changing society. This joining of theory and practice is called "praxis."[66]

Marx saw the history of all societies as the history of class struggles and viewed crime as a result of these class struggles.[67] He wrote in the *Communist Manifesto:*

> Freeman and slave, patrician and plebeian, lord and serf, guildmaster and journeyman, in a word, oppressor and oppressed, stood in constant opposition to one another, carried on an uninterrupted, now hidden, now open fight, a reconstruction of society at large, or in the common ruin of the contending classes.[68]

capitalism
An economic system in which private individuals or corporations own and control capital (wealth and the means of production) and in which competitive free markets control prices, production, and distribution of goods.

Emerging with each historical period, according to Marx's theory, is a new class-based system of ranking. Marx contended that with **capitalism**, "society as a whole is increasingly splitting up into two great classes directly facing each other—bourgeoisie [capitalist class] and proletariat [working class]."[69] The relations between the bourgeoisie and the proletariat become increasingly strained as the bourgeoisie comes to control more and more of the society's wealth and the proletariat is increasingly pauperized. In this relationship between the oppressive bourgeoisie and the pauperized proletariat lie the seeds of the demise of capitalism.[70]

Mark Colvin and John Pauly developed an integrated structural theory of delinquency, the purpose of which was to provide "a comprehensive theoretical approach to understanding the social production of serious patterned delinquent behavior," and using the empirical findings of others to support their model, they contended that the power relations to which most lower-class workers are subjected are coercive.[71]

Colvin and Pauly argued that the parents' experience of coerciveness in the workplace contributes to the development of coercive family control structures, which lead to alienated children. The coercive social milieu in which many people work reduces their capacity as parents to deal with their own children in anything other than a repressive fashion, frequently by using physical punishments—and this type of punishment hinders the development of positive bonds between children and their parents.[72]

The situation is exacerbated because juveniles with alienated parental bonds, according to Colvin and Pauly, are more likely to be placed in coercive school settings. Their alienation from both family and school encourages such juveniles to become involved with alienated peers, who form peer groups. These peer groups create two contrasting paths to delinquent involvement: In the first path, peer group coerciveness interacts with youngsters' earlier experiences of alienation to propel them into serious, patterned, violent delinquent behavior; in the second path, the experience of rewards from illegitimate sources builds a lasting attraction to serious and patterned delinquent behavior.[73]

Herman Schwendinger and Julia Siegel Schwendinger also stated that capitalism produces a marginal class of people who are superfluous from an economic standpoint.[74] They went so far as to say that "the historical facts are incontrovertible: capitalism ripped apart the ancient regime and introduced criminality among youth in all stations of life."[75]

The Schwendingers further argued that socialization agents within the social system, such as the school, tend to reinvent within each new generation the same class system: "The children of families that *have* more *get* more, because the public educational system converts human beings into potential commodities."[76] The schools tend to be geared toward rewarding and assisting those youths who exhibit early indications of achieving the greatest potential success in institutions of higher learning and later in the job market, but this selection is made at the expense of those who do not exhibit such potential in their early encounters with the educational system.[77]

In the Marxist perspective, the state and the law itself are ultimately tools of the ownership class and reflect mainly the economic interests of that class. Capitalism produces egocentric, greedy, and predatory human behavior. The ownership class is guilty of the worst crime: the brutal exploitation of the working class. Revolution is a means to counter this violence and is generally both necessary and morally justifiable. Conventional crime is caused by extreme poverty and economic disenfranchisement, products of the dehumanizing and demoralizing capitalist system.[78]

People In the Know
Interview with Richard Quinney

Question: Why do you believe that social justice is lacking in American society?

Quinney: Justice in a capitalist society is limited to the overall needs of a continuing capitalist system. Justice is largely limited to "criminal justice," a punitive model that does not deal with the inadequacies of the system. Social justice, on the other hand, would serve the needs of all people, including their economic well-being. The goal of social justice can be attempted in our capitalist society, but true social justice can be achieved only in a socialist society. The struggle for social justice is a struggle for the transformation of our present society in the United States.

Question: What are the chief contradictions of capitalism and how do they contribute to the extent and nature of crime in American society?

Quinney: There are many contradictions in capitalism. The basic contradiction is between the goal of progress and a better society, on the one hand, and the reality of the inability of capitalism

to ever attain this goal because of the inherent class structure of capitalism. The capitalist class owns and controls the means of production and distribution and, as such, assures that a subordinate class of workers and consumers will be dominated politically and economically— to assure the continuation of the capitalist system. Classes outside of the capitalist class commit crimes out of need, frustration, and brutalization. Members of the capitalist class commit crimes out of greed and power. The rates of crime under capitalism can never be substantially reduced. Capitalism generates its own crime and rates of crime.

Question: Why do you think that the capitalist state is oppressive and coercive?

Quinney: The capitalist state exists to perpetuate capitalist economics and the social relations of capitalism. It is the policy and enforcement arm of capitalist society. Thus, the actions carried out by the branches of the state are of a control nature, including the activities associated with dispensing education, welfare, and criminal justice. The state must also provide

(Continued)

benefits for those who suffer and fail under capitalist economics, but even these services have a control function, attempting to assure the continuation of the capitalist system.

Question: How does the early Quinney differ from the Quinney of today? Or how has your approach to the crime problem changed?

Quinney: I have moved through the various epistemologies and ontologies in the social sciences. After applying one, I have found that another is necessary for incorporating what was excluded from the former, and so on. Also, I have tried to keep my work informed by the latest developments in the philosophy of science. In addition, I have always been a part of the progressive movements of the time. My work is thus an integral part of the social and intellectual changes that are taking place in the larger society, outside of criminology and sociology. One other factor has affected my work in recent years: the search for meaning in my life and in the world.

Question: What direction do you anticipate the new criminology or the critical criminology will take?

Quinney: This is the time to substantiate the critical Marxist perspective through studies of specific aspects of crime. We know generally the causes of crime. Further work is in large part a political matter—showing others through the accepted means of research. In the long run, however, our interests must go beyond the narrow confines of criminology and sociology. The theoretical, empirical, political, and spiritual issues are larger than the issue of crime.

Question: Critical or new criminology theorists have written much less about delinquency than criminality in American society. What more needs to be contributed by Marxists in this area?

Quinney: Our society emphasizes youth and the youth culture while at the same time increasingly excluding youth from gainful and meaningful employment. Youth are being relegated to the consumption sector—without the economic means for consumption. Education—including college— has traditionally provided a place for youth that are not essential to a capitalist society. But with the widening of the economic gap between classes, will education be an outlet and opportunity for the majority of adolescents and young adults? We are approaching a structural crisis (and personal crises) that will require a solution beyond what is possible in a capitalist society. Our challenge is to understand the changes that are taking place around us and to have the courage to be a part of the struggle that is necessary.

Source: Richard Quinney received his Ph.D. from the University of Wisconsin, and he is emeritus professor of sociology at Northern Illinois University. *The Social Reality of Crime; Criminology, Class, State, and Crime; Providence: The Reconstruction of Social and Moral Order;* and *Social Existence* are some of the books that have brought Dr. Quinney's analyses of crime and social problems to the attention of readers throughout the world. This interview took place in February 1984 and is used with permission.

Note: Like other writers who reflect on their lifelong research and theories, Quinney tended to view his body of writings throughout his career as very connected and progressed from theme to theme and from publication to publication.[1] As he has suggested, his thinking has progressed from "the social constructionist perspective to phenomenology, from phenomenology to Marxist and critical philosophy, from Marxist and critical philosophy to liberation theology, from liberation theology to Buddhism and existentialism." And then to a more ethnographic and personal mode of thinking and being. It is necessary to note that in all of these intellectual travels, nothing was rejected or deleted from the previous states; rather each new state of development incorporated what had preceded it.[2] So, the Quinney reflected in this interview— and he was very influential at the time among American criminologists—is not the Quinney who continues to reflect on what it means to be human.

[1]John F. Wozniak, "Introduction to the Relevance of Richard Quinney's Writings on Peacemaking Criminology: Toward Personal and Social Transformation," in *Transformative Justice: Critical and Peacemaking Themes Influenced by Richard Quinney,* edited by John F. Wozniak, Michael E. Braswell, Ronald E. Vogel, and Kristie R. Blevins (Lanham, Md.: Lexington Books, 2008), pp. 167–89.

[2]R. Quinney, *Bearing Witness to Crime and Social Justice* (Albany: State University of New York Press, 2000), pp. x–xi.

Power and Authority Relationships

A second important dimension of conflict criminology is the focus on power and authority relationships. Max Weber, Ralf Dahrendorf, Austin T. Turk, and John Hagan have made contributions to this body of scholarship.

Weber's theory, like the Marxist perspective, contains a theory of social stratification that has been applied to the study of crime. Although Weber recognized the importance of the economic context in the analysis of social stratification, he did not believe that such a unidimensional approach could explain satisfactorily the phenomenon of social stratification. He added power and prestige to the Marxist emphasis on property and held these three variables responsible for the development of hierarchies in society. Weber also proposed that property differences led to the development of classes, power differences led to the creation of political parties and the development of classes, and prestige differences led to the development of status groups.

Further, Weber discussed the concept of "life chances" and argued that they were differentially related to social class; from this perspective, criminality exists in all societies and is the result of the political struggle among different groups attempting to promote or enhance their own life chances.[79]

Both Dahrendorf and Turk have extended the Weberian tradition in the field of criminology by emphasizing the relationships between authorities and their subjects. Dahrendorf contended that power is the critical variable explaining crime, arguing that although Marx built his theory on only one form of power, property ownership, a more useful perspective could be constructed by incorporating broader conceptions of power.[80]

Turk, constructing his analysis from the work of both Weber and Dahrendorf, argued that the social order of society is based on the relationships of conflict and domination between authorities and subjects.[81] Focusing on power and authority relationships, this perspective of conflict theory examines the relationships between the legal authorities who create, interpret, and enforce right–wrong standards for individuals in the political collectivity and those who accept or resist but do not make such legal decisions. Turk also made the point that conflicts between authorities and subjects take place over a wide range of social and cultural norms.[82]

John Hagan and his associates viewed the relationship between gender and nonserious delinquency as linked to power and control.[83] Using data collected in Toronto, Ontario, they suggested that the presence of power among fathers and the greater control of girls explain why boys are delinquent more often than girls. Unlike Hirschi's control theory, Hagan and colleagues' **power-control thesis** based the measurement of class on the authority that parents have in their positions at work, and they assumed that the authority of parents at work translates into conditions of dominance in the household and in the degree of their parental control over their children.

Robert M. Regoli and John D. Hewitt's **theory of differential oppression** contends that in the United States, authority is unjustly used against children, who must "adapt to adults' conceptions of what 'good children' are." Children experience oppression, in this view, because they exist in a social world in which adults look on them as inferior and in which they lack social power relative to adults. Oppression takes place when adults use their power to prevent children from attaining access to valued resources or to prevent them from developing a sense of self as a subject rather than an object. Accordingly, children must submit to the power and authority of adults, and when children react negatively or fail to conform to these pressures, a process begins that results in delinquent acts.[84]

The theory of differential oppression is organized around four principles:

1. Because children lack power on account of their age, size, and lack of resources, they are easy targets for adult oppression.

2. Adult oppression of children occurs in multiple social contexts and falls on a continuum ranging from benign neglect to malignant abuse.

3. Oppression leads to adaptive reactions by children. The oppression of children produces at least four adaptations: passive acceptance, exercise of illegitimate coercive power, manipulation of peers, and retaliation.

4. Children's adaptations to oppression create and reinforce adults' view of children as inferior subordinate beings and as troublemakers. This view enables adults to justify their role as oppressors and further reinforces children's powerlessness.[85]

Regoli and Hewitt recognized that the oppression of children falls along a continuum and that some children are oppressed to a greater degree than others. The very basis of their theory hinges on the belief that children who are reared in highly oppressive family conditions are more likely to become delinquent than those who are not raised in such aversive environments.[86]

power-control thesis
The view that the relationship between gender and delinquency is linked to issues of power and control.

theory of differential oppression
The view that in the United States, authority is unjustly used against children, who must adapt to adults' ideas of what constitutes "good children."

▲ These graffiti-covered row houses are in East Baltimore. According to the Marxist perspective, the very nature of capitalist society increases urban blight and contributes to the exploitation of lower-class youths, leading to an increased likelihood of crime.

■ Is this perspective valid? If so, how might capitalist societies lower their crime rates?

culture conflict theory
A perspective that delinquency or crime arises because individuals are members of a subculture that has conduct norms that are in conflict with those of the wider society.

conduct norms
The rules of a group governing the ways its members should act under particular conditions; the violation of these rules arouses a group reaction.

Group and Cultural Conflicts

Another dimension of conflict criminology is **culture conflict theory**, which focuses on group conflict. Thorsten Sellin and George B. Vold advocated this approach to the study of crime. Sellin argued that to understand the cause of crime, it is necessary to understand the concept of **conduct norms**,[87] which refers to the rules of a group concerning the ways its members should act under particular conditions. The violation of these rules arouses a group reaction.[88] Each individual is a member of many groups (family group, work group, play group, political group, religious group, and so on), and each group has its own particular conduct norms.[89] According to Sellin:

> The more complex a culture becomes, the more likely it is that the number of normative groups which affect a person will be large, [and] the greater is the chance that the norms of these groups will fail to agree, no matter how much they may overlap as a result of a common acceptance of certain norms.[90]

Sellin noted that an individual experiences a conflict of norms "when more or less divergent rules of conduct govern the specific life situation in which a person may find himself."[91] The act of violating conduct norms is "abnormal behavior," and crime represents a particular kind of abnormal behavior distinguished by the fact that crime is a violation of the conduct norms defined by criminal law.[92] Regarding criminal law, Sellin wrote:

> The criminal law may be regarded as in part a body of rules, which prohibit specific forms of conduct and indicate punishments for violations. The character of these rules ... depends upon the character and interests of those groups in the population which influence legislation. In some states these groups may comprise the majority, in others a minority, but the social values which receive the protection of criminal law are ultimately those which are treasured by the dominant interest groups.[93]

Sellin also has developed a theory of "primary and secondary culture conflict." Primary culture conflict occurs when an individual or group comes into contact with an individual or group from another culture and the conduct norms of the two cultures are not compatible; secondary culture conflict refers to the conflict arising whenever society has diverging subcultures with conduct norms.[94]

Vold, like Sellin (and in the tradition of Simmel), analyzed the dimension of group conflict. He viewed society "as a congeries [an aggregation] of groups held together in a shifting, but dynamic equilibrium of opposing group interests and efforts."[95] Vold formulated a theory of group conflict and applied it to particular types of crimes, but he did not attempt to explain all types of criminal behavior. He stated that group members are constantly engaged in defending and promoting their group's status. As groups move into each other's territory or sphere of influence and begin to compete in those areas, intergroup conflict is inevitable. The outcome of a group conflict results in a winner and a loser, unless a compromise is reached—but compromises never take place when one group is decidedly weaker than the other. Like Simmel, Vold believed that group loyalty develops and intensifies during group conflict.[96]

In sum, conflict criminologists can be divided into three basic groups: those emphasizing socioeconomic class, those emphasizing power and authority relationships, and those emphasizing group and cultural conflict. Those who emphasize socioeconomic class call themselves radical, Marxist, critical, humanist, or new criminologists and do not identify with the other two groups. Some significant differences do exist between radical criminologists and the other two groups: The non-Marxist conflict criminologists emphasize a plurality of interests and power and do not put a single emphasis on capitalism, as do the Marxist conflict criminologists, nor do the non-Marxist conflict criminologists reject the legal order as such or the use of legal definitions of crime.[97] Table 6–3 compares the three groups of conflict criminologists.

Library Extra 6–3
OJJDP's Juvenile Mentoring Program (JUMP)

Evaluation of Conflict Theory

Conflict criminology's critiques of the social order do contribute two important pieces to the puzzle of why juveniles commit delinquent acts. First, the various conflict criminology perspectives call attention to the macrostructural flaws that contribute to high rates of juvenile

TABLE 6–3
Comparisons of Conflict Perspectives

Perspective	Legal Definitions	Legal Order	Purpose of Conflict	Capitalism
Socioeconomic class (Marxist)	Rejection	Rejection	Revolution	Rejection
Power and authority relationships	Acceptance	Acceptance	Reform	Acceptance
Group and cultural conflict	Acceptance	Acceptance	Reform	Acceptance

delinquency. Second, radical humanism, also rooted in the structural inequalities of the social order, emphasizes the dignity of the person and is quick to identify instances where children experience oppression in the United States.[98]

Social Context of Delinquency: Restorative Justice and Peacemaking

For hundreds of years, community standards were passed to succeeding generations through interaction between adults and children in the community, and change in the standards came slowly. Conformity to those standards was enforced through both informal social mechanisms and the law. Because some of these standards enforced by the communities were sexist, racist, and classist and had nothing to do with the well-being of others or the community as a whole, the rebellion of the 1960s and 1970s attacked the potent existing informal social control mechanisms and began to rely more on the legal mechanisms for those standards essential for safe and fair communities.[99]

Advocates of restorative justice argue that after twenty-five years of relying on legal mechanisms, it is clear to many that legal standards are not sufficient to create healthy, ethical community behavior. The legal system is too distant from daily life to be effective and is too complicated and abstract for citizens to feel that they are a part of setting those standards or that they have responsibility for enforcing those standards in the community. In addition, because the legal system involves coercion and deprivation of liberty, it can set only minimum standards of behavior. Restorative-justice processes that encourage cooperation and voluntary engagement can establish standards for maximum behavior.[100]

One of the lessons of restorative justice taught to youths is empathy development. According to Kay Pranis and other proponents of restorative justice, we have allowed enormous distance to develop between ourselves and the children of others. We have not come to know them and have not invested emotionally, materially, and spiritually in their well-being. Moreover, we have not taught them by example to understand the interconnectedness of all things and the need to understand the impact of our actions on others.[101] The development of empathy requires (1) regular feedback about how our actions affect others, (2) relationships in which we feel valued and our worth is validated, and (3) experience of sympathy from others when we are in pain.[102]

Restorative justice also provides a framework for community members to reestablish a more appropriate relationship between community members and young people and to reduce the fear adults have of young people. The processes of restorative justice, especially face-to-face processes, involve the telling of personal stories in intimate settings. Stereotypes and broad generalizations about groups of people are difficult to sustain in the face of direct contact between youths and adults in a respectful setting. Restorative-justice processes assume value in every human being and therefore present individuals to one another in a respectful way, which draws out human dignity in everyone.[103]

▲ A teenager works at a part-time job in a fast-food restaurant. Youths who don't have jobs are more likely to find other ways to provide for what they want.

■ **What other ways might they choose?**

sentencing circles
A form of restorative justice that incorporates principles of ancient, aboriginal tribal justice to address the harm suffered by crime victims and their families, the responsibilities of offenders, and the role of community.

Community Conferencing and Sentencing Circles

Community conferences make it possible for victims, youths, and community members to meet one another to resolve issues raised by an offender's trespass.[104] A particularly promising form of community conferences is termed **sentencing circles**. Historically, sentencing circles were found in U.S. native and Canadian aboriginal cultures. These circles were then adopted by the criminal justice system in the 1980s as First Nations Peoples of the Yukon and local criminal justice officials endeavored to build more constructive ties between the criminal justice system and the grassroots community. In 1991, Judge Barry Stuart of the Yukon Territorial Court introduced sentencing circles in order to empower the community to participate in the justice process.[105]

One of the most intriguing developments in sentencing circles, as indicated by L. Parker, is the Hollow Water First Nations Community Holistic Healing Circle, which simultaneously addresses harm created by the offender, heals the victim, and restores community goodwill. Circles have been developed most extensively in the western provinces of Canada, and they have also experienced a resurgence in modern times among American Indian tribes (e.g., in the Navaho courts). Today circles may be found in most mainstream criminal justice settings. For example, in Minnesota, circles are used in a variety of ways for a variety of crimes and in varied settings[106]; a Hawaii minimum-security prison has a reentry restorative circles program that began in 2005.[107]

How does a sentencing circle work? Participants in healing or sentencing circles typically speak out while passing around a "talking piece." Separate healing circles are initially held for the victim and the offender; after the healing circles meet, a sentencing circle (with feedback from the family, the community, and the justice system) determines a course of action, and other circles then follow up to monitor compliance, whether that involves, for example, restitution or community service.[108]

Evaluation of Restorative Justice

Restorative justice is rapidly gaining acceptance in juvenile and adult justice systems. Instead of relying on legal intervention to deal with youths' misbehavior and community conflicts, restorative-justice groups are increasingly intervening and seeking to find reconciliation between offenders, victims, and the community. Its basic approach of valuing youngsters, affirming their strengths, and seeking communication with them has much in common with the Positive Youth Development (PYD) approach that was previously discussed.

Nancy Rodriguez used official juvenile court data from an urban area and found that youths who participated in a restorative-justice program were less likely to recidivate than juveniles in a comparison group. Her study further revealed that male and female juveniles with a minimal offense history exhibited the most success from participating in these programs.[109] Another study of the long-term impact of restorative-justice referrals on prevalence of reoffense, number of later official contacts, and seriousness of later offending behavior over several follow-up periods also found a positive impact of restorative-justice programs in all of these categories.[110] Gwen Robinson and Joanna Shapland saw the possibility for restorative justice to be able to reduce recidivism.[111] Restorative justice appears to be one of the most hopeful approaches to juvenile crime, especially with minor forms of juvenile delinquency. See Table 6–4 for an overview of restorative-justice theory and the programs that have been developed based on this approach.

Prevention of Delinquency
Promising Prevention Programs

The juvenile justice system has traditionally focused on youths after they have had initial contact with law enforcement authorities. The past twenty years, however, have witnessed the emergence of a proactive approach to preventing juvenile crime, an approach sometimes termed the "public health model of crime prevention."[112]

TABLE 6–4
Restorative Justice and Related Treatment Interventions

Theory	Treatment Interventions
Provides a framework for community members to establish a communication network with young people to resolve minor disputes.	Community Conferencing and Peacemaking
Makes it possible for victims, youths, and community members to resolve issues of youthful members' trespasses; following a healing circle, a sentencing circle decides on the behavioral consequences.	Community Conferencing and Sentencing
Uses the family group decision-making model in order to try to stop family violence.	Family Group Conferences (FGCs)
Involves a reparations program track designed for offenders who commit nonviolent offenses and who are considered at low risk for reoffense.	Reparation and Restitution
Enables in-kind or actual return of what has been lost; it can be viewed within the larger context of "making amends."	Restitution Programs
Encourages one-on-one victim–offender reconciliation facilitated through a mediator.	Victim–Offender Conferencing

This public health model, which grew out of the disease prevention efforts of a century ago, focuses on reducing risk and increasing opportunities for success. With its proactive emphasis on the prevention of social problems, the public health approach offers an appealing alternative to a reactive focus on rehabilitation or punishment. The public health approach employs the following four-step procedure to identify issues that need attention and to develop solutions: (1) Define the nature of the problem using scientific methods or data; (2) identify potential causes using analyses of risk and protective factors associated with the problem; (3) design, develop, and evaluate interventions; and (4) disseminate successful models as part of education and outreach.[113]

Some researchers have recently begun advocating a shift in the prevention field intended to concentrate exclusively on building resiliency rather than trying to reduce risks.[114] They contend that an emphasis on risks focuses primarily on deficits, whereas a prevention strategy can produce more significant outcomes by concentrating instead on building strengths. Research has shown, however, that delinquency prevention programs focusing too heavily on improving resiliency without addressing the source of the risks are largely unsuccessful.[115] The *Model Programs Guide* of the OJJDP argues that the design of effective prevention programs and strategies needs to consider the interrelationships between reducing risk factors and building resiliency (see Exhibit 6–2 for an introduction to the OJJDP guide).

The *Blueprints for Violence Prevention* report, developed by the Center for the Study and Prevention of Violence at the University of Colorado–Boulder and supported by the OJJDP, identified eleven model programs and twenty-one promising violence-prevention and drug abuse–prevention programs that have received rigorous evaluation.[116] Table 6–5 presents a complete list of the promising model programs the researchers identified, and the following discussion briefly describes the eleven model programs.

Big Brothers Big Sisters of America

With a network of more than five hundred local agencies throughout the United States that maintain more than 145,000 one-to-one relationships between youths and volunteer adults, Big Brothers Big Sisters of America (BBBSA) operates as the best-known and largest mentoring program in the nation. The program serves youths ages 6 to 18 years old, a significant number of whom are from single-parent and disadvantaged households.[117] An eighteen-month evaluation found that compared with a control group waiting for a

Exhibit 6–2
OJJDP *Model Programs Guide*

The Office of Juvenile Justice and Delinquency Prevention's *Model Programs Guide* (MPG) is designed to assist practitioners and communities in implementing evidence-based prevention and intervention programs that can make a difference in the lives of children and communities. The MPG database of evidence covers the entire continuum of youth services from prevention through sanctions to reentry. The MPG can be used to assist juvenile justice practitioners, administrators, and researchers to enhance accountability, ensure public safety, and reduce recidivism. The MPG is an easy-to-use tool that offers the first and only database of scientifically proven programs across the spectrum of youth services. The following prevention programs are assessed and presented in the guide:

Academic Skills Enhancement

Afterschool/Recreation

Alternative School

Classroom Curricula

Cognitive Behavioral Treatment

Community and Policy-Oriented Policing

Community Awareness/Mobilization

Drug, Alcohol Therapy/Education

Family Therapy

Gang Prevention

Leadership and Youth Development

Mentoring

Parent Training

School/Classroom Enhancement

Truancy Prevention

Vocational/Job Training

Wraparound/Case Management

CONCLUSION

The MPG contains summary information (program description, evaluation design, research findings, references, and contact information) on evidence-based delinquency prevention and intervention programs. Programs are categorized into exemplary, effective, and promising, based on a set of methodological criteria and the strength of the findings.

CRITICAL THINKING QUESTIONS

■ *Why is a program guide that includes treatment and prevention programs by state a potentially helpful resource for both policy makers and practitioners?*

Source: Adapted from *OJJDP Model Programs Guide,* http://www.dsgonline.com/mpg2.5/mpg_index.htm.

TABLE 6–5
Promising Model Programs and Age Groups of Targeted Juveniles

Blueprints Program	Pregnancy/ Infancy	Early Childhood	Elementary School	Junior High School	High School
Model Programs					
Big Brothers Big Sisters of America (BBBSA)			X	X	X
Bullying Prevention Program			X	X	
Functional Family Therapy (FFT)				X	X
Incredible Years	X	X			
Life Skills Training (LST)				X	
Midwestern Prevention Project (MPP)				X	
Multidimensional Treatment Foster Care (MTFC)				X	X
Multisystemic Therapy (MST)				X	X

TABLE 6–5 (*Continued*)
Promising Model Programs and Age Groups of Targeted Juveniles

Blueprints Program	Pregnancy/ Infancy	Early Childhood	Elementary School	Junior High School	High School
Nurse–Family Partnership	X				
Project Toward No Drug Abuse (Project TND)					X
Promoting Alternative Thinking Strategies (PATHS)			X		
Promising Programs					
Athletes Training and Learning to Avoid Steroids					X
Brief Strategic Family Therapy			X	X	X
CASASTART			X	X	
Fast Track			X		
Good Behavior Game			X		
Guiding Good Choices			X	X	
High/Scope Perry Preschool		X			
Houston Child Development Center	X	X			
I Can Problem Solve		X	X		
Intensive Protective Supervision				X	X
Linking the Interests of Families and Teachers			X		
Preventive Intervention				X	
Preventive Treatment Program			X		
Project Northland				X	
Promoting Action through Holistic Education				X	X
School Transitional Environmental Program				X	X
Seattle Social Development Project			X	X	
Strengthening Families Program: Parents and Children 10–14			X	X	
Student Training through Urban Strategies				X	X
Syracuse Family Development Program	X	X			
Yale Child Welfare Project	X	X			

Source: Table 1.1 in Sharon Mihalic et al., *Blueprints for Violence Prevention* (Washington, D.C.: Office of Juvenile Justice and Delinquency Prevention, 2004).

match, youths in this mentoring program were 46 percent less likely to start using drugs, 27 percent less likely to start drinking, and 32 percent less likely to hit or assault someone; they also were less likely to skip school and more likely to have improved family relationships.[118]

Bullying Prevention Program

This model program aims to restructure the social environment of primary and secondary schools in order to provide fewer opportunities for bullying and to reduce the peer approval and support that reward bullying behavior. Adults in the school setting are seen as the driving force of this program, and the program seeks to ensure that adults in schools are aware of bullying problems and are actively involved in their prevention.[119] This program has proved effective in large samples evaluated in South Carolina and Norway. In rural South Carolina, for example, children in thirty-nine schools in grades four through six who participated in the program reported that they experienced a 25 percent decrease in the frequency at which they felt bullied by other children.[120]

Functional Family Therapy

Functional Family Therapy (FFT) is a short-term family-based prevention and intervention program that has been successfully applied in a variety of contexts to treat high-risk youths and their families from various backgrounds. Specifically designed to help underserved and at-risk youths ages 11 to 18 years old, this multisystemic clinical program provides twelve one-hour sessions of **family therapy** spread over three months. More difficult cases may receive up to thirty hours of therapy.[121] The success of this program has been demonstrated and replicated for more than twenty-five years. Evaluations using controlled follow-up periods of one, three, and five years have demonstrated significant and long-term reductions, ranging from 25 to 60 percent.[122]

family therapy
A counseling technique that involves treating all members of a family; a widely used method of dealing with a delinquent's socially unacceptable behavior.

Incredible Years: Parent, Teacher, and Child Training Series

The Incredible Years model program has a comprehensive set of curricula designed to promote social competence and to prevent, reduce, and treat conduct problems in young children. The target population of this program is children ages 2 to 8 who exhibit or are at risk for conduct problems.[123] This program has received positive evaluations as meeting their original goals.[124]

Life Skills Training

Library Extra 6–4
OJJDP publication: *YouthBuild U.S.A.*

Life Skills Training (LST) lessons emphasize social resistance skills training to help students identify and resist pressures to use drugs. This intervention is meant to be implemented in school classrooms by teachers but also has been taught successfully by health professionals and peer leaders.[125] Using outcomes from more than a dozen studies, evaluators have found that LST can reduce tobacco, alcohol, and marijuana use by 50 to 75 percent in intervention students compared to control students.[126]

Midwestern Prevention Project

The Midwestern Prevention Project (MPP) targets peer group norms in schools in a comprehensive three- to five-year community-based prevention program aimed at reducing first-time use of alcohol, tobacco, and marijuana.[127] Researchers followed students from eight schools who were randomly assigned to treatment or to control groups for three years, and found that the program brought net reductions of up to 40 percent in adolescent smoking and marijuana use, with results maintained through high school graduation.[128]

Multidimensional Treatment Foster Care

Web Extra 6–2
FindYouthInfo
FindYouthInfo was formed by the Interagency Working Group on Youth Programs (IWGYP), which is composed of representatives from seventeen federal agencies that support programs and services focusing on youth.

Multidimensional Treatment Foster Care (MTFC) derives its name from the fact that the program is multifaceted, and provides intervention efforts through behavioral parent training for foster parents, skills training for youth, supportive therapy for youth, school-based behavioral interventions, and psychiatric consultation (when needed).[129] For adolescents who have had problems with chronic antisocial behavior, delinquency, and emotional disturbance, MTFC has been judged to be a cost-effective alternative to group or residential treatment, confinement, or hospitalization.[130] Evaluations of MTFC demonstrated that youths who participated in the program had significantly fewer arrests (an average of 2.6 offenses versus 5.4 offenses) and spent fewer days in lockup than youths placed in other community-based programs.[131]

Multisystemic Therapy

Multisystemic Therapy (MST) provides cost-effective community-based clinical treatment to chronic and violent juvenile offenders who are at high risk of out-of-home placement. MST specifically targets the multiple factors contributing to antisocial behavior. The overarching goal of the intervention is to help parents understand and help their children overcome their behavior problems. MST uses strengths in each youth's social network to promote positive change in his or her behavior.[132] Program evaluations have revealed 25 to 70 percent reductions in long-term rates of rearrest and 47 to 64 percent reductions in out-of-home placements. These and other positive results were maintained for nearly four years after treatment ended.[133]

Nurse–Family Partnership

Formerly called Prenatal and Infancy Home Visitation by Nurses, this model program, Nurse–Family Partnership, sends nurses to the homes of lower-income unmarried mothers, beginning during pregnancy and continuing for two years following the birth of the child.[134] Follow-up showed that this program's positive outcomes had long-term effects for both mothers and children[135]

Project Toward No Drug Abuse

The Project Toward No Drug Abuse program, or Project TND, targets high school youths (ages 14 to 19 years old) who are at risk for drug abuse.[136] It consists of twelve classroom-based sessions using the Socratic method, classroom discussions, skill demonstrations, role-playing, and psychodrama techniques.[137] At a one-year follow-up, participants in forty-two schools revealed reduced usage of cigarettes, alcohol, marijuana, and hard drugs.[138]

Promoting Alternative Thinking Strategies

A comprehensive program for promoting social and emotional competencies, Promoting Alternative Thinking Strategies (PATHS) focuses on the understanding, expression, and regulation of emotions. The yearlong curriculum is designed to be used by teachers and counselors with entire classrooms of children in kindergarten through fifth grade. Lessons include such topics as identifying and labeling feelings, assessing the intensity of feelings, expressing feelings, managing feelings, and delaying gratification.[139] Evaluations of this program have found positive behavioral changes related to peer aggression, hyperactivity, and conduct problems.[140]

These prevention programs are promising in their diversity and range of offerings. They work to prevent delinquency through school-based, peer group–based, and community-based interventions.

Delinquency across the Life Course: Labeling

One of the lessons to be learned from *Voices of Delinquency* is that those youngsters who were not apprehended and labeled by the juvenile justice system (first two sections) were able to move fairly easily from their adolescent behaviors into adult prosocial roles. Some had been deeply involved in drug use or drug trafficking, gang activities, and other forms of delinquency, but they did not have the disadvantage of the label "juvenile delinquent" or have the experiences of juvenile justice processing, including institutionalization. In contrast, those in the third and four sections of *Voices of Delinquency* were labeled. Some desisted in their late adolescence or early adulthood, but some went on to adult crime. Sadly, the final five stories were given by individuals who will spend the remainder of their lives in prison.

Certainly, more was involved than the label itself; there was the secondary response to the label. This secondary response sometimes included violent acts directed toward others.

Voices of Delinquency 6–3
Read "I Grew Up in New Orleans" for insight into how a youngster in an urban setting can be exposed to violence, drugs, and gangs on a regular basis.

Interestingly, when the lives of those who have committed serious and violent acts are examined, they have many other factors in common: They tend to be the children of the poor, the have-nots, who have been abused in a variety of ways and who have become a marginal class. For example, street gang activity is more frequently found in those social settings where poverty, unemployment, drugs, violence, and police encounters are commonplace. They see violence, sometimes on a regular basis, and anticipate that they will end up either in prison or dead at a young age.[141]

One of the major challenges is finding ways to break this cycle of the wasted lives of alienated youths going from the juvenile to the adult correctional system and frequently spending a majority of their lives in prison. Restorative justice is one possibility, PYD is another, and effective prevention programs would be a third possibility. In addition, those who work with youths in various types of programming—ranging from probation to residential treatment to institutional care—can sometimes be instrumental in helping youths turn their lives around.

Delinquency and Social Policy: The Conflict Perspective

The conflict perspective has several contributions to make to handling youth crime in America. Its emphasis on improving human rights is a reminder to policy makers, as well as to all interest groups for children, that the ability of youths to achieve their maximum potential in American society is very much affected by the larger issue of human rights. Whether or not racial justice and the ability to earn an adequate standard of living are guaranteed affects whether minority children and those from impoverished families face discrimination and poverty as they grow up. Similarly, women's rights affect the thousands of children across the nation reared in one-parent homes. Finally, children's rights promise that youths will be granted or guaranteed more of the basic rights that adults enjoy.

Conflict criminology also has much to teach children's advocacy groups about how power and domination affect the creation of policy. For example, these theories contend that in our society control is gained by those groups that wield the most power and resources; that once a group achieves dominance over others, it seeks to use the available societal mechanisms to its advantage to maintain that dominance; that laws are formulated in the interests of the dominant groups, with the result that those behaviors common to the less powerful groups may be restricted; and that the law enforcement and control systems operate to process disproportionately the less powerful members of society.

Third, the conflict perspective points out that the opportunity structure and the economic exploitation of a society become key variables in understanding lower-class youth crime. Societies in which economic exploitation is extreme and in which opportunity is limited can be expected to have high rates of delinquency. Therefore, an adequate standard of living for all Americans and increased employment opportunities for teenagers become critical issues in deterring youth crime. Many of the stories in the *Voices of Delinquency*, especially those of youths who have gone on to the adult correctional system, reveal backgrounds of economic deprivation and abuse; they felt powerless and dominated, and they struck out in retaliation. In "Forgotten Children," an example of this would be the inmate who is serving life without parole: "I was taught by society that I was one of the unworthy children of its blessings because of my skin color. I had been raised by society to be a child of destruction, and so the respect that I should have had for another's rights, person, or property became unimportant to me. What had been instilled in an undeveloped mind, hurting soul, and unloved heart was that what I wanted or needed I could attain by force or brutality."[142]

social injustice
According to many conflict-oriented criminologists, social injustice is found in apparent unfairness in the juvenile justice system arising from poor youths being disproportionately represented, female status offenders being subjected to sexist treatment, and racial minorities being dealt with more harshly than whites.

Finally, conflict criminologists argue that **social injustice** prevails in American society. These criminologists believe that the formal juvenile justice system, as well as the informal justice system, administers different sorts of justice to the children of the haves than to the children of the have-nots, to boys who commit delinquent offenses than to girls who commit "moral" offenses, and to white youths than to nonwhite youths.[143] Figure 6–2 describes the contributions that the conflict perspective can make to social policy.

FIGURE 6–2
Contributions of the Conflict Perspective to Social Policy

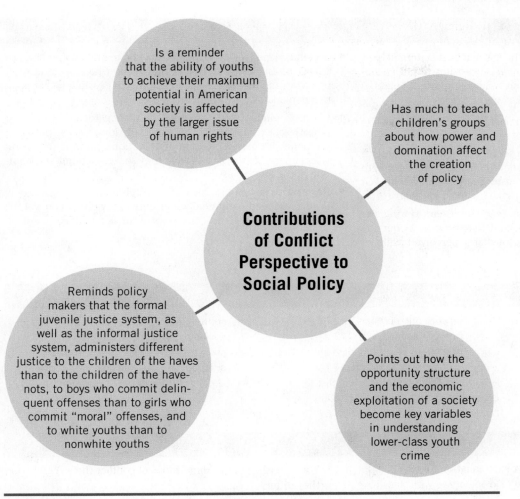

Is a reminder that the ability of youths to achieve their maximum potential in American society is affected by the larger issue of human rights

Has much to teach children's groups about how power and domination affect the creation of policy

Contributions of Conflict Perspective to Social Policy

Reminds policy makers that the formal juvenile justice system, as well as the informal justice system, administers different justice to the children of the haves than to the children of the have-nots, to boys who commit delinquent offenses than to girls who commit "moral" offenses, and to white youths than to nonwhite youths

Points out how the opportunity structure and the economic exploitation of a society become key variables in understanding lower-class youth crime

The Case

The Life Course of Amy Watters, Age 11

As Amy entered adolescence she began to question her self-worth. Although she was not consciously aware of it, the loss of her mother had contributed to a sense of rejection and personal inadequacy. Amy found it hard to believe that anyone loved her, especially her older sister, Jordan, with whom she was fighting constantly. Amy's father, Simon, was rarely around, as he still worked hard to support the family. Jordan had assumed many of the household duties that a mother might otherwise have performed—from keeping the house clean to preparing meals and doing the laundry. Much to Amy's disgust, her father had also told Jordan to "keep an eye" on Amy, and to assign her chores to perform.

The worst thing that happened to Amy in her eleventh year, however, was that a small group of bullies began picking on her. Amy was not part of the "in crowd" at school, and she didn't have the money to buy the kinds of clothes and electronic gadgets that might have led to greater social acceptance. As a result, some of the girls whom everyone seemed to look up to began harassing Amy, telling her that her hairstyle was an "unrecoverable disaster," and calling her names that really hurt.

Feeling unloved at home and threatened at school, Amy found acceptance with a crowd of adolescent troublemakers at her school. When she thought about it, which was only rarely, Amy told herself that she wasn't really like the people she found herself hanging out with, but reasoned that she needed their protection from the bullies. Sure enough, once it was known that Amy had become part of a tough crowd, the bullying ceased and she sensed that she had gained a new measure of respect among the kids at school.

Why does Amy resent Jordan? What might her father do to lessen the stress between the girls? Why did Amy turn to a "tough" crowd? What alternatives might she have pursued?

Learn More on the Web:

- A Life Course Theory of Cumulative Disadvantages: http://tinyurl.com/253rc39
- Anti-Bullying Programs for Schools: http://www.nobully.com

Follow the continuing Amy Watters saga in the next chapter.

SUMMARY

This chapter focuses on labeling theory, symbolic interactionist theory, conflict approaches to delinquency, restorative justice and peacemaking, and prevention programs. Some important points to remember are these:

- Reactions to deviance and crime play an important role in the creation of offender social identities.

- Reactions to deviance and crime occur within a social context, although the context may vary from the family to the group, to school settings, to official labeling by the justice system, and even to society's political decision-making mechanisms.

- In individual experiences, social reaction occurs during the process of everyday interaction, and that process frequently involves the application of labels to what is perceived as unacceptable behavior.

- Societal responses to deviant behavior may result in the application of negative labels to individuals who engage in such behavior, and those labels may limit future possibilities for positive personal accomplishment.

- Conflict criminologists relate delinquency to alienation and powerlessness among youths, especially lower-class youths; to the dominant class's creation of definitions of crime to control subordinate classes; and to what they see as economic exploitation of the lower classes.

- Restorative justice (and peacemaking) is an increasingly widely used method of communication between victims and youths and between youths and members of the community.

KEY TERMS

capitalism, p. 140
conduct norms, p. 144
conflict theory, p. 138
culture conflict theory, p. 144
family therapy, p. 150
labeling theory, p. 131

power-control thesis, p. 143
primary deviation, p. 132
process of becoming deviant, p. 132
radical criminology, p. 140
radical nonintervention, p. 133
secondary deviation, p. 132

sentencing circle, p. 146
social injustice, p. 152
social interactionist theory, p. 131
symbolic interactionist theory, p. 135
theory of differential oppression, p. 143

REVIEW QUESTIONS

1. What is the labeling perspective's explanation for why adolescents become delinquent? Do you agree with this interpretation?
2. How is the symbolic interactionist theory of delinquency an extension of, but different from, labeling theory?

3. What are the various dimensions of conflict theory? How do they differ?
4. What are the explanations of delinquency according to Marxist theory? Evaluate each of these explanations.

DISCUSSION QUESTIONS

1. Were you ever labeled when you were a young child or juvenile? What influence did it have on your subsequent attitudes and behavior? Did the labels you received become a self-fulfilling prophecy?
2. Can you identify any groups beyond young children among which official labels may be more likely to influence subsequent attitudes and behavior?
3. How would you illustrate the application of symbolic interactionist theory to decision making in youth gangs or in adolescent peer groups? How did such reference group norms affect your decision making and behavior as an adolescent?

4. Reintegrative shaming is a form of shaming, imposed by a sanction by the criminal justice system, that is thought to strengthen the moral bond between the offender and the community. Can you think of any other methods of shaming? How effective do you believe they are?
5. Does role taking influence delinquent/criminal behavior in gang members, compelling them to perform wrongful acts because they perceive that is what is expected of them? If so, who imposes the expectations, their peers or conventional society? Explain your responses.

GROUP EXERCISES

1. Have the students read Regoli and Hewitt's article "Holding Serious Juvenile Offenders Responsible: Implications from Differential Oppression Theory," accessible at http://www.jcjc.state.pa.us/jcjc/lib/jcjc/publications/newsletter/2003/mar03pdf. Then discuss the article in class.
2. Have the class debate/discuss the merits and weaknesses of labeling theory.

3. Have the class debate/discuss the merits and weaknesses of conflict theory.
4. Have the students discuss the Schwendingers' claim that "the historical facts are inconvertible: capitalism ripped apart the ancient regime and introduced criminality among youth in all stations of life."

NOTES

1. Iris Wagman Borowsky et al., "Teens Who Believe They'll Die Young Are More Likely to Engage in Risky Behavior," *Science Daily*, June 29, 2009, http://www.sciencedaily.com/releases/2009/06/090629081124.htm (accessed April 4, 2011).

2. Lening Zhang and Steven F. Messner, "The Severity of Official Punishment for Delinquency and Change in Interpersonal Relations in Chinese Society," *Journal of Research in Crime and Delinquency* 31 (November 1994), pp. 416–33.

3. Frank Tannenbaum, *Crime and the Community* (New York: Columbia University Press, 1938), pp. 19–20.

4. Ibid.

5. Edwin M. Lemert, *Social Pathology* (New York: McGraw-Hill, 1951).

6. Harold Finestone, *Victims of Change: Juvenile Delinquents in American Society* (Westport, Conn.: Greenwood Press, 1976).

7. Ibid., p. 198. For a discussion concerning the complexity of this process of moving from primary to secondary deviance, see Daniel L. Dotter and Julian B. Roebuck, "The Labeling Approach Re-Examined: Interactionism and the Components of Deviance," *Deviant Behavior* 9 (1988), pp. 19–32.

8. Finestone, *Victims of Change*.

9. Howard S. Becker, *Outsiders* (New York: Free Press, 1963), pp. 8–9.

10. Ibid.

11. Finestone, *Victims of Change*.

12. Edwin Schur, *Radical Nonintervention* (Englewood Cliffs, N.J.: Prentice-Hall, 1973), p. 155.

13. Zhang and Messner, "The Severity of Official Punishment for Delinquency," p. 418.

14. Francis Polymeria, Francis T. Cullen, and Joanne C. Gersten, "The Effects of Police and Mental Health Intervention on Juvenile Delinquency: Specifying Contingencies in the Impact of Formal Reaction," *Journal of Health and Social Behavior* 27 (1986), pp. 90–105.

15. Anthony Matarazzo, Peter J. Carrington, and Robert D. Hiscott, "The Effect of Prior Youth Court Dispositions on Current Disposition: An Application of Societal-Reaction Theory," *Theory of Quantitative Criminology* 17 (2001), pp. 169–200.

16. Jack P. Gibbs, "Conceptions of Deviant Behavior: The Old and the New," *Pacific Sociological Review* 9 (1966), pp. 9–14; Walter R. Gove, "Labeling and Mental Illness: A Critique," in *The Labeling of Deviance: Evaluating a Perspective*, 2d ed., edited by Walter R. Gove (Beverly Hills, Calif.: Sage, 1980), pp. 53–59; John Hagan, "Extra-Legal Attitudes and Criminal Sanctioning: An Assessment and a Sociological Viewpoint," *Law and Society Review* 8 (1974), pp. 357–83; Travis Hirschi, "Labeling Theory and Juvenile Delinquency: An Assessment of the Evidence," in *The Labeling of Deviance: Evaluating a Perspective*, 2d ed., edited by Walter R. Gove (Beverly Hills, Calif.: Sage, 1980), pp. 271–93; Charles R. Tittle, "Deterrence of Labeling?" *Social Forces* 53 (1975), pp. 399–410; and Charles F. Wellford, "Labeling Theory and Criminology: An Assessment," *Social Problems* 22 (1975), pp. 332–45.

17. Zhang and Messner, "The Severity of Official Punishment for Delinquency," p. 419. See also Tittle, "Deterrence of Labeling?" and Gove, "Labeling and Mental Illness."

18. Raymond Paternoster and Leeann Iovanni, "The Labeling Perspective and Delinquency: An Elaboration of the Theory and an Assessment of the Evidence," *Justice Quarterly* 6 (1989), p. 359. For a more recent article, see Mike Tapia, "U.S. Juvenile Arrests: Gang Membership, Social Class, and Labeling Effects," *Youth and Society* 43 (2011), pp. 1407–32.

19. Zhang and Messner, "The Severity of Official Punishment for Delinquency." For a more recent article, see Tapia, "U.S. Juvenile Arrests."

20. Ruth A. Triplett and G. Roger Jarjoura, "Theoretical and Empirical Specification of a Model of Informal Labeling," *Journal of Quantitative Criminology* 10 (1994), p. 243.

21. Raymond Paternoster and Ruth A. Triplett, "Disaggregating Self-Reported Delinquency and Its Implications for Theory," *Criminology* 26 (1988), p. 6. See also Lening Zhang, "Informal Reactions and Delinquency," *Criminal Justice and Behavior* 24 (March 1997), pp. 129–50.

22. John Braithwaite, *Crime, Shame and Reintegration* (Cambridge, England: Cambridge University Press, 1989). See also Toni Makkai and John Braithwaite, "Reintegrative Shaming and Compliance with Regulatory Standards," *Criminology* 32 (August 1994), pp. 361–85.

23. Triplett and Jarjoura, "Theoretical and Empirical Specification."

24. Ruth Ann Triplett, "Labeling and Differential Association: The Effects on Delinquent Behavior," Ph.D. dissertation, University of Maryland, 1990. For a model of informal labeling, see Triplett and Jarjoura, "Theoretical and Empirical Specification," pp. 241–76.

25. J. D. Orcutt, "Societal Reaction and the Response to Deviation in Small Groups," *Social Forces* 52 (1973), pp. 259–67.

26. Robert J. Sampson and John H. Laub, "A Life-Course Theory of Cumulative Disadvantage and the Stability of Delinquency," in *Developmental Theories of Crime and Delinquency*, edited by Terence P. Thornberry (New Brunswick, N.J.: Transaction Publishers, 1997), pp. 133–61.

27. Jon Gunnar Bernburg and Marvin D. Krohn, "Labeling, Life Chances, and Adult Crime: The Direct and Indirect Effects of Official Intervention in Adolescence on Crime in Early Adulthood," *Criminology* 41 (November 2003), pp. 1287–1313.

28. Jon Gunnar Bernburg, Marvin D. Krohn, and Craig J. Rivera, "Official Labeling, Criminal Embeddedness, and Subsequent Delinquency: A Longitudinal Test of Labeling Theory," *Journal of Research in Crime and Delinquency* 43 (February 2006), pp. 67–88.

29. G. Nettler, *Explaining Crime*, 3d ed. (New York: McGraw-Hill, 1984).

30. Donald J. Shoemaker, *Theories of Delinquency: An Examination of Explanations of Delinquency Behavior*, 6e. (New York: Oxford University Press, 2009).

31. Ross L. Matsueda, "Reflected Appraisals, Parental Labeling, and Delinquency: Specifying a Symbolic Interactional

Theory," *American Journal of Sociology* 97 (1992), pp. 1577–1611; Karen Heimer and Ross L. Matsueda, "Role-Taking, Role Commitment, and Delinquency: A Theory of Differential Social Control," *American Sociological Review* 59 (1994), pp. 365–90; Karen Heimer, "Gender, Race, and the Pathways to Delinquency," in *Crime and Inequality*, edited by John Hagan and Ruth D. Peterson (Stanford, Calif.: Stanford University Press, 1995), pp. 140–73; Karen Heimer and Ross L. Matsueda, "A Symbolic Interactionist Theory of Motivation and Deviance: Interpreting Psychological Research," in *Motivation and Delinquency*, Vol. 44 of the Nebraska Symposium on Motivation, edited by D. Wayne Osgood (Lincoln, Neb.: University of Nebraska Press, 1997), pp. 223–76; and Ross L. Matsueda and Karen Heimer, "A Symbolic Interactionist Theory of Role-Transitions, Role Commitments, and Delinquency," in *Advances in Criminological Theory*, edited by T. P. Thornberry (New Brunswick, N.J.: Transaction Publishers, 1997), pp. 163–213.

32. Matsueda, "Reflected Appraisals, Parental Labeling, and Delinquency."

33. Ibid.

34. Ibid.

35. Heimer, "Gender, Race, and the Pathways to Delinquency," p. 141.

36. Heimer and Matsueda, "A Symbolic Interactionist Theory of Role-Transitions."

37. Ibid.

38. Ibid.

39. The following discussion is based on ibid., pp. 1580–81.

40. George H. Mead, *Mind, Self and Society* (Chicago: University of Chicago Press, 1934).

41. Matsueda, "Reflected Appraisals, Parental Labeling, and Delinquency," p. 1580. See also Mead, *Mind, Self and Society*, and Herbert Blumer, *Symbolic Interactionism: Perspective and Method* (Englewood Cliffs, N.J.: Prentice-Hall, 1969).

42. Matsueda, "Reflected Appraisals, Parental Labeling, and Delinquency," p. 1581.

43. Matsueda, "Reflected Appraisals, Parental Labeling, and Delinquency."

44. Charles H. Cooley, *Human Nature and the Social Order*, rev. ed. (New York: Scribners, 1922).

45. Mead, *Mind, Self, and Society*.

46. Matsueda, "Reflected Appraisals, Parental Labeling, and Delinquency."

47. Ibid.

48. Ibid., p. 1602.

49. Ibid.

50. Ibid.

51. Heimer, "Gender, Race, and the Pathways to Delinquency," p. 145.

52. Ibid.

53. Ibid., p. 146.

54. Heimer and Matsueda, "Role-Taking, Role Commitment, and Delinquency."

55. David Shichor, "The New Criminology: Some Critical Issues," *British Journal of Criminology* 20 (1980), pp. 29–48.

56. Viktor Afanasyer, *Marxist Philosophy* (Moscow: Foreign Language Publishing House, n.d.).

57. This interpretation of Hegel's "thesis–antithesis–synthesis" paradigm is frequently questioned. See Ron E. Roberts and Robert Marsh Kloss, *Social Movements: Between the Balcony and the Barricade*, 2d ed. (St. Louis, Mo.: C. V. Mosby, 1979), p. 16.

58. Stephen Spitzer, "Toward a Marxian Theory of Deviance," *Social Problems* 22 (1975), pp. 638–51.

59. Georg Simmel, *Conflict*, translated by Kurt H. Wolf (Glencoe, Ill.: Free Press, 1955), p. 15.

60. Ralf Dahrendorf, "Out of Utopia: Toward a Reorientation of Sociological Analysis," *American Journal of Sociology* 64 (1958), pp. 115–27.

61. Richard Quinney, *Critique of Legal Order: Crime Control in Capitalist Society* (Boston: Little, Brown, 1974), p. 16.

62. William Bonger, *Criminality and Economic Conditions*, abridged ed. (Bloomington: Indiana University Press, 1969), p. 24.

63. See Larry Tifft and Dennis Sullivan, *Crime, Criminology, and Anarchism: The Struggle to Be Human* (Sanday, Orkney Islands, Scotland: Cienfuegos Press, 1980); Raymond J. Michalowski, *Order, Law, and Crime: An Introduction to Criminology* (New York: Random House, 1985); and Harold E. Pepinsky, "A Sociology of Justice," *Annual Review of Sociology* 12 (1986), pp. 93–108.

64. Tifft and Sullivan, *Crime, Criminology, and Anarchism*, and Michalowski, Order, Law, and Crime.

65. Pepinsky, "A Sociology of Justice."

66. Jonathan H. Turner, *The Structure of Sociological Theory* (Homewood, Ill.: Dorsey Press, 1978), p. 124.

67. Karl Marx and Frederick Engels, *The Communist Manifesto* (1848; reprint ed., New York: International Publishers, 1979).

68. Ibid., p. 9.

69. Ibid.

70. Ibid.

71. Mark Colvin and John Pauly, "A Critique of Criminology: Toward an Integrated Structural–Marxist Theory of Delinquency Production," *American Journal of Sociology* 89 (November 1983), pp. 513–51.

72. Ibid.

73. Ibid.

74. Herman Schwendinger and Julia S. Schwendinger, "Marginal Youth and Social Policy," *Social Problems* 24 (December 1976), pp. 84–91.

75. Herman Schwendinger and Julia Siegel Schwendinger, *Adolescent Subcultures and Delinquency* (New York: Praeger, 1985), p. 3.

76. Schwendinger and Schwendinger, "Marginal Youth and Social Policy."

77. Ibid.

78. David O. Friedrichs, "Victimology: A Consideration of the Radical Critique," *Crime and Delinquency* 29 (1983), pp. 283–94.

79. Max Weber, "Class, Status, Party," in *Class, Status and Power*, edited by Richard Bendix and S. M. Lipset (New York: Macmillan, 1953), pp. 63–75.

80. Ralf Dahrendorf, *Class and Class Conflict in Industrial Society* (Palo Alto, Calif.: Stanford University Press, 1959).

81. A. T. Turk, "Class, Conflict, and Criminalization," *Sociological Focus* 10 (August 1977), pp. 209–20.

82. Ian Taylor, Paul Walton, and Jock Young, *The New Criminology: For a Social Theory of Deviance* (Boston: Routledge and Kegan Paul, 1973).

83. John Hagan, A. R. Gillis, and John Simpson, "The Class Structure of Gender and Delinquency: Toward a Power-Control Theory of Common Delinquent Behavior," *American Journal of Sociology* 90 (1985) pp. 1151–78; John Hagan, John Simpson, and A. R. Gillis, "The Sexual Stratification of Social Control: A Gender-Based Perspective on Crime and Delinquency," *British Journal of Sociology* 30 (1979), pp. 25–38; John Hagan, John Simpson, and A. R. Gillis, "Class in the Household: A Power-Control Theory of Gender and Delinquency," *American Journal of Sociology* 92 (January 1987), pp. 788–816; John Hagan, A. R. Gillis, and John Simpson, "Clarifying and Extending Power-Control Theory," *American Journal of Sociology* 95 (1990), pp. 1024–37; and John Hagan, *Structural Criminology* (New Brunswick, N.J.: Rutgers University Press, 1989).

84. Robert M. Regoli and John D. Hewitt, *Delinquency in Society*, 8th ed. (Boston: Jones and Bartlett, 2010).

85. Beverly Kingston, Robert Regoli, and John D. Hewitt, "The Theory of Differential Oppression: A Developmental-Ecological Explanation of Adolescent Problem Behavior," *Critical Criminology* 11 (2003), pp. 237–60.

86. In *Social Sources of Delinquency: An Appraisal of Analytic Models* (Chicago: University of Chicago Press, 1978), Ruth Rosner Kornhauser includes the discussion of Sellin under cultural deviance theory.

87. In *Social Sources of Delinquency*, Ruth Rosner Kornhauser includes the discussion of Sellin under cultural deviance theory.

88. Thorsten Sellin, *Culture, Conflict, and Crime* (New York: Social Science Research Council, 1938).

89. Ibid.

90. Ibid., p. 29.

91. Ibid.

92. Ibid.

93. Ibid., p. 21.

94. Ibid.

95. George B. Vold, *Theoretical Criminology*, 2d ed., prepared by Thomas J. Bernard (New York: Oxford University Press, 1979), p. 283. For a more up-to-date analysis of Vold, see Thomas J. Bernard and Jeffrey B. Snipes, *Theoretical Criminology*, 4th ed. (New York: Oxford University Press, 1998), pp. 236–38.

96. Ibid.

97. Friedrichs, "Radical Criminology in the United States."

98. For a review of radical humanism, see Kevin Anderson, "Humanism and Anti-Humanism in Radical Criminological Theory," in *Perspectives on Social Problems* 3 (1991), pp. 19–38; and Kevin Anderson, "Radical Criminology and the Overcoming of Alienation: Perspectives from Marxian and Gandhian Humanism," in *Criminology as Peacemaking*, edited by Harold E. Pepinsky and Richard Quinney (Bloomington: Indiana University Press, 1991), pp. 14–29.

99. Kay Pranis, "Face to Face: Spaces for Reflective Community Dialog," *VOMA Connection* (Summer 2000).

100. Ibid.

101. Kay Pranis, "Empathy Development in Youth through Restorative Practices," *Public Service Psychology* 25 (Spring 2000), pp. 17–21.

102. Ibid.

103. Ibid.

104. S. Stuart, "Restorative Processes: Mediation, Conferencing, and Circles," http://www.restorativejustice.org.

105. L. Parker, "Circles," http://www.restorativejustice.org.

106. G. Bazemore and M. Umbreit, *A Comparison of Four Restorative Conferencing Models* (Washington, D.C.: U.S. Department of Justice, Office of Juvenile Justice and Delinquency Prevention, and U.S. Department of Justice, National Institute of Corrections, 2001).

107. Lorenn Walker, Ted Sakai, and Kat Brady, "Restorative Circles—A Reentry Process for Hawaii Inmates," *Federal Probation* 70 (2006), pp. 33–37, 86.

108. Ibid. See also P. McCold, "Overview of Mediation, Conferencing and Circles," paper presented at the 10th United Nations Congress on Crime Prevention and Treatment of Offenders, International Institute for Restorative Practices, Vienna, Austria, April 10–17, 1998.

109. Nancy Rodriguez, "Restorative Justice at Work: Examining the Impact of Restorative Justice Resolutions on Juvenile Recidivism," *Crime and Delinquency* 53 (2007), pp. 355–78.

110. Kathleen J. Bergseth and Jeffrey A. Bouffard, "The Long-Term Impact of Restorative Justice Programming for Juvenile Offenders," *Journal of Criminal Justice* 35 (2007), pp. 433–51.

111. Gwen Robinson and Joanna Shapland, "Reducing Recidivism: A Task for Restorative Justice," *British Journal of Criminology* 48 (2008), pp. 337–58.

112. *OJJDP Model Programs Guide*, p. 1, http://www/dsgonline.com/mpg2.5/prevention.htm (accessed July 28, 2012).

113. Ibid.

114. B. Bernard, *Fostering Resiliency in Kids: Protective Facts in the Family, School, and Community* (Portland, Ore.: Northwest Regional Educational Laboratory, 1991); and P. Benson, *All Kids Are Our Kids: What Communities Must Do to Raise Caring and Responsible Children and Adolescents*, 2d ed. (Hoboken, N.J.: Jossey-Bass, 2006).

115. J. Pollard, J. D. Hawkins, and M. Arthur, "Risk and Protection: Are Both Necessary to Understand Diverse Behavioral Outcomes in Adolescence?" *Social Work Research* 23 (1999), pp. 145–58.

116. Sharon Mihalic, Katherine Irwin, Abigail Fagan, Diane Ballard, and Delbert Elliott, *Successful Implementation: Lessons from Blueprints* (Washington, D.C.: Office of Juvenile Justice and Delinquency Prevention, 2004), p. 1.

117. Sharon Mihalic, Katherine Irwin, Abigail Fagan, Diane Ballard, and Delbert Elliott, *Blueprints for Violence Prevention* (Washington, D.C.: Office of Juvenile Justice and Delinquency Prevention, 2004), p. 55.

118. D. E. McGill, S. Mihalic, and J. K. Grotpeter, "Big Brothers Big Sisters of America," in *Blueprints for Violence Prevention: Book 2*, edited by D. S. Elliott (Boulder: University of Colorado, Institute of Behavioral Science, Center for the Study and Prevention of Violence, 1997), p. 55.

119. Mihalic et al., *Blueprints for Violence Prevention*, pp. 30–31.

120. M. A. Pentz, S. Mihalic, and J. K. Grotpeter, "The Midwestern Prevention Project," in *Blueprints for Violence Prevention: Book 1*, edited by D. S. Elliott (Boulder: University of Colorado, Institute of Behavioral Science, Center for the Study and Prevention of Violence, 1997), pp. 30–31.

121. Mihalic et al., *Blueprints for Violence Prevention*, pp. 26–27.

122. J. F. Alexander et al., "Functional Family Therapy," in *Blueprints for Violence Prevention: Book 3*, edited by D. S. Elliott (Boulder: University of Colorado, Institute of Behavioral Science, Center for the Study and Prevention of Violence, 2000), pp. 26–27.

123. Mihalic et al., *Blueprints for Violence Prevention*, pp. 22–23.

124. C. Webster-Stratton et al., "The Incredible Years: Parent, Teacher and Child Training Series," in *Blueprints for Violence Prevention: Book 11*, edited by D. S. Elliott (Boulder: University of Colorado, Institute of Behavioral Science, Center for the Study and Prevention of Violence, 2001), pp. 22–23.

125. Mihalic et al., *Blueprints for Violence Prevention*, p. 47.

126. G. Botvin, S. Mihalic, and J. K. Grotpeter, "Life Skills Training," in *Blueprints for Violence Prevention: Book 5*, edited by D. S. Elliott (Boulder: University of Colorado, Institute of Behavioral Science, Center for the Study and Prevention of Violence, 1998), p. 47.

127. Mihalic et al., *Blueprints for Violence Prevention*, pp. 31–33.

128. Pentz et al., "The Midwestern Prevention Project," pp. 31–33.

129. TFC Consultants, "MTFC Program Overview," http://www.mtfc.com/overview.html (accessed July 28, 2012).

130. Mihalic et al., *Blueprints for Violence Prevention*, pp. 56–58.

131. P. Chamberlain and S. Mihalic, "Multidimensional Treatment Foster Care," in *Blueprints for Violence Prevention: Book 8*, edited by D. S. Elliott (Boulder: University of Colorado, Institute of Behavioral Science, Center for the Study and Prevention of Violence, 1998), pp. 56–58.

132. Mihalic et al., *Blueprints for Violence Prevention*, pp. 27–28.

133. S. W. Henggeler et al., "Multisystemic Therapy," in *Blueprints for Violence Prevention: Book 6*, edited by D. S. Elliott (Boulder: University of Colorado, Institute of Behavioral Science, Center for the Study and Prevention of Violence, 2001), pp. 27–28.

134. Mihalic et al., *Blueprints for Violence Prevention*, pp. 18–20.

135. D. Olds et al., "Prenatal and Infancy Home Visitation by Nurses," in *Blueprints for Violence Prevention: Book 7*, edited by D. S. Elliott (Boulder: University of Colorado, Institute of Behavioral Science, Center for the Study and Prevention of Violence, 1998), pp. 18–20.

136. Mihalic et al., *Blueprints for Violence Prevention*, pp. 17–18.

137. Project Toward No Drug Abuse, "Introduction," http://tnd.usc.edu/preview.php (accessed July 28, 2012).

138. Mihalic et al., *Blueprints for Violence Prevention*, pp. 17–18.

139. Ibid.

140. M. Greenberg, M. Kusche, and S. Mihalic, "Promoting Alternative Thinking Strategies," in *Blueprints for Violence Prevention: Book 2*.

141. See Nan S. Park, Boom S. Lee, John M. Bolland, Alexander T. Vazsonyi, and Fei Sun, "Early Adolescent Pathways of Antisocial Behaviors in Poor, Inner-City Neighborhoods," *Journal of Early Adolescence* 28 (May 2008), pp. 185–205; and Robert Agnew, Shelley Keith Matthews, Jacob Bucher, Adria N. Welcher, and Corey Keyes, "Socioeconomic Status, Economic Problems, and Delinquency," *Youth & Society* 40 (2008), pp. 159–81.

142. Ibid., p. 159.

143. Some groups perceive greater injustice than others. See Kevin Buckler and James D. Unnever, "Racial and Ethnic Perceptions of Injustice: Testing the Core Hypotheses of Comparative Conflict Theory," *Journal of Criminal Justice* 36 (2008), pp. 270–78.

7 Gender and Delinquency

Chapter Objectives

After reading this chapter, you should be able to:

1. **Summarize why an understanding of gender differences is important in the study of delinquency.**
2. **Explain how gender roles impact girls' and boys' delinquency.**
3. **List the characteristics of female delinquents.**
4. **Explain the feminist theory of delinquency.**
5. **Summarize how gender bias impacts the processing of female delinquents.**
6. **Explain how male and female delinquent careers differ.**
7. **Describe the nature of a gender-responsive policy approach to delinquency prevention.**

There has been growing concern that while most juvenile arrests have been decreasing, the number of female juvenile arrests in some offense categories (such as drug and alcohol violations) continues to rise.

—Girls Study Group (Research Triangle Institute)

Introduction

On June 25, 2012, the FBI announced that its agents, working with local police officers in fifty-seven cities, had arrested 104 alleged pimps and rescued seventy-seven underage girls and two boys from lives of forced prostitution. The boys and girls, many of whom provided sexual services at truck stops, storefronts, casinos, and hotels, had been held against their will and were forced into prostitution by their adult captors who threatened to harm them and their families if they stopped cooperating. In announcing the arrests, FBI Assistant Director Kevin Perkins said, "Child prostitution remains a major threat to children across America. It is a violent and deplorable crime, and we are working with our partners to disrupt and put behind bars individuals and members of criminal enterprises who would sexually exploit children."[1]

Until recently, the study of delinquency had largely been the study of *male* delinquency. As early as 1973, two American sociologists, Carol Smart[2] and Dorie Klein,[3] called for the establishment of a feminist criminology because of the traditional neglect of the feminist perspective in classical delinquency theories. Klein appealed for "a new kind of research on women and crime—one that has feminist roots and a radical orientation." Fifteen years later, Meda Chesney-Lind, one of the country's most respected experts on female delinquency, issued a renewed call for attention to the problems of girls, and noted that the study of delinquency had long been gender biased, and that delinquency theories were still preoccupied with the delinquency of males. Consequently, she argued, what was known about delinquent offending and of the juvenile justice process had been shaped solely by male experiences and male understandings of the social world.[4]

While numerous studies of girl's delinquency followed the exhortations of feminists, things began to move much faster in 2003 when the federal Office for Juvenile Justice and Delinquency Prevention (OJJDP) awarded a grant to North Carolina's Research Triangle Institute (RTI) to study female delinquency and its consequences. Using funds provided by OJJDP, RTI formed the Girls' Study Group (GSG) with the avowed purpose of identifying sound theoretical strategies for combating female delinquency and violence.[5] Researchers and practitioners participating in the study group have been reviewing and analyzing existing literature as well as working to identify programs that effectively address the prevention and reduction of female offending. In recent years, the GSG has produced a number of publications and studies, some of which will be discussed later in this chapter.

Today's feminist criminologists agree on gender-based differences in adolescents' experiences, developmental rates, and the scope and motivation of male and female patterns of offending.[6] There is also general agreement that female adolescents enjoy greater social support and are more controlled than are males. Further, a review of available data shows that females are less disposed to crime than males and have fewer opportunities for certain types of crimes,[7] and researchers commonly accept that high self-esteem has the effect of discouraging favorable risk-taking situations among female adolescents while encouraging risk-taking situations in males.[8]

There is disagreement, however, in how to address the male-oriented approach to delinquency, thought by many to be both persistent and dominant. One approach focuses on the question of generalizability. Supporters of this gender-neutral position have examined such subjects as the family, social bonding, social learning, and delinquent peer relationships, and, to a lesser degree, deterrence and strain.[9] These theorists argue that little evidence has been found to date to suggest that separate theories are needed to account for male and female delinquency. They also claim that female delinquency tends to operate within similar surroundings and through the same factors as male delinquency, and add that empirical studies generally reveal that much more variation exists within each gender than between the sexes.[10] Thus, some feminist theorists would recommend that the subject of female delinquency be presented in textbooks as part of "a seamless whole rather than as a separate chapter."[11]

In contrast, other feminist theorists argue that new theoretical efforts are needed to understand female delinquency and women's involvement in adult crime. Sociologist Eileen Leonard, for example, questioned whether anomie, labeling, differential association, subculture, and Marxist theories can be used to explain the crime patterns of women and concluded that these traditional theories do not work and that they are basically flawed.[12] Chesney-Lind's application of male-oriented theories to female delinquency posited that existing delinquency theories are inadequate to explain female delinquency, and suggested that there is a need for a feminist model of delinquency because a patriarchal context has previously shaped all explanations and the handling of female delinquents and status offenders. She argued that the sexual and physical victimizations of adolescent females at home—and the relationship between these experiences and their crimes—have been systematically ignored.[13]

Leonard has argued that new theoretical efforts to understand women's crime must include an analysis of the links among gender, race, class, and culture.[14] After accusing some feminists of ignoring racial, class, ethnic, religious, and cultural differences among women, social philosopher Elizabeth V. Spelman concluded that it is only through an examination of such factors that oppression against women can be more clearly grasped and understood.[15] Chesney-Lind further extended this argument when she said that adolescent females and women are victims of "multiple marginality" because their gender, class, and race have placed them at the economic periphery of society. The labeling of a girl as delinquent takes place in a world, Chesney-Lind charged, "where gender still shapes the lives of young people in very powerful ways. Gender, then, matters in girls' lives and the way gender works varies by the community and the culture into which the girl is born."[16] (For an interview with Chesney-Lind see the *People In the Know* feature in this chapter.)

In the face of these two divergent positions—one seeking to explain away gender gaps and striving to be gender neutral, the other focusing on the importance of gender in understanding delinquency and crime—Darrell Steffensmeier and Emilie Allen attempted to put the two approaches together. In a now-classic paper, they contended that "[there] is no need for gender-specific theories," although they acknowledged that "qualitative studies reveal major gender differences in the context and nature of offending."[17] Steffensmeier and Allen went on to develop a "middle of the road position,"[18] which has not received much support in the literature.

In 2006, from the Ohio Serious Offender Study, Peggy C. Gipordano and her colleagues interviewed 109 young women when first incarcerated in a juvenile correctional facility, and followed them up to an average age of 29. Their research led them to conclude that "the either/or dichotomy suggested by the contrast between traditional and feminist frameworks is neither necessary nor helpful to the theory-building process."[19] They suggested that the Ohio study "indicates that the basic tenets of these seemingly opposing viewpoints are not in themselves fundamentally incompatible, and the results require a more integrated approach," finding that this was particularly true when the focus is on the small subgroup of girls with serious delinquent histories.[20]

Giordano and colleagues' follow-up of their study of this subgroup of serious female offenders suggested that a comprehensive understanding of their delinquent actions requires that we enlist the help of both classic explanations of delinquency and contemporary perspectives that emphasize uniquely gendered processes. Within the life histories of these girls, there is ample evidence of the types of social dynamics that support both approaches. Frequent themes within the narrative resulting from the study include disadvantaged neighborhoods, economic marginality, and an "excess of definitions favorable to the violation of law." At the same time, the study found, parents' criminal involvement and/or severe alcohol and drug problems can be identified early on, and they continued throughout the women's childhood and adolescent years. The adult follow-up study further supported the idea that some processes associated with continued crime or desistance seem to be "generic" (that is, they have a good fit with both women's and men's life experiences), whereas others appear to be more gender specific.[21]

People In the Know
Interview with Meda Chesney-Lind

Question: What gender differences can be identified in delinquency?

Chesney-Lind: The question now is whether the theories of delinquent behavior can be used to understand female crime, delinquency, and victimization. Will the "add women and stir" approach be sufficient to rescue traditional delinquency theories? My research convinces me that it will not work. Gender stratification or the patriarchal context within which both male and female delinquency is lodged has been totally neglected by conventional delinquency theory. This omission means that a total rethinking of delinquency as a social problem is necessary. The exclusion of girls from delinquency theory might lead one to conclude that girls are almost never delinquent and that they have far fewer problems than boys. Some might even suspect that the juvenile justice system treats the few girls who find their way into it more gently than it does the boys. Both of these assumptions are wrong. Current work on female delinquency is uncovering the special pains that girls growing up in male-dominated society face. The price one pays for being born female is upped when it is combined with poverty and minority status, but it is always colored by gender.

Consequently, sexual abuse is a major theme in girls' lives, and many girls on the run are running away from abusive and violent homes. They run to streets that are themselves sexist, and they are often forced to survive as women—to sell themselves as commodities. All of this is shaped by their gender as well as by their class and their color. You might ask, "How about the system's response to girls' delinquency?" First, there has been almost no concern about girls' victimization. Instead, large numbers of girls are brought into juvenile courts across America for noncriminal status offenses—running away from home, curfew, truancy, etc. Traditionally, no one in the juvenile justice system asked these girls why they were in conflict with their parents; no one looked for reasons why girls might run away from home. They simply tried to force them to return home or sentenced them to training schools.

The juvenile justice system, then, has neglected girls' victimization, and it has acted to enforce parental authority over girls, even when the parents were abusive. Clearly, the patterns described above require an explanation that places girls' delinquent behavior in the context of their lives as girls in a male-dominated society—a feminist model of delinquency if you will. That's what I'm working on these days.

Source: Meda Chesney-Lind is professor of sociology at the University of Hawaii at Manoa. Her articles have appeared in both criminal justice journals and edited criminal justice volumes, and she is widely acknowledged as one of the top authorities on female delinquency. Reprinted with permission from Meda Chesney-Lind.

Gender Ratio in Offending

gender ratio of crime
The comparison of rates of criminal offending by gender.

Important questions relate to the vastly different rates of criminal offending by gender, or what is known as the **gender ratio of crime**. Why are females dramatically less likely than males to be involved in most crimes? Conversely, why are males more crime-prone than females? What explains these gender differences in rates of offending?[22]

The issue of the gender ratio of crime immediately leads to an inquiry into the factors that block or limit girls' or women's involvement in crime. It can be argued that this inquiry "reflects an androcentric [male-centered] perspective that makes men's behavior the norm from which women appear to deviate through their limited offending."[23]

Some feminist theorists propose treating gender as a key element of social organization rather than as an individual trait, an approach that permits a more complex examination of the gender gap. Data on crime trends, for example, reveal that a gender gap is more persistent for some offenses than for others, fluctuates over time, and varies by class, race/ethnicity, and age.[24] Approaches that merely study the gender gap itself miss the opportunity to examine how causal factors differently shape men's and women's offending across important social dimensions. Miller and Mullins illustrated this point by noting evidence of a link between "underclass" conditions and African American women's offending—a link that fails to have explanatory power for women's offending in other social contexts.[25]

Karen Heimer and colleagues examined the "economic marginalization thesis," which proposes that "the gender gap in crime decreases and females account for a greater proportion of crime when women's economic well-being declines."[26] "Not only are women more likely to live in poverty than men," they added, "but also the gender gap in poverty rates for women in the most crime-prone group continues to increase."[27] They concluded that continued economic oppression, instead of enhanced economic opportunities for women, may be the root cause of the narrowing of the gender gap in crime that has taken place during the past four decades.[28]

A promising avenue for exploring the complexities of the gender ratio of offending is found in a conceptual scheme offered by Australian criminologist Kathleen Daly, and consists of these three areas of inquiry:

1. *Gendered pathways.* What trajectories propel females and males into offending? What social contexts and factors facilitate entrance to and desistance from offending, and how are they gendered?

2. *Gendered crime.* What are the ways in which street life, sex and drug markets, criminal opportunities, informal economics, and crime groups are structured by gender and other social features? What observed variation occurs in the sequencing and contexts of women's and men's law-breaking?

3. *Gendered lives.* How does gender affect the daily lives of females and males? How does gender structure identities and courses of action? How do these experiences intersect with lawbreaking?[29]

Social Context of Delinquency: Gender Roles and Delinquency

To a large degree, understandings of **gender** and gender-based roles are acquired through socialization. Children are socialized into preexisting gender arrangements and construct understandings of themselves and how they relate to others in terms of those frameworks. As Berkeley professor Barrie Thorne noted in her well-known early book on the subject, *Gender Play*:

> Parents dress infant girls in pink and boys in blue, give them gender-differentiated names and toys, and expect them to act differently. Teachers frequently give boys more classroom attention than girls. Children pick up the gender stereotypes that pervade books, songs, advertisements, TV programs, and movies. And peer groups, steeped in cultural ideas about what it is to be a girl or a boy, also perpetuate gender-typed play and interaction. In short, if boys and girls are different, they are not born but *made* that way.[30]

An empirically based landmark study by the American Association of University Women (AAUW), which included girls of color and all social classes, examined the behavior and treatment of girls in the classroom. The most striking finding in this research was that white girls tend to lose their sense of self-esteem as they advance from elementary school to high school; African American girls, in contrast, were found to maintain their self-esteem, but too often would become dissociated from school and schoolwork.[31]

Themes found to be unique to the high school–age girls in the AAUW study and in the girls described in the book *Schoolgirls*, by Peggy Orenstein, were obsession with physical appearance and popularity based on external characteristics rather than achievement, loss of freedom in later adolescence associated with budding sexuality, close attention to relationships, and intense mother–daughter patterns of communication. Inner-city African American and Latino girls were found to have somewhat unique issues related to life in tough neighborhoods, and the development of a tough exterior was seen as vital for their protection from gangs and violence; early pregnancy was a reality for many of them. In short, girls' victimization—from sexual harassment either at school or on the streets to full-blown sexual assaults—was a fact of girls' lives and had an important impact on their personalities and later development.[32]

In gender-specific guidelines written for the state of Oregon, P. Patton and M. Morgan suggested that while these statements may not be true of every girl and boy, generally speaking the following can be assumed:

- Girls develop their identity in relation to other people, whereas boys develop their identity in relation to the world.

- Girls resolve conflict based on relationships, whereas boys resolve conflict based on rules.

gender
The personal traits, social positions, and values and beliefs that members of a society attach to being male or female.

- Girls focus on connectedness and interdependence, whereas boys focus on independence and autonomy.
- Girls exhibit relational aggression, whereas boys exhibit overaggression.[33]

Although there has been a recent resurgence in recognizing the importance of biology in determining sex-linked behavior, children in today's society continue to be effectively socialized into **gender roles**. Thorne reminds her readers that children have an active role in society and that the social construction of gender—an active and ongoing process in their lives—is most visible in play. When she observed children in middle school, she could identify gender separation and integration taking place within the classroom, in the lunchroom, and on the playground. Children's active role in constructing gender could be seen as they formed lines, chose seats, gossiped, teased, and sought access to or avoided particular activities. Sociologist Barrie Thorne particularly found extensive self-separation by gender on the playground, where adults have little control.[34]

In addition to the social construction of gender roles, there appears to be considerable evidence that girls develop differently than boys. Marty Beyer, a clinical psychologist who has examined adolescent males and females across the nation since 1980, said recently that research "has identified different vulnerabilities and protective factors in girls."[35] Girls, for example, have a greater tendency to internalize their experiences, and they experience higher rates of anxiety, depression, withdrawal, and eating disorders than do boys. Girls are also more focused on relationships than boys, Beyer claimed.[36]

▲ A young woman looks at herself in the mirror of a cosmetics case on the streets of New York City's East Village.

■ **What gender differences does American delinquency display?**

gender role
A societal definition of what constitutes either masculine or feminine behavior.

The Female Delinquent

Recently, a growing body of research has been devoted to the study of the characteristics of delinquent girls.[37] Researchers have identified basic demographic and offense patterns as well as background characteristics such as family dysfunction, trauma, physical abuse, mental health issues, substance abuse, risky sexual behavior, academic problems, and delinquent peers as common features among girls in custody.[38]

The profile of at-risk adolescent females that emerges identifies common characteristics, including stories of victimization, unstable family life, school failure, repeated status offenses, and mental health and substance abuse problems.[39] B. Bloom and S. Covington have outlined a profile of a typical female juvenile offender that is shown in Figure 7–1.

The Girls' Study Group, referred to at the start of this chapter, examines issues such as patterns of offending among adolescents and how they differ for girls and boys; risk and protective factors associated with gender; and the causes and correlates of girls' delinquency. See Exhibit 7–1 for a 2010 report by this study group.

FIGURE 7–1
The Typical Female Juvenile Offender

Source: B. Bloom and S. Covington, "Effective Gender-Responsive Interventions in Juvenile Justice: Addressing the Lives of Delinquent Girls," paper presented at the annual meeting of the American Society of Criminology, Atlanta, GA, 2001.

- She is 13 to 18 years old.
- She has experienced academic failure, truancy, and dropping out.
- She has a history of repeated victimization, especially physical, sexual, and emotional abuse.
- She is from an unstable family background that includes involvement in the criminal justice system, lack of connectedness, and social isolation.
- She has a history of unhealthy dependent relationships, especially with older males.
- She has mental health issues, including a history of substance abuse.
- She is apt to be a member of a community of color.

Exhibit 7–1
Differences between Girls' and Boys' Delinquency

In April 2010, the Girls' Study Group, a collaborative project funded by the Office of Justice Programs at the U.S. Department of Justice, released a twenty-page report entitled "Causes and Correlates of Girls' Delinquency." That document summarized the findings of 1,600 of studies that had been conducted on girls' delinquency during the past two decades. A baker's dozen of some of the most interesting findings are listed below:

- Research conducted to date suggests that subtle differences in certain biological functions and psychological traits may contribute to gender-related variations in responses to certain environmental conditions.
- On the whole, girls' delinquent acts are typically less chronic and often less serious than those of boys.
- There is evidence that girls experience a greater number of negative life events during adolescence than boys do, and they may, in turn, be more sensitive to their effects, especially when they come from within the home.
- There is evidence that girls more often experience certain types of trauma, such as sexual abuse and rape, than boys do.
- Many studies of incidence of sexual abuse suggests that it is more pervasive among girls who engage in antisocial behavior, particularly those who engage in violent behavior, than among their male counterparts.
- In addition to gender differences in exposure to certain stressors, girls and boys may also vary in their sensitivity to the same stressor. For example, there are some suggestions that girls may be more sensitive to dysfunction and trauma within the home.
- Boys outnumber girls by a ratio of 3.1 in the diagnoses of attention deficit/hyperactivity disorder (ADHD) and other conduct disorders.

- Mental health problems linked to life stressors and experiences of victimization, such as anxiety, depression, and post-traumatic stress disorder, are diagnosed at much higher rates among girls than boys.
- Early maturation creates particular risks for girls because of the development of physical signs of maturity inconsistent with still largely undeveloped cognitive and emotional systems.
- Some studies have found that compared with other girls, early-maturing girls are more likely to engage in delinquency and other risk-taking behaviors. There is some evidence that early-maturing girls are at increased threat of various high-risk behaviors such as substance abuse, truancy, and running away.
- Early maturation in girls further appears to be a risk factor in exposure to intimate partner violence in adolescence.
- Early puberty, especially when coupled with disadvantaged neighborhoods and family conflict, is a key gender-related factor in predicting girls' delinquency.
- Complex family processes, such as parental supervision, attachment, and maltreatment, are important factors that help explain the difference in the onset of delinquency between girls and boys.

The entire publication can be found online at http://www.justicestudies.com/pubs/causes_girls.pdf.

Source: Margaret A. Zahn, Robert Agnew, Diana Fishbein, Shari Miller, Donna-Marie Winn, Gayle Dakoff, Candace Kruttschnitt, Peggy Giordano, Denise C. Gottfredson, Allison A. Payne, Barry C. Feld, and Meda Chesney-Lind, *Causes and Correlates of Girls' Delinquency* (Washington, D.C.: U.S. Department of Justice; Office of Juvenile Justice and Delinquency Prevention, 2010).

According to Joanne Belknap and Kristi Holsinger, "The most significantly and potentially useful criminological research in recent years has been the recognition of girls' and women's pathways to offending."[40] The first step along females' pathway into the juvenile justice system is victimization. The ages at which interviewed adolescent girls reportedly were most likely to be beaten, raped, stabbed, or shot were thirteen and fourteen years.[41] A large proportion of girls first entered the juvenile justice system as runaways, who frequently were attempting to escape abuse at home.[42]

Certain abuses follow these adolescent females into the juvenile justice system. Specific forms of abuse reportedly experienced by juvenile females include the consistent use of foul and demanding language by staff; inappropriate touching, pushing, and hitting by staff; placement in isolation for trivial reasons; and withholding of clean clothing. Some girls were strip-searched in the presence of male officers.[43]

A second step along females' pathway into the juvenile justice system involves substance abuse. Substance use in females is highly correlated with early childhood sexual victimization, especially among white females, with the literature consistently reporting a strong link between childhood abuse and the later development of alcoholism and other drug problems.[44] Significantly, at about the same age as the victimization occurred (usually when the girls were between thirteen and fourteen years old), the girls started using addictive substances.

A third step along females' pathway into the juvenile justice system involves girls acting out at home, in school, in sexual activity, in law-violating acts, and in gang involvement. The emotional problems troubled girls usually have tend to influence their negative behaviors;

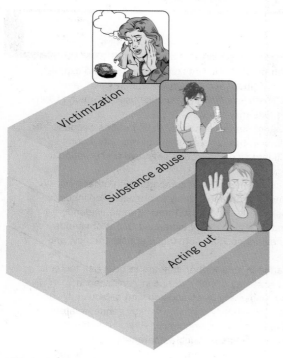

FIGURE 7–2
Pathways to Delinquency

Web Extra 7–1
Center on Juvenile and Criminal Justice: Girls
in the Criminal Justice System

Voices of Delinquency 7–1
Read "Walking Different Paths." Why was
Melissa not discovered in her various deviant
encounters? What would explain, in part,
Melissa's drug involvement? How did gender
affect her, and did it affect her escaping a
delinquent label?

Library Extra 7–1
OJJDP publication: *Juvenile Female Offenders: A Status of the States Report*

as a result, they do poorly in school, are sometimes suspended or expelled, or drop out. They run away from home and come before the juvenile court, or they are referred to the court for their involvement in gangs or delinquent behaviors. The three pathways to delinquency in this discussion of the female delinquent are depicted in Figure 7–2.

Explanations of Female Delinquency

Criminologists come to vastly different conclusions concerning the question of whether female juveniles commit delinquent acts for reasons different from those of young males. Early explanations of female delinquency, which viewed adolescent females as having certain biological characteristics or psychological tendencies that made them more receptive to certain kinds of delinquency, focused on biological and psychological factors thought common to females. Today, however, many criminologists question many biological and psychological explanations of delinquency, and instead see troublesome adolescent females as the product of a male-led patriarchal society. Consequently, many recent explanations of female delinquency have placed much greater emphasis on sociological factors.

Some criminologists challenge whether gender-specific explanations for delinquency and crime are even needed because, they say, existing social scientific theories can account for both males' and females' delinquency.[45] Still others argue for gender-specific explanations because, they say, traditional sociological theories of delinquent behavior fail to adequately explain the experience of being female. Gender-specific theories are discussed later in this chapter.

Biological and Constitutional Explanations

Although sociological theories remain in the forefront of the delinquency literature, the focus has shifted recently to biopsychological vulnerability factors that may be related to girls' delinquency. Five general categories of such factors have been considered: (1) stress and anxiety, (2) attention deficit/hyperactivity disorder (ADHD) and conduct disorder (CD), (3) intellectual deficits, (4) early pubertal maturation, and (5) mental health issues. These factors apply also to boys' delinquency, although in some cases, such as ADHD, boys have been labeled more often, but girls appear to have greater vulnerability when diagnosed.[46] For example, recently discovered gender-related differences may account for sex-related differences in reaction to stressors, and contribute to a heightened vulnerability to behavioral problems with females in responding to traumatic life events.[47] In other words, some recent research has led some to the conclusion that girls may indeed be more sensitive—and react with heightened emotion—to negative events in their lives than are boys.

Psychological Explanations

Psychological explanations of female delinquency vary between early and more recent explanations. Early studies addressed what was assumed to be "innate" female nature and its relationship to deviant behavior, but more recently the focus of study has been on social contexts as they contribute to female delinquency.

Gisela Konopka's early study of delinquent females, for example, linked a poor home life with a deep sense of loneliness and low self-esteem. Her conception of delinquency relied heavily on the notion of individual pathology, and she concluded that only a female who is "sick" can become delinquent.[48] Konopka identified four key factors contributing to female delinquency: (1) a uniquely dramatic biological onset of puberty, (2) a complex identification process because of a girl's competitiveness with her mother, (3) the changing cultural position of females and the resultant uncertainty and loneliness, and (4) the hostile picture that the world presents to some young females.[49]

A contemporary study, in contrast, focused on physical and sexual abuse of girls, and found that abused female delinquents tend to psychopathology, including post-traumatic stress disorder (PTSD), suicidal behavior, dissociative disorder, and borderline personality

Exhibit 7–2
The Sexualization of Girlhood

A 2010 American Psychological Association (APA) task force examined the sexualization of girls and girlhood in U.S. culture. The phrase "sexualization of girls" refers to the portrayal of girls as sexual objects, and in a sexual manner (i.e., dressed revealingly, and assuming bodily postures that imply sexual readiness). The APA task force was formed in response to the concerns of child advocacy organizations, journalists, psychologists, and parents, who have become alarmed over what they see as the increasing sexualization of girls in American society.

Healthy sexuality is an important component of both physical and mental health, fosters intimacy, bonding, and shared pleasure, and involves mutual respect between consenting partners. In contrast, several components of the process of sexualization set it apart from healthy sexuality. Sexualization occurs when:

- A person's value comes only from his or her sexual appeal or behavior, to the exclusion of other characteristics
- A person is held to a standard that equates physical attractiveness with being sexy
- A person is sexually objectified—that is, made into a thing for others' sexual use, rather than seen as a person with the capacity for independent action and decision making
- Sexuality is inappropriately imposed on a person.

The APA report proposed that the sexualization of girls occurs within the context of cultural norms, expectations, and values; is encouraged by family, peers, and others; and means that girls may treat and experience themselves as sexual objects. Further, if girls learn that sexualized behavior and appearance are generally approved of and rewarded by society and by their peers, then they will be likely to internalize these standards and engage in self-sexualization.

This report goes on to document the sexualization of girls in American society, including things such as:

- The media's treatment of girls, with wide sexual harassment taking place on prime-time programming

- Content analysis of music videos indicating that 44 to 81 percent contain sexual imagery
- References to relationships, romance, and sexual behavior common in popular music lyrics and videos
- A gross underrepresentation of girls in films with family-friendly content
- Anecdotal evidence that cartoons and animation contain sexualized images of girls and women
- Magazine portrayals of how girls attract the attention of boys by looking "hot" and "sexy"
- A large body of research that shows that media coverage of women's sports is minimal compared with the extensive coverage of men's sports
- Video/computer games that contain highly sexualized content and only a few strong female protagonists
- The Internet representations of female celebrities that are far more likely than male celebrities to be sexualized
- The sexualization of women in advertising
- Dolls, clothing, and cosmetic products that are marketed to girls that present sexualized images.

To address the problems associated with the sexualization of girls, APA researchers advocated for funding to support the development and implementation by public agencies, including schools, and private organizations of media literacy programs, including interactive media, that combat sexualization and objectification.

They also called for the inclusion of information about sexualization and objectification in health and other programs, including comprehensive sex education programs, and for the development of programming that may counteract damaging images of girlhood.

Source: American Psychological Association, Report of the APA Task Force on the Sexualization of Girls (Washington, D.C.: APA, 2010).

disorder.[50] In sum, recent studies of female delinquency have shifted away from the psychoanalytical perspective and begun to emphasize the social context of gendered behavior. Exhibit 7–2 discusses the sexualization of girlhood.

Sociological Explanations

Beginning in the late 1970s, numerous studies proceeded from the assumption that sociological processes traditionally related to males could also affect the delinquent involvement of females. General agreement exists among and between feminists and nonfeminists that literature approaching female delinquency from a sociological perspective appears to offer more promise than that which includes biological or psychological causes. Researchers have focused on sociological factors such as blocked opportunity, the women's liberation movement, social bonding, masculinity, power control, and peer group influence, among others. Research has discovered that the causal factors identified by these theories can explain much of the gender gap in delinquency.[51]

Library Extra 7–2
OJJDP publication: Guiding Principles for Promising Female Programming: An Inventory of Best Practices

General Strain Theory

Males may be more likely to become involved in delinquency than females because males tend to experience strains conducive to delinquency and cope with strains through delinquency. Females, in turn, may experience certain strains that may exhibit other-directed delinquency.

A teenage prostitute solicits a man near MacArthur Park in Los Angeles. Although the reasons offered for turning to prostitution may differ for white and African American juveniles, some feminist theorists contend that the fundamental reason is the same: the social and economic inequities of a patriarchal capitalist system.

■ Do you agree?

However, general strain theory explains female delinquency by contending that many females experience strains conducive to delinquency, such as harsh discipline, parental rejection, peer abuse, negative secondary school experiences, homelessness, and a strong need for money.[52]

Blocked Opportunity Theory

The role of blocked, or limited, opportunity has received considerable attention in the sociological analysis of male delinquency (see Chapter 4), but the usefulness of such variables in studying female delinquency has been largely ignored because males are seen as being concerned with achieving short- and long-term status and economic success, whereas juvenile females are viewed as possessing no such aspirations, instead being satisfied to occupy a role dependent on males.[53] Several studies found that the perception of limited opportunity was more strongly related to female delinquency than it was to male delinquency. Both African American and white female delinquents regarded their opportunities less positively than did the male delinquents in their sample; status offenders also perceived their opportunities as being less favorable than did nondelinquents.[54]

Social Learning Theory

Social learning theory contends that males have higher rates of delinquency than females primarily because they tend to be associated with delinquent peers and belong to gangs more often than do females. It is also argued that female peer groups are less conducive to delinquency than mixed-gender or all-male peer groups; males, in turn, have beliefs more favorable to delinquency than do females. However, according to social learning theory, some females are more likely than others to become involved in delinquent behavior because they tend to associate with others who provide exposure to delinquent models, reinforce delinquent behaviors, and teach identities that are favorable to delinquency.[55]

Social Control Theory

sex-role socialization
The process by which boys and girls internalize their culture's norms, sanctions, and expectations for members of their gender.

Proponents of social control theory contend that females are less involved in delinquency than males because **sex-role socialization** results in more ties and stronger social bonds for females than for males.[56] In addition, adolescent females may have less opportunity to engage in delinquent behavior because in general they are more closely supervised by parents. Females who are delinquent, according to social control theory, have less parental supervision, are less tied to their homes and families, are weakly bonded to parents and teachers, perform poorly in school, spend less time on homework, are involved in delinquent peer groups, and have less self-control.[57]

Differential Association Theory

Karen Heimer and Stacy De Coster found that emotional bonds to families were negatively related to the learning of violent definitions for girls but not for boys; coercive parental discipline and aggressive friends were positively related to the learning of violent definitions for boys but not for girls; and patriarchal beliefs about gender inhibited female violence without having any effect on male violence.[58]

Masculinity Hypothesis

masculinity hypothesis
The idea that as girls become more boylike and acquire more masculine traits, they become more delinquent.

Several studies of female delinquents have proposed a **masculinity hypothesis**. Freda Adler contended that as females become more malelike and acquire more masculine traits, they become more delinquent.[59] Francis Cullen and coworkers found that the more male and female adolescents possessed "male" personality traits, the more likely they were to become involved in delinquency but that the relationship between masculinity and delinquency was stronger for males than for females.[60] William E. Thornton and Jennifer James found a moderate degree of association between masculine self-expectations and delinquency but concluded that males were still more likely to be delinquent than were females, regardless of their degree of masculinity.[61]

Power-Control Theory

John Hagan and colleagues (discussed in Chapter 6) proposed a power-control theory to explain female delinquency.[62] Using a class-based framework and data collected in Toronto, Ontario, they contended that as mothers gain power relative to their husbands (usually by employment outside the home), daughters and sons alike are encouraged to be more open to risk taking. Parents in egalitarian families, then, redistribute their control efforts so that daughters are subjected to controls more like those imposed on sons; in contrast, daughters in patriarchal families are taught by their parents to avoid risks.[63] Hagan and colleagues concluded that "patriarchal families will be characterized by large gender differences in common delinquent behavior while egalitarian families will be characterized by smaller gender differences in delinquency."[64] Power-control theory thus concludes that when daughters are freed from patriarchal family relations, they more frequently become delinquent.[65]

Labeling Theory

Labeling theorists claim that males are more likely to be labeled as delinquents than females both because the male cultural stereotype views males as troublemakers and because males engage in more delinquency. Labeling theory does argue that some females are more delinquent than others because they have been informally labeled as delinquents by parents, teachers, and others as well as formally labeled by the juvenile justice system.[66]

Interactionist Theory of Delinquency

Heimer reported that delinquency for both females and males occurred through a process of role taking, in which youths considered the perspectives of significant others, and among both boys and girls, attitudes favoring deviance encouraged delinquency. She also found that "girls' misbehavior can be controlled by inculcating values and attitudes, whereas more direct controls may be necessary to control boys' deviance."[67]

Deterrence, Rational Choice, and Routine Activities Theories

The explanation as to why females see the costs of crime as high and the benefits as low is related to their higher level of supervision, their moral beliefs, more self-control, less time spent in unstructured and unsupervised activities with peers, less association with delinquent peers, and less prior delinquency. Some females who see the costs of crime as low and the benefits as high differ from other females; for example, they may spend more unstructured and unsupervised time with peers. This is particularly true of those females who run away from home and spend a lot of time on the streets.[68]

Evaluation of Explanations of Female Delinquency

The discussion of female delinquency readily leads to the conclusion that biological explanations are the less predictive factors. Personal maladjustment hypotheses may have some predictive ability in determining the frequency of delinquency in girls, but sociological theories appear to be able to explain more of female delinquency and do it far more adequately. Some feminists are satisfied with the conclusion of sociological studies positing that males and females are differentially exposed or affected by the same criminogenic associations.[69] Strain theory, general theory, social learning theory, social control theory, differential association theory, power-control theory, labeling theory, and symbolic interactionist theory all have received some support.[70] Other feminists (as the next two sections of this chapter will show) contend that the unique experiences of females require gender-specific theories. See Table 7–1 for a summary of selected explanations for female delinquency.

Feminist Theory of Delinquency

Historically, feminist theory has at least seven expressions: liberal feminism, phenomenological feminism, socialist feminism, Marxist feminism, radical feminism, third-wave feminism, and postmodern feminism. Chesney-Lind's radical feminist theory of delinquency, which is discussed in this chapter, is one of the most exciting efforts to explain delinquent behavior in adolescent females.

▲ A young jail inmate participates in an E-Visit, using a computer and an internet service to talk to family members. The program is part of a virtual visitation project designed to strengthen parent–child bonds.

■ **With increasing numbers of women being sent to prison, many children grow up without a mother at home. What else can be done to address this issue?**

TABLE 7–1
Summary of Types of Explanations of Female Delinquency

Types	Explanation
Biological and constitutional explanations	Biopsychological vulnerability factors related to girls' delinquency.
Psychological explanations	Focus on psychiatric disorders.
Sociological explanations	Focus on social structure and relationships among and between groups.
General strain theory	Females can experience strain, especially in the family and school, conducive to female delinquency.
Blocked opportunity theory	Some evidence has been found that the perception of limited opportunity is more strongly related to female delinquency than it is to male delinquency.
Social learning theory	Some females are more likely than others to become involved in delinquent behavior because of their exposure to delinquent models.
Social control theory	Females who are delinquent have less parental supervision and bonding to the school.
Differential association theory	Emotional bonds to families are negatively related to the learning of violent definitions for girls but not for boys.
Masculinity hypothesis	Some studies have found that as females become more malelike and acquire more masculine traits, they become more delinquent.
Power-control theory	When daughters are freed from patriarchal family relations, this theory concludes that they become more delinquent.
Labeling theory	Males are more likely to be labeled as delinquent than females, but some females—especially the more delinquent girls—can be informally labeled by parents, the school, and the justice system.
Interactionist theory of delinquency	For both males and females, delinquency occurs through a process of role taking.
Deterrence, rational choice, and routine activities theories	Some females see the costs of crime as low and the rewards as high. They usually spend more time in unstructured and unsupervised activities with peers.

feminist theory of delinquency
A theory that adolescent females' victimization at home causes them to become delinquent and that this fact has been systematically ignored.

The **feminist theory of delinquency** contends that girls' victimization and the relationship between that experience and girls' crime have been systematically ignored. Chesney-Lind, one of the main proponents of this position, stated that it has long been understood that a major reason for girls' presence in juvenile courts is their parents' insistence on their arrest. Researchers and those who work with female status offenders are discovering today that a substantial number are victims of both physical and sexual abuse.[71]

Chesney-Lind proposed that a feminist perspective on the causes of female delinquency include the following four propositions: First, girls are frequently the victims of violence and sexual abuse (estimates are that three-quarters of sexual abuse victims are girls), but unlike those of boys, girls' victimization and their response to that victimization are shaped by their status as young women. Second, their victimizers (usually males) have the ability to invoke official agencies of social control to keep daughters at home and vulnerable. Third, as girls run away from abusive homes characterized by sexual abuse and parental neglect, they are forced into the life of an escaped convict; unable to enroll in school or take a job to support themselves because they fear detection, female runaways are forced to engage in panhandling, petty theft, and sometimes prostitution to survive. Fourth, it is no accident that girls who are on the run from abusive homes or are on the streets because of impoverished homes

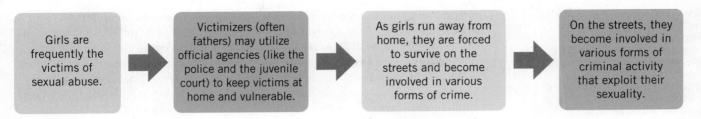

FIGURE 7–3
Chesney-Lind's Four Propositions on the Feminist Theory of Delinquency

become involved in criminal activities that exploit their sexuality. Because U.S. society has defined physically "perfect" young women as desirable, girls on the streets, who have little else of value to trade, are encouraged to utilize this resource. Not surprisingly, the criminal subculture also views them from this perspective.[72]

Considerable research supports the frequent victimization of adolescent females. Mimi Silbert and Ayala M. Pines found that 60 percent of the street prostitutes they interviewed had been sexually abused as juveniles.[73] R. J. Phelps and colleagues, in a survey of 192 female youths in the Wisconsin juvenile justice system, discovered that 79 percent of these youths (most of whom were in the system for petty larceny and status offenses) had been subjected to physical abuse that resulted in some form of injury.[74] Chesney-Lind's investigation of the backgrounds of adult women in prison underscored the links between their victimization as children and their later criminal careers, with interviews revealing that virtually all of these women were victims of physical and/or sexual abuse as youngsters. Chesney-Lind's four propositions on the feminist theory of delinquency are noted in Figure 7–3.

Gender Bias and the Processing of Female Delinquents

The underlying theme of this chapter is that adolescent females grow up in a culture that facilitates domination and control by males.[75] In this society, it is claimed that troublesome adolescent females are seen through lenses of discrimination, exploitation, and oppression.[76] Here are six corollaries:

1. *Adolescent females receive discriminatory treatment because of society's disapproval of sexual activity.*[77] Krohn, Curry, and Nelson-Kilger's analysis of ten thousand police contacts in a Midwestern city over a thirty-year period found that adolescent females who were suspected of status offenses were more likely than their male counterparts to be referred to juvenile court for such offenses during all three decades.[78] Some studies have found that police officers adopt a more paternalistic and harsher attitude toward younger females to deter any further violation or inappropriate sex-role behavior.[79] Several studies have indicated that juvenile females are treated more harshly than boys because of their sexual history.[80]

2. *Offering another perspective, Rosemary C. Sarri concluded that juvenile law has long penalized females.* She claimed that although the law may not be discriminatory on its face, the attitudes and ideologies of juvenile justice practitioners administering it may result in violations of the Equal Protection Clause of the Fourteenth Amendment by leading them to commit females to longer sentences than males under the guise of "protecting" the female juveniles.[81] She added that "females have a greater probability of being detained and held for longer periods than males, even though the overwhelming majority of females are charged with status offenses."[82]

3. *Juvenile females, as a number of studies have documented, receive punitive processing through the juvenile justice system.* This results in their staying longer in detention and having longer stays in juvenile institutions than males for similar offenses.[83]

Voices of Delinquency 7-2
Read "The Naïve Offender." Why did this youth, who had several offenses for which she could have come in contact with the justice system (engaging in sexual activity, transporting drug offenders, buying and using drugs), not come to the attention of the juvenile justice system? She is now working with troubled youths, but her life could have turned out much differently.

4. *According to another perspective, the oppressive treatment of adolescent females is hidden in the juvenile justice system.* Following the decriminalization of status offenses in 1979, Anne R. Mahoney and Carol Fenster reported that many girls appeared in court for criminal-type offenses that had previously been classified as status offenses, and they suggested that juvenile justice officials may have redefined these girls to be eligible for the kinds of protectionist sanctions that have been traditionally applied.[84]

5. *Another expression of the gender bias found in this "hidden justice" is that certain provisions of the Juvenile Justice and Delinquency Prevention Act provide that status offenders found in contempt of court for violating a valid court order may be placed in secure detention facilities, which permits juvenile judges to use their contempt power to confine repeat status offenders.* If a runaway girl, for example, was ordered by the court to remain at home but she chose to run away again, she might be found in contempt of court—a criminal-type offense. There is reason to believe that juvenile judges apply their contempt power more often to female status offenders than to their male counterparts.[85]

6. *The early studies, especially, found that police officers, intake personnel, and judges supported a sexual double standard.* Female status offenders, as previously indicated, were more likely than their male counterparts to be petitioned to formal court proceedings, to be placed in preadjudicatory detention confinements, and to be confined in juvenile institutions. But at the same time, males who committed delinquent acts frequently received harsher treatment than their female counterparts. Consistent with what is known as the "chivalry" or "paternalism" thesis, police were less likely to arrest females suspected of property or person crimes; if arrested, female delinquents were less likely than male delinquents to be formally charged with criminal offenses, and if charged, they were less likely than males to be incarcerated for their offenses.[86]

Figure 7–4 provides a summary of the six corollaries of gender bias and the processing of female delinquents.

On balance, some evidence does exist that the discriminatory treatment of female status offenders may be declining since passage of the Juvenile Justice and Delinquency Prevention Act.[87] No longer do many states send status offenders to training schools with delinquents. But the long tradition of sexism in juvenile justice will be difficult to change. Due process safeguards for female delinquents, as well as for female status offenders, must be established to ensure greater social justice for them in the juvenile justice system. The intrusion of extralegal factors into the decision-making process in the juvenile court has led to discrimination against the adolescent female that must become a relic of the past. See Exhibit 7–3 for information about the Amicus Girls Study, one state's attempt to pay attention to the welfare of girls in the juvenile justice system.

1. Society's disapproval of sexual activity results in discriminatory treatment of juvenile females.
2. Juvenile law has long overly penalized females.
3. Juvenile females are punitively processed throughout the juvenile justice system.
4. The oppressive treatment of adolescent females is hidden within the juvenile justice system.
5. Female status offenders are frequently found in contempt of court for violating a valid court order and then are placed in secure juvenile detention facilities.
6. Early studies found that police officers, intake personnel, and judges support a sexual double standard.

FIGURE 7–4
Six Corollaries of Gender Bias and the Processing of Female Delinquents

Exhibit 7–3
Amicus Girls Study

Amicus (Latin for "friend") is a Minnesota nonprofit organization with over forty-five years of experience in building positive relationships between juvenile and adult offenders and their communities. This study originated from a simple idea: Ask those individuals involved with girls throughout the juvenile justice system to share their thoughts on how the system is doing. Women incarcerated in the Minnesota Correctional Facility-Shakopee were also asked what could be learned from their experiences and lives to inform the work being done with the girls of today.

The study included information that was gathered from more than 220 individuals through focus groups and targeted interviews of girls, caregivers, professionals, and female prisoners, as well as a review of national and local studies. The girls themselves expressed a deep need to be "listened to and heard," adding that their stories do not always get told. They feel that many in the justice system do not communicate directly with them. As one girl in a focus group said when discussing her treatment in the justice system, "Sometimes they make it seem like we have no feelings, like what they say won't hurt us."

Amicus makes a number of broad recommendations based on the interviews with girls, women, their families and professionals, and conversations with various key stakeholders:

- *Recommendation—Apply what we know.* Promote existing standards of gender-responsive care and services, and provide training consistent with those standards. Professionals ask repeatedly for guidance on what to do and how to do it. Evidence-based standards exist and are included throughout this report.
- *Recommendation—Address racial, ethnic, and gender disparities.* Ensure that programming for girls responds to their individual and cultural needs. Continue to examine and address disproportionate minority contact.
- *Recommendation—Focus on prevention and early intervention.* Policy makers are encouraged to allocate more

resources for prevention and early intervention strategies. Wise investment in prevention and early intervention will decrease the need for costly intervention as girls grow older.
- *Recommendation—Integrate restorative justice values and practices.* Programming should focus on helping girls repair their relationships within the community and building connections to support them in living a safe and healthy life. Formulate policies and allocate resources in such a way that communities and programs are able to engage in and focus on restoring girls to the community.
- *Recommendation—Keep track of the girls.* In the process of trying to collect data on the numbers and demographic characteristics of girls in the justice system, Amicus found that data necessary to describe a continuum of services was not readily or consistently available through state and local agencies. Policy makers must know who the girls are, how they move through the system, and what works best with them if they are to allocate resources more efficiently and effectively.
- *Recommendation—Conduct a gender-responsive program assessment.* Amicus, through the feedback and requests of stakeholders, determined a need for an instrument that would help providers gauge their adherence to the standards of gender-responsive care. Although other useful assessments already exist, the decision was made that a juvenile-specific, Minnesota-specific instrument would better serve Minnesota service providers. The critical principles or elements of this assessment include being (1) responsive to the individual girl and her unique circumstances; (2) trauma sensitive and responsive; (3) family centered; (4) safe and nurturing; (5) culturally competent; (6) school based; (7) conducted by effective professionals; and (8) evidence based.

Source: Amicus Girls Study: Paying Attention to Girls in the Juvenile Justice System (Spring 2010), http://www.amicususa.org (accessed June 12, 2012).

Influence of Class

As part of the female delinquent's "multiple marginality," class oppression is another form of exploitation experienced by her.[88] In many ways, powerful and serious problems of childhood and adolescence related to poverty set the stage for a young person's entry into homelessness, unemployment, drug use, survival sex and prostitution, and ultimately even more serious delinquent and criminal acts. Even those adolescents coming from middle-class homes may be thrust into situations of economic survival if they choose to run away from abusive environments.

Traditional theories also fail to address the life situations of girls on the economic and political margins, because researchers typically fail to examine or talk with these girls. For example, almost all urban females identified by police as gang members have been drawn from low-income groups.[89] Lee Bowker and Malcolm Klein's examination of data on girls in gangs in Los Angeles stated the importance of classism as well as racism:

> We conclude that the overwhelming impact of racism, sexism, poverty and limited opportunity structures is likely to be so important in determining the gang membership and juvenile delinquency of women and girls in urban ghettos that personality variables, relations with parents and problems associated with heterosexual behavior play a relatively minor role in determining gang membership and juvenile delinquency.[90]

Class becomes important in shaping the lives of adolescent females in a number of other ways. Lower-class adolescent females tend to confront higher risk levels than middle- and upper-class adolescent females. They are more likely to have unsatisfactory experiences at school, to lack educational goals beyond high school, to experience higher rates of physical and sexual abuse, to deal with pregnancy and motherhood, to be involved in drug and alcohol dependency, to confront the risk of HIV/AIDS, and to lack supportive networks at home.[91] Although not all adolescent females at risk end up in the juvenile justice system, the likelihood of such a placement is greater for lower-class girls.[92]

Racial Discrimination

Young women of color, as well as other minority girls, often grow up in contexts very different from those of their white counterparts. An article by Lori D. Moore and Irene Padavic examines how gender-role ideology may affect racial/ethnic disparities, using data on African American, white, and Hispanic female juvenile offenders in Florida. As expected, they found that African American girls received harsher dispositions than white girls, but contrary to what might be expected, Hispanic girls' dispositions were no harsher than those of white girls. Further examination revealed that the effects of race/ethnicity depend largely on legal variables. Up to a certain threshold, white girls appear to be granted greater leniency than other racial groups, but as their offending severity and prior records increase, the juvenile justice system becomes increasingly intolerant. Sentencing decisions then become harsher for white girls than for African American girls.[93]

Because racism and poverty often go hand in hand, these girls are forced by their minority status and poverty to deal early and regularly with problems of abuse, drugs, and violence.[94] They also are likely to be attracted to gang membership.[95] H. C. Covey, Scott Menard, and R. Franzese summarized the effect of ethnicity on gang membership:

> Racial differences in the frequency of gang formation such as the relative scarcity of non-Hispanic, white, ethnic gangs may be explainable in terms of the smaller proportion of the non-Hispanic European American population that [lives] in neighborhoods characterized by high rates of poverty, welfare dependency, single-parent households, and other symptoms that characterize social disorganization.[96]

Minority girls' strategies for coping with the problems of abuse, drugs, violence, and gang membership, as Chesney-Lind has noted, "tend to place them outside the conventional expectations of white girls," and it also increases the likelihood that they will come to the attention of the juvenile justice system.[97]

The Whole Is Greater Than the Sum of Its Parts

An examination of the experience of African American women reveals the geometric effects of multiple forms of oppression involving gender, class, and race.[98] Diane Lewis has noted that because feminist theories of women's inequality "focused exclusively upon the effects of sexism, they have been of limited applicability to minority women subjected to the constraints of both racism and sexism."[99] Lewis further noted that "black women … tended to see racism as a more powerful cause of their subordinate position than sexism and to view the women's liberation movement with considerable mistrust."[100]

Daly summarized this argument by saying that "unless you consider all the key relations of inequality—class, race, gender (and also age and sexuality)—you have considered none," adding that "unless you consider the inseparability of these relations in the life of one person, you do not understand what we are saying."[101] Spelman conceptualized the independence and multiple natures of gender, class, and race by saying that "how one form of oppression is experienced is influenced by and influences how another form is experienced."[102]

This suggests that gender, class, and race are interlocking forms of oppression and that the whole is greater than its parts. Thus, female delinquents, like adult women, suffer the consequences of multiple types of oppression as they face processing by the justice system.[103]

Prevention of Delinquency

Formerly called the Girls Club of America, Girls Inc. is a nonprofit organization that inspires all girls to be strong, smart, and bold through a network of local organizations in the United States and Canada. Girls Inc. responds to the changing needs of girls and their communities through research-based programs and advocacy that empower girls to reach their full potential and to understand, assert, and value their rights. Girls Inc. sponsors a number of programs which are designed to enable young women to develop their capacities, which include the following:[104]

- *Preventing Adolescent Pregnancy.* Seeking to educate girls about the issues of sex and pregnancy, this program is designed to prepare girls to be able to decide when they want to engage in sexual practices.

- *Operation Start.* Aiming to increase the interest and abilities of girls in math, science, and technology, this program specifically seeks to prevent girls who show interest in these areas from adopting an attitude that technology and science are the exclusive arena of males and that females cannot excel in them.

- *Project Bold.* Teaching girls about violence and its prevention, this program is designed to help girls resist violence at home and the school. It further shows concrete examples of how to defend themselves.

- *Media Literacy.* Teaching girls to think critically about the images of women as presented by the media, this program focuses on issues such as body image and the dysfunctional manner to which the media portray the female body as a sexual object.

- *Economic Literacy.* Teaching girls how to handle money, this program presents the basic issues such as debt, credit-card practices, interest rates, and the value of savings. This program focuses on teaching girls how to plan and control their own economic future.

- *National Scholars.* Making it possible to provide scholarships for deserving young women, Lucille Miller Wright, a longtime supporter of Girls Inc., bequeathed $6.4 million from her estate to the organization to fund scholarships for young women members.

   With its commitment to provide girls with a strong and healthy self-concept so that they can grow into competent women, Girls Inc. has developed the Girls' Bill of Rights®. It states:

- Girls have the right to be themselves and to resist gender stereotypes.
- Girls have the right to express themselves with originality and enthusiasm.
- Girls have the right to take risks, to strive freely, and to take pride in success.
- Girls have the right to accept and appreciate their bodies.
- Girls have the right to have confidence in themselves and to be safe in the world.
- Girls have the right to prepare for interesting work and economic independence.

Delinquency across the Life Course: Gender and Delinquency

Jean Bottcher, in a study that targeted brothers and sisters of incarcerated teenagers, conceptualized gender as social practices and used these practices as the unit of analysis. Her study revealed social factors that intertwined with delinquent activities, limiting female delinquency while at the same time enabling and rewarding male delinquency: male dominance, differences in routine daily activities, variations in both sexual interests and transition to adulthood, and an ideology that defined both crime as male activity and child care as female activity.[105]

   Longitudinal studies reveal that delinquent careers differ by gender. Male careers tend to begin earlier and to extend longer into the adult years. Studies of youth gangs show that female members are more likely than male members to leave the gang if they have a child. According to Bottcher, conventional life patterns—especially marriage, parenting, and work—draw both males and females away from gangs and delinquency but do so more quickly and completely for females.[106]

Amy V. D'Unger, Kenneth C. Land, and Patricia L. McCall, in a follow-up of the second Philadelphia cohort study, found both life-course-persistent and adolescence-limited delinquency (see Terrie Moffitt's classification scheme in Chapters 2 and Chapters 3) among the males, with a high and low category for each group. Among the females in this study, there were comparable adolescence-limited groups, although with lower overall offending levels. The high-rate adolescence-limited female offenders did share marked similarities with low-rate chronic male offenders; however, the chronic or persistent category of offender was less prominent among the females.[107]

Rebecca S. Katz, using waves 1 and 7 of the National Longitudinal Survey of Youth, found that much as in other studies, childhood victimization, sexual discrimination, adult racial discrimination, and domestic violence largely explained women's involvement in crime and deviance. Katz found some support for revised strain theory as an explanation for female involvement in criminal behavior, but she concluded that female crime also may require a unique theoretical model that more directly takes into account females' social and emotional development in a racist and patriarchal society.[108] Alex R. Piquero, Robert Brame, and Terrie E. Moffitt, using data from the Cambridge study of males and from the Dunedin, New Zealand, birth cohort, found that the vast majority of both males and females never experience a conviction, and for those who do, the number of convictions is quite small. They also stated that boys, more than girls, tend to become involved in crime when measured by conviction experience and that boys, once they are involved, exhibit more variations in conviction activity than do girls; the data further revealed that boys can be separated into low-, medium-, and high-frequency offender groups, whereas girls can be separated into low- and medium-frequency groups. Finally, their analysis found that "the process of continuity in criminal activity is formed by the end of adolescence similarly for both males and females" and that "there appear to be more similarities than differences across gender in how adolescent and adult patterns of offending are linked."[109]

At least three studies have examined the desistance process among women. I. Sommers, D. R. Baskin, and J. Fagan found that quality marriages led women to desist from crime, with some variation depending on the class and race of the women being studied.[110] A later study by Sommers and Baskin revealed that the desistance process was quite different for inner-city women of color, who were more likely to desist when they received alcohol and drug treatment or because they grew tired or fearful of repeated imprisonments.[111] Finally, as discussed in Chapter 5, Peggy C. Giordano and colleagues followed up on a sample of serious adolescent female delinquents and found neither marital attachment nor job stability to be strongly related to female desistance; instead, desisters underwent a cognitive shift, or transformation, in which they experienced successful "hooks for change," which "facilitated the development of an alternative view of self that was seen as fundamentally incompatible with criminal behavior."[112]

Delinquency and Social Policy: Female Offenders

Another problem is that female offenders represents one of the least-serviced juvenile justice populations. There are only a few effective gender-specific programs nationally. The continuum of programs and services that are required to reduce females' entry into the juvenile justice system must be responsive both to gender and age and to developmental age.

A gender-responsive policy approach calls for a new vision for the juvenile justice system, one that recognizes the behavioral and social differences between female and male offenders that have specific implications for gender-responsive policy and practice.[113] Gender-responsive policy provides effective interventions that address the intersecting issues of substance abuse, trauma, mental health, and economic oppression, as Bloom and colleagues indicated; a focus on juvenile females' relationships with their family members is paramount as well (see Table 7–2).

> **TABLE 7–2**
> **Gender-Responsive Policies**

- Provide effective interventions that address the intersecting issues of substance abuse, trauma, mental health, and economic oppression.
- Focus on juvenile females' relationships with their family members.
- Provide intensive family-based programs tailored to the needs of adolescent females.
- Provide the opportunity for the development of positive relationships between female offenders and their children.
- Provide community-based services such as family counseling, substance abuse prevention, and educational services.

Source: B. Bloom, B. Owen, and S. W. Covington, "Woman Offenders and the Gendered Effects of Public Policy," *Review of Policy Research* 21 (2004), pp. 31–48.

Optimum environments for at-risk females of this age would be intensive family-based programs tailored to the needs of adolescent females.[114] Another possibility that has merit is a community-based all-girls school setting anchoring such services as family counseling, substance abuse prevention, specialized educational services (e.g., learning disabilities assessment), and mentoring services. A further gender-specific strategy is offering programs that provide the opportunity for the development of positive relationships between female offenders and their children.[115]

The Case

The Life Course of Amy Watters, Age 12

When Amy was 12, she made a terrifying discovery. One day, while undressing in front of the full-length mirror that her father had installed in her bedroom a few months earlier, she looked closely at one of the brackets holding the mirror in place on the wall. To her surprise she saw that a screw head on that bracket appeared to be missing. Upon further examination, she realized that what she was looking at was the lens of a tiny camera hidden within the bracket. Had someone been watching her as she undressed?

Amy hurriedly called her friends to talk about the discovery, and soon Sarah, Jake, and Mallory came over to her house to examine the mirror. Her father was away at work, and Jake disassembled the mirror, finding that Amy's suspicions had been correct. A small wireless camera, running on tiny batteries, was hidden in the mirror. When Jake, who was something of a geek, powered on her father's computer he quickly found that the wireless signal from the camera in the mirror fed into the home's router. Her father's computer screen displayed everything that went on in Amy's room, and provided an especially good close-up of activities taking place in front of the mirror.

Amy was horrified at the thought that her father had been watching her as she changed her clothes, and started thinking that he might have been selling live video feeds of her most intimate moments across the Internet. Before her friends could stop her, Amy packed a bag, gathered what money she could find in her father's desk drawers, and headed for the bus station. She didn't know where she was going, but she knew that she had to get away from home.

What emotional impact did the discovery of the hidden camera have on Amy? Could her relationship with her father ever be the same again? What alternatives did Amy have to running away? Why didn't she take them? How was this event likely influenced by Amy's gender?

Learn More on the Web:

- Fetal Distress Risk: http://usat.ly/aUj6R7
- Childhood Affection and Stress: http://usat.ly/bEknJB
- Causes and Correlates of Girls' Delinquency (Girls' Study Group): http://justicestudies.com/girls_study_group.pdf

Follow the continuing Amy Watters saga in the next chapter.

SUMMARY

This chapter examines issues of gender as they relate to delinquency. Some of the most important points include:

- Female delinquency, like all other social behaviors, takes place in a world where gender shapes the lives of adolescents in powerful ways.

- Feminist theory, on which this chapter builds, starts with the assumption that adolescent females are socially positioned in society in ways that make them especially vulnerable to male victimization, including physical and sexual abuse and the negative effects of poverty.

- Feminist theory proposes that the meaning of gender and the nature of gender-related behavior depend heavily on the social context in which they are found.

- One area of agreement among feminists and nonfeminists is that delinquency theories are primarily focused on why males commit delinquent acts and that not much attention has been given to the nature or causes of female delinquency.

- A major disagreement among theorists centers on whether separate perspectives are needed to explain female delinquency, with some writers charging that existing theories are inadequate to explain delinquency by females.

- Considerable evidence supports the position that female delinquency is produced by many of the same sociological factors as male delinquency and that more behavioral variation exists within genders than between them.

- An argument can be made that the relationship between the sexual and physical victimization of adolescent females at home and later law-violating behavior has been ignored and that new theoretical efforts are needed to deal with these experiences.

- Generally speaking, female delinquents are not treated more leniently by the juvenile justice system than are male delinquents when they commit status offenses, especially where disapproved sexual behavior is involved.

- Evidence shows that sexual offenses, incorrigibility, and running away from home do not make up the entire delinquent repertoire of girls; indeed, the offenses of male and female delinquents appear to be converging and are beginning to reflect similar patterns.

- Further examination of how gender, class, and race are interrelated will likely lead to additional insights into the problems facing female adolescents in the United States today.

KEY TERMS

feminist theory of delinquency, p. 170
gender, p. 163

gender ratio of crime, p. 162
gender roles, p. 164

masculinity hypothesis, p. 168
sex-role socialization, p. 168

JUVENILE DELINQUENCY VIDEOS

Peace Learning Program

In the *Peace Learning Program* video, a female juvenile facility is shown where the Peace Learning Program was established to handle the youths' needs. What is the Peace Learning Program? What are the goals of the Peace Learning Program? The coordinator of the program discusses the situation of one of the youth's and her involvement with the program. How is the program helping the youth with her individualized treatment needs? Can the values learned through the Peace Learning Program be transferred from the care facility to the real world? Why or why not?

REVIEW QUESTIONS

1. What are different ways to handle the study of female delinquency?
2. How is an understanding of gender learned? What does this mean?
3. What are the main explanations of female delinquency?

4. What is the feminist theory of delinquency?
5. What are the various types of feminist theories?
6. How do gender, class, and race contribute to the victimization of the female delinquent or status offender?

DISCUSSION QUESTIONS

1. Do you agree with Chesney-Lind's suggestion that a feminist model of delinquency is needed? Explain your response.
2. Which perspective should prevail in research, the one that pursues gender neutrality or the one that pursues gender specificity? If gender neutrality prevails, then would consistency demand race neutrality and ethnic neutrality as well? Explain your response.
3. Why is society seemingly so sensitive to the sexual behavior of adolescent girls?

4. Do you think these increased patterns of male domination and female subordination indicate emulation of behaviors observed in subcultural phenomena such as gangsta rap music videos? Explain your response.

5. Why is the relationship among gender, class, and race so important in understanding female delinquency?

GROUP EXERCISES

1. Try an anonymous poll of your students that asks the question: "During high school, were you greatly influenced, moderately influenced, or little influenced by peer pressure in making behavioral decisions?" Compile the results in male and female totals, and discuss the results in class.

NOTES

1. Michael Winter, "FBI: 79 Prostitutes Rescued, 104 Alleged Pimps Arrested," *USA Today*, June 25, 2012, http://content.usatoday.com/communities/ondeadline/post/2012/06/fbi-rescues-79-teen-prostitutes-arrests-104-alleged-pimps/1?csp=hf#.T-nxRXB8zOU (accessed June 26, 2012).

2. Carol Smart, *Women, Crime, and Criminology: A Feminist Critique* (London and Boston: Sage, 1976).

3. Dorie Klein, "The Etiology of Female Crime: A Review of the Literature," *Issues in Criminology* 8 (Fall 1973), pp. 3–30.

4. Meda Chesney-Lind, "Girls, Crime and Women's Place," *Crime and Delinquency* 35 (1988), pp. 5–29. See also Kathleen Daly and Meda Chesney-Lind, "Feminism and Criminology," *Justice Quarterly* 5 (1988), pp. 497–538.

5. See Margaret A. Zahn et al., *Girls Study Group: Understanding and Responding to Girl's Delinquency* (Washington, DC: Office of Juvenile Justice and Delinquency Prevention, 2010).

6. Office of Juvenile Justice and Delinquency Prevention, "Addressing Female Development in Treatment," in *Juvenile Female Offenders: A Status of the States Report* (Washington, D.C.: U.S. Department of Justice, 1998).

7. Paul Mazerolle, "Gender, General Strain, and Delinquency: An Empirical Examination," *Justice Quarterly* 15 (March 1998), pp. 65–91.

8. Karen Heimer, "Gender, Race, and the Pathways to Delinquency: An Interactionist Perspective," in *Crime and Inequality*, edited by J. Hagan and R. Peterson (Stanford, Calif.: Stanford University Press, 1994), pp. 140–73.

9. Jody Miller, *One of the Guys* (New York: Oxford University Press, 2001).

10. Kathleen Daly, "Looking Back, Looking Forward: The Promise of Feminist Transformation," in *The Criminal Justice System and Women: Offenders, Victims, and Workers* (New York: McGraw-Hill, 1995), pp. 443–57.

11. Josephina Figueira-McDonough and Elaine Selo, "A Reformulation of the 'Equal Opportunity' Explanation of Female Delinquency," *Crime and Delinquency* 26 (1980), pp. 333–43; John Hagan, A. R. Gillis, and John Simpson, "The Class Structure of Gender and Delinquency: Toward a Power-Control Theory of Common Delinquent Behavior," *American Journal of Sociology* 90 (1985), pp. 1151–78; and Douglas A. Smith and Raymond Paternoster, "The Gender Gap in Theories of Deviance: Issues and Evidence," *Journal of Research in Crime and Delinquency* 24 (1987), pp. 140–72.

12. Eileen Leonard, "Theoretical Criminology and Gender," in *The Criminal Justice System and Women*, pp. 55–70.

13. Chesney-Lind, "Girls, Crime and Women's Place." For an update of this article, see Meda Chesney-Lind, "Girls, Delinquency, and Juvenile Justice: Toward a Feminist Theory of Young Women's Crime," in *The Criminal Justice System and Women*, pp. 71–88.

14. Leonard, "Theoretical Criminology and Gender."

15. Elizabeth V. Spelman, *Inessential Woman: Problems of Exclusion in Feminist Thought* (Boston: Beacon Press, 1989).

16. Meda Chesney-Lind, *The Female Offender: Girls, Women, and Crime* (Thousand Oaks, Calif.: Sage, 1974), p. 4.

17. Darrell Steffensmeier and Emilie Allen, "Gender and Crime: Toward a Gendered Theory of Female Delinquency," *Annual Review of Sociology* 22 (1996), pp. 459–87.

18. Kathleen Daly, "Gender, Crime, and Criminology," in *The Handbook of Crime and Punishment*, edited by Michael Tonry (New York: Oxford University Press, 1998), p. 100.

19. P. C. Giordano, J. A. Deines, and S. A. Cernkovich, "In and Out of Crime: A Life Course Perspective on Girls' Delinquency," in *Gender and Crime: Patterns in Victimization and Offending*, edited by Karen Heimer and Candace Kruttschnitt (New York: New York University Press, 2006), p. 18.

20. Ibid.

21. Ibid.

22. Daly and Chesney-Lind, "Feminism and Criminology."

23. Jody Miller and Christopher W. Mullins, "Taking Stock: The Status of Feminist Theories in Criminology," in *The Status of Criminological Theory: Advances in Criminological Theory*, Vol. 15, edited by F. Cullen, J. P. Wright, with K. Blevins, F. Adler, and W. Laufer (series eds.) (New Brunswick, N.J.: Transaction, 2006), pp. 206–30.

24. D. Steffensmeier and J. Schwartz, "Trends in Female Criminality: Is Crime Still a Man's World?" in *The Criminal Justice System and Women: Offenders, Prisoners, Victims and Workers*, 3d ed., edited by B. R. Price and N. J. Sokoloff (New York: McGraw-Hill, 2004), pp. 95–111.

25. Miller and Mullins, "Taking Stock."

26. Karen Heimer, Stazcy Wittrock, and Unal Haline, "The Crimes of Poverty: Economic Marginalization and the Gender Gap in Crime," in *Gender and Crime: Patterns in Victimization and Offending*, p. 115.

27. Ibid., p. 121.

28. Ibid.

29. Daly, "Gender, Crime, and Criminology."

30. Barrie Thorne, *Gender Play: Girls and Boys in School* (New Brunswick, N.J.: Rutgers University Press, 1993), p. 2.

31. American Association of University Women (AAUW), *How Schools Are Shortchanging Girls* (Washington, D.C.: AAUW Educational Foundation, 1992).

32. P. Orenstein, *Schoolgirls* (New York: Doubleday, 1994).

33. Marcia Morgan and Pam Patton, *Oregon's Guidelines for Effective Gender-Specific Programs for Girls,* 2002, www.ncjrs.gov/App/publications/Abstract.aspx?id=19781.

34. Thorne, *Gender Play,* p. 157.

35. Marty Beyer, "Delinquent Girls: A Developmental Perspective," *Kentucky Children's Rights Journal* 9 (Spring 2001), p. 17.

36. Ibid.

37. C. S. Lederman, G. A. Dakof, M. A. Larreal, and L. Hua, "Characteristics of Adolescent Females in Juvenile Detention," *International Journal of Law and Psychiatry* 27 (2004), pp. 321–27; and M. Zahn, "The Causes of Girls' Delinquency and Their Program Implications," *Family Court Review* 45 (2007), pp. 456–65.

38. Lederman et al., "Characteristics of Adolescent Females in Juvenile Detention."

39. B. Bloom and S. Covington, "Effective Gender-Responsive Interventions in Juvenile Justice: Addressing the Lives of Delinquent Girls," paper presented at the annual meeting of the American Society of Criminology, Atlanta, GA, 2001.

40. Joanne Belknap and Karen Holsinger, "An Overview of Delinquent Girls: How Theory and Practice Failed and the Need for Innovative Changes," in *Female Offenders: Critical Perspectives and Effective Interventions*, edited by R. T. Zaplin (Gaithersburg, Md.: Aspen Publishers, 1998), p. 1.

41. Ibid.

42. Leslie Acoca, "Investing in Girls: A 21st Century Strategy," *Juvenile Justice* (October 1999), pp. 3–13.

43. Ibid.

44. W. R. Downs, T. Capshew, and B. Rindels, "Relationships between Adult Men's Alcohol Problems and Their Childhood Experiences of Parental Violence and Psychological Aggression," *Journal of Studies on Alcohol* (2004), pp. 336–45; National Center on Addiction and Substance Abuse at Columbia University (CASA), "Reducing Teen Smoking Can Cut Marijuana Use Significantly," http://www.casacolumbia.org/newsletter1457 (accessed November 2003).

45. Paul Mazerolle, "Gender, General Strain, and Delinquency: An Empirical Examination," *Justice Quarterly* 15, no. 65 (1998), pp. 65–91.

46. Diana Fishbein, Shari Miller, Donna Marie Winn, and Gayle Dakof, "Biopsychological Factors, Gender, and Delinquency," in *The Delinquent Girl*, edited by Margaret A. Zahn (Philadelphia: Temple University Press, 2008), pp. 84–106.

47. Ibid.

48. Gisela Konopka, *The Adolescent Girl in Conflict* (Englewood Cliffs, N.J.: Prentice-Hall, 1966).

49. These key factors from Gisela Konopka's *The Adolescent Girl in Conflict* are listed in Peter C. Kratcoski and John E. Kratcoski, "Changing Patterns in the Delinquent Activities of Boys and Girls: A Self-Reported Delinquency Analysis," *Adolescence* 18 (Spring 1975), pp. 83–91.

50. O. Miazad, *Human Rights Brief 10*, Washington College of Law, http://www.wel.american.edu/hrbrief/10-gender.cfm (accessed October 2007).

51. Robert Agnew, "The Contribution of 'Mainstream' Theories to the Explanation of Female Delinquency," in *The Delinquent Girl*, pp. 7–29.

52. Ibid.

53. Talcott Parsons, "Age and Sex in the Social Structure of the United States," *American Sociological Review* 7 (October 1942), pp. 614–16; James S. Coleman, *The Adolescent Society* (New York: Free Press, 1961); and Ruth Rittenhouse, "A Theory and Comparison of Male and Female Delinquency," Ph.D. dissertation, University of Michigan, Ann Arbor, 1963.

54. Susan K. Datesman, Frank R. Scarpitti, and Richard M. Stephenson, "Female Delinquency: An Application of Self and Opportunity Theories," *Journal of Research in Crime and Delinquency* 12 (1975), pp. 107–23; Jeffery O. Segrave and Douglas N. Hastad, "Evaluating Three Models of Delinquency Causation for Males and Females: Strain Theory, Subculture Theory, and Control Theory," *Sociological Focus* 18 (January 1985), pp. 1–17; and Stephen A. Cernkovich and Peggy C. Giordano, "Delinquency, Opportunity, and Gender," *Journal of Criminal Law and Criminology* 70 (1979), pp. 145–51.

55. Agnew, "The Contribution of 'Mainstream' Theories."

56. Travis Hirschi, *Causes of Delinquency* (Berkeley: University of California Press, 1969).

57. William E. Thornton, Jr., Jennifer James, and William G. Doerner, *Delinquency and Justice* (Glenview, Ill.: Scott Foresman, 1982).

58. Karen Heimer and Stacy De Coster, "The Gendering of Violent Behavior," *Criminology* 37 (1999), pp. 277–318.

59. Freda Adler, *Sisters in Crime* (New York: McGraw-Hill, 1975).

60. F. T. Cullen, K. M. Golden, and J. B. Cullen, "Sex and Delinquency: A Partial Test of the Masculinity Hypothesis," *Criminology* 15 (1977), pp. 87–104.

61. William E. Thornton and Jennifer James, "Masculinity and Delinquency Revisited," *British Journal of Criminology* 19 (July 1979), pp. 225–41.

62. John Hagan, John Simpson, and A. R. Gillis, "Class in the Household: A Power-Control Theory of Gender and Delinquency," *American Journal of Sociology* 92 (January 1987), pp. 788–816; and Hagan et al., "The Class Structure of Gender and Delinquency."

63. Hagan et al., "Class in the Household."

64. Ibid., p. 793.

65. Ibid.

66. Agnew, "The Contribution of 'Mainstream' Theories."

67. Karen Heimer, "Gender, Interaction, and Delinquency: Testing a Theory of Differential Social Control," *Social Psychology Quarterly* 59 (1996), p. 57.

68. Agnew, "The Contribution of 'Mainstream' Theories"; and J. Hagan and B. McCarthy, *Mean Streets and Homelessness* (Cambridge, Mass.: Cambridge University Press, 1997).

69. Ibid.

70. Giordano and Cernkovich, "Changing Patterns of Female Delinquency,." Report provided to the National Institute of Public Health, February 28, 1979), p. 24.

71. Chesney-Lind, "Girls, Crime and Women's Place."

72. Ibid.

73. Mimi Silbert and Ayala M. Pines, "Entrance into Prostitution," *Youth and Society* 13 (1982), pp. 471–500.

74. Cited in Chesney-Lind, "Girls, Crime and Women's Place."

75. Spelman, *Inessential Woman*.

76. Ibid.

77. Etta A. Anderson, "The 'Chivalrous' Treatment of the Female Offender in the Arms of the Criminal Justice System: A Review of the Literature," *Social Problems* 23 (1976), pp. 350–57. See also Meda Chesney-Lind, "Judicial Enforcement of the Female Sex Role: The Family Court and Female Delinquency," *Issues in Criminology* 8 (1973), pp. 57–59; Kristine Olson Rogers, "For Her Own Protection: Conditions of Incarceration for Female Juvenile Offenders in the State of Connecticut," *Law and Society Review* 7 (1973), pp. 223–46; and John M. MacDonald and Meda Chesney-Lind, "Gender Bias and the Juvenile Justice Revisited: A Multiyear Analysis," *Crime and Delinquency* 47 (2001), pp. 173–98.

78. Marvin D. Krohn, James P. Curry, and Shirley Nelson-Kilger, "Is Chivalry Dead?" *Criminology* 21 (1983), pp. 417–39.

79. Christy A. Visher, "Gender, Police Arrest Decisions, and Notions of Chivalry," *Criminology* 21 (1983), pp. 5–28; and Chesney-Lind, "Judicial Enforcement of the Female Sex Role."

80. Jean Strauss, "To Be Minor and Female: The Legal Rights of Women under Twenty-One," *Ms.* 1 (1972), pp. 70–75; Yona Cohn, "Criteria for Probation Officers' Recommendations to Juvenile Court," *Crime and Delinquency* 1 (1963), pp. 272–75; Rogers, "For Her Own Protection"; Chesney-Lind, "Judicial Enforcement of the Female Sex Role"; and Laurie Schaffner, "Female Juvenile Delinquency: Sexual Solutions and Gender Bias in Juvenile Justice," paper presented at the annual meeting of the American Society of Criminology in Washington, DC, November 1998.

81. Rosemary C. Sarri, "Juvenile Law: How It Penalizes Females," in *The Female Offender*, edited by Laura Crites, pp. 67–85 (Lexington, Mass.: D. C. Heath and Co., 1977).

82. Ibid., p. 76.

83. Randall G. Shelden and John Horvath, "Processing Offenders in a Juvenile Court: A Comparison of Males and Females," paper presented at the annual meeting of the Western Society of Criminology, Newport Beach, CA, February–March, 1986, cited in Coramae Richey Mann, *Female Crime and Delinquency* (Tuscaloosa: University of Alabama Press, 1984); Meda Chesney-Lind, "Girls and Status Offenses: Is Juvenile Justice Still Sexist?" *Criminal Justice Abstracts* 20 (March 1988), pp. 144–65; Randall R. Beger and Harry Hoffman, "The Role of Gender in Detention Dispositioning of Juvenile Probation Violaters," *Journal of Crime and Justice* 21 (1998), pp. 173–86; Robert Terry, "Discrimination in the Police Handling of Juvenile Offenders by Social Control Agencies," *Journal of Research in Crime and Delinquency* 14 (1967), pp. 218–30; Rogers, "For Her Own Protection;" and Clemens Bartollas and Christopher M. Sieverdes, "Games Juveniles Play: How They Get Their Way," unpublished report, 1985.

84. Anne Rankin Mahoney and Carol Fenster, "Family Delinquents in a Suburban Court," in *Judge, Lawyer, Victim, Thief: Woman, Gender Roles and Criminal Justice*, edited by Nicole Hahn and Elizabeth Anne Stanko (Boston: Northeastern University Press, 1982), pp. 22–54.

85. Donna M. Bishop and Charles E. Frazier, "Gender Bias in Juvenile Justice Processing: Implications of the JJDP Act," *Journal of Criminal Law and Criminology* 82 (1992), pp. 1132–52; and Carla P. Davis, "At Risk Girls and Delinquency Career Pathway," *Crime and Delinquency* 53 (July 2007), pp. 408–35.

86. Ibid.

87. Ibid.

88. Chesney-Lind, *The Female Offender*.

89. Ibid.

90. Lee Bowker and Malcolm Klein, "The Etiology of Female Juvenile Delinquency and Gang Membership: A Test of Psychological and Social Structural Explanations," *Adolescence* 13 (1983), pp. 750–51.

91. For many of these findings, see Joy G. Dryfoos, Adolescents at Risk: Prevalence and Prevention (New York: Oxford University Press, 1990).

92. Michele R. Decker, Anita Raj, and Jay G. Silverman, "Sexual Violence against Girls: Influences of Immigration and Acculturation," *Violence against Women* (May 2007), pp. 498–513.

93. Lori D. Moore and Irene Padavic, "Racial and Ethnic Disparities in Girls' Sentencing in the Juvenile Justice System," *Feminist Criminology* 5 (2010), pp. 263–85.

94. Chesney-Lind, *The Female Offender*.

95. Finn-Aage Esbensen and L. Thomas Winfree, "Race and Gender Differences between Gang and Nongang Youths: Results from a Multisite Survey," *Justice Quarterly* 15 (September 1998), pp. 505–26.

96. H. C. Covey, Scott Menard, and R. Franzese, *Juvenile Gangs*, 2d ed. (Springfield, Ill.: Charles C. Thomas, 1997), p. 240.

97. Chesney-Lind, *The Female Offender*, p. 23.

98. Spelman, *Inessential Woman*.

99. Diane K. Lewis, "A Response to Inequality: Black Women, Racism, and Sexism," *Signs: Journal of Women in Culture and Society* 3 (1977), p. 339. For this discussion on African American women, I am indebted to Kathleen Daly, "Class–Race–Gender: Sloganeering in Search of Meaning," *Social Justice* 20 (1993), p. 58.

100. Lewis, "A Response to Inequality," p. 339.

101. Daly, "Class–Race–Gender," p. 58.

102. Spelman, *Inessential Woman*, p. 123.

103. Ibid.

104. The material in this section is adapted from Girls Inc. www.girlsinc.org/ Accessed October 25, 2012.

105. Jean Bottcher, "Social Practices of Gender: How Gender Relates to Delinquency in the Everyday Lives of High-Risk Youths," *Criminology* 39 (2001), pp. 905–25.

106. Bottcher, "Social Practices of Gender."

107. Amy V. D'Unger, Kenneth C. Land, and Patricia L. McCall, "Sex Differences in Age Patterns of Delinquent/Criminal Careers: Results from Poisson Latent Class Analyses of the Philadelphia Cohort Study," *Journal of Quantitative Criminology* 18 (December 2002), pp. 349–75.

108. Rebecca S. Katz, "Explaining Girls' and Women's Crime and Desistance in the Context of Their Victimization Experiences," *Violence against Women* 6 (June 2000), pp. 633–60.

109. Alex R. Piquero, Robert Brame, and Terrie E. Moffitt, "Extending the Study of Continuity and Change: Gender Differences in the Linkage between Adolescent and Adult Offending," *Journal of Quantitative Criminology* 21 (June 2005), pp. 219–43.

110. I. Sommers, D. R. Baskin, and J. Fagan, "Getting Out of the Life: Crime Desistance by Female Street Offenders," *Deviant Behavior* 15 (1994), pp. 125–49.

111. I. Sommers and D. R. Baskin, "Situational or Generalized Violence in Drug Dealing Networks," *Journal of Drug Issues* 27 (1997), pp. 833–49.

112. Peggy C. Giordano, Stephen A. Cernkovich, and Jennifer L. Rudolph, "Gender, Crime, and Desistance: Toward a Theory of Cognitive Transformation," *American Journal of Sociology* 107 (January 2002), p. 1038.

113. B. Bloom, B. Owen, and S Covington, "Women Offenders and the Gendered Effects of Public Policy," *Review of Policy Research* 21 (2004), pp. 31–48.

114. Ibid.

115. Ibid.

8 Families and Delinquency

Chapter Objectives

After reading this chapter, you should be able to:

1. Explain how problems in the family affect adolescents and list the factors in the family that are most likely to promote the likelihood of delinquent behavior.

2. Describe the relationship between the impact of family transitions and problem behaviors.

3. Explain how the mass media can influence adolescent behavior.

4. Explain how neglect and child abuse contribute to delinquency.

5. List the sequence of events that occurs as the community responds to child maltreatment.

6. Summarize the family-related risk factors for delinquency.

The number of abused and neglected children has special significance for the juvenile justice system because many of these children end up in the system.

—Federal Advisory Committee on Juvenile Justice

Introduction

On January 12, 2012, a Fort Wayne, Indiana, mother drew national attention because of her unconventional form of child discipline. She forced her fourteen-year-old son to wear a sign around his neck listing his lawbreaking behavior—and stand on a street corner for two hours. The sign read: "I lie, I steal, I sell drugs, I don't follow the law." The mother justified her action by saying, "He broke the law again today and they only gave him a few hours community service. So I decided that he is going to wear a sign."

The form of punishment that the mother chose to use was infuriating to some while it was enlightening to others. One parent said, "Boy, that seems awfully harsh." Another agreed, "I think that's a little extreme." A third person supported the mother, saying, "Sometimes you have to do something drastic so that he gets the point."

Occasionally, however, creative punishment can cross the line and get parents into trouble with the law. Last year, for example, a Staten Island mother dropped her 6-year-old daughter off at a police station as a scare tactic, but was later charged by the police with child endangerment.[1]

socialization

The process by which individuals come to internalize their culture; through this process, an individual learns the norms, sanctions, and expectations of being a member of a particular society.

The family is the primary agent for the **socialization** of children. It is the first social group a child encounters and is the group with which most children have their most enduring relationships. The family gives a child his or her principal identity, even his or her name; teaches social roles, moral standards, and society's laws; and disciplines any child who fails to comply with those norms and values. The family either provides for or neglects children's emotional, intellectual, and social needs; the neglect of these basic needs can have a profound effect on the shaping of a child's attitudes and values.

This chapter discusses adolescents and family problems; the relationship between the family and delinquency; and the types and impact of child abuse and neglect, both at the time of their occurrence and across the life course.

Impact of Families on Delinquency

The importance of the family in understanding delinquent behavior can be seen in the fact that most theories of delinquency rely heavily on the parent–child relationship and parenting practices to explain delinquency.[2] Social disorganization theories, subcultural theories, social control theories, and life-course theories all have this emphasis.[3] The theoretical emphasis on family processes, in turn, is supported by findings that family relationships and parenting skills are directly or indirectly related to delinquent behavior.[4]

A structure versus function controversy has been one of the important and continuing debates on the relationship between family and delinquency. The structural perspective focuses on factors such as parental absence, family size, and birth order, whereas the functional or quality-of-life view argues for the significance of parent–child interaction, the degree of marital happiness, and the amount and type of discipline.[5]

In 2011, Abigail Fagan and colleagues, using data from 18,512 students in grades six, eight, ten, and twelve, found that family factors were significantly related to delinquency and drug use for both girls and boys and for all grades. This study also revealed that across grades, parents treated girls and boys differently, but neither seemed to receive preferential treatment, and younger children reported more positive and active parenting than older students. In addition, this study indicated complexities in parent–child interactions that must be taken into account when examining the causes of adolescent offending and when planning strategies to prevent the development of problem behaviors.[6]

Family Factors

A number of family factors have been identified as being associated with delinquency behavior. These factors are covered in the following sections.

Broken Homes

broken home

A family in which parents are divorced or are no longer living together.

The early research found a direct relationship between **broken homes** and delinquency[7]; later studies, however, questioned the relationship between broken homes and delinquency.[8]

Researchers have shed further light on this debate. It has been reported that the factor of broken homes affects adolescent females more than males,[9] that broken homes have a larger impact on delinquency among African Americans than on other racial groups,[10] and that the connection between broken homes and delinquency is more evident for status offenses than it is for more serious offenses.[11]

Single-Parent Homes

More recently, there has been an examination of the fact that juvenile delinquents appear to come disproportionately from single-parent homes. The family structure in the United States is now changing dramatically; over a third (34 percent) of all children are raised in single-parent households.[12] Besides frequent poverty as a circumstance of family life, single parents must often deal with lack of governmental assistance for things like child care or after-school programs. Additional issues, such as the lack of in-home help from an adult partner, also contribute to the difficulties that single parents face.[13] However, although a more recent study found that adolescents in broken homes tend to be more delinquent than youth in intact homes, the process of family dissolution is not associated with concurrent increases in offending.[14]

Birth Order

Some evidence supports the significance of **birth order** in that delinquent behavior is more likely to be exhibited by middle children than by first or last children. The first child, according to this view, is more likely to receive the undivided attention and affection of both parents, and the last child benefits from the parents' experience in raising children as well as from the presence of other siblings, who serve as role models.[15]

Family Size

Research findings on **family size** reveal that children from large families generally engage in more delinquency than do children from smaller families.[16] Some evidence exists that delinquent siblings learn delinquency from other family members.[17] Similarly, recent research has substantiated the relationship between **delinquent siblings** or criminal parents and the likelihood of children's delinquent behavior.

Quality of Home Life

Studies have generally reported that poor quality of home life, measured by marital adjustment and harmony within the home, affects the rate of delinquent behavior among children more than whether or not the family is intact. Nye found the happiness of the marriage to be the key to whether or not children become involved in delinquent behavior.[18] Similarly, several studies have found a significant relationship between **rejection by parents** and delinquent behavior.[19]

Discipline in the Home

Inadequate **supervision and discipline** in the home have been commonly cited to explain delinquent behavior. John Paul Wright and Francis T. Cullen, using data from the National Longitudinal Survey of Youth, advanced the concept of "parental efficacy" as an adaptation of Robert J. Sampson and colleagues' "collective efficacy" (see Chapter 4)." Wright and Cullen developed the concept of parental efficacy because they wanted to evaluate the relationship between parental controls and other forms of support in reducing delinquency with children. They found that parental support and parental control enhance the effects of one another, and that both can significantly reduce children's inappropriate behaviors.[20]

Library Extra 8–1
NIJ-sponsored publication: *Communitywide Strategies to Reduce Child Abuse and Neglect: Lessons from the Safe Kids/Safe Streets Program*

birth order
The sequence of births in a family and a child's position in it, whether firstborn, middle, or youngest child.

Web Extra 8–1
Center on Child Abuse and Neglect website

family size
The number of children in a family, a possible risk factor for delinquency.

delinquent sibling
A brother or sister who is engaged in delinquent behaviors; an apparent factor in youngsters' involvement in delinquency.

rejection by parents
The disapproval, repudiation, or other uncaring behavior directed by parents toward children.

supervision and discipline
The parental monitoring, guidance, and control of children's activities and behavior.

▲ A sixteenth-century inscription on a plaque on the wall of Venice's Pieta church discouraging parents from abandoning their unwanted babies.

■ **What led some early writers to say that broken homes are possibly the single most important cause of delinquency? Do you agree?**

▲ A pregnant girl in high school.

■ **Why do children born to young mothers face greater risks?**

Ronald L. Simons and colleagues, using data from a sample of several hundred African American caregivers and their children, found that increases in collective efficacy (i.e., the ability of a group to clearly state its goals) within a community over time were associated with increases in authoritative parenting—which is defined as parents combining warmth and support with firm monitoring and control. Both authoritative parenting and collective efficacy, they added, served to deter affiliation with deviant peers as well as involvement in delinquent behavior, and this deterrent effect of authoritative parents was enhanced when it took place within a community with high collective efficacy.[21]

Conclusions

Conflicting findings make drawing conclusions about the relationship between delinquency and the family difficult, but the following seven observations have received wide support:

1. Family conflict and poor marital adjustment are more likely to lead to delinquency than is the structural breakup of the family.

2. Children who are intermediate in birth order and who are part of large families appear to be involved more frequently in delinquent behavior, but this is probably related more to parents' inability to provide for the emotional and financial needs of these children than to birth position or family size.

3. Children who have delinquent siblings or criminal parents may be more prone to delinquent behavior than those who do not.

4. Rejected children are more prone to delinquent behavior than those who have not been rejected, and children who have experienced severe rejection are probably more likely to become involved in delinquent behavior than those who have experienced a lesser degree of rejection.

5. Consistency of discipline within the family seems to be important in deterring delinquent behavior.

6. Lack of mother's supervision, father's and mother's erratic/harsh discipline, parental rejection, and lack of parental attachment appear to be the most important predictors of serious and persistent delinquency.[22]

7. The rate of delinquency appears to increase with the number of unfavorable factors in the home; that is, multiple risk factors within the family are associated with a higher probability of juvenile delinquency than are single factors.[23]

See Figure 8–1 for a representation of family factors and their relationship to delinquency.

Voices of Delinquency 8–1
Read "It Has Been Quite a Ride." How did the chaos of this young woman's family life affect her? Why did she prevail in the midst of what seemed to be overwhelming problems?

Transitions and Delinquency

Divorced and single-parent families, blended families, out-of-wedlock births, homelessness, unemployment, alcohol and drug abuse, and violence are some of the family problems that affect adolescents today. Adolescents experiencing such problems are at a high risk of becoming involved in socially unacceptable behaviors.

The high divorce rate in the United States translates into an increasing number of single-parent families. In 2009, 70 percent of children below the age of eighteen years lived with two married parents, 26 percent with one parent, and 4 percent with no parents (see Figure 8–2).[24] Divorce typically affects African American families more than Caucasian families: As many as 40 percent of Caucasian children and 75 percent of African American children will experience divorce or separation in their family before they reach sixteen years of age. Many of these same children will experience multiple family disruptions over the course of their childhood.[25]

FIGURE 8–1
Family Factors and Their Relationship
to Delinquency

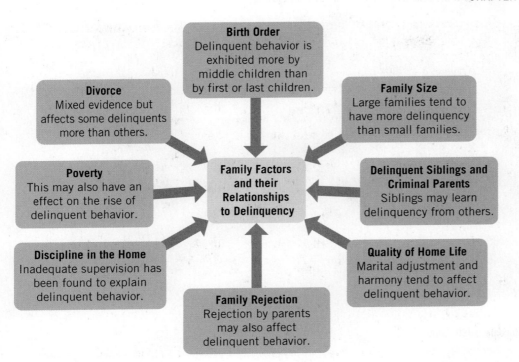

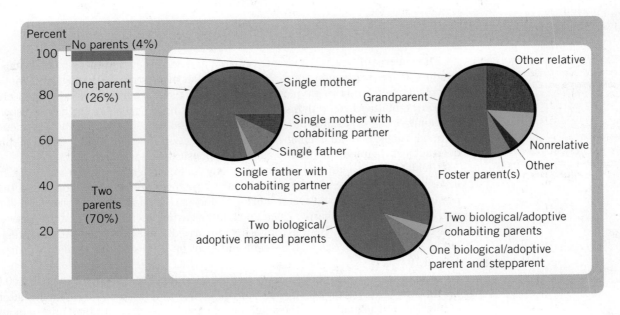

FIGURE 8–2
Percentage of Children, Ages Zero to Seventeen, Living in Various Family Arrangements

Source: Forum on Child and Family Services, *America's Children in Brief: Key Indicators of Well-Being* (Washington, D.C.: Federal Interagency Forum on Child and Family Statistics, 2010), p. 6.

Poverty is a serious problem in the lives of children. In 2008, 16 percent of all children living in female-headed families (with no husband present) continued to experience a higher poverty rate (42 percent) than their counterparts living in married-couple families (8 percent).[26] Economic hardship and lack of access to opportunity tend to undermine marital and parental functioning; furthermore, adolescents who experience family transitions may have difficulty managing anger and other negative emotions that may contribute to their involvement with delinquency or drugs. See Figure 8–3 for percentages of children under eighteen years of age living in poverty, based on family type.

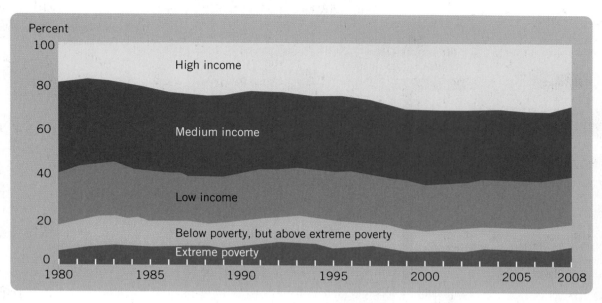

FIGURE 8–3
Percentage of American Children by Family Income, 1980–2008

Source: Forum on Child and Family Services, *America's Children in Brief: Key Indicators of Well-Being* (Washington, D.C.: Federal Interagency Forum on Child and Family Statistics, 2010), p. 6.

Library Extra 8–2
NIJ-sponsored publication: *Co-Occurring Intimate Partner Violence and Child Maltreatment*

The majority of divorced parents remarry, and adolescents in these families must learn to adjust to a new parental figure. Blended families place stress on biological parents, step-parents, and children. In a typical blended family, the mother has custody of her children, and the stepfather lives with his wife's children; his biological children (if any) usually visit the home on an occasional or regular basis. Few adolescents escape the experience of a blended family without feeling resentment, rejection, and confusion. Some stepparents even subject their stepchildren to emotional, physical, or sexual abuse.

Childbearing is a life experience that many American female adolescents have. In some instances, children are wanted and adolescent mothers are married; more often than not, however, pregnancy in adolescence leads to abortion or adoption. The birth rate of unmarried women has risen sharply since 2002, after having been relatively stable between the mid-1980s and 2002.[27] The birth rate for unmarried teenagers fifteen to seventeen years old in 2006 rose from 62 to 92 percent and went up from 40 to 81 percent for those ages 18 and 19.[28]

Homelessness is a phenomenon that shapes the lives of an estimated 500,000 to 1.3 million young people each year. Many homeless youths leave their families after years of physical and sexual abuse, the addiction of a family member, strained interpersonal relations, and parental neglect. Homelessness, regardless of a child's age, is likely to expose him or her to settings permeated by substance abuse, promiscuity, pornography, prostitution, and crime.[29]

Unemployment also affects some family units in the United States. In 2011, the number of people sixteen years old and older officially designated unemployed was 8.9 percent. In 2011, the unemployment rate for whites sixteen years and older was 7.9; the unemployment rate was for African American men sixteen years and older was 16.1 percent; and the unemployment rate for Hispanics sixteen years and older was 11.3 percent.[30] The bad news for African-American and Hispanic families is that from 11 to 16 percent of the population is still experiencing unemployment and its ill consequences.[31]

Adolescents whose family members have substance abuse problems also have their sad stories to tell. Neglect, abuse, and economic hardship are common factors in family settings where alcohol misuse and substance abuse are ordinary behavior. Arrest data in *Crime in the United States 2010* reflect the nationwide scope of this problem in the general population. But while the prevalence of substance abuse is unarguable, its actual impact on adolescents is not easily measurable, since it is simply not possible to display the impact on a "one abuse instance = one adverse impact on one or more adolescent(s)" basis.[32] The impact is clearly visible, however, in the behaviors of the youths it affects.

Violence has long been a major characteristic of the problem family, and it is no stranger to family life today. Marital violence is a pervasive problem that affects nearly one-third of the married population. Numerous studies also show that some parents act out their aggression on their children,[33] and some families use physical violence for disciplinary purposes. Karen Heimer found that coercive discipline strategies teach youths to rely on force and coercion to resolve problems.[34]

Web Extra 8–2
Child Welfare League of America website

Other Expressions of Family Life

The foster family; the adopted child; children with lesbian, gay, bisexual, and transgender parents; and cohabiting parents provide other family contexts for children.

The Foster Family

Foster care can be defined as 24-hour substitute care for children outside their own homes. Foster care settings include, but are not limited to, relative foster homes (whether payments are being made or not), nonrelative foster family homes, emergency shelters, residential facilities, and preadoptive homes. The publication *Foster Care Statistics 2010* reveals a number of key findings (see Figure 8–4 for the number of children who enter and leave foster care):

- On September 30, 2010, there were an estimated 408,425 children in foster care.
- More than a quarter (26 percent) were in the homes of relatives, and nearly half (48 percent) were in nonrelative foster family homes.
- About half (51 percent) had the goal of reunification with their families.
- About half (51 percent) of the children left the system to be reunited with their parents or primary caretakers.
- Close to half of the children (46 percent) who left foster care in fiscal year 2010 were in care for less than one year.[35]

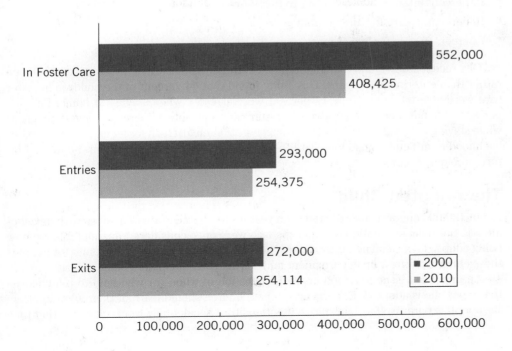

FIGURE 8–4
Number of Children Entering and Exiting Foster Care, FY 2000 and FY 2010

Source: Child Welfare Information Gateway, *Foster Care Statistics 2010* (Washington, D.C.: Children Bureau, May 2012), p. 3.

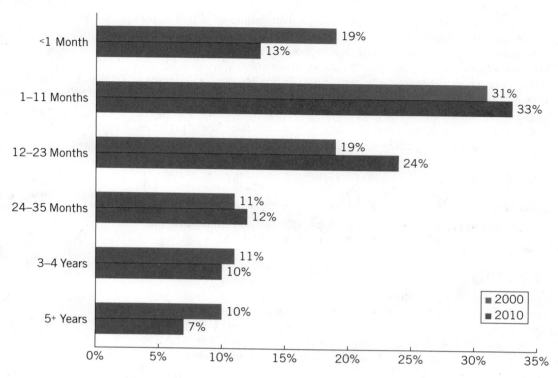

FIGURE 8–5
Length of Stay for Children Exiting Foster Care, FY 2000 and FY 2010
Source: Child Welfare Information Gateway, *Foster Care Statistics 2010* (Washington, D.C.: Children Bureau, May 2012), p. 3.

The 254,114 children who exited foster care during fiscal year 2010 spent time in care as follows (see Figure 8–5):

- 13 percent in care less than one month
- 33 percent in care for one to eleven months
- 24 percent in care for twelve to twenty-three months
- 12 percent in care for twenty-four to thirty-five months
- 10 percent in care for three to four years
- 7 percent in care for five or more years.[36]

One recent study found that children had better outcomes when they remained at home rather than entering foster care. This study found that 44 percent of the children in foster care were arrested, while only 14 percent were arrested when staying at home. Fifty-six percent of females became pregnant in foster care, but only 33 percent became pregnant while staying at home.[37] This study also suggests that children on foster care have a greater likelihood of difficult adjustments later in life and will require additional intervention if future problems occur.

The Adopted Child

About 120,000 children are adopted each year in the United States. Children with developmental, physical, or emotional handicaps who were once considered unadoptable are now being adopted ("special needs adoptions"). Adoptions provide the opportunity for many of these children to grow up in permanent families instead of in foster homes or institutions.[38]

An important issue in adoptions is the question of when (or whether) to tell children that he or she is adopted. Experts agree that children should learn of their adoption from the adoptive parents. If a child learns intentionally or accidentally from someone other than his or her adopted parents, the child may feel anger and mistrust toward the parents and, as a result, may view the adoption as shameful or bad because it was kept a secret. The struggle with their own identify, which is normal for all adolescents, may be even more intense for those children adopted from other countries or cultures. In addition, the adopted child may have an increased interest in his or her birth parents.[39] Some adoptive children may develop emotional or behavioral problems, which may or may not relate to insecurities related to being adopted.[40]

Children with Lesbian, Gay, Bisexual, and Transgender Parents

Millions of children in the United States have gay, lesbian, bisexual, and/or transgender (LGBT) parents. Some of these children were conceived in heterosexual relationships or marriages. An increasing number of LGBT parents have conceived children and/or raised them from birth, either in ongoing committed relationships or as single parents.[41]

In contrast to what is commonly believed, children of LGBT parents:

- Are not more likely to be gay than children with heterosexual parents.
- Do not reveal differences in whether they think of themselves as male or female (gender identity).
- Are not more likely to be sexually abused.
- Do not show differences in their male and female behaviors (gender role behavior).[42]

Although research shows that children with gay and lesbian parents are often as well adjusted as children who have heterosexual parents, they can still face challenges. Some LGBT families face discrimination in their communities and children may be teased or bullied by their peers. Parents can help their children cope with such pressures by preparing them to handle questions about their background or family, by helping the child come up with and practice appropriate responses to teasing or mean remarks, and by considering living in a community where diversity is more accepted.[43]

Cohabitating Parents

The rates of divorce are going down, and the numbers of cohabiting parents are rapidly increasing. Before twelve years of age, children are more likely to live with unmarried parents than to have married parents separate or divorce.[44] See Figure 8–6.

Some children must deal with a variety of partners, usually mothers' boyfriends, moving into or out of the home. Over time, the child's parent may have lived with dozens or even hundreds of partners. Some stay a short period of time, while others may be a part of the child's life for years. Eventually the relationship may lead to marriage.

Another recent study found that a quarter of American women with multiple children conceived them with multiple partners.[45] Psychologist John Gottman, a coauthor of the study, says such instability can have a negative impact on kids in various ways. He claims that children of cohabitating parents tend to externalize aggression more as well as depression.[46] Another study found that cohabitation is associated with children's simultaneous increases in offending.[47]

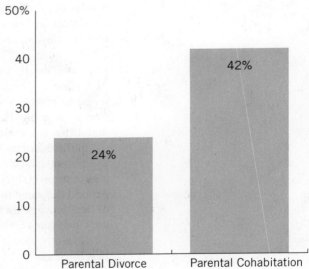

FIGURE 8–6
Percent of Children Experiencing Divorce/Separation and Cohabitation, 2002-2007

Source: Stephanie d'Otreppe, Sheela Kennedy, and Larry Bumpass, *National Survey of Family Growth*, 2011.

Mass Media and Delinquent Behavior

Part of the challenge of being a parent today is dealing effectively with the influence that the mass media have on children. For our purposes, the term *mass media* refers to the Internet, radio, television, commercial motion pictures, videos, CDs, music, and the press (newspapers, journals, and magazines).

▲ Three pre-teens playing video games.

■ **Some people think that violent video games can lead to violent behavior. Do you agree?**

Violent TV Programs and Movies

Most people today watch a lot of television, and many seem to depend on media programming for their understandings of the surrounding world.[48] Consequently, criminologists have shown considerable interest in assessing the relationship between delinquent behavior and the exposure to violence viewed on television. Researchers in the area of delinquency generally conclude that TV violence is most likely to negatively impact the behavior of those children who are already predisposed toward violence and that it seems to have much less influence on young people who are not so predisposed.[49]

The influence of television and motion pictures also extends to the phenomenon of contagion. An example of the contagion effect of motion pictures can be seen in the movie *Colors*, whose showing in theaters across America led gang members nationwide to begin wearing their groups' colors; prior to seeing the movie, most gang members had not been wearing their gang colors.[50]

Some evidence exists to indicate that there is a connection between parental responsibility and the access children have to violent media content. Gregory Zimmerman and Greg Pogarsky's study investigated differences in parent and child estimates of the child's exposure to violence. Using data from the Project on Human Development in Chicago Neighborhoods, most parents (66 percent) underestimated their children's exposure to violence and its impact on the child's psychosocial functioning. Parental underestimates of children's exposure to violence reflected lower levels of family support, which led to more internalizing and externalizing problems and delinquency for the child.[51]

Violent Video Games

Video games involving violent scenarios, such as "Halo 2," "Grand Theft Auto," and "Asheron Call 2," are the focus of considerable controversy today. Some people accuse video game makers of promoting values that support violence. Not surprisingly, the software entertainment industry, with its annual $28 billion in sales paced by a nation's thirst for action, claims that their games are offered only for entertainment purposes.[52]

In August 2005, members of the American Psychological Association (APA) adopted a resolution calling for less violence in video and computer games marketed to children. One APA panelist, Kevin M. Kieffer, reported research that shows playing violent video games tends to make children more aggressive and less prone to helping behaviors.[53] Craig A. Anderson, one of the pioneers of research in this area, adds, "There really isn't any room for doubt that aggressive game playing leads to aggressive behavior."[54]

In the fall of 2005, the Federal Trade Commission (FTC) launched an investigation into the system used for rating video games, particularly what some saw as undeservedly low ratings that made the violent and sexually themed game "Grand Theft Auto" available to teens. Around the same time, a group of bipartisan senators proposed that the National Institutes of Health oversee a comprehensive $90 million study on the effects of violent media, including video games, on children's development.[55]

Recently, researchers C. L. Olson and D. W. Warner conducted focus groups with forty-two boys ages 12 to 14 to determine how children are influenced by violent interactive games. Boys, they found, typically used games to fantasize about power and fame, to work through angry feelings or relieve stress, and to explore and master what they perceived as exciting and realistic environments. The boys in this study group did not believe that they had been negatively impacted by violent games, although they were concerned that younger children might imitate game behavior, particularly swearing.[56]

Internet-Initiated Crimes

Internet access is easily available to nearly everyone in the United States today, but the Web has become a new frontier for innovative forms of cybercrime. One source of Internet-initiated crime is the supremacist and hate groups that target young people through the Web. In like manner, youthful perpetrators of violent crimes are sometimes influenced by information collected or contacts made on the Internet, and child sexual abuse, where initial contacts are made through the Web, now accounts for up to 4 percent of all arrests for sexual assaults against juveniles.[57] See Exhibit 8–1 for a discussion of Internet-initiated sex crimes against minors.

Gangsta Rap

Gangsta rap is a form of hip-hop music that some believe negatively influences young people by devaluing human life, the family, religious institutions, schools, and the justice system.[59] Gangsta rap, pioneered by Ice-T and other rappers influenced by Schoolly D's hard-core rap, portrays the lifestyles of inner-city gang members, and its lyrics relate stories of violence-filled lives. Guns play a prominent part in those lyrics and are frequently depicted as a means for attaining manhood and status.

Exhibit 8–1
Internet-Initiated Sex Crimes against Minors

The goals of the 2004 National Juvenile Online Victimization (N-JOV) Study were to survey police agencies within the United States in order to document and enumerate arrests for Internet-related sex crimes committed against minors and to describe the offenders' characteristics. One area studied was the availability of child pornography (CP) on the Internet; key findings follow:

- Law enforcement agencies made an estimated 1,713 arrests for Internet-related crimes involving the possession of child pornography during the twelve months beginning July 1, 2000.
- Almost all of those arrested for CP possession were male; 91 percent were white, and 86 percent were older than age 25. Only 3 percent were younger than age 18.
- Most arrestees had images of prepubescent children (83 percent) and images graphically depicting sexual penetration (80 percent).
- Approximately one in five arrested CP possessors (21 percent) had images depicting sexual violence involving children, such as bondage, rape, and torture.
- About 39 percent of those arrested were in possession of at least one video containing moving images of child pornography.
- Roughly 53 percent of the cases involving pornography came to the attention of the justice system as CP possession cases, 31 percent could be classified as cases of child sexual victimization, and 16 percent were cases involving Internet sexual solicitations of undercover investigators posing as children.
- CP possession cases originated at all levels of law enforcement, with 25 percent beginning in federal agencies, 11 percent in Internet Crimes against Children (ICAC) Task Forces (which were not yet fully operational during the time frame covered by the study), 60 percent in other state and local agencies, and 3 percent in other agencies such as international law enforcement.
- Of the arrested CP possessors, 40 percent were "dual offenders" who sexually victimized children and also possessed child pornography, with both crimes uncovered during the same investigation; an additional 15 percent were dual offenders who attempted to sexually victimize children by soliciting undercover investigators who posed online as minors.
- One in six investigations beginning with allegations or investigations of CP possession discovered dual offenders.
- In the overall N-JOV Study, 39 percent of arrested offenders who met victims online and 43 percent of offenders who solicited undercover investigators were dual offenders.
- Almost all arrested CP possessors (96 percent) were convicted or pleaded guilty, and 59 percent were incarcerated.
- Victims in these crimes were primarily thirteen- to fifteen-year-old adolescent girls who met adult offenders (76 percent of such offenders were older than age 25) in Internet chat rooms.
- The majority of offenders did not deceive victims about the fact that they were adults who were interested in sexual relationships.
- Most victims met and had sex with the adult offenders on more than one occasion, and half of the victims were described as feeling a close bond or being in love with the offenders.
- Almost all cases with male victims involved male offenders.
- Offenders used violence in 5 percent of the episodes recorded.[58]

CRITICAL THINKING QUESTIONS

■ *Why would an adolescent girl respond to an Internet solicitation and meet an adult who made it clear that he wanted to have a sexual relationship? Why would such a high percentage (half) develop a close relationship with the adult, with some of the victims describing themselves as "in love"? How are Internet-initiated sex crimes related to the failure of parents to assume responsibility for their children's well-being?*

Sources: Janis Wolak, David Finkelhor, and Kimberly J. Mitchell, *Child-Pornography Possessors Arrested in Internet-Related Crimes: Findings from the National Juvenile Online Victimization Study* (Washington, D.C.: National Center for Missing and Exploited Children), pp. vii–viii; and Janis Wolak, David Finkelhor, and Kimberly J. Mitchell, "Internet-Initiated Sex Crimes against Minors: Implications for Prevention Based on Findings from a National Study," *Journal of Adolescent Health* 35 (2004), p. 424.

Today's rap music has its origins in the hip-hop culture of young, urban, working-class African-Americans.[60] The subject matter of this music, which is available to children via television (especially MTV), the Internet, radio (including satellite radio), and retail CDs and DVDs, has created considerable controversy, with critics charging that the messages it espouses include misogyny, homophobia, racism, and materialism. Gangsta rappers usually defend themselves by pointing out that they are describing the reality of inner-city life and claim that when they are rapping, they are merely playing a character.[61]

Brown University Professor Tricia Rose's 2006 book *Hip-Hop Wars* claims that hip-hop is in crisis, because its lyrics are becoming increasingly saturated with themes involving thugs, pimps, black gangsters, and 'hos. She raises a number of important questions about hip-hop: Does hip-hop cause violence, or does it merely reflect a violent ghetto culture? Is hip-hop sexist, or are its detractors merely anti-sex? Does the portrayal of black culture in hip-hop undermine black social advancement? Rose calls for a more accurate reflection in the music of a richer cultural space, including anger, politics, and sex than the current images in sound and video provide.[62]

In summary, today's parents must face the reality that their children's minds are being bombarded with extensive disturbing stimuli. Violence permeates movies and TV screens; video games are no less violent, and the most popular ones among teenagers are probably the most violent. Supremacist and hate groups are targeting young people through their websites; the Internet offers opportunities for the sexual abuse of vulnerable adolescent males and females. Finally, gangsta rap is filled with violence, appears to devalue human life, and contains lyrics promoting homophobia, misogyny, racism, and materialism. Figure 8–7 summarizes the types of media and how they can influence adolescent behavior.

Neglect and Child Abuse

Neglect and **child abuse**, like the other family problems addressed in this chapter, have a profound influence on shaping the behavior and attitudes of adolescents and adults.[63] Various categories of child abuse and neglect, also referred to as *child maltreatment*, are identified in Table 8–1.

Cathy Spatz Widom's initial study of abuse and neglect found that 29 percent of those abused and neglected as children had a nontraffic criminal record as adults, compared with 21 percent of the control group.[64] Widom and Michael G. Maxfield's updated study, which followed 1,575 cases from childhood through adolescence and into young adulthood, was able to examine the long-term consequences of abuse and neglect[65]:

1. Being abused or neglected as a child increased the likelihood of arrest as a juvenile by 59 percent, as an adult by 29 percent, and for a violent crime by 30 percent.
2. Maltreated children were younger at the time of their first arrest, committed nearly twice as many offenses, and were arrested more frequently.

neglect
A disregard for the physical, emotional, or moral needs of children. Child neglect involves the failure of the parent or caregiver to provide nutritious food, adequate clothing and sleeping arrangements, essential medical care, sufficient supervision, access to education, and normal experiences that produce feelings of being loved, wanted, secure, and worthy.

child abuse
The mistreatment of children by parents or caregivers. Physical abuse is intentional behavior directed toward a child by the parent or caregiver to cause pain, injury, or death. Emotional abuse involves a disregard of a child's psychological needs. Sexual abuse is any intentional and wrongful physical contact with a child that entails a sexual purpose or component, and such sexual abuse is termed *incest* when the perpetrator is a member of the child's family.

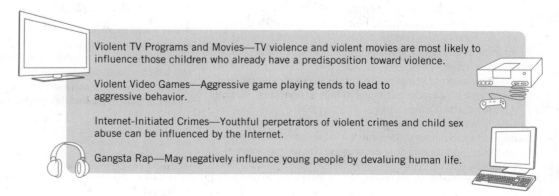

Violent TV Programs and Movies—TV violence and violent movies are most likely to influence those children who already have a predisposition toward violence.

Violent Video Games—Aggressive game playing tends to lead to aggressive behavior.

Internet-Initiated Crimes—Youthful perpetrators of violent crimes and child sex abuse can be influenced by the Internet.

Gangsta Rap—May negatively influence young people by devaluing human life.

FIGURE 8–7
Mass Media and Delinquent Behavior

TABLE 8–1
Definitions of Child Maltreatment and Severity Ratings

Types of Maltreatment	Brief Definition	Examples of Least and Most Severe Cases
Physical abuse	A caregiver inflicts a physical injury on a child by other than accidental means.	*Least*—Spanking results in minor brusing. *Most*—A child's injuries require hospitalization, cause permanent disfigurement, or lead to a fatality.
Sexual abuse	Sexual contact or attempted sexual contact occurs between a caretaker (or responsible adult) and a child for the purposes of the caretaker's sexual gratification or financial benefit.	*Least*—A child is exposed to pornographic materials. *Most*—A caretaker uses force to make a child engage in sexual relations or prostitution.
Physical neglect	A caretaker fails to exercise a minimum degree of care in meeting a child's physical needs.	*Least*—Food is not available for a child's regular meals, a child's clothing is too small, or a child is not kept clean. *Most*—A child suffers from severe malnutrition or severe dehydration due to gross inattention to his or her medical needs.
Lack of supervision or moral neglect	A caretaker does not take adequate precautions (given a child's particular emotional and developmental needs) to ensure his or her safety in and out of the home.	*Least*—An eight-year-old is left alone for short periods of time (e.g., less than three hours) with no immediate source of danger in the environment. *Most*—A child is placed in a life-threatening situation without adequate supervision.
Emotional maltreatment	Thwarting of a child's basic emotional needs (such as the need to feel safe and accepted) occurs persistently or at an extreme level.	*Least*—A caretaker often belittles or ridicules a child. *Most*—A caretaker uses extremely restrictive methods to bind a child or places a child in close confinement such as a closet or trunk for two or more hours.
Educational maltreatment	A caretaker fails to ensure that a child receives an adequate education.	*Least*—A caretaker allows a child to miss school up to 15 percent of the time when the child is not ill and there is no family emergency. *Most*—A caretaker does not enroll a child in school or provide any educational instruction.
Moral–legal maltreatment	A caretaker exposes a child to or involves a child in illegal or other activities that may foster delinquency or antisocial behavior.	*Least*—A child is permitted to be present for adult activities, such as drunken parties. *Most*—A caretaker causes a child to participate in felonies such as armed robbery.

Source: Adapted from Barbara Tatem Kelley et al., "In the Wake of Childhood Maltreatment," *Juvenile Justice Bulletin* (Washington, D.C.: U.S. Department of Justice, Office of Juvenile Justice and Delinquency Prevention, 1997), p. 4.

3. Physically abused and neglected (versus sexually abused) children were the most likely to be arrested later for a violent crime.

4. Abused and neglected females also were at increased risk of arrest for violence as juveniles and adults.

5. Abused and neglected white children were no more likely to be arrested for a violent crime than their nonabused and nonneglected white counterparts; in contrast, African American abused and neglected children showed significantly increased rates of violent arrests compared with African American children who were not maltreated.[66]

Extent and Nature of the Problem

The passage of legislation in all fifty states in the late 1960s requiring mandatory reporting of child abuse and neglect cases focused attention on abuse and neglect, as did the passage by Congress of the Child Abuse Prevention and Treatment Act and the establishment of the National Office on Child Abuse and Neglect in 1974. As an indication of the extent of

Web Extra 8–3
National Center for Missing and Exploited Children

Web Extra 8–4
Child Welfare Information Gateway

Voices of Delinquency 8-2
Read "A Small-Town Boy." How did his father's condition affect what happened to this young man? How did his mother affect what took place in his life? Are you surprised that he committed the crime he did?

Web Extra 8–5
Child Exploitation and Obscenity Section of the U.S. Department of Justice's Criminal Division

maltreatment of children, an estimated 3.3 million maltreatment referrals involving approximately 6 million children were made to child protective services (CPS) during fiscal year 2008. Of that number, 772,000 children were estimated to be victims.[67]

Victimization Statistics

The following figures are from a 2010 U.S. Department of Health and Human Services publication:

* More than 70 percent of child maltreatment victims experienced neglect.
* More than 15 percent were physically abused.
* Fewer than 10 percent were sexually abused.
* Fewer than 10 percent were psychologically maltreated.[68]

  See Figure 8–8 for victimization rates by maltreatment types.

  Younger children make up the largest percentage of victims. Nearly 33 percent of all victims of maltreatment were younger than 4 years of age, an additional 23.6 percent were ages 4 to 7, and 18.9 percent were ages 8 to 11 (see Figure 8–9 for ages of victims). Victimization was split almost evenly between the sexes: 51.5 percent of the victims were girls and 48.2 percent were boys. Nearly one-half (46.1 percent) of all victims were white, one-fifth (21.7 percent) were African American, and one-fifth (20.8 percent) were Hispanic.

  Child fatalities represent the most tragic consequences of maltreatment. These statistics were reported for 2008:

* An estimated 1,760 children died due to child abuse or neglect.
* The overall rate of child fatalities was 2.35 deaths per 100,000 children.
* More than 30 percent (31.9 percent) of child fatalities were attributed to neglect only, but physical abuse was also a major contributor to child fatalities.
* More than three-quarters (79.8 percent) of the children who died because of child abuse and neglect were younger than four years old.
* Infant boys (younger than one year) had the highest rates of fatalities at 19.31 deaths per 100,000 boys of the same age in the national population.
* Infant girls less than one year of age had a rate of 17.32 deaths per 100,000 girls of the same age.[69]

Perpetrators of Maltreatment

Web Extra 8–6
Institute on Violence, Abuse, and Trauma website

In 2008 nearly 80 percent of child maltreatment victims were abused by their parents, with another 6.5 percent abused by other relatives. Women comprised a larger percentage of perpetrators than men—56.2 percent compared to 42.6 percent. Nearly 75 percent of all perpetrators were younger than age 40.[70]

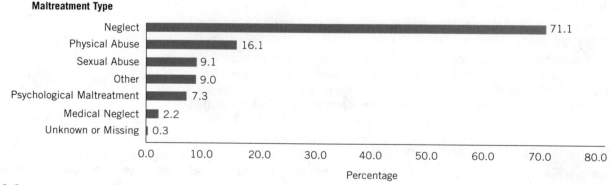

FIGURE 8–8
Child Victimization Rates by Maltreatment Type, 2008

Source: Children's Bureau, *Child Maltreatment 2008* (Washington, D.C.: U.S. Department of Health and Human Services, 2010), p. 27.

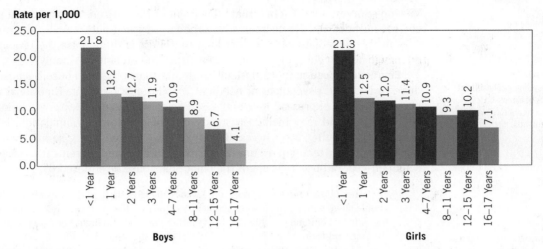

FIGURE 8–9
Child Maltreatment by Age and Sex
Source: Children's Bureau, *Child Maltreatment 2008* (Washington, D.C.: U.S. Department of Health and Human Services, 2010), p. 26.

Neglect

The word *neglect* generally refers to disregard for the physical, emotional, or moral needs of children or adolescents. The Children's Division of the American Humane Association established a comprehensive definition of neglect, stating that physical, emotional, and intellectual growth and welfare are jeopardized when a child can be described in the following terms:

- Malnourished, ill-clad, dirty, without proper shelter or sleeping arrangement
- Unsupervised, unattended
- Ill, lacking essential medical care
- Denied normal experiences that produce feelings of being loved, wanted, secure, and worthy (emotional neglect)
- Failing to attend school regularly
- Exploited, overworked
- Emotionally disturbed due to constant friction in the home, marital discord, or mentally ill parents
- Exposed to unwholesome, demoralizing circumstances.[71]

Defining neglect in legal or social terms, nevertheless, does not begin to capture an accurate picture of the neglected child. Such children must be seen if an observer is to realize the true hopelessness of their existence.[72] Newspapers frequently report the deaths of young children due to neglect or child abuse. As tragic as these cases are, however, Crosson-Tower asked, "But what happens to the children who survive? The babies abandoned on streets or in hospitals, children left unattended for days without food in filthy roach-infested apartments, or children brutally abused?"[73]

Child Abuse

There are several types of child abuse, including physical, emotional, and sexual abuse. The term *physical abuse* refers to intentional behavior directed toward a child by the parent or caretaker to cause pain, injury, or death.

Murray A. Straus has been one of the strongest proponents of defining corporal punishment as physical abuse. Straus examined the extent of physical abuse using data from a number of sources, notably the 3,300 children and 6,000 couples in the National Family

Web Extra 8–7
National Center for Children Exposed to Violence

emotional abuse
A disregard for the psychological needs of a child, including lack of expressed love, withholding of contact or approval, verbal abuse, unrealistic demands, threats, and psychological cruelty.

sexual abuse
The intentional and wrongful physical contact with a person, with or without his or her consent, that entails a sexual purpose or component.

incest
Any intrafamily sexual abuse that is perpetrated on a child by a member of that child's family group and that includes not only sexual intercourse but also any act designed to stimulate a child sexually or to use a child for sexual stimulation, either of the perpetrator or of another person.

▲ Jerry Sandusky, the former Penn State assistant football coach who was found guilty on 45 counts of child sexual abuse in 2012.

■ **Although cases involving sexual predators seem to appear in the news almost daily, national statistics show that the sexual abuse of children has declined significantly in the last decade or two. What might account for that decline?**

Violence Survey, and he found that 90 percent of U.S. citizens used physical punishment to correct misbehavior. He claimed that although physical punishment may produce conformity in the immediate situation, its long-run effect is to increase the probability of delinquency in adolescence and violent crime inside and outside the family.[74]

Emotional abuse is more difficult to define than physical abuse because it involves a disregard for the psychological needs of a child or adolescent. Emotional abuse encompasses a lack of expressed love and affection as well as deliberate withholding of contact and approval and may include a steady diet of put-downs, humiliation, labeling, name-calling, scapegoating, lying, demands for excessive responsibility, seductive behavior, ignoring, fear-inducing techniques, unrealistic expectations, and extreme inconsistency.[75] Randy, a sixteen-year-old boy, tells about the emotional abuse he suffered:

> My father bought me a baby raccoon. I was really close to it, and it was really close to me. I could sleep with it, and it would snug up beside me. The raccoon wouldn't leave or nothing. A friend of mine got shots for it. My father got mad one night because I didn't vacuum the rug, and there were seven or eight dishes in the sink. He said, "Go get me your raccoon." I said, "Dad, if you hurt my raccoon I'll hate you forever." He made me go get my raccoon, and he took a hammer and killed it. He hit it twice on the head and crushed its brains. I took it out and buried it.[76]

Nature of Child Abuse

Stephanie Amedeo and John Gartrell's study of 218 abused children found that the characteristics of parents, including being mentally ill and having been abused themselves when they were young, have the greatest ability to predict abuse. Their study also revealed that triggers or stressors, such as alcohol and drug use, often precipitate abuse.[77]

Research findings disagree concerning the age at which a child is most vulnerable to parental abuse. The National Incidence and Prevalence of Child Abuse and Neglect study found that the incidence of physical abuse increased with age.[78] David G. Gil found that half the confirmed cases of abuse involved children over six years of age and that nearly one-fifth were teenagers.[79] Yet while many adolescents may experience child abuse, the more serious cases still occur with infants and young children, who are more susceptible to injury; indeed, according to some researchers, three months to three years of age is the most dangerous period in a child's life.[80] Teenagers are more physically durable, are able to protect themselves better, and can leave the home if parents become too abusive.

Child abuse also seems to be more prevalent in urban areas than in suburban or rural settings. Urban areas having better resources to detect child abuse does not entirely explain why so many more cases are reported to urban police. Obviously, the congested populations and poverty of the city, which lead to other social problems, partly account for abuse being predominantly an urban problem.

The abusive situation is often characterized by one parent who is aggressive and one who is passive. The passive parent commonly defends the aggressive one, denies the realities of the family situation, and clings to the intact family and to the abusive partner. The passive parent behaves as though he or she is a prisoner in the relationship, condemned to a life sentence, and usually does not consider the option of separating from the aggressive partner because he or she is committed to the relationship, no matter how miserable the home situation may be.[81]

Children and adolescents may be victimized by either nonfamilial sexual abuse or incestuous sexual abuse. **Sexual abuse** of a child is intentional and wrongful physical contact with a child that entails a sexual purpose or component. Oral–genital relations, fondling of erogenous areas of the body, mutual masturbation, and intercourse are typical sexually abusive acts.[82]

Incest, according to the Office on Child Abuse and Neglect, is "intrafamily sexual abuse which is perpetrated on a child by a member of that child's family group and includes not only sexual intercourse, but also any act designed to stimulate a child sexually or to use a child for sexual stimulation, either of the perpetrator or of another person."[83] Incestuous sexual abusers may include a parent, grandparent, stepparent, sibling, aunt, uncle, or other member of the child's extended family. Nonfamilial sexual abusers may include any unrelated adult the child encounters outside the home (e.g., at school, church, recreational venues).

Recently, the number of sexual abuse cases substantiated by child protective service agencies in the United States underwent a dramatic 40 percent reduction between 1992 and 2000, with opinion being divided as to why the estimated annual incidence dropped from 150,000 to 89,500 cases. The trend has occurred in the majority of states; of forty-nine states, thirty-nine experienced a total decline of 30 percent or more in substantiated cases of sexual abuse from their peak year to 2004.[84]

Incest reportedly occurs most frequently between a biological father or stepfather and a daughter but also may involve brother and sister, mother and son, and father and son.[85] Father–daughter incest usually is a devastating experience for the girl and sometimes has lifelong consequences. Stepfathers also sexually victimize stepdaughters, but biological fathers appear to be involved in more cases of sexual abuse than are stepfathers. Angela Browne and David Finkelhor's review of the literature on sexual abuse revealed that abuse by fathers or stepfathers has a more negative impact than abuse by others and that experiences involving genital contact and force seem to result in more trauma for the victim.[86] The average incestuous relationship lasts about three and one-half to four years.[87] The completed act of intercourse is more likely to take place with adolescents than with younger children.

Helen, a sixteen-year-old, was sexually victimized by her father for three years, and she had great difficulty getting anyone to believe that her father was committing incest. When the father was finally prosecuted, she made this statement:

> When I was thirteen, my father started coming into my room at night. He usually did it when he was drinking. He would force me to have sex with him. I told my mother. I told my teachers at school. But nobody would believe me.[88]

Some evidence exists that **brother–sister incest** takes place more frequently than **father–daughter incest**, but its long-term consequences are usually less damaging because it does not cross generational boundaries and often occurs as an extension of sex play.[89] But brother–sister incest can have damaging consequences for the sister if the act is discovered and she is blamed for being sexually involved with her brother. If the girl feels she has been seduced or exploited, then the damage may be even greater.

Mother–son incest is less common and only rarely reported, largely because of the strong stigmas and taboos attached to the idea of sex between boys and their mothers.[90] Mother–son incest usually begins with excessive physical contact, which eventually becomes sexually stimulating. "Don't leave me" or "Don't grow up" messages are communicated to the son as the mother seeks ways to prolong physical contact with him by sleeping with him, bathing him, or dressing him.[91]

Father–son incest also is rarely reported, largely because it violates both the moral code against incest and the taboo against homosexuality. The stress of an incestuous relationship, as well as the threat to masculinity, often results in serious consequences for the boy when father–son incest does occur. Sons who are involved in father–son incest usually experience acute anxiety because they feel damaged, dirty, and worthless, and they may cope by retreating into their own world and losing contact with reality.[92]

The National Center on Child Abuse and Neglect has identified five factors that are usually present when father–daughter incest takes place: (1) the daughter's voluntary or forced assumption of the mother's role, (2) the parents' sexual incompatibility, (3) the father's reluctance to seek a partner outside the family unit, (4) the family's fear of disintegration, and (5) the unconscious sanctioning by the mother.[93]

Neglect, Child Abuse, and Delinquency

Research findings have revealed that a neglected or abused child is more likely to become involved in delinquency or status offenses. Neglect or abuse may have a negative impact on the emotional development of the child; it may lead to truancy and disruptive behavior in

brother–sister incest
Sexual activity that occurs between brother and sister.

father–daughter incest
Sexual activity that occurs between a father and his daughter. Also refers to incest by stepfathers or the boyfriend(s) of the mother.

mother–son incest
Sexual activity that occurs between a mother and her son. Also refers to incest by stepmothers or the girlfriend(s) of the father.

father–son incest
Sexual activity between father and son. Also refers to incest by stepfathers or the boyfriend(s) of the mother.

Voices of Delinquency 8–3
Read "A Sixteen-Year-Old Sexual Predator." Did this individual's sexual victimization contribute to his sexual deviancy? Do you believe that he belongs on a sex offender registry?

school or running away from home or may generate so much pain that alcohol and drugs are sometimes viewed as a needed escape. Neglect or abuse may cause so much self-rejection, especially in victims of incest, that these youths may vent their self-destructiveness through prostitution or may even commit suicide. Neglect or abuse may also create so much anger that abused youngsters later commit aggressive acts against others.

Emotional Trauma of Neglect and Child Abuse

Victims of neglect and child abuse often have low self-esteem, considerable guilt, high anxiety, mild to serious depression, and high internal conflict.[94] Physically, they may experience disturbances in sleeping patterns, weight loss or gain, or continual illnesses, and they also tend to have poor social relationships.[95] A longitudinal sample of five hundred juveniles confined to forty-eight correctional facilities in twenty states was assessed to examine the relationship between having been subjected to child maltreatment and experiencing anxiety and depression. The analysis revealed that confined youths who had experienced greater levels of child maltreatment had higher levels of both anxiety and depression and that higher levels of maltreatment were associated with increased depression over time.[96]

Runaways

Teenagers who have been abused frequently run away from home.[97] One sexually abused girl explained: "I never thought about where I was running to—only what I was running from."[98] **Running away** becomes a way of coping with the pain of neglect, physical abuse, and sexual abuse. The youth often sees running away as the only way to manage an unmanageable problem, or parents sometimes tell the child to get out because they want to rid themselves of the problems that the abusive situation has created. When abused adolescents are placed in foster homes, their running away may not stop because they often choose to reject their new family rather than risk the possibility of being rejected again. Unfortunately, sometimes children are removed from abusive homes only to experience abuse all over again in a foster home.

Disruptive and Truant Behavior in School

Several studies have found that neglected and abused children have greater difficulty in school than children who are not maltreated.[99] According to R. S. Kempe and C. H. Kempe, "Many of these children become academic and social failures almost immediately upon entering school."[100] Neglected and abused school-age children tend to have deficiencies in language development,[101] are more frequently placed in special education classes,[102] are more likely to be assigned to classes for children with disabilities,[103] have more learning problems,[104] are more disobedient and have greater difficulty accepting authority,[105] and have more conflict with peers.[106]

Drug and Alcohol Abuse

In an effort to blot out their pain and isolation, many abused children turn to drug and alcohol abuse.[107] Widom found that neglected and abused adolescent females were at increased risk for drug offenses,[108] and S. D. Peters found an association between sexual abuse and later alcohol abuse.[109] Richard Dembo and colleagues, in an examination of a sample of youths in a detention center, reported that sexual victimization had a direct effect on drug use, whereas physical abuse had an indirect and direct effect on drug use.[110] Abused children often feel they have nothing to lose by taking drugs; they are concerned only with forgetting their insecurity, anxiety, and lack of confidence. A type of loving and trusting relationship that they have never had with people before sometimes develops through drugs, so they can finally belong, experiencing closeness and security with peers who also take drugs.

Barbara L. Myers, former director of Christopher Street, Inc., and a victim of sexual abuse as an adolescent, tells why she turned to drugs:

> I was eleven years old when I first discovered that drugs could make the terrible world around me disappear. . . . When I was on drugs, I felt high, happy, and in control of my life. When I was high, I had peers; I finally belonged somewhere—in a group with other

running away
The act of leaving the custody and home of parents or guardians without permission and failing to return within a reasonable length of time; a status offense.

kids who took drugs. Whatever the others were taking, I took twice as much or more. I wasn't aware like the rest of them; I got high without worrying about how much I could handle or what it would do to me. It made me feel big and powerful because I didn't care what happened to me.

People said that taking too many drugs would burn out your brains. I used to think that I could become a vegetable if only I could succeed in burning out my brains. I wanted to be a vegetable. I used to picture myself as a head of lettuce. I used to look at mentally retarded people and think that they were so happy and didn't care about anything. I envied them because you could spit at them, and they would smile; they didn't seem to understand what hurt was.[111]

▲ Children playing in the South Bronx, New York City.

■ **What social and economic factors might lead to an increased incidence of child neglect?**

Sexual Behavior

A study of 535 young women who became pregnant as teenagers found that 66 percent had been sexually abused as children.[112] Considerable evidence shows that sexual abuse victims themselves often become involved in deviant sexual behavior; for example, promiscuity appears to be high among female sexual abuse victims.[113] Many female sexual abuse victims also become involved in prostitution,[114] and sexual abuse is frequently a part of the background of male prostitutes.[115] It is not surprising that female sexual abuse victims are attracted to prostitution, because they have come to see themselves as shamed, marked, and good only for delivering sex. The self-destructive aspect of prostitution serves as another way of expressing rage for never having been loved and for having been sexually and/or physically abused. In prostitution, sexual abuse victims take control by making strangers pay for sex. Detachment has already been learned in childhood; therefore, it is relatively easy for them to disassociate themselves from brief sexual encounters.[116] One recent study found that girls who experienced sexual abuse had more negative mental health, school difficulties, substance abuse, and risky sexual behavior as well as high rates of involvement with the juvenile justice system.[117]

Violence and Abuse

The idea that violence begets violence is firmly entrenched in the minds of both professionals and the general public. There is considerable support for the finding that abused and neglected male victims are more likely to express their anger in ways that hurt others, whereas female victims of mistreatment are more likely to become self-destructive.[118] There is also substantial support for the finding that those who have been abused or neglected in the past are more likely to abuse or neglect their children than those who have not experienced abuse or neglect. For example, in reviewing the research on family violence, Richard J. Gelles noted: "One of the consistent conclusions of domestic violence research is that individuals who have experienced violent and abusive childhoods are more likely to grow up and become child and spouse abusers than individuals who have experienced little or no violence in their childhood."[119]

Several studies have found a positive relationship between neglect and abuse and later violent criminal acts. Thornberry, using data from the Rochester Youth Development Study, found that 69 percent of youths who were maltreated as children reported later involvement in violence, compared to 57 percent of those who were not maltreated.[120] See Table 8–2 for the connection between child neglect and abuse and delinquency.

There is some evidence that childhood maltreatment that does not persist into adolescence has minimal correlation with adolescent delinquency.[121] The negative influence of severe maltreatment, such as sexual abuse by parents or caretakers, is commonly seen as carrying into adulthood and perhaps even throughout the life course. However, Peggy C. Giordano, Stephen A. Cernkovich, and Jennifer L. Rudolph's study of women across the life course is a reminder that female offenders who suffered extremely abusive childhoods can still have cognitive transformations as adults and can desist from criminal behaviors.[122]

> **TABLE 8–2**
> **The Connection Between Child Neglect and Abuse and Delinquency:**
> **Consequences of Abuse and Neglect**

- Victims of child abuse and neglect often show psychological damage.
- Victims of child abuse and neglect frequently run away from home.
- Some research supports that neglected and abused children have greater difficulty in school.
- Many abused and neglected children turn to drug and alcohol abuse.
- Evidence exists that sexual abuse victims themselves may become involved in deviant sexual behavior.
- Children who have experienced abusive and violent childhoods are likely to grow up and express violent behavior.

Child Abuse and the Juvenile Justice System

The term *child protective services* usually refers to services that are provided by an agency authorized to act on behalf of a child when parents are unwilling or unable to do so. In all states, these agencies are required by law to conduct assessments or investigations of reports of child abuse and neglect and to offer treatment services to families where maltreatment has taken place or is likely to occur.[123]

Although the primary responsibility for responding to reports of abuse and neglect rests with state and local child protective services agencies, the prevention and treatment of child maltreatment can involve professionals from many organizations and disciplines. Jurisdictions do differ in their procedures, but community responses to child maltreatment generally include the following sequence of events:

Identification

- Individuals who are likely to identify abuse are often those in a position to observe families and children on a regular basis. These include educators, medical professionals, police officers, social services personnel, probation officers, day-care workers, and the clergy. Family members, friends, and neighbors also may be able to identify abuse.

Reporting

- Some individuals—educators, child-care providers, medical and mental health professionals, social services providers, police officers, and clergy—often are required by law to report suspicions of abuse and neglect. Some states require such reporting by any person who has knowledge of abuse or neglect.

- Child protective services or law enforcement agencies generally receive the initial report of alleged abuse or neglect. This initial report may include the identity of the child and information about the alleged maltreatment, the parent or other caretaker of the child, the setting in which maltreatment took place, and the person making the report.

Intake and Investigation

- Protective services staff are required to determine whether the report constitutes an allegation of abuse or neglect and how urgently a response is needed. The initial investigation involves gathering and analyzing information about the child and family. Protective services agencies may work with law enforcement during this intake investigation.

- In some jurisdictions, a police officer always accompanies the social worker on the child abuse or neglect investigation to protect the social worker, to help if the parents become

▲ The U.S. Supreme Court building in Washington, D.C. In 2005, the Court considered the right of parents to be notified when their minor children seek abortions. The case, *Ayotte* v. *Planned Parenthood*, centered on New Hampshire's Parental Notification Prior to Abortion Act. The Court did not issue a definitive ruling and sent the case back to lower courts for further consideration.

■ **Should parents be notified when their minor children seek abortions?**

assaultive, to use legal authority to take the child out of an abusive home if necessary, to gather evidence and take pictures if admissible evidence is present, and to permit the social worker to focus on the family rather than being preoccupied with the legal investigation.

- Caseworkers usually respond to reports of abuse and neglect within two to three days. An immediate response is required if it is determined that the child is at imminent risk of injury or impairment. If the intake worker makes the decision that the referral does not constitute an allegation of abuse or neglect, the case may be closed. If there is substantial risk of serious harm to the child or lack of supervision, state law allows the child to be removed from the home.

- If the decision is to take the child out of the home, the juvenile court judge must be called for approval as soon as the social worker and police officer leave the house. If the child has been taken out of the home, a temporary removal hearing normally is held in the juvenile court within three to five days. At this hearing, the juvenile judge can decide to leave the child in the temporary placement—a foster home, youth shelter, or group home—or return the child to the parent(s).

- Following the initial investigation, the protective services agency usually draws one of the following conclusions: (1) There is sufficient evidence to support or substantiate the allegation of maltreatment or risk of maltreatment; (2) there is insufficient evidence to support maltreatment; or (3) maltreatment or the risk of maltreatment appears to be present, although there is insufficient evidence to conclude or substantiate the allegation. When sufficient evidence does not exist, additional services may be provided if it is believed that there is risk of abuse or neglect in the future.

Assessment

- Protective services staff are responsible for identifying the factors that contributed to the maltreatment and for addressing the most critical treatment needs.

Case Planning

- Case plans are developed by protective services, other treatment providers, and the family to alter the conditions and/or behaviors that result in child abuse or neglect.

Treatment

- Protective services and other treatment providers have the responsibility to implement a treatment plan for the family.

Evaluation of Family Progress

- After implementing the treatment plan, protective services and other treatment providers evaluate and measure changes in family behavior and conditions that led to child maltreatment. They also assess changes in the risk of maltreatment and determine when services are no longer required.

Case Closure

- Some cases are closed because the family resists intervention efforts and the child is seen as being at low risk of harm. Other cases are closed when it has been determined that the risk of abuse or neglect has been eliminated or reduced to the point that the family can protect the child from maltreatment without additional intervention.

- If the determination is made that the family will not protect the child, the child may be removed from the home and placed in foster care. If the decision is made that a child cannot be returned home within a reasonable time, parental rights may be terminated so that permanent alternatives can be found for the child.

Involvement of Juvenile or Family Court

- An adjudication (fact-finding) hearing is held if a petition of abuse or neglect has been filed by the department of social services. Juvenile courts hear about 150,000 child abuse and neglect cases a year. Usually present at the adjudication hearing are the assistant district, state, or county attorney; the youth and his or her attorney; the parents and their attorney; the social worker assigned to the case; and the police officer who conducted the investigation. After the evidence has been presented, the juvenile court judge decides whether the petition charging neglect or abuse has been substantiated; if it has, a disposition hearing is set for about four weeks later.

- States vary in the standard of proof needed to substantiate allegations of child abuse and neglect: six states rely on the caseworker's judgment; eighteen states, on some credible evidence; eleven states, on credible evidence; twelve states, on the preponderance of evidence; and three states have no official reporting means. About 30 percent of all child abuse and neglect reports in the country are substantiated, which varies somewhat by type of maltreatment and by state.[124] For example, in Massachusetts, allegations were confirmed in 55 percent of investigations in 2002, whereas in New Hampshire, only 9 percent were substantiated.[125]

Termination of Parental Rights

- In the most serious cases of child maltreatment, the state moves to terminate parental rights and to place a child for adoption. In 2000, parents of 64,000 children across the country had their parental rights terminated. However, not all terminations of parental rights resulted from child maltreatment; the overall rate of parental rights termination for substantiated child maltreatment cases is about 8 percent.[126]

Prosecution of Parents

- The prosecution of parents in criminal court depends largely on the seriousness of the injury to the child and on the attitude of the district, county, or state attorney's office toward child abuse. The cases most likely to be prosecuted are those in which a child has been seriously injured or killed and those in which a father or stepfather has sexually abused a daughter or stepdaughter. The most common charges in prosecutions are simple assault, assault with intent to commit serious injury, and manslaughter or murder. See Figure 8–10 for the sequence of events from child abuse to court processing.

Prevention of Delinquency in the family

Parental training and family-based intervention programs are now used as means of preventing delinquency in the family.

Parental Training

Parental training is consistently viewed as one of the most effective means of preventing delinquency and bringing treatment to young children who have conduct problems.[127] The most common form of parental training is Parent Management Training (PMT). This intervention teaches parents social learning techniques useful in shaping their children's behaviors. The goals of PMT are to improve parental control and monitoring as well as to improve the quality of the parent–child relationship. PMT programs can be implemented in a variety of formats and settings, which contributes to their accessibility and popularity.[128]

There are at least four promising model programs that work with adolescent and preadolescent juvenile offenders and use a parent-training component:

- *Functional Family Therapy (FFT):* This family-system approach focuses on the functions that problems serve within the family and for individual family members. Studies show that recidivism rates among youths participating in family systems and behavioral parent-training approaches are about half those of youths participating in client-centered relationship therapy, psychodynamic therapy, and no treatment comparison groups.

- *Multisystemic Therapy (MST):* This is a family- and home-based treatment model that is based on research demonstrating the multidimensional causes of delinquent behavior. MST is a highly individualized family- and community-based therapeutic approach that views behavior as the end product of the interactions among individuals with their interconnected systems: family, peer group, school, and community.

Identification
Those individuals who are likely to identify abuse.

Reporting
The initial report of alleged abuse or neglect is made to child protective services.

Intake and Investigation
The initial investigation involves gathering and analyzing information about the child and family.

The decision is made to support or substantiate the allegation of maltreatment or there is insufficient evidence to support the allegation.

A decision may be made to take the child out of the home.

Assessment
Protective services staff must identify the factors contributing to the maltreatment of the child and address the most critical needs.

Case Planning
Case plans are developed to alter the conditions and/or behaviors resulting in child abuse or neglect.

Treatment
Protective services are responsible for implementing a treatment plan.

Evaluation of Family Progress
After implementing the treatment plan, protective services evaluate and measure changes in family behavior and conditions that led to child maltreatment.

Case Closure
Some cases are closed because of progress in the home. Other times it is necessary to remove the child from the home.

Involvement of Juvenile or Family Court
Case is referred to the juvenile court, which hears about 150,000 cases a year.

Termination of Parental Rights
In serious cases, the state moves to terminate parental rights and to place a child for adoption.

Prosecution of Parents
The cases most likely to be prosecuted are those in which a child has been seriously injured or killed.

- *Adolescent Transitions Program (ATP):* This intervention has evolved into a school-based prevention program that targets family management practices and deviant peer influence.
- *Strengthening Families Program (SFP):* The program's seven-week curriculum includes parent-only sessions, family sessions, and child-only sessions. Studies at one and a half to four years after program completion reveal that, compared to control groups, the program produced substantial reductions in substance use, school truancy, conduct problems, and affiliation with antisocial peers. Culturally sensitive curriculums have been developed for use with Hispanic and African American populations.[129]

The leading problem in implementing parent-training programs has been the recruitment and retention of parents. Nonetheless, parent-training programs can be highly effective as a preventive measure in reducing later delinquency.[130]

Family-Based Intervention Programs

A number of family programs have identified themselves as being effective in the prevention of delinquency:

- *Nurse-Family partnership (NFP):* NFP is probably the most widely recognized of these programs. This program provides first-time, low-income mothers with family visitation from public health nurses. These nurses work with families in their homes during pregnancy and during the first two years of a child's life.[131]
- *Perry Preschool:* This preschool enrichment program provides high-quality education for disadvantaged children ages 3 to 4. The purpose of this program is to improve their capacity for future success in school as well as in life. A follow-up to age 27 reveals that those who received this enrichment experience had fewer arrests, including those for drug manufacturing and distribution offenses, and that significantly fewer of those who experienced this program were chronic offenders.[132]
- *PeaceBuilders:* Another program highlighted in the OJJDP Model Programs Guide, PeaceBuilders is a violence prevention program for elementary and middle schools. The program is designed to promote prosocial behavior among students and faculty. Children learn such principles as (1) praise people, (2) avoid put-downs, (3) seek people with good judgment as advisers and friends, (4) correct hurts that you cause, (5) right wrongs, and (6) help others.[133] Flannery and colleagues' study identified an 89 percent decrease in physical aggression and an 82 percent decrease in verbal aggression.[134]

Delinquency across the Life Course: Family-Related Risk Factors for Delinquency

With the emergence of the life-course perspective, there has been increased empirical and theoretical interest in the role played by family relations both in fostering and in protecting against delinquency and drug involvement. Studies have documented the family-related risk factors that increase delinquency propensity. Researchers have most frequently explored the impact on delinquency of the informal social control exercised by parents and within families.[135]

Michael R. Gottfredson and Travis Hirschi's self-control theory argues that the principal cause of individuals' low self-control is ineffective parenting. Ineffective parents are those who fail to monitor their children, to recognize deviant behavior when it takes place, and to punish such deviance. They are likely to have children who are low in self-control and therefore are more delinquent.[136] Carter Hay's findings from a sample of urban high school students generally supported Gottfredson and Hirschi's position, linking ineffective parenting, low self-control in children, and higher rates of delinquency.[137]

Some research has examined the links between corporal punishment and adolescent delinquent behavior or drug use. Ronald L. Simons and colleagues found that when parents engage in severe forms of corporal punishment coupled with the absence of parental involve-ment and warmth, children tend to feel angry and unjustly treated, resist parental authority, and are likely to become involved in delinquent behavior.[138] As mentioned earlier, Heimer also found that families who use coercive discipline merely teach their children that force and violence are appropriate tactics for solving problems; children thus learn definitions favor-able to violence, which encourages them to be more prone to violent delinquent behavior.[139]

Shannon E. Cavanagh, using a sample drawn from the National Longitudinal Study of Adolescent Health, found that family structure at adolescence best predicted later emo-tional distress and that family structure at adolescence, along with cumulative family insta-bility across childhood, best predicted current marijuana use.[140] Jennifer E. Lansford and colleagues, in a longitudinal study of 574 children followed from age 5 to age 21, found that individuals who had been physically abused in the first five years of life were at greater risk for being arrested as juveniles for violent, nonviolent, and status offenses. Moreover, physi-cally abused youths were less likely to have graduated from high school and more likely to have been fired in the past year, to have been a teenage parent, and to have been pregnant or to have impregnated someone in the past year while not married.[141]

Robert J. Sampson, John H. Laub, and Christopher Wimer followed a sample of five hundred high-risk boys from adolescence to age 32 and found that being married is as-sociated with an average reduction of about 35 percent in the odds of crime compared to a nonmarried status. The data consisted of criminal histories and dated records for all five hundred men along with personal interviews (using a life-history calendar), with a stratified subsample of fifty-two men who were followed to age 70. They concluded that "the results are robust, supporting the inference that the status of marriage causally [inhibits] crime over the life course."[142]

Delinquency and Social Policy: Child Maltreatment

Child maltreatment is a serious issue in the United States. This maltreatment can take place in a variety of contexts: from abusive or neglectful parents, from caretakers, from the Inter-net (in terms of child pornography), in the school, or even from religious leadership. We do know that some children are at greater risk of victimization than others:

- Children with allegations of multiple types of maltreatment were nearly three times more likely to be determined by authorities to be maltreated than were children with al-legations of physical abuse.

- Children reported to be victims of sexual abuse were about 71 percent more likely to be considered victims than children with allegations of physical abuse only.

- Children who were reported to be disabled were 68 percent more likely to be a victim of maltreatment than children who were not disabled.

- Children who were reported by educational personnel were twice as likely to be consid-ered maltreated as children reported by social and mental health personnel.

- Findings of victimization were inversely related to the age of a child. Children who were younger than four years old were most likely determined to be maltreated compared to all other age groups.[143]

We also know that child maltreatment can be an influential factor leading to such un-desirable outcomes as emotional trauma, running away, disruptive and truant behavior in school, drug and alcohol abuse, sexual behavior, and violence and abuse. The more serious the maltreatment of a child, the more likely it is that he or she will become involved in these behaviors, which can have such negative consequences on his or her life course. The abused child, if seriously abused, can even become involved in taking a parent's life.

To reduce the extent of child abuse and neglect in the United States, a number of strate-gies or interventions are needed. Widom recommended the following six principles:

1. "The earlier the intervention, the better."
2. "Don't neglect neglected children."

3. "One size does not fit all," which means that "what works for one child in one context may not work for a different child in the same setting, the same child in another setting, or the same child in another period in his or her development."

4. "Surveillance is a double-edged sword," meaning intervention agents must be sensitive to the possibilities of differential treatment on the basis of race or ethnic background and take steps to avoid such practices.

5. "Interventions are not one-time efforts."

6. "Resources should be accessible."[144]

THE CASE

The Life Course of Amy Watters, Age 13

After she left home, Amy spent almost a year on the run. During that time she didn't attend school and had no contact with her father. She lived under a highway overpass in a city about an hour away from her home with new "friends" that she had made. They were other kids who, like herself, had left home for one reason or another. During that time she became especially close to Damon, a fifteen-year-old boy who had left a Mormon family in Utah and spent his days earning a small income doing odd jobs for people who didn't ask about his background. Physical closeness had been natural, as staying warm at night meant snuggling up with Damon. After only a couple of nights, Amy found herself having sex. It quickly turned into a regular occurrence and Amy, who had begun menstruating a year earlier, became concerned that she would get pregnant. At the same time, she didn't want to disappoint Damon who seemed to greatly enjoy their encounters, and she soon learned to find pleasure in their nightly activities. Not long after they had pledged themselves to one another, however, Amy learned that Damon had begun to sell sexual services to men that he met by hanging around bars in the city's seedy downtown district. One of the men, Damon told her, wanted to take naked pictures of him and sell them on the Internet. The money was sure to be good, Damon said.

What is the likely relationship between Amy's early sexual activity and other forms of delinquency? Generally speaking, why might early sex and delinquency be associated with one another?

Learn More on the Web:
Some studies have shown that early sexual activity may lead teens into delinquency.

- Early Sex May Lead Teens to Delinquency: http://researchnews.osu.edu/archive/adoldel.htm
- Developmental Patterns in Exposure to Violence: http://justicestudies.com/developmental.pdf

Family issues such as inconsistent or lax supervision and various forms of abuse are some of the most studied links to juvenile delinquency. Researchers on the family believe that girls have stronger connections to the family than do boys throughout life. This connection can serve as a protective factor for girls, unless it is damaged or severed. For more information see the following sites:

- Women, Crime and Society: http://www.ncjrs.gov/App/abstractdb/AbstractDBDetails.aspx?id=85249
- In a Different Voice: http://courseweb.stthomas.edu/sjlaumakis/Reading%204-GILLIGAN.pdf

Follow the continuing story of Amy Watters in the next chapter.

SUMMARY

As this chapter notes, the family is the most important social institution in the lives of most young children. This chapter also makes some additional points:

- Studies of the relationship between the family and delinquency have generally concluded that the quality of life within the home is a more significant deterrent of delinquent behavior than the presence of both parents; that parental rejection is associated with delinquent behavior; and that inconsistent, lax, or severe discipline is associated with increased delinquency.

- Similar research concludes that delinquent behavior among children increases proportionately with the number of problems within the family. Divorced and single-parent families, blended families, births to unmarried women, alcohol and drug abuse, poverty, and violence are problems that some families encounter.

- Adolescents are exposed to a variety of seemingly negative media influences, including violent movies, TV shows, and video games; Internet pornography; and gangsta rap and other forms of music carrying violent themes.

- Research findings show at least a partial link between child abuse and neglect and delinquent behavior and status offenses.
- Children who have been neglected and abused may experience psychological problems, run away from home, become involved in truancy and disruptive behavior in school, and turn to drug and alcohol abuse.
- Some neglected and abused youngsters become involved in deviant sexual behavior and assume an aggressive stance toward others.

- In many cases of child maltreatment, authorities are reluctant to intervene unless severe physical injury, gross neglect, or sexual abuse can be demonstrated.
- The failure of a family to provide for the needs of its children can have an effect on the attitudes and behaviors of those children that can last into their adult years—and even for the rest of their lives.

KEY TERMS

birth order, p. 185
broken home, p. 184
brother–sister incest, p. 199
child abuse, p. 194
delinquent sibling, p. 185
emotional abuse, p. 198

family size, p. 185
father–daughter incest, p. 199
father–son incest, p. 199
incest, p. 198
mother–son incest, p. 199
neglect, p. 194

rejection by parents, p. 185
running away, p. 200
sexual abuse, p. 198
socialization, p. 184
supervision and discipline, p. 185
inconsistant

JUVENILE DELINQUENCY VIDEOS

Child Abuse

Child Abuse shows a family's interaction with the juvenile justice system dealing with child abuse. The father explains his side of the story; how does the social worker deal with the possibility of child abuse? Why does the social worker take custody of the other two children? When brought before the court, what programs must the parents attend in order to keep custody of the children? Based on the video and the readings, what types of treatment and programs are used to handle this type of delicate family situation? Discuss.

REVIEW QUESTIONS

1. How is the family the primary agent for the socialization of children?
2. What are the most serious problems facing the American family today? What are their effects on children?
3. What conditions within the family are more likely to result in delinquent behavior?
4. What is neglect? What are some examples of neglect within the home?
5. What are physical and emotional abuse? What are some examples of physical and emotional abuse within the home?
6. What is incest? What different kinds of incest exist? What type of father is most likely to become involved in incest?
7. How are child abuse and neglect related to status offenses and delinquent behavior?

DISCUSSION QUESTIONS

1. Why do you think children born in the middle of the birth order are more likely to exhibit delinquent behavior?
2. Some advocate such dramatic measures as revocation of parental rights, removal of children from the home, and even forced sterilization of parents convicted of felony abuse or neglect. What is your position on the issue?
3. What factors do you think contribute to the fact that the rate of maltreatment by mothers alone is more than twice the rate of fathers acting alone?
4. Do you agree with Strauss's contention that corporal punishment legitimizes violence in children? Explain your response.
5. If you were a social worker, how would you handle the emotional abuse case described in the story of Randy and his raccoon?
6. Would you support or oppose legislation designating sexual abuse committed by a foster care provider a more egregious offense than other forms of sexual abuse and calling for more severe penalties? (Remember that legislation on hate crimes has established precedent for such unique categorization of especially reprehensible offenses.)

GROUP EXERCISES

1. Have students research data for their city and state on teen pregnancies, births, and abortions. Use the findings to guide a class discussion.
2. Take an anonymous poll of your students to determine how many came from broken homes. Ask volunteers to relate how being from a broken home has affected their participation in or rejection of delinquent behavior.
3. (a) Have one student research his or her state's law regarding the parental right to impose corporal punishment. (b) Then ask how many students believe corporal

punishment is an appropriate way to discipline minor children and how many believe it is inappropriate. (c) Guide a discussion of the students' views on corporal punishment. During the discussion, have the lone researcher inform his or her classmates of what is permissible under state law.
4. Have the students read the case of the Menendez brothers, accessible at http://www.trutv.com/library/crime/notorious_murders/famous/menendez/index_1.html; then have students discuss the case.

NOTES

1. "Fed Up Mom Deals Peculiar Punishment to Troubled 14-Year-Old Son: Forces Her Boy to Wear a Sign on a Street Corner Naming His Many Wrongs," *CBS New York*, January 12, 2012, http://newyork.cbslocal.com/2-012/01/12/fed-up-mom-deals-peculaiar-punishment-to-trou8bled-14-year-old-son
2. Marvin D. Krohn, Susan B. Stern, Terence P. Thornberry, and Sung Joon Jang, "The Measurement of Family Process Variables: The Effect of Adolescent and Parent Perceptions of Family Life on Delinquent Behavior," *Journal of Quantitative Criminology* 8 (1992), p. 287. For these theories of delinquency, see Travis Hirschi, *Causes of Delinquency* (Berkeley: University of California Press, 1969); Marvin Krohn, "The Web of Conformity: A Network Approach to the Explanation of Delinquent Behavior," *Social Problems* 33 (1986), pp. 81–93; Gerald Patterson, *Coercive Family Process* (Eugene, Ore.: Castilia Press, 1982); and Terence Thornberry, "Toward an Interactional Theory of Delinquency," *Criminology* 25 (1987), pp. 863–92.
3. Kristin Y. Mack, Michael J. Lieber, Richard A. Featherstone, and Maria A. Monserud, "Reassessing the Family-Delinquency Association: Do Family Types, Family Processes, and Economic Factors Make a Difference?" *Journal of Criminal Justice* 35 (2007), pp. 51–67.
4. Krohn et al., "The Measurement of Family Process Variables." For studies supporting the proposition that family relationships and parenting skills are related to delinquency, see D. Elliott, D. Huizinga, and S. Ageton, *Explaining Delinquency and Drug Use* (Beverly Hills, Calif.: Sage, 1985); Walter R. Gove and R. Crutchfield, "The Family and Juvenile Delinquency," *Sociological Quarterly* 23 (1982), pp. 301–19; M. Krohn and J. Massey, "Social Control and Delinquent Behavior: An Examination of the Elements of the Social Bond," *Sociological Quarterly* 21 (1980), pp. 337–49; J. Laub and R. Sampson, "Unraveling Families and Delinquency: A Reanalysis of the Gluecks' Data," *Criminology* 26 (1988), pp. 355–80; R. Loeber and M. Stouthamer-Loeber, "Family Factors as Correlates and Predictors of Juvenile Conduct Problems and Delinquency," in *Crime and Justice: An Annual Review of Research*, edited by M. Tonry and

N. Morris (Chicago: University of Chicago Press, 1986), pp. 29–149; W. J. McCord, J. McCord, and Irving Zola, *The Origins of Crime* (New York: Columbia University Press, 1959); F. I. Nye, *Family Relationships and Delinquency Behavior* (New York: John Wiley, 1958); G. R. Patterson and T. J. Dishion, "Contributions of Families and Peers to Delinquency," *Criminology* 23 (1985), pp. 63–79; and M. D. Wiatrowski, D. B. Griswold, and M. K. Roberts, "Social Control and Delinquency," *American Sociological Review* 46 (1981), pp. 524–41.
5. Lawrence Rosen, "Family and Delinquency: Structure or Function," *Criminology* 23 (1985), pp. 553–73.
6. Abigail A. Fagan, M. Lee Van Horn, Susan Antaramin, and J. David Hawkins, "How Do Families Matter? Age and Gender Differences in Family Influences on Delinquency and Drug Use," *Youth Violence & Juvenile Justice* 9 (2011), pp. 150–70.
7. W. D. Morrison, *Juvenile Offenders* (London: T. Fisher Unwin, 1896); Sophonisba P. Breckenridge and Edith Abbott, *The Delinquent Child and the Home* (New York: Russell Sage Foundation, 1912); William Healy, *The Individual Delinquent* (Boston: Little, Brown, 1915); William Healy and Augusta Bronner, *Delinquents and Criminals: Their Making and Unmaking* (New York: Macmillan, 1926); and Ernest H. Shideler, "Family Disintegration and the Delinquent Boy in the United States," *Journal of Criminal Law and Criminology* 8 (January 1918), pp. 709–32.
8. Nye, *Family Relationships and Delinquent Behavior*; and R. A. Dentler and L. J. Monroe, "Social Correlates of Early Adolescent Theft," *American Sociological Review* 28 (1961), pp. 733–43.
9. Richard S. Sterne, *Delinquent Conduct and Broken Homes* (New Haven, Conn.: College and University Press, 1964); J. Toby, "The Differential Impact of Family Disorganization," *American Sociological Review* 22 (1957), pp. 505–12; T. P. Monahan, "Family Status and the Delinquent Child: A Reappraisal and Some New Findings," *Social Forces* 35 (1957), pp. 250–58; and T. P. Monahan, "Broken Homes by Age of Delinquent Children," *Journal of Social Psychology* 51 (1960), pp. 387–97.

10. Ross L. Matsueda and Karen Heimer, "Race, Family Structure, and Delinquency: A Test of Differential Association and Social Control Theories," *American Sociological Review* 52 (1987), pp. 826–40.

11. Marvin D. Free Jr., "Clarifying the Relationship between the Broken Home and Juvenile Delinquency: A Critique of the Current Literature," *Deviant Behavior* 12 (1991), pp. 109–67.

12. Annie E. Casey Foundation, *Kids Count Data Center, 2010,* htttp://datacenter.kidcount.org/data/acrossstates/Rankings .Aspx?ind=106.

13. W. D. Manning and K. A. Lamb, "Adolescent Well-Being in Cohabiting, Married, and Single-Parent families," *Journal of Marriage and Family* 65 (2003), pp. 876–83.

14. Ryan Schroeder, Aurea Osgood, and Michael Oghia, "Family Transitions and Juvenile Delinquency," *Sociological Inquiry* 80 (2010), pp. 579–606.

15. Sheldon Glueck and Eleanor Glueck, *Unraveling Juvenile Delinquency* (Cambridge, Mass.: Harvard University Press for the Commonwealth Fund, 1950); Nye, *Family Relationships and Delinquent Behavior*; and W. J. McCord, J. McCord, and Irving Zola, *The Origins of Crime* (New York: Columbia University Press, 1959).

16. Loeber and Stouthamer-Loeber, "Family Factors as Correlates and Predictors of Juvenile Conduct Problems and Delinquency."

17. Glueck and Glueck, *Unraveling Juvenile Delinquency.*

18. Nye, *Family Relationships and Delinquent Behavior*; Glueck and Glueck, *Unraveling Juvenile Delinquency*; McCord et al., *The Origins of Crime*; R. C. Audry, *Delinquency and Parental Pathology* (London: Methuen, 1960); Randy L. Lagrange and Helen R. White, "Age Differences in Delinquency: A Test of Theory," *Criminology* 23 (1985), pp. 19–45; Paul Howes and Howard J. Markman, "Marital Quality and Child Functioning: A Longitudinal Investigation," *Child Development* 60 (1989), pp. 1044–51; and Joan McCord, "Family Relationships, Juvenile Delinquency, and Adult Criminality," *Criminology* 29 (August 1991), pp. 11–23.

19. Glueck and Glueck, *Unraveling Juvenile Delinquency.*

20. John Paul Wright and Francis T. Cullen, "Parental Efficacy and Delinquent Behavior: Do Control and Support Matter?" *Criminology* 39 (2001), pp. 677–705.

21. Ronald L. Simons, Leslie Gordon Simons, Callie Harbin Burt, Gene H. Brody, and Carolyn Cutrona, "Collective Efficacy, Authoritative Parenting and Delinquency: A Longitudinal Test of a Model Integrating Community- and Family-Level Processes," *Criminology* (November 2005), pp. 989–1029.

22. Glueck and Glueck, *Unraveling Juvenile Delinquency.*

23. See Glueck and Glueck, *Unraveling Juvenile Delinquency,* pp. 91–92.

24. *America's Children in Brief: Key National Indicators of Well-Being 2010* (Washington, D.C.: Federal Interagency Forum on Child and Family Statistics, 2011).

25. Terence P. Thornberry, Carolyn A. Smith, Craig Rivera, David Huizinga, and Magda Stouthamer-Loeber, "Family Disruption and Delinquency," *Juvenile Justice Bulletin* (September 1999).

26. *America's Children in Brief.*

27. Ibid.

28. Ibid.

29. National Coalition for the Homeless, *Homeless Youth: NCH Fact Sheet #13* (Washington, D.C.: National Coalition for the Homeless, 2006).

30. Labor Force Statistics from the Current Population Survey, http0:P//www.bls.gov/web/empsit/cpseea36.htm.

31. Ibid.

32. Federal Bureau of Investigation, *Crime in the United States 2007* (Washington, D.C.: U.S. Department of Justice, 2008).

33. Michael Hershorn and Alan Rosenbaum, "Children of Marital Violence: A Closer Look at the Unintended Victims," *American Journal of Orthopsychiatry* 55 (April 1985), pp. 169–84. See also R. L. McNeely and Gloria Robinson-Simpson, "The Truth about Domestic Violence: A Falsely Framed Issue," *Social Work* 32 (November–December 1997), pp. 485–90.

34. Karen Heimer, "Socioeconomic Status: Subcultural Definitions and Violent Delinquency," *Social Forces* 75 (1997), pp. 799–833.

35. Child Welfare Information Gateway, *Foster Care Statistics 2010* (Washington, D.C.: Children Bureau, May 2012), p. 3

36. Ibid.

37. Joseph Drake, "Child Protection and Child Outcomes: Measuring the Effects of Foster Care," *American Economy Review* (2008), http://www.mit.edu/-jjdoyle/doyle_fosterIt_ march07_aer.pdf (accessed June 18, 2012).

38. American Academy of Child & Adolescent Psychiatry, *Facts for Families,* March 2011, http://ascap.org/page.ww?name= The+Adopted+Child&section+Facts+for+families (accessed June 18, 2012).

39. Ibid.

40. Ibid.

41. American Academy of Child & Adolescent Psychiatry, *Fact for Families: Children with Lesbian, Gay, Bisexual and Transgender Parents,* August 2011, http://www.aacap.org/ cs/root/facts_for_families_withlesbian_gay_bisexual_and_ transgender_parents (accessed June 18, 2012).

42. Ibid.

43. Ibid.

44. Jennifer Ludden, *Study: Are Cohabiting Parents Bad for Kids?,* August 16, 2011. http://wwwo.npr.org/2011/08/ 16/139651077/study-are-cohabiting-parents-bad-for-kids (accessed June 18, 2012).

45. John Guttsman has spent over thirty five years investigating this subject. See. www.gottman.com/49853/Research-FAQs .html.

46. Ibid.

47. Schroeder et al., "Family Transitions and Juvenile Delinquency," pp. 579–604.

48. Comments made by Mike Carlie in the *Into the Abyss: A Personal Journey into the World of Street Gangs,* Chapter 12. See http://www.faculty.missouristate.edu/M/ MichaelCarlie/what_I_learned_about/media.htm.

49. This is the general consensus of the vast amount of research done on this topic.

50. See Walter B. Miller, *The Growth of Youth Gang Problems in the United States: 1970–98* (Washington, D.C.: U.S. Department of Justice, Office of Juvenile Justice and Delinquency Prevention, 2001).

51. Gregory Zimmerman and Greg Pogarsky, "The Consequences of Parents' Underestimation and Overestimation of Youth Exposure to Violence," *Journal of Marriage and Family* 73 (2011), pp. 194–208.

52. *Experts Debate Effects of Violent Video Games*, September 26, 2005, http://homepage.mac.com/iajukes/blogwavestudio/LH20050626175144/ LHA2005092622.

53. Ibid.

54. Ibid.

55. Ibid.

56. C. L. Olson and D. W. Warner, "The Role of Violent Video Game Content in Adolescent Development: Boys' Perspectives," *Journal of Adolescent Research* 23 (2008), pp. 55–75.

57. CATTA, *Protecting Our Children against Internet Perpetrators* (Sonoma: Sonoma State University, California Institute of Human Services, 2006).

58. Adapted from Janis Wolak, David Finkelhor, and Kimberly J. Mitchell, *Child-Pornography Possessors Arrested in Internet-Related Crimes*: *Findings from the National Juvenile Online Victimization Study* (Washington, D.C.: National Center for Missing and Exploited Children), pp. vii–viii; and Janis Wolak, David Finkelhor, and Kimberly J. Mitchell, "Internet-Initiated Sex Crimes against Minors: Implications for Prevention Based on Findings from a National Study," *Journal of Adolescent Health* 35 (2004), p. 424.

59. Becky Blanchard, "The Social Significance of Rap and Hip-Hop Culture," *Edge: Ethics of Development in a Global Environment,* http://www.stanford.edu/class/e297c/poverty_prejudice/mediarace/socialsignificance.htm (accessed January 8, 2013).

60. Ibid.

61. Ibid.

62. Tricia Rose, *Hip-Hop Wars: What We Talk About When We Talk About Hip-Hop and Why It Matters* (Jackson, Tenn.: Basic Civitas Books, 2008).

63. Matthew T. Zingraff and Michael J. Belyea, "Child Abuse and Violent Crime," in *The Dilemmas of Punishment,* edited by Kenneth C. Haas and Geoffrey P. Alpert (Prospect Heights, Ill.: Waveland Press, 1986), pp. 49–53.

64. Cathy Spatz Widom, "Child Abuse, Neglect, and Violent Criminal Behavior," *Criminology* 27 (1989), pp. 251–71. See also Cathy Spatz Widom, *The Cycle of Violence* (Washington, D.C.: National Institute of Justice, 1992), p. 3.

65. Cathy S. Widom and Michael G. Maxfield, "An Update on the 'Cycle of Violence,'" *Research in Brief* (Washington, D.C.: National Institute of Justice, 2001).

66. Ibid. For other support for the relationship between abuse and neglect and later violent behavior, see Carlos E. Climent and Frank R. Erwin, "Historical Data on the Evaluation of Violent Subjects: A Hypothesis-Generating Study," *American Journal of Psychiatry* 27 (1972), pp. 621–24; Dorothy O. Lewis, Shelly S. Shanok, Jonathan H. Pincus, and Gilbert H. Glaser, "Violent Juvenile Delinquents: Psychiatric, Neurological, Psychological and Abuse Factors," *Journal of the American Academy of Child Psychiatry* 18 (1979), pp. 307–19; and Mark Monane, "Physical Abuse in Psychiatrically Hospitalized Children and Adolescents," *Journal of the American Academy of Child Psychiatry* 23 (1984), pp. 653–58.

67. Children Bureau, *Child Maltreatment 2008* (Washington, D.C.: U.S. Department of Health and Human Services, 2010), p. 27.

68. Ibid.

69. Ibid.

70. Ibid.

71. *In the Interest of Children: A Century of Progress* (Denver: American Humane Association, Children's Division, 1966).

72. Norman A. Polansky, Christine Deaix, and Shlomo A. Sharlin, *Child Neglect: Understanding and Reaching the Parent* (New York: Welfare League of America, 1972), pp. 21–52. See also Cynthia Crosson-Tower, *Understanding Child Abuse and Neglect* (Boston: Allyn and Bacon, 1999).

73. Crosson-Tower, *Understanding Child Abuse and Neglect.*

74. Murray A. Straus, "Discipline and Deviance: Physical Punishment of Children and Violence and Other Crime in Adulthood," *Social Problems* 38 (May 1991), pp. 103–23.

75. James Garbarino and Gwen Gilliam, *Understanding Abusive Families* (Lexington, Mass.: D. C. Heath, 1980).

76. Interviewed in May 1981.

77. Stephanie Amedeo and John Gartrell, "An Empirical Examination of Five Theories of Physical Child Abuse," paper presented at the Annual Meeting of the American Society of Criminology, Reno, NV, November 1989.

78. The National Incidence Study, *Third National Study of Child Abuse and Neglect* (Washington, D.C.: Child Welfare Information Gateway, 1996), pp. 1–10.

79. David G. Gil, *Violence against Children: Physical Abuse in the United States* (Cambridge, Mass.: Harvard University Press, 1970).

80. C. Henry Kempe et al., "The Battered-Child Syndrome," *Journal of the American Medical Association* 181 (July 1962), pp. 17–24; B. Fontana, *Somewhere a Child Is Crying: Maltreatment—Causes and Prevention* (New York: Macmillan, 1973); and R. Galdston, "Observations of Children Who Have Been Physically Abused by Their Parents," *American Journal of Psychiatry* 122 (1965), pp. 440–43.

81. Leontine Young, *Wednesday's Children: A Study of Child Neglect and Abuse* (New York: McGraw-Hill, 1964).

82. Blair Justice and Rita Justice, *The Broken Taboo: Sex in the Family* (New York: Human Sciences Press, 1979).

83. Ibid., p. 27.

84. David Finkelhor and Lisa M. Jones, *Explanations for the Decline in Child Sexual Abuse Cases* (Washington, D.C.: Office of Juvenile Justice and Delinquency Prevention, 2004).

85. For a more extensive discussion of the four types of incest possible within a family unit, see Crosson-Tower, *Understanding Child Abuse and Neglect*, pp. 155–62.

86. Angela Browne and David Finkelhor, "Impact of Child Abuse: A Review of the Research," *Psychological Bulletin* 99 (1986), pp. 66–77.

87. K. C. Meiselman, *Incest: A Psychological Study of Causes and Effects with Treatment Recommendations* (San Francisco: Jossey-Bass, 1978); and Christine A. Curtois, *Adult Survivors of Child Sexual Abuse* (Milwaukee, Wis.: Families International, 1993).

88. Interviewed as part of a court case with which the author was involved.

89. Justice and Justice, *The Broken Taboo.*

90. A. Nicholas Groth, "Patterns of Sexual Assault against Children and Adolescents," in *Sexual Assault of Children and Adolescents,* edited by Ann Wolbert Burgess, A. Nicholas Groth, Lynda Lytle Holmstrom, and Suzanne M. Sgroi (Lexington, Mass.: D. C. Heath, 1978).

91. Justice and Justice, *The Broken Taboo.*

92. Ibid.

93. Office on Child Abuse and Neglect, *Child Sexual Abuse.*

94. Eli H. Newberger and Richard Bourne, "The Medicalization and Legalization of Child Abuse," *American Journal of Orthopsychiatry* 48 (October 1977), pp. 593–607; and Straus, Gelles, and Steinmetz, *Behind Closed Doors: Violence in the American Family* (Garden City, NY: Anchor Books, 1981).

95. Garbarino and Gilliam, *Understanding Abusive Families.*

96. Angela R. Gover and Doris Layton MacKenzie, "Child Maltreatment and Adjustment to Juvenile Correctional Institutions," *Criminal Justice and Behavior* 30 (2003), pp. 374–96. See also Angela R. Gover, "Native American Ethnicity and Childhood Maltreatment as Variables in Perceptions and Adjustment to Boot Camps v. Traditional Correctional Settings," in *Rehabilitation Issues: Problems and Prospects in Boot Camps* (New York: Haworth Press, 2005), pp. 177–98; and Kimberly J. Mitchell, Michele Ybara, and David Finkelhor, "The Relative Importance of Online Victimization in Understanding Depression, Delinquency, and Substance Abuse," *Child Maltreatment* 12 (2007), pp. 314–24.

97. Meda Chesney-Lind, "Girls' Crime and Women's Place: Toward a Feminist Model of Juvenile Delinquency," paper presented at the Annual Meeting of the American Society of Criminology, Montreal, Canada, 1987; M. Geller and L. Ford-Somma, *Caring for Delinquent Girls: An Examination of New Jersey's Correctional System* (Trenton: New Jersey Law Enforcement Planning Academy, 1989).

98. *Incest: If You Think the Word Is Ugly, Take a Look at Its Effects* (Minneapolis: Christopher Street, 1979), p. 10.

99. For a review of these studies, see Diane D. Broadhurst, "The Effect of Child Abuse and Neglect in the School-Aged Child," in *The Maltreatment of the School-Aged Child,* edited by Richard Volpe, Margot Breton, and Judith Mitton (Lexington, Mass.: D. C. Heath, 1980), pp. 19–41.

100. R. S. Kempe and C. H. Kempe, *Child Abuse* (Cambridge, Mass.: Harvard University Press, 1978), p. 125.

101. Florance Blager and H. P. Martin, "Speech and Language of Abused Children," in *The Abused Child: A Multi-disciplinary Approach in Development Issues and Psychological Problems,* edited by H. P. Martin (Cambridge, Mass.: Ballinger, 1976).

102. D. F. Kline and J. Christiansen, *Educational and Psychological Problems of Abused Children* (Logan: Utah State University Department of Special Education, 1975).

103. H. P. Martin, "Neurological Status of Abused Children," in *The Abused Child,* edited by H. P. Martin (Cambridge, Mass.: Ballinger, 1976), pp. 67–82.

104. Ibid.

105. M. Halperin, *Helping Maltreated Children* (St. Louis, Mo.: C. V. Mosby, 1979).

106. Kline and Christiansen, *Educational and Psychological Problems.*

107. T. Houten and M. Golembiewski, *A Study of Runaway Youth and Their Families* (Washington, D.C.: Youth Alternatives Project, 1976); J. Streit, "A Test and Procedure to Identify Secondary School Children Who Have a High Probability of Drug Abuse," *Dissertation Abstracts International* 34 (1974), pp. 10–13; and Danya Glaser and Steven Frosh, *Child Sexual Abuse* (London, MacMillian Education, 1993).

108. Widom, "Child Abuse, Neglect, and Violent Criminal Behavior." See also Ilene R. Bergsmann, "The Forgotten Few: Juvenile Female Offenders," *Federal Probation* 53 (March 1989), p. 74.

109. S. D. Peters, "The Relationship between Childhood Sexual Victimization and Adult Depression among Afro-American and White Women," unpublished doctoral dissertation, University of California, Los Angeles, 1984.

110. Richard Dembo, Max Dertke, Lawrence La Voie, Scott Borders, Mark Washburn, and James Schmeidler, "Physical Abuse, Sexual Victimization and Illicit Drug Use: A Structural Analysis among High Risk Adolescents," *Journal of Adolescence* 10 (1987), pp. 13–34; and Rosie Teague, Paul Mazerolle, Margot Legosz, and Jennifer Sanderson, "Linking Childhood Exposure to Physical Abuse and Adult Offending: Examining Mediating Factors and Gendered Relationships," *Justice Quarterly* 25 (2008), pp. 313–48.

111. Barbara Meyers, "Incest: If you Think the World is Ugly, Take a Look at its Effects," in Barbara McComb Jones, Linda L. Jenstrom, and Kee MacFarlane, eds., *Sexual Abuse of Children: Selected Readings* (Washington, D.C.: National Center on Child Abuse and Neglect, 1980), p. 100.

112. Sarah Nordgren, "Experts Find Links between Teen Mothers, Sexual Abuse," *Waterloo Courier,* September 11, 1995.

113. David Finkelhor, *Sexually Victimized Children* (New York: Free Press, 1979).

114. J. James and J. Meyerding, "Early Sexual Experiences as a Factor in Prostitution," *Archives in Sexual Behavior* 7 (1977), pp. 31–42.

115. Justice and Justice, *The Broken Taboo.*

116. See *Incest: If You Think the Word Is Ugly,* p. 13.

117. Star Goodkind, Irene Nq, and Rosemary C. Sari, "The Impact of Sexual Abuse in the Lives of Young Women Involved or at Risk of Involvement with the Juvenile Justice System,"

Violence against Women 12 (May 2006), pp. 456–77. See also Melissa Jonson-Reid and Ineke Way, "Adolescent Sexual Offenders: Incidence of Childhood Maltreatment, Serious Emotional Disturbance, and Prior Offenses," *American Journal of Orthopsychiatry* 71 (January 2001), pp. 120–30.

118. Widom, "Child Abuse, Neglect, and Violent Criminal Behavior." See also Todd I. Herrenkohl, Cynthia Souse, Emiko A. Tajima, Roy C. Herrenkohl, and Carrie A. Moylan, *Trauma Violence Abuse* 9 (2008), pp. 84–99.

119. Richard J. Gelles, "Violence in the Family: A Review of Research in the Seventies," *Journal of Marriage and the Family* (November 1980), pp. 467–479.

120. Terence P. Thornberry, *Violent Families and Youth Violence* (Washington, D.C.: U.S. Department of Justice, 1994).

121. Timothy O. Ireland, Carolyn A. Smith, and Terence P. Thornberry, "Developmental Issues in the Impact of Child Maltreatment on Later Delinquency and Drug Use," *Criminology* 40 (May 2002), pp. 359–401.

122. Peggy C. Giordano, Stephen A. Cernkovich, and Jennifer L. Rudolph, "Gender, Crime, and Delinquency: Toward a Theory of Cognitive Transformation," *American Journal of Sociology* 107 (January 2002), pp. 1000–03.

123. The first part of the following section is modified from Howard N. Snyder and Melissa Sickmund, *Juvenile Offenders and Victims: 1999 National Report* (Washington, D.C.: Office of Juvenile Justice and Delinquency Prevention, 1999), pp. 43–44. See also David Finkelhor, Theodore P. Cross, and Elise N. Cantor, "How the Justice System Responds to Juvenile Victims: A Comprehensive Model, *Juvenile Justice Bulletin* (December 2005).

124. Finkelhor et al., "How the Justice System Responds to Juvenile Victims."

125. U.S. Department of Health and Human Services, Administration on Children, Youth, and Families, *Child Maltreatment 2002: Reports from the States to the National Child Abuse and Neglect Data System* (Washington, D.C.: U.S. Government Printing Office, 2004).

126. Children's Bureau, *The Adoption and Foster Care Analysis Reporting System Preliminary Report* (Washington, D.C.: U.S. Department of Health and Human Services, Administration on Children, Youth, and Families, 2001).

127. Carrie F. Mulford and Richard E. Redding, "Training the Parents of Juvenile Offenders: State of the Art and Recommendations for Service Delivery, *Journal of Child Family Studies* 17 (2008), pp. 629–48.

128. Ibid., p. 632.

129. Ibid, pp. 638–40.

130. Ibid., p. 643.

131. Sharon Mihalic, Katherine Irwin, Abigail Fagan, Diane Ballard, and Delbert Elliott, *Blueprints for Violence Prevention* (Washington, D.C.: Office of Juvenile Justice and Delinquency Prevention, 2004).

132. See OJJDP Model Programs Guide.

133. Ibid.

134. Ibid.

135. Timothy O. Ireland, Carolyn A. Smith, and Terence P. Thornberry, "Developmental Issues in the Impact of Child Maltreatment on Later Delinquency and Drug Use," *Criminology* 40 (May 2002), pp. 360–63. See also Robert J. Sampson and John H. Laub, "Crime and Deviance in the Life Course," in *Life-Course Criminology,* edited by Alex Piquero and Paul Mazerolle (Belmont, Calif.: Wadsworth/ Thompson Learning, 2001), pp. 21–42.

136. Michael R. Gottfredson and Travis Hirschi, *A General Theory of Crime* (Stanford, Calif.: Stanford University Press, 1990).

137. Carter Hay, "Parenting, Self-Control, and Delinquency: A Test of Self-Control Theory," *Criminology* 39 (August 2001), pp. 707–36.

138. Ronald L. Simons, Chyi-In Wu, Kuei-Hsui Lin, Leslie Gordon, and Rand D. Conger, "A Cross-Cultural Examination of the Link between Corporal Punishment and Adolescent Antisocial Behavior," *Criminology* 38 (January 2000), pp. 47–79.

139. Karen Heimer, "Socioeconomic Status, Subcultural Definitions, and Violent Delinquency," *Social Forces* 75 (1997), pp. 799–833.

140. Shannon E. Cavanagh, "Family Structure History and Adolescent Adjustment," *Journal of Family Issues* 29 (2008), pp. 944–80.

141. Jennifer E. Lansford, Shari Miller-Johnson, Lisa J. Berlin, Kenneth A. Dodge, John E. Bates, and Gregory S. Pettit, "Early Physical Abuse and Later Violent Delinquency: A Prospective Longitudinal Study," *Child Maltreatment* 12 (2007), pp. 233–45.

142. Robert J. Sampson, John H. Laub, and Christopher Wimer, "Does Marriage Reduce Crime? A Counterfactual Approach to Within Individual Casual Effects," *Criminology* 44 (2006), p. 20.

143. Children's Bureau, *Child Maltreatment 2004* (Washington, D.C.: U.S. Department of Health and Human Services, 2004).

144. Cathy Spatz Widom, "Child Victims: Searching for Opportunities to Break the Cycle of Violence," *Applied and Preventive Psychology*, Vol. 7, No. 4 (Winter 1998), pp. 225–234.

Chapter Objectives

After reading this chapter, you should be able to:

1. **Summarize the evolution of education in the United States.**
2. **Summarize the problems of vandalism, violence, and school bullying and the facts that influence these problems.**
3. **Explain the relationship between delinquency and school failure.**
4. **Summarize the major theoretical perspectives on the school experience and delinquency.**
5. **Summarize school students' rights.**
6. **Summarize the factors that influence students' tendency to drop out of school.**
7. **Summarize various school interventions that appear to have a positive impact on delinquency.**

If a child cannot go to school without fear of being raped, robbed, or even murdered, then nothing else the government does really matters.

—National Policy Forum

▲ Olympic Gold Medalist Claressa Shields prepares to walk through metal detectors during her first day as a high school senior at Northwestern High School in Flint, Michigan. Shields won the gold medal for Women's Middleweight boxing at the 2012 Summer Olympics in London.

■ **What can be done to make schools safer still?**

Introduction

On December 14, 2012, 20-year-old Adam Lanza fatally shot twenty young children and six adult staff members at the Sandy Hook Elementary School in the small city of Newtown, Connecticut. Before his killing rampage, Lanza had gone to his Newtown home and shot his 52-year-old mother, Nancy, to death. The weapons used in the school shooting, two pistols and a semi-automatic assault rifle, belonged to his mother and had been stolen from the house. Lanza committed suicide by shooting himself in the head as first responders arrived. He was later identified as an awkward kid who wore the same clothes almost every day (green shirt and khaki pants). He liked tinkering with computers and enjoyed playing violent video games.[1]

Prior to the Newtown shooting, the two most deadly school shootings had taken place on April 16, 2007, at Virginia Tech in which 33 people were killed, and at Columbine High School on April 20, 1999, in which 13 people died.

Schools have been the setting for some horrific shootings that have shocked the nation. Experts offer explanations for school killings which range from "merely an aberration," to a lack of impulse control in children today, to the breakdown of the family, to the abundance of guns in the hands of young people, and too much violence on television. Whatever their cause, school killings have focused attention on violence in school settings.

There is no question that an examination of delinquency in the United States must take a long look at the school experience. A longitudinal study conducted by J. Feldhusen, J. Thurston, and J. Benning found school relationships and experiences to be the third most predictive factor in delinquency, exceeded only by family and peer group relationships.[2] Delbert S. Elliott and Harwin L. Voss stated that "the school is the critical social context for the generation of delinquent behavior."[3] Arthur L. Stinchcombe believed that failure in school leads to rebelliousness, which leads to more failure and negative behaviors.[4] More recently, Eugene Maguin and Rolf Loeber's meta-analysis found that children with lower academic performance offend more frequently, commit more serious and violent offenses, and persist in their offending.[5]

In sum, there is considerable evidence that the school has become an arena for learning delinquent behavior. This chapter will look at the history of education in the United States, at the nature of crime in the schools, at different aspects of the relationship between the school setting and delinquent behavior, at the issue of students' rights, and at interventions used by some schools to prevent and control delinquency within school settings.

Brief History of American Education

The U.S. Constitution says nothing about public schools, but by 1850 nearly all of the northern states had enacted laws mandating free education. By 1918, education was both free and compulsory in nearly every state of the union. The commitment to public education arose largely from the growing need for a uniform approach to socialization of the diverse groups immigrating to this country. Joel H. Spring, a historian, writes of this movement:

> Education during the nineteenth century has been increasingly viewed as an instrument of social control to be used to solve the social problems of crime, poverty, and Americanization of the immigrant. The activities of public schools tended to replace the social training of other institutions, such as the family and church. One reason for the extension of school activities was the concern for the education of the great numbers of immigrants arriving from eastern and southern Europe. It was feared that without some form of Americanization immigrants would cause a rapid decay of American institutions.[6]

During most of the nineteenth century, U.S. schools were chaotic and violent places where teachers unsuccessfully attempted to maintain control over unmotivated, unruly, and unmanageable children through novel and sometimes brutal disciplinary methods.[7] For example, Horace Mann reported in the 1840s that in one school with 250 pupils, he saw 328 separate floggings in one week of five school days, an average of over 65 floggings a day.[8]

Widespread dissatisfaction with the schools at the turn of the twentieth century was one of the factors leading to the Progressive education movement. Its founder, John Dewey, advocated reform in classroom methods and curricula so students would become more questioning, creative, and involved in the process of their own education. Dewey was much more concerned about individualism and personal growth than rigid socialization.[9]

The 1954 U.S. Supreme Court decision that ruled racial segregation in public schools unconstitutional was a pivotal event in the history of American education—it obligated the federal government to make certain that integration in schools was achieved "within a reasonable time limit."[10] The busing of children to distant schools, which arose out of the Supreme Court decision and which has resulted in the shift from neighborhood schools, remains a hotly debated issue.

During the 1960s, open classrooms, in which the teacher served as a "resource person" who offered students many activities from which to choose, were instituted as an alternative to the earlier teacher-oriented classrooms. As was the case with the Progressive education movement, the concept of the open classroom was accepted more widely in private schools than in public schools.

The baby boom of the 1950s resulted in increased enrollments and more formalized student–teacher contacts in public schools in the 1960s and early 1970s. Public education also became more expensive in the 1970s, because the increasing numbers of children in the classroom meant that more equipment (including expensive items such as computers, scientific equipment, and audiovisual aids) had to be purchased. At the same time, teachers' unions took a firmer stance during contract talks, and many larger cities experienced teachers' strikes during this decade.

Since at least the mid-1980s, instead of optimism, dire warnings have been issued by all sides concerning the state of education. An expert on schools put it this way in 1984:

> American schools are in trouble. In fact, the problems of schooling are of such crippling proportions that many schools may not survive. It is possible that our entire public education system is nearing collapse. We will continue to have schools, no doubt, but the basis of their support and their relationship to families, communities and states could be quite different from what we have known.[11]

Figure 9–1 provides a timeline showing major issues that have faced American schools during the past two hundred years.

TIMELINE

1850	1896	1900	1918	1954
Nearly all of the northern states had enacted mandatory free education.	**John Dewey's** advocation of reforms led to the Progressive education movement.	**Schools were** chaotic and violent places where teachers used sometimes brutal measures to maintain control.	**Education was** both free and compulsory in nearly every state in the union.	**The U.S. Supreme Court** ruled racial segregation in public schools was unconstitutional.

1960s	1970s	1980s	2010s
Open classrooms in which teachers served as resource persons were instituted as an alternative to the teacher-oriented classrooms.	**Increased enrollments** and more formalized student-teacher contacts grew out of the baby boom.	**Public education** became more expensive.	**Dire warnings** began to be issued concerning the state of education.	**That American schools** are in trouble is an increasingly articulated position.

FIGURE 9–1
Major Issues American Schools Have Faced during Various Time Periods

School Crime

Crime in the schools, especially public schools, is a serious problem now facing junior and senior high schools across the nation. This high crime rate expresses itself through **vandalism**, **violence**, drug trafficking, and gangs. Vandalism and violence are examined in this section, and Chapters 10 and 11 will explore the difficulties that youth gangs and drugs bring to the school setting.

Vandalism and Violence

There are two major reasons why so much youth crime is taking place in our schools. First, while urban schools are frequently criticized for failing to provide safe, orderly environments, the communities around these schools suffer from serious levels of crime and disorder. Unsafe schools, in other words, are lodged within unsafe neighborhoods. The level of school crime and violence is also dependent on the community context because most of the students are members of the community. For example, if a community has a large number of adolescent drug dealers, runners, and lookouts; youth gang leaders and followers; chronically disruptive youths; and juvenile property offenders, then local schools are likely to have high rates of youth crime. Similarly, schools with little vandalism or violence are usually lodged in supportive communities that have low rates of criminal or delinquent behavior.[12]

Second, schools' authoritarian atmosphere and the likelihood of failure by many students, especially those with limited learning abilities, create bored, frustrated, dissatisfied, and alienated students. In one study, students consistently rated themselves as more bored in school than in any other setting.[13] The repressive methods of education, as Martin Gold noted, make school one of the most difficult experiences for adolescents in American society.[14] Urie Bronfenbrenner added that "the schools have become one of the most potent breeding grounds of alienation in American society."[15] Exhibit 9–1 lists recent indicators of school crime and safety.

vandalism
The act of destroying or damaging, or attempting to destroy or damage, the property of another without the owner's consent or destroying or damaging public property (except by burning).

violence
A forceful physical assault with or without weapons. It includes many kinds of fighting, rape, other attacks, gang warfare, and so on.

Exhibit 9–1
Indicators of School Crime and Safety

VIOLENT DEATHS AT SCHOOL
- From July 1, 2009, through June 30, 2010, there were seventeen homicides and one suicide of school-age youths (ages 5 to 18) at school.

NONFATAL STUDENT VICTIMIZATION
- In 2010, students ages 12 to 18 were victims of about 828,000 nonfatal crimes at school, including thefts and violent crimes.
- In 2010, more students ages 12 to 18 experienced total victimization (theft and violent crime) at school than away from school.
- In 2010, about 10 percent of male students in grades nine through twelve reported being threatened or injured with a weapon on school property in the past year, compared to 5 percent of female students.

NONFATAL TEACHER VICTIMIZATION
- A greater percentage of secondary school teachers (8 percent) reported being threatened with injury by a student than elementary school teachers (7 percent). However, a greater percentage of elementary school teachers (6 percent) reported having been physically attacked than secondary school teachers (2 percent).

SCHOOL ENVIRONMENT
- In 2009–2010, 85 percent of public schools reported one or more serious violent incidents, amounting to an estimated 1.9 million crimes. This figure translates into a rate of 40 crimes per one thousand students enrolled in 2009–2010.
- In 2009, 28 percent of public schools reported that student bullying was a daily or weekly problem, and 6 percent reported having been cyberbullied. A higher percentage of females (20 percent) than males (13.4 percent) reported being the subject of rumors in 2009, and a higher percentage of females (8 percent) than males (4 percent) reported being excluded from activities on purpose.
- During the 2009–2010 school year, 39 percent of public schools (about thirty-two thousand schools) took at least one serious disciplinary action against a student for specific offenses. Of the 433,800 serious disciplinary actions taken during the 2009–2010 school year, 74 percent were suspension for five days or more, 20 percent were transferred to

- specialized schools, and 6 percent were removed with no services for the remainder of the school year.
- Between the 1999–2000 and 2009–2010 school years, there was an increase in the percentage of public schools reporting the use of the following safety and security measures: controlled access to the building during school hours (from 75 to 92 percent); controlled access to school grounds during school hours (from 34 to 46 percent); faculty required to wear badges or picture IDs (from 25 to 63 percent); the use of one or more security cameras to monitor the school (from 19 to 61 percent); the provision of telephones in most classrooms (from 45 to 74 percent); and the requirement that students wear uniforms (from 12 to 19 percent).
- In 2009, a higher percentage of students ages 12 to 18 reported that they were afraid of attack or harm at school (4 percent) than away from school (3 percent) during the school year.

- In 2009, 29 percent of students ages 12 to 18 reported that street gangs were present at their school.
- The percentage of students in grades nine through twelve who reported that drugs had been offered, sold, or given to them decreased from 32 percent in 1985 to 23 percent in 2009.
- In 2009, about 9 percent of students ages 12 to 18 reported being targets of hate-related words at school and 29 percent of students reported seeing hate-related graffiti at school.

CRITICAL THINKING QUESTIONS

■ *Why do so many teachers feel unsafe in the school setting? What can be done to make public schools even safer?*

Source: Simone Robers, Jijun Zhang, Jennifer Truman, and Thomas D. Snyder, *Indicators of School Crime and Safety: 2011* (Washington, D.C.: U.S. Departments of Education and Justice, U.S. Government Printing Office, 2012), pp. iii–vi.

The need to establish a safe learning atmosphere is a serious issue in public education today. Schools have adopted a variety of measures, including suspensions, expulsions, corporal punishment, and increased law enforcement involvement, to establish a safer environment, which will be discussed in the next section.

In sum, it can be argued that schools are safer for children than other areas because children experience higher rates of violence away from school than they experience when they are at school (as well as coming to or leaving school). There has also been some decline in violence from 1992 to 2011. Yet students still experience high rates of disorder in some schools, especially public urban schools.[16] Students are more fearful of being attacked at school than away from school.[17] Some students avoid certain areas of their schools, and more students are faced with intimidation from bullies. Weapons, gangs, and drugs in schools are further indicators of school disorder.[18]

Library Extra 9–1
OJJDP Fact Sheet: *Overcoming Barriers to School Reentry*

Library Extra 9–2
Bureau of Justice Statistics (BJS) publication: *Indicators of School Crime and Safety*

bullying
The hurtful, frightening, or menacing actions undertaken by one person to intimidate another (generally weaker) person, to gain that person's unwilling compliance and/or to cause him or her to be fearful.

School Bullying

Bullying in school is a worldwide problem. Even though most of the research on bullying has taken place in Great Britain, Japan, and Scandinavian countries, it has been noted and discussed wherever formal schooling environments are found. Bullying consists of such direct behaviors as teasing, threatening, taunting, hitting, and stealing that have been initiated by one or more aggressive students against a weaker victim. In addition to such direct attacks, bullying may also be more indirect, causing a student to be socially isolated through intentional exclusion. Boys typically are involved in more direct bullying methods, whereas girls utilize more subtle strategies, such as spreading rumors and enforcing social isolation. Whether the bullying is direct or indirect, its key component is repeated physical or psychological intimidation that creates an ongoing pattern of harassment and abuse.[19] See Exhibit 9–2 for the story of nine adolescents who were charged after the suicide of a classmate.

According to 2010 bullying statistics, about 2.7 million students are bullied each year by about 2.1 students taking on the role of the bully. These bullying statistics further reveal that about one in seven students in grades kindergarten through twelfth grade is either a bully or has been a victim of bullying. A teen or child who has been bullied may in turn become the bully as a way to retaliate. Physical bullying increases in elementary school, peaks in middle school, and declines in high school; verbal abuse, on the other hand, tends to remain constant.[20]

▲ A teenage girl bullying another girl. Students report being more afraid of attacks at school than when they are away from school.

■ **What can be done to reduce such fears?**

Cyberbullying

cyberbullying
The use of the Internet and related technologies to harm other people, in a deliberate, repeated, and hostile manner.

Cyberbullying is a form of teen violence that can do lasting harm to young people. Cyberbullying involves using technology, such as cell phones and the Internet, to bully or harass another person. Cyberbullying can take many forms:

- Spreading rumors online or through texts
- Sending mean messages or threats to a person's e-mail account or cell phone
- Stealing a person's account information to break into his or her account and send damaging messages
- Posting hurtful or threatening messages on social networking sites or web pages
- Pretending to be someone else online to hurt another person
- Sexting, or circulating sexually suggestive pictures or messages about a person
- Taking unflattering pictures of a person and spreading them via cell phone or the Internet.[21]

Cyberbullying can lead to depression, anxiety, or suicide. Also, once things have circulated on the Internet, they may never disappear and, hence, can resurface at later times to renew the pain of cyberbullying.

Bullying and Suicide

Suicide continues to be one of the leading causes of death among children under the age of fourteen; "bullycide" is a term used to describe suicide as the result of bullying. And there is evidence that there is a strong connection between bullying, being bullied, and suicide.[22]

Bullying of Gay Teens

According to recent gay bullying statistics, gay and lesbian teens are two to three times more likely to commit suicide than other youths. About 30 percent of all completed suicides have been related to sexual identity crisis. Students who fall into the gay, bisexual, lesbian, or transgendered identity groups report being five times more likely to miss school because they feel unsafe after being bullied due to their sexual orientation. About 28 percent of these students claim that this is the reason they dropped out of school.[23]

Exhibit 9–2
Nine Adolescents Charged After Suicide of Classmate

In 2010, a prosecutor brought charges against nine juveniles at the South Hadley High School in western Massachusetts who subjected a classmate to relentless taunting and physical threats. This bullying, according to the prosecutor, led the freshman, Phoebe Prince, to hang herself from a stairwell at her home following school. In this case, of the nine charged adolescents, seven girls and two boys, ages 16 to 18, face a variety of felony charges including statutory rape, violation of civil rights with bodily injury, harassment, stalking, and disturbing a school assembly. Prince's family had recently moved to the United States from Ireland. Investigators found that the abuse took place in the school library, the lunchroom, and the hallways. Phoebe went to school officials, but she told a friend that no action was taken. This pattern of abuse included text messages, Facebook postings, threats, and efforts to corner Phoebe, whose actions were described as fearful, distraught, and panicked. She endured three months of it, and then hanged herself.

CRITICAL THINKING QUESTIONS

■ *Why do you think that school administrators did nothing about this ongoing abuse? Do you think that this lack of response is a typical response of school administrators? How frequently do you believe that students' lives are made miserable by bullies at school? What punishment do you believe the bullies in this case should receive?*

Source: Carlin DeGuerin Miller, "Phoebe Prince's Final Days: Bullied Girl Suffered 'Intolerable" Abuse before Suicide, Say Court Documents," http://www.cbsnews.com/8301-504083_162-20002132-504083.html (accessed February 13, 2012); Helen Kennedy, "Phoebe Prince, South Hadley High School 'New Girl,' Driven to Suicide by Teenage Cyber Bullies," *Daily-News*, March 29, 2010; and Erik Eckholm and Katie Zezima, "9 Teenagers Are Charged after Suicide of Classmate," *The New York Times*, March 30, 2010, A14.

Billy Lucas, age 15, of Greensburg, Indiana, hanged himself from the rafters of his family's barn; Seth Walsh, 13, of Tehachapi, California, hanged himself from a tree in his yard; Tyler Clementi, 18, a Rutgers University freshman, jumped off the George Washington Bridge in New York City; Asher Brown, 13, of Houston, Texas, shot himself in the head. What these teens had in common was that they had been bullied in school and apparently came to the same conclusion: if you are gay or thought to be gay, life just is not worth living.[24]

Bullying and School Shootings

There is some evidence that revenge for bullying is one of the strongest motivations for school shootings. A reported 61 percent of students said they believe students shoot others at school because they have been victims of physical violence at school or at home. [25]

Bullying and Student Disabilities

A further study found that students with mild disabilities were more likely to be perceived as bullies by both teachers and peers; in addition, teachers rated students with mild disabilities as being bullied by their peers significantly more often. Academically gifted students were seen by teachers as having the lowest rates of both bullying and being bullied.[26]

Bullying and Race

The data from a survey of 24,345 youths on the evidence of racial/ethnic differences in children's self-report of being a victim of bullying revealed that African American youths who were victimized tended to underreport being a victim of bullying.[27]

Web Extra 9–1
Anti-Bullying Network

Web Extra 9–2
Bullying.org

Video 9–1 Travis Hirschi

Delinquency and the School

Lack of academic achievement, low social status at school, school failure, and dropping out are factors frequently cited as being related to involvement in delinquency. This section looks at the first three factors, and dropping out is considered later in the chapter.

Academic Achievement

Considerable evidence indicates that, whether measured by self-report or by official police data, both male and female delinquency is associated with poor **academic performance** at school.[28] Travis Hirschi claimed that the causal chain shown in Figure 9–2 may eventually lead to delinquent behavior.[29] Numerous researchers have pointed out that delinquents' lack of achievement in school is related to other factors besides academic skills. For example, several studies have found that delinquents are more rejecting of the student role than are nondelinquents.[30] Delinquents' performance in school may be further affected by their relationships with classmates and teachers; several studies have concluded that the relationship between school performance and delinquency is mediated by peer influence.[31] Maguin and Loeber's meta-analysis of studies of academic performance and delinquency relationships found that children with lower academic performance committed more delinquent acts, committed more serious delinquent acts, and had a longer offending history than those with higher academic performance, an association that was stronger for males than for females and for whites than for African Americans, and that academic performance also predicted delinquent involvement independent of socioeconomic status.[32]

academic performance
Achievement in schoolwork as rated by grades and other assessment measures. Poor academic performance is a factor in delinquency.

Video 9–2 Albert K. Cohen

FIGURE 9–2
Hirschi's Causal Chain

Source: Adapted from Travis Hirschi, *Causes of Delinquency* (Berkeley: University of California Press, 1969), pp. 131–32, 156.

▲ A high school graduate with her mother after a Seattle ceremony.

■ **Studies have shown that delinquents tend to perform poorly at school. What factors contribute to poor school performance?**

Ann Arnett Ferguson spent three and a half years observing a middle school classroom in a western state and found that the classroom experience was anything but positive for many African American children.[33] However, Richard B. Felson and Jeremy Staff, using the National Education Longitudinal Study, concluded that academic performance and delinquency have a spurious relationship.[34]

Low Social Status

Albert K. Cohen's influential study of delinquent boys was one of the most comprehensive analyses ever undertaken of the role of the school in the development of delinquent subcultures. According to Cohen's theory, working-class boys (as discussed in Chapter 4) feel status deprivation when they become aware that they are unable to compete with middle-class youths in the school. Although avoiding contact with middle-class youths might solve the problem, working-class boys cannot do this because they are forced to attend middle-class schools established on middle-class values; consequently, they reject middle-class values and attitudes and form delinquent subcultures that provide them with the status denied in school and elsewhere in society.[35] Jackson Toby's study, based on a variation of Cohen's thesis, contended that a lower-class background makes school success difficult because lower-class youths lack verbal skills and encouragement from home.[36] John C. Phillips proposed steps by which low status in school can lead to deviant behavior (see Figure 9–3).[37] However, the proposed relationship between social class and delinquency in the school has been challenged. For example, one study found that any adolescent male who does poorly in school, regardless of class background, is more likely to become involved in delinquent behavior than one who performs well in school.[38]

In short, most of the evidence points to three conclusions: Lack of achievement in school is directly related to delinquent behavior, most delinquents want to succeed in school, and the explanations for poor academic achievement are more complex than lack of general aptitude or intelligence. Although the existence of a relationship between social class and delinquency in the school has mixed support, a relationship between school achievement and delinquency is much clearer.

School Failure

A number of statements can be made about the relationship between school failure and delinquency. First, it can be claimed that school failure is directly related to delinquency. Those adolescents who fail in school seek out peers who also are not succeeding in school. School failure brings disapproval from family and teachers. Second, school failure can create psychological problems with youth, and these negative feelings toward self are the real cause of the delinquent acts. Third, school failure and delinquency, it can be argued, share a common cause, such as poverty, drugs, family disruption, or gangs. Fourth, the school has a role in school failure. The school can contribute to student's alienation, and many have charged that school tracking—which is dividing students into groups according to achievement level and ability—has been a contributing cause of school failure.

The stories in the *Voices of Delinquency* mention the school only to say they were bored, got "high" in school, and were involved with gangs in the school setting. Boredom, of course, will result in alienation. As one youth said, who later committed a homicide when he was fifteen:

> Right about that time [turned nine and third grade] my grades started to get bad. I couldn't concentrate. I was bored. I was always daydreaming and asking to go to the bathroom, anything but my school work. I stopped doing my homework. Even when I tried, I couldn't concentrate for long. I was lectured and told to do better, but I just continued to do more of the same. I was lucky to receive a passing grade for the year.[39]

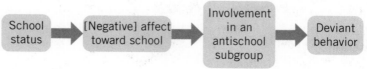

FIGURE 9–3
Phillips's Steps Leading to Deviant Behavior

School failure is one of the major contributing causes of dropping out of school, and the high rate of school dropouts is one of the most serious issues facing schools in the United States. School dropouts, as discussed later in this chapter, contribute to high rates of unlawful behaviors and delinquency across the life course.

Theoretical Perspectives on School and Delinquency

Most major theories of delinquency see the school as a factor contributing to delinquent behavior. Blocked opportunity theory, strain theory, cultural deviance theory, social control theory, labeling theory, radical criminology, general theory of crime, and interactionist theories all make contributions to understanding delinquency in schools.

The majority of studies focusing on blocked opportunity have found that those most likely to commit delinquent acts are young people who do poorly in school or who believe that they have little chance of graduation. Observers say that when youthful offenders are unable to perform satisfactorily in school, they become disruptive, decide to drop out, or are suspended—all of which further reinforces involvement in deviant behavior.[40] Strain theorists contend that youngsters from certain social classes are denied legitimate access to culturally determined goals and opportunities and that the resulting frustration leads to either the use of illegitimate means to obtain society's goals or the rejection of those goals. Strain theory views the school as a middle-class institution in which lower-class children are frequently unable to perform successfully; these youths then turn to delinquency to compensate for feelings of status frustration, failure, and low self-esteem.[41]

Cultural deviance theorists argue that children learn delinquent behavior through being exposed to others and by mimicking or modeling others' actions—children may come to view delinquency as acceptable because of their exposure to others whose definitions of such behavior are positive. Because schools tend to reflect the characteristics of the community of which they are a part, attending school in high-crime areas increases the likelihood of association with delinquent peers.[42]

Social control theorists believe that delinquency varies according to the strength of a juvenile's bond to the social order. Social control theorists also posit that the school is one of the major socializing institutions, providing youths with structure, incentives, expectations, and opportunities for social bonding, and that delinquency is likely to result when a strong bond to school does not develop.[43]

Labeling theorists argue that once students are defined as deviant, they adopt a deviant role in response to their lowered status. Early on, schools attach labels on the basis of achievement and behavior, and these labels may influence the subsequent treatment of youths. For example, when students are labeled as aggressive, difficult to manage, or slow learners at an early stage, they may be put in a slow track for the remainder of their schooling. According to labeling theorists, this differential treatment contributes to delinquent identities and behaviors.[44]

Some radical criminologists view the school as a means by which the privileged classes maintain power over the lower classes. Subjected to the controlling forces of the state, lower-class children are exploited as they experience powerlessness and alienation, and they are more likely than middle- and upper-class children to be placed in the lowest tracks, to receive poor grades, to be suspended for disciplinary reasons, and to drop out of school. According to radical theorists, lower-class children are essentially being trained to accept menial roles in the social order.[45]

In the general theory of crime, once self-control has formed in childhood, it affects adolescents in the choices they make in peer relations, school conduct and achievement, drug and alcohol use, and delinquent activities. Thus, students with self-control will be able to abstain from activities in school that would affect teachers' negative evaluations; from unwholesome peer relations in and out of school that would affect their desire to succeed, including gang participation; and from behaviors that would garner the attention of the police and juvenile justice system officials.[46]

Interactional theory, as developed by Thornberry and colleagues, is an integrated theory that can be applied to the school. It originally stated that attachment to parents and commitment to school are important buffers against delinquency, so adolescents who are

TABLE 9–1
Theoretical Perspectives on School and Delinquency

Blocked Opportunity Theory	Those most likely to commit delinquent acts are those who do poorly in school or who believe they have little chance of graduation.
Strain Theory	The school is viewed as a middle-class institution in which lower-class children are frequently unable to perform successfully, and they turn to delinquency to compensate for feelings of status frustration, failure, and low self-esteem.
Cultural Deviance Theory	Because schools tend to reflect the characteristics of the community of which they are a part, attending school in high-crime areas increases the likelihood of association with delinquent peers.
Social Control Theory	The school is seen as one of the major socializing institutions, providing students with structure, incentives, expectations, and opportunities for social bonding; delinquency is likely to result when a strong bond to school does not develop.
Labeling Theory	This theory argues that once students are defined as deviant, they adopt a deviant role in response to their lowered status.
Radical Criminology	Some radical criminologists view the school as a means by which the privileged classes maintain power over the lower classes.
General Theory of Crime	Students with self-control are able to abstain from activities in school that would attract them to delinquent behavior and that would gain the negative attention of teachers and the juvenile justice system.
Interactional Theory	Delinquency behavior reduces the strength of the bonds to family and school, thereby establishing a behavioral trajectory toward increased delinquency.

emotionally bonded to parents and who succeed at school are unlikely candidates for serious delinquency. Later versions of this theory have found that while weakened bonds to family and school do cause delinquency, delinquent behavior further reduces the strength of the bonds to family and school, thereby establishing a behavioral trajectory toward increasing delinquency.[47]

Another integrated theory related to the school is one developed by Wayne N. Welsh, Jack R. Greene, and Patricia H. Jenkins that draws on control theory, school climate theory, and social disorganization theory to examine the influence of individual, institutional, and community factors on misconduct in Philadelphia middle schools. One of the strong conclusions reached by these researchers is that the simplistic assumption that bad communities typically produce "bad children" or "bad schools" is unwarranted.[48] (See Table 9–1 for the theoretical perspectives of school and delinquency.)

Students' Rights

in loco parentis
The principle according to which a guardian or an agency is given the rights, duties, and responsibilities of a parent in relation to a particular child or children.

The school's authority over students comes from two principal sources: the concept of **in loco parentis** and state-enabling statutes.[49] E. Edmund Reutter, Jr., summarized *in loco parentis* as follows:

The common law measure of the rights and duties of school authorities relative to pupils attending school is the *in loco parentis* concept. This doctrine holds that school authorities stand in the place of the parent while the child is at school. Thus, school personnel may establish rules for the educational welfare of the child and may inflict punishments for disobedience. The legal test is whether a reasonably knowledgeable and careful parent might so act. The doctrine is used not only to support rights of school authorities ... but to establish their responsibilities concerning such matters as injuries that may befall students.[50]

State-enabling statutes authorize local school boards to establish reasonable rules and regulations for operating and keeping order in schools, which do not necessarily have to be in written form.[51] A classic statement on this type of authority was made in the 1966 case of *Burnside* v. *Byars*:

> The establishment of an educational program requires the formulation of rules and regulations necessary for the maintenance of an orderly program of classroom learning. In formulating regulations, including those pertaining to the discipline of schoolchildren, school officials have a wide latitude of discretion. But the school is always bound by the requirement that the rules and regulations must be reasonable. It is not for us to consider whether such rules are wise or expedient but merely whether they are a reasonable exercise of the power and discretion of the school authorities.[52]

The courts have become involved with schools in a number of important areas: procedural due process, freedom of expression, hair and dress codes, school searches, and safety.[53]

Procedural Due Process

Dixon v. *Alabama State Board of Education* (1961) was a major breakthrough for students' rights because the appeals court held for the first time that due process requires a student to receive notice and some opportunity for a hearing before being expelled for misconduct.[54] In 1969, the U.S. Supreme Court issued its far-reaching decision in *Tinker* v. *Des Moines Independent School District*, declaring that students do not shed their constitutional right of freedom of speech at the schoolhouse door. The issue that was involved in this case was whether students had the right to wear black armbands to protest the Vietnam War, and the Court ruled that school authorities did not have the right to deny free speech, even the expression of an unpopular view, unless they had reason to believe that it would interfere with the school operations.[55] In the 1986 *Bethel School District No. 403* v. *Fraser* case, the Court upheld a school system's right to suspend or discipline a student who uses profane or obscene language or gestures, reasoning that the use of lewd and offensive speech undermined the basic educational mission of the school.[56] In a 1988 decision, *Hazelwood School District* v. *Kuhlmeier*, the Court ruled that the principal could censor articles having to do with pregnancy and parental divorce in a student publication; the Court's majority justified this censorship because such publications were perceived to be part of the educational curriculum of the school.[57]

In January 1975, the U.S. Supreme Court took up the problem of **due process rights** in the schools, stating in *Goss* v. *Lopez* that schools may not summarily suspend students, for even one day, without following fundamentally fair fact-finding procedures.[58] In suspensions of ten days or less, a student is entitled to oral or written notice of the charges, an explanation of the evidence, and an opportunity to be heard. The *Wood* v. *Strickland* ruling, issued a month after the *Goss* decision, found that school officials may be subject to suit and held financially liable for damages if they deliberately deprive a student of his or her clearly established constitutional rights.[59]

The issue of corporal punishment came before the U.S. Supreme Court in the 1975 *Baker* v. *Owen* and *Ingraham* v. *Wright* cases.[60] Although *Baker* v. *Owen* merely affirmed a lower-court ruling, *Ingraham* v. *Wright* held that reasonable corporal punishment is not cruel and unusual punishment under the Eighth Amendment to the U.S. Constitution.[61]

due process rights
The constitutional rights that are guaranteed to citizens—whether adult or juvenile—during their contacts with the police, their proceedings in court, and their interactions with the public schools.

Freedom of Expression

Several court cases have defined students' rights to freedom of religion and expression in schools. In *West Virginia State Board of Education* v. *Barnette*, the Supreme Court held that students could not be compelled to salute the flag if that action violated their religious rights.[62] In *Tinker*, the wearing of black armbands was declared symbolic speech and therefore within the protection of the First Amendment.[63]

Hair and Dress Codes

Court cases testing the power of school administrators to suspend students for violations of hair and dress codes were widespread in the late 1960s and early 1970s. In *Yoo* v. *Moynihan*, a student's right to style his or her hair was held to be under the definition of the constitutional right to privacy[64]; then in *Richards* v. *Thurston*, the Court ruled that a student's right to wear long hair derived from his interest in personal liberty.[65] In *Crossen* v. *Fatsi*, a dress code prohibiting "extreme style and fashion" was ruled unconstitutionally vague and unenforceable as well as an invasion of the student's right to privacy.[66] Other decisions have held that schools cannot prohibit the wearing of slacks,[67] dungarees,[68] or hair "falling loosely about the shoulders."[69]

School Searches

The use of drugs and weapons is changing the nature of police–student relations in schools. In the 1990s, the police began to enforce the 1990 federal Gun-Free School Zones Act and increasingly, in communities across the nation, to enforce drug-free school zone laws. Drug-free zones usually include the school property along with the territory within a thousand-foot radius of its perimeter. Alabama has the most aggressive law in this nation: Territory within three miles of a school is declared drug free.[70]

school search
The process of searching students and their lockers to determine whether drugs, weapons, or other contraband is present.

The use of drug-sniffing dogs, Breathalyzers, hidden video cameras, and routine **school searches** of students' pockets, purses, school lockers, desks, and vehicles on school grounds appears to be increasing as school officials struggle to regain control over their schools. In some cases, school officials conduct their own searches; in other cases, the police are brought in to conduct the searches.

In the *New Jersey* v. *T.L.O.* decision (1985), the U.S. Supreme Court examined the issue of whether Fourth Amendment rights against unreasonable searches and seizures apply to the school setting.[71] On March 7, 1980, a teacher at Piscataway High School in Middlesex County, New Jersey, discovered two adolescent females smoking in a bathroom. He reported this violation of school rules to the principal's office, and the two females were summoned to meet with the assistant vice principal. When one of the females, T.L.O., claimed that she had done no wrong, the assistant principal demanded to see her purse; on examining it, he found a pack of cigarettes and cigarette rolling papers, some marijuana, a pipe, a large amount of money, a list of students who owed T.L.O. money, and letters that implicated her in marijuana dealing. T.L.O. confessed later at the police station to dealing drugs on school grounds.[72]

The juvenile court found T.L.O. delinquent and sentenced her to a year's probation, but she appealed her case to the New Jersey Supreme Court on the grounds that the search of her purse was not justified under the circumstances of the case. When the New Jersey Supreme Court upheld her appeal, the state appealed to the U.S. Supreme Court, which ruled that school personnel have the right to search lockers, desks, and students as long as they believe that either the law or school rules have been violated. The legality of a search, the Court stated, need not be based on obtaining a warrant or on having probable cause that a crime has taken place; rather, the legality of the search depends on its reasonableness, considering the scope of the search, the student's gender and age, and the student's behavior at the time.[73]

The significance of this decision is that the Supreme Court opened the door for greater security measures because it gave school officials and the police the right to search students who are suspected of violating school rules.[74] Of eighteen cases in the years 1985 through 1991 that were decided by state appellate decisions applying the *T.L.O.* decision, school officials' intervention was upheld in fifteen of them.[75]

In its 1995 *Vernonia School District 47J v. Acton* decision, the U.S. Supreme Court extended schools' authority to search by legalizing a random drug-testing policy for student athletes. This decision suggests that schools may employ safe-school programs, such as drug-testing procedures, as long as the policies satisfy the reasonableness test.[76]

In the 2002 *Board of Education of Independent School District No. 92 of Pottawatomie County v. Earls* decision, the U.S. Supreme Court reversed the judgment of the court of appeals and upheld the right of the school district to test students who participated in extracurricular activities; the Court found this to be a "reasonably effective means of addressing the School District's legitimate concerns in preventing, deterring, and detecting drug use by students."[77] The Court in Pottawatomie expanded the *Vernonia* decision by extending the drug testing of student athletes to the testing of students involved in extracurricular activities, which is an especially important issue, given the recent concern over steroid use on the part of professional, college, and high school athletes. See Figure 9–4.

- Investigating Incidents
- Identifying Suspects
- Controlling Campus Access
- Searching for Drugs and Weapons

FIGURE 9–4
The Changing Role of the School Resource Officer

Safety

Court-imposed limitations on schools concerning the rules under which youths can be disciplined (*Tinker*) and the requirements for procedural due process relating to school administrators taking disciplinary action (*Goss*, *Ingraham*, and others) have made local school authorities increasingly wary of using tough methods to discipline students. Principals have become reluctant, for example, to suspend youths for acts such as acting insubordinate, wearing outlandish clothing, loitering in halls, and creating classroom disturbances; only a few decades earlier, such conduct would have drawn a quick notice of suspension. Increased judicial intervention in the academic area has contributed to (though not caused) an increase in unruly behavior, thereby reducing the safety of students in the public schools.[78]

In sum, judicial intervention in schools during the past three decades has had both positive and negative impacts. Students' rights are less likely to be abused than in the past because the courts have made it clear that students retain specific constitutional rights in school settings. However, school administrators who perceive themselves as handcuffed by court decisions have become reluctant to take firm and forceful action against disruptive students, and violence and delinquency in the schools continue to be a problem. See Table 9–2 for a summary of landmark cases about students' rights and the following Evidence-Based Practice for a discussion of best practices in the school setting.

TABLE 9–2
Summary of Landmark Cases and Students Rights

Category of Rights	Name and Date of Case	Summary of the Case and Decision
Procedural Due Process	*Dixon v. Alabama State Board of Education* (1961)	This case specified that due process requires a student to receive notice and opportunity for a hearing before being expelled for misconduct.
Procedural Due Process	*Tinker v. Des Moines Independent School District* (1969)	The issue was whether students had the right to wear black armbands to protest the Vietnam War. The U.S. Supreme Court ruled that school authorities did not have the right to deny free speech, even the expression of an unpopular view, unless they had reason to believe that it would interfere with the school operations.
Procedural Due Process	*Bethel School District No. 403 v. Fraser* (1986)	The Court upheld a school system's right to suspend or discipline a student who uses profane or obscene language or gestures, reasoning the use of lewd and offensive speech undermined the basic educational mission of the school.
Freedom of Expression	*West Virginia State Board of Education v. Barnette* (1943)	Students could not be compelled to salute the flag if the action violated their religious rights.
Hair and Dress/Clothes	*Yoo v. Moynihan* (1969)	A student's right to style his or her hair was held to be under the definition of the constitutional right to privacy.

(Continued)

TABLE 9–2
Summary of Landmark Cases and Students Rights (*Continued*)

Category of Rights	Name and Date of Case	Summary of the Case and Decision
School Searches	*New Jersey* v. *T.L.O.* (1985)	School personnel have the right to search lockers, desks, and students as long as they believe that either the law or school rules have been violated. The significance of this decision is that the Supreme Court opened the door for greater security measures because it gave school officials and the police the right to search students who are suspected of violating school rules.
School Searches	*Vernonia School District 47J* v. *Acton* (1995)	Supreme Court extended schools' authority to search by legalizing a random drug-testing policy for student athletes. This decision suggests that schools may employ safe-school programs, such as drug testing procedures, as long as the policy satisfies the reasonableness test.
School Searches	*Board of Education of Independent School District No. 92 of Pottawatomie County* v. *Earls* (2002)	The Court reversed the judgment of the court of appeals and upheld the right to test students of the district who participated in extracurricular activities.

Evidence-Based Practice
Best Practice in the School Setting

Grover J. Whitehurst, as assistant secretary for educational research and improvement at the U.S. Department of Education, defined evidence-based education as "the integration of professional wisdom with the best available empirical evidence in making decisions about how to deliver instruction." Evidence-based education permits educators and family members to adapt to specific circumstances or environments in an area in which research evidence may be absent or incomplete. However, without at least some empirical evidence, education will be unable to resolve competing approaches, generate cumulative knowledge, and avoid fads and personal biases. The State Education Resource Center lists nine standards for evidence-based education:

- *1: A Clear and Common Focus.* In high-performing schools, administrators, teachers, students, and parents share and commit to clearly articulated and understood common goals based on the fundamental belief that all students can learn and improve their performance. There is clear evidence of school practices to support this belief.
- *2: High Standards and Expectations.* High-performing schools show evidence that each teacher believes "all students can learn and I can teach them." Staff members are dedicated to helping every student achieve challenging state and local standards. All students are engaged in an appropriately ambitious and rigorous course of study in which the high standards of performance are clear and consistent and the conditions for learning are modified and differentiated. This results in all students being prepared for success in the workplace, postsecondary education, and civic responsibilities.
- *3: Strong Leadership.* School leadership is focused on enhancing the skills, knowledge, and motivation of the people in the organization and creating a common culture of high expectations based on the use of skills and knowledge to improve the performance of all students. Leadership fosters a collaborative atmosphere between the school and the community while establishing positive systems to improve leadership, teaching, and student performance.
- *4: Supportive, Personalized, and Relevant Learning.* In high-performing schools, supportive learning environments provide positive personalized relationships for all students while engaging them in rigorous and relevant learning.
- *5: Parent/Community Involvement.* In high-performing schools, parents and community members help develop, understand, and support a clear and common focus on core academic, social, and personal goals contributing to improved student performance and have a meaningful and authentic role in achieving these goals. The school community works together to actively solve problems and create win–win solutions. Mentoring and outreach programs provide for two-way learning between students and community/business members.
- *6: Monitoring, Accountability, and Assessment.* In high-performing schools, teaching and learning are continually adjusted on the basis of data collected through a variety of valid and reliable methods that indicate student progress and needs. The assessment results are interpreted and applied appropriately to improve individual student performance and the instructional program.
- *7: Curriculum and Instruction.* High-performing schools have aligned curriculum with core learning expectations to improve the performance of all students. Students achieve high standards through rigorous, challenging learning. Staff delivers an aligned curriculum and implements research-based teaching and learning strategies. Students are actively involved in their learning through inquiry, in-depth learning, and performance assessments.
- *8: Professional Development.* Ongoing professional development aligned with the school's common focus and high

expectations to improve the performance of all students is critical in high-performing schools. These professional development offerings are focused and informed by research and school/classroom-based assessments. Appropriate instructional support and resources are provided to implement approaches and techniques learned through professional development.

• *9: Time and Structure.* High-performing schools are flexibly structured to maximize the use of time and accommodate

the varied lives of their students, staff, and community in order to improve the performance of all students. The structure of programs extends beyond the traditional school day and year as well as beyond the school building. The program draws on the entire community's resources to foster student achievement.

Source: State Education Resource Center, *Best Practices in Education* (Middletown, Conn.: State Education Resource Center) (website accessed, June 15, 2012).

The goal is for more states to meet these standards. As this chapter has repeatedly said, educational achievement and engagement, as well as school dropouts, have a significant effect on a youth's involvement in delinquency as well as crime in adult years. For example, using a sample of 4,147 delinquents released from Florida correctional institutions, Thomas Bloomberg and colleagues' analysis yielded two findings: (1) Youths with above-average academic achievement while incarcerated were significantly more likely to return to school postrelease, and (2) youths with above-average attendance in public school were significantly less likely to be rearrested within the one-year postrelease period. Although the academic gains were pronounced among African American males, the preventive effects of school attendance are similar across race and sex. What this suggests is that education can be part of a larger preventive effort that assists youthful offenders in successful community reentry.[79]

School Discipline

Both public and private schools have a responsibility to provide a safe environment for students and teachers and to promote an environment conducive to learning. It is sometimes necessary to discipline those students who endanger others or create a negative learning environment.

Security Measures

Schools typically have a number of security measures to address things such as fights on campus, vandalism, theft, drugs, alcohol, weapons, bomb threats, teacher safety, parking lot problems, fire alarms, and outsiders on campus. Each of these situations usually has a number of subsecurity measures associated with them. For example, counter-drug measures may include drug detection dogs, random searches, locker searches, vapor detection of drugs, and drug detection swipes.

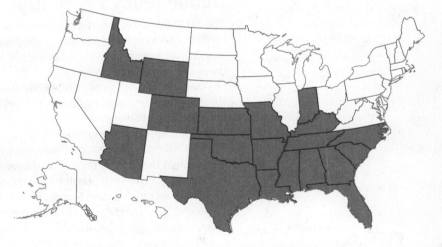

■ States that allow corporal punishment in schools

FIGURE 9–5
The Status of In-School Corporal Punishment in the States

Source: The Center for Effective Discipline, http://www.stophitting.com/index.php?page=statesbanning.

Corporal Punishment

An important discipline issue concerns whether a teacher or school official can legitimately inflict corporal punishment on a misbehaving child. By law, more than half of the states do not permit corporal punishment. Even so, the U.S. Supreme Court upheld the use of corporal punishment in public schools as a legitimate disciplinary measure.[80] Still, in those states that permit corporal punishment, school officials are understandably concerned about its use. (See Figure 9–5 for a state-by-state analysis of corporal punishment in schools).

Room Detention

After-school detention normally is served in one-hour increments and is held in a designated area. In general, students can be placed on after-school detention, which can typically be assigned by any staff member or substitute teacher. Classroom detention is usually assigned by a teacher and is to be served in a specific classroom. Saturday school, when it is held by a school, usually takes place in a study hall, generally for four hours.

Out-of-School Suspensions

Between 79 and 94 percent of schools have policies known as "zero tolerance"—the term that is given to a school or district policy that mandates certain punishments for various students' offenses.[81] In 2009–2010, California schools administered four hundred thousand out-of-school suspensions. In that school year, 7 percent of California schoolchildren and 18 percent of African American schoolchildren were suspended at least once. Students with disabilities were more than twice as likely to be suspended as students without disabilities. A 2011 study by the Council of State Government found that students who were suspended or expelled were at a higher risk of repeating a grade, coming into contact with the juvenile justice system, and dropping out of school.[82]

Expulsion from School

The main difference between suspension and expulsion is the amount of time that a student must stay out of school. A suspension may only last for a few days, but an expulsion can extend up to one year. The local board of education makes expulsion decisions and will usually appoint an impartial hearing officer when expulsion is being considered. Typical charges leading to expulsion are:

1. Possessing a gun or other deadly weapon on school grounds or at a school activity
2. Using a firearm or other deadly weapon to commit a crime off school grounds
3. Selling or attempting to sell illegal drugs, on or off school grounds.[83]

Delinquency Prevention

The OJJDP has reviewed a number of delinquency prevention programs in schools. These include alternative schools, mentoring, parent training, school classroom engagement, community awareness models, drug/alcohol therapy and education, truancy prevention, aftercare, and responsive classrooms.

One of the most promising of the interventions listed in the OJJDP's Program Guide is the Responsive Classroom approach, which is a multicomponent approach to instruction and classroom management designed to promote prosocial behavior and academic functioning in elementary school students. The approach was developed with the goals of increasing student investment, responsibility, and learning and decreasing problem behaviors. This approach is based on educational theories regarding the importance of learning as a social activity. That is, the Responsive Classroom program stresses the importance of how children learn with an emphasis on learning through interaction, of teachers getting to know the students and their families on a personal level, and of teaching social skills such as cooperation, responsibility, and self-control.[84]

The program's six components, developed by educators, concentrate on classroom organization, morning meetings, rules and consequences, academic choice, guided discovery, and communication with parents.

Evaluation Methodology

A pretest/post-test, quasi-experimental design was used to assess the program's effectiveness on students' social and academic functioning. A total of 301 ethnically diverse, urban students in grades one through five in two schools participated in the study. Participants came from a low-socioeconomic background in which 95.4 percent of the students qualified for reduced or free lunches. The treatment condition consisted of 253 students who were exposed to the Responsive Classroom approach (RC); the control condition included 48 students (drawn from a third school) who were not exposed to the program (NRC). To test the program's effectiveness, quantitative and qualitative teacher-, parent-, and student-rated indices were used. Dosage and fidelity to the program were attended to.

Evaluation Outcome

Three unpublished studies have evaluated the Responsive Classroom approach with white, African American, and Latino students from prekindergarten through sixth grade. In several studies of Responsive Classroom, the program was perceived to have a positive effect on increasing social skills and on limiting problem behaviors in students. The longest study included six months of the intervention. In this study, results indicate that the Responsive Classroom approach had a positive impact on students' social and academic behaviors. Teachers, parents, and students in the RC condition reported positive changes in the average frequency of social skills from fall to spring compared with NRC reports, which indicated virtually no change or a decrease in social skills during the same period.

Regarding academic improvement, scores on a basic skills test showed significantly greater improvement for the RC students. Furthermore, statistical analyses suggested that social skills may function as academic enablers for students. Teachers reported that they liked the approach and perceived it to be effective but found it difficult to implement. It was suggested that this approach takes time to learn to implement.

Delinquency across the Life Course: Factors Involved in Dropping Out of School

High school **dropout** rates have become a major issue in the United States, with one student in five dropping out of school prior to graduation. Today, nearly 5 million eighteen- to twenty-four-year-olds lack a high school diploma. In addition, the United States currently ranks twentieth out of twenty-eight industrialized democracies in high school graduation rates.[85] Students tend to drop out of school for four reasons, which are frequently interrelated: (1) academic failure, which involves failing courses; (2) disinterest in school, which often results in poor attendance; (3) problematic behavior inside or outside of the school setting that interferes with learning, and (4) life events, such as getting a job, becoming pregnant, or caring for an ill family member.[86]

dropout
A young person of school age who, of his or her own volition, no longer attends school.

One study that related the school to a life-course perspective was undertaken by Zengyin Chen and Howard B. Kaplan. Using a longitudinal panel data set collected at three developmental stages (early adolescence, young adulthood, and middle adulthood), Chen and Kaplan investigated how early school failure influenced status attainment at midlife, concluding that "early negative experiences set in motion a cascade of later disadvantages in the transition to adulthood, which, in turn, influences SES [socioeconomic status] attainment later in the life course."[87]

Wendy Schwartz analyzed information from the Educational Resource Information Center and determined the following:

- In the past twenty years, the earnings level of dropouts doubled while it nearly tripled for college graduates.
- Recent dropouts will learn $200,000 less than high school graduates and over $800,000 less than college graduates over the course of their lives.
- Dropouts comprise nearly half of the nation's prison population
- Dropouts comprise nearly half of all heads of households on welfare. [88]

Robert Sampson and John Laub have demonstrated that high school can be a turning point in an individual's life course (see Chapter 2).[89] Richard Arum and Irenee R. Beattie assessed the effects of high school educational experiences on the likelihood of adult incarceration.[90] Using event history analysis and the National Longitudinal Survey of Youth data, they found that high school educational experiences have a lasting effect on an individual's risk of incarceration. This study offered specifications of the high school context to identify how high school experiences can serve as a defining moment in an adolescent's life trajectory.[91]

Previous research has found that peer status in adolescence is positively associated with school achievement and adjustment. However, subculture theories of delinquency suggest that (1) disadvantaged boys frequently are able to gain some form of peer status through violence and (2) membership in violent groups undermines educational attainment. Data from the National Longitudinal Study of Adolescent Health were examined to see whether peer status within highly violent groups increases a male's risk of becoming a high school dropout. This study found that disadvantaged boys with high status in violent groups are at much greater risk of becoming high school dropouts than other students.[92]

Kimberly Henry and colleagues' 2012 article, using data from the Rochester Youth Development Study, found that school disengagement is a warning sign that is robustly related to dropping out as well as to serious problem behaviors across the developmental stages of middle adolescence, late adolescence, and early adulthood. In other words, school disengagement is a predictor of dropout, delinquency, and problem substance use during adolescence and early adulthood.[93]

In sum, dropping out of school has serious consequences for an adolescent that includes greater difficulty with gaining employment and lowered earnings, peer relationships, substance abuse, and delinquent behavior. Some evidence also exists that the effects of dropping out of school can affect an individual for the duration of his or her life.

Delinquency and Social Policy: The Most Promising Strategies in the School Setting

Several intervention strategies promise to benefit schools in the United States: improved quality of the school experience; increased use of mentors for students who are encountering difficulties or experiencing problems; greater use of alternative schools for students who cannot adapt to the traditional education setting; reduction of crime control and its punitiveness in public schools; development of a comprehensive approach to school success that includes home, school, church/synagogue, parents, and other institutions and persons who participate in school processes affecting students' lives; effective school-based violence prevention programs; and more effective programs to prevent dropping out of school.

Improving the Quality of the School Experience

Library Extra 9–3
Office of Community Oriented Policing Services (COPS) publication: *Bullying in Schools*

As mentioned earlier in this chapter, a close relationship exists between school performance and academic achievement, and later life consequences. Various studies have found that:

* Good teaching is one of the first lines of defense against misbehavior. Good teaching can make students feel wanted and accepted and can encourage students to have more positive and successful experiences in the classroom.
* Education must be oriented more toward the individual.
* Achievement should be defined in terms of a student's individual progress, not that of others in the class. This is particularly important for low achievers, who need the best facilities and the most effective teachers to allow them to realize their potential.
* Tracking systems, which classify students according to their ability, should be avoided as much as possible.
* Safety is one of the most important prerequisites of involvement in the educational system.

- Students have a right to be involved in the operation of the school. Youths too frequently see themselves as immersed in an educational system that is beyond their control and unresponsive to their needs.
- Finally, schools should adopt more flexible hours and schedules so that students can become oriented to the world of work.

Mentoring Relationships

In 2005, three million adults had formal one-to-one mentoring relationships with young people, an increase of 19 percent since 2002.[94] Youth development experts generally agree that mentoring is a critical component in a child's social, emotional, and cognitive development and that it has the potential to build a sense of industry and competency, boost academic performance, and broaden horizons.[95] School-based mentoring is one of the most promising types of youth mentoring taking place today and is experiencing rapid growth.

Alternative Schools

Disruptive behavior is a very serious problem in many of this nation's classrooms. School administrators often suspend or expel students who cause trouble[96]; however, a policy of swift suspension may stigmatize troublemakers as failures and reinforce their negative behaviors. **Alternative schools** are deemed a much more satisfactory way of dealing with young people whom public schools cannot control, or who are doing unsatisfactory work in a public school setting. The juvenile court sometimes requires disruptive students to attend an alternative school, but more frequently, students are referred by the public school system. In 2000–2001, 39 percent of public school districts had alternative schools and programs and served approximately 613,000 at-risk students in about 10,900 alternative schools and programs in the United States. In addition to dealing more effectively with disruptive students than the public school does, alternative schools tend to reduce absenteeism and dropout rates.[97]

Positive School–Community Relationships

In contrast to efforts at reducing delinquency in the school by investing in hardware and preventive technology, an alternative intervention strategy is the development of a comprehensive, or multicomponent, approach that includes home, school, and other persons and institutions that participate in the social processes affecting the students' lives. Delinquency and the quality of the public school experience, then, must be analyzed within the larger context of school–community relationships.[98]

School-Based Violence Prevention Programs

Schools, as this chapter has repeatedly stated, must be safe for students. They must feel safe, both on their way to school and on their way home from school. Students must be protected from victimization in any form, including bullying. It is inexcusable for teachers to avoid or fail to respond to students who are being violated in any way by others.

From Correctional Contexts to School Settings

A new priority in juvenile justice is an emphasis on the role of schools in the transition of juvenile offenders from institutional confinement to life in the community. When an institutionalized delinquent returns to the public school setting, there are potential problems, and the needs of juvenile offenders, fellow students, teachers, and the community must all be considered.[99]

Library Extra 9–4
OJJDP Fact Sheet: *Addressing the Problem of Juvenile Bullying*

Library Extra 9–5
OJJDP publication: *Juvenile Mentoring Program: A Progress Review*

Web Extra 9–3
National Education Association website, School Safety section

Web Extra 9–4
National Youth Violence Prevention Resource Center website

disruptive behavior
Unacceptable conduct at school. It may include defiance of authority, manipulation of teachers, inability or refusal to follow rules, fights with peers, destruction of property, use of drugs in school, and/or physical or verbal altercations with teachers.

alternative school
A facility that provides an alternative educational experience, usually in a different location, for youths who are not doing satisfactory work in the public school setting.

▲ A police dog checks student lockers for contraband. In an attempt to provide a safe learning environment, some schools have adopted stringent security measures, leading some critics to compare today's public schools to prisons.

■ **Are such strict measures necessary?**

Reduce the Number of High School Dropouts

A 2009 National Governors Association publication, *Achieving Graduation for All*, offers a number of action steps to establish a more effective dropout prevention and recovery agenda. The action steps are (1) promoting high school graduation for all, (2) targeting youth at risk of dropping out, (3) reengaging youth who have dropped out of school, and (4) providing rigorous, relevant options for earning a high school diploma.[100]

Reduction of the Crime Control Model in Public Schools

Despite decreases in student delinquency, student drug use, violent school victimization, and school-related deaths, formal social control has intensified in public schools during the past two decades. According to a recent article in the journal *Criminology*:

* Schools have become too much like prisons. Like prisons, many urban high schools have stark, impersonal architecture and drab interiors; humiliate the pupil whose behavior is unacceptable; insist on movement in lines; restrict movement within the building; and sometimes regulate personal appearance through dress codes.

* The need to establish a safe learning atmosphere is a serious issue in public education today, but the added security features of many public schools make them appear even more like prisons. Uniformed police are stationed in many schools; other schools have their own security staff. Some schools submit students to metal detector searches before they are allowed to enter. Electronically locked doors are appearing in more and more schools. Locker searches for drugs and weapons are everyday occurrences in many schools. Identification tags or photo ID badges for students and silent panic buttons for teachers are other means schools are using to regain control of the environment.[101]

* The crime control model is the guiding principle found in most urban public schools. The actions of rule-breakers and troublemakers are frequently defined with criminal justice language. Students are sometimes called "suspects" or "repeat offenders," and they are subjected to "investigations," "interrogations," and "searches by dogs" or by security who at times "need backup." Students may be placed on in-school suspension, which is related at least in part to solitary confinement. In fact, a thirteen-year-old boy in Georgia in 2008 hanged himself during an in-school suspension, in a "security room" that resembled a prison cell. Furthermore, out-of-school suspensions are compared to incarceration, expulsions are likened to execution, and zero tolerance policies function in the school equivalent of mandatory-minimum criminal sentencing sanctions.[102]

* A serious issue is that African American students are disciplined more frequently and more severely than others for similar behaviors. This practice seems to reflect how African American criminals are subjected to harsher criminal punishments than other offenders for similar crimes (although it may be impossible to control for all differences in background or extenuating circumstances in studies). Disadvantaged, urban schools with a greater African American, poor, and Hispanic student population seem to be more likely to respond to behavior in a punitive manner and less likely to respond in a restorative manner.[103]

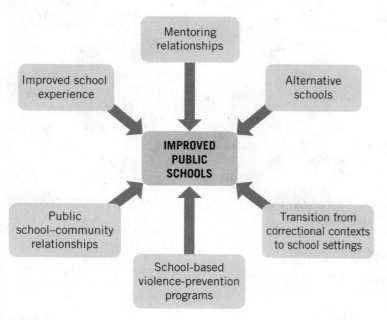

FIGURE 9–6
Intervention Strategies to Improve Schools

See Figure 9–6 for an overview of intervention strategies that can be used to improve schools.

The Case

The Life Course of Amy Watters, Age 14

Amy's life as a runaway came to an abrupt end on a cold February night, when Damon didn't come back to her as he normally did. Earlier, he had told her that he was going out on a "photo shoot," as he liked to call the time he spent posing for photographers pandering to portions of the gay community's desire for images of underage boys. Desperately cold and hungry, Amy made her way to a homeless shelter, where workers quickly identified her as a runaway and called social services workers. A lady with the Florida Department of Children and Families (DCF) interviewed Amy, determined her identity, and made a few phone calls to some of Amy's relatives. Following a hot meal and a one-night stay at the shelter, Amy was put on a bus for the two-hour trip to her Aunt Ellen's place. When she got there, Ellen was waiting at the bus station for her, and took her under her wing with many kind loving words. Ellen was Amy's father's sister, and after a few days spent with Ellen, Amy's father arrived to take her home.

Amy and her father never spoke about why Amy had run away, nor did the topic of the camera hidden in the mirror ever come up. Amy was thankful to get back to her own home and, after a night spent in her own bed, did a thorough search of her room for hidden viewing devices. Satisfied that there were none, she settled back into a somewhat normal routine and resumed her schooling.

Amy was now in junior high school, however, and the atmosphere at the school was far different from what it had been at the school she had left. Many of the students seemed haughty and boastful, while others were outright troublemakers. Very few students seemed concerned about their grades, and all of them hung in small gangs that didn't accept outsiders. Amy wasn't a member of any particular group, and she soon found herself being picked on by girls her own age that made fun of her on any pretext. One day they taunted Amy because of the clothes she wore, saying that they were "Walmart's finest." On another day, they criticized her looks, telling her that she was ugly and that it was a waste of renewable resources (a topic that was under study in class) having her on the planet. Amy felt socially isolated and soon became distraught. Although she wanted to, she was unable to concentrate on her studies until she remembered her experience of three years earlier when she had had to join a tough crowd in order to end the bullying to which she had been subjected. Given the sexual experience she had gained as a runaway, Amy found it easy to gain favor among the school's most admired athletes. With surprisingly little effort, Amy soon became the girlfriend of the football team's star running back, who people called CJ. CJ, who had failed his freshman year and was seventeen years old, had a rough-and-tumble personality that attracted Amy. "I was never the kind of person to play by the rules," he told her one day. "The more someone tells me not to do something the more I want to do it." The word soon went out on campus, "Don't nobody touch this girl; she belongs to CJ." In no time, the girls who had taunted Amy were seeking her attention.

How could the school environment have been better structured so as to protect Amy from bullying? Generally speaking, are there aspects of the high school environment that inadvertently contribute to (or support) delinquent activity?

Learn More on the Web:

- Toward Safe and Orderly Schools—The National Study of Delinquency Prevention in Schools: http://justicestudies.com//delinquency_in_schools.pdf
- School Discipline and Delinquency Prevention in Texas: http://www.texaspolicy.com/pdf/2011-SchoolDiscipline-CEJ-ml.pdf

Follow the continuing Amy Watters saga in the next chapter.

SUMMARY

The costs of delinquency in schools can be measured in lost future earnings, reduction of a sense of safety in the school environment, and disruption of school activities. This chapter also points out the following:

- Delinquent behavior can be best understood as the product of complex socialization processes operating at many different levels within the school system.

- A student's lack of school achievement appears to be directly related to the likelihood of his or her delinquent behavior.

- Court decisions have mandated provision of specific constitutional rights to students, such as free speech and due process, in the school environment.

- Some school administrators perceive themselves as being handcuffed by court decisions and are reluctant to take firm and forceful action against disruptive students.

The school has long been acknowledged as important in the socialization of children, but public education is facing many sharp criticisms today:

- Public schools are failing to effectively educate and properly socialize American youths.
- Since the 1970s, vandalism, violence, and drug trafficking have become serious problems in many schools.
- High rates of school crime create unsafe conditions and an unwholesome environment for learning.

For schools to improve, a number of changes need to take place:

- Elevating the quality of the school
- Reducing the effects of bullying
- Increasing the use of mentoring
- Providing more effective alternative school experiences for disruptive students
- Finding ways to renew urban schools
- Developing more positive school–community relationships
- Making schools safe from violence.

KEY TERMS

academic performance, 221
alternative school, 233
bullying, 219
cyberbullying, 220

disruptive behavior, 233
dropout, 231
due process rights, 225
in loco parentis, 224

school search, 226
vandalism, 218
violence, 218

REVIEW QUESTIONS

1. What crimes exist in public schools?
2. What factors are related to failure in school?
3. What theoretical explanations deal with delinquency and the school experience?

4. What rights do students have?
5. What interventions were mentioned that could be useful in reducing delinquency in the public schools?

DISCUSSION QUESTIONS

1. Although schools may well be avenues for learning delinquent behavior, that behavior likely does not include shooting or bombing as an acceptable response to ordinary conflicts. Where are today's youths learning that resorting to such violence is an appropriate course of action?
2. Were you victimized by a bully, or did you observe violence during your elementary or secondary schooling? Relate the incidents.
3. What are the consequences of vandalism and violence in public schools?

4. Is increased criminality among dropouts a predictable result as they confront the economic realities of their limited earning capacities?
5. Do you think a program designed to reduce bullying in schools would have any effect on school violence and victimization?
6. Do you believe the various theoretical perspectives discussed here are useful for explaining the relationship between schools and delinquency?

GROUP EXERCISES

1. Show the film *Bowling for Columbine*, and then have a discussion of the incident.
2. Have the students research material related to the February 2009 shooting death of a six-year-old classmate named Kayla Rolland in a Michigan elementary school; then discuss this incident, including the fact that the young shooter's father was a cocaine dealer.
3. Have the students research their county and state data on academic performance by adjudicated delinquents,

comparing those data to the data on students not adjudicated as delinquent.
4. Have students research their county and state dropout rates.
5. Have the class review the University of Colorado at Boulder's "Evaluation of School-Based Violence Prevention Programs," accessible at www.colorado.edu/cspv/publications/factsheets/school/violence/FS-SV08.html; then discuss the material.

NOTES

1. CBS, "Alleged Oakland School Shooter One L. Goh Pleads Not Guilty," http://www.cbsnews.com/8301-2-01_162-57424546/alleged-oakland-school-shooter-one-1-goh-pleads-not-guilty (accessed June 13, 2012).

2. John F. Feldhusen, John R. Thurston, and James J. Benning, "A Longitudinal Study of Delinquency and Other Aspects of Children's Behavior," *International Journal of Criminology and Penology* 1 (1973), pp. 341–351.

3. Delbert S. Elliott and Harwin L. Voss, *Delinquency and Dropout* (Lexington, Mass.: Lexington Books, 1974).

4. Arthur L. Stinchcombe, *Rebellion in a High School* (Chicago: Quadrangle Press, 1964).

5. Eugene Maguin and Rolf Loeber, "Academic Performance and Delinquency," in *Crime and Justice: A Review of Research*, edited by Michael Tonry (Chicago and London: University of Chicago Press, 1996), p. 145.

6. Joel H. Spring, *Education and the Rise of the Corporate State* (Boston: Beacon Press, 1972), p. 62.

7. Joan Newman and Graeme Newman, "Crime and Punishment in the Schooling Process: A Historical Analysis," in *Violence and Crime in the Schools*, edited by Keith Baker and Robert J. Rubel (Lexington, Mass.: Lexington Books, 1980), pp. 729–68.

8. Horace Mann and the Reverend M. H. Smith, *Sequel to the So-Called Correspondence between the Rev. M. H. Smith and Horace Mann* (Boston: W. B. Fowle, 1847).

9. John Dewey, "My Pedagogic Creed" (1897), reprinted in *Teaching in American Culture*, edited by K. Gezi and J. Meyers (New York: Holt, Rinehart, and Winston, 1968), pp. 408–11.

10. *Brown* v. *Board of Education of Topeka, Kansas* (1954), 347 U.S. 483.

11. John Goodlad, *A Place Called School* (New York: McGraw-Hill, 1984), p. 1.

12. Julius Menacker, Ward Weldon, and Emanuel Hurwitz, "Community Influences on School Crime and Violence," *Urban Education* 25 (1990), pp. 68–80.

13. Mihaly Csikszentmihalyi, Reed Larson, and Suzanne Prescott, "The Ecology of Adolescent Activities and Experience," *Journal of Youth and Adolescence* 6 (1977), pp. 281–94.

14. Martin Gold, "School Experiences, Self-Esteem, and Delinquent Behavior: A Theory for Alternative Schools," *Crime and Delinquency* 24 (1978), pp. 322–35.

15. Urie Bronfenbrenner, "The Origins of Alienation," *Scientific American* 231 (1973), p. 53.

16. For a discussion of school disorder, see Wayne N. Welsh, "Effects of Student and School Factors on Five Measures of School Disorder," *Justice Quarterly* 18 (December 2001), pp. 911–47.

17. This finding is from J. P. DeVoe, K. Kaufman, P. Ruddy, S. A. Miller, A. K. Planty, M. Snyder, T. D. Duhart, and M. R. Rand, *Indicators of School Crime and Safety: 2002* (Washington, D.C.: U.S. Departments of Education and Justice, 2002). For a discussion of students' fear, see Lynn A. Addington, "Students' Fear after Columbine: Findings from a Randomized Experiment," *Journal of Quantitative Criminology* 19 (December 2003), pp. 367–87.

18. For a discussion of weapons in school, see Pamela Wilcox and Richard R. Clayton, "A Multilevel Analysis of School-Based Weapons Possession," *Justice Quarterly* 18 (September 2001), pp. 510–39.

19. Ron Banks, "Bullying in Schools," *ERIC Digest*, http://www.ericdigests.org/1997–4bullying/bullying.htm.

20. *Bullying Statistics 2010,* http://www.bullyinstatistics.org/content/bullying-stgatistics-2010.htm

21. Ibid.

22. Ibid.

23. Ibid.

24. *Gay Bullying Statistics*, http://www.bullyingstatistics.org/content/gay-bullying-statgistics.htm.

25. Kenneth Miller, *Gay Teens Bullied to the Point of Suicide*, http://www.lhj.com/relationships/family/raising-kids/gay-teens-bullied-to-suicide (accessed June 17, 2012).

26. David B. Estell, Thomas W. Farmjer, Matthew J. Irvin, Amity Crowther, Patrick Akos, and Daniel J. Boudah, "Students with Exceptionalities and the Peer Group Context of Bullying and Victimization in Late Elementary School," *Journal of Child Family Studies* 18 (2009), pp. 136–50.

27. Anne L. Sawyer, Catherine P. Bradshaw, and Lindsey M. O'Brennan, "Examining Ethnic, Gender, and Developmental Differences in the Way Children Report Being a Victim of 'Bullying' on Self-Report Measures," *Journal of Adolescent Health* 43 (2008), pp. 106–14.

28. LaMar T. Empey and S. G. Lubeck, *Explaining Delinquency* (Lexington, Mass.: Lexington Books, 1971); M. Gold, *Status Forces in Delinquent Boys* (Ann Arbor: Institute for Social Research, University of Michigan, 1963); Martin Gold and D. W. Mann, "Delinquency as Defense," *American Journal of Orthopsychiatry* 42 (1972), pp. 463–79; T. Hirschi, *Causes of Delinquency* (Berkeley: University of California Press, 1969); H. B. Kaplan, "Sequel of Self-Derogation: Predicting from a General Theory of Deviant Behavior," *Youth and Society* 7 (1975), pp. 171–97; and A. L. Rhodes and A. J. Reiss Jr., "Apathy, Truancy, and Delinquency as Adaptations to School Failure," *Social Forces* 48 (1969), pp. 12–22.

29. Hirschi, *Causes of Delinquency*.

30. M. L. Erickson, M. L. Scott, and L. T. Empey, *School Experience and Delinquency* (Provo, Utah: Brigham Young University, 1964); R. J. Havighurst et al., *Growing Up in River City* (New York: John Wiley and Sons, 1962); W. Healy and A. F. Bronner, *New Light on Delinquency and Its Treatment* (New Haven, Conn.: Yale University Press, 1963); and W. C. Kvaraceus, *Juvenile Delinquency and the School* (New York: World Book Company, 1945).

31. J. David Hawkins and Denise M. Lishner, "Schooling and Delinquency," in *Handbook on Crime and Delinquency Prevention* (Westport, Conn.: Greenwood Press, 1987), pp. 23–54.

32. Maguin and Loeber, "Academic Performance and Delinquency."

33. Ann Arnett Ferguson, *Bad Boys: Public Schools in the Making of Black Masculinity* (Ann Arbor: University of Michigan Press, 2000). For other accounts with similar findings, see John D. Hull, "Do Teachers Punish According to Race?" *Time*, April 4, 1994, pp. 30–31; Minnesota Department of Children, Families, and Learning, *Student Suspension and Expulsion: Report to the Legislature* (St. Paul: Minnesota Department of Children, Families, and Learning, 1996); Commission for Positive Change in the Oakland Public Schools, *Keeping Children in Schools: Sounding the Alarm on Suspensions* (Oakland, Calif.: Commission for Positive Change in the Oakland Public Schools, 1992).

34. Richard B. Felson and Jeremy Staff, "Explaining the Academic Performance and Delinquency Relationship," *Criminology* 44 (2006), pp. 299–320.

35. Albert K. Cohen, *Delinquent Boys: The Culture of the Gang* (Glencoe, Ill.: Free Press, 1955).

36. Jackson Toby, "Orientation to Education as a Factor in the School Maladjustment of Lower-Class Children," *Social Forces* 35 (1957), pp. 259–66.

37. John C. Phillips, "The Creation of Deviant Behavior in American High Schools," in *Violence and Crime in the Schools*, edited by Keith Baker and Robert J. Rubal (Lexington, Mass.: Lexington Books, 1980), pp. 115–27.

38. Kenneth Polk and F. Lynn Richmond, "Those Who Fail," in *Schools and Delinquency* (Englewood Cliffs, N.J.: Prentice-Hall, 1972), pp. 59–69.

39. "The Thinker," story 21 of the *Voices of Delinquency*.

40. For this discussion, see LaMar T. Empey, Mark C. Stafford, and Carter H. Hay, *American Delinquency: Its Meaning and Construction* (Belmont, Calif.: Wadsworth, 1999), p. 195.

41. Cohen, *Delinquent Boys*.

42. Walter B. Miller, "Lower-Class Culture as a Generating Milieu of Gang Delinquency," *Journal of Social Issues* 14 (1958), pp. 5–19.

43. Hirschi, *Causes of Delinquency*. See also Kevin M. Beaver, John Paul Wright, and Michael O. Maumem, "The Effects of School Classroom Characteristics on Low Self-Control: A Multilevel Analysis," *Journal of Criminal Justice* 36 (2008), pp. 174–81.

44. Edwin M. Lemert, *Social Pathology* (New York: McGraw-Hill, 1951).

45. Mark Colvin and John Pauly, "A Critique of Criminology: Toward an Integrated Structural-Marxist Theory of Delinquency Production," *American Journal of Sociology* 89 (November 1983), pp. 513–51.

46. Michael R. Gottfredson and Travis Hirschi, *A General Theory of Crime* (Palo Alto, Calif.: Stanford University Press, 1990).

47. Terence P. Thornberry, "Toward an Interactional Theory of Delinquency," *Criminology* 25 (1987), pp. 862–91.

48. Wayne N. Welsh, Jack R. Greene, and Patricia H. Jenkins, "School Disorder: The Influence of Individual, Institutional, and Community Factors," *Criminology* 37 (February 1999), pp. 73–116.

49. Stephen Goldstein, "The Scope and Sources of School Board Authority to Regulate Student Conduct and Status: A Non-constitutional Analysis," 117 U. Pa. L. Rev. 373, 1969.

50. E. Edmund Reutter Jr., *Legal Aspects of Control of Student Activities by Public School Authorities* (Topeka, Kan.: National Organization on Legal Problems of Education, 1970).

51. *Hanson* v. *Broothby*, 318 F. Supp. 1183 (D. Mass., 1970).

52. *Burnside* v. *Byars*, 363 F.2d 744 (5th Cir. 1966).

53. This section on the rights of students is derived in part from Robert J. Rubel and Arthur H. Goldsmith, "Reflections on the Rights of Students and the Rise of School Violence," in *Violence and Crime in the Schools*, pp. 73–77.

54. *Dixon* v. *Alabama State Board of Education*, 294 F.2d 150, 158 (5th Cir. 1961; cert. denied, 368 U.S. 930).

55. *Tinker* v. *Des Moines Independent School District*, 383 U.S. 503.

56. *Bethel School District No. 403* v. *Fraser*, 478 U.S. 675, 106 S.Ct. 3159, 92 L.Ed.2d 549 (1986).

57. *Hazelwood School District* v. *Kuhlmeier*, 488 U.S. 260, 108 S.Ct. 562, 98 L.Ed.2d 592 (1988).

58. *Goss* v. *Lopez*, 419 U.S. 565.

59. *Wood* v. *Strickland*, 420 U.S. 308.

60. *Baker* v. *Owen*, 423 U.S. 907, affirming 395 F. Supp. 294 (1975); and *Ingraham* v. *Wright*, 430 U.S. 651 (1975).

61. 423 U.S. 907, affirming 395 F. Supp. 294 (1975).

62. *West Virginia State Board of Education* v. *Barnette*, 319 U.S. 624.

63. *Tinker* v. *Des Moines Independent School District*.

64. *Yoo* v. *Moynihan*, 20 Conn. Supp. 375 (1969).

65. *Richards* v. *Thurston*, 424 F.2d 1281 (1st Cir. 1970).

66. *Crossen* v. *Fatsi*, 309 F. Supp. 114 (1970).

67. *Scott* v. *Board of Education*, U.F. School District #17, Hicksville, 61 Misc. 2d 333, 305 N.Y.S.2d 601 (1969).

68. *Bannister* v. *Paradix*, 316 F. Supp. 185 (1970).

69. *Richards* v. *Thurston*.

70. Ronald D. Stephens, "School-Based Interventions: Safety and Security," in *The Gang Intervention Handbook*, edited by Arnold P. Goldstein and C. Ronald Huff (Champaign, Ill.: Research Press, 1993), pp. 257–300.

71. *New Jersey* v. *T.L.O.*, 469 U.S. (1985).

72. Ibid.

73. Ibid.

74. For an extensive discussion of the relevant issues and court decisions related to the police in the schools, see Samuel M. Davis, *Rights of Juveniles: The Juvenile Justice System* (St. Paul, Minn.: Thompson Publishing, 2003), Sections 3–19 to 3–34.3.

75. J. M. Sanchez, "Expelling the Fourth Amendment from American Schools: Students' Rights Six Years after T.L.O.," *Law and Education Journal* 21 (1992), pp. 381–413.

76. *Veronia School District 47J* v. *Action*, 115 S.Ct. 2394 (1995).

77. *Board of Education of Independent School District No. 92 of Pottawatomie County et al.* v. *Earls*, 536 U.S. 822 (2002).

78. Rubel and Goldsmith, "Reflections on the Rights of Students."

79. Thomas Bloomberg, William Bales, and Alex Piquero, "Is Educational Achievement a Turning Point for Incarcerated Delinquents Across Race and Sex?" *Journal of Youth & Adolescence* 41 (2012), pp. 202–16.

80. *Bounds* v. *Smith*, 430 U.S. 817 (1977).

81. Committee on School Health, "Out-of-School Suspension and Expulsion," *Pediatrics* 112 (2003), pp. 1206–09.

82. Kay Murphy, "Report Spotlights Out-of-School Suspensions in California," *Oakland Tribune,* April 10, 2012.

83. *Texas' School-to-Prison Pipeline: School Expulsion,* Texas Appleseed's Mission, 2010. For the effect of severe functions, see David Maimon, Olena Antonaccio, and Michael T. French, "Severe Sanctions, Easy Choice? Investigating the Role of School Sanctions in Preventing Adolescent Violent Offending," *Criminology* 50 (May 2012), pp. 495–524.

84. OJJDP Model Program Guide.

85. Daniel Princiotta and Ryan Reyna, *Achieving Graduation for All: A Governor's Guide to Dropout Prevention and Recovery* (Washington, D.C.: National Governor Association Center for Best Practices, 2009), p. 3.

86. Ibid., p. 4.

87. Zeng-yin Chen and Howard B. Kaplan, "School Failure in Early Adolescence and Status Attainment in Middle Adulthood: A Longitudinal Study," *Sociology of Education* 76 (April 2003), pp. 110–27.

88. Wendy Schwartz, After-School and Community Technology Programs for Low-Income Families (Washington, D.C.: Educational Resource Information Center Clearinghouse on Urban Education, 2003).

89. Robert Sampson and John Laub, *Crime in the Making: Pathways and Turning Points through Life* (Cambridge, Mass.: Harvard University Press, 1993).

90. Richard Arum and Irenee R. Beattie, "High School Experience and the Risk of Adult Incarceration," *Criminology* 37 (August 1999), pp. 515–39.

91. Ibid.

92. Jeremy Staff and Derek Kreager, "Too Cool for School? Violence, Peer Status and High School Dropout," *Social Forces* 87 (2008), pp. 445–71.

93. Kimberly Henry, Kelly Knight, and Terence Thornberry, "School Disengagement as a Predictor of Dropout, Delinquency, and Problem Substance Use during Adolescence and Early Adulthood," *Journal of Youth & Adolescence* 41 (2012), pp. 156–66.

94. *Mentoring in America 2005: A Snapshot of the Current State of Mentoring* (2005). http://www.mentoring.org/program _staff/evaluation/2005_national_poll.php.

95. National Mentoring Center, *School-Based Mentoring,* http://www.nerel.org/mentoring/topic_school.html.

96. Public Alternative Schools for At-Risk Students, *Indicators* 27 (2003), http://165.224.221.98/programs/coe/2003/section4/indicator27.asp.

97. Ibid.

98. Jacqueline R. Scherer, "School–Community Relations Network Strategies," in *Violence and Crime in the Schools,* pp. 61–70.

99. Ibid.

100. Princiotta and Reyna, *Achieving Graduation for All.*

101. Allison Ann Payne and Kelly Welch, "Modeling the Effects of Racial Threat on Punitive and Restorative School Discipline," *Criminology* 48 (2010), p. 1021.

102. Ibid.

103. Ibid.

10 Gangs and Delinquency

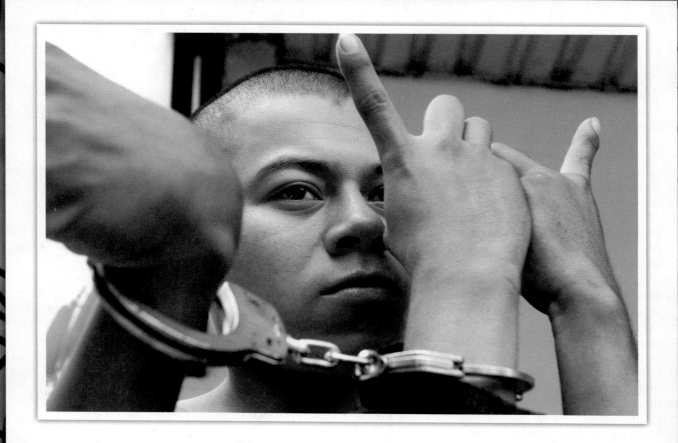

Chapter Objectives

After reading this chapter, you should be able to:

1. **Summarize the development of gangs in the United States.**

2. **Describe the nature and extent of gang activity in the United States.**

3. **Name various theories about why youths join gangs.**

4. **Explain the life-course perspective regarding the study of gangs and their members.**

5. **Summarize effective strategies for prevention and controlling of gangs.**

Gang members' mutual support of criminal activities, and possession of a value system which condones such behavior, distinguishes gang members and gangs from all other offenders and groups.

—Michael K. Carlie, *Into the Abyss*

Introduction

During the past 30 years, urban street gangs, armed with Israeli-made Uzis, Soviet AK-47s, diverted U.S. military M16s, and other automatic weapons, have evolved into small criminal empires fighting for control of thriving narcotics, auto theft, prostitution, gunrunning, and extortion operations. Illegal drugs form the backbone of most gang moneymaking criminal operations, with the manufacture and sale of **crack**, or rock cocaine, providing the bulk of the business. The crack trade, more than anything else, transformed street gangs into ghetto-based for-profit criminal organizations. Although most urban or street gangs are led by adults, juveniles often play a central role in their day-to-day activities.[1]

As street gangs have become more business-like, a few have formed associations with other organized crime groups, including Mexican drug cartels, Asian criminal groups, and Russian organized crime families. Gangs and their members are also becoming more sophisticated in their use of technology, including computers, cell phones, and the Internet. These new high-tech tools are frequently used to facilitate criminal activity and avoid detection by the police. Although some sources say that the number of gang members is in decline across the United States, some Hispanic gangs, such as *Mara Salvatrucha* (MS-13) and 18th Street (MS-18), are experiencing an influx of new members.[2]

This chapter focuses on youths who are involved in gangs. Youth gangs have become a problem in many nations and are widespread in the United States in urban, suburban, and rural areas.

crack
A less expensive but more potent form of cocaine.

Library Extra 10–1
OJJDP publication: *Co-Offending and Patterns of Juvenile Crime*

Video 10–1 *Uniform Crime Report*

Development of Gangs in the United States

Gangs have existed in this nation for centuries. In the War of 1812, for example, Jean Laffite led his band of pioneers and smugglers against the British in support of Andrew Jackson. The Younger and James gangs, two infamous gangs of the Wild West, have long been folk heroes.[3] Youth gangs, as we know them, also originated in the early decades of this nation's history. Some evidence indicates that youth gangs may have existed as early as the American Revolution[4]; other data suggest that they first emerged in the Southwest following the Mexican Revolution in 1813.[5] Youth gangs seemed to have spread into New England in the early 1800s, primarily because of the shift from agrarian to industrial society. Youth gangs, which began to flourish in Chicago and other large cities in the nineteenth century as immigration and population shifts reached peak levels, were primarily Irish, Jewish, and Italian.[6] During the twentieth century, the makeup of youth gangs changed rather significantly in nearly every decade.

Gangs and Play Activity: The 1920s through the 1940s

Frederick Thrasher's 1927 study, titled *The Gang: A Study of 1,313 Gangs in Chicago*, was a pioneering and as-yet unsurpassed work on gangs.[7] Thrasher viewed gangs as a normal part of growing up in ethnic neighborhoods. Adolescents who went to school together and played together in the neighborhood naturally developed a strong sense of identity, which led to their forming close-knit groups. Thrasher saw these gangs, evolving from neighborhood play groups, as bonded together without any particular purpose or goal and as largely transitory social groupings, typically with fewer than thirty members. They were generally organized in three concentric circles: a core composed of a leader and lieutenants, the rank-and-file membership, and a few occasional members. Finally, although each gang was different, the protection of turf was universally expected gang behavior.[8]

What is clear is that youth gangs emerged early on in Chicago because they fulfilled the social needs of adolescent boys. They offered a rite of passage from adolescence into adulthood, and it was from gang participation that youths were prepared to go into the next phase of their lives, including the assumption of adult responsibilities.

▲ A *Mara Salvatrucha* (MS-13) gang member displays his tattoos. MS-13 is one of the nation's most violent gangs.

■ **What are the attractions of gangs like MS-13 for their members?**

West Side Story Era: The 1950s

From the late 1940s through the 1950s, teenage gangs became more established in urban areas, such as Boston, New York, and Philadelphia. In addition to the time they spent hanging out, they partied together, and when necessary, they fought other gangs together. The musical *West Side Story*, later made into a movie, presented a picture of two 1950s New York youth gangs singing, dancing, and battling over turf; the Sharks, recent immigrants from Puerto Rico, defended their neighborhood, while the Jets defended theirs, and territorial lines were confined to neighborhood ethnic boundaries.

The 1950s gangs did not have the lethal weapons that today's gangs have, but they were very capable of violent behavior. One of the authors was hired to work with a white gang in Newark, New Jersey, in 1960–1961. The job became available because his predecessor, who had been on the job for two weeks, had a knife held to his chest, cutting his shirt and drawing a little blood. The predecessor was warned that bad things would happen if he did not quit, so he chose to resign. The author received quite an education in how gangs operated that year, and unlike his predecessor, he did not have any threatening experiences.

Millions of dollars in federal, state, and local money were spent on projects and programs designed to prevent and control the behavior of these fighting gangs. For example, according to Walter Miller, the detached workers program, one of the most widely funded efforts, sent professional workers into the community to work with gang youths but it proved to have little or no positive effect on reducing gangs' rates of delinquent behavior.[9] However, J. Hodgkinson and colleagues' 2009 systematic review of comprehensive gang programs found the actual impact to be larger than Miller's original analysis suggested.[10]

These gangs continued to meet the social needs of adolescent youth. Gang youths spent their time together usually milling around and finding ways to entertain themselves. They occasionally become involved in violence toward other gangs, but the fighting with other gangs was usually done with fists rather than with guns or knives.

Development of the Modern Gang: The 1960s

In the midst of a rapidly changing social and political climate in the 1960s, drugs influenced gang activity for the first time, "supergangs" emerged in several cities, and gangs became involved in social betterment programs and political activism.

Drugs led to reduced gang activity in some urban areas, and when gangs began to reduce their activities or even to disappear from some urban areas in the middle and late 1960s, some observers thought that the problem was coming to an end. New York City was one of the urban areas in which gang activity decreased significantly in the 1960s, with the major reason offered for this apparent reduction of activity being the use of hard drugs. Lesser reasons included the civil rights movement, urban riots, the growth of militant organizations, the war in Vietnam, and an exodus from the ghettos.[11]

A leader of a large Bronx gang in New York City reflected on the lack of gangs in the 1960s: "You can't keep a brother interested in clicking [gang activities] if he's high or nodding."[12] A college student who was a heroin addict for several years in Spanish Harlem in New York City during the 1960s also blamed drugs for the lack of gang activity:

> My brother was a big gang member. But we did not go for that kind of thing. Man, we were on drugs. That was cool. We were too busy trying to score to fool around with gang activity. It was everybody for himself.[13]

The 1960s was also the decade in which the major supergangs developed. Some neighborhood gangs became larger and more powerful than other gangs in surrounding neighborhoods, and they forced these groups to become part of their gang organization. Eventually a few gangs would control an entire city. For example, in the 1960s, the Crips, an African American supergang, began as a small clique in a section of south Los Angeles.[14] By 1972, there were eighteen Crips and Bloods gangs in Los Angeles, and they were the largest gangs of the more than five hundred active gangs in the city.[15] In Chicago, the Vice Lords, Blackstone Rangers, and Gangster Disciples, all major supergangs today, also had their beginnings during that decade. (See Exhibit 10–1 for an explanation of how the Gangster Disciples developed at this time.)

Exhibit 10–1
Origins of the Gangster Disciples

Larry Hoover, the chief of the Gangster Disciples, provides the following information on the beginnings of this gang.

I remember how close I came to death when I was 17. It was the night I was standing near the front of the Sarah Harrison Lounge drinking Wild Irish Rose, and David Barksdale, who was the sole leader of the Disciples, and his main people confronted me. I don't know how they got into my neighborhood that fast. They had me surrounded. There were only two of us, and there must have been 50 of them.

As David and I faced each other, I noticed he held a beer can in his hand. The next thing I knew, his fist was in my face. The 180 pounds of muscular raw power sternly admonished, "You are not going with Charlie Atkins. You guys are going to be Disciples." I firmly stated, "I am not going to be a Disciple." Guns were made visible. I thought, I will do anything to get out of this alive, but that is not what I said. For some reason, they didn't shoot us. That still surprises me.

My 20 soldiers and I became members of the Double 6 King Cobras, a faction of the Cobrastones led by Charles Atkins. Charlie was tough, dangerous, and very lethal. His slight build didn't discourage him from quickly losing his temper. This began a three-year period from 1966 to 1969 where we were always fighting the Disciples. Out of the bloodbaths, two gangs emerged with tremendous power—the Blackstones and the Disciples.

Jeff Fort tried to make a deal with me to become a part of the Blackstone Nation. There were somewhere around 75 gang factions that made up the Nation. I did attend a few of their meetings, but he didn't offer to make me one of the Main 21. I remained bound to the Double 6 King Cobras until one night, [when] David and his main leaders got out of their cars holding their hands in the air. This indicated there would be no shooting. They offered to form a treaty with us. We agreed to stop fighting the Disciples.

It wasn't long after that he asked me if we could merge and each have the same amount of power. We would share the power, two kings, coexisting in one land. Neither of us would be higher or more important. He would lead the Devil Disciples. I would conduct the Gangster Disciples. The merger left us 6,000 strong. It was then that I realized my sovereign power. I was a king, and I was only 19 years old.

Source: Courtesy of Linda Dippold Bartollas.

During the late 1960s, the three Chicago supergangs became involved in social and political activism. The Vice Lords moved further than any of the other Chicago street gangs toward programs of community betterment.[16] Their involvement in social action began in the summer of 1967 when leaders of the Vice Lords attended meetings at Western Electric and Sears, Roebuck. Operation Bootstrap, which resulted from these meetings, formed committees for education and recreation as well as law, order, and justice. A grant from the Rockefeller Foundation in February 1967 enabled the Vice Lords to found a host of economic and social ventures, and they also worked with Jesse Jackson on Operation Breadbasket and, in the summer of 1969, joined with the Coalition for United Community Action to protest the lack of African American employees on construction sites in African American neighborhoods.

In 1968, all three street gangs worked against the reelection of Mayor Richard Daley's Democratic machine, and this political activism brought increased strain to their relationship with the Democratic Party's organization.[17] The interrelationships between the legal and political contexts became apparent on the streets of Chicago as street gangs experienced what they perceived as harassment from the police. As soon as he began a new term, Mayor Daley announced a crackdown on gang violence, and the state's attorney, Edward Hanrahan, followed by appraising the gang situation as the most serious crime problem in Chicago. The courts complied with this crackdown on gangs by increasing dramatically the number of gang members sent to prison in Illinois.[18]

Also, in the 1960s some gangs became involved in the Civil Rights struggle. That support, however, largely came to an end with a disparaging remark about gangs made by Martin Luther King, Jr., at Soldiers Field in Chicago. As King was speaking, gang-affiliated youth showed their displeasure by standing up and leaving.[19] Consequently, gang youth in Chicago became increasingly involved in the Black Panthers and Black Nationalists groups, following their loss of interest in the mainstream Civil Rights struggle.

The social roots of the emergence of gangs can be seen in the "social betterment" programs that the Blackstone Rangers and Vice Lords conducted in their neighborhoods. Using funds from federal and local grants, there was an attempt to improve the neighborhoods. It was not long, however, before Jeff Fort and the Blackstone Rangers were charged with improper use of funds, and funding support quickly dried up.

Expansion, Violence, and Criminal Operations: The 1970s and Early 1980s

In the 1970s and 1980s, as leadership roles were assumed by adults, street gangs became responsible for an even bigger portion of muggings, robberies, extortions, and drug-trafficking operations in the United States. One city after another reported serious problems with gangs in the early 1970s, and it became apparent that the gangs of the 1970s and early 1980s were both more violent than the gangs of the 1950s and more intent on making money from crime; furthermore, they were systematic in their efforts to extort local merchants, engage in robberies, shake down students for money, intimidate local residents, and sell stolen goods.

Some gangs became so sophisticated that the police regarded their activities as organized crime. Those gangs kept attorneys on retainer—some even printed business cards to further their careers in extortion, and they sold the cards to businesses to provide "protection" and to warn away rivals.[20]

The mid-1980s were a turning point for many ghetto-based street gangs. Important economic factors that played a role in the emergence of gangs became evident during this period. Gangs began to focus on making money from crime, and drug trafficking became the means of much of the gang's activity. Crack cocaine had hit the streets and urban street gangs competed with one another for the drug trade.

For example, several Los Angeles gangs established direct connections to major Colombian smugglers, which ensured a continuous supply of top-quality cocaine; in some Chicago neighborhoods, heavily armed teams sold drugs openly on street corners, using gang "pee-wees" (youngsters) as police lookouts.

Since the 1980s a task force in Los Angeles has focused on gang-related criminal activities. The task force believes that traditional street gangs are not just a local problem but that these urban gangs can be linked to international or transnational gangs and drug-trafficking organizations. It is further believed that Los Angeles's gangs can potentially be used by international terrorists seeking to bring violence or mass destruction to the city.[21]

Development of Emerging Gangs: The Late 1980s and 1990s

In 1988–1989 and through the early 1990s, an upsurge of youth gangs suddenly occurred throughout the United States. Some of these youth gangs used the names of the national urban gangs, such as the Bloods and Crips from Los Angeles or the Gangster Disciples, Vice Lords, and Latin Kings from Chicago. Other gangs made up their own names, based on neighborhoods or images they wanted to depict to peers and the community. By the mid-1990s, nearly every city, many suburban areas, and even some rural areas across the United States experienced the reality of youths who considered themselves gang members. The growth of these emerging gangs peaked by the early 1990s and began to decline by the end of the 1990s.

The Present

The number of gangs, as well as membership in these gangs, began to decline in the mid-1990s and has continued to decline overall throughout the United States, with the exception to this decline being the recent growth of some ethnic gangs, such as MS-13. At the same time, federal law enforcement has had success in breaking up such urban gangs as the Gangster Disciples and the El Rukns. The street gang traditionally has been a cultural by-product in the United States, but ganglike structures are now being reported in numerous cities worldwide. Cities in Asian/Pacific nations reporting gangs are Beijing, Hong Kong, Melbourne, Papua New Guinea, and Tokyo, and European cities with gangs include Berlin, Frankfurt, London, Madrid, Manchester, and Zurich. There have also been indications that gang activity is taking place in Canada, Russia, and South America.[22] See Figure 10–1 for a timeline on the development of gangs.

TIMELINE

1920s–1940s	1940s–1950s	1960s
Gangs were largely transitory social groups in Chicago and elsewhere, and gang membership was a type of rite of passage.	**Teenage gangs** became established in Boston, New York, and Philadelphia. Members hung out together, partied together, and gangs fought each other over "turf."	**Drugs began** to influence gang activity, "supergangs" in Chicago and Los Angeles emerged, and some Chicago gangs became involved in social betterment programs.

1970s–1988	1989–1999	2000–present
Leadership of gangs was assumed by adults, street gangs became involved in more unlawful behaviors and drug trafficking, and gangs became increasingly more violent.	**The number of** youth gangs exploded across the United States.	**Gang membership** and the number of gangs have begun to slightly decline, with some ethnic gangs skyrocketing in numbers. Gangs have spread worldwide.

FIGURE 10–1
Development of Gangs in the Twentieth and Early Twenty-First Centuries

Nature and Extent of Gang Activity

The *Highlights of the 2010 National Youth Gang Survey* estimated that the United States has 29,400 gangs and 756,000 gang members.[23] The 2010 survey focused on gang problems and gangs, but according to the 2009 National Youth Gang Survey, the number of gang members in the United States has averaged about 775,000 during the past fourteen years. Following a decline from 1996, annual estimates have remained relatively steady in the past five years (Figure 10–2). The estimated number of total gangs in the fourteen-year survey has averaged around 26,000 (Figure 10–3). Larger cities and suburban areas were more likely to report higher numbers of gangs from 2002 to 2009 (Figure 10–4).

Knowledge of the gang world requires an examination of gangs and (1) consideration of the profile of gang members, (2) an understanding of gangs' intimidation of the school environment, (3) the structure and leadership of street gangs, (4) the process of gang emergence in small towns and cities, (5) the racial and ethnic backgrounds of gang members, and (6) female delinquent gangs. See the *People In the Know* interview with Sam Dillon, former gang leader of the Black P-Stone Nation, which sheds some light on at least a few of these issues. Exhibit 10–2 lists a number of the individuals who have been pioneers in helping us understand youth gangs.

Definitions of Gangs

Considerable disagreement exists about what parameters define a **gang**, but the U.S. Department of Justice defines a gang by applying the following criteria:

1. an association of three or more individuals;
2. whose members collectively identify themselves by adopting a group identity which they use to create an atmosphere of fear or intimidation frequently by employing one

gang
A group of youths who are bound together by mutual interests, have identifiable leadership, and act in concert to achieve a specific purpose that generally includes the conduct of illegal activity.

▲ Four Cambodian male gang members flash gang signs on a Long Beach, California, porch. Youth gangs have been spreading throughout the country, and gang are now active in many small towns.

■ **What accounts for this spread?**

FIGURE 10–2
Estimated Number of Gang Members in the United States, 1996–2009

Source: National Gang Center, *National Youth Gang Survey Analysis: Measuring the Extent of Gang Problems* (Washington, D.C.: Office of Juvenile Justice and Delinquency Prevention, 2011), p. 4.

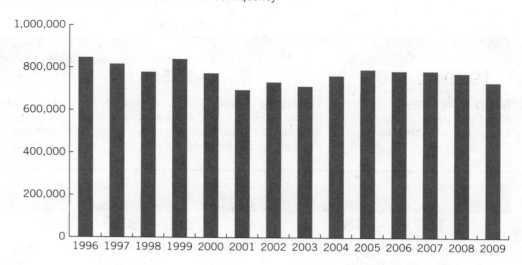

FIGURE 10–3
Estimated Number of Gangs in the United States, 1996–2009

Source: National Gang Center, *National Youth Gang Survey Analysis: Measuring the Extent of Gang Problems* (Washington, D.C.: Office of Juvenile Justice and Delinquency Prevention, 2011), p. 1.

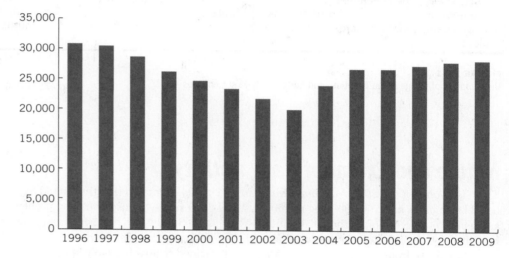

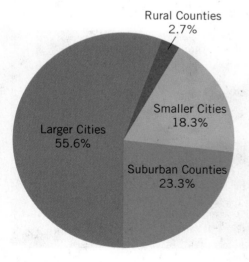

FIGURE 10–4
Distribution of Gang Members by Area Type, 2009

Source: National Gang Center, *National Youth Gang Survey Analysis: Measuring the Extent of Gang Problems* (Washington, D.C.: Office of Juvenile Justice and Delinquency Prevention, 2011), p. 5.

or more of the following: a common name, slogan, identifying sign, symbol, tattoo or other physical marking, style or color of clothing, hairstyle, hand sign or graffiti;

3. the association's purpose, in part, is to engage in criminal activity and the association uses violence or intimidation to further its criminal objectives;

4. its members engage in criminal activity, or acts of juvenile delinquency that if committed by an adult would be crimes;

5. with the intent to enhance or preserve the association's power, reputation, or economic resources;

6. the association may also possess some of the following characteristics:

a. the members employ rules for joining and operating within the association;
b. the members meet on a recurring basis;
c. the association provides physical protection of its members from other criminals and gangs;
d. the association seeks to exercise control over a particular location or region, or it may simply defend its perceived interests against rivals; or
e. the association has an identifiable structure.[24]

People In the Know
Interview with Sam Dillon

Question: Tell me about your former leadership position in the Black P-Stone Nation.

Dillon: I was a member of the "Main 21" of the Blackstone Rangers. We later became the Black P-Stone Nation. The Main 21 were the enforcers of the Black P-Stone Nation. If someone violated or stepped out of line, they had to deal with us. I was responsible for controlling the North Side and parts of Woodlawn.

Question: I understand that you were pretty "bad."

Dillon: I've been shot and stabbed on different occasions, and this tended to make me very ruthless. Life became very cheap for me. As I look back on the things I used to do, it sometimes frightens me.

Question: You did time in prison. How did that come about?

Dillon: I was sentenced to fourteen to twenty years for murder. I did nine years and three months. I was released and continued my involvement with the gang. A year later I was charged with a double homicide, and I went on the run for eight years. I even made the television show *America's Most Wanted*.

Question: What turned you around? What was your turning point?

Dillon: My faith in God. I had a religious experience and came to know that God was indeed real. I also realized that the list of people who needed to be dealt with became too long.

Question: Did gangs provide any positive contributions in your life? What is your evaluation of gangs today?

Dillon: Gangs are based on raw power. Gangs are an indigenous creation of the people on the street. Gangs are people who claim power for people who have no power. But gangs have gotten out of control. Kids can't be kids. The children are normally the future of this nation, but gangs destroy children. Therefore, they destroy a nation.

Question: Tell me about your work with gangs in recent years.

Dillon: I have developed a gang model that is designed to make kids think about their actions. This model is specifically designed for gang kids.

I teach kids about the realities of gang life. I try to warn children not to make the mistakes I have and to become the way I have. I've wasted over half my life in jails and prisons, and I try to prevent that from happening to kids today.

Source: Interviewed in June 2012. Sam Dillon has worked at the Boys Training School in Eldora, Iowa. Sam has also worked with gang youth in an urban high school in Chicago.

Exhibit 10–2
Gang Scholars

A number of individuals have been pioneers in our understanding of youth gangs.

Pioneers	Contributors
Frederick Thrasher	Thrasher's 1927 study was one of the first to define a youth gang and his examination of more than a thousand gangs in Chicago identified the role that gangs played in these youths' lives.
Martín Sánchez Jankowski	His study of thirty-seven gangs in both New York and Los Angeles over a decade provide much of our understanding of how the urban poor became involved in urban gangs.
Walter B. Miller	Beginning with his analysis of the Mid-City Project in Boston in the early 1960s to his death in 2004, Miller became one of the giants with his analysis of the growth and changes in gangs. He died before his monumental gang study of twenty-one street gangs was published.
Joan Moore	Moore studied both Mexican American male and female gangs in the barrios in Los Angeles. Her study of female gangs is one of the most important of the twentieth century. It reveals the evolution of female gangs as well as their greater involvement in criminal activity.
James Diego Vigil	He has examined the self-identity and survival of Chicago gang members as they deal with life in the barrio.
James F. Short, Jr.	Beginning with his research on Chicago gangs in the 1950s, Short has continued to study gangs and our understanding of gangs.
Irving Spergel	Long a contributor to our understanding of Chicago gangs, Spergel is especially well known for his role in the Comprehensive Community-Wide Approach to Gang Prevention, Intervention, and Suppression Program.

Profiles of Gang Members

Gang profiles have at least six important dimensions: age of gang membership, race and ethnicity of gang members, size of the gang, commitment to the gang, impact of the gang on its members, and attraction of the gang.

Age of Gang Membership

The smaller the community, the more likely it is that gang members will be juveniles. Esbensen and colleagues, in their examination of gang members in eleven locations, found that youth make up the following percentage of gang members: Milwaukee, Wisconsin, 15.4 percent; Phoenix, Arizona, 12.6 percent; Omaha, Nebraska, 11.4 percent; Las Cruces, New Mexico, 11.0 percent; Kansas City, Missouri, 10.1 percent; Orlando, Florida, 9.6 percent; Philadelphia, Pennsylvania, 7.7 percent; Terrance, California, 6.3 percent; Providence, Rhode Island, 6.0 percent; Pocatello, Idaho, 5.6 percent; and Will County, Oregon, 3.8 percent.[25]

Juveniles become involved at as young as eight years of age, running errands and carrying weapons or messages. They are recruited as lookouts and street vendors and join an age-appropriate junior division of the gang. Gangs use younger and smaller members to deal cocaine out of cramped "rock houses," which are steel-reinforced fortresses. Gangs have long known that youngsters are invaluable because their age protects them against the harsher realities of the adult criminal justice system[26] (see Figure 10–5).

Race and Ethnicity of Gang Members

According to the 2008 National Gang Center Survey, 50 percent of all gang members are Hispanic/Latino, 32 percent are African American, 11 percent are white, and 8 percent are classified as other. The most conspicuous trend is the greater representation of Hispanic/Latino gang members compared to African American and white gang members (see Figure 10–6).

FIGURE 10–5
Age of Gang Members in the United States, 1996–2008

Source: National Gang Center, 2010 online survey analysis.

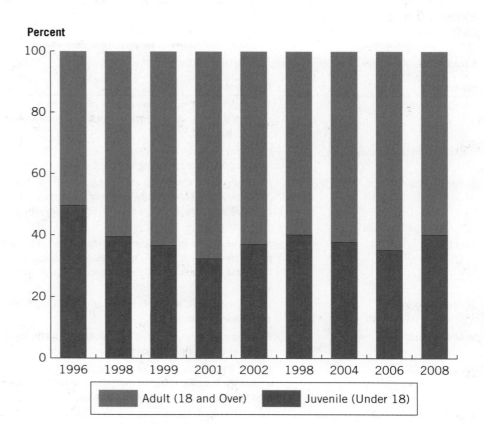

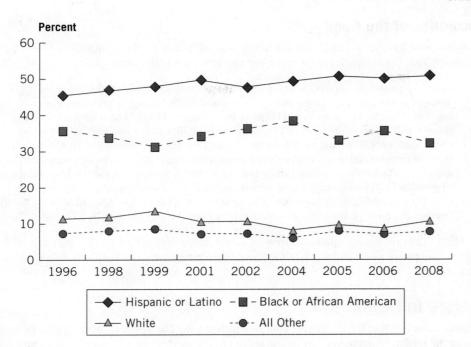

Percent

FIGURE 10–6
Race/Ethnicity of U.S. Gang Members, 1996–2008
Source: National Gang Center, 2010 online survey analysis.

- ◆— Hispanic or Latino
- -■- Black or African American
- △— White
- --●- All Other

Size of the Gang

Gangs vary in size depending on whether they are traditional or specialty gangs in urban areas or emerging gangs in smaller cities. Large and enduring traditional (territorial) gangs in urban areas average about 180 members, whereas drug-trafficking gangs average only about 25 members. Some urban gangs (e.g., the supergangs of Chicago) have thousands of members, but gangs in emerging areas usually number less than 25 or so members.

Web Extra 10–1
National Youth Gang Center website

Commitment to the Gang

Gang members have varying degrees of commitment to the gang. J. D. Vigil[27] and Vigil and J. M. Long[28] identified four basic types of gang involvement:

1. *Regulars.* The regulars are strongly attached to the gang and have few interests outside of the gang. The regulars are the hard-core members of the inner clique who make key decisions, set standards, are the key recruiters, and enforce the sanctions against violators of group norms.

2. *Peripheral members.* The peripheral members are also strongly attached to the gang but participate less often than the regulars because they have other interests besides the gang.

3. *Temporary members.* The temporary members are marginally committed, joining the gang at a later age than the regulars and peripherals; they also tend to remain in the gang for only a short time.

4. *Situational members.* The situational members are very marginally attached, generally participate only in certain activities, and avoid violent activities whenever possible.[29]

Impact of the Gang on Youth

Jorja Leap has worked with gangs for many years and has seen the emotional damage that gang involvement brings to the individual. She claims that the majority of gang members have backgrounds in which they have been beaten, sexually abused, neglected, or some combination of the three. "Kids," according to Leap, "aren't running toward something. They are running away from something." For those gang members who are able to leave the gang, she adds, they frequently must deal with post-traumatic stress disorder (PTSD).[30]

Voices of Delinquency 10–1
Read "From Gang Member to College Football Star." What was the attraction of gangs for this youth? How did he get out of the gang?

Attraction of the Gang

Why do young people join gangs? Willie Lloyd, legendary leader of a gang called the Almighty Unknown Vice Lords, explained why he became involved with gangs:

> I grew up on the streets of Chicago. When I was growing up, the Lords had a big impact on me. I never saw it as a gang but a cohesive and unified principle on which a person could organize his life. Even as a kid of nine, I was intrigued by the Lords when I first saw them outside of the Central Park Theater. It was the first time I had ever witnessed so many black people moving so harmoniously together. They were motored by the same sense of purpose and they all wore similar dress and insignia. There were over a hundred guys, all in black, with capes and umbrellas. To my young eyes, it was the most beautiful expression I had ever seen. They all seemed so fearless, so proud, so much in control of their lives. Though I didn't know one of them at the time, I fell in love with all of them. In retrospect, I made up my mind the very first time I saw the Vice Lords to be a Vice Lord.[31]

Mike Carlie, in his national overview of youth gangs, expanded on the question of why youths join gangs, asking why gangs form and what gangs offer to those who join them (see Table 10–1).

Gangs in Schools

Schools have become fertile soil for violent youth gangs. The violence perpetrated by gangs across the nation tends to vary from one school to the next, depending on the economic and social structures of the community, the gang tradition within that school, the gang's stage of development, and the extent of drug trafficking taking place.

Gangs perpetrate school violence in a number of ways; for example, gang members are likely to bring concealed weapons into schools. Moreover, because more than one gang is

TABLE 10–1
Attraction of Gangs

Why Gangs Form	What Gangs Offer	Why Youths Join
Social discrimination or rejection	Acceptance	To avoid being discriminated against and to seek acceptance and a sense of belonging
Absence of a family and its unconditional love, positive adult role models, and proper discipline	Surrogate family	To be in a family and to have unconditional love, positive adult role models, and discipline
Feelings of powerlessness	Power	To overcome their powerlessness
Abuse, fear, and lack of security	Security	To reduce their feelings of fear and to feel secure
Economic deprivation	Means of earning money	To gain economically
School failure and delinquency	Alternative to school	To vent their frustration
Low self-esteem	Opportunities to build high self-esteem	To acquire high self-esteem
Lack of acceptable rites of passage into adulthood	Rite of passage to adulthood	To accomplish their passage from childhood to adulthood
Lack of legitimate free-time activities	Activity	To keep from being bored
Pathological needs	Setting in which to act out aggression	To vent their anger
Influence of migrating gang members	Any of the aforementioned	To get any of the aforementioned
Mass media portrayals of gangs and gang members	Any of the aforementioned	To get any of the aforementioned
Choice to follow in others' footsteps	Any of the aforementioned	To follow tradition and to gain acceptance
Ability to join	Any of the aforementioned	To get any of the aforementioned

Source: Adapted from Mike Carlie, *Into the Abyss: A Personal Journey into the World of Street Gangs,* http://www.faculty.missouristate.edu/m/mkc0961. Reprinted with permission from Michael K. Carlie.

typically present in a high school, conflict among gangs takes place on a regular basis. This conflict may be based on competition over the drug market, or it may relate to individual gangs within the school that are seeking to expand their turf. Fights may erupt in the school hallways, in the cafeteria, or during dances. Warring gang youths sometimes start a mass riot, with stabbings and shootings occurring during these altercations. The use of deadly weapons, of course, increases the likelihood of injuries or fatalities.

Finally, conflict among rival gangs in different schools also perpetrates violence. Fights commonly take place during athletic contests between competing schools. A drive-by shooting is the most serious violence that can erupt among rival gangs in the school setting. What usually occurs is that a gang youth is killed, and the victim's gang deems it necessary to retaliate, so before school, during lunch recess, or following school, a car speeds by, its occupants spraying bullets.[32]

A Portland, Oregon, high school head football coach told of an incident in which a group of Crips, dressed in blue, came speeding through the school's field house parking lot. His team was standing by him when he shouted, "Slow it down, fellas." They slowed down, pulled out a semiautomatic weapon, and pointed it at the coach and his team. The coach hit the deck and ordered his team to drop for cover. The coach said, "I thought I had bought the farm. Fortunately, they didn't pull the trigger. In my 20 years of teaching, I have never been afraid until this year."[33]

Web Extra 10–2
National Gang Crime Research Center (NGCRC) website

Gangs in schools today have an economic base (drug dealing), which was not true in earlier years. Gangs have a number of techniques for selling drugs in schools. In some schools, gang members prop doors open with cigarette packs and then signal from windows to nonstudents waiting to enter the building.[34] Some gang members sell drugs in the bathrooms, in the lunchrooms, or in parking lots. Gangs also use younger children in their drug trafficking: The children first serve as lookouts, but as they get older, they can become couriers (runners), who work as conduits between dealers and buyers.[35]

Urban Street Gangs

In urban settings, street gangs have become quasi-institutionalized and compete for status and authority within schools and other social institutions. Violence in schools and nearby neighborhoods has encouraged students to seek protection in gang membership. Youths hope that wearing the proper color and style of clothes and flashing the correct gang sign will keep them safe.

Urban gangs are sometimes able to effectively take control of schools, which permits them to collect fees from other students for the privilege of attending school, traversing the corridors, and avoiding gang beatings. Fear and intimidation keep both students and faculty from reporting gang activities to authorities. Many urban schools have had to adopt extreme security measures to protect themselves from gang violence and drug trafficking.

M. S. Jankowski contended that "one of the reasons that society does not understand gangs or the gang phenomenon very well is that there have not been enough systematic studies undertaken as to how the gang works as an organization," and he suggested that the most important organizational features of urban gangs are leadership, recruitment, initiation rites, role expectations and sanctions, migration patterns, and staying with the gang.[36]

Leadership

There are three types of gang leadership:

1. *Vertical/hierarchical type.* The vertical/hierarchical type divides leadership hierarchically into several levels, with authority and power being related to the position in the line of command.

2. *Horizontal/commission type.* Each horizontal/commission type is made up of several officeholders who share equal authority over the members and who share duties as well as power and authority.

3. *Influential type.* The influential types assign no written duties or titles to their leadership positions, but they usually have two to four members who are considered the leaders of the group and whose authority is based on their charisma.[37]

Three gang recruitment strategies

1. In the "fraternity" type of recruitment, the gang presents itself as an organization that is the "in" thing to join.

2. The "obligation" recruitment strategy involves members who attempt to persuade potential members that it is their duty to join.

3. The "coercive" type of recruitment strategy uses physical and/or psychological pressure on potential members and threatens that either they or their family will be attacked if they fail to join.

FIGURE 10–7
Three Gang Recruitment Strategies

Source: Martin Jankowski, *Islands in the Street* (Berkeley: University of California Press, 1991).

The most conspicuous example of the vertical/hierarchical type of leadership is found in the Chicago-based gangs. The best known of these gangs—the Gangster Disciples, the Vice Lords, the Black Disciples, and the El Rukns—have leaders who command great respect among gang members. Jeff Fort of the El Rukns (formerly Blackstone Rangers and Black P-Stone Nation), David Barksdale of the Disciples, and Larry Hoover of the Gangster Disciples are the three most legendary leaders of past decades. Exhibit 10–3 reveals some of the power that Jeff Fort had in the 1960s with the gang that was then called the Blackstone Rangers. The Bloods and the Crips, the two most notorious Los Angeles gangs, are representative of the horizontal/commission type. They are confederations among hundreds of subgroups or sets; the sets are formed along neighborhood lines, and most sets have twenty to thirty members.[38] Gangs in emerging gang communities, which are discussed later in the chapter, are examples of the third form of gang leadership, the influential type.

Recruitment

Gangs regularly go on recruiting parties, using three basic recruitment strategies (see Figure 10–7).

The recruitment of younger members is generally easy, because the life of a gang member looks very glamorous. Recruitment begins early in the grade school years; adolescent males are most vulnerable in the junior high years.[39] But even if a youth has enough support systems at home to resist joining a gang, it is very difficult to live in a neighborhood that is controlled by a street gang and not join. A gang leader explained: "You had two choices in the neighborhood I grew up in—you could either be a gang member or [be] a mama's boy. A mama's boy would come straight home from school, go up to his room and study, and that was it."[40]

1. In the "fraternity" type of recruitment, the gang presents itself as an organization that is the "in" thing to join.

2. The "obligation" type involves members who attempt to persuade potential members that it is their duty to join.

3. The "coercive" type uses physical and/or psychological pressure on potential members and threatens that either he or his family will be attacked if he fails to join.[41]

Initiation Rites

Urban gangs have several methods of initiation:

- A new member may be "blessed-in" to a gang. Those who are blessed-in to a gang usually have older brothers, fathers, mothers, or other relatives who are already in the gang.

- A new male member more typically must be "jumped-in," that is, he must fight other members. He may have to fight a specified number of gang members for a set period of time and demonstrate that he is able to take a beating and fight back, or he may have to either stand in the middle of a circle and fight his way out or run between lines of gang members as they administer a beating (under the latter circumstances, he is expected to stay on his feet from one end of the line to the other).

Exhibit 10–3
Jeff Fort and the Rise of the Blackstone Rangers

In 1959 a scrawny young boy by the name of Jeff Fort turned twelve years old in Woodlawn (Chicago) on the West Side. He and a few friends hung around the street corners, but nobody noticed. In the beginning they stole hubcaps and groceries, dividing the proceeds among themselves. The gang became the brightest light their young minds had ever dared to believe in, flickering through the darkness of the nights poisoned by danger, degradation, and despair. They were christened the Blackstone Rangers, and the light swelled brighter from its name alone.

Jeff Fort called twenty-one leaders to him, giving them responsibility and power, understanding intuitively that sharing his power would only make him stronger. They became known as the Main 21, but the gangs were well aware that they were the Enforcers. Bull, Mad Dog, Stone, Lefty, Thunder, Tom Tucker, Leto, Hutch, Bosco, Clark, Mickey Cogwell, Porgy, A. D., Old Man, Caboo, Moose, Dog, Crazy Paul, Bop Daddy, Cool Johnnie, and Sandman handled the problems that needed to be taken care of. The code dictated behavior. Punishment was meted out for not honoring the code. Everyone understood this. They could tell you to fight Louis, and out of sheer fear you would do it in a heartbeat.

Jeff and the Main 21 held meetings in the First Presbyterian Church at 6400 South Kimbark, where a large gymnasium held thousands of Blackstones. The Main 21 [members] were seated in a semicircle across the stage at the end of the gym. A microphone and podium were ready for the entrance of the awaited leader. He appeared out of nowhere, purposefully calm, controlled, loose, milking the crowd slowly, letting the heart rates increase steadily and build with the anticipation of what his next move would be.

He raised his fist, jerking it back hard, with power they all knew him to have. He yelled, "Blackstone," and together, as if one voice came from thousands of bodies, the thunderous roar resounded back: "Blackstone."

The spotlight circled the Main 21 [members]; then a second light appeared, dancing symmetrically with the first, increasing the rhythm, picking up a swaying motion that the bodies in the gym began to recognize and move to. A third spotlight flashed on, holding Jeff Fort in its sight, suggesting that the best was yet to come. It was.

Jeff, with his arms hanging loosely by his sides, began to feel the anticipation grow like a living thing. His breath quickening, nostrils [flaring], hair standing up on the back of his neck, his head slowly rotating back and forth [as he looked] across the crowd as if singling out each and every Stone in the audience, [his] piercing eyes [would hold them one at a time], looking directly at them.

In a deep, booming voice that sent static flying across the gym, he demanded, "Stones Run It!"

As if an electrical shock wave made its way through each nervous system, the brain registered a flight response translating to a simultaneous forward movement of thousands of bodies rising in a sea of exultation. There were thousands of voices singing praises to their master as they claimed, "Stones Run It!"

Jeff roared back, "Stones Run It!"

"Stones Run It!" they fired back.

Strangling the microphone, tap dancing to the energy bombarding off the four walls, Jeff screamed in a hoarse, rasping voice, "Blackstones!" moving the Main 21 [members] into action as they deliberately made their way down the stage onto the auditorium floor among the Stones, fists pounding in and out of the air above them, as if forcing it to perform with them, directing the Stones to thunder over and over and over again, "Blackstones, Blackstones, Blackstones!"

The Stones were literally everywhere in the late 1960s, incorporating other gangs into the nation like a confederacy under one flag. Known as America's most powerful gang, [its members] reveled in the notoriety acquired as a nation of Stones. Members were arrested for crimes ranging from reckless conduct and resisting arrest to armed robbery and murder.

CRITICAL THINKING QUESTIONS

■ *Why do you think those who experienced this style of gang leadership responded with such enthusiasm? Why was Jeff Fort skillful in setting the stage for such a response?*

Source: Reprinted with permission from Linda Dippold Bartollas.

- A female is usually initiated into male-dominated gangs by providing sexual services for one or more gang members.
- A new member is often expected to participate in illegal acts, such as committing thefts or larcenies.
- A new member is frequently expected to assist in trafficking drugs.
- A new member in some gangs is expected to participate in "walk-up" or "drive-by" shootings.
- A new member is sometimes expected to commit a gang-assigned murder. Completing the procedure has sometimes been called a "blood-in" but is rarely part of initiation rites today.[42]

Role Expectations and Sanctions

A street gang's clothing, colors, and hand signs have traditionally been held sacred by gang members. In the world of gangs, warfare can be triggered by the way someone wears his hat, folds his arms, or moves his hands. Gang identity includes following codes for dress and

representing
The use by criminal street gangs of secret handshakes and special hand signs.

Web Extra 10–3
Mike Carlie's *Into the Abyss: A Personal Journey into the World of Street Gangs*

behavior, making certain that the gang's name and symbol are scrawled in as many places as possible. Each gang has its own secret handshakes and hand signs, known as **representing**. Rival groups sometimes display the signs upside down as a gesture of contempt and challenge.[43] In recent years, however, urban gang members have been much less open about their membership in an organization and are less likely to identify themselves by clothing, colors, and hand signs than in the past.

What has not changed is the expectation that members will be loyal to their gang. Loyalty involves not giving up information about the gang to other gangs or law enforcement officials, doing what you are asked to do, and respecting other members (especially leaders) of the gang. If a gang member violates certain norms or expectations of the gang, he or she receives a violation. A violation usually means a physical beating; the second or third violation could result in the gang member being killed.

Migration Patterns

Another feature of urban gangs is gang migration, which can take place in at least three ways: (1) the establishment of satellite gangs in another location, (2) the relocation of gang members with their families, and (3) the expansion of drug markets.

Several studies have been unable to document the establishment of satellite gangs in other locations.[44] Cheryl Maxson and colleagues, in surveying law enforcement agencies in over 1,100 cities nationwide, found that 713 reported some gang migration; the most typical pattern of this gang migration was the relocation of gang members with their families (39 percent), and the next most typical pattern was the expansion of drug markets (2 percent).[45]

Staying with the Gang

In recent decades, more juveniles have remained with urban gangs into their adult years. The major reasons for this continuation of gang activity into the adult years are the changing structure of the economy, resulting in the loss of unskilled and semiskilled jobs, and the opportunities to make money from the lucrative drug markets.

Library Extra 10–2
OJJDP Fact Sheet: *Highlights of the 2010 National Youth Gang Survey*

Those juveniles who do leave their urban gangs do it for many of the same reasons as other juveniles who mature out of committing delinquent behavior. Their leaving may involve the influence of a girlfriend, a move to another neighborhood or city, or the fear of arrest and incarceration in the adult system.[46] See Figure 10–8 for the major organizational characteristics of urban gangs.

FIGURE 10–8
Major Organizational Characteristics of Urban Gangs

Law-Violating Behaviors and Gang Activities

Despite the fluidity and diversity of gang roles and affiliations, it is commonly agreed that core members are involved in more serious delinquent acts than are situational or fringe members.[47]

In the 2007 National Youth Gang Survey, many agencies with gang problems reported a decrease in gang-related crime (see Figure 10–9), but by 2009 most agencies reported that gang-related problems were "staying about the same."[48]

The 2010 National Youth Gang Survey reported that highly populated areas accounted for the vast majority of gang-related homicides. Among the large cities, the number of reported gang-related homicides increased 13 percent from 2009 to 2010. In 2010, more than half of the seven hundred total homicides that occurred in Chicago, Illinois, and Los Angeles, California, were reported to be gang related.[49]

Gangs are increasingly using technology in the commission of crime. The most frequently reported use of technology involves cell phones with walkie-talkie or push-to-talk functions. Walkie-talkie cell phones enable gang members to alert one another to the presence of law enforcement officers or rival gang members. Gang members also use pay-as-you-go cell phones and call forwarding to insulate themselves from police; in addition, gang members make use of police scanners, surveillance equipment, and equipment for detecting microphones or bugs to insulate their criminal activity and to impede police investigations.[50]

Gangs are also making increased use of computers and the Internet. According to the *2011 National Gang Threat Assessment,* gangs use personal computers, laptops, and personal digital assistants to produce ledgers and maintain records of their criminal enterprises.[51] In addition, some evidence exists that gangs are using the Internet to track court proceedings and to identify witnesses; armed with publicly available records of legal proceedings, gangs can then identify and victimize witnesses. The Internet is sometimes used for soliciting sexual acts (a form of Internet-supported prostitution), and it provides a venue for the sale of gang-related clothing, music, and other paraphernalia; gangs are also using the Internet to become more involved in the pirating of movies and music.[52] See Exhibit 10–4, "Keeping Gangs Off the Streets," for anti-gang efforts by communities.

A final dimension of law-violating behaviors of urban street gangs is the extent to which they are becoming organized crime groups. Scott Decker, Tim Bynum, and Deborah Weisel

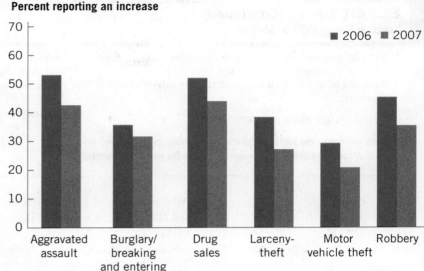

Percent reporting an increase

■ 2006 ■ 2007

FIGURE 10–9
Change in Reported Gang-Related Crime, 2006–2007

Source: National Gang Center, *National Youth Gang Survey Analysis: Gang-Related Offenses* (Washington, D.C.: National Gang Center, 2008).

EXHIBIT 10–4
Keeping Gangs Off the Streets

Gang injunctions and public nuisance controls have been used in some urban areas to control the congregation of and behavior of gangs. A gang injunction is a restraining order against a group or, more specifically, a civil court order declaring the gang's public behavior a nuisance and requiring the gang to cease those activities.

Gang injunctions have been particularly utilized in California, and a current list of such injunctions can be seen on the Los Angeles City Attorney's Office website at http://atty.lacity.org/our_office/criminaldivision/ganginjunctions/index.htm. To see an injunction in detail, visit http://www.justicestudies.com/pubs/injunction.pdf, which details an injunction against the Rolling 40 Crips and other named Los Angeles gangs.

Los Angeles first experimented with gang injunctions in the 1980s, against the West Los Angeles–based Playboy Gangsta Crips. It was followed by injunctions in the cities of San Jose, Burbank, San Diego, Westminster, Pasadena, Redondo Beach, Modesto, and Oxnard. Today, 150 gang injunctions have been issued in California; Los Angeles alone has dozens of gang injunctions covering fifty-seven gangs and eleven thousand gang members.

In 2011, Matthew O'Deane's investigation examined the effectiveness of gang injunctions in California. The purpose of this research was to determine if gang injunctions actually reduce crime. In evaluating twenty-five gang injunctions from four California counties, it was found that gang injunctions can be a very beneficial tool if used and implemented correctly and that injunctions can have a corresponding impact on reducing gang crime in the communities where they are implemented.

However, gang injunctions—which are part of what can be referred to as the "suppression model" of law enforcement—are expensive and require increased policing. The vagueness of gang injunctions, according to critics, can lead to a system of policing that uses racial profiling to target potential gang members. Urban youth of color (often African Americans or Latino) become the targets of gang injunctions. Baggy clothing, gang-affiliated colors, beanies or sports caps, tattoos, and hoodies constitute reasonable evidence for the police to harass and run the youth off the streets.

A public nuisance law is another means to avoid the congregating of gang youth. The crime of "making a public nuisance" is typically defined as an offense against, or interfering with, the comfortable enjoyment of life or property by a neighborhood or considerable number of people A city or state government can target gang activities when police officers determine that gang members are:

- Confronting, intimidating, annoying, harassing, threatening, provoking, or assaulting any residents in groups of three or more
- Standing, sitting, walking, driving, or gathering with any known gang members
- Using words, phrases, gestures, clothing, or symbols commonly known as gang signs
- Using or possessing pagers or beepers in a manner tending to indicate participation in the possession and/or sale of narcotics
- Trespassing or encouraging others to trespass

(Continued)

EXHIBIT 10–4   *(Continued)*
Keeping Gangs Off the Streets

- Blocking free access or egress to sidewalks, streets, driveways, or doorways
- Signaling to or acting as a lookout to warn others of police approach.

CRITICAL THINKING QUESTIONS

■ *There are those who oppose injunctions and public nuisance laws because they can result in police unnecessarily harassing youths and running*

them off the streets. And there are those who contend that the injunctions and public nuisance laws protect the community and reduce the danger of gangs. What do you think?

Sources: Matthew O'Deane, "The Evaluation of the Effectiveness of Gang Injunctions in California," *Journal of Criminal Justice Research* (March 2011); and *Crime Against Public Order and Morals*, http://faculty.newc.edu/instevens/293/293lect13.htm.

---

interviewed members of African American and Hispanic gangs in San Diego and Chicago and found that only the Gangster Disciples in Chicago are assuming the attributes of organized crime groups.[53] It can be argued that aspects of organized crime groups are found in such drug-trafficking gangs as the Bloods and Crips in Los Angeles, the Miami Boys of southern Florida, and the Jamaican Posses of New York and Florida. (See the *People In the Know* interview with Jorja Leap for more about the gangs in Los Angeles.) Beginning in the mid-1980s, these street gangs appeared to become criminal entrepreneurs, supplying illicit drugs, and in a brief period of several years, many of these street gangs developed intrastate and interstate networks for the purpose of expanding their illegal drug-market sales.

People In the Know
Interview with Jorja Leap

Question: Can you give us some background on how Los Angeles earned its reputation as "ground zero for gangs"?

Leap: California in general and Los Angeles in particular are often viewed as "ground zero" for gangs. What makes Los Angeles unique is that due to different social, cultural, and economic conditions, many major black and brown gangs got their start in the Southern California landscape. It's also important to keep in mind that although many gangs got their start in Los Angeles, they have migrated—both nationally and internationally—and as they have moved they have changed. Gangs are survival machines—they adjust to different regional surroundings, culture, language, and law enforcement reaction.

The many factors that have contributed to Los Angeles indeed being "ground zero" for gangs include the large urban sprawl that has been dotted with the largest public housing developments or "projects" west of the Mississippi. These projects traditionally offered both black and brown gangs a fertile environment for both organizing themselves and intimidating groups of people. The car culture of southern California facilitated drive-by crime and ensured ready access to the U.S.–Mexican border, which facilitated the easy transfer of both undocumented immigrants, drugs, and weapons. Over the years that gang crime developed—including the aptly labeled "decade of death" that spanned the mid-1980s to 1990s—the ability of law enforcement to adequately ensure the safety of Los Angeles was seriously hindered by lack of funding: Only 7,000 officers were available to patrol the 465 square miles of the city, compared with 40,000 officers who regularly patrolled the 304 square miles of New York City. The fragmenting of families due to drugs and mental disorder coupled with the deterioration of public schools in the wake of a dwindling tax base also contributed to the demise of public safety and the rise of gangs. This could be contrasted with the incredible growth of

the California prison system where gang members were incarcerated. The heavy hand of the criminal justice system had an unintended consequence: Imprisonment actually helped strengthen gang organization. For example, the rise of the Mexican Mafia guaranteed that gangs would be more structured and ultimately more deadly.

Finally—and in some ways most importantly—both policy makers and practitioners did not adequately grasp the origins, diagnosis, and treatment of gang violence for many years, buying gangs time and ensuring their growth and development. It took until the twenty-first century for lawmakers, activists and police officers to agree, "We can't arrest our way out of the gang problem." At that point, in the city of Los Angeles alone, there were 40,000 known gang members. However, beyond Los Angeles, there were gangs represented as far away as Australia and in as unlikely institutions as the U.S. military.

Question: Tell me about your experiences with gang interventionists? Do they make a difference? What do you feel is needed or required to solve the problem of gang violence and gang membership in the U.S.?

Leap: The gang problem is multifaceted and, logically, the solution should also be multifaceted. It's often surprising to me that policy makers or community practitioners or even law enforcement will suggest a one-dimensional answer. I have had tremendous experiences working with community interventionists and policy advocates—everyone from Father Greg Boyle to Big Mike Cummings to Constance Rice—and the most important thing I have learned is that it is going to take a multiplicity of approaches all working together. First, schools are where the most effective gang prevention and early intervention take place. I've worked for years on so much ethnography and community-based research to finally see that schools all too often miss the boat on providing kids an alternative to gang life. But schools alone are not enough. Instead, there needs to be a seamless transition to after-school programs that need to last not just until 5:00 but late into the night. Gangs don't observe bankers' hours and neither should after-school programs. The success of programs like "Summer Night Lights" proves that this approach works in fighting crime—but it needs to be more than a summertime effort, The lights should be on and games should be played all year round.

Prevention is a major part of dealing with gangs; the other part is effective gang intervention and community reentry. I would never dispute the significance of "violence interruption" but the real challenge is then what? Gang members need something in place of their neighborhoods, which all too often serve as a de facto employment service. Gang members, particularly those returning to the community after incarceration along with those who have expressed the wish to stop violent activity, need jobs,

vocational training, therapy, and mentoring. They need to learn that they can be fathers and mothers—working, raising their children and helping to heal their communities. The works of places like Homeboy Industries in Los Angeles, Youth Uprising in Oakland, Roca in Chelsea, and countless other organizations that devote themselves to helping to both heal and train former gang members stand as examples that there are long lasting solutions to the problem of gangs. As one former gang member implored, "We just need someone to show us another path—we want to walk on that path, we just need someone to show us the way."

Source: Interviewed in June 2012. Dr. Leap is on the faculty of the University of California at Los Angeles. She is a recognized expert in gangs, violence, and crisis intervention. She is currently the senior policy adviser on Gangs and Youth Violence for the Los Angeles County Sheriff. She has recently published *Jumped In: What Gangs Taught Me about Violence, Drugs, Love, and Redemption* (Boston: Beacon Press, 2012).

Gangs in Small Communities

Since the early 1990s, nearly every city, many suburban areas, and even some rural areas across the nation have experienced the reality of youths who consider themselves gang members. This nationwide expansion began in the late 1980s and appeared to be fueled by four different situations. First, in some communities it took place when ghetto-based drug-trafficking gangs sent ranking gang members to a community to persuade local youths to sell crack cocaine; second, gang-related individuals began to operate on their own established drug-trafficking networks among community youths. Third, urban gang members whose families had moved to these communities were instrumental in developing local chapters of urban gangs, and fourth, youths in communities with little or no intervention from outsiders developed their own versions of gangs. The latter two types were less likely to become involved in drug trafficking than were the first two types.

Several individuals have speculated how these groups, which are called **emerging gangs** in this discussion, but could be called "started groups," are formed. One of the authors studied this process of gang formulation in the late 1980s and saw this process taking place in many jurisdictions.

Behind the first wave of nationwide gang expansion was urban gang leaders' knowledge that a lot of new markets were ripe for exploitation and that crack cocaine would command a high price in these new areas. To introduce the drug in these new markets, the representatives of most urban gangs promised the possibility of a gang satellite, that is, the emerging local gang would be connected by both name and organizational ties to the parent gang. However, urban gangs had neither the intent nor the resources to develop extensions of themselves in the emerging gang community, and the promise of being a gang satellite was only a carrot to persuade local youths to sell crack cocaine for the urban gang. The development of emerging gangs involved in drug trafficking throughout the nation has seven possible stages, and the degree and seriousness of gang activity in a community depend on the gang's stage of development[54] (Figure 10–10):

1. *Implementation.* The first stage begins when an adult gang member, usually a high-ranking officer, comes to a city that has no gangs. On arriving, this gang member goes to a low-income minority neighborhood where he recruits several juveniles to sell crack and be members of the new gang. The recruited juveniles are assured of a percentage of the money they make from the sale of crack; although the exact percentage seems to vary from gang to gang, it is typically about 10 percent.[55] The representative from the urban gang returns on a regular basis to supply drugs and pick up the money.

2. *Expansion and conflict.* In the second stage, the adult who came to the community tells the recruited juveniles enough about his gang that they are able to identify with it.

emerging gang
Any youth gang that formed in the late 1980s and early 1990s in communities across the nation and that is continuing to evolve.

FIGURE 10–10
Stages of Gang Development

They start to wear the proper clothing, learn gang signs, and experience a sense of camaraderie, yet their primary motivation is still to make money from selling drugs. One Midwestern youth claimed that he was making $40,000 a month selling crack for the Unknown Vice Lords when he was arrested and institutionalized.[56] Conflict inevitably arises as drug-trafficking gangs attempt to expand their markets, usually in the same neighborhoods. Fights may break out during school functions, at athletic events and shopping centers, and in parks and other common gathering places. Weapons may be used at this time, and the number of weapons increases dramatically in the community.

3. *Organization and consolidation.* In stage 3, youths identifying with a certain gang attempt to develop a group culture. The leadership is assumed by one or more members of the core group as well as by young adult males from the community. The increased visibility of the gang attracts a sizable number of "wannabes." The gang may be larger but is still relatively unorganized, consisting primarily of a group of males hanging around together. Recruitment is emphasized, and considerable pressure is put on young minority males to join the gang. One of these males noted, "If you are black, age 12 or so, they really put pressure on you to join. It's hard not to."[57]

4. *Gang intimidation and community reaction.* Several events typically take place during stage 4. Some whites join the minority gangs, and other whites form gangs of their own. One youth represented the spirit of this white reaction when he said, "The blacks ain't going to push us around."[58] Minority gangs are still more likely to wear their colors and to demonstrate gang affiliation. Drugs are also increasingly sold in the school environment, and gang control becomes a serious problem in the school. A high school teacher expressed her concern: "I've never had any trouble teaching in this school. Now, with these gang kids, I'm half afraid to come to school. It's becoming a very serious situation."[59] Gangs become more visible in shopping centers, and older people begin to experience some fear of shopping when gang youths are present. Equally disturbing—and much more serious in the long run—is that gangs become popular among children in middle school, with some allegiance being given to gangs among young children in first and second grades.

5. *Expansion of drug markets.* Drugs are openly sold in junior and senior high schools, on street corners, and in shopping centers during the fifth stage. Crack houses are present in some minority neighborhoods. Extortion of students and victimization of both teachers and students take place frequently in the public schools. The gangs are led by adults who remain in the community, the organizational structure is more highly developed, and the number of gang members shows a significant increase. Outsiders have been present all along, but during this stage they seem to be continually coming into and going out of the community. Men in their mid-twenties roll into the community driving high-status automobiles, wearing expensive clothes and jewelry, and flashing impressive rolls of money.

6. *Gang takeover.* Communities that permit the gangs to develop to stage 6 discover that gangs are clearly in control in minority neighborhoods, in the schools, at school events, and in shopping centers. The criminal operations of gangs also become more varied and now include robberies, burglaries, aggravated assaults, and rapes. Drive-by shootings begin to occur on a regular basis, and citizens' fear of gangs increases dramatically. The police, whose gang units usually number several officers, typically express an inability to control drug trafficking and violence.

7. *Community deterioration.* The final stage is characterized by the deterioration of social institutions and the community itself because of gang control. Citizens move out of the city, stay away from shopping centers, and find safer schools for their children. When an emerging gang community arrives at this stage of deterioration, it is fully experiencing the gang problems of urban communities.

In sum, while a community's reaction greatly affects the seriousness of the problem, nongang and sometimes low-crime communities across the nation in the late 1980s and early 1990s began to experience the development of gangs. These emerging gangs developed along different trajectories, but the most toxic to a community was the process that would take hold when ghetto-based drug-trafficking gang members were able to persuade minority youths to sell crack cocaine for them, and these youths, in turn, developed what they thought would be a satellite to the parent gang.

Once gangs are established in a community, several steps are usually involved with children becoming part of a gang. Vigil, for example, has identified seven steps that may be involved. It begins in elementary school and by middle school, where children have carved out their niches, some will begin to gravitate toward gang groups. The most vulnerable children with poor achievement and family strain, according to Vigil, are those most receptive to gangs. By the end of middle school, these youths look to those who promise to provide protection. They then spend more time with gang members, and mutual acceptance is followed by an initiation—where the young person becomes committed to the gang.[60]

Racial and Ethnic Gangs

Hispanic/Latino, African American, Asian, Caucasian, and Native American gangs constitute the basic types of racial and ethnic gangs in the United States. Hispanic/Latino and African American gangs are generally more numerous and have more members than other racial/ethnic gangs. In 2010, due to the steady increase in the percentage of Hispanic/Latino members, the numbers of members in these gangs approached nearly one-half of all reported gang members.

Hispanic/Latino Gangs

Hispanic/Latino gangs are divided into Mexican American (or Chicano), Cuban, Puerto Rican, Dominican, Jamaican, and Central American members. According to the *2011 National Gang Threat Assessment*, law enforcement agencies across the nation reported that the most prominent Hispanic/Latino gangs in their jurisdictions were the Los Surenos (Sur 13), Latin Kings, MS-13, 18th Street, Nortenos, and La Raza, with more than 50 percent of reporting agencies indicating that Sur 13 was present in their jurisdiction and nearly 40 percent reporting moderate to high Sur 13 gang activity (Sur 13 was found to be present in 35 states).[61] Hispanic/Latino gang members frequently dress distinctively, display colors, communicate through graffiti, use monikers, and bear tattoos.[62]

African American Gangs

African American gangs have received more attention in this chapter than any other racial or ethnic group because most of the ghetto-based drug-trafficking gangs that have established networks across the nation are African American. For example, the Bloods and Crips from Los Angeles, the People and Folks from Chicago, and the Detroit gangs are all mostly African American. African American gangs usually identify themselves by adopting certain colors in addition to other identifiers, such as common hand signs (see Figure 10–11).

Asian Gangs

The various Asian gangs in California include Chinese, Vietnamese, Filipino, Japanese, and Korean groups. The Chinese gangs, especially, have spread to other major cities in this nation, and some of the other gangs also are active outside California. Asian gangs tend to be more organized and to have more of an identifiable leadership than is true of other street gangs. Ko-Lin Chin's examination of Chinese gangs found them to be involved in some of the nation's worst gang-related violence as well as heroin trafficking, but unlike other ethnic gangs, Chinese gangs are closely tied to the social and economic life of their rapidly developing and economically robust communities.[63] A study of Vietnamese youth gangs in southern California found that these youths experienced much marginality but attained the American dream by robbing Vietnamese families of large amounts of cash that such families keep at home.[64]

FIGURE 10–11
People and Folk Nations Gang Signs

Source: Information gathered from Durham (N.C.) Police Department, *Gang Awareness Booklet*, http://www.durhampolice.com/pdf/gang_awareness_booklet.pdf.

Caucasian Gangs

Until the closing decades of the twentieth century, most gangs were made up of white youths. Student surveys generally reveal a much larger representation of white adolescents among gang members than other types of studies show.[65] For example, a survey of nearly six thousand eighth-graders at eleven sites showed that 25 percent of the whites said they were gang members.[66] In the 1990s, the West Coast saw the solidification of lower- and middle-class white youths into groups who referred to themselves as *stoners*. These groups frequently abused drugs and alcohol and listened to heavy metal rock music, and some members practiced satanism, which included grave robbing, desecration of human remains, and sacrifice of animals.[67] Stoner groups can be identified by their mode of dress: colored T-shirts with decals of their rock music heroes or bands, Levis, and tennis shoes. They may also wear metal-spiked wrist cuffs, collars, and belts as well as satanic jewelry. The emerging white gangs across the nation have used many of the symbols of the stoner gangs, especially the heavy metal rock music and the satanic rituals, but they are not as likely to call attention to themselves with their dress, may refer to themselves as neo-Nazi skinheads, and are involved in a variety of hate crimes in addition to drug trafficking.[68]

Native American Gangs

Attention also has been given to Navajo youth gangs.[69] In 1997, the Navajo Nation estimated that about sixty youth gangs existed in Navajo country. Gang values have encouraged such risky behaviors as heavy drinking and drug use, frequently leading to mortality from injuries and alcohol. A small percentage of Navajo male youths were involved in these groups, and at most 15 percent were peripherally affiliated with gangs. Many gang activities involved hanging around, drinking, and vandalizing, but gang members also robbed people, bootlegged alcohol, and sold marijuana.[70]

Female Delinquent Gangs

Traditional sociologists once considered the female gang almost a contradiction in terms.

- A few studies have identified female gangs in Philadelphia and New York, with some of the gangs being extremely violent.[71] A number of studies have found that adolescent females are connected to adolescent male gangs. The planning is done by the males, who usually exclude the females, but the female gang members would participate in violent crimes and drug-related gang activities.[72] Loyalty to the gang rivaled loyalty to the family, and most friends came from within the gang. The gang, according to J. C. Quicker, offered warmth, friends, loyalty, and socialization as it insulated its members from the harsh environment of the barrio.[73] Finn-Aage Esbensen and colleagues found from their analysis of the Denver Youth Survey that girl gang participants committed a wide variety of offenses at only a slightly lower frequency than boys involved in gangs,[74] and Carl S. Taylor found that women were frequently represented in drug-trafficking gangs in Detroit.[75]

- Beth Bjerregaard and Carolyn Smith determined that involvement in gangs for both females and males was associated with increased levels of delinquency and substance abuse.[76] Joan Moore and John Hagedorn's 2001 summary of the research on female gangs reported that delinquency rates of female gang members are lower than those of male gang members but higher than those of nongang females and males.[77]

- Esbensen and colleagues' findings also failed to support the notion that girls involved in gangs were mere sex objects and ancillary members, and they also showed that girls aged out of gangs before boys and that girls received more emotional fulfillment from their involvement with gang activity.[78]

- From research conducted in St. Louis and Columbus, Ohio, Jody Miller found that a female in a mixed-gender gang, an environment that supports gender hierarchies and the exploitation of young women, must learn to negotiate to survive in the gang milieu.[79] Gang involvement does expose young women to risks of victimization. Young women can choose to be "one of the guys" and expose themselves to higher risks of being arrested, injured, or even killed in conflicts with rival gangs[80]... Or they can use gender to decrease their risk of being harmed by not participating in "masculine" activities such as fighting and committing crime; however, females who opt out of violence and crime are then viewed as lesser members and may expose themselves to greater risks of victimization within their gangs.[81]

In sum, most studies found that female gangs still serve as adjuncts to male gangs, yet an increasing number of important studies show that female gangs provide girls with the necessary skills to survive in their harsh communities while allowing them a temporary escape from the dismal future awaiting them.[82] What these studies revealed is that females join gangs for the same basic reasons that males do—and share with males in their neighborhood the hopelessness and powerlessness of the urban underclass.[83] See Table 10–2 for a summary of the various types of gangs.

Theories of Gang Formation

The classical theories about the origins of juvenile gangs and gang delinquency date from research done in the 1950s and were formulated by Herbert A. Bloch and Arthur Niederhoffer; Richard Cloward and Lloyd Ohlin; and Albert Cohen, Walter B. Miller, and Lewis Yablonsky.

▲ Detained female members of the Mara 18 gang flash hand signs while shouting insults at rival gang members.

■ **What roles do females play in street gangs?**

- Bloch and Niederhoffer's theory was based on the idea that joining a gang is part of the experience male adolescents need to grow up to adulthood, so the basic function of the gang is to provide a substitute for the formalized puberty rites that are found in other societies.[84]

- Cloward and Ohlin's theory used the notion that lower-class boys interact with and gain support from other alienated individuals and that these youngsters pursue illegitimate means to achieve the success they cannot gain through legitimate means.[85]

- Cohen's theory stated that gang delinquency represents a subcultural and collective solution to the problem that faces lower-class boys of acquiring status when they find themselves evaluated according to middle-class values in the schools.[86]

TABLE 10–2
Characteristics of Various Types of Gangs

Type of Gang	Description
Urban	Located in urban areas, made up largely of adults, and involved in all forms of law-violating activities, including drug trafficking
Emerging	Located in smaller cities and communities across the nation, made up almost entirely of juveniles, and focused on hanging-out and some law-violating activities
Racial and Ethnic	Hispanic/Latino, African American, Asian, Caucasian, and Native American constitute the main type of racial/ethnic gangs. These gangs tend to be made up of adults and their law-breaking activities differ from one type of racial and ethnic gang to another.
Female Delinquent	These gangs are found primarily in urban areas and are made up more of adults than juveniles. Most of the female gangs serve as adjuncts to male gangs.

- Miller held that there is a definite lower-class culture and that gang behavior is an expression of that culture; he saw gang leadership as based mainly on smartness and toughness and viewed the gang as very cohesive and highly conforming to delinquent norms.[87]

- Finally, Yablonsky suggested that violent delinquent gangs arise out of certain conditions, like those found in urban slums, that encourage the development of the sociopathic personality in adolescents, and such sociopathic individuals become the core leadership of these gangs.[88]

These classical theories of gangs focused on sociological variables such as strain (Cloward and Ohlin), subcultural affiliation (Miller and Cohen), and social disorganization (Yablonsky). Cohen, Cloward and Ohlin, and Miller also stressed the importance of the peer group for gang membership.[89] Each of the five theories of gang formation has received both support and criticism, but research into current expressions of gang activity is needed, because the existing theories were based primarily on 1950s gangs.[90]

Other theories of gangs are associated with social disorganization theory.[91] This theory is based on the assumptions that poor economic conditions cause social disorganization, that there is a deficiency of social control, and that this lack of social control leads to gang formation and involvement because youths in low-income neighborhoods seek the social order and security that gangs offer.[92]

More recently, underclass theory has been widely used to explain the origins of gangs.[93] In the midst of big-city ghettos and barrios filled with poverty and deprivation, it is argued, gangs are a normal response to an abnormal social setting.[94] Part of the underclass's plight, according to Fagan, is being permanently excluded from participating in mainstream labor market occupations, so members of the underclass are forced to rely on other economic alternatives, such as low-paying temporary jobs, part-time jobs, some form of welfare, or involvement in drug trafficking, prostitution, muggings, and extortion.[95] Hagedorn documented the loss of manufacturing jobs in Milwaukee during the 1980s, resulting in an increasingly segmented labor force in which minorities were consigned low-wage or even part-time work, welfare, and the illegal economy.[96] Vigil found that people who join gangs are pushed into these groups by their condition of poverty and their status as minorities—marginal to the wider society, their communities, and their families, they are subject to difficulties in all areas, and this multiple marginality makes them the most likely candidates for gang membership, because in a real sense, they have little else going for them—and he added that this "dialectic of multiple marginality [also] applies to why females now are more active in gangs."[97]

Jankowski contended that gang violence and the defiant attitude of young men are connected with the competitive struggle in poor communities and that being a product of their environment, they adopt a "Hobbesian view of life in which violence is an integral part of the state of nature."[98] The operations and survival rates of gangs vary greatly but, according to Jankowski's theory, can be accounted for by the interaction of four elements:

> [These four elements are] (1) inequality, and individual responses to reduce inequality; (2) the ability of the gang (both leadership and rank and file) to manage the desires and behavior of people with defiant individualist characters; (3) the degree to which a collective of individuals has been capable of developing a sophisticated organization to carry out its economic activities; and (4) the extent to which it has been able to establish ties to institutions belonging to the larger society.[99]

Moreover, Decker and Van Winkle stated that an explanation of why youths join gangs must be seen in the larger context of pulls and pushes.[100] Pulls relate to the attractiveness and benefits that the gang is perceived to offer a youth, and the benefits frequently cited are enhanced prestige or status among friends, excitement, and monetary profits from drugs. These personal advantages make gang involvement appear to be a rational choice. The pushes of gang membership come from the social, economic, and cultural forces of the larger society. Youths' experiences in response to these forces may include needing protection from other gangs, seeking an identity to overcome feelings of marginality, being recruited or coerced into gangs, or growing up in a neighborhood in which gang membership is a tradition.

Michael F. de Vries proposed that researchers need an integrated approach to understand why juveniles become involved with gangs, stating that for African American youths, strain theory is "the heart of why African Americans find gang associations worthwhile." Gangs offer deprived African American youths some opportunities to obtain status and financial gain that are denied to them in the larger culture. Asian immigrants, he argued, are also experiencing such strain: Although African Americans are more "likely to engage in illicit drug distribution to counteract their inherited inferior position in society, Asians are more apt to engage in home invasions, theft, and intimidation as their way of coping with a similar strain." According to de Vries, subcultural theory appears to be helpful in explaining Hispanic gangs, which are largely separated from Anglo American culture by their own traditions; he stated that "this subcultural group places a high degree of value on an individual's prowess (machismo), territorial identity, pride, and loyalty to their own group identity." Control theory, especially for middle-class whites, helps explain why these youths become involved in gang activity—social bonds are coming under attack as the family unit is becoming weaker.[101] See Table 10–3 for a summary showing theories of why juveniles join gangs.

Delinquency Prevention

Surveys of youth gangs across the nation reveal that the numbers of gangs and gang members had been decreasing but now are starting to rise again. There is no question that youth gangs are still a serious social problem. Gang involvement affects the quality of life for many youngsters and for most communities across the United States.

Even when gang youths are causing considerable problems at schools and in neighborhoods, communities have a tendency to deny that they have a gang problem.[102] Then, if a dramatic incident occurs—such as the killing of an innocent victim or a shoot-out in which one or more gang youths are killed—what began as denial becomes repression, or the collective phenomenon of making the gangs "invisible." Meanwhile, despite such efforts as establishing gang units in police departments (or increasing the size of existing units) and harassing gang members at every opportunity, gangs begin an inexorable process of intimidation and terror that ultimately touches all aspects of community life.

TABLE 10–3
Theories of Why Juveniles Join Gangs

Type of Theory	Proponents	Brief Description
Normal part of growing up	Block and Niederhoffer	Joining the gang is part of the experience adolescents need to grow up to adulthood.
Strain theory	Cloward and Ohlin	Youngsters pursue gangs to achieve the success they cannot achieve through legitimate means.
Subcultural affiliation and strain theory	Cohen	Gang delinquency represents a subcultural and collective solution to the problems facing lower-class boys.
Subcultural affiliation	Miller	There is a definite lower-class culture and gang behavior is an expression of that culture.
Social disorganization	Yablonsky	Violent delinquent gangs arise out of certain conditions, which are found in urban slums.
Underclass theory	Fagan and others	Excluded from participation in labor market occupations, members of the underclass are attracted to other economic alternatives, such as gangs.
Larger context of pulls and pushes	Decker and Van Winkle	Pulls relate to the attractiveness of gangs, and pushes come from the social, economic, and cultural forces of the larger society.

Another reason for seeking successful interventions is that gangs are destructive to their members. Gangs that originate as play groups frequently become involved in dangerous, even deadly, games. Joining a gang may be a normal rite of passage for a youth, but gangs minister poorly to such basic adolescent needs as preparation for marriage, employment, and adaptation to the adult world. Adolescent males who join gangs for protection are often exposed to dangers that most nongang youths are able to avoid, and adolescent females who join because they are attracted to male members are often sexually exploited. Gang members are more likely both to commit delinquent acts and to become victims of crime than are youths who do not join gangs.[103] Finally, joining a gang may provide status and esteem in the present, but gang membership frequently leads to incarceration in juvenile and/or adult facilities.

Irving Spergel and colleagues' report on forty-five cities with gang problems identified five strategies of intervention: (1) community organization, mobilization, and networking; (2) social intervention, focusing on individual behavioral and value change; (3) opportunities provision, emphasizing the improvement of basic education, training, and job openings for youths; (4) suppression, focusing on arrest, incarceration, monitoring, and supervision of gang members; and (5) organizational development and change, or the creation of special units and procedures.[104]

In examining the implementation of these strategies, Spergel and colleagues found that suppression was most frequently used (44 percent), followed by social intervention (31.5 percent), organizational development (10.9 percent), community organization (8.9 percent), and opportunities provision (4.8 percent).[105] Community organization was more likely to be used by programs in emerging gang cities, whereas social intervention and opportunities provision tended to be favored strategic approaches in cities with chronic gang problems, but only seventeen of the forty-five cities saw any evidence of improvement in their gang situation.[106]

Spergel and colleagues, in developing a model for predicting general effectiveness in intervention strategies, stated:

> A final set of analyses across all cities [indicates] that the primary strategies of community organization and provision of opportunity along with maximum participation by key community actors [are] predictive of successful efforts at reducing the gang problem.[107]

Spergel and colleagues expanded their approach into the Comprehensive Community-Wide Approach to Gang Prevention, Intervention and Suppression Program. This model contains several program components for the design and mobilization of community efforts by school officials, employers, street outreach workers, police, judges, prosecutors, probation and parole officers, and corrections officers.[108] The Gang Violence Reduction Program, an early pilot of this model, was implemented in Chicago, and after three years of program operations, the areas assessed in the preliminary evaluation of this project—lower levels of gang violence, fewer arrests for serious gang crimes, and hastened departures of youths from gang activities—were positive among the targeted group.[109]

The program was later implemented in five jurisdictions: Mesa, Arizona; Tucson, Arizona; Riverside, California; Bloomington, Illinois; and San Antonio, Texas.[110] These sites initially undertook the process of community mobilization as they identified or assessed the nature and extent of the gang problem; they then planned for program development and implementation in a problem-solving framework. It was not long thereafter that they began to implement appropriate interrelated strategies to target gang violence and its causes while they continued to reassess the changing nature and extent of the gang problem. Their strategies consisted of a combination of community mobilization, social intervention and outreach, provision of social and economic opportunities for youths, suppression or social control, and organizational change and development.[111]

What these efforts by Spergel and colleagues demonstrate is that only an integrated, multidimensional community-oriented effort is likely to have any long-term effect in preventing and controlling gangs in the United States. Such gang prevention, intervention, and control models must have several components: (1) The community must take responsibility for developing and implementing the model; (2) the model must take very seriously the structural hopelessness arising from the unmet needs of underclass children; (3) prevention programs, especially in the first six years of school, must be emphasized; (4) supporters must coordinate all the gang intervention efforts taking place in a community; and (5) sufficient financial resources must be available to implement the model.

Delinquency across the Life Course: Gang Membership

The life-course perspective offers a number of insights regarding the study of gangs and their members. The most basic is that gang membership can be thought of as a trajectory, with some youngsters entering this trajectory and some not. Those who do enter it stay for varying lengths of time and become more or less involved in gang activities and behaviors. If gang membership is conceived as a trajectory with behavioral consequences, why some people enter it and some do not is an important consideration. The life-course perspective is a reminder that the origins of gang membership are found in several domains, are multidimensional, and include childhood risk factors, the social structural position of the family, family relationships, and the unfolding influences of adolescence. Moreover, the life-course orientation suggests that for many people gang membership may act as a turning point with the potential to alter or redirect basic life-course pathways. Finally, the life-course perspective suggests that the duration of gang membership should intensify its consequences.[112]

Thornberry and colleagues contributed an important life-course orientation in their analysis of the gang behavior of Rochester youths as they aged into their young adult years. Following the sample in the Rochester Youth Development Study from ages 13 to 22, these researchers were able to separate selection effects (the extent to which delinquents seek out the gang) from facilitation effects (the extent to which the gang fosters delinquent behavior in its members). They have done this analysis for a variety of illegal behaviors related to gang activity, delinquency, drug use, drug selling, violence, and gun carrying and use and have found that gang membership seems to have a pronounced impact on facilitating all of these behaviors.[113]

Thornberry and colleagues also explored the longer-term consequences of joining a street gang. Does involvement in this strongly deviant form of adolescent social network exact a toll in the later life of the person, or is gang membership merely a transitory adolescent phenomenon with few (if any) long-term consequences? The researchers concluded that "gang membership appears to have a pernicious impact on many aspects of life-course development. In addition, while the pattern of onset and duration of gang membership varies somewhat by gender, it has negative impacts on the life course of adolescent girls, as it does on adolescent boys."[114]

Marvin D. Krohn and colleagues' 2011 study of adolescent gang involvement across the life course sought to understand how gang involvement in adolescence influences life chances and later criminal behavior. Krohn's study found that gang involvement leads to an increase in the number of life transitions experienced by gang members that result in both economic hardship and criminal involvement in adulthood. Continuing failures in the economic and family realms, according to these researchers, contribute to further involvement in either street crime or lead to arrest in adulthood.[115]

Delinquency and Social Policy

A number of communities are addressing the prevention and control of gangs across the United States. The following list provides details about some of the efforts now under way:

- The National Gang Center has recognized the Child Development Community Policing Program as providing an effective structure for linking youth exposed to violence with needed resources. Developed by the Yale Child Study Center in New Haven,

Voices of Delinquency 10–2
Read "From a Latino Gang Member to a Teacher in an Alternative School." Why was this youth able to make the transition from a gang to a nongang way of life? Why is he so motivated to work with gang youths as an adult?

Video 10–2 Gangs: Community Prevention

Library Extra 10–3
Solutions to Address Gang Crime

▲ Members of the Miami Police Department's anti-gang task force monitor the city's annual Calle Ocho festival.
■ **What can the police do to combat the growing influence of street gangs?**

Connecticut, in 1992, it has been replicated in many communities across the United States. It teams police with mental health clinicians in providing interdisciplinary intervention to families and children who are victims, witnesses, or perpetrators of violent crimes. There are also interventions based in hospital emergency rooms to help break the cycle of gang retaliatory violence.[116]

- In Richmond, Virginia, the one-stop resource centers make services accessible and available to the community. These services include prenatal and infant care, after-school activities, truancy and dropout prevention, and job programs. The One-Stop Resource Center is located in the middle of an apartment complex that houses more than four thousand residents. Housed in the center is a free health clinic and computer lab for area youth.[117]

- The PanZOu Project in North Miami Beach, Florida, serves at-risk and gang-involved or high-risk (mainly Haitian) youth and their families. Its purpose is to provide a safe place for the youth to come together and become involved in healthy prosocial activities. The services it provides include strengthening families classes, intensive case management, job skills placement and development, conflict resolution, and life skills.[118]

- Homeboy Industries was founded in 1992 by Father Greg Boyle, S. J. This program is designed to assist high-risk youth, former gang members, and ex-offenders with a variety of free programs, such as legal services, mental health counseling, tattoo removal, curriculum and education classes, employment services, and work-readiness training. Most distinctive about Homeboy Industries are its small businesses, which gives hard-to-place individuals an opportunity for employment in transitional jobs in a supportive and safe environment. These businesses include the Homeboy Bakery, Homegirl Café & Catering, Homeboy/Girl Merchandise, Homeboy Farmers Markets, The Homeboy Dinner at City Hall, Homeboy Silkscreen & Embroidery, Homeboy Grocery, and Homeboy Café & Bakery in the American Airlines terminal at Los Angeles International Airport. Homeboy Industries is recognized as the largest gang intervention program in the United States and is seen as a national model. Exhibit 10–5 discusses Father Greg Boyle and his vision.

EXHIBIT 10–5
Father Greg Boyle, S. J.—A Man with a Vision

One of the most remarkable and influential people who has ever worked in gang intervention is Father Greg, as he is known. He was born in Los Angeles, one of eight children, and after graduating from high school in Los Angeles, he decided to become a Jesuit and was ordained a priest in 1984.

While he was a priest in a small congregation at Dolores Mission Church, Father Greg and the local community developed positive alternatives to gang membership, including establishing a day care program and an elementary school and finding legitimate employment for youth.

In 1982, as a response to civil unrest in Los Angeles, Father Greg launched the first business, Homeboy Bakery. One of its purposes was to enable rival gang members to work side by side. The success of the bakery laid the groundwork for the other businesses that followed.

Father Greg is a nationally renowned speaker, and in 2005 was a featured speaker at the White House Conference on Youth at the personal invitation of Mrs. George Bush. In addition to all of the committees he serves on, he has received much recognition and many awards, including the California Peace Prize, on behalf of Homeboy Industries and for his work with former gang members. In 2008, he received the Civic Medal of Honor from the Los Angeles Chamber of Commerce. In 2010, he published *Tattoos on the Heart: The Power of Boundless Compassion*, recalling his twenty some years in the barrio of Los Angeles.

Father Greg, like others across the nation, is attempting to make a difference by giving gang youth hope and providing a means of support for them to leave the gang.

Source: Carol Ann Morrow, "Jesuit Greg Boyle, Gang Priest," *St. Anthony Messenger*, http://www.americancatholic.org/Messenger/Aug1999/feature1.asp (accessed July 18, 2012).

THE CASE

The Life Course of Amy Watters, Age 14

Amy soon learned that her new boyfriend, CJ, was a member of a street gang whose influence extended throughout the school. The gang was called the Splitter Boyz, and rumor had it that the Boyz made a lot of money by selling marijuana and other drugs to students throughout the city. Most sales took place during the school day and handoffs of money and drugs were concealed in exchanges of backpacks, lunches, and homework folders; and even secreted into laptops, iPads, and the like.

Amy soon learned that the Boyz were led by a man called Jake. Jake, whom CJ had never actually met, was said to be in his thirties and to be wealthy beyond belief. "He can buy anything—or ANYONE—he wants," CJ told her. "I'm going to be like that some day," he said. Right now, however, CJ was pretty low in the gang's hierarchy, and was striving to work his way up. CJ's assignment, said to have been handed down directly from Jake, was to turn as many of the school's football team into regular customers as he could. Thanks to CJ, marijuana was soon the recreational drug of choice at team parties and pep rallies, although one golden rule remained. "No smoking before games," Jake told her. "Sex," he told her, "well, now that's a different story."

Other than marijuana, some team members were anxious to purchase steroids, which CJ made available to them at what he called "discount prices." Amy once asked CJ if he ever used steroids. "Hell no," he answered. "Who knows what's in that sh*t!"

Why is CJ affiliated with a gang? Generally speaking, what is the attraction of street gangs for young people? How do gangs contribute to delinquency?

Learn More on the Web:

- National Gang Center: http://www.nationalgangcenter.gov
- National Gang Threat Assessment: http://www.fbi.gov/stats-services/publications/national-gang-threat-assessment-2009-pdf

Follow the continuing Amy Watters saga in the next chapter.

SUMMARY

The relationship between gang membership and delinquency is clearly documented in the literature, with both incidence and persistence of delinquency being directly tied to a youth's gang involvement. This chapter also explains the following:

- Young people derive meaning from and have their social needs met through contact with family members, peers, teachers, leaders, and participants in churches, community organizations, and school activities.

- Some youngsters find little reason to become involved in law-violating activities, whereas others become involved with various forms of delinquent behavior—often through the negative influence of peers.

- Some delinquents, with frustrated needs and nowhere else to find hope, become attracted to gangs. For these youths, gangs become quasi-families and offer acceptance and status, as well as a sense of purpose and self-esteem.

- Youth gangs are widespread throughout the United States; even small towns and rural areas are contending with the problem of gangs.

- Although youth gangs are not a recent phenomenon, many of today's gangs seem especially violent, and more than a few are characterized by the widespread use of automatic and semiautomatic weapons.

- Although gangs have historically trafficked in illicit drugs, drug trafficking provides a central focus for many of today's gangs.

- Drug gangs, or those whose primary purpose involves trafficking in illegal drugs, are much more prevalent today than in the past.

- Youth gangs of the past often transformed into street gangs, particularly in urban areas, with control of each gang in the hands of adults.

- In some urban areas, juveniles now constitute a minority of gang members.

- Many gang experts say that gangs thrive because of the poverty and lack of opportunity facing those who live in many of our nation's urban neighborhoods.

- The hopelessness of inner-city environments makes drug trafficking attractive and gang membership desirable for many young people, even in the face of a high possibility of being injured, imprisoned, or killed.

- Grassroots community groups have had some success in working with gang members, but gang reduction depends on providing children of the underclass with more positive options than they have today.

KEY TERMS

crack, p. 241
emerging gang, p. 257

gang, p. 245
representing, p. 254

REVIEW QUESTIONS

1. Why are gangs so popular among young people?
2. How have street gangs changed through the years?
3. What are the main organizational characteristics of gangs?
4. How do various racial/ethnic gangs differ?
5. What are some different ways that adolescent females can become involved in gangs?

6. What are the seven possible stages of development that an emergent gang may go through? How does the gang's stage of development relate to the degree and seriousness of gang activity in the community?

JUVENILE DELINQUENCY VIDEOS

Gang Counseling

Gang Counseling depicts a specialized gang unit within a detention facility. What is the perspective of gang involvement from the correctional officer? From the child psychiatrist? From the juveniles in the facility? Based on the video and the readings from this chapter, what types of programs are available to handle youths associated with gangs? The psychiatrist explains that early intervention is a key aspect in keeping youths out of gangs. From the readings, what early diversionary programs are set up to prevent juveniles from entering gangs?

Former White Supremacy Member

The *Former White Supremacy Member* video features a former gang member within a juvenile institution. How did the youth become involved with the gang? The youth explains the benefits of being locked up. According to the youth what are some of the "upsides" of being incarcerated? Another juvenile in the institution compares the juvenile facility to the adult facility. Why does the youth say he would rather be in the adult prison? Discuss. Based on the video and the readings from this chapter, do institutions offer treatment programs for gang members who plan on being released back into the public? Discuss.

DISCUSSION QUESTIONS

1. Discuss the development of gangs in recent years in your community. At what stage are they? What gang activities are evident? If gangs have not yet developed in your community, analyze why this is so.
2. In your community or nearby communities, what activities are females involved in with male youth gangs? Are there any separate female gangs?
3. Why have adults taken over so many youth gangs? With adults in leadership roles, what roles are reserved for youths?

4. Why is denial such a favorite strategy of police chiefs, school superintendents, and public officials for dealing with gangs? How much has this strategy been used in the community where you live or in a situation you know of?
5. What do you think is the most effective way to break up street gangs?
6. Are there any ways in which gangs could have a positive impact on adolescents?

GROUP EXERCISES

1. You have an opportunity to work with eight male gang members who are between fourteen and sixteen years of age. You have decided to design the twenty sessions around the theme of hopelessness. What would you do in these sessions to help instill more hope in the lives of these young men?
2. A particularly heinous crime has been committed by gang youths in your community. The community, which has been in a state of denial, is now alarmed. Community leaders invite you to speak to a group of concerned and leading citizens to develop a community-based plan to deal with gangs. You gather some friends together and develop a gang-prevention and gang-control plan for that community. What do you think will be the main steps in the plan that you and your group develop?

NOTES

1. Robert Walker, "Mara Salvatrucha MS-13, *Gangs OR Us*, http://www.gangsorus.com/marasalvatrucha13.html (accessed September 10, 2006).

2. Ibid.

3. Carl S. Taylor, *Dangerous Society* (East Lansing: Michigan State University Press, 1990).

4. Luc Sante, *Low Life: Lures and Snares of Old New York* (New York: Vintage Books, 1991).

5. Robert Redfield, *Folk Culture of Yucatán* (Chicago: University of Chicago Press, 1941).

6. James C. Howell, *Youth Gangs: An Overview* (Washington, D.C.: Office of Justice Programs, Office of Juvenile Justice and Delinquency Prevention, 1998); and Sante, *Low Life.*

7. Frederick Thrasher, *The Gang: A Study of 1,313 Gangs in Chicago* (Chicago: University of Chicago Press, 1927).

8. Ibid.

9. See Walter B. Miller, "The Impact of a Total Community Delinquency Control Project," *Social Problems* 10 (Fall 1962), pp. 168–191.

10. J. Hodgkinson, S. Marshall, G. Berry, P. Reynolds, M. Newman, E. Burton, K. Dickson and J. Anderson, "Reducing Gang-Related Crime: A Systematic Review of 'Comprehensive' Interventions," *Summary Report* (London: EPPI Centre, Social Science Research Unit, Institute of Education, University of London, 2009).

11. H. Craig Collins, "Youth Gangs of the 70s: An Urban Plague," *Police Chief* 42 (September 1975), pp. 50–54.

12. Ibid., p. 50.

13. Interview with student in March 1974.

14. John C. Quicker and Akil S. Batani-Khalfani, "Clique Succession among South Los Angeles Street Gangs: The Case of the Crips," paper presented to the Annual Meeting of the American Society of Criminology, Reno, NV, November 1989.

15. J. D. Vigil, *A Rainbow of Gangs: Street Cultures in the Mega-City* (Austin: University of Texas Press, 2002).

16. See David Dawley, *A Nation of Lords: The Autobiography of the Vice Lords* (Garden City, N.Y.: Anchor Books, 1973).

17. James Jacobs, *Stateville: The Penitentiary in Mass Society* (Chicago: University of Chicago Press, 1977).

18. Ibid.

19. Dr. Nehemiah Russell, who was present in Soldier Field that night, reported to one of the authors what had taken place.

20. Paul Weingarten, "Mean Streets," *Chicago Tribune Magazine* 19 (September 1982), p. 12.

21. Jorja Leap, *Jumped In: What Gangs Taught Me about Violence, Drugs, Love, and Redemption* (Boston: Beacon Press, 2012).

22. For an excellent review of gangs in the United States, see Chapter 1 in James C. Howell, *Gangs in America's Communities* (Los Angeles: Sage, 2012).

23. Arlen Egley, Jr., and James C. Howell, *Highlights of the 2010 National Youth Gang Survey* (Washington, D.C.: Office of Juvenile Justice and Delinquency Prevention, 2012), p. 1.

24. U.S. Department of Justice, *About Violent Gangs*, http://www.justice.gov/criminal/ocgs/gangs (accessed July 5, 2012).

The USDOJ notes that "this definition is not intended to include traditional organized crime groups such as La Cosa Nostra, groups that fall within the Department's definition of 'international organized crime'; drug trafficking organizations or terrorist organizations."

25. F. Esbensen, D. Peterson, T. J. Taylor, and A. Freng, *Youth Violence: Sex and Race Differences in Offending, Victimization, and Gang Membership* (Philadelphia: Temple University Press, 2010), p. 74.

26. For the role behavior of juveniles in gangs, see Mike Carlie, *Into the Abyss: A Personal Journal into the World of Street Gangs*, http://www.faculty.missouristate.edu/m/mkc096f.

27. J. D. Vigil, "Cholos and Gangs: Culture Change and Street Youths in Los Angeles," in *Gangs in America,* edited by C. Ronald Huff (Newbury Park, Calif.: Sage, 1990), pp. 146–152.

28. J. D. Vigil and J. M. Long, "Emic and Etic Perspectives on Gang Culture: The Chicano Case," in *Gangs in America*, pp. 55–68.

29. Discussion of Vigil and Long's typology is based on Randall G. Shelden, Sharon K. Tracy, and William B. Brown, *Youth Gangs in American Society* (Belmont, Calif.: Wadsworth, 1997), pp. 69–70.

30. Leap, *Jumped In,* pp. 90, 116, 175.

31. Interview in 1982 at the Iowa State Penitentiary at Fort Madison, Iowa.

32. For more information on drive-by shootings, see William B. Sanders, *Gangbangs and Drive-Bys: Grounded Culture and Juvenile Gang Violence* (New York: Aldine de Gruyter, 1994).

33. Ronald D. Stephens, "School-Based Interventions: Safety and Security," in *The Gang Intervention Handbook*, edited by Arnold P. Goldstein and C. Ronald Huff (Champaign, Ill.: Research Press, 1993), pp. 222–223.

34. See "Dope Fiend Teaches Algebra at Austin High," *Austin Voice* 9 (March 1 and March 8, 1994).

35. Patricia Wen, "Boston Gangs: A Hard World," *Boston Globe*, Tuesday, May 10, 1988. For a description of the various roles within gang drug trafficking, see Felix M. Padilla, *The Gang as an American Enterprise* (New Brunswick, N.J.: Rutgers University Press, 1992).

36. Martín Sánchez Jankowski, *Islands in the Street: Gangs and American Urban Society* (Berkeley: University of California Press, 1991). For a more up-to-date article by Sanchez Jankowski, see "Gangs and Social Change," *Theoretical Criminology* 7 (2003), pp. 191–216.

37. Ibid.

38. Joan Moore, Diego Vigil, and Robert Garcia, "Residence and Territoriality in Chicano Gangs," *Social Problems* 31 (December 1985), pp. 182–94.

39. Elaine S. Knapp, *Embattled Youth: Kids, Gangs, and Drugs* (Chicago: Council of State Governments, 1988), p. 13.

40. Interview with gang leader in 1995.

41. Jankowski, *Islands in the Street.*

42. Carlie, *Into the Abyss*.

43. Ibid.

44. John M. Hagedorn, *People and Folks: Gangs, Crime and the Underclass in a Rustbelt City*, 2d ed. (Chicago: Lake View Press, 1988); C. Ronald Huff, "Youth Gangs and Public Policy," *Crime and Delinquency* 35 (October 1989), pp. 524–537; and Dennis P. Rosenbaum and Jane A. Grant, *Gangs and Youth Problems in Evanston* (Chicago: Northwestern University, Center for Urban Affairs, 1983).

45. Cheryl Maxson, Malcolm W. Klein, and Lea C. Cunningham, *Street Gangs and Drug Sales*, (Washington, D.C.: National Institute of Justice, 1993). See also Cheryl L. Maxson, "Gang Members on the Move," *Juvenile Justice Bulletin* (Washington, D.C.: Office of Justice Programs, Office of Juvenile Justice and Delinquency Prevention, 1998).

46. See Ira Reiner, *Gangs, Crime and Violence in Los Angeles: Findings and Proposals from the District Attorney's Office* (Arlington, Va.: National Youth Gang Information Center, 1992).

47. Jeffrey Fagan, "Social Processes of Delinquency and Drug Use among Urban Gangs," in *Gangs in America*, pp. 182–219. See also Jeffrey Fagan, "The Social Organization of Drug Use and Drug Dealing among Urban Gangs," *Criminology* 27 (1989), pp. 633–64.

48. Arlen Egley, Jr., and James C. Howell, *Highlights of the 2009 National Youth Gang Survey* (Washington, D.C.: Office of Juvenile Justice and Delinquency Prevention, 2012).

49. Egley and Howell, *Highlights of the 2010 National Youth Gang Survey*.

50. National Gang Intelligence Center, *2011 National Gang Threat Assessment* (Washington, D.C.: Bureau of Justice Statistics, 2011).

51. Ibid.

52. Ibid.

53. Scott H. Decker, Tim Bynum, and Deborah Weisel, "A Tale of Two Cities: Gangs as Organized Crime Groups," *Justice Quarterly* 15 (September 1998), pp. 395–425.

54. This seven-stage development scheme was developed from conversations with a variety of individuals, ranging from gang leaders and gang members to police administrators, school officials, and newspaper reporters, across the nation.

55. Gang youths were very reluctant to talk about the percentage.

56. Interview with youth in August 1990.

57. Interview with adolescent in February 1991.

58. Interview with gang member in October 1989.

59. Comment made by a teacher to the author following a gang seminar he presented in March 1990.

60. J. D. Vigil, "The Established Gang," in *Gangs: The Origins and Impact of Contemporary Youth Gangs in the United States*, edited by S. Cummings and D. J. Monti (Albany: State University of New York Press, 1993), pp. 95–112.

61. National Gang Intelligence Center, *2011 National Gang Threat Assessment*.

62. For an examination of Chicano gangs, see James Diego Vigil, *Barrio Gangs: Street Life and Identity in Southern California* (Austin: University of Texas Press, 1988); and Joan Moore, *Home Boys: Gangs, Drugs, and Prison in the Barrios of Los Angeles* (Philadelphia: Temple University Press, 1978).

63. See Ko-Lin Chin, "Chinese Gangs and Extortion," in *Gangs in America*, pp. 129–145.

64. James Diego Vigil and Steve Chong Yun, "Vietnamese Youth Gangs in Southern California," in *Gangs in America*, pp. 146–162.

65. Howell, *Youth Gangs*.

66. Finn-Aage Esbensen and D. W. Osgood, *National Evaluation of G.R.E.A.T.: Research in Brief* (Washington, D.C.: Office of Justice Programs, National Institute of Justice, 1997).

67. For an examination of the seriousness of the problem of satanism among American youths, see Philip Jenkins and Daniel Maier-Katkin, "Satanism: Myth and Reality in a Contemporary Moral Panic," revised paper presented at the American Society of Criminology, Baltimore, MD, November 1990.

68. See Pete Simi, Lowell Smith, and Ann M. S. Reiser, "From Punk Kids to Public Enemy Number One," *Deviant Behavior* 29 (2009), pp. 753–74.

69. See Eric Henderson, Stephen J. Kunitz, and Jerrold E. Levy, "The Origins of Navajo Youth Gangs," *American Indian Culture and Research Journal* 23 (1999), pp. 243–64.

70. Ibid.

71. See Freda Adler, *Sisters in Crime: The Rise of the New Female Criminal* (New York: McGraw-Hill, 1975); W. B. Miller, "The Molls," *Society* 11 (1973), pp. 32–35; E. Ackley and B. Fliegel, "A Social Work Approach to Street Corner Girls," *Social Work* 5 (1960), pp. 29–31; and Peggy C. Giordano, "Girls, Guys and Gangs: The Changing Social Context of Female Delinquency," *Journal of Criminal Law and Criminology* 69 (1978), p. 130.

72. Lee Bowker and M. W. Klein, "Female Participation in Delinquent Gang Motivation," *Adolescence* 15 (1980), pp. 508–19; J. C. Quicker, *Home Girls: Characterizing Chicano Gangs* (San Pedro, Calif.: International University Press, 1983).

73. Quicker, *Home Girls*.

74. Finn-Aage Esbensen, Elizabeth Piper Deschenes, and L. Thomas Winfree, Jr., "Differences between Gang Girls and Gang Boys: Results from a Multisite Survey," *Youth Society* 31 (1999), pp. 27–53.

75. Carl S. Taylor, *Girls, Gangs, Women and Drugs* (East Lansing: Michigan State University Press, 1993).

76. Beth Bjerregaard and Carolyn Smith, "Gender Differences in Gang Participation, Delinquency, and Substance Abuse," *Journal of Quantitative Criminology* 9 (1993), pp. 329–55.

77. Joan Moore and John Hagedorn, "Female Gangs: A Focus on Research," *Juvenile Justice Bulletin* (Washington, D.C.: Office of Juvenile Justice and Delinquency Prevention, 2001).

78. Esbensen et al., "Differences between Gang Girls and Gang Boys."

79. Jody Miller, "Gender and Victimization Risks among Young Women in Gangs," *Journal of Research in Crime and Delinquency* 35 (November 1968), pp. 429–453; Jody Miller and Rod K. Bronson, "Gender Dynamics in Youth Gangs:

Comparison of Female and Female Accounts," *Justice Quarterly* 17 (September 2000), pp. 420–447; and Jody Miller, *One of the Guys: Girls, Gangs, and Gender* (New York: Oxford University Press, 2001).

80. Miller, *One of the Guys*.
81. Miller and Bronson, "Gender Dynamics in Youth Gangs," pp. 443–445.
82. Karen Joe and Meda Chesney-Lind, "Just Every Mother's Angel: An Analysis of Gender and Ethnic Variations in Youth Gang Membership," paper presented at the Annual Meeting of the American Society of Criminology, Phoenix, AZ, November 1993.
83. Ibid.
84. H. A. Bloch and A. Niederhoffer, *The Gang: A Study in Adolescent Behavior* (New York: Philosophical Library, 1958).
85. Richard A. Cloward and Lloyd E. Ohlin, *Delinquency and Opportunity: A Theory of Delinquent Gangs* (New York: Free Press, 1960).
86. Albert K. Cohen, *Delinquent Boys: The Culture of the Gang* (Glencoe, Ill.: Free Press, 1955).
87. Walter B. Miller, "Lower-Class Culture as a Generating Milieu of Gang Delinquency," *Journal of Social Issues* 14 (1958), pp. 5–19.
88. Lewis Yablonsky, *The Violent Gang* (New York: Macmillan, 1962).
89. Bjerregaard and Smith, "Gender Differences in Gang Participation, Delinquency, and Substance Use."
90. See Patrick G. Jackson, "Theories and Findings about Youth Gangs," *Criminal Justice Abstracts* (June 1989), pp. 322–23.
91. See Gerald D. Suttles, *The Social Order of the Slum: Ethnicity and Territory in the Inner City* (Chicago: University of Chicago Press, 1968); and Thrasher, *The Gang*.
92. Jankowski, *Islands in the Street*.
93. See William Julius Wilson, *The Truly Disadvantaged: The Inner City, the Underclass, and Public Policy* (Chicago: University of Chicago Press, 1987).
94. G. David Curry and Irving A. Spergel, "Gang Homicide, Delinquency, and Community," *Criminology* (1988), pp. 381–405.
95. J. E. Fagan, "Gangs, Drugs, and Neighborhood Change," in *Gangs in America*, pp. 39–74.
96. Hagedorn, *People and Folks*.
97. Vigil, *Barrio Gangs: Family, Friends, Violence (West Nyack, N.Y.: Cambridge University, 1996)*, p. 101.
98. Jankowski, *Islands in the Street*, p. 139.
99. Ibid.
100. Scott H. Decker and Barrik Van Winkle, *Life in the Gang*.
101. Correspondence from Michael F. de Vries. See also R. E. Johnson, A. C. Marcos, and S. J. Bahr, "The Role of Peers in the Complex Etiology of Adolescent Drug Use," *Criminology* 25 (1987), pp. 323–40.
102. See Huff, "Youth Gangs and Public Policy."
103. James Short, Jr., "Gangs, Neighborhood, and Youth Crime." *Criminal Justice Bulletin* 5 (Washington, D.C.: Department of Justice, 1965), pp. 1–11. See also Terence J. Taylor, Dana Peterson, Finn-Aage Esbensen, and Adrienne Freng, "Gang Membership as a Risk Factor for Adolescent Violent Victimization," *Journal of Research in Crime and Delinquency* 44 (2007), pp. 251–380.
104. I. A. Spergel, G. D. Curry, R. A. Ross, and R. Chance, *Survival of Youth Gang Problems and Programs in 45 Cities and Sites, Report 2, National Youth Gang Suppression and Intervention Project* (Chicago: University of Chicago School of Social Service Administration, 1989), p. 211.
105. Ibid., p. 212.
106. Ibid., p. 216.
107. Ibid., p. 218.
108. Ibid.
109. Howell, "Youth Gangs."
110. Ibid.
111. Ibid.
112. Terence P. Thornberry and James H. Burch II, "Gang Members and Delinquent Behavior," *Juvenile Justice Bulletin* (Washington, D.C.: Office of Justice Programs, Office of Juvenile Justice and Delinquency Prevention, 1997).
113. Terence P. Thornberry, Marvin D. Krohn, Alan J. Lizotte, and Carolyn A. Smith, *Gangs and Delinquency in Developmental Perspective* (Cambridge, England: Cambridge Press, 2003).
114. Ibid., p. 3.
115. Marvin D. Krohn, Jeffrey A. Ward, Terence P. Thornberry, Alan J. Lizotte, and Rebekah Chu, "The Cascading Effects of Adolescent Gang Involvement Across the Life Course," *Criminology*, 49 (November 2011), pp. 991–1028.
116. Office of Juvenile Justice and Delinquency Prevention, "Innovative Local Law Enforcement and Community Policing Programs for the Juvenile Justice System," *Juvenile Justice Bulletin* (Washington, D.C.: U.S. Department of Justice, Office of Juvenile Justice and Delinquency Prevention, 1996).
117. National Gang Center, *Best Practices to Address Community Gang Problems* (Washington, D.C.: U.S. Department of Justice, Office of Juvenile Justice and Delinquency Prevention, 2010).
118. Ibid., p. 1.

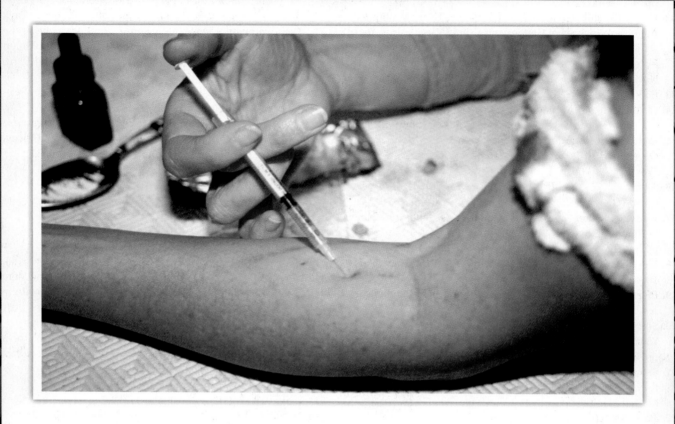

Chapter Objectives

After reading this, you should be able to:

1. Differentiate between drug use and drug abuse.
2. Summarize recent trends in adolescent drug use.
3. List the drugs used most often by adolescents.
4. Explain the relationship between drug abuse and delinquency.
5. Differentiate between the types of juveniles who sell drugs.
6. Summarize the various theories about why some juveniles use drugs.
7. Describe the impact that drug use as a juvenile may have on a person's life.
8. Summarize the effectiveness of various approaches to preventing and controlling drug use among adolescents.

For the foreseeable future, American youngsters will be aware of the psychoactive potential of many drugs and, in general, will have relatively easy access to them.

—*Monitoring the Future* study

Introduction

A 2011 report by the Office of Juvenile Justice and Delinquency Prevention (OJJDP) drew attention to the fact that research has consistently found that substance abuse among adolescents is linked to serious juvenile offending.[1] That finding was further supported by research from the ongoing OJJDP-sponsored *Pathways to Desistance* study. The "pathways" study is a large collaborative, multidisciplinary project that is currently following 1,354 serious juvenile offenders (both male and female) ages 14 to 18 for seven years after their adjudication as delinquent. The study is exploring factors that lead youths who have committed serious offenses to continue offending, or to desist from offending. Some of those factors include individual maturation, drug involvement, life changes, and involvement with the criminal justice system. A significant major finding of the study to date is that substance abuse treatment reduces both the use of illegal substances and criminal offending.

The adolescent offenders profiled in the *Pathways to Desistance* study initially self-reported very high levels of substance use and substance abuse problems. The use of illegal substances was linked to other illegal activities that were also engaged in by the study participants. As such, substance abuse was found to be "a strong, prevalent predictor of offending." The presence of a drug or alcohol disorder and the level of substance use were both shown to be strongly and independently related to the level of self-reported offending and the number of arrests. "The good news," say researchers involved in the study, "is that treatment appears to reduce both substance use and offending." According those authors, "Youth whose treatment lasted for at least 90 days and included significant family involvement showed significant reductions in alcohol use, marijuana use, and offending over the following 6 months."

Drug and alcohol use and juvenile delinquency have been identified as the most serious problem behaviors of adolescents. The good news is that substance abuse among adolescents has dropped dramatically since the late 1970s. Another piece of good news is that alcohol use, especially occasions of heavy drinking, continued on a long-term gradual decline among adolescents, reaching historically low levels in 2011. The bad news is that marijuana use among teens rose in 2011 for the fourth straight year. Daily marijuana use is now at a thirty-year peak among high school seniors.[2] More bad news is that drug use has significantly increased among high-risk youths and is becoming commonly linked to juvenile law-breaking. More juveniles are also selling drugs than ever before in the history of the United States. Furthermore, the spread of AIDS within populations of intravenous drug users and their sex partners adds to the gravity of the substance abuse problem.

Young people usually prefer substances that are not too costly. Beer and marijuana meet this criterion better than hard drugs do. Availability and potency are also important in drug use, because the substances are generally used as a means to other ends, such as achieving excitement. For example, marijuana and alcohol are used at rock concerts, parties, dances, football games, and outings to add to the excitement that is already present in such activities or to produce excitement when it seems to be lacking. In addition to enhancing excitement, substances can promote exploring new social spheres, sexual relationships, and unfamiliar places. Users also ingest narcotic substances to escape or retreat from the external world into their private inner selves. See Exhibit 11-1 for the drug classification schema established by the federal Controlled Substances Act.

There is a difference between drug use and drug abuse. Drug use can be viewed as a continuum that begins with nonuse and includes experimental use, culturally endorsed use, recreational use, and compulsive use.[3] As an example of culturally endorsed use, peyote has been used sacramentally in the Native American church for centuries, and twenty-three states exempt this sacramental use of peyote from criminal penalties.[4]

Adolescent drug use becomes abuse only when the user becomes dysfunctional (e.g., is unable to attend or perform in school or to maintain social and family relationships; exhibits dangerous, reckless, or aggressive behavior; or endangers his or her health). The drug-dependent compulsive user's life usually revolves around obtaining, maintaining, and using a supply of drugs.[5] And as this chapter will show, drug use not only causes harm in itself but also is closely linked to delinquency.

EXHIBIT 11–1
Controlled Substance Schedules

The drugs and other substances that are considered controlled substances under the CSA are divided into five schedules. A listing of the substances and their schedules is found in the **DEA regulations, 21 C.F.R. Sections 1308.11 through 1308.15**. A controlled substance is placed in its respective schedule based on whether it has a currently accepted medical use in treatment in the United States and its relative abuse potential and likelihood of causing dependence. Some examples of controlled substances in each schedule are outlined below.

NOTE: Drugs listed in schedule I have no currently accepted medical use in treatment in the United States and, therefore, may not be prescribed, administered, or dispensed for medical use. In contrast, drugs listed in schedules II–V have some accepted medical use and may be prescribed, administered, or dispensed for medical use.

SCHEDULE I CONTROLLED SUBSTANCES

Substances in this schedule have a high potential for abuse, have no currently accepted medical use in treatment in the United States, and there is a lack of accepted safety for use of the drug or other substance under medical supervision.

Some examples of substances listed in schedule I are: heroin, lysergic acid diethylamide (LSD), marijuana (cannabis), peyote, methaqualone, and 3,4-methylenedioxymethamphetamine ("ecstasy").

SCHEDULE II CONTROLLED SUBSTANCES

Substances in this schedule have a high potential for abuse which may lead to severe psychological or physical dependence.

Examples of single entity schedule II narcotics include morphine and opium. Other schedule II narcotic substances and their common name brand products include: hydromorphone (Dilaudid®), methadone (Dolophine®), meperidine (Demerol®), oxycodone (OxyContin®), and fentanyl (Sublimaze® or Duragesic®).

Examples of schedule II stimulants include: amphetamine (Dexedrine®, Adderall®), methamphetamine (Desoxyn®), and methylphenidate (Ritalin®). Other schedule II substances include: cocaine, amobarbital, glutethimide, and pentobarbital.

SCHEDULE III CONTROLLED SUBSTANCES

Substances in this schedule have a potential for abuse less than substances in schedules I or II and abuse may lead to moderate or low physical dependence or high psychological dependence.

Examples of schedule III narcotics include combination products containing less than 15 milligrams of hydrocodone per dosage unit (Vicodin®) and products containing not more than 90 milligrams of codeine per dosage unit (Tylenol with codeine®). Also included are buprenorphine products (Suboxone® and Subutex®) used to treat opioid addiction.

Examples of schedule III non-narcotics include benzphetamine (Didrex®), phendimetrazine, ketamine, and anabolic steroids such as oxandrolone (Oxandrin®).

SCHEDULE IV CONTROLLED SUBSTANCES

Substances in this schedule have a low potential for abuse relative to substances in schedule III.

An example of a schedule IV narcotic is propoxyphene (Darvon® and Darvocet-N 100®).

Other schedule IV substances include: alprazolam (Xanax®), clonazepam (Klonopin®), clorazepate (Tranxene®), diazepam (Valium®), lorazepam (Ativan®), midazolam (Versed®), temazepam (Restoril®), and triazolam (Halcion®).

SCHEDULE V CONTROLLED SUBSTANCES

Substances in this schedule have a low potential for abuse relative to substances listed in schedule IV and consist primarily of preparations containing limited quantities of certain narcotics. These are generally used for antitussive, antidiarrheal, and analgesic purposes.

Examples include cough preparations containing not more than 200 milligrams of codeine per 100 milliliters or per 100 grams (Robitussin AC® and Phenergan with Codeine®).

Source: Drug Enforcement Administration, *Controlled Substance Schedules,* http://www.deadiversion.usdoj.gov/schedules/index.html (accessed August 4, 2012).

Drug Use among Adolescents

Library Extra 11–1
COPS publication: *Underage Drinking*

Society focuses on youths' use of harder drugs, although alcohol remains the drug of choice for most adolescents. Drug use among adolescents was extremely high during the late 1960s and into the 1970s, reaching epidemic proportions. Overall rates of illicit drug use appeared to peak sometime around 1979 and then leveled off, but even with the leveling off that took place, rates of illicit drug use among youths remained high for some time. Then, in 2001, there was a significant downturn in drug-use levels.[6] According to the 2011 *Monitoring the Future* study, overall illicit drug use by youths continued to decline until 2008, after which increased use of some drugs began to occur.[7]

According to the 2010 National Survey on Drug Use and Health, an estimated 22.6 million Americans ages 12 or older were current (past-month) illicit drug users, which means they had used an illicit drug during the month prior to the survey interview. Illicit drugs include marijuana/hashish, cocaine (including crack), heroin, hallucinogens, inhalants, and prescription-type psychotherapeutic drugs used for nonmedical purposes. This is an increase of 4 percent from 21.8 million in 2010.[8]

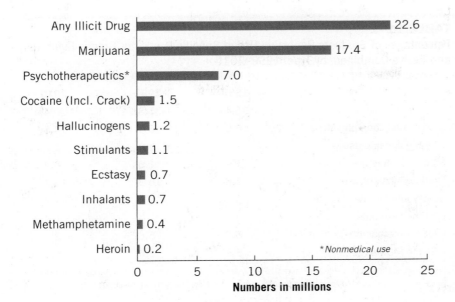

Any Illicit Drug	22.6
Marijuana	17.4
Psychotherapeutics*	7.0
Cocaine (Incl. Crack)	1.5
Hallucinogens	1.2
Stimulants	1.1
Ecstasy	0.7
Inhalants	0.7
Methamphetamine	0.4
Heroin	0.2

*Nonmedical use

Numbers in millions

FIGURE 11–1
Past Month Illicit Drug Use Among People Ages 12 or Older in the United States, 2010

Source: Adapted from Lloyd D. Johnston, Patrick M. O'Malley, Jerald G. Bachman, and John E. Schulenberg, *Monitoring the Future: National Results on Adolescent Drug Use* (Washington, D.C.: National Institutes of Health, 2010), *Tables 5, 6, and 7.*

The National Survey on Drug Use and Health documents increases in the specific categories of prescription drugs, marijuana, MDMA (Ecstasy), and methamphetamine. The increase in the use of illicit drugs from 2009 to 2010 was driven by a significant increase in current use of marijuana (from 5.8 to 6.9 percent). Figure 11–1 shows users of illicit drugs in 2010.

Table 11–1 lists the 2010 percentages of students in grades eight, ten, and twelve reporting drug use in 1999, 2001, and 2010; Table 11–2 shows percentages for drug use by students in those same grades in the past month, in the past year, and over their lifetime. In 2010, males had higher rates of illicit drug use among persons ages 12 or older than females (11.2 versus 6.8 percent, respectively). Males were more likely than females in the past month to use marijuana (9.1 versus 4.7 percent), but males and females had similar rates for stimulants, methamphetamine sedatives, and nonmedical use of psychotherapeutic drugs.

Current illicit drug use among persons ages 12 or older varied by race/ethnicity in 2010; the lowest rate was among Asians (3.5 percent). Rates were 12.5 percent for persons who reported being of two or more races, 10.7 percent for African Americans, 12.1 percent for Native Americans or Alaska natives, 9.1 percent for Caucasians, 5.4 percent of Native Hawaiians or Other Pacific Islands, and 8.1 percent for Hispanics.

Adolescents vary, of course, in terms of how frequently they use drugs and the type of drugs they use. The variables of age, gender, urban or rural setting, social class, and availability strongly affect the types of drugs used and have some effect on the frequency of drug use. Some users take drugs only at parties and on special occasions, some reserve them for weekends, and some use drugs every day.

Studies indicate that although fewer adolescents appear to be experimenting with drugs, those who use them tend to do so more frequently. Heavy users tend to be those who are male and white as well as youths who do not plan to attend college, and in school, lower achievers abuse drugs more than do high achievers. Substance abuse is more common on the East and West Coasts than in the middle of the country. In sum, although drug use among adolescents peaked during the late 1970s, rates of illicit drug use in this nation remain high, especially among high-risk youths.

THE FIRST CIGARETTE.——A SKETCH FROM MODERN LIFE, DRAWN EXPRESSLY FOR THE "DAYS' DOINGS."

▲ In this 1871 engraving, a young boy is encouraged to smoke his first cigarette by two older girls while a shocked lady intrudes upon the scene. The use of drugs—both "soft" and "hard"—has a long history in our society, complicating efforts to identify the roots of modern-day drug abuse.

■ **Why do people use drugs?**

TABLE 11–1

Percentages of Students Reporting Use of Specific Drugs, for Grades Eight, Ten, and Twelve Combined, by Type, 1999–2010

	1999	2001	2010
Lifetime marijuana use	36.4%	35.3%	30.4%
30-day marijuana prevalence	16.9	16.6	14.8
Lifetime cocaine use	7.2	5.9	3.9
30-day cocaine prevalence	1.9	1.5	0.9
Lifetime inhalant use	17.5	15.3	12.1
30-day inhalant prevalence	3.3	2.8	2.4
Lifetime heroin use	2.2	1.7	1.4
Lifetime methamphetamine use	6.5	5.8	2.2
Lifetime MDMA (Ecstasy) use	5.3	8.0	5.5

Source: Adapted from Lloyd D. Johnston, Patrick M. O'Malley, Jerald G. Bachman, and John E. Schulenberg, *Monitoring the Future: National Results on Adolescent Drug Use* (Washington, D.C.: National Institutes of Health, 2011), Tables 1, 3, and 7.

TABLE 11–2

Percentages of High School Students Reporting Drug Use, 2010

Student Drug Use	Eighth Grade	Tenth Grade	Twelfth Grade
Past-month use	9.5%	18.5%	23.8%
Past-year use	16.0	30.2	38.3
Lifetime use	21.4	37.0	48.2

Source: Adapted from Lloyd D. Johnston, Patrick M. O'Malley, Jerald G. Bachman, and John E. Schulenberg, *Monitoring the Future: National Results on Adolescent Drug Use* (Washington, D.C.: National Institutes of Health, 2010), Tables 5, 6, and 7.

Types of Drugs

The licit and illicit drugs used by adolescents, in decreasing order of frequency, are alcohol, tobacco, marijuana, cocaine, methamphetamine, inhalants, sedatives, stimulants (amphetamines and hallucinogens), steroids, prescription drugs, and heroin. The licit drugs are those permitted for users who are of age (age 18 and older for tobacco and age 21 and older for alcohol); the illicit drugs are those forbidden by law (exceptions being drugs prescribed by a physician and marijuana in jurisdictions that permit the use of this drug). Exhibit 11–2 provides information on various drug names and categories. A number of illicit drugs take control of adolescents' lives when they become addicted. **Drug addiction**, according to noted drug-abuse researcher James A. Inciardi, is "a craving for a particular drug, accompanied by physical dependence, which motivates continuing usage, resulting in tolerance to the drug's effects and a complex of identifiable symptoms appearing when it is suddenly withdrawn."[9]

Alcohol and Tobacco

The reaction to Prohibition in the early twentieth century fostered the view of alcohol use as acceptable behavior that should be free from legal controls because the public did not perceive alcohol as a dangerous drug then (nor does it now). What makes **alcohol** so dangerous is that it relaxes inhibitions, and adolescents participate in risky behavior while under its influence. Adolescents' alcohol use can be linked to property destruction, fights, academic failure, occupation problems, and conflict with law enforcement officials.[10] Youths who are under the influence of alcohol may commit delinquent acts that they otherwise would not.

drug addiction
The excessive use of a drug, which is frequently characterized by physical and/or psychological dependence.

alcohol
A drug made through a fermentation process that relaxes inhibitions.

Web Extra 11–1
Underage Drinking Enforcement Training Center website

Web Extra 11–2
Mothers Against Drunk Driving (MADD) website

Exhibit 11–2
Drugs: What's In a Name?

Drug names have been a source of confusion for many who have attempted to understand the drug problem. One drug may have a dozen or more names. Drugs may be identified by brand name, generic name, street name, or psychoactive category.

BRAND NAME

The name that a manufacturer gives a chemical substance is its brand name. Brand names are registered and are frequently associated with trademarks. This brand name identifies a drug in the pharmaceutical marketplace and may not be used by other manufacturers. Psychoactive substances without any known medical application or experimental use are not produced by legitimate companies and, as a result, have no brand name.

GENERIC NAME

The generic name is the chemical or other identifying name of a drug. Generic names are frequently used by physicians when they write prescriptions because generic drugs are usually less costly than brand-name drugs. Generic names are further used in most drug-abuse legislation at the federal and state levels to specify controlled substances. Generic names are sometimes applicable to the psychoactive chemical substances in drugs and not to the drugs themselves. For example, marijuana has the chemical tetrahydrocannabinol, or THC, as the active substance.

STREET NAME

Street names are slang terms. Many of them originated with the 1960s pop culture, and others continue to be produced in modern-day subculture. The street names for marijuana, cocaine, methamphetamine, and heroin are found elsewhere in this chapter.

PSYCHOACTIVE CATEGORY

Psychoactive drugs are categorized according to their effects on the human mind. Stimulants, narcotics, depressants, and hallucinogens are typical psychoactive categories.

EXAMPLE

PCP and angel dust are street names for a veterinary anesthetic marketed under the brand name Sernylan. Sernylan contains the psychoactive chemical phencyclidine, which is classified as a depressant under the Controlled Substances Act.

Source: Frank Schmalleger, *Criminal Justice Today*, 12th ed., © 2013, p. 634. Reprinted by permission of Pearson Education, Inc., Upper Saddle River, N.J.

The seriousness of alcohol use among adolescents can be seen in the data from the 2011 *Monitoring the Future* (MTF) study, which is funded by the National Institute on Drug Abuse, part of the National Institutes of Health. According to the MTF, binge drinking (five or more drinks in a row during the prior two-week interval) has also been declining.[11]

The use of cigarettes by adolescents is also a national public health concern. Due largely to efforts designed to steer young people away from the use of tobacco, cigarette smoking has declined sharply among American adolescents since the mid-1990s. Figure 11–2 shows the past-year cigarette initiates among persons ages 12 or older.

Voices of Delinquency 11–1
Read "Feeding the Monster." How did the addiction to alcohol and drugs control this person's life? The individual described in this story may be the best student that one of the authors ever had. How could such a capable person spend most of his life fighting addictions?

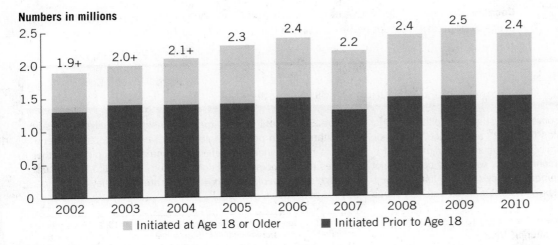

Numbers in millions

FIGURE 11–2
Past-Year Cigarette Initiates among Persons Ages 12 or Older, by Age at First Use, 2002–2010

Source: Adapted from Lloyd D. Johnston, Patrick M. O'Malley, Jerald G. Bachman, and John E. Schulenberg, *Monitoring the Future: National Results on Adolescent Drug Use* (Washington, D.C.: National Institutes of Health, 2010), Tables 5, 6, and 7.

Web Extra 11–3
National Clearinghouse for Alcohol and Drug Information website

Tobacco use is often neglected in a discussion of drugs because nicotine is not considered a mind-altering drug, yet there is considerable evidence that tobacco users suffer severe health consequences from prolonged use and that they subject others to the same consequences. The adverse health effects from cigarette smoking account for an estimated 443,000 deaths, or nearly one of every five deaths, each year in the United States. More deaths are caused each year by tobacco use than by all deaths from illegal drug use, alcohol use, human immunodeficiency virus (HIV), motor vehicle injuries, suicides, and murders combined.[12]

Marijuana

marijuana
The most frequently used illicit drug; usually smoked, it consists of dried hemp leaves and buds.

Marijuana, made from dried hemp leaves and buds, is the most frequently used illicit drug. An interesting indicator of the popularity of marijuana is the number of street terms that have been used to designate the substance: *A-bomb, Acapulco Gold, African black, ashes, Aunt Mary, baby, bammy, birdwood, California red, Colombian gold, dope, giggle-weed, golden leaf, grass, hay, joints, Mexican brown, Mexican green, Panama gold, pot, reefer, reefer weed, seaweed, stinkweed, Texas tea*, and *weed*.[13]

Heated debates about the hazards of using marijuana have waged for some time. Some medical experts in the United States contend that marijuana has some demonstrable medical benefits while other medical studies argue that it does not. A nonprofit, nonpartisan research clearing house—PRO-Con—has compiled over a hundred peer-reviewed studies on marijuana, analyzing studies for and against its use. Although the scientific debate continues, marijuana is one of the few drugs that has gained "medical usage" status in various states. Connecticut passed medical marijuana legislation in mid-2012, becoming the seventeenth state to do so.

Voices of Delinquency 11–2
Read "Walking Away from Drugs Isn't Easy." Why does this person who graduated with a 3.9 grade-point average from college say that it is hard to walk away from drugs? Why did she keep going back to drug use, regardless of the cost?

Note also that there is considerable debate over whether marijuana should be legalized, not only for medical purposes, but in order for the government to regulate it, tax its use, and profit from it. Ultimately, some interest groups hope that the legalization of marijuana will begin the process of decreasing the illegal trafficking and the escalating violence of the drug lords in Mexico and throughout Latin America.

The fact is that the resurgence in marijuana use among teens in recent years means that fewer teens report seeing much danger associated with it, even with regular use. Evidence also exists that teens' disapproval of marijuana use has fallen from 2009 to 2012.[14] In recent years, substances known as synthetic marijuana have made an appearance. See Exhibit 11–3 for a discussion of synthetic marijuana.

Cocaine

cocaine
A coca extract that creates mood elevation, elation, grandiose feelings, and feelings of heightened physical prowess.

Cocaine, the powder derivative of the South American coca plant, is replacing other illegal drugs in popularity. Street names for cocaine include *coke, lady snow, nose candy, Super*

Exhibit 11–3
Synthetic Marijuana

Sometimes sold online, in convenience stores, gasoline stations, or head shops, under names like "K-2" and "Spice," synthetic marijuana is meant to mimic the effects of marijuana. It frequently contains synthetic cannabinoid, which originally did not appear on the Drug Enforcement Agency's (DEA's) list of scheduled substances. Makers spray their chemicals onto dry herbs and plants.

Synthetic marijuana makers have tried to stay ahead of law enforcement by continually altering their substances with new ones that have similar properties.

In February 2011, the DEA used it temporary emergency powers to declare a number of chemicals used in such products to be Schedule I drugs—that is, unsafe and highly abused substances with no legitimate medical use. In addition, twenty states have banned synthetic marijuana and a number of other states have pending legislation to ban it. In 2011, 11.4 percent of high school seniors nationwide indicated that they had used it in the prior twelve months.

Source: L. D. Johnston, P. M. O'Malley, J. G. Bachman, and J. E. Schulenberg, *Monitoring the Future: National Results on Adolescent Drug Use: Overview of Key Findings, 2011* (Ann Arbor: Institute for Social Research, University of Michigan, 2012).

Fly, and *toot*. The major source of cocaine is Colombia, and its distribution is a major diplomatic issue in many Central and South American countries.

Snorting (inhaling) is the most common method of using cocaine, but freebasing (smoking) cocaine became popular in the 1980s. Freebase cocaine is derived from a chemical process in which the purified cocaine is crystallized; the crystals are crushed and smoked in a special heated glass pipe. Smoking freebase cocaine provides a quicker, more potent rush and a more powerful high than regular cocaine. Intravenous cocaine use also occurs, producing a powerful high, usually within fifteen to twenty seconds. The method of speedballing (the intravenous use of cocaine in combination with another drug) intensifies the euphoric effect but can be quite dangerous.[15]

A less expensive but more potent version of cocaine—crack—achieved great popularity in the 1980s and 1990s. Crack apparently arrived in inner-city neighborhoods in Los Angeles, Miami, and New York between 1981 and 1983[16]; then it spread throughout the nation. Crack is known by users as *boulders, bricks, crumbs, doo-wap (two rocks), eight-ball (large rocks), flavor*, and *white (hard white)*. Crack is most typically smoked in special glass pipes or makeshift smoking devices and is also smoked with marijuana in cigarettes, which are called *geek joints, lace joints*, or *pin joints*. A shotgun, which is secondary smoke exhaled from one crack user into the mouth of another, also provides the desired high.[17] Crack is frequently smoked in "crack houses," which may be abandoned buildings or the homes of crack dealers or users.

The addiction to crack by adolescent boys and young men can lead to abusive treatment of others; denial of responsibilities to family, school, and work; and increased rates of delinquent and criminal behavior. In addition to high rates of prostitution, other consequences of the addiction of adolescent girls and adult women to crack are widespread child abuse and child neglect and the toxic effects of crack during pregnancy.[18] The use of crack during pregnancy contributes to the premature separation of the placenta from the uterus, which results in stillbirths and premature infants, and infants who survive cocaine use in utero suffer withdrawal symptoms at birth and are at greater danger for strokes and respiratory ailments.[19] There is also a greater risk of sudden infant death syndrome (SIDS) among cocaine-exposed infants; such infants have a 17 percent incidence of SIDS, compared with 1.6 percent in the general population.[20] Furthermore, cocaine-exposed infants are more likely to experience emotional disorders, learning disabilities, and sensorimotor problems.[21]

One of the major issues relating to crack is that the penalty has been much harsher than for powdered cocaine, and many minorities believe that this was a racist policy—given that crack was more prevalent in minority communities, whereas powder was more prevalent in white communities.

The current use of cocaine powder among all eighth, tenth, and twelfth graders is far less than the annual prevalence rates in the mid-1980s or during the resurgence in use in the mid-1990s. The use of crack cocaine has also been in decline for some years after reaching peak levels around 1998 or 1999. In 2011, the annual prevalence rate of cocaine use for all three grades combined fell significantly.[22]

Methamphetamine

Methamphetamine is a synthetic drug otherwise known by its street names: *chalk, crank, crystal meth, glass, ice*, and *meth* (to name just a few). It is a highly addictive stimulant, which can be injected, smoked, or snorted. Its effects last up to eight hours, with an initial rush at the beginning and a less intense high for the duration. This drug makes a user feel awake, aware, and happy but also agitated and paranoid. Methamphetamine is one of many of the so-called club drugs (see Exhibit 11–4). See Table 11–3 for the percentage of students reporting the use of methamphetamine in 2004 and 2010.

The use of methamphetamine is growing. It originally was concentrated in California (especially in the San Diego area) but has widely spread to other states in the West and to states in the South and the Midwest.

▲ A crystal meth pipe being displayed by a DEA agent.

■ **How much drug use is there among adolescents in American society today?**

Exhibit 11–4
A Risky Process

The following comes from an interview with a college student and former meth user, who recalls what it was like to use meth.

COOKING AND DEALING METH

Let me tell you about a drug I was addicted to for a long time. I even sold and manufactured this drug. Meth is made of common household products. Anyone can make it. It's really simple. You can buy the ingredients at Wal-Mart, hardware stores, and gas stations. When my boyfriend and I were cooking, we tried to play it smart, though. We'd buy ingredients from different people in different states in order to not get caught, because the authorities pay attention to people who make large purchases of the ingredients for the drug and would track them down. It is even worse now. If you go to Wal-Mart in my hometown, for example, and buy three things of drain cleaner or two packages of lithium batteries, your picture gets automatically taken at the register, and it is likely that the store will call the police on you.

The cooking process is complicated by the fact that you sometimes have to rely on a handful of people to assemble all the ingredients, and everyone wants a cut of the profit. One person might go to a farmer's field and steal anhydrous out of his tanks, another might buy ephedrine pills, and another might get the batteries or drain cleaner. If you do this all yourself, you increase the likelihood that you will get caught. Police are getting smarter all the time; they have even started setting up and monitoring anhydrous tanks on local farms.

Although it is made out of common household ingredients and is easy to cook, meth is very dangerous to make. I know people who have been burned and people who have had it blow up in their faces. It is really a risky process. You have to cover your face so that you don't breathe any of the materials; if you leave your face uncovered, you won't be happy (you will feel pain every time you breathe in). You also have to be careful what it touches. If any gets on your clothes, for example, it will burn holes right through your shirt, pants, shoes, or whatever fabric it comes in contact with.

Meth also stinks like mad when it is being made, which is why the Midwest and West are prime places for manufacturing the drug. With so many abandoned farmhouses, empty barns, and trailers and with so much land, it is much easier to find a safe place to cook. It would be virtually impossible to cook meth in New England because there is very little open space. If you were stupid and tried to cook it in a hotel or in your kitchen (as many

have done), your neighbors would smell it, you would call attention to yourself, and it is likely that you would be busted.

As simple as it is, not just anyone can cook meth. You have to learn how. Most cookers learn by being "taken in" by another cooker/dealer. It usually works like this. You start using, you use more frequently, and you get to know the person you buy from. If the person you buy from is also a cooker and you can earn his or her trust or become a friend, he or she might show you how to cook. Once someone like that takes you under his or her wing, you are "in"—you are part of the inner circle. Being "taken in" is a very delicate process because meth makes people so paranoid. I remember thinking helicopters were following me, people were on my roof, and other crazy [stuff], and I always thought my friends were narcs. Everyone who used, cooked, or sold was constantly accusing each other of being narcs. This often led to violence in the ranks of the users—people getting jumped, beaten, stolen from, or threatened with guns or other violence.

Once you're in, though, once you're dealing, you don't want to be out. You have everyone's respect, everyone wants to talk to you, everyone wants what you have, everyone looks up to you, and you are making a lot of money. Add all of this to the physical addiction of the drug, and you might be able to begin to understand why people get "sucked in" once they are part of this lifestyle. This is what made it so hard for me to "leave the field." I was addicted to the drug and addicted to the money I was making. But when my best friend got busted cooking at age 20 (it was his first time getting in trouble *ever*) and got sent to prison for 91 years, I did not have to think twice—I have been sober and out of the "scene" for years.

METH AND THE "DRUG PROBLEM"

No one can deny that meth is a very serious problem in the Midwest. Kids here are into it. From what I've seen and according to national drug-use data, more people are using meth and the users are getting younger and younger. Anyone from upper-class kids to kids from the "other side of the tracks" is using it. Jocks, cheerleaders, debate team members, and drama club kids are just as likely to use it as a high school dropout. Meth is increasingly popular. It is not as popular as marijuana yet, but it is just as easy to get; it is everywhere. It is just as easy to get meth as it is to buy pot or to find someone to buy you alcohol if you are underage, if you know the right people.

Source: Personal interview with one of the authors.

Inhalants

inhalant
A volatile liquid that gives off a vapor, which is inhaled, producing short-term excitement and euphoria followed by a period of disorientation.

Many types of **inhalants** are used by adolescents, but what these drugs have in common is that youths have to inhale the vapors to receive the high that they seek. One frequently used inhalant is butyl nitrite, commonly called *RUSH*, which is packaged in small bottles and can often be found in adult bookstores as well as on the street. Other inhalants that are easier for young drug users to obtain are chlorohydrocarbons and hydrocarbons, which can be inhaled directly from gasoline, paint thinner, glue, or aerosol cans.

Library Extra 11–2
OJJDP Fact Sheet: *Substance Abuse: The Nation's Number One Health Problem*

The use of these drugs brings about a feeling of excitement that is often followed by disorientation accompanied by slurred speech and a feeling of sleepiness. The use of inhalants can also be followed by mild to severe headaches and/or nosebleeds. Chronic use of some inhalants is associated with neurological damage and injury to the liver and kidneys.[23]

TABLE 11–3
Percent of Students Reporting Methamphetamine Use, 2004 and 2010

	Eighth Grade		Tenth Grade		Twelfth Grade	
	2004	2010	2004	2010	2004	2010
Past-month use	0.6%	0.7%	1.3%	0.7%	1.4%	0.5%
Past-year use	1.5	1.2	3.0	1.6	3.4	1.0
Lifetime use	2.5	1.8	5.3	2.5	3.4	2.3

Source: Monitoring the Future: National Results on Adolescent Drug Use, 1975–2011 (Washington, D.C.: National Institutes of Health, 1975–2011).

Sedatives

Like inhalants, many different **sedatives**, or barbiturates, are used by young people. The common factors among all sedatives is that they are taken orally and that they affect the user by depressing the nervous system and inducing a drowsy condition. On the street, they are known by the color of their capsule; for example, Seconal pills are known as *reds*, Amytals are called *blue devils*, and Tuinals are known as *rainbows*. Another popular sedative is methaqualone, which is known as *Quaaludes* or *Ludes* on the street.

Adolescents often abuse prescription drugs. Benzodiazepines (minor tranquilizers or sedatives) are among the most widely prescribed of all drugs. Valium, Librium, and Equanil are commonly prescribed for anxiety or sleep disorders, so to obtain them, some adolescents simply raid their parents' medicine cabinets. Adolescents can also get these prescription drugs from older teens or young adults or purchase them from Internet-based sources. The National Association of Boards of Pharmacy has identified about two hundred websites that dispense prescription drugs but do not offer online prescribing services. According to a recent *Chicago Tribune* article that was cited by the American Medical Association, at least four hundred websites both dispense and offer a prescribing service, and half of these sites are located in foreign countries.[24] Some adolescents have broken into pharmacies and stolen the drugs they want, whereas others obtain them through online trades in illicit clearinghouses called "pharms."

Amphetamines

Amphetamines were first made in Germany in the 1880s, but it was not until World War II that they were used by Americans. All the military branches issued Benzedrine, Dexedrine, and other types of amphetamines to relieve fatigue and anxiety, especially under battle conditions. Amphetamines became more readily available after the war and were widely used by students studying for examinations, by truck drivers trying to stay alert for extended periods of time, by people attempting to lose weight, and by people seeking relief from nasal congestion. Street names for the amphetamines that were used at the time included *bennies, black beauties, King Kong pills, pinks,* and *purple hearts.*[25]

In the 1990s, **Ecstasy**, the common name for MDMA, became popular on college campuses and with adolescents and was widely used at parties. Ecstasy is usually ingested orally in tablet or capsule form, is sometimes snorted, and is occasionally smoked; it is reported to produce profound pleasurable effects, such as acute euphoria and positive changes in attitude and self-confidence.[26] Ecstasy and various other substances are sometimes called **club drugs** (Exhibit 11–5).

sedative
A drug that is taken orally and affects the user by depressing the nervous system, causing drowsiness.

amphetamine
A stimulant drug that occurs in a variety of forms.

Ecstasy
A form of amphetamine (MDMA) that began to be used by adolescents in the United States in the 1980s and 1990s and is now rather widespread.

club drug
A synthetic psychoactive substance often found at nightclubs, bars, raves, and dance parties. Club drugs include MDMA (Ecstasy), ketamine, methamphetamine (meth), gamma hydroxybutyrate (GHB), phencyclidine (PCP), and Rohypnol.

Web Extra 11–4
Clubdrugs.org

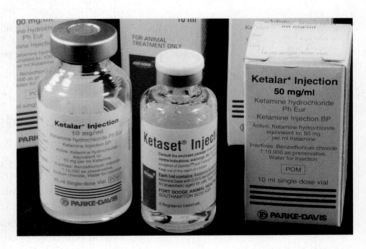

▲ Pharmaceutical ketamine intended for injection. Ketamine, which is frequently dried and sold illegally as a powder for abuse, is a rapid-acting general anesthetic whose effects are similar to those of PCP. People who use it report feeling detached or disconnected from their surroundings.

■ **What other kinds of drugs are popular with young people today?**

Exhibit 11–5
Club Drugs

The term *club* drug is a general one used for certain illicit substances (primarily synthetic) that are usually found at nightclubs, bars, and raves (all-night dance parties). Substances that are often used as club drugs include, but are not limited to, gamma hydroxybutyrate (GHB), ketamine, MDMA (Ecstasy), methamphetamine, and Rohypnol. Street names are *Special K, vitamin K, jet* (ketamine), *G liquid, Ecstasy, soap* (GHB), and *roofies* (Rohypnol). Meth and LSD (acid) are also considered club drugs.

To some, club drugs seem harmless; in reality, however, these substances can cause serious psychological and physical problems, including death. The parties (sometimes called "raves") where these drugs are used are often promoted as alcohol-free events, which gives parents a false sense of security that their children will be safe attending such parties.

But the effects of club drugs include the following:

- Ketamine can distort perception and produces feelings of detachment from the environment and self. High doses of ketamine can cause delirium and amnesia.
- GHB abuse can cause coma and seizures.

- Rohypnol can incapacitate users and cause amnesia and, especially when mixed with alcohol, can be fatal. GHB and Rohypnol are often connected with drug-facilitated sexual assault, rape, and robbery.
- MDMA can cause a user's blood pressure and heart rate to increase to dangerous levels and can lead to kidney failure. It can also cause severe hyperthermia from the combination of the drug's stimulant effect and the often hot, crowded atmosphere of a rave.
- MDMA users may suffer long-term brain injury. Research has shown that MDMA can cause damage to the parts of the brain that are critical to thought and memory.

CRITICAL THINKING QUESTIONS

- *Have you ever been to parties where club drugs were available? How do you explain their popularity?*

Source: National Institute on Drug Abuse, *Club Drugs*, http://www.drugabuse.gov/drugs-abuse/club-drugs (accessed June 18, 2012).

Hallucinogens

A parade of hallucinogens has been available over the years to adolescents interested in embracing mind-expanding experiences. Leading the parade in the 1960s was D-lysergic acid diethylamide, popularly known as LSD. Public antagonism arose in the late 1960s against LSD and other psychedelic substances, and its use dramatically declined in the 1970s.

Phencyclidine (PCP), a nervous system excitant that has analgesic, anesthetic, and hallucinogenic properties, was introduced in the late 1960s and became popular during the 1970s. First marketed as the PeaCe Pill, PCP was also known as *angel dust, animal tank, aurora borealis, buzz, devil dust, DOA, dummy dust, elephant, elephant juice, goon, rocket fuel,* and *THC*. Concern over PCP mounted during the 1970s, as its dangerousness became apparent.[27] In 1987, for example, hospital emergency rooms reported eight thousand incidents involving PCP, sometimes in combination with other drugs.[28] Use of PCP declined during the 1980s, with national samples of high school seniors who had used PCP at least once dropping from 13 percent in 1979 to less than 3 percent by 1990.[29]

Anabolic Steroids

Currently, one hundred different types of anabolic steroids have been developed, and each requires a prescription to be used legally in the United States. Street terms include *Arnolds, gym candy, juice, pampers, stackers,* and *weight trainers*. Anabolic steroids can be taken orally, injected intramuscularly, or rubbed on the skin in the form of creams or gels. Steroids are often used in patterns called *cycling*, which involves taking multiple doses of the drugs over a period of time, stopping for a period, and then starting again; users also often combine several different types of steroids in a process known as *stacking*. The reason for this, according to users, is that they believe the steroids will interact to produce a greater effect on muscle size than would happen using each drug individually.[30] A further method of steroid use is called *pyramiding*, a process in which users slowly escalate steroid use, reaching a peak amount at midcycle and gradually lowering the dose toward the end of the cycle.[31]

Results from the 2010 *Monitoring the Future* study, which surveyed students in eighth, tenth, and twelfth grades, showed that 1.1 percent of eighth graders, 1.6 percent of tenth graders, and 2.0 percent of twelfth graders reported using steroids at least once in their lifetime. See Table 11–4.

The percentage of twelfth graders indicating that steroids are "fairly easy" or "very easy" to obtain in 2010 was 27.3 percent. Anabolic steroid abuse has been associated with a wide

TABLE 11–4
Reported Steroid Use by Grade Level

	Eighth Grade	Tenth Grade	Twelfth Grade
Past-month use	0.3%	0.5%	1.1%
Past-year use	0.5	1.0	1.5
Lifetime use	1.1	1.6	2.0

Source: Adapted from Lloyd D. Johnston, Patrick M. O'Malley, Jerald G. Bachman, and John E. Schulenberg, *Monitoring the Future: National Results on Adolescent Drug Use* (Washington, D.C.: National Institutes of Health, 2009), Tables 1, 3, and 7.

range of adverse effects, ranging from those that are physically unattractive, such as breast development in men and acne, to others that are life threatening. Although most of the effects are reversible if the abuser quits taking the drug, some can be permanent. In addition to their physical effects, anabolic steroids can cause increased irritability and aggression.[32] Furthermore, other health consequences occurring in both males and females using steroids include heart attacks, liver cancer, and elevated cholesterol levels, and those who inject steroids run the risk of contracting or transmitting bloodborne diseases, including HIV.[33]

Heroin

Opium, which is derived from certain poppy species, is the source of heroin, morphine, paregoric, and codeine, some of which are still used medically today. **Heroin**, a refined form of morphine, was introduced about the turn of the twentieth century, and its street names include *black tar; boy, brown, H, harry, Henry, horse, shit*, and *smack*.[34]

heroin
A refined form of morphine that was introduced around the beginning of the twentieth century.

Chronic heroin use, unlike the use of most other drugs, appears to produce relatively minor direct or permanent physiological damage. Nevertheless, street heroin users typically neglect themselves and, as a result, report such disorders as heart and lung abnormalities, scarred veins, weight loss, malnutrition, endocarditis (a disease of the heart valves), stroke, gynecological problems, hepatitis, local skin infections, and abscesses.[35]

Table 11–5 lists the major types of drugs along with a description of each. The table is organized from top to bottom in terms of most commonly abused drugs to those that are least commonly abused.

TABLE 11–5
Drug Use by Decreasing Order of Frequency

Type of Drug	Description
Alcohol and tobacco	Both are considered illicit drugs because their use by juveniles is prohibited. Their wide use is considered a serious social problem.
Marijuana	The most frequently used illicit drug, marijuana is known by a variety of street names and is usually smoked.
Cocaine	Snorting (inhaling) is the most common method of using cocaine, but freebasing (smoking) cocaine has gained some popularity.
Methamphetamine	This highly addicting stimulant can be injected, smoked, or snorted. This is one of the many so-called club drugs.
Inhalants	With these drugs, youths need to inhale the vapors to receive the high they seek.
Sedatives	The common factor of sedatives is that they are taken orally and depress the nervous system, inducting a drowsy condition.
Ecstasy	Sometimes called a club drug, Ecstasy can be ingested orally, is sometimes snorted, and is occasionally smoked.
Hallucinogens	LSD was used in the 1960s and 1970s, but PCP, a nervous system excitant has been more recently used by adolescents.
Anabolic steroids	It is believed that steroids can produce an effect on muscle size; the one hundred different types can be taken orally, injected intramuscularly, or rubbed on the skin in the form of creams or gels.

Drug Use and Delinquency

An issue that has long been debated is whether drugs cause delinquency or delinquency leads to drug use or whether some other factors precede both delinquency and the onset of drug use.[36] Considerable research has found that delinquency tends to precede the use of drugs.[37] Other research suggests that what might appear to be a causal association is in fact a product of shared antecedents.[38] It is possible that a common factor, or syndrome, exists that underlies both delinquent behavior and drug use; this common factor may explain the frequency and type of drug use.[39]

Since the early 1990s, consensus has been increasing on the findings that explain the onset and continuing use of illicit drugs:

Web Extra 11–5
Office of National Drug Control Policy website

- There is widespread agreement that there is a sequential pattern of involvement in drug use during adolescence.[40] Denise B. Kandel and colleagues, using cross-sectional research and longitudinal data, proposed a developmental model for drug-use involvement: Alcohol use follows a pattern of minor delinquency and exposure to friends and parents who drink; the use of marijuana follows participation in minor delinquency and adoption of beliefs and values that are consistent with those held by peers but opposed by parents' standards; and adolescents' drug use proceeds to other illicit drugs if relationships with parents are poor and there is increased exposure to peers who use a variety of illegal drugs.[41] In examining drug use, it is important to identify in which of three major groups users belong. In the first group, youths or adults experiment once or twice and then discontinue drug use, whereas members of the second group continue drug use into young adulthood but do not allow drug use to interfere with their lives in any major ways; those in the third group become addicted or dependent on drugs, their entire lifestyle is likely to be designed around acquiring drugs daily, and they frequently commit crimes to maintain their drug supply.

Library Extra 11–3
OJJDP Fact Sheet: *Assessing Alcohol, Drug, and Mental Disorders in Juvenile Detainees*

- A number of risk factors appear to be related to delinquency and drug use. Early factors consist of perinatal difficulties, minor physical abnormalities, and brain damage, and later developmental risk factors are found in the family environment, including a family history of alcoholism, poor family management practices, and family conflict; other risk factors are early antisocial behavior and academic failure. Community risk factors include living in economically deprived areas and disorganized neighborhoods. According to J. David Hawkins, Richard F. Catalano, and Devon D. Brewer, the more of these risk factors a child has, the more likely it is that he or she will become involved in drug abuse.[42]

- There is little debate that youths who use hard drugs are more likely to engage in chronic delinquent behavior.[43] Delbert S. Elliott and D. Huizinga found that nearly 50 percent of serious juvenile offenders were also multiple drug users, that 82 percent of these offenders reported use (beyond experimentation) of at least one illicit drug, that rates of alcohol use among serious offenders were four to nine times those of nonoffenders, and that rates of marijuana use among serious offenders were fourteen times those of nonoffenders.[44] Jeffrey Fagan and colleagues' survey of inner-city youths also determined that heavy substance use was more prevalent and frequent among serious delinquents but that the type of substance used was more strongly associated with delinquency than was the frequency of drug use.[45]

Drug-Trafficking Juveniles

Drug-trafficking juveniles can be divided into several groups. There are those who occasionally sell small amounts of drugs, usually to support their own drug appetites, but they commit few (if any) delinquent acts. They are most likely to sell marijuana to friends and classmates and usually avoid coming to the attention of the police or the juvenile justice system.

Another group of drug-trafficking juveniles sells drugs frequently and may get their drugs from adult suppliers; they sell drugs in public places, such as on street corners, and are more

▲ Packages of Spice and K2, herbal marijuana alternatives.

■ **Should such herbal formulations be outlawed?**

likely to be arrested by the police and to be referred to the juvenile court. This group typi-cally sells drugs independently of any gang affiliation, especially in suburban settings.[46]

A third group sells drugs as part of their gang affiliation (especially in urban settings). Unlike the first two groups, drug trafficking within this group is controlled by adults, and participants in this group often end up in training schools or adult prisons. A student on academic scholarship in college told about his role in a gang's drug-trafficking operation:

> I must have been ten or eleven, and I was told to show up on this street corner. When I got there, they gave me a gun and told me to keep watch. If anyone came around, they told me to shoot them. They were taking care of business inside the crack house. Fortunately, no-body came around because I would have shot them. It surely would have changed my life.[47]

Explanations for the Onset of Drug Abuse

Some adolescents never use drugs, others use drugs from time to time on an experimental or recreational basis, and still others go through a period of experimentation with substance use and become committed to continuous use. This latter group is physically and/or emo-tionally addicted to the continued use of drugs.

At least two issues can help us understand juveniles who use drugs. The first is deter-mining whether it is the onset of drug use, the escalation of drug use, the addiction to drug use, or the cessation of drug use that is being addressed. We might ask: Why do some juve-niles never try drugs? Why do some juveniles experiment with drugs from time to time but do not become addicted? Why do other adolescents go from the beginning stages of drug use to more serious stages? Why do still other juveniles become addicted to drugs? Why are some of those who become addicted able to quit, whereas other addicts seem unable or unwilling to terminate drug use?

The second issue is that there is no single comprehensive picture of what causes ado-lescents' use of drugs. R. L. Simons, R. D. Conger, and L. B. Whitbeck made this point when they said that "while research has established a number of correlates of drug use, no theo-retical model has been developed which specifies the causal ordering of these associations and explicates their relationship to each other."[48] To express this another way, we might be aware of many of the reasons why juveniles become involved in drug use, but we do not know how all of the pieces of the puzzle fit together.[49]

The following sections specifically address adolescents' initial use of drugs by focusing on theories that attempt to explain substance use among adolescents.

Cognitive-Affective Theories

A number of theories have focused on how perceptions about the costs and benefits of drug use contribute to adolescents' decisions to experiment with these substances. Such mod-els share two assumptions: (1) The decision to use substances rests in substance-specific expectations and perceptions held by adolescents, and (2) the effects of all other variables (e.g., adolescents' personality traits or their involvement with peers who use substances) are mediated through substance-specific cognitions, evaluations, and decisions.[50] The theory of reasoned action, which holds that the most important determinant of a person's behavior is behavioral intent, is the most encompassing of these cost/benefit decision-making models.[51]

Addictive Personality Theory

Another explanation for the onset and continued use of drugs says that the typical addict has an addiction-prone personality and suffers from some deep-rooted personality disorder or emotional problem.

Stress Relief Theory

The desire to get high, which is seen as a way to relieve stress, depression, or the boredom of everyday life, is common in adolescent peer culture. The desire to drink alcohol and get high is very much related to the desire to feel good, to be comfortable in social situations,

Voices of Delinquency 11–3
Read "A Juvenile Drug Dealer." Why did this youth go from using to selling drugs? How could his life have turned out much differently?

Library Extra 11–4
National Drug Intelligence Center publica-tion: *National Drug Threat Assessment*

and to gain acceptance in peer culture. This explanation for the appeal of substance abuse says that stress relief provides a sought-after high or peak experience.

Social Learning Theory

Social learning theory posits that an adolescent's involvement in substance abuse has three sequential effects: It begins with the observation and imitation of substance-specific behaviors; it continues with social reinforcement, such as encouragement and support for drug use; and it culminates in a juvenile's expectation of positive social and physiological consequences from continued drug use. These anticipated consequences might be primarily social in nature, such as acceptance or rejection by peers, during experimental use and then become largely physiological in nature, such as positive or negative physiological reactions to the substances themselves, during subsequent stages. Social learning theory essentially says that an adolescent who anticipates that using substances will produce more personal benefits than costs will be at risk for continued use.[52]

Social Control Theories

Travis Hirschi's social control theory and J. D. Hawkins and J. G. Weis's social development model both assume that emotional attachments to peers who use substances is a primary cause of substance abuse. Unlike social learning theories, however, these two approaches pay specific attention to weak conventional bonds to society and to the institutions and individuals who might otherwise discourage deviant behavior.[53] Hirschi asserted that the deviant impulses that most adolescents share are held in check or controlled by strong bonds to conventional society, families, schools, and religions; however, adolescents who do not have such controlling influences will not feel compelled to adhere to convention or to engage in socially acceptable behaviors.[54]

The social development model proposes that adolescents become attached to substance-using peers if they feel uncommitted either to conventional society or to positive role models. Unlike Hirschi's social control theory, which focuses largely on social systems, the social development model focuses more on individuals—their social development and their social interactions. This focus shifts developmentally, with parents dominating the preschool years, teachers dominating the preadolescent phase, and peers dominating the adolescent stage.[55]

Social Disorganization Theory

Social disorganization theory explains the onset and escalation of adolescents' drug use by claiming that a bleak economic environment for certain disenfranchised groups has created a generation of young adults in urban inner cities who regularly experience doubt, hopelessness, and uncertainty. According to this perspective, the hopelessness of the poor leads them to seek relief. Hence, drug use and alcohol abuse provide an immediate fix for hopelessness but, in the long run, create other problems.[56]

Integrated Theories

Elliott and colleagues offer a model that expands traditional strain, social control, and social learning theories into a single perspective that accounts for delinquent behavior and drug use.[57] They describe the mechanisms by which neighborhood disorganization, attachment to families, and social values contribute to involvement with drugs.[58] This model was initially created to explain the causes of delinquency, but it was later more fully developed to explain adolescents' drug-using behavior.[59]

Web Extra 11–6
National Drug Intelligence Center website

The attempt to explain a social phenomenon with a single theory has a long history in sociology, but substance abuse theory (like delinquency theory) owes its origins to several theoretical perspectives. For some individuals, drugs are an escape from the dreariness and toxicity of their home environments; for others, substance abuse is an attempt to escape from emotionally crippling problems; and for still others, substance abuse arises rather normally as part of peer influences. Integrated or interactionist models combining the effects of

Exhibit 11–6
Explanations for the Onset of Drug Abuse

- *Cognitive-Affective Theories*—These theories relate to how the perceptions about the costs and benefits of drug use contribute to adolescents' decisions to experiment with these substances.
- *Addictive Personality Theory*—The typical addict has an addiction-prone personality and suffers from some deep-rooted personality disorder or emotional problems.
- *Stress Relief Theory*—The desire to get high—as a means to relieve stress, depression, or the boredom of everyday life—is common in adolescent culture.
- *Social Learning Theory*—This theory postulates that an adolescent's involvement in substance abuse begins with observation and imitation of substance-specific behaviors,

continues with social reinforcement, and cultivates in a juvenile's expectation of positive social and physiological consequences from continued drug use.
- *Social Control Theories*—Emotional attachment to peers who use substances is a primary cause of substance abuse.
- *Social Disorganization Theory*—The bleak economic environment has resulted in those situated in these settings experiencing doubt, hopelessness, and uncertainty, and, as a result, they seek relief in drugs.
- *Integrated Theories*—Elliott and colleagues use strain, social control, and social learning theories to form a perspective that accounts for delinquent behavior and drug use.

strain, control, and social learning theories probably make the most sense in explaining why adolescents start using alcohol and drugs.[60] The theories regarding the onset of drug abuse are summarized in Exhibit 11–6.

Delinquency across the Life Course: Drug Use

Two basic pathways are possible for substance-abusing youths. They may restrict themselves to substance abuse and not become involved in other delinquent activities; these offenders may desist from substance abuse after their adolescent years or continue to use drugs as adults. Alternatively, substance-abusing youths who also participate in other delinquent activities may desist from one or both types of activity during adolescence or continue to be involved in one or both as adults.

There is some evidence that about two-thirds of substance-abusing youths continue to use drugs after reaching adulthood but that about half desist from other forms of criminality. Researchers in the 1980s found that drug abusers who persisted in both crime and substance abuse as adults typically came from poor families, did poorly in school, used multiple types of drugs, were chronic offenders, and had an early onset of both drug use and delinquent behavior.[61]

Marvin D. Krohn, Alan J. Lizotte, and Cynthia M. Perez, in their 1997 analysis of the Rochester data, found that the use of alcohol and drugs in early adolescence increases a youngster's risk of becoming pregnant or impregnating someone, becoming a teenage parent, dropping out of school, and prematurely living independently from parents or guardians; in turn, the process of experiencing these early transitions increases the chances that individuals will use alcohol and drugs when they become young adults.[62] Krohn and colleagues suggested that the cumulative impact of experiencing various early transitions may be detrimental to the successful movement, or transition, to adult status and adult roles.[63] It is not surprising that an early or unsuccessful transition in one area will have implications for other trajectories.[64] Off-time and out-of-order transitions can be especially disruptive because the individual may not be prepared for the added responsibilities and obligations that frequently accompany these transitions, and precocious transitions can further lead to problematic consequences because of the increased economic burdens and reduced economic prospects facing those who experience them. For example, teenage parenthood can disrupt the order of transitions by leading youths to enter full-time employment before completing high school, which can derail career development. The person who leaves school before graduation may not have any choice but a low-paying unskilled job, which in turn produces job instability and ongoing economic disadvantages.[65]

Web Extra 11–7
Drug Enforcement Administration (DEA) website

Gary M. McClelland, Linda A. Teplin, and Karen M. Abram highlighted several generalizations about drug use and adolescent development that are widely recognized and accepted:

- Substance use commonly follows a sequence from tobacco and alcohol to marijuana and then to more dangerous substances.
- Substance use and abuse that begin in early adolescence are associated with more serious delinquency and longer deviant careers, antisocial personality disorders in later life, and more numerous risky behaviors.
- Substance abuse is associated with poor academic performance.
- More severe substance abuse and dependence are associated with serious criminal offenses in general.
- Substance use and abuse are associated with higher rates of psychiatric disorders and with disorders of greater severity.[66]

In 2012, Helene R. White and colleagues examined the association of alcohol use with the persistence and desistance of serious violent offending among African American and Caucasian young men from adolescence into adulthood. Five violent groups were identified: nonviolent, late-onsetters, desisters, persisters, and one-time offenders. Alcohol use trajectories were identified for those groups 12 through 24/25 years of age. Both persisters and desisters showed the highest levels of drinking at thirteen years of age, but by twenty-four or twenty-five years of age the persisters drank less than the nonviolent and one-timer groups. No evidence was found to show that the association between drinking and violence differed for African Americans and Caucasians, but the findings do suggest that change in alcohol use could provide clues for preventing violent offending.[67]

Drug addicts, like those with a history of delinquency and criminality, sometimes have a turning point, or change, when they walk away from drug use, but those who were deeply entrenched in the drug world as adolescents and continue this activity in their adult years find it particularly difficult to give up drugs. Those who are able to stay with the straight life typically have had a religious experience or have had an extremely positive experience in a therapeutic community for drug addicts.[68] (See Exhibit 11–7 for one person's account of how he walked away from his addiction to alcohol and drugs after several decades of dependency.)

D. B. Kandel and J. A. Logan reported that significant status changes, including marriage and parenthood, were correlated with the cessation of marijuana smoking among users in their middle to late twenties.[69] L. A. Goodman and W. H. Kruskal found that reasons for cessation involved the imposition of both internal controls and external controls.[70]

Exhibit 11–7
Overcoming Chemical Dependency

In a May 2004 interview, a former addict told his story.

My dad was an African American. During his prime years, he was rated as one of the ten best baseball players in the country. He was always on the road; I didn't get to see him much. He finally stopped traveling when I was in the eighth grade, but all that did was put him in the nightclub business. He didn't take much interest in my life. I can count the number of extracurricular activities he went to; he would show up late or not at all. He would say that he would pick me up from school, but he wouldn't. The animosity I had for my dad continued up until the day he passed.

My mom is white. She was divorced and had two children from her first marriage. She married my father while he was in prison. He was in prison for writing bad checks. She stayed married to him for as long as she could, and then they divorced. I saw so little of my dad that I was raised in a white society. But when I stepped out of that door, I was a black man. I had quite a time adjusting to the two societies. There were a lot of days I had to fight to get home from school.

I can remember one time when I was eight or nine and I was laying on the bed and crying. I couldn't understand why people would treat me the way they did. My mom really couldn't explain it because she was a white female trying to educate a black young boy about racism within both the white community and the black community.

I felt a lot of pressure as a kid. Due to the fact that my dad owned clubs, I had access to alcohol. I didn't start drinking until I was 15 or 16 years old. But when I did start drinking, I really drank. I also began to smoke marijuana.

I went away to college on an academic scholarship. I didn't like school and only drank and smoked more pot. My alcohol intake was soaring, and my smoking was also increasing. I joined the military and for five years drank a lot of alcohol.

I got out of the military, got married, and had three children. My drug and alcohol use increased dramatically from 1985 to 1990. When crack came around, I got into that. I was what you call a weekend crack addict. That lasted until one day I went to a college football game with a cousin of mine. I cashed my check, and that weekend I smoked my whole paycheck up.

I didn't know what to tell my wife. I committed myself to an inpatient treatment program. I went in on a Monday, and as I was walking down the hall on a Thursday after Recreation, this warm feeling came over my body. I had to hold on to the wall because I almost lost my balance. It was like it was washed out of me. And since that day to the day right now, I haven't had a drink. I haven't smoked marijuana. I haven't done cocaine. I haven't smoked cigarettes.

Unfortunately, my wife had had it with me. She divorced me, but I have spent a lot of time with my children. I want to be a good father, something my father was not to me.

I do not define myself as an alcoholic. I do not consider myself to be a drug addict. I am a chemically dependent person. When I go to the doctor, I tell him not to prescribe anything that will ever be addictive to me.

Source: Personal interview with author.

L. Thomas Winfree, Jr., Christine S. Sellers, and Dennis L. Clason examined the reasons for adolescents' cessation of and abstention from substance use and determined that social learning variables clearly distinguished abstainers from current users, but they were less able to distinguish former users from current users or former users from abstainers.[71] Ryan D. Schroeder, Peggy C. Giordano, and Stephen A. Cernkovich investigated the effect of drug use on desistance processes using a sample of previously institutionalized youths and found that social network effects, particularly partner criminality, explain some of the negative impacts of drug use on life-course patterns of criminal offending.[72]

Voices of Delinquency 11–4
Read "Selling Drugs Was My Downfall." Unlike the story in Voices of Delinquency 11-3, this does not have a positive outcome. Can you identify why the life course of these two individuals ended up so differently?

Delinquency and Social Policy: Solutions to the Drug Problem

Prevention programs, treatment interventions, strict enforcement, and harm reduction are all possible means of controlling drug use among adolescents. Prevention, which has already been discussed, and treatment appear to be the most effective means of controlling drug abuse, and there is abundant evidence that deterrence tactics, such as the federal "war on drugs" (involving mostly strict enforcement), have been largely ineffective with both juveniles and adults.

Prevention Programs

The 1990s saw dramatic developments in drug prevention programs. The Center for the Study and Prevention of Violence at the University of Colorado began an initiative called Blueprints for Violence Prevention, in which researchers evaluated six hundred programs designed to prevent violence and drug abuse and to treat youths with problem behaviors.[73] The investigators were able to identify eleven model programs and twenty-one promising programs. Some of the more noteworthy include (1) Life Skills Training (LST), which is designed to prevent or reduce the use of "gateway" drugs such as tobacco, alcohol, and marijuana[74]; (2) Midwestern Prevention Project (MPP), which is a comprehensive three- to five-year community-based prevention program targeting gateway use of alcohol, tobacco, and marijuana[75]; and (3) Project Toward No Drug Abuse (Project TND), which targets high school youths who are at risk for drug abuse.[76] Significantly, Blueprints for Violence Prevention researchers reported that both model programs and promising programs had positive outcome assessments when evaluated over a period of several years.[77]

Police departments across the country conduct at least three substance abuse prevention programs in schools: Drug Abuse Resistance Education (D.A.R.E.), School Program to Educate and Control Drug Abuse (SPECDA), and Project Alert. The D.A.R.E. program is a widely replicated effort to prevent substance abuse. Although Chapter 13 notes that recent evaluations of D.A.R.E. are less than encouraging, it is the most popular school-based drug education program in the United States and operates in about 70 percent of our nation's school districts, reaching 25 million students; it has also been adopted in forty-four other countries.[78] New York City's SPECDA, a collaborative project of the city's police department and board of education, is another highly praised drug prevention program.[79] Project Alert, a program originating in middle schools in California and Oregon, appears to have had some success in teaching students to avoid drugs and to resist peer pressure to use tobacco and alcohol.[80]

Library Extra 11–5
General Counterdrug Intelligence Plan

Library Extra 11–6
University of Michigan's *Monitoring the Future survey*

Effective programs need to incorporate early childhood and family interventions, school-based interventions, and comprehensive community-wide efforts. The important dimension of drug prevention interventions, as is continually emphasized throughout this text, is a multidimensional approach centering on the family, school, and community.

Treatment Interventions

Treatment for drug abusers takes place in psychiatric and hospital settings for youngsters whose parents can afford it or have third-party insurance benefits. Other youths, especially those substance abusers who have committed minor forms of delinquency, receive treatment in privately administered placements, which vary tremendously in the quality of program design and implementation. Substance abusers who are involved in serious forms of delinquency will likely be placed in county or state facilities whose basic organizational goals are custodial and security oriented, and they generally receive some substance abuse counseling, especially in group contexts.

Library Extra 11–7
Office of National Drug Control Policy: *National Drug Control Strategy, 2009*

Substance-abusing youths with typical multiple problems may be more malleable than adult offenders, but there is little evidence that the majority of substance abuse programs are any more successful than those for adult substance abusers. Élan in Maine; Rocky Mountain in Colorado; Provo Canyon in Utah; and Cascade, Cedu, and Hilltop in California are privately administered therapeutic schools or emotional growth programs that may be better than the average substance abuse program for juveniles.[81]

Drug courts are another fairly recent treatment innovation for those who have a history of drug use (see Chapter 12). To address alcohol and drug problems, treatment services in drug courts have been based on formal theories of drug dependence and abuse. They also attempt to employ the best therapeutic tools and to provide participants with the opportunities needed to build cognitive skills. Research findings generally show that drug courts can reduce recidivism and promote other positive outcomes, but research has been unable to uncover which court processes affect which outcomes and for what types of offenders.[82]

The balanced restorative-justice model has been used as a form of treatment intervention with drug- and alcohol-abusing adolescents. It forms the guiding philosophy in twelve states and builds on restorative-justice conferencing that takes place in informal settings where voluntary negotiating encounters include victims, offenders, and their relevant communities.[83] Restorative-justice conferencing can also use more coerced restorative obligations, such as restitution or community service imposed by formal proceedings. What makes these processes and obligations "restorative," rather than rehabilitative or retributive, is the restorative intent underlying their imposition.[84]

Drug and alcohol abuse interventions have also been developed in a number of community-based and institutional settings. Some training schools, for example, conduct group sessions for those with histories of drug use. A social worker may conduct ongoing drug and alcohol abuse groups, and members from outside groups, such as Alcoholics Anonymous (AA) or Narcotics Anonymous (NA), may come into the institution and hold sessions.

Strict Enforcement

The "war on drugs" has not been won with juveniles any more than it has with adults. A disastrous consequence of this "war" is that increasing numbers of minority youths who were involved in using or selling crack cocaine have been brought into the justice system for extended periods of time. Some have even argued that the war on drugs has been a factor contributing to the spread of youth gangs.[85] Strict enforcement, however, has seemed to make a difference in several ways:

▲ Teen representatives of Drug Free Youth in Town are introduced at a Miami, Florida, workshop.

■ **How can the success of drug prevention programs be measured?**

- The destruction of overseas drug-producing crops has probably had some impact on the availability of drugs in the United States, raising prices and making some drugs harder to find.

- Heavy penalties associated with the sale of illicit drugs appear to have been at least somewhat effective in deterring both juvenile and adult offenders.

- Law enforcement's targeting of dealers has had some success in getting those offenders off the streets.

- The policing of the sale of tobacco products, especially cigarettes, at convenience stores and other places has made it more difficult for minors to purchase or obtain tobacco products.

- The strict enforcement of no-drug zones around schools has discouraged or at least reduced the number of persons trafficking drugs to school-age children.

- Strict enforcement of adolescent drug trafficking at school and in neighborhoods may have reduced the availability of drugs to young people.

Harm Reduction

Harm reduction is an approach designed to reduce the harm done to youths by drug use and by the severe penalties resulting from drug use and sales. A number of harm-reduction strategies have been employed:

- Programs in which health professionals administer drugs to addicts as part of a treatment and detoxification regimen

- Drug-treatment facilities that are available for those drug addicts wishing to enter treatment

- Needle exchange programs that are intended to slow the transmission of HIV and that provide educational resources about how HIV is contracted and spread.

Juvenile drug users generally find a wide variety of treatment programs and facilities. Treatment programs are usually more readily available to middle- and upper-class youths than to lower-class youths, partially because wealthier parents can afford to pay for the care of their dependent children. The legalized administration of drugs to addicts and needle exchange programs are more typically found when working with adult drug users than with juveniles. Table 11–6 summaries the proposed solutions to the drug problem.

TABLE 11–6
Proposed Solutions to the Drug Problem

Type of Effort	Brief Description	Evaluation
Prevention programs	More than six hundred programs have been developed to prevent and treat drug abuse.	A few have promise, but most have been ineffective.
Treatment interventions	These usually take place in psychiatric and hospital settings for parents who can afford it or have third-party insurance benefits.	There is little evidence of success.
Strict enforcement	The "war on drugs" campaign waged against juveniles.	With juveniles no evidence of success, but it has had some impact in deterring drug trafficking
Harm reduction	This approach was designed to reduce the harm done to youths by drug use and by the severe penalties resulting from drug use and sales.	Programs like these are more widely spread with adults than with juveniles.

The Case

The Life Course of Amy Watters, Age 15

Amy's father, Simon, had always been a drinker. He had consumed both alcohol and marijuana for as long as she could remember, and he was often tipsy or high, and sometimes clearly drunk. He made no excuses for his behavior, and frequently told Amy that his father had given him his first drink when he was only eight years old. Children who learned to drink early, he said, had far less trouble handling alcohol and other substances later in life than those to whom alcohol was forbidden.

One night when her father was clearly intoxicated, he asked Amy if she'd like to have a drink with him. Until now, he'd separated the part of his life that involved drinking from Amy— except, of course, for the unintended influence that it had had on her to see him drunk. Now, however, he told Amy that it was always nice to have a drinking partner, and that she was old enough to drink, anyway. Of course, alcohol was not new to Amy and she had sometimes engaged in binge drinking while away from home. Amy was no stranger to illicit drugs, either, having smoked marijuana and experimented with cocaine with her former boyfriend, Damon, on quite a few occasions.

So, after a few more words of encouragement from her father, she sat down in front of the television and started drinking Scotch—her father's drink of choice. As the evening wore on she became increasingly intoxicated and passed out on the couch.

She woke up the next day with a headache, but feeling strangely liberated—as though she had somehow entered an adult world in which she had the freedom to make choices previously unavailable to her. Or at least choices that were somehow now acceptable. Alcohol itself, she realized, was also liberating, and she vaguely remembered telling her father closely guarded secrets that she had kept to herself since running away.

What kind of a role model is Amy's father? Why are alcohol consumption and delinquency closely associated?

Learn More on the Web:

Studies have shown that children of heavy drinkers are at greater risk of having emotional problems than are children whose parents are not alcoholics. Moreover, most children of alcoholics have experienced various forms of neglect and abuse.

- American Academy of Child and Adolescent Psychiatry, *Children of Alcoholics*:
  www.aacap.org/galleries/FactsForFamilies/17_children_of_alchoholics.pdf

Follow the continuing Amy Watters saga in the next chapter.

SUMMARY

This chapter has discussed drug and alcohol use by adolescents. Some of the key points of the chapter are as follows:

- Drug use and alcohol abuse are forms of problem behavior, and their onset, duration, and termination are determined by the dynamics of the interplay between the environment and particular young people, which varies over developmental periods.

- The good news is that drug use appears to have declined significantly since the late 1970s, with perhaps slight increases since the early 1990s.

- It is also good news that the use of cigarettes has declined among American adolescents.

- The bad news is that alcohol abuse remains high among American adolescents and shows no signs of decreasing.

- The data seem to show that high-risk children are becoming increasingly involved in substance abuse.

- Although the use of crack cocaine may be declining across the nation, it remains the drug of choice for many disadvantaged youths.

- It is disconcerting that teenagers have increased their use of marijuana in the past decade.

- Recent increasing use of methamphetamine by adolescents may also be viewed as a matter of social concern.

- A number of theories examine why juveniles use drugs, but integrated theories appear to provide the most adequate forms of explanation.

- Early prevention efforts in schools and in other social contexts appear to be making headway with low-risk children.

- The fact that substance abuse is usually one of several problems for high-risk youths makes it more difficult to achieve substantial success through therapeutic interventions.

KEY TERMS

alcohol, p. 276
amphetamine, p. 281
club drug, p. 281
cocaine, p. 278

drug addiction, p. 276
Ecstasy, p. 281
heroin, p. 283
inhalant, p. 280

marijuana, p. 278
sedative, p. 281

REVIEW QUESTIONS

1. What drug remains the drug of choice for most adolescents? Why?
2. What drugs are used by adolescents? Why are some more widely used than others?
3. What is the debate about the relationship between drug use and delinquency?
4. What is known about drug-trafficking juveniles?
5. What are the various theories for the onset of drug use among adolescents and adults?
6. What is the relationship between drug use and the life course?
7. What approaches have been tried to solve the drug problem?

DISCUSSION QUESTIONS

1. Why is drug use so popular in American society?
2. Why does the typical drug user use drugs up to a certain point and then go no further? At the same time, why do other youths who seem to be as committed to this stopping point continue using drugs?
3. Do you think cultural drug use should be exempted from criminal penalties? Explain your reasoning.
4. Should nicotine be added to the list of controlled substances? Explain your reasoning.
5. Why would a youth pursue only the drug pathway rather than the delinquency/drug pathway?
6. What factors do you think contribute to low drug-use rates among African American and Asian adolescents?
7. Why do college students drink as much as they do? How is their drinking related to the subject matter of this chapter?

GROUP EXERCISES

1. Invite a medical expert to address the class regarding the short- and long-term health effects of the use of the various drugs discussed in this chapter.
2. Invite a leader of the local MADD chapter to address the class.
3. Invite a member of your local police department's drug enforcement unit to address the class regarding drug-use patterns in your city and state.
4. Have the students clip newspaper or web articles related to Ecstasy use in your city and state, and have them share the articles with the class.
5. Invite a recovering addict from a local narcotics support group to address the class regarding his or her experiences in the postaddiction phase of his or her life.
6. Invite a drug counselor to address the class regarding his or her experiences trying to assist drug users.

CHAPTER RESOURCES

Go to mycrimekit.com to explore the following study tools and resources specific to this chapter:

- **Practice Quiz:** Practice with multiple-choice, true/false, short-answer, and essay questions.
- **WebQuests:** Do web activities about child and family statistics and their relevance to juvenile crime and delinquency.
- **Flashcards:** Use 10 flashcards to test your knowledge of the chapter's key terms.
- **Career Center:** Check out the hot links to interesting careers in criminal justice, criminology, and juvenile justice.
- **Research Center:** Check out the Cybrary and MySearchLab for even more resources.

NOTES

1. Jeff Slowikowski, *Highlights from Pathways to Desistance: A Longitudinal Study of Serious Adolescent Behavior* (Washington, D.C.: Office of Juvenile Justice and Delinquency Prevention, March 2011).

2. L. D. Johnston, P. M. O'Malley, J. G. Bachman, and J. E. Schulenberg, *Monitoring the Future: National Results on Adolescent Drug Use: Overview of Key Findings, 2011* (Ann Arbor: Institute for Social research, University of Michigan, 2012).

3. Howard Abadinsky, *Drugs: An Introduction*, 4th ed. (Belmont, Calif.: Wadsworth/Thompson Learning, 2001).

4. In 1990, the U.S. Supreme Court ruled 6–3 in an Oregon case that states can prohibit the use of peyote by members of the Native American church [*Employment Division, Department of Human Resources of Oregon* v. *Smith*, 494 U.S. 872 (1990)]. But Congress enacted a statute providing a defense for those who use the substance "with good faith practice of a religious belief."

5. Abadinsky, *Drugs*.

6. *Juveniles and Drugs* (Washington, D.C.: Office of National Drug Control Policy, 2004).

7. L. D. Johnston, P. M. O'Malley, J. G. Bachman, and J. E. Schulenberg, *Monitoring the Future: National Results on Adolescent Drug Use: Overview of Key Findings, 2011* (Bethesda, Md.: National Institute on Drug Abuse, 2012).

8. Substance Abuse and Mental Health Services Administration, *Results from the 2010 National Survey on Drug Use and Health: National Findings* (Rockville, Md.: office of Applied Studies, 2011).

9. James A. Inciardi, *The War on Drugs II* (Mountain View, Calif.: Mayfield, 1992), p. 62.

10. Public Health Service, *Healthy People 2000: National Health Promotion and Disease Prevention Objectives—Full Report with Commentary* (Washington, D.C.: U.S. Department of Health and Human Services, 1991).

11. Johnston et al., *Monitoring the Future, 2011*.

12. Centers for Disease Control and Prevention, *Health Effects of Cigarette Smoking*, http://www.cedc.gov/tobacco/data_statistics/fact_sheets/health_effects/effects_cig_smoking (accessed June 20, 2012).

13. For many other names, see Inciardi, *The War on Drugs II*.

14. Johnson et al., *Monitoring the Future, 2011*.

15. Inciardi, *The War on Drugs II*.

16. Gordon Witkin, "The Men Who Created Crack," U.S. News & World Report (August 29, 1991), pp. 44–53. See also Malcolm W. Klein, Cheryl L. Maxson, and Lea C. Cunningham, "'Crack,' Street Gangs, and Violence," Criminology 29 (November 1991), pp. 623–50.

17. Inciardi, *The War on Drugs II*.

18. Ibid.

19. Ibid.

20. "Cocaine Abuse," *NIDA Capsules* (November 1989).

21. James N. Hall, "Impact of Mother's Cocaine Use," *Street Pharmacologist* 11 (October 1987).

22. Johnson et al., *Monitoring the Future, 2011*.

23. T. M. McSherry, "Program Experiences with the Solvent Abuser in Philadelphia," in *Epidemiology of Inhalant Abuse: An Update*, NIDA Research Monograph 85, edited by R. A. Crider and B. A. Rouse (Washington, D.C.: National Institute on Drug Abuse 1989), pp. 106–20.

24. U.S. Food and Drug Administration, *Frequently Asked Questions*, http://www.fed.gov/oc/buyonline/faqs.html.

25. Inciardi, *The War on Drugs II*.

26. Abadinsky, *Drugs*.

27. Bureau of Justice Statistics, *Drug Enforcement Report* (Washington, D.C.: U.S. Department of Justice, January 3, 1990).

28. Substance Abuse and Mental Health Services Administration, *Preliminary Estimates from the 1997 National Household Survey on Drug Abuse*.

29. University of Michigan News and Information Services, January 24, 1991.

30. *NIDA Infofax: Steroids (Anabolic-Androgenic)* (Washington, D.C. National Institute on Drug Abuse, 1999).

31. Ibid.

32. National Institute on Drug Abuse, *Research Report: Anabolic Steroid Abuse* (Washington, D.C.: U.S. Department of Justice, April 2000).

33. Ibid.

34. Inciardi, *The War on Drugs II*.

35. For an overview of medical complications associated with heroin addiction, see Jerome J. Platt, *Heroin Addiction: Theory, Research, and Treatment* (Malabar, Fla.: Robert E. Krieger, 1986), pp. 80–102.

36. David M. Altschuler and Paul J. Brounstein, "Patterns of Drug Use, Drug Trafficking, and Other Delinquency among Inner-City Adolescent Males in Washington, D.C.," *Criminology* 29 (1991), p. 590.

37. Lloyd D. Johnson et al., "Drugs and Delinquency: A Search for Causal Connections," in *Longitudinal Research on Drug Use: Empirical Finds and Methodological Issues*, edited by Denise B. Kandel, Ronald C. Kessler, and Rebecca Z. Margulies (Washington, D.C.: Hemisphere, 1978), pp. 137–56; J. C. Friedman and A. S. Friedman, "Drug Use and Delinquency among Lower Class, Court Adjudicated Adolescent Boys," in *Drug Use in America* 1 (Washington, D.C.: National Commission on Marijuana and Drug Abuse: Government Printing Office, 1973); J. A. Inciardi, "Heroin Use and Street Crime," *Crime and Delinquency* 25 (1979), pp. 335–46; and L. N. Robins and G. E. Murphy, "Drug Use in a Normal Population of Young Negro Men," *American Journal of Public Health* 57 (1967), pp. 1580–96.

38. Altschuler and Brounstein, "Patterns of Drug Use, Drug Trafficking, and Other Delinquency"; Richard Jessor and Shirley L. Jessor, *Problem Behavior and Psychosocial Development: A Longitudinal Study of Youth* (New York: Academic Press, 1977); R. L. Akers, "Delinquent Behavior, Drugs and Alcohol: What Is the Relationship?" *Today's Delinquent* 3 (1984), pp. 19–47; D. S. Elliott and D. Huizinga, *The Relationship between Delinquent Behavior and ADM*

Problems (Boulder, Colo.: Behavior Research Institute, 1985); and Delbert S. Elliott, David Huizinga, and Scott Menard, *Multiple Problem Youth: Delinquency, Substance Use, and Mental Health Problems* (New York: Springer-Verlag, 1989). See also Richard Felson, Jukka Savolainer, Mikko Aaltonen, and Heta Moustgaard, "Is the Association between Alcohol Use and Delinquency Causal or Spurious?" *Criminology* 46 (2008), pp. 786–808.

39. See Marc Le Blanc and Nathalie Kaspy, "Trajectories of Delinquency and Problem Behavior: Comparison of Social and Personal Control Characteristics of Adjudicated Boys on Synchronous and Nonsynchronous Paths," *Journal of Quantitative Criminology* 14 (1998), pp. 181–214; and Helene Raskin White, "Marijuana Use and Delinquency: A Test of the 'Independent Cause' Hypothesis," *Journal of Drug Issues* (1991), pp. 231–56.

40. Bureau of Justice Statistics, *Drugs, Crime, and the Justice System* (Washington, D.C.: Government Printing Office, 1993).

41. Kandel et al., *Longitudinal Research on Drug Use*.

42. J. David Hawkins, Richard F. Catalano, and Devon D. Brewer, "Preventing Serious, Violent, and Chronic Juvenile Offending," in *A Sourcebook: Serious, Violent and Chronic Juvenile Offenders*, edited by James C. Howell, Barry Krisberg, J. David Hawkins, and John J. Wilson (Thousand Oaks, Calif.: Sage, 1995).

43. Delbert S. Elliott, David Huizinga, and Suzanne S. Ageton, *Explaining Delinquency and Drug Use* (Beverly Hills, Calif.: Sage, 1985).

44. D. S. Elliott and D. Huizinga, "The Relationship between Delinquent Behavior and ADM Problem Behaviors," paper prepared for the ADAMHA/OJJDP State of the Art Research Conference on Juvenile Offenders with Serious Drug/Alcohol and Mental Health Problems, Bethesda, MD, April 17–18, 1984.

45. J. Fagan, J. Weis, and Y. Cheng, "Delinquency and Substance Use among Inner-City Students," *Journal of Drug Abuse* (1990), pp. 351–402.

46. Klein et al., "'Crack,' Street Gangs, and Violence."

47. Based on an interview in April 1995.

48. R. L. Simons, R. D. Conger, and L. B. Whitbeck, "A Multistage Social Learning Model of the Influence of Family and Peers upon Adolescent Substance Abuse," *Journal of Drug Issues* 18 (1988), p. 293.

49. John Petraitis, Brian R. Flay, and Todd Q. Miller, "Reviewing Theories of Adolescent Substance Use: Organizing Pieces in the Puzzle," *Psychological Bulletin* 117 (1995), pp. 67–86. See also W. Alex Mason, Julia E. Hitchings, Robert J. McMahon, and Richard L. Spoth, "A Test of Three Alternative Hypotheses Regarding the Effects of Early Delinquency on Adolescent Psychosocial Functioning and Substance Involvement," *Journal of Abnormal Child Psychology* 35 (2007), pp. 831–43; and David B. Henry and Kimberly Kobus, "Early Adolescent Social Networks and Substance Use," *Journal of Early Adolescence* 27 (2007), pp. 346–62.

50. Ibid.

51. I. Ajken and M. Fishbein, *Understanding Attitudes and Predicting Social Behavior* (Englewood Cliffs, N.J.: Prentice-Hall, 1980).

52. Petraitis et al., "Reviewing Theories of Adolescent Substance Use." See also Joan L. Neff and Dennis E. Waite, "Male versus Female Substance Abuse Patterns among Incarcerated Juvenile Offenders: Comparing Strain and Social Learning Variables," *Justice Quarterly* 24 (March 2007), pp. 106–32.

53. Travis Hirschi, *Causes of Delinquency* (Berkeley: University of California Press, 1969); J. D. Hawkins and J. G. Weis, "The Social Development Model: An Integrated Approach to Delinquency Prevention," *Journal of Primary Prevention* 6 (1985), pp. 73–97; Jayne A. Fulkerson, Keryn E. Pasch, Cheryl L. Perry, and Kelli Konro, "Relationships between Alcohol-Related Informal Social Control, Parental Monitoring and Adolescent Problem Behaviors among Racially Diverse Urban Youth," *Journal of Community Health* 33 (2008), pp. 425–33.

54. Hirschi, *Causes of Delinquency*.

55. J. D. Hawkins, R. F. Catalano, and J. Y. Miller, "Risk and Protective Factors for Alcohol and Other Drug Problems in Adolescence and Early Adulthood," *Psychological Bulletin* 112 (1992), pp. 64–105.

56. Radical theorists have made this a theme of their research on poor adolescents, especially minority ones. See Chapter 6.

57. Elliott et al., *Explaining Delinquency and Drug Use*.

58. D. S. Elliott, D. Huizinga, and S. Menard, *Multiple Problem Youth: Delinquency, Substance Abuse Mental Health Problems* (New York: Springer-Verlag, 1989).

59. Ibid.

60. Peter W. Greenwood, "Substance Abuse Problems among High-Risk Youth and Potential Interventions," *Crime and Delinquency* 38 (October 1992), pp. 444–58. For the reciprocal relationships that interactional theory posits among drug use, association with drug-using peers, and beliefs about drug use, see Marvin D. Krohn, Alan J. Lizotte, Terence P. Thornberry, Carolyn Smith, and David McDowall, "Reciprocal Causal Relationships among Drug Use, Peers, and Beliefs: A Five-Wave Panel Model," *Journal of Drug Issues* 26 (1996), pp. 405–28.

61. Marcia Chaiken and Bruce Johnson, *Characteristics of Different Types of Drug-Involved Youth* (Washington, D.C.: National Institute of Justice, 1988).

62. Marvin D. Krohn, Alan J. Lizotte, and Cynthia M. Perez, "The Interrelationships between Substance Use and Precocious Transitions to Adult Status," *Journal of Health and Social Behavior* 38 (March 1997), pp. 87–101.

63. Ibid.

64. Glen H. Elder, Jr., "Time, Human Agency, and Social Change: Perspectives on the Life Course," *Social Psychology Quarterly* 57 (1994), pp. 4–15.

65. Krohn et al., "The Interrelationships between Substance Use and Precocious Transitions."

66. Gary M. McClelland, Linda A. Teplin, and Karen M. Abram, *Detention and Prevalence of Substance Use among Juvenile Detainees* (Washington, D.C.: Office of Juvenile Justice

and Delinquency Prevention, 2004); see the report for the citations supporting each generalization.

67. Helene R. White, Chioun Lee, Eun-Young Mun, and Rolf Loeber, "Developmental Patterns of Alcohol Use in Relation to the Persistence and Desistance of Serious Violent Offending Among African American and Caucasian Young Men," *Criminology* 50 (May 2012), pp. 391–426.

68. The author has interviewed a number of adult former drug addicts and staff of therapeutic communities, and these explanations were typically given for why a drug addict went straight and stayed clean.

69. See D. B. Kandel and J. A. Logan, "Patterns of Drug Use from Adolescence to Young Adulthood: Periods of Risk for Initiation, Continued Use, and Discontinuation," *American Public Health* 74 (1984), pp. 660–66.

70. L. A. Goodman and W. H. Kruskal, *Measures of Association for Cross Classification* (New York: Springer-Verlag, 1979).

71. L. Thomas Winfree, Jr., Christine S. Sellers, and Dennis L. Clason, "Social Learning and Adolescent Deviance Abstention: Toward Understanding the Reasons for Initiating, Quitting, and Avoiding Drugs," *Journal of Quantitative Criminology* 9 (1993), pp. 101–25.

72. Ryan D. Schroeder, Peggy C. Giordano, and Stephen A. Cernkovich, "Drug Use and Processes," *Criminology* 45 (2007), pp. 192–222.

73. Sharon Mihalic, Katherine Irwin, Abigail Fagan, Diane Ballard, and Delbert Elliott, *Blueprint for Violence Prevention* (Washington, D.C.: Office of Juvenile Justice and Delinquency Prevention, 2004).

74. G. Botvin, S. Mihalic, and J. K. Grotpeter, "Life Skills Training," in *Blueprint for Violence Prevention: Book 5*, edited by D. S. Elliott (Boulder: University of Colorado, Institute of Behavioral Sciences, Center for the Study and Prevention of Violence, 1998).

75. Mihalic, *Blueprint for Violence Prevention.*

76. Ibid.

77. Ibid.

78. National Institute of Justice, *The D.A.R.E. Program: A Review of Prevalence, User Satisfaction, and Effectiveness* (Washington, D.C.: U.S. Department of Justice, 1994).

79. William DeJong, *Arresting the Demand for Drugs: Police and School Partnership to Prevent Drug Abuse* (Washington, D.C.: National Institute of Justice, 1987).

80. Phyllis Ellickson, Robert Bell, and K. McGuigan, "Preventing Adolescent Drug Use: Long-Term Results of a Junior High Program," *American Journal of Public Health* 83 (1993), pp. 856–61.

81. Deanna Atkinson, an administrator in the Élan program, suggested this list of noteworthy programs in a September 1995 telephone conversation. The Elan School closed in 2011.

82. *Drug Courts: The Second Decade* (Washington, D.C.: National Institute of Justice, 2006).

83. Gordon Bazemore and Lode Walgrave, "Restorative Juvenile Justice: In Search of Fundamentals and an Outline for Systemic Reform," in *Restorative Juvenile Justice: Repairing the Harm of Youth Crime*, edited by Gordon Bazemore and Lode Walgrave (Monsey, N.Y.: Criminal Justice Press, 1999), pp. 45–74.

84. Ibid.

85. Thomas J. Dishion, Deborah Capaldi, Kathleen M. Spracklen, and Li Fuzhong, "Peer Ecology of Adolescent Drug Use," *Development and Psychopathology* 7 (1995), pp. 803–24.

Chapter Objectives

After reading this chapter, you should be able to:

1. Summarize the development of the juvenile justice system.

2. Summarize the development of community-based corrections and institutions for juveniles.

3. Describe various programs that divert juveniles from the juvenile justice system.

4. Summarize the structure of the juvenile justice system.

5. Summarize the stages of delinquency case processing.

6. Compare the juvenile and adult justice systems.

7. Explain the nature of graduated sanctions in juvenile justice.

8. Summarize the reasons for racial and ethnic differences in juvenile offending and confinement.

9. Describe how delinquency might be prevented and enumerate some strategies for delinquency prevention.

10. Summarize possible future trends in juvenile justice.

The current [juvenile justice] system, a relic from a more innocent time, teaches youthful offenders that crime pays and that they are totally immune and insulated from responsibility.

—*National Policy Forum*

Introduction

In 2011 the New York–based Vera Institute of Justice released a report on New York City's risk assessment instrument (RAI), a tool that had been created in 2007 to help family court judges make informed decisions about whether arrested youth are likely to reoffend or fail to appear if allowed to go home before their cases could be adjudicated in court. The Vera study came amidst a crisis in the city's ability to place children awaiting final disposition by the court. The crisis began in 2006, when the New York City Department of Probation shut down the city's only alternative to juvenile detention—a program that provided schooling, counseling, and supervision to youths who had been ordered to remain at home until their cases had been heard. That program had been built around alternative to detention (ATD) centers, which operated daily from eight in the morning until four o'clock in the afternoon. The ATDs closed, however, after claims that they were not reaching the right juveniles, and that youths were being held in the program for much longer than needed. The city's juvenile court judges were left with no alternative but to detain offenders whom they deemed at risk prior to adjudicatory hearings.

Five years after the closing of the ATD centers, the Vera report found that under the new RAI "the overall rate of rearrest for youth during the time their cases are pending … dropped by about one-third." Researchers also noted that far fewer low-risk youth were being ordered into detention at their first court appearance. "The RAI," says Annie Salsich, director of Vera's Center on Youth Justice, "gives judges objective data to consider when making detention decisions."[1]

Society has long considered how best to process and treat juvenile offenders and how to determine at what age a person is able to form the mental intent necessary for the commission of a crime. Many observers suggest young children are too immature to form the mental "evilness" required to plan and commit certain acts of violence and therefore deserve compassion if arrested and processed by the juvenile justice system.[2] However, in support of the recent "get tough with juveniles" position, the argument is frequently made that society has some fifteen-, sixteen-, and seventeen-year-old youthful offenders who function on adult levels. Some say that traditional handling, in which the best interests of the child guide the juvenile justice system, does not necessarily offer much promise in dealing with these kids.

The juvenile justice system is responsible for controlling and correcting the behavior of law-violating juveniles. The system's inability to accomplish its basic mission has resulted in massive criticism from all sides. Indeed, both conservatives and liberals want to reduce the scope of the juvenile court's responsibilities: Conservatives want to refer serious youthful offenders to the adult court, whereas some liberals recommend divesting the juvenile court of its jurisdiction over status offenders.

Development of the Juvenile Justice System

This chapter examines juvenile justice through the lenses of the past, the present, and the future. Beginning with the development of juvenile justice in the United States, its structures, functions, and issues are discussed, and future possibilities are suggested.

Origins of the Juvenile Court

The first juvenile court was founded in Cook County (Chicago), Illinois, in 1899 when the Illinois legislature passed the Juvenile Court Act. The *parens patriae* doctrine provided a legal catalyst for the creation of the juvenile court, furnishing a rationale for the use of informal procedures for dealing with juveniles and for expanding state power over children. *Parens patriae* was also used to justify the juvenile court's authority to determine the causes of delinquent behavior and to make decisions on the disposition of cases. The kindly parent, the state, could thus justify relying on psychological and medical examinations rather than on trial by evidence. Once the *parens patriae* rationale was applied to juvenile proceedings, the institution of the juvenile court followed.

In his book *The Child Savers*, Anthony Platt discussed the political context of the origin of the juvenile court, claiming that the juvenile court was established in Chicago and later elsewhere because it satisfied several middle-class interest groups. He saw the juvenile court as an expression of middle-class values and of the philosophy of conservative political groups. In denying that the juvenile court was revolutionary, Platt charged:

> The child-saving movement was not so much a break with the past as an affirmation of faith in traditional institutions. Parental authority, education at home, and the virtues of rural life were emphasized because they were in decline at this time. The child-saving movement was, in part, a crusade which, through emphasizing the dependence of the social order on the proper socialization of children, implicitly elevated the nuclear family and, more especially, the role of women as stalwarts of the family. The child savers were prohibitionists, in a general sense, who believed that social progress depended on efficient law enforcement, strict supervision of children's leisure and recreation, and the regulation of illicit pleasures. What seemingly began as a movement to humanize the lives of adolescents soon developed into a program of moral absolutism through which youths were to be saved from movies, pornography, cigarettes, alcohol, and anything else which might possibly rob them of their innocence.[3]

Platt contended that the behaviors the **child savers** deemed worthy of penalty—such as engaging in sex, roaming the streets, drinking, fighting, frequenting dance halls, and staying out late at night—were found primarily among lower-class children. Therefore, juvenile justice from its inception, he argued, reflected class favoritism that resulted in the frequent processing of poor children through the system while middle- and upper-class children were more likely to be excused.[4]

The children of the poor were a particular problem to the child savers because the juvenile court emerged in the wake of unprecedented industrial and urban development in the United States. This process was closely connected with large-scale immigration to urban centers of people who had different backgrounds from the indigenous population. These immigrants brought new social problems to Chicago and other urban centers, and the child savers were determined to "rescue" the immigrant children and to protect them from their families.[5]

Emergence of Community-Based Corrections

The first application of community-based corrections for juveniles grew out of juvenile aftercare, or parole, used to supervise juveniles after their institutionalization. Such programs are nearly as old as juvenile correctional institutions. By the 1820s, superintendents of houses of refuge had the authority to release juveniles when they saw fit; some juveniles were returned directly to their families, and others were placed in the community as indentured servants and apprentices who could reenter the community as free citizens once they finished their terms of service. This system became formalized only in the 1840s, when states set up inspection procedures to monitor the supervision of those with whom youths were placed.

Juvenile **aftercare** was influenced by the development of adult parole in the late 1870s. Zebulon Brockway, the first superintendent of Elmira Reformatory in New York State, permitted parole for carefully selected prisoners. When they left the institution, parolees were instructed to report to a guardian on arrival, to write immediately to the superintendent, and to report to the guardian on the first of each month.

Juvenile aftercare programs spread throughout the United States in the early decades of the twentieth century and took on many of the features of adult parole. Juveniles were supervised in the community by aftercare officers, whose jobs were similar to those of parole officers in the adult system. The parole board did not become a part of juvenile corrections, for in more than two-thirds of the states, institutional staff continued to decide when youths would return to the community.

Probation as an alternative to institutional placement for juveniles arose from the effort of John Augustus, a Boston cobbler, in the 1840s and 1850s. Augustus, who is called "the father of probation," spent considerable time in the courtroom and in 1841 persuaded a judge to permit him to supervise an offender in the community rather than sentencing the offender to an institution. During the next two decades, Augustus worked with nearly two thousand individuals, including both adult and juvenile offenders. As the first probation

▲ Lionel Tate walks down a hallway with Broward County (Florida) sheriff's officers during his sentencing hearing in 2006. At age fourteen Tate was the youngest person to be convicted and sentenced to life in prison. Tate was later released on parole and held up a pizza delivery person with a gun.

■ **Do you think he should get another chance?**

child savers
A name given to an organized group of progressive social reformers of the late nineteenth and early twentieth centuries who promoted numerous laws aimed at protecting children and institutionalizing an idealized image of childhood innocence.

aftercare
The supervision of juveniles who are released from correctional institutions so that they can make an optimal adjustment to community living; also, the status of a juvenile conditionally released from a treatment or confinement facility and placed under supervision in the community.

probation
A court-ordered nonpunitive juvenile disposition that emphasizes community-based services and treatment and close supervision by an officer of the court. Probation is essentially a sentence of confinement that is suspended as long as the probationer meets the conditions imposed by the court.

officer, Augustus initiated several services still used in probation today: investigation and screening, supervision, educational and employment services, and provision of aid and assistance.[6]

Expansion and Retrenchment in the Twentieth Century

In the twentieth century, probation services spread to every state and were administered by both state and local authorities. The use of volunteer probation workers had disappeared by the turn of the twentieth century, only to return in the 1950s. Probation became more treatment oriented: Early in the twentieth century, the medical treatment model was used; later, in the 1960s and 1970s, probation officers became brokers who delivered services to clients. The upgrading of standards and training also was emphasized in the 1960s and 1970s.

residential program
A program conducted for the rehabilitation of youthful offenders within community-based and institutional settings.

Residential programs, the third type of community-based juvenile corrections to appear, had their origins in the Highfields Project, a short-term guided-interaction group program. Known officially as the New Jersey Experimental Project for the Treatment of Youthful Offenders, this project was established in 1950 on the former estate of Colonel and Mrs. Charles Lindbergh. The Highfields Project housed adjudicated youths who worked during the day at the nearby New Jersey Neuro-Psychiatric Institute and met in two guided-interaction groups five evenings a week at the Highfields facility. Similar programs were initiated in the 1960s at South Fields in Louisville, Kentucky; Essexfields in Newark, New Jersey; Pinehills in Provo, Utah; the New Jersey centers at Oxford and Farmingdale for boys and at Turrell for girls; and the START centers established by the New York City Division for Youth.

In the late 1980s and 1990s, a decline in federal funding, along with the "get-tough" mood of society, meant the closing of some residential and day-treatment programs. Although probation remained the most widely used judicial disposition, both probation and aftercare services were charged to enforce a more hard-line policy with juvenile offenders. Figure 12–1 shows a timeline of the most important events in the evolution of community-based corrections for juveniles.

Development of Juvenile Institutions

Before the end of the eighteenth century, the family was commonly believed to be the source or cause of deviancy, so the idea emerged that perhaps the well-adjusted family could provide the model for a correctional institution for children. The house of refuge, the

TIMELINE

1820s	1840s	1841
Superintendents of houses of refuge had the power to release juveniles from the institution.	**States set up** inspection procedures to supervise those with whom juveniles were placed.	**John Augustus** began to supervise juvenile and adult offenders in Boston.

1869	1890	1950	1980s–present
The Commonwealth of Massachusetts established a visiting probation agent system that supervised youthful offenders.	**Juvenile probation was** established statewide in Massachusetts.	**The Highfields** Project was established.	**Retrenchment** took place in community-based corrections.

FIGURE 12–1
Timeline of Community-Based Corrections for Juveniles in the United States

first juvenile institution, reflected the family model wholeheartedly; it was designed to bring order, discipline, and care of the family into institutional life. The institution was to become the home; the peers, the siblings; and the staff, the parents.[7]

The New York House of Refuge, which opened on January 1, 1825, with six girls and three boys, is usually acknowledged as the first house of refuge. Several similar institutions already existed in England and Europe.[8] During the next decade or so, Boston, Philadelphia, Bangor (Maine), Richmond, Mobile, Cincinnati, and Chicago followed suit in establishing houses of refuge for males; twenty-three schools were chartered in the 1830s and another thirty in the 1840s. Some houses of refuge were established by private philanthropists, some by the state government or legislature, and some jointly by public authorities and private organizations. The vast majority of the houses of refuge were for males. The average capacity was 210, but the capacity ranged from 90 at Lancaster, Massachusetts, to 1,000 at the New York House of Refuge for Boys.[9]

The development of the **cottage system** and the construction of these juvenile institutions outside cities were two reforms of the mid-nineteenth century. The cottage system, which was introduced in 1854 and quickly spread throughout the nation, housed smaller groups of youths in separate buildings, usually no more than twenty to forty youths per cottage. Early cottages were log cabins; later cottages were built from brick or stone. Now called **training schools** or industrial schools, these juvenile facilities were usually constructed outside cities so that youths would be reformed through exposure to the simpler rural way of life. It was presumed that residents would learn responsibility and new skills as they worked the fields and took care of the livestock, and their work would enable the institution, in turn, to provide its own food and perhaps even realize a profit.

cottage system
A widely used treatment practice that places small groups of training school residents into cottages.

training school
A correctional facility for long-term placement of juvenile delinquents; may be public (run by a state department of corrections or youth commission) or private.

Twentieth-Century Changes

Several significant changes occurred in juvenile institutionalization during the first several decades of the twentieth century. One change was that reformers advocated treatment on several fronts. Case studies were used to prescribe treatment plans for residents; reception units were developed to diagnose and classify new admissions; individual therapies, such as psychotherapy and behavior modification, were used; and group therapies, such as guided-interaction groups, became popular means of transforming the inmate subculture. Institutional programs also became more diverse. Confined juveniles could graduate from state-accredited high school programs; home furloughs and work-release programs were permitted in many training schools and included printing, barbering, welding, and repairing automobiles. Furthermore, the types of juvenile correctional facilities increased to include ranches and forestry camps as well as the traditional prison-like training schools. Finally, several experimental forms of training schools developed that offered the promise of changing juvenile corrections.

In spite of the improvements in many reform schools, as well as the truly experimental efforts in a few, the story of the twentieth-century training school is one of scaled-down prisons for juveniles.[10] In the 1960s and 1970s, reformers began to accuse training schools of being violent, inhumane, and criminogenic.[11] Widespread criticism of training schools, various court decisions, and pressure groups in state legislatures led to a number of reforms in the mid- and late 1970s. These innovations included the decision to no longer confine status offenders with delinquents in training schools, an increase in staff training programs, the growing acceptance of grievance procedures for residents, and the establishment of coeducational facilities.

In the late 1980s and 1990s, a number of disturbing changes took place in juvenile institutionalization. Training schools became overcrowded and more violent. Members of minorities made up a greater proportion of the population of juvenile correctional institutions, especially for drug offenses. Status offenders and juveniles who had committed nonserious delinquent acts continued to be committed to private training schools, but private placements also began to admit youngsters who had committed serious delinquent offenses. More youths were transferred to adult court for violent crimes and received long-term prison sentences. Figure 12–2 shows a timeline for the development of juvenile institutionalization.

TIMELINE

1825	1854	1850s–1860s	1880–1899
The New York House of Refuge was opened.	**The cottage** system was introduced.	**Juvenile facilities** were called training schools or industrial schools.	**The public became** disillusioned, realizing that training schools were primarily custodial institutions and not rehabilitative.

1900–1950s	1960s–1970s	Late 1970s	Late 1980s–present
Training schools underwent a period of reform, especially with the introduction of varied methods of treatment.	**Training schools** came under great criticism for not reforming juveniles under their care.	**Training schools** underwent another period of reform.	**Training schools** became overcrowded, grew more violent, and confined increased numbers of minority youths.

FIGURE 12–2
Timeline of Juvenile Institutionalization

Diversion from the Juvenile Justice System

diversion programs
Dispositional alternatives for youthful offenders that exist outside of the formal juvenile justice system.

In the late 1960s and early 1970s, **diversion programs** sprouted up across the nation. *Diversion* is a term that refers to keeping juveniles outside the formal justice system, and typically makes use of a variety of programs intended to keep troubled youth out of custody. The diversion process, which is usually initiated by the courts or the police, means that (1) the justice subsystem retains control over youthful offenders, and (2) youths who fail to respond to diversion usually will be returned to the juvenile court for continued processing in the system. In the 1990s, new forms of diversion developed in the United States and included community courts, alternative dispute resolution, gun courts, youth courts, and drug courts. Youth courts and drug courts are described in more detail in what follows.

Youth Courts

Youth courts, also known as *teen courts, peer courts,* or *student courts*, are juvenile justice programs in which youths are sentenced by their peers (see Figure 12–3 for a brief history of youth courts). Established and administered in a variety of ways, most youth courts are used as a sentencing option for first-time offenders ages 11 to 17 years old who are charged with nonviolent misdemeanor offenses. The offender has typically acknowledged his or her guilt and participates in a youth court voluntarily rather than going through the more formal juvenile justice procedures.[12] In 2005, more than 110,000 youths volunteered to hear more than 115,000 juvenile cases, and more than 20,000 adults volunteered to be facilitators for peer justice in youth court programs; 1,158 youth court programs in forty-nine states and the District of Columbia provided restorative justice for youthful offenders.[13] Figure 12–4 shows four possible case-processing models used in juvenile court.

Youth courts usually handle first-time offenders who are charged with offenses such as theft, misdemeanor assault, disorderly conduct, and possession of alcohol. The majority of these teen courts (87 percent) reported that they rarely or never accepted any juveniles with prior arrest records. The most common disposition used by these courts is community service, followed (in level of use) by victim apology letters (86 percent), apology essays (79 percent), teen court jury duty (75 percent), drug/alcohol classes (59 percent), and monetary restitution (34 percent).[14]

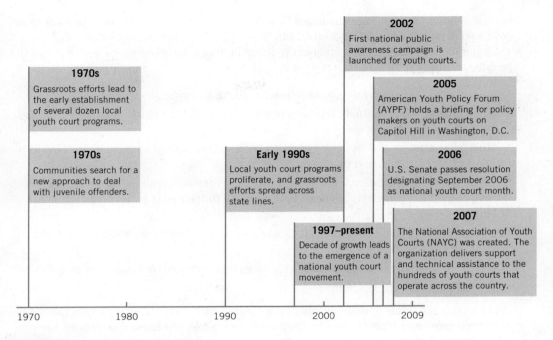

FIGURE 12–3
A Brief History of Youth Courts

Source: Adapted from Scott B. Peterson and Jill Beres, "History of Youth Courts," *Report to the Nation, 1993 to 2008: The Global Youth Justice Movement—15 Year Update on Youth Courts and Teen Courts.* Courtesy of Scott B. Peterson.

1. *Adult judge.* An adult serves as judge and rules on legal terminology and courtroom procedures. Youths serve as attorneys, jurors, clerks, bailiffs, and so forth.

2. *Youth judge.* This is similar to the adult judge model except that a youth serves as the judge.

3. *Tribunal.* Youth attorneys present the case to a panel of three youth judges, who decide the appropriate disposition for the defendant. A jury is not used.

4. *Peer jury.* This model does not use youth attorneys. The case is presented to a youth jury by a youth or adult, and the youth jury then questions the defendant directly.

FIGURE 12–4
Youth Courts: Four Possible Case-Processing Models

Source: Adapted from Scott B. Peterson and Jill Beres, "History of Youth Courts," *Report to the Nation, 1993 to 2008: The Global Youth Justice Movement—15 Year Update on Youth Courts and Teen Courts.* Courtesy of Scott B. Peterson.

The Juvenile Drug-Court Movement

By 2007, approximately two thousand juvenile drug courts were functioning across the nation. The juvenile drug-court movement grew out of an expanding adult drug-court movement that was stimulated by Title V of the Violent Crime Control and Law Enforcement Act of 1994. That act authorized the U.S. attorney general to make grants to various agencies to establish drug courts. These agencies include states, state and local courts, units of local government, and Indian tribal governments.[15]

A number of strategies are common to juvenile drug courts compared with traditional juvenile courts, and include:

- Much earlier and much more comprehensive intake assessments
- Much greater focus on the functioning of the juvenile and the family throughout the juvenile court system
- Much closer integration of the information obtained during the assessment process as it relates to the juvenile and the family
- Much greater coordination among the court, the treatment community, the school system, and other community agencies in responding to the needs of the juvenile and the court
- Much more active and continuous judicial supervision of the juvenile's case and treatment process
- Increased use of immediate sanctions for noncompliance and incentives for progress for both the juvenile and the family[16]

Currently six states operate juvenile drug courts, with the greatest activity in California (two programs) and Florida (four programs). For example, the Escambia County Juvenile Drug Court in Pensacola, Florida, began operating in April 1996. It is a twelve-month three-phase approach to treating substance use and abuse, with Phase I lasting about two months, Phase II lasting four months, and Phase III lasting six months. The drug-court judge supervises treatment of up to forty offenders by reviewing reports from treatment personnel to determine the need for either positive or negative incentives to encourage participation and involvement.[17]

A 2010 study of juvenile drug courts compared 1,120 youths handled by juvenile drug courts in multiple jurisdictions with 1,120 youth not in juvenile drug court, but who participated in adolescent outpatient drug treatment. The juvenile drug courts appeared to do a better job (compared to treatment alone) of helping youth reduce symptoms of their emotional problems and reduce their substance abuse. Other findings of this study included the following:

recidivism
The repetition of delinquent behavior by a youth who has been released from probation status or from training school.

- Juvenile drug-court proceedings were less likely than youth in treatment-only situations to begin treatment within two weeks of intake, which is significant because it has been found that initiation of treatment within two weeks is a major protective factor against relapse and **recidivism**.
  - Juvenile drug courts are one of several ways of getting significantly impaired youth into treatment early and reliably achieving positive outcomes.[18]

Diversion: Pros and Cons

The most positive characteristic of diversion programs is that they minimize the penetration of youthful offenders into the justice system, but empirical studies of diversion generally have not demonstrated that doing something (treatment or services) is necessarily better than doing nothing. Researchers warn that the overlooked negative consequences of diversion challenge the viability of this concept.[19] Some of these negative effects include widening the net of juvenile justice by increasing the number of youths under the control of the system, increasing the size of the system (budget and staff), ignoring clients' due process rights or constitutional safeguards, and labeling minor offenders.[20] See Figure 12–5 for types of diversion programs.

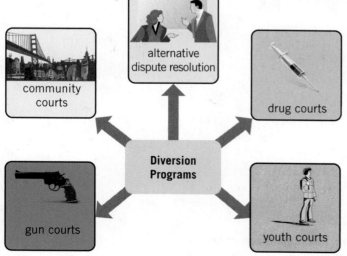

FIGURE 12–5
Types of Diversion Programs

The Juvenile Justice System Today

Like most systems (private or public), the juvenile justice system is most concerned with maintaining its equilibrium and surviving. The system is able to survive by maintaining internal harmony while simultaneously managing environmental inputs. The police and the juvenile court, juvenile probation, residential and day-treatment programs, detention facilities, long-term juvenile institutions, and aftercare are all closely interrelated, so changes in one organization have definite consequences elsewhere within the system.

Structure and Functions

The juvenile justice system is made up of three basic subsystems—police, juvenile court, and corrections—that consist of between ten thousand and twenty thousand public and private agencies, with annual budgets totaling hundreds of millions of dollars. Many of the forty thousand police departments across the nation have juvenile divisions, and more than three thousand juvenile courts and about one thousand juvenile correctional facilities exist in the United States.[21] Of the fifty thousand employees in the juvenile justice system, more than thirty thousand are employed in juvenile correctional facilities, sixty-five hundred are juvenile probation officers, and the remaining personnel are aftercare (parole) officers and staff who work in residential programs. In addition, several thousand more employees work in diversion programs and private juvenile correctional systems.[22]

The functions of the three subsystems are somewhat different. The basic work of the police is maintaining order and enforcing the law. The function of maintaining order, which occupies most of police officers' time, involves such responsibilities as settling family disputes, providing emergency ambulance service, directing traffic, furnishing information to citizens, preventing suicides, finding shelter for homeless people or substance abusers, and checking the homes of families on vacation. The law enforcement function requires that the police deter crime, make arrests, obtain confessions, collect evidence for strong cases that can result in convictions, and increase crime clearance rates. The police must also deal with juvenile lawbreaking and provide services juveniles need.

The juvenile courts are responsible for disposing of cases referred to them by intake divisions of probation departments (see Chapter 15), supervising juvenile probationers, making detention decisions, dealing with cases of child neglect and dependency cases, and monitoring the performance of youths who have been adjudicated delinquent or status offenders. *The parens patriae* philosophy of the juvenile court charges the court with treating rather than punishing youngsters appearing before juvenile judges, but the treatment arm of the juvenile court goes only so far, and youths who commit serious crimes or persist in juvenile lawbreaking may be sent to training schools or transferred to adult court.

The corrections system is charged with the care of youthful offenders sentenced by the courts. Juvenile probation, the most widely used judicial disposition, supervises offenders released to probation by the courts, ensuring that they comply with the conditions of probation imposed by the courts and desist from delinquent behavior in the community. Day-treatment and residential programs (see Chapter 15) are charged with preparing youths for their return to the community, with preventing unlawful behavior in the program or in the community, and with providing humane care for youths directed to the programs. Long-term juvenile correctional institutions have similar responsibilities, but the officials of these programs also are charged with deciding when each youth is ready to be released to the community. Officials of long-term institutions must also ensure that residents receive their constitutional and due process rights. Aftercare officers, the final group in the juvenile justice system, have the responsibility of supervising youths released from long-term juvenile correctional institutions; like probation officers, aftercare officers are expected to make certain that youthful offenders fulfill the terms of their aftercare agreements and avoid delinquent behavior. (See Figure 12–6.)

▲ Dr. Jerome G. Miller is seen in this 1972 photo. In the early 1970s, Miller undertook a radical social experiment, closing down virtually all of Massachusetts' training schools and dispersing delinquent children to community-based programs.
■ **What would be the consequences of such an action today?**

Library Extra 12–1
OJJDP publication: *Juvenile Offenders and Victims: 2006 National Report (Chapter 4)*

Library Extra 12–2
OJJDP publication: *How the Justice System Responds to Juvenile Victims: A Comprehensive Model*

Subsystem   Function

Police

Maintaining order and enforcing the law

Juvenile Court

Disposing of cases referred to them by intake divisions of probation departments, supervising juvenile probationers, making detention decisions, dealing with cases of child neglect and dependency, monitoring the performance of youths who have been adjudicated delinquent or status offenders

Corrections

Caring for youthful offenders sentenced by the courts, supervising offenders released to probation by the courts, and using day-treatment and residential programs, as well as short- and long-term juvenile facilities, to prepare youths for release to the community

FIGURE 12–6
Basic Subsystems of the Juvenile Justice System

Web Extra 12–1
OJJDP PowerPoint presentation: *Juvenile Justice System Structure and Process*

▲ A mother consoles her daughter as they stand in front of a judge after the child was charged with truancy.

■ **How does the juvenile justice system differ from the adult criminal justice system?**

Stages in the Juvenile Justice Process

The means by which juvenile offenders are processed by juvenile justice agencies are examined throughout this text. The variations in the juvenile justice systems across the nation make it difficult to describe this process, but Figure 12–7 is a general flowchart of the juvenile justice system. The process begins when a youth is referred to the juvenile court. Some jurisdictions permit a variety of individuals or agencies to refer the juvenile, whereas in others only the police are charged with this responsibility. The more common procedure is that the youth whose alleged offense has already been investigated on the basis of a citizen complaint is taken into custody by the police who have made the decision to refer the juvenile to the juvenile court.

The intake officer, usually a probation officer (see Chapter 15), must decide whether the juvenile should remain in the community or be placed in a shelter or detention facility. The intake officer has a variety of options in determining what to do with a youth, but in more serious cases, the juvenile generally receives a petition to appear before the juvenile court.

The juvenile court judge (or the referee in many jurisdictions) hears the cases of juveniles referred to the court. If the juvenile is to be transferred to adult court, this must be done before any juvenile proceedings take place; otherwise, an adjudicatory hearing, the primary purpose of which is to determine whether the juvenile is guilty of the delinquent acts alleged in the petition, takes place. The court hears evidence on these allegations. The case of *In re Gault* (see Chapter 16) usually is interpreted to guarantee to juveniles the right to representation by counsel, freedom from self-incrimination, and the right to confront and cross-examine witnesses, and some states also give juveniles the right to a jury trial.

A disposition hearing takes place when a juvenile has been found delinquent in the adjudicatory stage. Most juvenile court codes now require that the adjudicatory and disposition hearings be held at different times. The number of dispositions juvenile judges have available to them varies from one jurisdiction to the next. In addition to the standard dispositions of warning and release, placement on juvenile probation, or adjudication to the department of youth services or corrections, some judges can place juveniles in a publicly or privately administered day-treatment or residential program, and some jurisdictions even grant juvenile judges the authority to send a juvenile to a particular correctional facility.

The juvenile adjudicated to a training school is generally treated somewhat differently in small states than in large states. In small states with one training school for males and (usually) one for females, a youth adjudicated to a training school usually is sent directly to the appropriate school, but large states that have several facilities for males and perhaps more than one for females may send the youth to a classification (or diagnostic) center to determine the proper institutional placement. Training school residents currently are not confined as long as they were in the past and frequently are released within a year. Institutional release takes place in a variety of ways, but the juvenile released from the training school is generally placed on aftercare status. To be released from this supervision, the juvenile must fulfill the rules of aftercare and must avoid unlawful behavior.

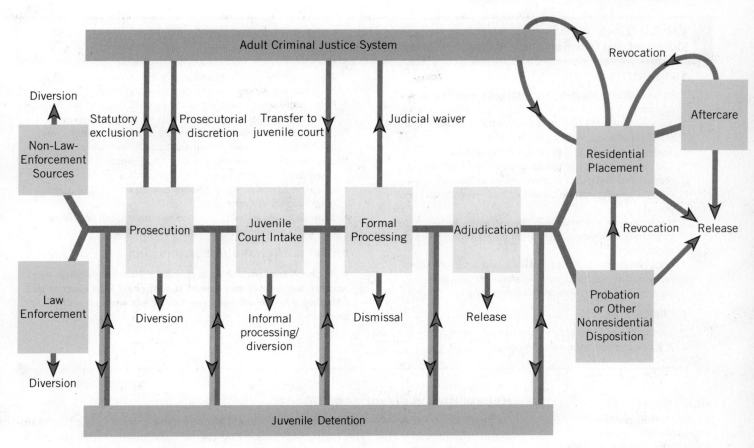

Note: This chart gives a simplified view of case flow through the juvenile justice system. Procedures vary among jurisdictions.

FIGURE 12–7
Stages of Delinquency Case Processing in the Juvenile Justice System

Source: Adapted from Howard N. Snyder and Melissa Sickmund, *Juvenile Offenders and Victims: 2006 National Report* (Washington, D.C.: Office of Juvenile Justice and Delinquency Prevention, 2006), p. 205.

Comparison of the Juvenile and Adult Justice Systems

There is much similarity between the juvenile and adult justice systems. Both systems are made up of three basic subsystems (police, court, and corrections) and numerous inter-related agencies. The flow of justice in both is supposed to progress from law violation to police apprehension, judicial process, judicial disposition, and rehabilitation in correctional agencies. The basic vocabulary is usually the same in the juvenile and adult systems, but even when the vocabulary differs, the intent remains the same (see Table 12–1).

Both juvenile and adult systems are under fire to "get tough on crime," especially on offenders who commit violent crimes. Both must deal with case overloads and institutional overcrowding; both must operate on fiscal shoestrings; and both face the ongoing problems of staff recruitment, training, and burnout. There are, however, some differences between the two systems; see Exhibit 12–1 for a list of some similarities and differences.

BASIC CORRECTIONAL MODELS

To correct the behavior of the juvenile delinquent, four basic correctional models have traditionally been applied to the juvenile justice system: (1) the rehabilitation model, (2) the justice model, (3) the crime control model, and (4) the balanced and restorative model. An emerging model in juvenile justice, which is based more on a balanced approach between treatment and punishment, is much more focused on punishment and accountability than has been the case in juvenile justice in the past.

Exhibit 12–1
Similarities and Differences between the Juvenile and Adult Justice Systems

SIMILARITIES

- Police officers use discretion with both juvenile and adult offenders.
- Juvenile and adult offenders receive *Miranda* warnings and other constitutional rights at time of arrest.
- Juveniles and adults can be placed in pretrial facilities.
- The juvenile court and the adult court use proof beyond a reasonable doubt as the standard for evidence.
- Plea bargaining may be used with both juvenile and adult offenders.
- Convicted juvenile and adult offenders may be sentenced to probation services, residential programs, or institutional facilities.
- Boot camps are used with juvenile and adult offenders.
- Released institutional juvenile and adult offenders may be assigned to supervision in the community.

DIFFERENCES

- Juveniles can be arrested for acts that would not be criminal if they were adults (status offenses).
- Age determines the jurisdiction of the juvenile court; age does not affect the jurisdiction of the adult court.
- Parents are deeply involved in the juvenile process but not in the adult process.
- Juvenile court proceedings are more informal, whereas adult court proceedings are formal and open to the public.
- Juvenile court proceedings, unlike adult proceedings, are not considered criminal. Juvenile records are generally sealed when the age of majority (usually age 16 or 17) is reached. Adult records are permanent.
- Juvenile courts cannot sentence juveniles to jail or prison; only adult courts may issue such sentences.

CRITICAL THINKING QUESTIONS

■ *How much harm would it do to juveniles if juvenile proceedings were abolished and juveniles were handled in adult court? What would be the advantages if juvenile offenders were handled with adult proceedings and procedures?*

Rehabilitation (Treatment) Model

rehabilitation model
A correctional model whose goal is to change an offender's character, attitudes, or behavior so as to diminish his or her delinquent propensities. The medical, adjustment, and reintegration models are variants of this model because they are all committed to changing the offender.

adjudicatory hearing
The stage of juvenile court proceedings that usually includes the youth's plea, the presentation of evidence by the prosecution and by the defense, the cross-examination of witnesses, and a finding by the judge as to whether the allegations in the petition can be sustained.

commitment
A determination made by a juvenile judge at the disposition stage of a juvenile court proceeding that a juvenile is to be sent to a juvenile correctional institution.

detention
The temporary restraint of a juvenile in a secure facility, usually because he or she is acknowledged to be dangerous either to self or to others.

dispositional hearing
The stage of the juvenile court proceedings in which the juvenile judge decides the most appropriate placement for a juvenile who has been adjudicated a delinquent, a status offender, or a dependent child.

juvenile court officer
A probation officer who serves juveniles (the term is used in some but not all probation departments).

Parens patriae, the philosophical basis of the **rehabilitation model**, emerged with the founding of the juvenile court. The state, represented by the juvenile court, was to deal with children differently than it did with adults by substituting a more informal and flexible procedure. In the juvenile court, a fatherly and benevolent juvenile judge would gently, and in a friendly manner, probe the roots of the child's difficulties. The court, acting in lieu of a child's parents, was to engage in individualized justice; delinquency was viewed as a symptom of some underlying social or family problem.

The juvenile court, then, was to serve as a social clinic. Its task was to call up the scientific expert to provide the necessary treatment for the child. *Child-saving reformers*, a term used by Anthony Platt, were confident that the combination of *parens patriae* philosophy and the treatment provided by the scientific expert would lead to the salvation of wayward children.[23]

TABLE 12–1
Juvenile and Adult Justice System Terminology

Juvenile Terminology	Adult Terminology
Adjudicatory hearing	Trial
Aftercare	Parole
Commitment	Sentence to confinement
Detention	Holding in jail
Dispositional hearing	Sentencing hearing
Juvenile court officer	Probation officer
Offender	Defendant
Petition	Indictment
Petitioner	Prosecutor
Respondent	Defense attorney
Taking into custody	Arrest

The rehabilitation model is based on the belief that the basic mission of juvenile justice is to rehabilitate youthful offenders. The treatment model also proposes that the legal definition of delinquency should be broad and that victimless crimes and status offenses, as well as crimes against victims, should remain on the books. Proponents of this model do not believe in the frequent use of detention facilities; these facilities should be reserved for children who need special care and custody.

How Does the Rehabilitation Model Work?

The mental, physical, and social needs of the child are the focus of the treatment model, and many rehabilitation efforts are implemented before the juvenile is processed into the system. Police officers may recommend community programs to youths and their parents that help youths in need with their specific problems. Intake officers, probation officers, prosecutors, judges, and aftercare officers also may either informally or formally request that juveniles, status as well as delinquent offenders, attend drug and alcohol, tutoring, anger management, and other after-school programs; youths who are institutionalized also often receive drug and alcohol, sexual offending, and other treatment modalities. The treatment model has encountered considerable criticism in the late twentieth century, but it is experiencing a resurgence of research and interest in the early twenty-first century.

The Justice Model

The *parens patriae* philosophy has been challenged by advocates of due process since the very founding of the juvenile court. Those promoting the due process approach wanted to give juveniles better protection through due process provisions and procedural safeguards. In the 1970s, proponents of due process were troubled by the contradictions of juvenile justice philosophy and by the inequities and inadequacies of juvenile justice law, policy, and practice.[24] These reformers turned to David Fogel's **justice model** and its concept of **just deserts**. Fogel believed that both juvenile and adult offenders are volitional and responsible human beings and, consequently, deserve to be punished if they violate the law. The punishment they receive, however, must be proportionate to the seriousness of the offense. Fogel also proposed the end of the indeterminate sentence and parole, the initiation of uniform sentencing, and the establishment of correctional programming based solely on the compliance of inmates.[25] Fogel reasons, "If we cannot coercively treat with reliability, we can at least be fair, reasonable, humane, and constitutional in practice."[26]

How Does the Justice Model Work?

Proponents of the justice model are now advocating a number of changes to bring more fairness to juvenile justice:

- Limit the enormous discretion granted to juvenile justice practitioners.
- Divert increasing numbers of youthful offenders from the justice system to voluntary services.
- Remedy common deficiencies in due process to ensure greater fairness in the transactions among the justice system, the family, and the juvenile offender.
- Curb the indeterminate sentencing practices of juvenile courts and give juveniles a fixed sentence by the court at the time of disposition.
- Decriminalize status offenses.
- Change the governing principle of sentencing to one of *proportionality*, which means that there must be a relationship between the seriousness of the offense committed and the severity of the sanction imposed.
- Make training schools safer and more humane.
- Allow programs offered in training schools to be voluntary in nature and to have nothing to do with the release of a youth.
- Require restitution and community service sanctions of more juvenile lawbreakers; these sanctions have the potential for fairness because they give youthful offenders opportunities to atone or make amends for the damage or harm they have inflicted on others.[27]

petition
A document filed in juvenile court alleging that a juvenile is a delinquent and asking that the court assume jurisdiction over the juvenile or asking that an alleged delinquent be waived to criminal court for prosecution as an adult.

petitioner
In the juvenile justice system, an intake officer (prosecutor) who seeks court jurisdiction over a youthful offender.

respondent
The defense attorney in the juvenile court system.

taking into custody
The process of arresting a juvenile for socially unacceptable or unlawful behavior.

justice model
A contemporary model of imprisonment based on the principle of just deserts.

just deserts
A pivotal philosophical underpinning of the justice model that holds that juvenile offenders deserve to be punished and that the punishment must be proportionate to the seriousness of the offense or the social harm caused.

The mandatory sentencing law for violent juvenile offenders in the state of New York, the determinate sentencing law for juveniles in the state of Washington, and the institutional release policy adopted in the state of Minnesota are other indicators of the national acceptance of the justice model.

The Crime Control Model

crime control model
A correctional model supporting discipline and punishment as the most effective means of deterring youth crime.

The **crime control model** emphasizes punishment as the remedy for juvenile misbehavior. Punishment philosophy actually originated well before the eighteenth century, but it gained popularity in the 1970s because of the assumed rise of youth crime. Although this approach has had different connotations at various times, supporters today maintain that punishment is beneficial because it is educative and moral. Offenders are taught not to commit further crimes, whereas noncriminal citizenry receive a demonstration of what happens to a person who breaks the law; punishment, proponents believe, deters crime.

The supporters of punishment as a means of crime control claim that the juvenile court has wrongly abandoned punishment in favor of an emphasis on individual rehabilitation. They argue for severity and certainty of punishment and advocate a greater use of incarceration. Other fundamental assumptions of punishment philosophy propose that those who become involved in unlawful behavior are abnormal and few in number; that this unlawful behavior reflects a character defect that punishment can correct; that punishment can be helpful in teaching a youth to be responsible, diligent, and honest; and that the deterrence of youth crime depends on the juvenile justice system apprehending and punishing youthful offenders with greater speed, efficiency, and certainty.

How Does the Crime Control Model Work?

The crime control model holds that the first priority of justice should be to protect the life and property of the innocent. Accordingly, proponents of this model support the police and are quick to isolate juvenile offenders, especially those who have committed serious crimes, in detention homes, jails, and training schools. The increased use of transfers to adult court and the adoption of mandatory sentencing laws specifying extended confinements for serious crimes are recent crime control policies. Many states are now using a combination of the crime control and justice models to deal with violent and hard-core juvenile offenders.

Library Extra 12–3
OJJDP Juvenile Justice Bulletin: "Restorative Justice Conferences as an Early Response to Young Offenders"

Balanced and Restorative Model

balanced and restorative model
An integrative correctional model that seeks to reconcile the interests of victims, offenders, and communities through programs and supervision practices.

A traditional New Zealand approach to juvenile offending, the **balanced and restorative model**, is rapidly expanding throughout the United States and, indeed, throughout the world. "Balanced" refers to system-level decision making by administrators to "ensure that resources are allocated equally among efforts to ensure accountability to crime victims, to increase competency in offenders, and to enhance community safety." These three goals are summarized in the terms *accountability*, *competency*, and *community protection*.[28]

Accountability refers to a sanctioning process in which offenders must accept responsibility for their offenses and the harm caused to victims, and make restitution to the victims, assuming that community members are satisfied with the outcome. *Competency* refers to the rehabilitation of offenders, that is, when offenders improve their educational, vocational, emotional, social, and other capabilities and can perform as responsible adults in the community. *Community protection* refers to the ability of citizens to prevent crime, resolve conflict, and feel safe because offenders have matured into responsible citizens. Subsequently, the overall mission of the balanced and restorative justice model is to develop a community-oriented approach to the control of offenders rather than rely solely either on punishment by confinement or on individual rehabilitation through counseling. The juvenile justice system, in implementing this model, meets the needs of the community, the victim, and the offender in the most cost-effective manner possible.

How Does the Balanced and Restorative Justice Model Work?

This approach is an alternative to processing youths through the juvenile justice systems of their communities. Once a juvenile is identified as being a perpetrator of a delinquent act, a police officer, probation officer, community volunteer, or other designated person initiates the restorative process. The victim, the offender, the offender's family, a law enforcement representative, or a volunteer brings all the parties together to begin discussing the problem at hand.

This model, in other words, calls for a new framework of community organization and a restructuring of practitioner roles throughout the juvenile justice system. It calls for a new set of values that emphasize a commitment to all—the offender, the victim, and the community. Importantly, offenders are viewed as clients whose crime is a symptom of family breakdown, community disorganization, and community conflict, and these problems must be addressed if juvenile crime is to be reduced.

Comparison of the Four Models

The treatment model is most concerned that juvenile offenders receive therapy rather than institutionalization. The crime control model emphasizes punishment because it argues that juveniles must pay for their crimes. Proponents of this model support long-term, rather than short-term, confinements for juvenile offenders. The justice model strongly supports the granting of procedural safeguards and fairness to juveniles who have broken the law. Yet proponents of this model also believe that the punishment of juveniles should be proportionate to the gravity of their crimes. The balanced and restorative justice model also contends that juveniles have free will and know what they are doing and, therefore, should receive punishment for their antisocial behavior. The advantages of this model, according to its proponents, are that it includes the punishment approach of the crime control and justice models, supports the due process emphasis of the justice model, and places consequences on behavior to encourage juveniles to become more receptive to treatment.

Each of the models has supporters. The crime control model, or the hard line, is used with violent and repetitive juvenile offenders. The treatment model, or the soft line, is primarily used with status offenders and minor offenders. Some jurisdictions show support for the justice model in juvenile justice, but the balanced and restorative justice model is making the most extensive advances. Nevertheless, on a day-to-day basis, juvenile justice practitioners continue to pick and choose from each of the four models in designing how they work with juvenile offenders. These conflicting approaches, as well as the intolerance of those who follow a different course of action, create inefficiency and confusion in juvenile justice. Table 12–2 compares the key elements of the rehabilitation, justice, crime control, and balanced and restorative models.

TABLE 12–2
Corrections Models Compared

	Models			
Elements	**Rehabilitation**	**Justice**	**Crime Control**	**Balanced and Restorative**
Theory of why delinquents offend	Behavior is caused or determined; based on positivism	Free will; based on the classical school	Free will; based on the classical school	Free will; based on the classical school
Purpose of sentencing	Change in behavior or attitude	Justice	Restoration of law and order	Community protection
Type of sentencing advocated	Indeterminate	Determinate	Determinate	Determinate
View of treatment	Goal of correctional process	Voluntary but necessary in a humane system	Ineffective and actually coddles offenders	Voluntary but necessary in a humane system
Crime control strategy	Use therapeutic intervention to eliminate factors causing crime	Provide fairness for victims, for offenders, and for practitioners in the system	Declare war on youth crime by instituting "get-tough" policies	Make juvenile offenders accountable for their behavior

Source: Reprinted with permission from Clemens Bartollas.

Treatment in Juvenile Justice

This section presents a selection of therapeutic methods—both individual and group—that have been used nationally in juvenile community-based and correctional facilities. It also identifies some of their more salient features.

Individual-Level Treatment Programs

The number of different individual techniques include insight-based therapy, behavioral therapy, and cognitive-behavioral therapy. These are reviewed below.

Insight-Based Therapy

It is common for training schools today to employ insight-based therapy techniques for the treatment of mental and emotional disorders. There are many different types of **insight-based therapy** techniques, but in general the therapist utilizes insight, persuasion, suggestion, reassurance, and instructions so that residents can see themselves and their problems more realistically and can develop a desire to cope effectively with their fears and problems. See Table 12–3 for a summary of the various types of insight-based therapies.

Psychiatrists, clinical psychologists, and psychiatric social workers have used various forms of insight-based therapies in training schools since the early twentieth century. Residents are encouraged to talk about past conflicts that cause emotional problems. The insight that residents gain from this therapy supposedly helps resolve the conflicts and unconscious needs that drove them to crime. At the conclusion of therapy, it is hoped that the resident will become responsible for his or her own behavior.

Insight-based therapies have some fundamental limitations in a training school context. Residents usually do not see themselves as having emotional problems and are reluctant to share their inner thoughts.

Behavioral Therapy

A second form of individual treatment, behavioral therapy, rests on the assumption that desirable behaviors that are rewarded immediately and systematically will increase, while undesirable behaviors that are not rewarded or punished will diminish or be extinguished. Behavioral therapy uses what it terms "positive and negative reinforcement" in order to encourage desirable and extinguish undesirable behavior. **Behavioral modification** is the principal technique used in behavioral therapy, and it is practiced informally in a great many

insight-based therapy
Treatment designed to encourage communication of conflicts and insight into problems, with the goal of symptoms relief, change in behavior, and personality growth.

behavioral modification
A technique in which rewards of punishments are used to change a person's behavior.

TABLE 12–3
Insight-Based Therapies

Type	Treatment Goal	Qualifications of Therapist	Length of Treatment Period	Response from Offenders
Psychotherapy	Lead inmates to insight	Psychiatrist, psychologist, social worker	Long term	Will examine individual problems with therapist
Transactional analysis	Lead inmates to insight	Psychiatrist, psychologist, trained non-professional, staff	Usually several months	Will examine individuals problems in a group context and will learn a new approach to interpersonal relationships
Reality therapy	Help inmates to obtain basic needs	Psychiatrist, psychologist, trained non-professional staff	Short period of time	Will learn to cope with reality, model responsible behavior, and determine right from wrong

training schools. It works like this: Residents receive additional privileges as they become more accepting of the institutional rules and procedures, and as they demonstrate more positive attitudes. Conversely, bad attitudes and bad behavior result in loss of privileges.

Cognitive-Behavioral Therapy

Cognitive-behavioral therapy (CBT) for offenders is based on the assumption that the foundations for criminal behavior are dysfunctional patterns of thinking. The intent is that by altering routine misinterpretations of life events, offenders can modify antisocial aspects of their personality and consequential behavior. The goal of these interventions is to identify cognitive deficits linked to delinquency, such as impulsivity, personal impairments, self-defeating behavior, egocentricity, inability to reason critically, interpersonal problem-solving skills, and a preoccupation with self (see Exhibit 12–2).[29]

CBT in offender treatment targets the thoughts, choices, attitudes, and meaning systems that are associated with antisocial behavior as well as deviant lifestyle. It generally uses a training approach to teach new skills in areas where offenders showed deficits, such as generating alternative solutions, rather than reacting on first impulse; interpersonal problems awareness; opening up and listening to other perspectives; evaluating consequences; resisting; soliciting feedback; taking others' well-being into account; and deciding on what is the most beneficial course of action.[30]

The most widely adopted of the cognitive-behavioral interventions is the **Cognitive Thinking Skills Program (CTSP)** developed by Robert Ross and Elizabeth Fabiano, which is now a core program in the Canadian correctional system and has been implemented in the United States, New Zealand, Australia, and some European countries.[31]

> **Cognitive-Behavioral Therapy (CBT)**
> Therapy based on the assumption that the foundations for criminal behavior are dysfunctional patterns of thinking.

> **Cognitive Thinking Skills Program (CTSP)**
> A cognitive-behavioral intervention program designed to improve offenders' thinking processes.

Exhibit 12–2
Definition of Thinking Errors

1. *Closed Channel*—The criminal communicates from a closed position.
   a. When he talks, he controls what others know about him.
   b. When he listens, he lacks receptivity.
   c. When he evaluates, it is from a position of self-righteousness, faulting, or blaming others.
2. *Fragmentation*—Fluctuations in interests, attitudes and goals ... result in the criminal making good starts and poor finishes.
3. *Uniqueness*—The criminal tends to think about himself as different than others, usually superior.
4. *Superoptimism*—The criminal tends to think that he will be successful in all he undertakes because of his uniqueness; therefore, preparation and effort are not needed. Superoptimism is absolutely essential prior to and during criminal activity.
5. *Pride*—The criminal takes pride in his ability to live by his wits, to do what others are fearful of doing and [in] his "tough guy" view of himself.
6. *Pretentiousness*—[There is] a component of power and control whereby the criminal displays his inflated, "big shot" image in an effort to impress the world.
7. *Failure to Assume Obligations*—The criminal views an obligation as something that controls him. Failing to assume an obligation results in hardship for people who depend on him, i.e., child, spouse, employer.
8. *Ownership*—[There is] an attitude whereby the criminal assumes possession of other people's property and domination over other people.
9. *Failure to Make an Effort or Endure Adversity*—Because of his uniqueness thinking, and superoptimism thinking, the criminal doesn't believe he should have to put forth effort or endure hardship to accomplish a goal.
10. *Lack of Time Perspective*—The criminal's time frame is mainly in the present. There is little learning from the past or using the present to prepare for the future.
11. *Poor Decision Making*—[This is] the outcome of poor reasoning, failure to find out facts or consider the future from a responsible perspective.
12. *Lack of Trust*—The criminal demands [that] others trust him but objects to trusting others.
13. *Anger*—The criminal [uses] anger to control and regain control of others.
14. *I Can't*—The criminal [says] "I can't" when he really means "I don't want to" or "I am not going to," [which] results in rejecting responsible behavior.
15. *Victimstance*—The criminal uses this thinking pattern when being held accountable for wrongdoing in an attempt to avoid punishment.

CRITICAL THINKING QUESTIONS

■ *How would you go about identifying these thinking errors in youthful offenders? What would you recommend a youth to change his or her thinking errors?*

Source: Materials used as part of staff training at Four Oaks, Inc., in Iowa.

CTSP was developed through a systematic review of all published correctional programs that were associated with reduced criminal recidivism. The researchers identified one hundred evaluations of effective programs and discovered they all were designed to target offenders' thinking. Rigid thinking could be minimized by teaching participants creative thinking skills and providing them with prosocial alternatives to use when reporting on or responding to interpersonal problems. A core component of CTSP is the belief that teaching offender techniques of self-control could improve their social adjustments.[32]

A review of the literature leads to the conclusion that combining elements of cognition and behavior approaches is found in the principle of self-reinforcement. This concept says that behavior and cognitive changes reinforce each other. When cognitive changes lead to changes in behavior, what results is a sense of well-being that strengthens positive thinking and, as a result, further strengthens behavioral changes. This self-reinforcing feedback process is key to the cognitive-behavior approach and is a basis for helping offenders understand the cognitive-behavior process.[33]

CBT Effectiveness

A considerable amount of research shows positive effects for the use of cognitive-behavioral approaches with offenders[34]:

- A meta-analysis of sixty-nine studies covering both behavioral and cognitive-behavioral problems determined that the cognitive-behavioral programs are more effective in reducing rates of recidivism than the behavioral programs. The mean reduction was about 39 percent for treated offenders.[35]

- Another meta-analysis of correctional treatment concluded that cognitive-behavioral methods constituted critical aspects of effective correctional treatment.[36]

- Another study determined that the most effective interventions are those that employed cognitive-behavioral techniques to improve cognitive function.[37]

- There is strong evidence that positive results are more likely to take place among certain subgroups. For example, CTSP seems to be more effective with offenders over age 25 and with property offenders.[38]

Group Programs

In addition to individual-level therapies, most training schools maintain group counseling programs. The most popular of these programs are guided group interaction, positive peer culture, and drug and alcohol treatment programs.

Guided Group Interaction

Guided Group Interaction (GGI)
A treatment modality based on the assumption that youths can confront their peers and force them to face the reality of their behavior more effectively than staff can. GGI is the most widely used treatment modality in juvenile corrections.

Guided group interaction (GGI) is probably the most widely used treatment modality. It has been used in at least eleven states: Florida, Georgia, Illinois, Kentucky, Maryland, Michigan, Minnesota, New Hampshire, New Jersey, South Dakota, and West Virginia. Since the 1950s, when this modality was first used, it has been based on the assumption that youths could confront their peers and force them to face the reality of their behavior more effectively than could staff.

The GGI approach is characterized by a nonauthoritarian atmosphere, intensity of interaction, group homogeneity, and an emphasis on group structure. Residents in many residential GGI programs, for example, are given considerable say in when a group member will be released, granted a home furlough, or approved for off-campus visits; in how a group will be punished; and in whether the outside door will be locked or left open at night.

Giving residents responsibility for decision making, of course, is a different approach to child care from that followed in most correctional settings. The adult leader constantly refers the decision making back to the group. When informed by a youth that a group member planned to run away, for example, one staff member retorted: "So what do you want me to do? He's your buddy; he's part of your group. You can talk to him if you have to; but it's up to all of you to help one another."[39]

Although the research findings on GGI have been mixed, the general picture that emerges is that a GGI experience in a nonresidential program is at least as effective as and much less costly than confinement in a state facility and that a GGI experience in an institutional program seems to have more positive impact on less delinquent youngsters.[40]

Positive Peer Culture

The concept of **positive peer culture (PPC)** generated considerable excitement in juvenile corrections, especially in the 1970s. Developed by Harry Vorrath and associates as an outgrowth of GGI, PPC has been implemented in all of the juvenile state institutions in Michigan, Missouri, and West Virginia.[41]

Vorrath believes that PPC "is a total system for building positive youth subcultures."[42] The main philosophy of PPC is to "turn around" the negative peer culture and to mobilize the power of the peer group in a positive way. PPC does this by teaching group members to care for one another; caring is defined as wanting what is best for a person. Vorrath believes that once caring becomes "fashionable" and is accepted by the group, "hurting goes out of style."[43]

Although Vorrath believes that the basic assumptions of these youths can be changed, few people change many of their background assumptions over the period of a lifetime—much less when they are stripped of their freedom and are in therapy. For this modality to be properly evaluated more research is needed. But its present successes should remind both followers and critics that PPC remains one of the most promising ways to treat, change, correct, and rehabilitate juvenile offenders.

Positive Peer Culture (PPC)
A total system for building positive youth subcultures. Its main goal is to turn around negative peer cultures and to mobilize the power of the peer group in positive ways.

Drug and Alcohol Abuse Interventions

Drug and alcohol abuse by juveniles, as well as their involvement in drug trafficking in the community, constitutes a serious social problem today. A director of guidance in a training school acknowledged the seriousness of the problem when he said, "Rarely do we get a boy who doesn't have some history of drug or alcohol abuse in his background."[44]

Drug and alcohol abuse interventions increasingly are being developed in community-based and institutional settings to assist those who need help with such problems. These groups are being conducted in training schools in at least three ways: First, institutionalized juveniles assessed to have a problem with alcohol and/or drugs are placed in a separate cottage or in a chemical-abuse group. Specialized staff are hired to work in these cottages or lead these groups. Second, in other training schools, the social worker or another cottage staff member conducts ongoing drug and alcohol abuse groups. Third, outside groups, such as Alcoholics Anonymous (AA) or Narcotics Anonymous (NA), come into the institution and hold sessions for interested residents.

Considering the extensiveness of the problem of drug use and trafficking among juvenile offenders, there are still too few programs being offered in juvenile placements. The programs that are offered tend to be relatively unsophisticated and lacking in adequate theoretical design, treatment integrity, and evaluation follow-up. Treatment studies conducted on prison populations have found that when drug programs are well integrated and use effective program elements that have been implemented carefully, these programs:

- Reduce relapse
- Reduce criminality
- Reduce inmate misconduct
- Reduce mental illness
- Reduce behavioral disorders
- Increase the level of the inmates' stake in societal norms
- Increase levels of education and employment upon return to the community
- Improve health and mental health symptoms and conditions
- Improve relationships.[45]

Unquestionably, development of effective alcohol and drug abuse programs represents one of the most important challenges of juvenile justice today.

What Works for Whom and in What Context

The overall quality of treatment in the juvenile justice system is not impressive. Enforcing offender rehabilitation has sometimes resulted in making delinquents worse rather than better through treatment. The frequent criticism that offender rehabilitation is defective in theory and is a disaster in practice has been true on too many occasions. Program designs often have given little consideration to what a particular program can realistically accomplish with a particular group of offenders and frequently have relied on a single cure for a variety of complex problems. In addition, programs generally have lacked integrity, because they have not delivered the services they claimed with sufficient strength to accomplish the goals of treatment. Furthermore, the research on offender rehabilitation generally has been inadequate, with many projects and reports on rehabilitation almost totally lacking in well-developed research designs.[46]

Still, some progress has been made. Various meta-analyses and literature reviews from the 1980s indicated that treatment programs had somewhat more positive findings than earlier studies had revealed.[47] The emerging picture that received increased support in the 1990s was that "something" apparently works, though no generic method or approach, as distinct from individual programs, especially shines.[48] Or, to state this differently, several methods appear promising, but none had produced major reductions in recidivism.

Beginning in the 1990s and continuing until the present day, evidence-based programs and practices have been increasingly produced and circulated. The federal Office of Juvenile Justice and Delinquency Prevention was one of the most enthusiastic supporters of evidence-based programs. Throughout this text, including in this chapter, examples of evidence-based programs are discussed. It is anticipated that these increasing numbers of evidence-based programs will give the field a better understanding of what works.

The fact still remains that correctional treatment must discover what works for which offenders in what context. In other words, correctional treatment could be more effective if amenable offenders were offered appropriate treatments by matched workers in an environment that is conducive to producing positive effects.

To match up individual offenders with the treatments most likely to benefit them will be no easy task. Only through well-planned and soundly executed research with the necessary information be gained. Back in the 1970s, the Panel of Rehabilitative techniques recommended the use of the "template matching technique." This technique creates a set of descriptors, or a "template," of the kinds of people who are most likely to benefit from a particular treatment according to the theory or basic assumptions underlying it.[49] The treatment resources are greater than they have been in the past, and it is hoped that treatment in juvenile justice will have much better outcomes.

Graduated Sanctions in Juvenile Justice

In adult corrections, increased attention has been given to intermediate sanctions and in recent decades these intermediate sanctions have included a system of graduated sanctions, ranging from fines, daily reporting centers, and drug courts to intensive probation and residential placement.

This same movement has gained some momentum in juvenile justice, but in juvenile justice the system of graduated sanctions is focused on serious, violent, and chronic juvenile offenders. These offenders are moving along a continuum through a well-structured system that addresses both their needs and the safety of the community. At each level, juvenile offenders are subject to more severe sanctions if they continue in their delinquent offenses.[50]

Core Principles of a System of Graduated Sanctions

A model "graduated system" combines youth discipline with humane, reasonable, and appropriate sanctions. It offers a continuum of care that consists of diverse programs. Included in this continuum are intermediate sanctions within the community both for first-time nonviolent offenders and for more serious offenders, secure care programs for the most violent offenders, and aftercare programs that provide high levels of both social control and treatment services.

Each of the graduated sanctions is intended to consist of graduations, or levels, that together with appropriate services constitute an integrated approach. This approach is designed to stop the youthful offender's further participation in the system by inducing law-abiding behavior as early as possible through the commendation of treatment sanctions and appropriate interventions. The family must be involved in each level in the continuum. Aftercare must be actively involved in supporting the family and in integrating the youth into the community. Programs will need to use risk and needs assessments to determine appropriate placement for the offender. The effectiveness of interventions depends on their being swift and certain, and incorporating increased sanctions, including the possible loss of freedom. As the severity of the sanctions increases, so must the intensity of the treatment. Such sanctions could ultimately mean confinement in a secure setting, ranging from a secure community-based facility to a public or private training school, camp, or ranch. The programs are most effective for hard-to-handle youth and address key areas of risk in their lives, provide adequate support and supervision, and offer youths a long-term stake in the community.

Race and Juvenile Justice

One of the most disturbing issues facing the juvenile justice system today is the long-standing and pronounced disparities in the processing of white and minority youths. Northeastern University's Donna Bishop concluded: "Despite decades of research, there is no clear consensus on why minority youths enter and penetrate the juvenile justice system at such disproportionate rates."[51] According to Bishop, two explanations have been given: "The first is that minority overrepresentation reflects race and ethnic differences in the incidence, seriousness, and persistence of delinquent involvement (the 'differential offending' hypothesis)" and "the second is that overrepresentation is attributable to inequities—intended or unintended—in juvenile justice practice (the 'differential treatment' hypothesis)."[52]

University of Missouri–St. Louis Professor Janet L. Lauritsen, in examining what is known about racial and ethnic differences in juvenile offending, offered the following conclusions that have wide support in the literature:

Web Extra 12–2
American Bar Association's Juvenile Justice Committee

- Rates of juvenile homicide are higher for minorities than for white youthful offenders. Similarly, variations exist in rates of lethal violence between minority groups.

- Official data suggest disproportionate involvement in nonlethal violence on the part of African American youths. When arrest data are restricted to specific forms of nonlethal violence, African American youths appear to be disproportionately involved in robbery, aggravated assault, and rape.

- Juvenile property crime data show that African American youths are slightly more involved in such offenses than white youths, although the level of involvement varies by type of property crime.

- Arrest data show that white youths are disproportionately involved in alcohol offenses and that American Indian youths are slightly more likely than African American or Asian American youths to be arrested for these crimes.

- African American youths are disproportionately arrested for drug abuse violations and illicit drug use, but self-report data from juveniles on their own drug involvement do not confirm the differences between African American and white youths suggested by arrest data. In fact, white youths are somewhat more likely to report using marijuana, selling any drug, and selling marijuana.

- Weapons violations arrest data indicate that African American youths are disproportionately likely to be arrested for weapons possession or use.[53]

- Although the most commonly occurring crimes exhibit few group differences, the less frequent and serious crimes of violence show generally higher levels of African American and Latino American involvement.[54]

Lauritsen concluded that this kind of empirical evidence suggests that the relationship between race and ethnicity and juvenile involvement in delinquency is complex and contingent on the type of offense. In contrast, Bishop suggested that minority overrepresentation in the juvenile justice system is attributable to inequities in system practices rather than differences in the incidence, seriousness, or persistence of offending.

Minorities are overrepresented among youths held in secure detention, petitioned to juvenile court, and adjudicated delinquent. Among those who are adjudicated delinquent, minorities are more often committed to the "deep end" of the juvenile system: When confined, they are more likely to be housed in large public institutions rather than in privately run specialized treatment facilities or group homes, and prosecutors and judges seem quicker to relinquish jurisdiction over minorities, transferring them to criminal court for prosecution and punishment.[55]

Disproportionate Minority Confinement

Carl E. Pope and William H. Feyerherm's highly regarded assessment of the issue of discrimination against minorities revealed that two-thirds of the studies they examined found "both direct and indirect race effects or a mixed pattern (being present at some stages and not at others)."[56] They added that selection bias can take place at any stage and that small racial differences may accumulate and become more pronounced as minority youths are processed into the juvenile justice system.[57]

The Coalition for Juvenile Justice (then the National Coalition of State Juvenile Justice Advisory Groups) brought national attention to the problem of **disproportionate minority confinement** in its 1988 annual report to Congress. In that same year, Congress responded to evidence of disproportionate confinement of minority juveniles in secure facilities by amending the Juvenile Justice and Delinquency Prevention Act (JJDPA) of 1974 to provide that states must determine whether the proportion of minorities in confinement exceeded their proportion in the population of the state; if there was overrepresentation, states must demonstrate efforts to reduce it.[58]

During the 1992 reauthorization of the JJDPA, Congress substantially strengthened the effort to address disproportionate confinement of minority youths in secure facilities. Elimination of disproportionate minority confinement was elevated to the status of a "core requirement" alongside deinstitutionalization of status offenders, removal of juveniles from adult jails and lockups, and separation of youthful offenders from adults in secure institutions. The 2002 reauthorization of the JJDPA also changed the disproportionate minority confinement (DMC) mandate to reduce minority contact with the system.

Web Extra 12–3
Coalition for Juvenile Justice website

Disproportionate Minority Confinement (DMC)
The court-ordered confinement, in juvenile institutions, of members of minority groups in numbers disproportionate to their representation in the general population.

Web Extra 12–4
OJJDP: *DMC Chronology*

Library Extra 12–4
OJJDP publication: *Disproportionate Minority Contact*

Library Extra 12–5
NIJ article: *Brick by Brick: Dismantling the Border between Juvenile and Adult Justice*

Prevention of Delinquency

Comprehensive Delinquency Prevention Strategy

Based on research spearheaded and funded by the OJJDP, a consensus developed that the most effective strategy for juvenile corrections is to focus comprehensive prevention and diversion efforts on high-risk juveniles who are involved in violence; these juveniles—the ones whom officials are quick to dump into the adult system—commit the most frequent and more serious delinquent acts. At the same time that the seriousness of their behaviors was affecting changes in juvenile codes across the nation, research was beginning to find that these high-risk youths can be impacted by well-equipped and well-implemented prevention and treatment programs.[59]

Such programs are based on the assumption that the juvenile justice system does not see most serious offenders until it is too late to intervene effectively.[60] This strategy also presumes that if the goal is to reduce the overall violence in American society, it is necessary to successfully intervene in the lives of high-risk youthful offenders, who commit about 75 percent of all violent juvenile offenses.[61]

Several general characteristics are found in these comprehensive programs: They address key areas of risk in youths' lives, they seek to strengthen the personal and institutional factors contributing to healthy adolescent development, they provide adequate support and supervision, and they offer youths a long-term stake in the community.[62] These prevention programs for high-risk youths must be integrated with local police, child welfare, social services, school, and family preservation programs because comprehensive approaches to delinquency prevention and intervention require strong collaborative efforts between the juvenile justice system and other service provision systems, including health, mental health, child welfare, and education. An important component of a community's comprehensive plan is to develop mechanisms that effectively link these service providers at the program level.[63]

The comprehensive or multisystemic aspects of these programs are designed to deal simultaneously with many aspects of youths' lives. They are intensive, often involving weekly or even daily contacts with at-risk youths, and build on youths' strengths rather than focusing on their deficiencies. These programs operate mostly (though not exclusively) outside the formal justice system under a variety of public, nonprofit, or university auspices. Finally, they combine accountability and sanctions with increasingly intensive rehabilitation and treatment services, which are achieved through a system of graduated sanctions in which an integrated approach is used to stop the penetration of youthful offenders into the system.[64] Figure 12–8 provides an overview of this comprehensive prevention strategy.

In 1996, three communities—Lee and Duval Counties in Florida and San Diego County in California—collaborated with the OJJDP to apply the processes and principles set forth in OJJDP's comprehensive strategy statement; initial evaluations of the three pilot projects reported that each of the three sites had benefited significantly from the comprehensive planning process.[65] The following were among the accomplishments identified in a 2000 report:

- Enhanced community-wide understanding of prevention services and sanction options for juveniles
- Expanded networking capacity and better coordination among agencies and service providers
- Institution of performance measurement systems
- Hiring of staff to spearhead ongoing comprehensive strategy planning and implementation efforts
- Development of comprehensive five-year strategic action plans.[66]

FIGURE 12–8
A Comprehensive Delinquency Prevention Strategy

Source: Mark A. Matese and John A. Tuell, *Update on the Comprehensive Strategy for Serious, Violent, and Chronic Juvenile Offenders* (Washington, D.C.: Office of Juvenile Justice and Delinquency Prevention, 1998, 2003, and 2009), p. 1.

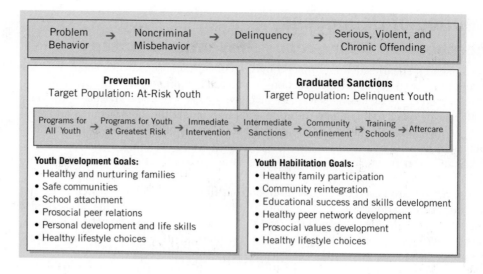

Voices of Delinquency 12–1
Read "I Want to Stay Out of Places Like This." Why is the justice experience such a negative experience for youths?

Delinquency across the Life Course: Effects of the Juvenile Justice System on Juvenile Offenders

Early cohort studies certainly did not present a favorable picture of the effect of the juvenile justice process on juvenile delinquents. The Philadelphia studies found that the probability of becoming an adult offender increased dramatically for individuals with a record of juvenile delinquency. The Philadelphia, Racine, and Columbus cohort studies found that stricter punishments by the juvenile justice system were likely to encourage rather than to eliminate recidivism (further delinquent behavior).[67] The Racine cohort studies found that an increase in frequency and seriousness of misbehavior typically occurred in the periods following the administration of sanctions by the justice system and that those who had police contacts as juveniles were more likely to have police contacts as adults.[68] The Columbus cohort study further found that the impact of institutional treatment was basically negative; in fact, after institutionalization, the length of time between arrests decreased dramatically.[69] These studies found that the probabilities of continuing with juvenile crime and going on to adult crime increased for individuals who were brought to the attention of the juvenile justice system.

More recent longitudinal studies have not been more positive about the impact of the juvenile justice system. As Chapter 3 revealed, the earlier youths come to the attention of the juvenile justice system, the more likely they are to continue with juvenile crime; the more time they spent in the juvenile justice system, the more likely they are to go on to adult crime; and the deeper they go into the system, the higher the rates of recidivism when they leave and the more serious crimes they tend to commit as adults.

Delinquency and Social Policy: The Importance of Early Intervention

Research seems to show that the younger a child is when first involved with the juvenile justice system, the more likely it is that the child will persist in delinquency; that the more contact a juvenile has with the juvenile justice system, the more likely it is that he or she will persist in delinquent behavior; and that the further a youngster is processed into the juvenile justice system, the less chance there is that he or she will be diverted successfully from the system.[70] These findings readily lead to the conclusion that primary (or early) prevention is much more desirable than later means of delinquency control.

There is also common agreement among experts on a number of concepts. First, no one solution exists to the delinquency prevention problem; that is, no one program component is available that by itself can alter the outcomes for all high-risk children. Second, high-risk behaviors are interrelated, so prevention programs should have broad and comprehensive goals. Third, each community requires a package of services that involve community-wide planning. Fourth, the focus of prevention should be on changing institutions rather than on changing individuals. Fifth, the timing of interventions is critical in achieving a successful outcome; preschool and middle school periods are when problems develop and ought to receive more focus in prevention interventions. Finally, a continuity of efforts must be maintained because one-shot efforts have little or no effect.[71] Exhibit 12–3 is a reminder of the importance of early intervention.

The social development model implies the following six principles for the prevention of delinquency in those neighborhoods characterized by high rates of serious and violent delinquency:

1. A key to delinquency prevention is community organization against delinquency.
2. Community control of prevention efforts and other services for youth should be encouraged.

Exhibit 12–3
Delinquency Prevention

The desirable goal is for a child not to become involved in delinquent behavior, but if that goal cannot be achieved in a child's life, then the next desirable goal is for his or her delinquent behavior to be minor and limited to a few acts. If that goal cannot be achieved, then the next goal is for the delinquency to be confined to a youth's adolescent years. The purpose of prevention ultimately is for a child to live a productive and fulfilling life.

In *Voices of Delinquency*, each individual describes the pain of a wasted life, a life in which each has also taken other lives, with the result that most will spend the remainder (or most) of their lives in prison and one will be executed by the state. Reading these final stories in *Voices of Delinquency* is a vivid reminder of the importance of delinquency prevention to this society.

STORIES FROM VOICES OF DELINQUENCY

"The Thinker"

"I still long for freedom but have accepted my fate. If I could change it, I would, but I don't dwell on freedom like some guys do…. I'll never give up hope or the dream of freedom, but I'm not going to obsess over it. I have my life, and I'll get as much out of it as I can."

"Forgotten Children"

"With thirty-two days before being released, I was charged with two counts of murder, tried, convicted, and sentenced to two life sentences. Since that time, some twenty-six years have passed. Here I sit in prison seeking to overcome the need for attention and seeking to overcome the deprivations of my childhood."

"A Small-Town Boy"

"One evening I made a terrible decision while under the influence of this drug combination [alcohol and tranquilizers]. It resulted in the death of a girlfriend and cost me the rest of my life in prison. I truly regret my actions."

"My Father Was an Alcoholic"

"I have come to the realization that the beatings were only a small part of my childhood. My abusive background certainly influenced my life of crime, but there is more to it than that. My mental disability has no doubt influenced my life of crime. There were also all those drugs I took. I guess I will never know what really went wrong inside of me. What I do know is that I am now the living dead."

"Selling Drugs Was My Downfall"

"So I went to the store to get a pack of cigarettes, and I saw him pumping gas at the same point. I pointed and aimed, and I shot and killed this young man. To this day I wish I could definitely turn the clock back. I have a few friends who have been gunned down, and it makes me depressed that I have put myself in that pair of shoes. It does not make me feel very good about myself at all."

Individuals have human agency (i.e., they exercise free choice), and in spite of the social environment in which they live, they still make choices about what they are going to do with their lives—including whether they will become involved in delinquent acts or not. Human agency (choice) is still available, regardless of what pathway they take through their adolescent and adult years. For prevention efforts to work in their lives, they need support from a variety of sources, and viable prevention programs can also be helpful to them as they receive reinforcement for the positive decisions they make.

3. The participation of youths, as well as adults, should be encouraged.

4. Delinquent groups and gangs should be co-opted into constructive activities or disbanded.

5. Access to legitimate opportunities should be restricted, and legitimate educational, employment, and social activities should be accessible to all youths.

6. Efforts to improve the control mechanisms of the family should be directed at enhancing its direct control function and its ability to develop self-control among children.[72]

Trends for the Future

Several changes are taking place in juvenile justice today and will likely continue in the future:

- *Expansion of restorative justice.* As mentioned in several chapters of this text, restorative justice is one of the most exciting movements in corrections today, and it has recently been coupled with intermediate sanctions. From the grassroots level to local and state headquarters, restorative justice is rapidly gaining momentum within the United States. Victim–offender conferencing (sometimes called mediation) is the oldest and most widely used expression of restorative justice, with more than thirteen hundred programs in eighteen countries.[73] While stressing accountability for offenses committed, restorative strategies operate with the goal of repairing injuries to victims and to communities in which crimes have taken place. Whether these conferences occur before, during, or after adjudication, they promote education and transformation within a context of respect and healing. These models are neither mutually exclusive nor compete in and of themselves and can be combined or adapted depending on the special situation at hand.[74]

- *Increased use of technology.* Rather than rely on traditional methods of security and control, the correctional system is now entering a new phase of technocorrections, which involves using technology rather than personnel to monitor probation, aftercare, and institutional populations. Today, technology-driven security is designed to maintain security, both in the community and in institutions. Community corrections has relied for quite some time on technology to monitor offenders; for example, electronic monitoring (EM) has been increasingly used in probation services. Now, new methods of technology are being explored to provide probation and parole officers with tools to better manage their caseloads and do their jobs more effectively and efficiently.

▲ A counselor (right) talks with a teenage girl and her parents during a therapy session in Los Angeles, California.

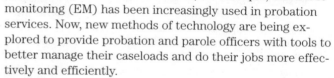

■ **What are the goals of the balanced and restorative model of corrections?**

- *Greater use of evidence-based practice principles and approaches.* Evidence-based practice is increasingly used in juvenile justice today. As Donna M. Bishop of Northeastern University notes, meta-analyses have identified effective generic strategies as well as principles-based approaches useful in delinquency prevention, and knowledge about these effective strategies and principles is being disseminated throughout the field.[75]

- *Legislatures are likely to become more rather than less involved in juvenile court law.* One of the purposes of this increased involvement will be to raise penalties against gang members and those who try to recruit children into gangs. At the same time, youth gangs will continue to persist as a serious problem in the twenty-first century because they provide a significant support system for those who lack support in other social settings. Some critics content that this trend signals a shift toward punishing juveniles and adults on the basis of who they are rather than what they have done.

- *The issue of gun control will be revisited.* Gun control may be the most serious problem facing juvenile justice in the early decades of the twenty-first century. Significant gun-control efforts made in urban areas during the past few decades to reduce the availability of gun to juveniles will likely continue.

- *It is likely that the juvenile justice system will continue in its present form.* Although the system may receive criticism, it is unlikely that the country will give up on the century-long experience with a separate system for juveniles.

The Case

The Life Course of Amy Watters, Age 15

It never occurred to Amy (not seriously, at least) that she might be arrested. One day, however, after smuggling drugs into the school in a couple of tampon containers that she carried in her purse, Amy was called to the office. When she got there, she was ushered into the principal's conference room, where she faced the principal, a school counselor, and a female deputy sheriff. Her boyfriend, CJ, was also seated at the table looking very uncomfortable.

The sheriff's office, Amy was told, had been conducting a county-wide investigation into the use of illegal drugs in the county's high schools. Video surveillance, it turned out, had implicated both Amy and CJ in a series of drug transfers. She was shown one of the videos, a black-and-white stream from an overhead camera in one of the school's hallways, that clearly showed her handing freezer bags full of what looked like marijuana (the pictures were a bit grainy) to CJ.

Although the investigators did not yet know the extent of her involvement, it quickly became clear to Amy that she and CJ had been caught red-handed. Amy was told that her backpack was being confiscated by deputies, and that it would be searched for drugs or drug residue. Her father was on his way to the school, the principal told her, along with CJ's parents, and once they got there she and CJ were to be questioned by the female officer.

Amy and CJ were told to go to a small area off of the conference room to await the arrival of their parents. While there, the two talked about their situation, and Amy told CJ that it would be best if they admitted what they had been doing. CJ was adamant in proclaiming that he would deny everything. He had to protect the Boyz at all costs, he said. He would never rat them out. Besides, he said, "I'm eighteen now, and a senior. If I get busted, I'm going to criminal court."

Why hadn't Amy realistically considered the possibility of arrest? Should young people placed under arrest have all of the same rights as an adult? Why or why not?

Learn More on the Web:
- Juvenile Justice Case Flow Processing: http://www.ojjdp.gov/ojstatbb/structure_process/case.html
- Juvenile Court Chronology: http://criminal.findlaw.com/crimes/juvenile-justice/le2_9.html

Follow the continuing Amy Watters saga in the next chapter.

SUMMARY

The juvenile justice system is responsible for controlling and correcting the behavior of law-violating juveniles. Of special note are the following points:

- It can be argued that the juvenile justice system has improved since the mid-1970s, but the improvements hardly seem to have scratched the surface in terms of designing a justice system that will effectively deal with juvenile delinquency in the United States.

- The problem of continued serious juvenile delinquency in the United States challenges the juvenile justice system to mobilize a coordinated and effective approach to dealing with youth crime.

- Racial and ethnic inequities represent one of the most serious issues facing the juvenile justice system today.

- Conflicting philosophies and strategies for dealing with youth crime and a fragmented juvenile justice system that varies from one jurisdiction to another make it nearly impossible for the juvenile justice process to handle delinquency cases effectively.

- The balanced and restorative model is rapidly gaining acceptance in more and more jurisdictions as a promising modality that should be employed in the fight against juvenile crime.

- Efforts to coordinate a continuum of increasing sanctions for violent and chronic youthful offenders offer hope and represent positive directions for the juvenile justice system.

KEY TERMS

adjudicatory hearing, p.308

aftercare, p. 299

balanced and restorative model, p. 310

behavioral modification, p. 312

child savers, p. 299

cognitive-behavioral therapy (CBT),
    p. 313

Cognitive Thinking Skills Program
    (CTSP), p. 313

commitment, p. 308

cottage system, p. 301

crime control model, p. 310

detention, p. 308

dispositional hearing, p. 308

disproportionate minority confinement,
    p. 318

diversion programs, p. 302

guided group interaction (GGI), p. 314

insight-based therapy, p. 312

just deserts, p. 309

justice model, p. 309

juvenile court officer, p. 308

petition, p. 308

petitioner, p. 308

positive peer culture (PPC), p. 315

probation, p. 299

recidivism, p. 304 *Repeat offense*

rehabilitation model, p. 308

residential program, p. 300

respondent, p. 308

taking into custody, p. 308

training school, p. 301

JUVENILE DELINQUENCY VIDEOS

At a Glance: The Juvenile Justice Process

At a Glance depicts a youth offender starting through the juvenile justice system beginning with the intake process. Based on the readings in this chapter, discuss which steps of the justice system are present in the video. How are these processes designed to protect the rights of the child while also reaching the goals of the court? Are these processes established by *parens patriae*? Why or why not?

Entering the Juvenile Justice System

Entering the Juvenile Justice System follows a juvenile with a record of arrests as he enters the juvenile justice system through

the intake process. The intake officers are very concerned with the youth's drug use; why is this an important factor at the intake process? Notice the questions asked by the officer when filing the intake report. Discuss the importance of these questions and how they relate to the youth's criminal record, medical history, and drug and alcohol habits. Does the intake process do a reliable job in assessing the juvenile's immediate needs? Why or why not? How would the intake process be handled if the juvenile admitted to being on drugs at the time? Discuss.

REVIEW QUESTIONS

1. What were the origins of the American juvenile justice system?
2. How did community-based corrections for juveniles develop?
3. How did juvenile probation develop, and what programs exist to divert juveniles from formal handling by the system?
4. How is the juvenile justice system structured? What are its main components?
5. What are the stages of delinquency case processing?
6. How do the juvenile and adult justice systems differ?
7. What are graduated sanctions? How do they work in the juvenile justice system?
8. What racial and ethnic differences in the juvenile justice system can be identified? Why do they exist?
9. How might delinquency be prevented? What are some strategies useful in delinquency prevention.
10. What are some future trends for juvenile justice?

DISCUSSION QUESTIONS

1. The juvenile justice system uses four ways to deal with delinquency: the rehabilitation model, the justice model, the crime control model, and the balanced and restorative model. Which do you think works best? Why? Why is the balanced and restorative model gaining such popularity nationwide?
2. After reading this chapter, do you feel encouraged or discouraged about the ability of society to deal effectively with delinquency? Why?
3. Does society really need a juvenile justice system that is separate from the adult system used with criminals? Be able to defend your explanation.
4. Some suggest today's youths are far more sophisticated than were the youths of earlier generations, so they should be held responsible for their behavior at an earlier age. Do you agree? Explain your response.
5. Should terminologies be standardized for the adult and juvenile justice systems? Explain your response.

GROUP EXERCISES

1. Have students research their county and state data to determine how many juveniles are currently incarcerated and how many are currently on probation. Discuss their findings.
2. Have students research their county and state data to determine the applicable juvenile recidivism rate. Discuss their findings.

3. Appoint teams to research juvenile justice processing in the ten most populated countries (excluding the United States and Germany); then have each team prepare and present a briefing to the class.

NOTES

1. Jennifer Fratello, Annie Salsich, and Sara Moqulescu, *Juvenile Detention Reform in New York City: Measuring Risk through Research* (New York: Vera Institute of Justice, 2011).
2. Elizabeth S. Scott and Thomas Grisso, "The Evolution of Adolescence: A Developmental Perspective on Juvenile Justice Reform," *Journal of Criminal Law & Criminology* 88 (1997), pp. 137–89.
3. Anthony M. Platt, *The Child Savers*, 2nd ed. (Chicago: University of Chicago Press, 1977), p. 3.
4. Ibid. For interpretations similar to Platt's, see also Sanford J. Fox, "Juvenile Justice Reform: An Historic Perspective," *Stanford Law Review* 22 (1970), p. 1187; and Douglas Rendleman, "Parens Patriae: From Chancery to the Juvenile Court," *South Carolina Law Review* 28 (1971), p. 205.
5. David Shichor, "Historical and Current Trends in American Juvenile Justice," *Juvenile and Family Court Journal* 34 (August 1983), pp. 61–75.
6. John Augustus, *First Probation Officer* (Montclair, N.J.: Patterson-Smith Company, 1972).
7. David J. Rothman, *The Discovery of the Asylum* (Boston: Little, Brown, 1971).
8. Steven Schlossman, "Delinquent Children: The Juvenile Reform School," in *The Oxford History of the Prison*, edited by Norval Morris and David J. Rothman (New York: Oxford University Press, 1995), pp. 325–49.
9. Rothman, *The Discovery of the Asylum.*
10. Schlossman, "Delinquent Children."
11. See Howard Polsky, *Cottage Six: The Social System of Delinquent Boys in Residential Treatment* (New York: Russell Sage Foundation, 1963); Clemens Bartollas, Stuart J. Miller, and Simon Dinitz, *Juvenile Victimization: The Institutional Paradox* (New York: Halsted Press, 1976); Barry C. Feld, *Neutralizing Inmate Violence: The Juvenile Offender in Institutions* (Cambridge, Mass.: Ballinger, 1977); and Kenneth Wooden, *Weeping in the Playtime of Others: America's Incarcerated Children* (New York: McGraw-Hill, 1976).
12. Scott B. Peterson and Jill Beres, *Report to the Nation 1993 to 2008: The Global Youth Justice Movement, 15 Year Update on Youth Courts and Teen Courts* (Cleveland, Ohio: Global Issues Resource Center, Cuyahoga Community College, 2008).
13. Ibid.
14. T. M. Godwin, *Peer Justice and Youth Empowerment: An Implementation Guide for Teen Court Programs* (Lexington, Ky.: American Probation and Parole Association, 1998).
15. C. W. Huddleston, C. West, Douglas B. Barlowe, and Rachel Casebold, *Painting the Current Picture: A National Report on Drug Courts and Other Problems—Solving Court Programs in the United States* (Washington, D.C.: Bureau of Justice Statistics, 2008), pp. 1–16.
16. Marilyn Roberts, Jennifer Brophy, and Caroline Cooper, *The Juvenile Drug Court Movement* (Washington, D.C.: Office of the Juvenile Justice and Delinquency Prevention, 1997).
17. Ibid.
18. Melissa L. Ives, Ya-Fen Chan, Kathryn C. Modisette, and Michael L. Dennis, "Needs, Services, and Outcomes of Youths in Juvenile Treatment Drug Courts as Compared to Adolescent Outpatient Treatment," *Drug Court Review*, pp. 10-12, 2010, http://www.reclaimingfutures.org/sites/blog.reclaimingfutures .org/files/userfiles/Ives%20et%20al%202010%20JTDC%20 quasi%20experiment-1.pdf (accessed October 31, 2012).
19. Andrew Rutherford and Robert McDermott, *National Evaluation Program Phase Report: Juvenile Diversion* (Washington, D.C.: U.S. Government Printing Office, 1976).
20. Carolyn Hardin and Jeffrey N. Kusher, *Quality Improvement for Drug Courts: Evidence-Based Practices* (Washington, D.C.: National Drug Court Institute, 2008.
21. For specific numbers of staff in juvenile corrections, see Timothy J. Flanagan and Kathleen Maguire, *Sourcebook of Criminal Justice Statistics—1999* (Washington, D.C.: U.S. Government Printing Office, 2000).
22. Ibid.
23. Platt, *The Child Savers.*
24. Charles Shireman, "The Juvenile Justice System: Structure, Problems and Prospects," in *Justice as Fairness*, edited by David Fogel and Joe Hudson (Cincinnati: W. H. Anderson, 1981), 136–41.
25. David Fogel, ". . . We Are the Living Proof . . .": The Justice Model for Corrections* (Cincinnati: W. H. Anderson, 1975).
26. Fogel, "Preface," in *Justice as Fairness*, viii.
27. Adapted from Shireman, "The Juvenile Justice System."
28. Adapted from D. Maloney, D. Romig, and T. Armstrong, "Juvenile Probation: The Balanced Approach," *Juvenile and Family Court Journal* 39 (1988), 5; G. Bazemore, "On Mission Statements and Reform in Juvenile Justice: The Case for the Balanced Approach," *Federal Probation* 56 (1992), 64–70; G. Bazemore, "What's 'New' about the Balanced Approach?" *Juvenile and Family Court Journal* 48 (1997), pp. 2, 3.
29. Gerald G. Gaes, Timothy J. Flanagan, Lawrence L. Motiuk, and Lynn Steward, "Adult Correctional Treatment," in *Crime and Justice, 26th Edition: Prisons*, edited by Michael Tonry and Joan Petersilia (Chicago: University of Chicago Press, 1999), 374-375.

30. Harvey Milkman and Kenneth Wanberg, *Cognitive-Behavioral Treatment: A Review and Discussion for Correctional Professionals* (Washington, D.C.: National Institute of Corrections, 2007), 5.

31. Patricia van Voorhis, Lis M. Spruance, P. Neal Richey, Shelley Johnson Listwan, and Renita Seebrook, "The Georgia Cognitive Skills Experiment: A Replication of Reasoning and Rehabilitation," *Criminal Justice and Behavior* 31 (2004), 282–305.

32. Ibid.

33. Ibid.

34. Ibid.

35. Frank S. Pearson, Douglas S. Lipton, Charles M. Cleland, and Dorline S. Yee, "The Effects of Behavioral/Cognitive-Behavioral Programs on Recidivism," *Crime and Delinquency* 48 (2002), 476-496.

36. Milkman and Wanberg, *Cognitive-Behavioral Treatment,* xix.

37. Ibid.

38. Pearson, Lipton, Cleland, and Yee, "The Effects of Behavioral/cognitive-Behavioral Programs on Recidivism."

39. Interview with Harry Vorrath quoted in Oliver J. Keller, Jr., and Benedict S. Alper, *Halfway Houses: Community Centered Correction and Treatment* (Lexington, Mass.: D.C. Heath, 1970), 55.

40. Ibid.

41. The following materials are adapted from Harry H. Vorrath and Larry K. Brendtro, *Positive Peer Culture* (Chicago: Aldine, 1974).

42. Ibid.

43. Ibid.

44. Interviewed in 1986 in a Midwestern training school.

45. See the Federal Bureau of Prisons, *Substance Abuse Treatment,* http://www.bop.gov/inmate_PROGRAMS_SUBSTANCE.JSP (accessed May 18, 2012).

46. Lee Scherest, Susan O. White, and Elizabeth D. Brown, eds., *The Rehabilitation of Criminal Offenders* (Washington, D.C.: National Academy of Sciences, 1979), Susan Martin, Lee Sechrest, and Robin Redner, eds., *Rehabilitation of Criminal Offenders: Directions for Research* (Washington, D.C.: National Academy of Sciences, 1981).

47. For an examination of the meta-analyses, see Ted Palmer, *The Re-Emergence of Intervention* (Beverly Hills, Calif.: Sage, 1999), pp. 48–76.

48. Palmer, *The Re-Emergence of Intervention,* p. 48.

49. Sechrest et al., *The Rehabilitation of Criminal Offenders,* pp. 35–37.

50. Barry Krisberg, et al., *Guide for Implementing the Comprehensive Strategy for Serious, Violent, and Chronic Juvenile offenders* (Washington, D.C.: Office of Juvenile Justice and Delinquency Prevention, 1995), p. 133.

51. Donna M. Bishop, "The Role of Race and Ethnicity in Juvenile Justice Processing," in *Our Children, Their Children: Confronting Racial and Ethnic Differences in American Juvenile Justice,* edited by Darnell F. Hawkins and Kimberly Kempf-Leonard (Chicago: University of Chicago Press, 2005), p. 23.

52. Ibid.

53. Janet L. Lauritsen, "Racial and Ethnic Differences in Judicial Offending," in *Our Children, Their Children*, pp. 91–95.

54. Ibid.

55. Bishop, "The Role of Race and Ethnicity in Juvenile Justice Processing."

56. Carl E. Pope and William Feyerherm, *Minorities and the Juvenile Justice System* (Washington, D.C.: Office of Juvenile Justice and Delinquency Prevention, 1995), pp. 2–3.

57. Ibid. See also Donna M. Bishop and Charles E. Frazier, *A Study of Race and Juvenile Processing in Florida, Report Submitted to the Florida Supreme Court Racial and Ethnic Bias Study Commission, 1990*; and Carl E. Pope, Rick Ovell, and Heidi M. Hsia, *Disproportionate Minority Confinement: A Review of the Research Literature from 1989 through 2001* (Washington, D.C.: Office of Juvenile Justice and Delinquency Prevention, 2002).

58. Harold M. Snyder and Melissa Sickmund, *Juvenile Offenders and Victims*: 2006 National Report (Washington, D.C.: National Center for Juvenile Justice, 2006).

59. James C. Howell, ed., *Guide for Implementing the Comprehensive Strategy for Serious, Violent, and Chronic Juvenile Offenders* (Washington, D.C.: Office of Juvenile Justice and Delinquency Prevention, 1995).

60. Ibid.

61. Ibid.

62. Ibid.

63. Ibid.

64. Ibid.

65. Kathleen Coolbaugh and Cynthia J. Hansel, "The Comprehensive Strategy: Lessons Learned from the Pilot Sites," *Juvenile Justice Bulletin* (2000).

66. Ibid.

67. Marvin E. Wolfgang, Robert M. Figlio, and Thorsten Sellin, *Delinquency in a Birth Cohort* (Chicago: University of Chicago Press, 1972).

68. Lyle W. Shannon, *Assessing the Relationships of Adult Criminal Careers to Juvenile Careers: A Summary* (Washington, D.C.: U.S. Government Printing Office, 1982).

69. Donna Martin Hamparian et al., *The Violent Few: A Study of Dangerous Juvenile Offenders* (Lexington, Mass.: Lexington Books, 1980).

70. These results are consistently found in the professional literature of delinquency.

71. Joy G. Dryfoos, *Adolescents at Risk: Prevalence and Prevention* (New York: Oxford University Press, 1990).

72. Joseph G. Weis and John Sederstrom, *The Prevention of Serious Delinquency: What to Do* (Washington, D.C.: National Institute for Juvenile Justice and Delinquency Prevention, 1981).

73. M. Coates, R. Coates, and B. Vos, "The Impact of Victim–Offender Mediation—Two Decades of Research," *Federal Probation* 65 (2001), pp. 29–36.

74. Katherine van Wormer and Clemens Bartollas, *Women and the Criminal Justice System*, 4d ed. (Upper Saddle River, N.J.: Prentice-Hall, 20 13).).

75. Donna M. Bishop, "Evidence-Based Practice and Juvenile Justice," *Criminology and Public Policy* 11, no. 3 (2012), pp. 483–89.

Chapter Objectives

After reading this chapter, you should be able to:

1. **Describe the factors that influence juveniles' attitudes toward the police.**

2. **Describe the factors that influence the disposition of juveniles and the types of formal and informal dispositions.**

3. **Summarize the legal rights of juveniles in encounters with police.**

4. **Summarize various police efforts to prevent delinquency.**

5. **Summarize the findings of evaluation of Project D.A.R.E.**

The vast majority of youth are good citizens who have never been arrested for any type of crime.

—Shay Bilchik, President, Child Welfare League of America

Introduction

In April 2011, an eight-year-old boy named Aiden was pepper sprayed by Lakewood, Colorado, police officers responding to a call for assistance from teachers at Glennon Heights Elementary School. Aiden, it seems, had flown into a violent rage, throwing furniture and threatening to kill his teachers. When police arrived they found him wielding a sharp piece of wooden trim that he had torn off of a wall like a spear—threatening to stab those around him. Rather than risk a physical encounter, responding officers sprayed the boy with pepper spray. The incident was the third time that police had been called to deal with Aiden's apparent temper tantrums. Even so, the boy's mother criticized police for using what she saw as excessive force. They treated him "like a common criminal," she later told reporters.[1]

Juvenile crime represents one of the most demanding and frustrating areas of police work. A common complaint of police officers is that arrested juvenile offenders are back on the streets before the officers have had a chance to complete the necessary paperwork. Also, with the rise of youth gangs and with increased numbers of juveniles carrying weapons, policing juveniles is much more dangerous than it used to be. Finally, police departments give little status to those dealing with youth crime because they regard arresting a juvenile as a poor "bust."

Policing juveniles is similar in some ways to policing adults, yet in other ways it is quite different. It is similar in that both juveniles and adults have constitutional protections; that juveniles can be as hostile to the police as adults can be; that armed juveniles, of course, are as dangerous as armed adults; that both juveniles and adults are involved in gangs, some of which are involved in drug trafficking; and that alcohol and drugs affect the functioning of both juveniles and adults. A major difference is the belief that juveniles are more salvageable than adults—few would argue against the widely held tenet that juveniles are more likely than adults to experience a turning point where they can walk away from crime.

Accordingly, the importance of police–juvenile relations cannot be minimized (Figure 13–1). The police are usually the first contact a youth has with the juvenile justice system. As the doorway into the system, the police officer can use his or her broad discretion to either detour youths or involve them in the system. In a real sense, the police officer becomes an on-the-spot prosecutor, judge, and correctional system when dealing with a juvenile offender.

The History of Police–Juvenile Relations

The earliest Puritan communities in the United States used informal methods of controlling juveniles. Probably the most effective of these informal methods was *socialization*, by which youths were taught the rules of society from the time they were born until the rules became internalized. If a youth violated a law, the family, church, and community stepped in to bring the youth back into line. The family was expected to punish the youth, and if the family failed, church and community elders turned to other punishments.

The industrialization and urbanization that began in the late 1700s reduced the effectiveness of informal social controls. As the population increased and cities grew, the traditional tight-knit family and community structures became disorganized and street crime increased. Religious, ethnic, and political violence also increased, leading the society to look for other methods of social control.[2] Police forces were created to help solve the problem (Figure 13–2).

In the 1830s and 1840s, full-time police forces were established in larger cities, such as Boston, New York, and Philadelphia; by the 1870s, all the major cities had full-time forces, and many of the smaller cities had part-time forces. Social control had moved from the family to police officers walking the beat. The police emerged as a coercive force employed to keep youthful criminals, gangs, ethnic minorities, and immigrants in line.

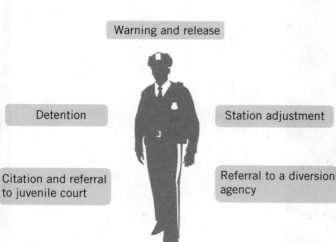

Warning and release

Detention

Station adjustment

Citation and referral to juvenile court

Referral to a diversion agency

FIGURE 13–1
Police Activities to Combat Delinquency

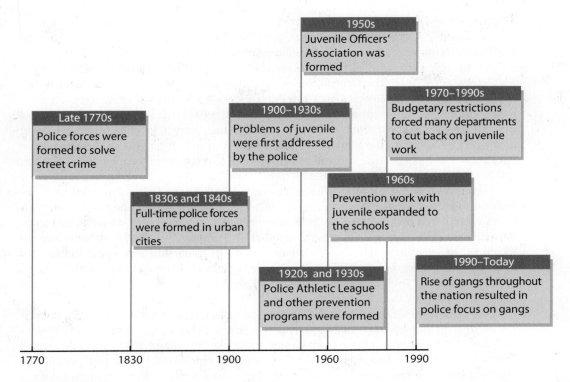

FIGURE 13-2
Juveniles and the Police

Police officers had the power to arrest juveniles, but they still used many informal techniques of social control. Some officers undoubtedly were effective in striking up friendships with juveniles and convincing them to mend their ways. In other cases, police reprimanded juveniles verbally or turned them over to their parents or parish priests. Unfortunately, the power of police officers at this time was virtually unlimited; some officers talked abusively to children, roughed them up, or beat them in alleys. The result was that, added to the corruption found in many police departments, considerable tension existed between police officers and the communities they patrolled. Few, if any, efforts to remedy this problem occurred before the 1900s.

In the first three decades of the twentieth century, the Portland, Oregon; New York City; and Washington, D.C., police departments started to address the problem of juvenile crime. Police chiefs began to think in terms of prevention instead of mere control. Policewomen were hired to deal with delinquents and runaway and truant children by patrolling amusement parks, dance halls, and other places where juveniles might be corrupted. The job of these officers was to dissuade the youths from engaging in a life of crime.[3]

The idea of prevention was so popular that 90 percent of the nation's largest cities had instituted some type of juvenile program by 1924.[4] The Police Athletic League was launched in the 1920s, and by the 1930s, most large police departments had either assigned welfare officers to difficult districts, initiated employment bureaus for youthful males, and assigned officers to juvenile courts, or set up special squads to deal with juvenile crime.[5] Other innovative actions included instituting relief programs, giving poor children gifts at Christmas, and developing programs whereby police spoke to various groups of youths, such as Boy Scouts and Campfire Girls.[6]

A major development occurred in the mid-1920s. Until this time, departments had not effectively organized their juvenile crime prevention efforts. Chief August Vollmer of the Berkeley, California, Police Department is credited with being the first chief to bring together the various segments of a police force to form a youth bureau.[7] The concept spread to other urban areas, and soon youth bureaus, often called *youth aid bureaus, juvenile*

juvenile officer
In some police departments, a police officer who has received specialized training to work effectively with juveniles and who is tasked primarily with such work.

bureaus, juvenile control bureaus, juvenile divisions, or *crime prevention bureaus,* were founded throughout major cities in the United States. The police in these bureaus were the forerunners of the modern **juvenile officers**.

Two developments formalized the increasingly important role of juvenile officers in the United States. In 1955, the Central States Juvenile Officer's Association was formed, followed soon after by the International Juvenile Officer's Association in 1957. Meetings were held by these and similar groups at regional, national, and international levels. For the first time, the responsibilities, standards, and procedures necessary in juvenile work were being developed. In addition, the increase in social science research on youths highlighted the necessity of training juvenile officers better, because these officers were expected to help, rather than punish, youthful offenders.

Preventive police work with juveniles continued through the 1960s. Programs were developed to reduce delinquency and to improve the way youths viewed the police. Police officers volunteered to speak to elementary, junior high, and high school students, and some departments developed special programs for these purposes. The Police Athletic League expanded its athletic programs and set up courses in leadership and moral training for youths. Furthermore, some police agencies helped youths find jobs and worked with schools to reduce truancy. Programs to fight drugs and alcohol and to show the consequences of drinking and driving were also developed.

In the 1970s, 1980s, and 1990s, severe budgetary restrictions forced many police departments to reduce their emphasis on juvenile programs. Some dropped their juvenile divisions altogether, whereas others limited their activity to dependent, neglected, and abused children in response to the increasingly recognized problems of domestic violence. By the late 1990s and the first decade of the twenty-first century, some police departments were experimenting with community-based or **problem-oriented policing** as well as restorative justice practices.

problem-oriented policing
A contemporary policing strategy through which police agencies place more emphasis on addressing the fundamental circumstances that create juvenile crime rather than focusing exclusively on incidents of delinquency.

Beginning in the late 1980s and continuing to the present, youth gangs have developed in nearly every urban and suburban area of the nation, as well as in some rural areas. The problems that these gangs have created have resulted in the police being given the responsibility of identifying and controlling these gangs. Gang divisions were developed in many departments, and other law enforcement emphases were placed on controlling gangs.

Juveniles' Attitudes toward the Police

The subject of juveniles' attitudes toward the police has received considerable attention in recent decades:

- Several studies have reported that juveniles who have had contact with the police have more negative attitudes toward them than those who have not had contact.[8] This seems to be especially true of African American youth whose cultural-accepted view of police is independent of their arrest experience.[9]

- Scott H. Decker's 1981 review of literature on attitudes toward the police concluded that youths had more negative attitudes toward the police than did older citizens and that race, the quality of police services, and previous experiences with the police also affected citizens' attitudes.[10]

- Komanduri S. Murty, Julian B. Roebuck, and Joann D. Smith found in a 1990 Atlanta study that "older, married, white-collar, highly educated, and employed respondents reported a more positive image of the police than did their counterparts—younger, single, blue-collar, poorly educated, unemployed/underemployed respondents."[11]

- Michael J. Leiber, Mahesh K. Nalla, and Margaret Farnworth challenged the traditional argument that juveniles' interactions with the police are the primary determinant of their attitudes toward law enforcement officers. Instead, they saw juveniles' attitudes toward authority and social control developing in a larger sociocultural context, and global attitudes toward police affect youths' assessment of specific police contacts.[12]

- Data from the *Monitoring the Future* survey of high school seniors from the late 1980s through the mid-1990s indicated that high school seniors' attitudes toward the police became more negative during that period across all subsets of the sample. However, the *Monitoring the Future* data for 2007 revealed that when high school seniors were asked their opinions of the police and other law enforcement agencies, 35.8 percent (up from 26.6 percent in 1996) responded either "good" or "very good." If the 30.2 percent of "fair" responses were added to the "good" and "very good" categories, roughly 61 percent of high school seniors could be considered to have a positive attitude toward law enforcement.[13]

- Susan Guarino-Ghezzi and Bryan Carr contend, on the basis of a study conducted in Boston, "that the way police interact with juveniles alienates youths who are already alienated from the wider society, and that the results are incorporated into the youths' subculture. This sets the stage for what Guarino-Ghezzi and Carr call a **cycle of alienation**.[14]

- Research continues today into subcultural theory and the relations of juveniles with the police. Terry Nihart and colleagues predictably find that juveniles' attitudes toward the police are positively correlated with the youths' attitudes toward parents and teachers.[15] In a different type of study, Yolander G. Hurst found that rural youths are more positive toward the police than are urban youths with whites not significantly more positive than African Americans.[16]

In general, most youths appear to have positive attitudes toward the police. Younger juveniles are more positive than older ones, white juveniles are more positive than African Americans, and female juveniles are more positive than males. A positive attitude also seems to be influenced by social class, because middle-class youths tend to be more positive than lower-class youths. Generally, juveniles who have not had contact with the police are more positive than those who have had police contact. The most hostile attitudes are typically those of youths with extensive histories of law-violating activities, who have had contact with the police, or who are involved in youth gangs. See Table 13–1.

▲ A police officer questions a handcuffed juvenile.

■ **What is the "cycle of alienation"? How can it be avoided?**

cycle of alienation
The process of police–juvenile interaction that further alienates youth who are already only loosely bound to the wider society.

Processing of Juvenile Offenders

When responding to juvenile lawbreakers, police are influenced by a variety of individual, sociocultural, and organizational factors. They can choose a more or less restrictive response to an individual offender.

Factors Influencing Police Discretion

Police discretion can be defined as the choice a police officer makes between two or more possible means of handling a situation. Discretion needs to be both professional and personal. Discretion is important, because the police actually act as a court of first instance in initially categorizing a juvenile. The police officer thus becomes a legal and social traffic director who can use his or her wide discretion to detour juveniles from the justice system or involve them in it.

Police discretion has come under attack because many believe the police abuse their broad discretion, but most police contacts with juveniles are impersonal and nonofficial and consist simply of orders to "Get off the corner," "Break it up," or "Go home." Studies

police discretion
A police officer's ability to choose from among a number of alternative dispositions when handling a situation.

Web Extra 13–1
State Bar of Texas: Juvenile Law Section

TABLE 13–1
Attitudes toward the Police

Favorable Attitudes toward Police	Less Favorable Attitudes toward Police
Younger children	Older children
Caucasians	African Americans
Girls	Boys
Middle- and upper-class youngsters	Lower-class youngsters

generally estimate that only 10 to 20 percent of police–juvenile encounters become official contacts.[17] In 2004, Stephanie M. Myers, reporting on data collected for the Project on Policing Neighborhoods (POPN), a study of police in Indianapolis, Indiana, and St. Petersburg, Florida, found that 84 (13 percent) of the 654 juvenile suspects were arrested.[18]

The point can also be made that the juvenile justice system could not function without police discretion. Urban courts, especially, are overloaded; probation officers' caseloads are entirely too high; and many juvenile correctional institutions are jammed to capacity. If police were to increase by two to three times the number of youths they referred to the system, the resulting backlog of cases would be unmanageable.

The police officer's disposition of the juvenile offender is mainly determined by eleven factors: (1) offense, (2) citizen complaints, (3) gender, (4) race, (5) socioeconomic status, (6) individual characteristics of the juvenile, (7) police–juvenile interactions, (8) demeanor, (9) police officer's personality, (10) departmental policy, and (11) external pressures (see Table 13–2).

Offense

The most important factor determining the disposition of the misbehaving juvenile is the seriousness of the offense.[19]

Citizen Complaints

A number of studies have found that the presence of a citizen or the complaint of a citizen is an important determining factor in the disposition of an incident involving a juvenile.[20] If a citizen initiates a complaint, remains present, and wishes the arrest of a juvenile, chances are that the juvenile will be arrested and processed.[21] If the potential arrest situation results from police patrol, the chances are much greater that the youth will be warned and released.

Gender

Traditionally, girls have been less likely than boys to be arrested and referred to the juvenile court for criminal offenses, but there is some evidence of the erosion of police "chivalry" in the face of youthful female criminality.[22] Yet, as Chapter 7 noted, girls are far more likely to be referred to the court if they violate traditional role expectations for girls through behaviors such as running away from home, failing to obey parents, or being sexually promiscuous.[23]

TABLE 13–2
Factors Influencing Disposition

Individual Factors
Personality characteristics of the juvenile
Personality characteristics of the police officer
Interaction between the police officer and the juvenile
Sociocultural Factors
Citizen complaints
Gender of the juvenile
Race/ethnicity of the juvenile
Socioeconomic status of the juvenile
Influence of cultural norms in the community and values of the wider society on both juveniles and police officers
External pressures in the community to arrest certain types of juvenile offenders
Organizational Factors
Nature of the offense
Departmental policy

Race

Studies differ on the importance of race in determining juvenile disposition. On the one hand, several studies (after results were corrected to account for offense seriousness and prior record) have found that the police are more inclined to arrest minority juveniles[24]; the strongest evidence showing race as a determining factor is found in the Philadelphia cohort study.[25] However, several other studies failed to find much evidence of racial bias. It is difficult to appraise the importance of race in the disposition of cases involving juveniles, because African Americans and members of other minority groups appear to be involved in serious crimes more often than whites. Nonetheless, it does seem that racial bias makes minority juveniles special targets of the police.[26]

Socioeconomic Status

Substantiating the effect of class on the disposition of cases involving juveniles is difficult because most studies examine race and socioeconomic status together, but lower-class youngsters, according to many critics of the juvenile justice system, receive different "justice" than middle- or upper-class youths.

Individual Characteristics of the Juvenile

Such individual factors as prior arrest record, previous offenses, age, peer relationships, family situation, and conduct of parents also have a bearing on how the police officer handles each juvenile.[27] A juvenile who is older and has committed several previous offenses is likely to be referred to the juvenile court.[28] The family of the juvenile is also an important variable.

▲ A white police officer questions a handcuffed African American juvenile.

■ **What constitutes racial profiling? Is racial profiling ever justified?**

Police–Juvenile Interactions and Demeanor

A number of studies have found that a juvenile's behavior toward a police officer is a significant factor in determining disposition.[29] As would be expected, they show that juveniles who act with disrespect are most likely to be arrested.[30]

Police Officer's Personality

Police officer personalities have also been studied to see how they shape the nature of police–juvenile interactions. An officer who has little tolerance for adolescents may more frequently become involved in a confrontation that leads to arrest and official processing by the justice system.

Departmental Policy

Police departments vary in their policies on handling misbehaving juveniles.[31] James Q. Wilson found that the more professional police departments had higher numbers of juveniles referred to the juvenile court, because they used discretion less often than departments that were not as professional.[32]

External Pressures

The attitudes of the press and the public, the status of the complainant or victim, and the philosophy and available resources of referral agencies usually influence the disposition of juvenile lawbreakers.

In sum, sufficient studies have been done to provide an outline of an empirical portrait of the policing of juveniles. Of the eleven factors influencing police officers' dispositions of juveniles, the seriousness of the offense and complaints by citizens appear to be more important than the other factors. However, individual factors, departmental policy, and external pressures also are highly influential in determining how police–juvenile encounters are handled.

Informal and Formal Dispositions

Studies on police discretion reveal many inconsistencies. There is common agreement that the fair handling of juveniles should not be influenced by factors such as the friendliness of juveniles, their race, sex, social class, or community reputations. Nevertheless, personal biases do sometimes influence individual police officers.

Unquestionably, police typically come into contact daily with many different types of juveniles in various situations. Some youths have mental illnesses; some come from families torn apart by alcohol, drugs, and other addictive disorders; some youths are neglected; and some are abused physically, emotionally, or sexually. Some youths have no family members to turn to in times of need, and some find school a frightening, frustrating, and valueless experience. Conversely, many find gang experiences rewarding and emotionally satisfying, and use them as a way to gain the respect of peers. Police officers must deal effectively with all of these types of youths.

Informal and Formal Dispositions

A patrol officer or juvenile officer has at least five options when investigating a complaint against a juvenile or arriving at the scene of law-violating behavior:

1. *Warning and release.* The least severe sanction is applied when the patrol officer decides merely to question and release the youth. Commonly, this occurs when a juvenile is caught committing a minor offense.

2. *Station adjustment.* The juvenile can be taken to the station, where the juvenile will have his or her contact recorded, will be given an official reprimand, and then will be released to the parents. In a **station adjustment**, the first thing the department does when the juvenile is brought to the station is to contact the parents. [33]

3. *Referral to a diversion agency.* The juvenile can be released and referred to a diversion agency. In some jurisdictions, the police operate their own diversion program; more typically, juveniles are referred to agencies such as Big Brothers Big Sisters, a runaway center, or a mental health agency.

4. *Citation and referral to juvenile court.* The police officer can issue a **citation** and refer the youth to the juvenile court. Law enforcement agencies refer more than fourth-fifths of the delinquency cases handled by juvenile courts. Table 13–3 gives the percent of delinquency cases referred to juvenile court by police agencies in 2006.

5. *Detention.* The police officer can issue a citation, refer the youth to the juvenile court, and take him or her to a detention center. An intake worker at the detention center then decides whether the juvenile should be returned to the parents or left at the detention center. A juvenile is left in detention when he or she is thought to be dangerous to self or others in the community or has no care in the home. Taking youths out of their own homes and placing them in detention facilities clearly must be a last resort.

station adjustment
One of several disposition options available to a police officer whereby a juvenile is taken to the police station following a complaint, the contact is recorded, and the juvenile is given an official reprimand and then released to his or her parents or guardians.

citation
A summons to appear in juvenile court.

TABLE 13–3
Percentages of Delinquency Cases Referred by Law Enforcement, 2006

Most Serious Offense	Percent
Delinquency	82%
Person	87
Property	91
Drugs	90
Public order	61

Source: Howard N. Snyder and Melissa Sickmund, *Juvenile Offenders and Victims: 2006 National Report* (Washington, D.C.: National Center for Juvenile Justice, Office of Juvenile Justice and Delinquency Prevention, 2006), p. 157.

Informal Options: On the Streets

Police view youths within the context of their community. This means that officers see how youths interact in their neighborhoods with friends and family and witness the many different ways that youths socialize. The good beat officer knows who belongs to various peer groups and gangs, who is stable and who is unstable, who is belligerent and who is not; and these officers often know the circumstances of youths' lives. Such factors affect how the police process a particular event or incident. For example, some of the following police actions are informal responses to youthful misbehavior and no permanent record of the incident will be kept, nor will juveniles be held for further actions by the juvenile court:

- Kids clowning around on the sidewalk are simply ignored by a passing officer.
- Police officers suggest that youths take their sidewalk soccer game into a nearby play-ground or vacant lot if they are bothering people, if someone could get hurt, or if a citizen has complained.
- An officer might talk to a youth bullying others and suggest that the bully change his or her ways.
- Some officers strike up friendships with local youths, sit and talk with them, and sometimes go to their school or sporting events.
- Officers who see youths fighting or stealing something might talk to them about the harm they are causing and how they might get into trouble as a result.
- An officer might write down the juvenile's name and address on a notepad for future reference.

Informal Options: At the Station (Station House Adjustment)

- Youths are taken to the police station, where their situation is discussed with them and their parents; the youths are then sent home with their parents.
- In larger departments, youths are sent to a police youth bureau, which consists of specially trained officers or other personnel who counsel the youths and their parents but who permit the youths to remain in the community.
- Police officers or youth bureau personnel unofficially refer or direct youths and/or their parents or guardians to anger management classes, vocational training programs, shelters, or counseling programs for alcohol, drug, mental illness, or other problems.
- Police or youth service personnel contact and work with school personnel in getting truant youths back in schools or into special programs. (School personnel may initiate these contacts, and special programs may be set up in cooperation with police departments.)
- Police contact the probation department informally to access probation department programs for a youth in question. (The probation department also handles many cases informally.)
- Police unofficially contact children and youth services to get proper care for dependent and neglected or other children in need of supervision.

Combined Informal and Formal Processing

- A youth is taken into custody or arrested; he or she is then booked, talked to, and released without further action.
- A youth is taken into custody or arrested and booked and then released with the firm warning that any further problems will be dealt with by arrest and prosecution.
- Once a youth is in custody, officers officially notify community agencies such as children and youth services that a youth needs their services and either send the youth to the agency or have the agency pick up the youth.

Formal Processing: At the Station

- The parents of arrested youths are called to the police station and, after booking, have their child released to their care and supervision. The case may end at that point or may be referred to juvenile court for further consideration.

- The youth is taken into custody, booked, fingerprinted, and then referred to juvenile intake, which has both informal and formal options. After evaluation by either the police or the court intake personnel, youths may be placed in secure detention awaiting their preliminary hearing and trial. This secure detention may, in some cities, be in the local jail or a youth detention center.

- Police in states with legislative waiver will, after arresting and booking a youth, automatically waive the youth directly to adult court, which further evaluates the youth.

The further youths are processed into the system, the less discretionary authority the police have. On the street, the amount of discretion of police officers is considerable; in states with legislative waiver, police discretion is limited, especially with violent crimes. In addition, police discretion is governed to a considerable extent by departmental policy.

The Legal Rights of Juveniles

Juveniles were at the mercy of the police for much of the twentieth century. Few or no laws protected juveniles in trouble because of the rehabilitative ideal in juvenile justice. Police officers, whose primary mission was to maintain law and order, used whatever tactics seemed appropriate to restore the peace. Friendliness, persuasion, threats, coercion, and force were all used to gain the compliance of juveniles. If these tactics failed, juveniles were taken into juvenile court or, depending on the laws of the state and the seriousness of the crimes, to adult court for prosecution. Few protections were granted to juveniles in the areas of search and seizure, interrogation, fingerprinting, lineups, or other procedures (see Figure 13–3).

In the 1960s, the U.S. Supreme Court's decisions began to change this relationship between the police and juveniles. Although not all police departments have endorsed or adhered to the guidelines laid down by the courts, most departments have made a conscientious effort to abide by the standards of justice and fairness implied by these decisions.[34]

Search and Seizure

search and seizure
The police procedure used in the investigation of crimes for the purpose of gathering evidence.

The Fourth Amendment to the Constitution of the United States protects citizens from unauthorized **search and seizure**. This amendment states:

> The right of the people to be secure in their persons, houses, papers, and effects, against unreasonable searches and seizures, shall not be violated, and no Warrants shall issue, but upon probable cause, supported by Oath or affirmation, and particularly describing the place to be searched, and the persons or things to be seized.

TIMELINE

1936	1948	1966	1967	1979	1989
Brown v. Mississippi: This case established that confessions cannot be physically coerced by the police.	**Haley v. Ohio:** Held that methods used in obtaining juvenile's confession violated the Due Process Clause of the Fourteenth Amendment.	**Miranda v. Arizona:** This case prohibited the use of a confession in court unless the individual was advised of his or her rights before interrogation.	***In re* Gault:** This case made the right against self-incrimination and the right to counsel applicable to juveniles.	**Fare v. Michael C.:** This case applied the "totality of the circumstances" approach to the interrogation of juveniles.	**Commonwealth v. Guyton:** An underage caregiver can not act as an interested adult (acting *in loco parentis*).

FIGURE 13–3
Important U.S. Supreme Court Cases on the Police Interrogation of Juveniles

The issue here is the right to privacy. All citizens are guaranteed the right by the Constitution to feel secure in their person and home. Law enforcement officers may not abridge that right without following very strict due process guidelines. In 1961, the Supreme Court decision in *Mapp* v. *Ohio* affirmed Fourth Amendment rights for adults. This decision stated that evidence gathered in an unreasonable search and seizure— that is, evidence seized without probable cause and without a proper search warrant— is inadmissible in court.[35] This inadmissibility of illegally obtained evidence is referred to as the *exclusionary rule*. In the 1967 *State* v. *Lowery* case, the Supreme Court applied the Fourth Amendment ban against unreasonable searches and seizures to juveniles:

> Is it not more outrageous for the police to treat children more harshly than adult offenders, especially when such is violative of due process and fair treatment? Can a court countenance a system, where, as here, an adult may suppress evidence with the usual effect of having the charges dropped for lack of proof, and, on the other hand, a juvenile can be institutionalized—lose the most sacred possession a human being has, his freedom—for "rehabilitative" purposes because the Fourth Amendment right is unavailable to him?[36]

Juveniles, therefore, are protected from unreasonable searches and seizures. Juveniles must be presented with a valid search warrant unless they have either waived that right, have consented to having their person or property searched, or have been caught in the act. If these conditions have not been met, courts have overturned rulings against the juveniles. For example, evidence was dismissed in one case when police entered a juvenile's apartment at 5:00 a.m. without a warrant to arrest him.[37] In another case, Houston police discovered marijuana on a youth five hours after he had been stopped for driving a car without lights and a driver's license. Confined to a Texas training school for this drug offense, the youth was ordered released by an appellate court because the search took place too late to be related to the arrest.[38] The least right to privacy is on the street, followed generally by the automobile and school; the greatest right to privacy is in the home.[39]

When a crime is committed in the community, the job of the police officer is to solve the crime and make an arrest. The officer must, however, follow legal rules that guarantee that the alleged offender is treated fairly. How do police proceed?

An example is that of the police approaching a youth with a specific and articulable suspicion that the juvenile is armed and possibly dangerous. The law enforcement experience of the police officer, a high-drug-dealing area of town, an obvious bulge in clothing, or the presence of another officer who may have arrested the youth previously and found a weapon on the youth may all lead to reasonable suspicion justifying a pat down search of the person. In this case, the officer may do a *Terry* search; that is, pat down the youth's outer clothing in a search for weapons only.[40] Police may not do pat downs as part of their routine stops or in order to find contraband. The pat down is for weapons only. However, in doing the pat down, if the police find an illegal weapon, they may take the weapon and arrest the youth for possessing it; then, they legally may search the youth for other contraband.[41]

A second scenario illustrates another type of concern. A police officer temporarily detains a youth on the street or takes the youth to the station. When is the juvenile actually under arrest? Some jurisdictions consider an **arrest** as occurring whenever the person stopped does not feel free to leave the presence of the police officer. Indeed, youths in any of the above examples could be taken or asked to come to the police station, be interviewed, and then be allowed to leave; this would be perfectly legal and within the juveniles' rights in some states and jurisdictions. The clearest indicator, of course, is when an offender officially is charged with a crime and given notice to appear at further hearings. A juvenile may, in fact, ask the officer if it is permissible to leave. The options for the police officer here are to release the juvenile immediately, detain the juvenile longer and let him or her go after further questioning and satisfying their concerns, or arrest the youth. For further examples of police decision making, see Exhibit 13–1.

arrest
The process of taking a person into custody for an alleged violation of the law. Juveniles who are under arrest have nearly all the due process safeguards accorded to adults.

Exhibit 13–1
Decisions Police Officers Make

In what follows, a police detective describes how she decides on a course of action in an incident involving a juvenile.

Let's take an incident: A juvenile male is involved in some form of criminal mischief. He causes a little damage to a house (for example, egging, spray painting) and his basic intention was not to do any major danger, but primarily as a prank.

How I would handle this depends on several factors: How much damage was done, what kind of damage, the juvenile's intent, and how the victim feels. If the damage is minor, and the victim does not want to press charges, but still wants some type of restitution, the juvenile may be asked to come back and clean up the damage and/or pay for the damage himself. Along with that is the juvenile's intent and attitude. Was it just a prank and the juvenile is apologetic for it, or does he have the attitude that

he won't go back and clean it up and does not feel remorseful for the damage? Finally, how much support does the juvenile have at home? Are the parents supportive of the police and victim, and will they hold the juvenile accountable for his actions? Or is there no support at home? If the attitude of the juvenile is poor and if the juvenile is not going to be held accountable for the damage by his parents, then I would most likely have to handle it in a more formal way with charges.

CRITICAL THINKING QUESTIONS

■ *Do you feel this kind of decision-making is reasonable? What do some of the stories in* **Voices of Delinquency** *suggest is a real advantage of not being arrested and processed through the justice system?*

Interrogation Practices

The Fourteenth Amendment of the Constitution affirms that police must adhere to standards of fairness and due process in obtaining confessions. Current standards also require that the courts must take into consideration the totality of circumstances under which a confession was made in determining the appropriateness of the confession.

The Supreme Court decision *Haley* v. *Ohio* is an early example of excesses in **police interrogation**. In the *Haley* case, a fifteen-year-old youth was arrested at his home five days after a store robbery in which the owner was shot. Five or six police officers questioned the boy for about five hours; he then confessed after being shown what were alleged to be the confessions of two other youths. No parent or attorney was present during the questioning. The Supreme Court invalidated the confession, stating:

> The age of the petitioner, the hours when he was grilled, the duration of his quizzing, the fact that he had no friend or counsel to advise him, the callous attitude of the police toward his rights combine to convince us that this confession was wrung from a child by means which the law should not sanction. Neither man nor child can be allowed to stand condemned by methods which flout constitutional requirements of due process of law.[42]

police interrogation
The process of interviewing a person who has been arrested with the express purpose of obtaining a confession.

Miranda v. Arizona
The landmark 1966 U.S. Supreme Court ruling that suspects taken into police custody must, before any questioning can take place, be informed that they have the right to remain silent, that anything they say may be used against them, and that they have the right to legal counsel.

The Supreme Court also ruled in *Brown* v. *Mississippi* that police may not use force to obtain confessions[43]; in this case, police had used physical force to extract a confession. Other confessions have been ruled invalid because the accused was too tired; was questioned too long; and/or was not permitted to talk with spouse, friends, or lawyer either while he or she was being interrogated or until he or she confessed.[44]

Juveniles taken into custody are entitled to the rights stated in the 1966 decision of **Miranda v. Arizona**. This Supreme Court decision prohibits the use of a confession in court unless the individual was advised of his or her rights before interrogation, especially the right to remain silent, the right to have an attorney present during questioning, and the right to be assigned an attorney by the state if the individual could not afford one.[45] *In re Gault* (see Chapter 14) made the right against self-incrimination and the right to counsel applicable to juveniles.[46] However, the *Gault* decision failed to clarify whether or not a juvenile could waive the protection of the *Miranda* rules and also failed to specify what is necessary for a juvenile to waive his or her *Miranda* rights intelligently and knowingly. For example, is a juvenile's ability to waive *Miranda* rights impaired if the youth is under the influence of drugs or alcohol or in a state of shock?

▲ A police officer places a juvenile under arrest.

■ **What rights do juvenile offenders have when facing processing by the juvenile justice system?**

The 1979 *Fare* v. *Michael C.* decision applied the "totality of the circumstances" approach to the interrogation of juveniles. The circumstances behind this case were that Michael C. was implicated in a murder that took place during a robbery, so the police arrested the sixteen-year-old youth and brought him to the station. After he was advised of his *Miranda* rights, he requested to see his probation officer; when this request was denied, he proceeded to talk to the police officer, implicating himself in the murder. The Supreme Court ruled in this case that Michael C. appeared to understand his rights and that when his request to talk with his probation officer was denied, he expressed his willingness to waive his rights and continue the interrogation.[47]

Thomas Grisso, who studied juveniles interrogated by the St. Louis police in 1981, found that virtually all of them had waived their *Miranda* rights, so he questioned whether juveniles were even "capable of providing a meaningful waiver of the rights to avoid self-incrimination and to obtain legal counsel." After surveying a sample of juveniles, Grisso found that almost everyone younger than fourteen years of age and half the juveniles in the fifteen- to sixteen-year-old age bracket had less than adequate understanding of what their *Miranda* rights entailed.[48]

Several court cases have held that the minority status of a juvenile is not an absolute bar to a valid confession. A California case upheld the confession of two juveniles from Spanish-speaking families; although both had been arrested before, one had an IQ of 65–71, with a mental age of ten years and two months.[49] Similarly, a North Carolina court of appeals approved the confession of a twelve-year-old youth who was charged with shooting out a window in a camper truck.[50] A Maryland appellate court approved the confession of a sixteen-year-old youth, a school dropout with an eighth-grade education, who was charged with firebombing and burning both a store and a school during a racial confrontation.[51]

To protect juveniles against police interrogation excesses, many jurisdictions have a statutory requirement that a parent, someone acting *in loco parentis* for the child, or counsel for the child must be present at police interrogation in order for a confession to be admissible. In *Commonwealth* v. *Guyton* (1989), the Massachusetts court held that no other minor, not even a relative, can act as an interested adult.[52] Other courts have ruled that the interested adult may be a child's relative.[53] Some states attempt to protect the juvenile by requiring that the youth be taken to the juvenile detention center or to juvenile court if he or she is not returned immediately to the parents' custody, obviously preferring that police interrogation take place within juvenile facilities rather than at a police station.[54]

Fingerprinting

Fingerprinting, along with other pretrial identification practices, has traditionally been highly controversial in juvenile corrections. Some juvenile court statutes require that a judge approve the taking of fingerprints of juveniles, control access to fingerprint records, and provide for fingerprint destruction under certain circumstances.[55] In many other jurisdictions, the police department determines policy, with some police departments routinely fingerprinting all juveniles taken into custody and suspected of serious wrongdoing. The Juvenile Justice and Delinquency Prevention Act of 1974 recommended that fingerprints be taken only with the consent of the judge, that juvenile fingerprints not be recorded in the criminal section of the fingerprint registry, and that the records be destroyed after their purpose has been served.

A 1969 Supreme Court decision that reversed a Mississippi ruling is the most important case dealing with juvenile fingerprints. In this case, the U.S. Supreme Court ruled, among other things, that fingerprints taken by the police could not be used as evidence. The youth in question was detained by the police without authorization by a judicial officer, was interrogated at the time he was first fingerprinted, and was fingerprinted again at a later date; the Court ruled that the police should not have detained the youth without authorization by a judicial officer, that the youth was unnecessarily fingerprinted a second time, and that the youth should not have been interrogated at the first detention when he was fingerprinted.[56]

fingerprinting
A pretrial identification procedure used with both juveniles and adults following arrest.

Pretrial Identification Practices

pretrial identification practices
The procedures such as fingerprinting, photographing, and placing juveniles in lineups for the purpose of identification prior to formal court appearance.

Among other **pretrial identification practices**, both photographing and placing juveniles in lineups are highly controversial. Another recent practice is to notify the school district regarding juveniles who have been convicted of serious or violent crimes.

A lineup consists of the police placing a number of suspects in front of witnesses or victims, who try to identify the person who committed the crime against them. If no one can be identified, the suspects are released to the community, but if one of the persons is identified as the perpetrator, the police then proceed with their prosecution. The courts have been careful to set standards for the police to follow because innocent youths could end up labeled as delinquents and confined in an institution; one important standard is that the offender must have an attorney at the initial identification lineup in order to ensure that the identification of the offender is not tainted.

In one important case, *United States* v. *Wade* (1967), the Supreme Court ruled that the accused has a right to have counsel present at postindictment lineup procedures.[57] In *Kirby* v. *Illinois* (1972), the Court went on to add that the defendant's right of counsel during postindictment lineup procedures goes into effect as soon as the complaint or the indictment has been issued.[58] In the *In re Holley* decision (1970), a juvenile accused of rape had his conviction reversed by the appellate court because of the lack of counsel during the lineup identification procedure.[59]

At the end of 1997, forty-five states and the District of Columbia had statutes permitting photographing of juveniles under certain circumstances for criminal history record purposes, and juvenile codes in forty-two states allowed names—and sometimes even pictures and court records—of juveniles who were involved in delinquency proceedings to be released to the media.[60] Since 1997, still more states have permitted similar pretrial identification practices.

Photographs also can play an important part in the identification of offenders. For example, in one case, a rape victim was shown a photograph of one suspect only, and she could not identify the offender from that photograph but then later identified her attacker in a probation office. A California appellate court noted that permitting the identification of offenders on the basis of only one photograph was inappropriate because it could prejudice the victim.[61]

Another problem with photographs is their permanency and potential stigmatizing effects on youths in the community. Because photographs are filed and frequently reviewed by police officers, the police examine these photographs whenever something happens in the community, so innocent youths may never be able to escape the stigma of such labeling. For these reasons, some states require that judges give the police written consent to take photographs, that the photographs not be published in the media, and that the photographs be destroyed when the youths become adults. See Table 13–4.

TABLE 13–4
Legal Rights of Juveniles

Category	Brief Description of Juvenile Rights within Each Category
Search and seizure	Juveniles, like adults, are protected from unauthorized search and seizure.
Interrogation practices	Police must adhere to standards of fairness and due process in obtaining confessions.
Fingerprinting	Police handle the fingerprinting of juveniles in a wide variety of ways; however, there is more consistency in how they destroy the records after their purpose has been served.
Pretrial identification practices	The photographing and placing of juveniles in lineups are controversial but are more frequently taking place today than in the past.

Social Context of Delinquency: The Police and the Prevention of Juvenile Offenses

Three ways in which police departments are attempting to implement community-based policing in the prevention and deterrence of youth crime are through community-based, school-based, and gang-based interventions (see Figure 13–4).

Community-Based Interventions

Community relations are a major focus of police officers who work with juveniles. They must cultivate good relations with school administrators and teachers, with the staff of community agencies, with the staff of local youth organizations and youth shelters, with the juvenile court, and with merchants and employees at popular juvenile hangouts. Of course, juvenile police officers also must develop good relations with parents of youthful offenders as well as with the offenders themselves. The officer who has earned the respect of the youths of the community will be aware of what is happening in the community and will be called on for assistance by youths in trouble.

One of the important challenges the police face today is finding missing children. The AMBER Alert system began in 1996 when Dallas–Fort Worth broadcasters teamed with local police departments to develop an early-warning system to assist in finding abducted children, which they called the Dallas AMBER Plan. AMBER, which stands for America's Missing: Broadcast Emergency Response, was named in memory of nine-year-old Amber Hagerman, who was kidnapped while riding her bicycle and brutally murdered in Arlington, Texas, in 1996. Other states and communities soon set up their own alert plans, and the AMBER Alert network was adopted nationwide.[62] Exhibit 13–2 describes AMBER Alerts.

The police are called on to intercede in a variety of juvenile problems. These include enforcing the curfew ordinances that more and more communities across the nation are passing,[63] enforcing drug laws,[64] preventing hate crimes committed by teenagers against minority groups (Jews, other ethnic groups, and homosexuals),[65] focusing attention on serious habitual offenders, enhancing the quality and relevance of information that is exchanged through active interagency collaboration, and controlling gun-related violence in the youth population.

Voices of Delinquency 13–1
Read "What Would I Say to Urban Gang Kids?" In this story, a former gang member, who is now a university graduate and a police officer working with youths (including gang youths), relates a speech that he makes to these youths. Is this likely to be an effective presentation?

Library Extra 13–1
Police Encounters with Juvenile Suspects

▲ A police officer talks to a preschool class about home safety in Port Angeles, Washington. Establishing good community relations is crucial for police officers who work with juveniles.

■ **What are these children likely to remember from this experience?**

Community-Based
Community relations are a major focus of police officers who work with juveniles.

School-Based
Developing effective delinquency prevention programs in schools is one of the most important challenges facing the police today.

Gang-Based
The number of street gangs rose dramatically across the nation beginning in the late 1980s.

FIGURE 13–4
Policing to Deter Delinquency

Exhibit 13–2
AMBER Alert

The following material, which describes the AMBER Alert system in a question-answer format, comes from the federal Office of Justice Programs.

HOW DOES PROJECT AMBER WORK?

Once law enforcement has determined that a child has been abducted and the abduction meets the AMBER Alert criteria, law enforcement notifies broadcasters and state transportation officials. AMBER Alerts interrupt regular programming and are broadcast on radio and television and appear on highway signs. AMBER Alerts can also be issued on lottery tickets, to wireless devices such as mobile phones, and over the Internet. Through the coordination of local, state, and regional plans, the Department of Justice (DOJ) is working toward the creation of a seamless national network.

HOW EFFECTIVE HAS IT BEEN?

AMBER Alert has been very effective. The programs have helped save the lives of two hundred children nationwide.

Over 84 percent of those recoveries have occurred since October 2002, when President George W. Bush called for the appointment of an AMBER Alert Coordinator at the first-ever White House Conference on Missing, Exploited, and Runaway Children.

AMBER Alerts serve as deterrents to those who would prey on children. Program data have shown that some perpetrators release the abducted child after hearing the AMBER Alert on the radio or seeing it on television.

NOW THAT ALL 50 STATES HAVE AMBER ALERT PLANS, HOW DOES THIS HELP CHILDREN AND FAMILIES?

The establishment of AMBER Alert plans in all fifty states marks an important milestone in the efforts to prevent child abductions. No matter where a child is abducted, communities and law enforcement work together to recover missing children quickly and safely. The numbers of recovered children speak for themselves. In 2001, only two children were recovered via AMBER Alert; in 2004, that number rose to seventy-one. Interstate expansion has had a marked impact in saving children's lives.

WHAT ARE THE CRITERIA FOR ISSUING AMBER ALERTS?

Each state AMBER Alert plan has its own criteria for issuing alert notices. The PROTECT Act, passed in 2003, which established the role of AMBER Alert Coordinator within the DOJ, calls for the

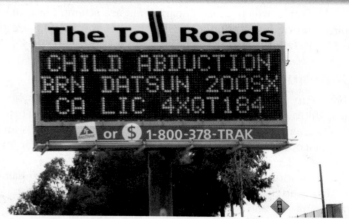

▲ An AMBER Alert sign informs motorists of a child abduction incident in Orange County, California.

■ How does the AMBER Alert system work?

DOJ to issue minimum standards or guidelines for AMBER Alerts that states can adopt voluntarily. The DOJ's Guidance on Criteria for Issuing AMBER Alerts follows:

* Law enforcement must confirm that an abduction has taken place.
* The child is at risk of serious injury or death.
* There is sufficient descriptive information of the child and the captor or captor's vehicle to issue an alert.
* The child must be seventeen years old or younger.
* It is recommended that AMBER Alert data be immediately entered into the FBI National Crime Information Center. Text information describing the circumstances surrounding the abduction of the child should be entered, with the case flagged as "child abduction."

Most states' guidelines adhere closely to DOJ's recommended guidelines.

CRITICAL THINKING QUESTIONS

■ *What is the significance of the AMBER Alert program for local communities and for the nation? How do local media and national law enforcement networks serve as a deterrent to those who might consider abducting children?*

Source: Adapted from http://www.amberalert.gov/faqs.html.

In many larger cities, police departments form juvenile units to handle youth crime. A 2000 survey of law enforcement agencies (those with one hundred or more sworn officers) reported that a large proportion of these agencies had special units targeting juvenile justice concerns (see Table 13–5).[66]

School-Based Interventions

Library Extra 13–2
OJJDP Juvenile Justice Bulletin: "Effective Intervention for Serious Juvenile Offenders"

Developing effective delinquency prevention programs in schools is one of the most important challenges facing the police at the present time. Community predelinquent programs have included courses in high school, junior high school, and elementary school settings addressing school safety, community relations, drug and alcohol abuse, city government, court

TABLE 13–5
Special Units Targeting Juvenile Justice Concerns

	Type of Agency	
Type of Special Unit	Local Police	State
Drug education in schools	70%	30%
Juvenile crime	62	10
Gangs	45	18
Child abuse	46	8
Domestic violence	45	10
Missing children	48	31
Youth outreach	33	6

Source: Howard N. Snyder and Melissa Sickmund, *Juvenile Offenders and Victims: 2006 National Report* (Washington, D.C.: National Center for Juvenile Justice, Office of Juvenile Justice and Delinquency Prevention, 2006), p. 153.

procedures, bicycle safety, and juvenile delinquency. The Officer Friendly Program and the McGruff "Take a Bite Out of Crime" program were established throughout the nation to develop better relations with younger children.

More recently, popular prevention programs have included Gang Resistance Education and Training (G.R.E.A.T.) and Law-Related Education (LRE). Since the program began in 1991, more than twelve thousand law enforcement officers have been certified as G.R.E.A.T. instructors and close to 6 million students have graduated from the G.R.E.A.T. program.[67] This program is found in all fifty states and in the District of Columbia and is used in more than five hundred communities across the United States. During 1999–2000, the program underwent an extensive program and curriculum review. The original program was expanded to thirteen lessons and placed more emphasis on active learning and increased teacher involvement. The G.R.E.A.T. program currently consists of a thirteen-week middle-school curriculum, an elementary curriculum, a summer program, and family training.

Evaluations have been done in 1999, 2001, 2004, and another one—of the new curriculum—concludes in 2012. From all the surveys conducted, the consistent finding was that G.R.E.A.T. has not reduced youths involvement in gangs and delinquent behavior, but it did help young people to develop positive relations with law enforcement.[68]

Law Enforcement Education (LRE), another popular prevention program, is designed to teach students the fundamental principles and skills needed to become responsible citizens in a constitutional democracy.[69] A 1985 national curriculum survey reported that LRE had been added to the curriculum in more than half of the forty-six states involved in the study.[70] One of the few studies evaluating LRE programs found that these programs, when properly conducted, can reduce tendencies toward delinquent behavior and improve a range of attitudes related to responsible citizenship and that successful students were also less likely to associate with delinquent peers and to use violence as a means of resolving conflict.[71] See Exhibit 13–3 on the police sending court citations of students.

Today, the need for substance abuse prevention programs demands creativity and involvement on the part of the police. The Drug Abuse Resistance Education (D.A.R.E.) program (discussed in the section on social policy below) is a widely replicated effort by the police to prevent substance abuse. New York City's School Program to Educate and Control Drug Abuse (Project SPECDA), which is a collaborative effort of the city's police department and board of education, is another highly praised drug-prevention program; in this project, a sixteen-session curriculum, with the units split evenly between fifth and six grades, imparts basic information about the risks and effects of drug use, makes students aware of the social pressures that cause drug use, and teaches acceptable methods of resisting peer pressure to experiment with drugs.[72]

Exhibit 13–3
L.A. School Police, District Agree to Rethink Court Citations of Students

Records show that the police in Los Angeles issued an average of thirty citations a day, 40 percent to kids who were ten to fourteen years old.

The Center for Public Integrity and the Los Angeles-based Community Strategy Center each performed their own analysis recently of citation records obtained from the Los Angeles Unified School District Police Department, the nation's largest police force. The center found that between 2009 and the end of 2011, Los Angeles school police officers issued more than 33,500 tickets to students ages 18 and younger, with more than 40 percent handed out to children ten to fourteen years old. This was an average of about thirty tickets a day, a large portion of which was for young children for disturbing the peace, which can mean a physical fight or using threatening or disruptive language.

A spokesperson for LA Unified said in a statement that "the LASPD is committed to reviewing the data and analyzing incident types in which alternative strategies can be feasibly developed, especially in areas such as truancy."

The center's analysis also revealed that citations to middle-class students were heavily concentrated in Los Angeles's most heavily Latino and African American neighborhoods.

Critics contend that introducing students to the juvenile justice system for low-level offenses actually pushes many away from the school and increases the possibility of their dropping out. The areas where student ticketing is heaviest corresponds to neighborhoods where Los Angeles's dropout rates have been the highest. Critics further charge that a heavier police presence in lower-income neighborhoods leads to unequal police involvement in school life.

CRITICAL THINKING QUESTIONS

■ *What is your position on police issuing so many tickets from school?*

Source: The Center for Public Integrity, "L.A. School Police, District Agree to Rethink Court Citations of Students," June 12, 2012.

In addition to drug-prevention programs, the police respond to incidents ranging from student fights and assaults to drug and weapon possession. Officers also regularly drive by schools during night and weekend patrol to prevent vandalism and burglary to school property, and the police are responsible for providing security and safety to the school. In some schools, this requires conducting searches of students as they come into the school, monitoring the halls, doing conflict mediation when necessary, and protecting students as they come to and go home from school. The police are frequently called on to assist the school in searching for weapons and drugs on school property and are charged to enforce drug-free school zone laws and the federal Gun-Free School Zones Act. The police are also expected to enforce school attendance programs in a few school districts across the nation.

The federal Office of Community Oriented Policing Services (COPS) has awarded almost $715 million to more than 2,900 law enforcement agencies to fund more than 6,300 school resource officers (SROs) through the COPS in Schools (CIS) program. In addition, COPS has appropriated nearly $21 million to train COPS-funded SROs and school administrators in partnering schools or school districts to work more collaboratively through the CIS program. SROs in schools can serve in a variety of ways: They may function not only as law enforcement officers but as problem solvers, LRE educators, and community liaisons; they may teach classes in crime prevention, substance abuse awareness, and gang resistance; they may monitor and assist troubled students through mentoring programs; and they may promote social and personal responsibility by encouraging student participation in community service activities. Moreover, these officers help schools develop policies to address delinquent activity and school safety.[73]

Voices of Delinquency 13-2
Read "Feeding the Monster." In this story, the writer tells how the police enhanced their department's reputation in the community. He says, "Hell, the cops were doing more for our egos than we were." How likely is this to occur elsewhere?

Library Extra 13–3
NIJ-sponsored publication: *Children in an Adult World: Prosecuting Adolescents in Criminal and Juvenile Jurisdictions*

Gang-Based Interventions

The number of street gangs rose dramatically across the nation beginning in the late 1980s. The characteristics of these gangs vary widely from one city to another. Some of the gangs are simply groups of adolescents who hang around together and who seldom get into any serious trouble, other gangs engage in extensive drug activity, and some have become involved in violent drive-by shootings in which innocent citizens have been killed.

Drugs and violence have made gangs a problem for the police. For example, police officers caught a group of Los Angeles Crips conducting a drug sales seminar in St. Louis, Missouri.[74] Once a community becomes aware of the seriousness of the gang problem—usually after a violent gang incident has taken place—then pressure is typically put on the police to solve the problem. Police departments have frequently responded to this pressure by setting up one of three types of intervention units to work with gangs.[75]

The Youth Service Program, which is one such unit, is formed to deal with a specific gang problem and is not a permanent unit within the police department; officers continue to perform their regular duties and are not exclusively concerned with gang problems. The gang detail is a second type of unit, and the officers in these units generally are pulled from detective units or juvenile units. The gang detail differs from the Youth Service Program in that its officers are assigned solely to gang problems and do not routinely work on other assignments. The **gang unit** is the third type of unit, and the members of these permanent units see themselves as specialists who are working on gang problems; for example, many gang units will develop extensive intelligence networks with gang members in the community.[76]

gang unit
A specialized unit established by some police departments to address the problem of gangs.

Delinquency across the Life Course: Effects of Police Discretion

The police are the first line of contact with law-violating juveniles. They frequently have the discretion to divert a youth or refer him or her to the attention of the juvenile justice system, especially when the juvenile is involved in a minor offense. As repeatedly stated in this text, there is no question that the juvenile who has an early onset of crime and comes to the attention of the justice system is more likely to be involved with the justice system longer and go on to the adult system more than the youth who is diverted from the system or begins his or her onset of crime at a later date in adolescence. With that in mind, it is important to recognize that the police must try everything possible to avoid contributing to the ongoing delinquency and later criminality of individuals.

Delinquency and Social Policy: Project D.A.R.E.

The most popular school-based drug-education program in the nation is Drug Abuse Resistance Education (D.A.R.E.), a program that receives over $200 million annually in public funding despite strong evidence of its ineffectiveness. This program is designed to equip elementary school children with skills for resisting peer pressure to experiment with tobacco, drugs, and alcohol. Using a core curriculum consisting of seventeen hour-long weekly lessons, D.A.R.E. gives special attention to fifth and sixth graders to prepare them for entry into junior high and high school, where they are most likely to encounter pressure to use drugs. Since it was founded, D.A.R.E. has expanded to encompass programs for middle and high school students, gang prevention, conflict resolution, parent education, and after-school recreation and learning. As the most popular school-based drug-education program in the United States, it is administered in about 75 percent of this nation's school districts, reaching 26 million, and has been adopted in more than fifty countries.[77]

It has been widely evaluated, and there are several disappointing findings:

- The D.A.R.E. program has some immediate beneficial effects on student knowledge of drugs, social skills, attitudes about drug use, and attitudes toward the police.
- These effects dissipate quickly and are typically gone within one to two years.
- The effects of D.A.R.E. on drug-use behavior (measured in numerous ways) are extremely rare.
- The identified effects tend to be small in size and also dissipate quickly.[78]

Dennis Rosenbaum summarized this collective evidence:

In sum, the results were very disappointing despite high expectations for the program. Across more than 30 studies, the collective evidence from evaluations with reasonably good scientific validity suggests that the core D.A.R.E. program does not prevent drug use in the short term, nor does it prevent drug use when students are ready to enter high school or college. Students who receive D.A.R.E. are indistinguishable from students who do not participate in the program.[79]

Rosenbaum raised a question that has been widely raised elsewhere—"How can we reconcile this state of knowledge with the reality of worldwide support for D.A.R.E.?"—and goes on to say, "The irony for the drug prevention field (and other fields as well) is that a program known to be ineffective receives millions of dollars in support, whereas programs known to be effective or promising are sidelined and remain unfunded."[80]

Dozens of communities in the 1990s and early 2000s have dropped the D.A.R.E. program, but the debate whether to continue funding has been waged both nationally and internationally. Proponents of D.A.R.E. are a strong interest group and presently are able to maintain federal funding for this drug-prevention program.

THE CASE

The Life Course of Amy Watters, Age 16

Things had not gone well when Amy and CJ were questioned by the deputy. To ensure fairness all around, the deputy had said, a tripod-based video camera would be used to create a record of the interviews. First the deputy interviewed Amy while she had CJ wait in a separate room—one well out of ear-shot of the interrogation room. Before the session started, however, Amy was advised of her rights in front of her father and asked whether she wanted to continue to answer questions. Her father was also told he could stop the interview process at any time and hire a lawyer to represent his daughter; the process would then resume at a later time.

Amy's father talked briefly with his daughter, and began to suggest that Amy stay silent, as was her right. Amy protested, however, saying that she wanted to admit her involvement in the scheme to bring drugs into the school. "Dad," she said to her father, "I didn't take any money for anything. I'm really not THAT guilty of doing anything wrong."

Amy's father didn't want to argue with his daughter, and wasn't sure that he could afford a lawyer anyway, so he went along with her request. So, as he watched, the deputy proceeded to ask Amy a series of questions, and Amy slowly admitted her involvement in the drug smuggling scheme—eventually revealing what she knew of its scope and the extent of CJ's involvement in it. CJ, she said, wasn't really making any money from drug sales, and everybody on the football team wanted the marijuana that he sold them. The officer seemed unconvinced by her attempts to minimize the harm done, and told her that dealing drugs on school grounds was a serious offense. That night Amy slept in a juvenile confinement facility, waiting to be taken for a hearing before a juvenile court judge the next day.

Why did Amy decide to confess? What would have happened if she hadn't?

Learn More on the Web:

- Police Encounters with Juvenile Suspects: http://www.ncjrs.gov/pdffiles1/nij/grants/205124.pdf
- The Police Handling of Juveniles: http://law.jrank.org/pages/1667/Police-Handling-Juveniles.html

Follow the continuing Amy Watters saga in the next chapter.

SUMMARY

This chapter focused on the relationship between the police and juveniles in U.S. society. Policing juveniles is similar in some ways to policing adults, yet in other ways it is quite different:

- Because the police usually represent the first contact a juvenile has with the justice system, effective police–juvenile relations are vitally important.

- In the late nineteenth and early twentieth centuries, the policing of juveniles came to be viewed differently than the policing of adults. This change, which coincided with reforms in community-based and institutional care of delinquents, emphasized the importance of delinquency prevention.

- Specialized police units were soon created in many of our country's large cities and were charged with delinquency prevention and the apprehension of juveniles who broke the law.

- In the late 1970s and early 1980s, budgetary constraints led to reduced police involvement in delinquency prevention and in diversionary programs for juveniles.

- By the late 1980s and early 1990s, however, a rise in juvenile violence, growing juvenile drug abuse, and proliferation of youth gangs again led to an expanded police emphasis on delinquency prevention and to an examination of the problems faced by juveniles.

- Juveniles today generally demonstrate a better attitude toward the police than in the past, and police officers today are typically more positive about the handling of juveniles, showing that efforts to enhance police–juvenile relations have been at least partly successful.

- The most important elements in understanding police–juvenile relations today may be the public's expectation that the police should address the problems of juvenile crime and prevent youth crime in rich and poor communities alike.

- Today's police have wide discretion in dealing with juvenile lawbreakers, and several studies have found that 80 to 90 percent of police–juvenile encounters result in diversion from official processing by the juvenile justice system.

- Although a number of factors influence how police officers respond to juvenile offenders, the most important element influencing police discretion and disposition of the juvenile offender is the nature of the offense committed.

- Over time, juveniles have been granted a number of significant due process rights by the courts, and those rights have placed increased requirements on the police for the proper handling of juveniles.

- Of special concern today is the need for the police to deal with the problem of violent youth crime—a challenge made all the more difficult by the fact that many juveniles possess handguns, gangs are widespread, juvenile drug abuse remains at significant levels, and some juveniles have become involved in hate crimes.

KEY TERMS

arrest, p. 337

citation, p. 334

cycle of alienation, p. 331

fingerprinting, p. 339

gang unit, p. 345

juvenile officer, p. 330

Miranda v. *Arizona*, p. 338 — 1966

police discretion, p. 331

police interrogation, p. 338

pretrial identification practices, p. 340

problem-oriented policing, p. 330

search and seizure, p. 336

station adjustment, p. 334

JUVENILE DELINQUENCY VIDEOS

Calling the Police

In *Calling the Police*, the formal and informal interactions between juveniles and law enforcement are discussed. How can these interactions have an impact on the at-risk juvenile? Discuss the living situations that the law enforcement officers emphasize is a common factor in many of these children's lives. How does the home life of a child have an impact on his or her involvement with criminal behavior? What would cause a parent to call the police about a child? What are the aims of the police in dealing with at-risk and delinquent children?

Police Perspective

Police Perspective shows police officers discussing the differences between handling children and adults. How does law enforcement deal with juveniles? Based on the video and the readings from this chapter, how does police discretion factor into juvenile interactions with law enforcement? The officers mention the different backgrounds that juveniles can come from; how does the background of a child affect an officer's decision when interacting with the juvenile? Discuss.

REVIEW QUESTIONS

1. Overall, how do juveniles feel about the police?
2. What are the most important factors affecting the processing of juveniles?
3. What disposition alternatives are available to the police when dealing with juveniles?
4. What are the most important legal rights of juveniles?
5. How do the police attempt to prevent and deter delinquency?

DISCUSSION QUESTIONS

1. Why do the attitudes of minority and white youths toward the police tend to differ? Why would youthful offenders feel differently toward the police than nonoffenders? Have your experiences with the police made a difference in how you feel about the police?
2. What are the rights of a juvenile taken into custody?
3. What is your evaluation of D.A.R.E.? Did you participate in a D.A.R.E. program in high school? If so, did it make a difference in your using or not using drugs?
4. Why is the police role in working with juveniles more difficult today than it was in the past?
5. Do you think police discretion leads to discriminatory decision making?
6. Is "by-the-book" policing the wisest course of action to prevent charges of discrimination? Explain your response.

GROUP EXERCISES

1. Have students research data from their county and state to determine how many police departments have dedicated juvenile crime units or officers.
2. Invite a two- or three-member panel from your local police department, including at least one supervisor (sergeant or lieutenant), to discuss police discretion with the class.
3. Invite a member of your local police department's juvenile crime unit to address the class regarding juvenile justice issues in your community.
4. Invite a member of your local police department's gang unit to address gang issues in your community.

NOTES

1. "Police Forced to Pepper Spray Unruly Second-Grader; Mother Claims Excessive Force," *The Daily Mail*, April 6, 2011, http://policelink.monster.com/news/articles/152776-police-forced-to-pepper-spray-unruly-second-grader-mother-claims-excessive-force?utm_source=nlet&utm_content=pl_c1_20110407_pepperspray_mem (accessed April 7, 2011).
2. David R. Johnson, *Policing the Urban Underworld: The Impact of Crime on the Development of the American Police, 1800–1887* (Philadelphia: Temple University Press, 1979), pp. 78–89.
3. Robert M. Fogelson, *Big-City Police* (Cambridge, MA: Harvard University Press, 1977), pp. 86–87.
4. Ibid.
5. Ibid.
6. Ibid.
7. Ibid.
8. Winfree and Griffiths, "Adolescents' Attitudes Toward the Police," pp. 79–99.
9. Rusinko et al., "The Importance of Police Contact in the Formulation of Youths' Attitudes Toward Police," 65.
10. Scott H. Decker, "Citizen Attitudes Toward the Police: A Review of Past Findings and Suggestions for Future Policy," *Journal of Police Science and Administration* 9 (1981), pp. 80–87.
11. Komanduri S. Murty, Julian B. Roebuck, and Joann D. Smith, "The Image of Police in Black Atlanta Communities," *Journal of Police Science and Administration* 17 (1990), pp. 250–57.
12. Michael J. Leiber, Mahesh K. Nalla, and Margaret Farnworth, "Explaining Juveniles' Attitudes Toward the Police," *Justice Quarterly* 15 (March 1998), pp. 151–71.
13. J. G. Bachman, L. D. Johnson, P. M. O'Malley, *Monitoring the Future: Questionnaire Responses from the Nation's High School Seniors*, 2007 (Ann Arbor, MI: Institute for Social Research). Roughly 13 percent of the youths had no opinion on the question. Data for 2001 were provided by Johnston et al., *Monitoring the Future Project*.
14. Susan Guarino-Ghezzi and Bryan Carr, "Juvenile Offenders v. the Police: A Community Dilemma," *Caribbean Journal of Criminology and Social Psychology* 1 (July 1996), pp. 24–43.
15. Terry Nihart et al., "Kids, Cops, Parents and Teachers: Exploring Juvenile Attitudes Toward Authority Figures," *Western Criminology Review* 6 (2005), pp. 79–88.
16. Yolander G. Hurst, "Juvenile Attitudes Toward the Police," *Criminal Justice Review* 32 (2007), pp. 121–41.
17. James Q. Wilson, "Dilemmas of Police Administration," *Police Administration Review* 28 (September–October 1968), pp. 407–17.
18. Stephanie M. Myers, *Police Encounters with Juvenile Suspects: Explaining the Use of Authority and Provision of Support* (Washington, D.C.: National Institute of Justice, 2004).
19. Donald J. Black and Albert J. Reiss Jr., "Police Control of Juveniles," *American Sociological Review* 35 (February 1979), pp. 63–77.
20. Robert M. Terry, "Discrimination in the Handling of Juvenile Offenders by Social Control Agencies," *Journal of Research in Crime and Delinquency* 4 (July 1967), pp. 218–30; Nathan Goldman, *The Differential Selection of Juvenile Offenders for Court Appearance* (New York: National Council on Crime and Delinquency 1963); Black and Reiss, "Police Control of Juveniles"; and Irving Piliavin and Scott Briar, "Police Encounters with Juveniles," *American Journal of Sociology* 70 (September 1964), pp. 206–14.
21. Terry, "Discrimination in the Handling of Juvenile Offenders"; Black and Weiss, "Police Control of Juveniles"; and Robert M. Emerson, *Judging Delinquents: Context and Process in Juvenile Court* (Chicago: Aldine, 1969).
22. Gail Armstrong, "Females under the Law—Protected but Unequal," *Crime and Delinquency* 23 (April 1977), pp. 109–20; Meda Chesney-Lind, "Judicial Paternalism and the Female Status Offender," *Crime and Delinquency* 23 (April 1977), pp. 121–30; and Meda Chesney-Lind, "Girls and Status Offenses: Is Juvenile Justice Still Sexist?" *Criminal Justice Abstracts* (March 1988), pp. 144–65.
23. Meda Chesney-Lind, "Juvenile Delinquency: The Sexualization of Female Crime," *Psychology Today* 8 (July 1974), pp. 43–46; and I. Richard Perleman, "Antisocial Behavior of the Minor in the United States," in *Society, Delinquency, and Delinquent Behavior*, edited by Harwin L. Voss (Boston: Little, Brown, 1970), pp. 35–43.
24. Theodore N. Ferdinand and Elmer C. Luchterhand, "Inner-City Youths, the Police, the Juvenile Court, and Justice," *Social Problems* 17 (Spring 1970), pp. 510–27; Goldman, *The Differential Selection of Juvenile Offenders*; and Piliavin and Briar, "Police Encounters with Juveniles."

25. Marvin E. Wolfgang, Robert M. Figlio, and Thorsten Sellin, *Delinquency in a Birth Cohort* (Chicago: University of Chicago Press, 1972).

26. Philip W. Harris, "Race and Juvenile Justice: Examining the Impact of Structural and Policy Changes on Racial Disproportionality," paper presented at the 39th Annual Meeting of the American Society of Criminology, Montreal, Quebec, Canada, November 13, 1987.

27. James T. Carey et al., *The Handling of Juveniles from Offense to Disposition* (Washington, D.C.: U.S. Government Printing Office, 1976); A. W. McEachern and Riva Bauzer, "Factors Related to Disposition in Juvenile–Police Contacts," in *Juvenile Gangs in Context*, edited by Malcolm W. Klein (Englewood Cliffs, N.J.: Prentice-Hall, 1967), pp. 148–60; Thorsten Sellin and Marvin E. Wolfgang, *The Measurement of Delinquency* (New York: John Wiley & Sons, 1964); and Ferdinand and Luchterhand, "Inner-City Youths."

28. Merry Morash, "Establishment of Juvenile Police Record," *Criminology* 22 (February 1984), pp. 97–111.

29. Piliavin and Briar, "Police Encounters with Juveniles."

30. Carl Werthman and Irving Piliavin, "Gang Members and Police," in *The Police*, edited by David J. Bordua (New York: Wiley, 1967), pp. 56–98; and Richard J. Lundman, Richard E. Sykes, and John P. Clark, "Police Control of Juveniles: A Replication," *Journal of Research in Crime and Delinquency* 15 (January 1978), pp. 74–91.

31. Goldman, *The Differential Selection of Juvenile Offenders. Differential Selection of Juvenile Offenders.*

32. Wilson, "Dilemmas of Police Administration."

33. Howard N. Snyder and Melissa Sickmund, Juvenile Offenders and Victims, 2006 (Washington, D.C.: National Center for Juvenile Justice, 2006).

34. For a discussion of the Constitution and Supr[34] For a discussion of the Constitution and Supreme Court decisions relevant to the schools, see Reed B. Day, *Legal Issues Surrounding Safe Schools* (Topeka, KS: National Organization on Legal Problems of Education, 1994).

35. *Mapp* v. *Ohio*, 367 U.S. 643 (1961); Day, *Legal Issues Surrounding Safe Schools*, 25–38.

36. *State* v. *Lowery*, 230 A. 2d 907 (1967).

37. *In re Two Brothers and a Case of Liquor,* Juvenile Court of the District of Columbia, 1966, reported in *Washington Law Reporter* 95 (1967), 113.

38. *Ciulla* v. *State*, 434 S.W. 2d 948 (Tex. Civ. App. 1968).

39. For a good general discussion of search and seizure law see http://law.enotes.com/everyday-law-encyclopedia/search-and-seizure. Among the Supreme Court cases relevant to privacy are *Katz* v. *U.S.*, 389 U.S. 347, 88 S. Ct. 507. 19 L. Ed. 2d 576 (1967) and *Hester* v. *U.S.*, 265 I.S. 57, 44 S. Ct. 445, 68 L. Ed. 898 (1924). See also Judge David Demers, "Search and Seizure Outline," 2002, http://www.judges.com/Demers/page153-179.htm.

40. *Terry* v. *Ohio*, 392 U.S. 1, 20 L 2d 889, 911 (1968) at http://urban75.org/legal/rights.html.

41. Ibid.

42. *Haley* v. *Ohio*, 332 U.S. 596 (1948).

43. *Brown* v. *Mississippi*, 399 F.2d 467 (5th Cir. 1968).

44. Samuel M. Davis, *Rights of Juveniles*: *The Juvenile Justice System*, 2d ed. (New York: Thompson, 2005), Sections 3–45.

45. *Miranda* v. *Arizona*, 384 U.S. 436 (1966).

46. *In re Gault*, 387 U.S. (1967).

47. *Fare* v. *Michael C.*, 442 U.S. 23, 99 S.Ct. 2560 (1979).

48. T. Grisso, *Juveniles' Waiver of Rights and Psychology: Legal and Psychological Competence* New York: Plenum Press, 1981).

49. *People* v. *Lara*, 62 Cal. Rptr. 586 (1967); cert. denied, 392 U.S. 945 (1968).

50. *In re Mellot,* 217 S.E. 2d 745 (C.A.N. Ca. 1975).

51. *In re Dennis P. Fletcher*, 248 A.2d. 364 (Md. 1968); cert. denied, 396 U.S. 852 (1969).

52. *Commonwealth* v. *Guyton,* 405 Mass. 497 (1989).

53. *Commonwealth* v. *McNeil*, 399 Mass. 71 (1987).

54. Gisli H. Gudjonsson, Jon Fridrik Sigurdsson, Inga Dora Sigfusdottir, and Bryndis Bjork Asgeirsdottir, "False Confession and Individual Differences: The Importance of Victimization among Youth," *Personality and Individual Differences* 45 (2008), pp. 801–05.

55. Elyce Z. Ferster and Thomas F. Courtless, "The Beginning of Juvenile Justice, Police Practices, and the Juvenile Offender," *Vanderbilt Law Review* 22 (April 1969), pp. 598–601.

56. Howard N. Snyder and Melissa Sickmund, *Juvenile Offenders and Victims: 2006 National Report* (Washington, D.C.: National Center for Juvenile Justice, Office of Juvenile Justice and Delinquency Prevention, 2006).

57. *United States* v. *Wade*, 388 U.S. 218, 87 S.Ct. 1926 (1967).

58. *Kirby* v. *Illinois*, 406 U.S. 682, 92 S.Ct. 1877 (1972).

59. *In re Holley*, 107 R.I. 615, 268 A.2d 723 (1970).

60. Snyder and Sickmund, *Juvenile Offenders and Victims: 2006.*

61. *In re Carl T.*, 81 Cal. Rptr. 655 (2d C.A., 1969).

62. Office of Justice Programs, *America's Missing: Broadcast Emergency Response: Frequently Asked Questions on AMBER Alert,* http://www.amberalert.gov/faqs.html.

63. Snyder and Sickmund, *Juvenile Offenders and Victims: 2006.*

64. Ibid. H

65. See Mark S. Hamm, *American Skinheads: The Criminology and Control of Hate Crime* (Westport, Conn.: Praeger, 1993).

66. Snyder and Sickmund, *Juvenile Offenders and Victims: 2006 National Report.*

67. G.R.E.A.T, *History of the G.R.E.A.T. Program, 2012,* http://www.great.ca-org/Organizatioln/Histlory.Aspx, accessed on June 12, 2012.

68. F. A. Esbensen and D. W. Osgood, "Gang Resistance Education and Training (G.R.E.A.T.): Results from the National Evaluation," *Journal of Research in Crime and Delinquency* 36 (1999), pp. 194–225; F. A. Esbensen, D. W. T. J. Taylor, D. Peterson, and A. Frenger, "How Great Is G.R.E.A.T."? Results from a Longitudinal Quasi- Experimental Design," *Criminology and Public Policy* 1 (2001),

87–118; and J. Achcroft, D. J. Daniels, and S. V. Hart, *Evaluating G.R.E.A.T.: A School-Based Gang Prevention Program* (Washington, D.C.: U.S. Department of Justice, 2004).

69. Norman D. Wright, *From Risk to Resiliency: The Role of Law-Related Education* (pamphlet) (Des Moines, Iowa: Institute on Law and Civil Education, June 20–21, 1995).

70. Carole L. Hahn, "The Status of the Social Studies in Public School in the United States: Another Look," *Social Education* 49 (1985), pp. 220–23.

71. Judith Warrent Little and Frances Haley, *Implementing Effective LRE Programs* (Boulder, Colo.: Social Science Education Consortium, 1982).

72. William DeJong, *Arresting the Demand for Drugs: Police and School Partnership to Prevent Drug Abuse* (Washington, D.C.: National Institute of Justice, 1987).

73. *COPS in Schools: The COPS Commitment to School Safety* (Washington, D.C.: Office of Community-Oriented Policing Services, n.d.). For how police resource officers spend their time, see Richard Lawrence, "The Role of Police–School Liaison Officers in School Crime Prevention," paper presented at the Annual Meeting of the Academy of Criminal Justice Sciences, Albuquerque, NM, March 11, 1998.

74. Ronald D. Stephens, "School-Based Interventions: Safety and Security," in Arnold P. Goldstein and Ronald C. Huff, eds., *The Gang Intervention Handbook* (Champaign, IL: Research Press, 1993), pp. 219–56.

75. Jerome A. Needle and William Vaughn Stapleton, "Police Handling of Youth Gangs," in *Reports of the National Juvenile Justice Assessment Centers* (Washington, D.C.: U.S. Department of Justice, 1983).

76. Ibid.

77. National Institute of Justice, *The D.A.R.E. Program: A Review of Prevalence, User Satisfaction, and Effectiveness* (Washington, D.C.: U.S. Department of Justice, 1994).

78. Dennis P. Rosenbaum, "Just Say No to D.A.R.E.," *Crime and Public Policy* 6 (2007), pp. 815–24.

79. Ibid.

80. Ibid.

14 Juvenile Court

Chapter Objectives

After reading this chapter, you should be able to:

1. **Summarize the three positions concerning the role of the juvenile court.**
2. **Summarize the evolution of juvenile courts and the key Supreme Court decisions that have contributed to changes.**
3. **Summarize the pretrial procedures involved in juvenile court proceedings.**
4. **Summarize juvenile trial proceedings.**
5. **Distinguish between determinate and indeterminate sentencing structures.**
6. **Explain how transfer to the adult court impacts juvenile offenders.**
7. **Describe the key principles for excellence in juvenile court.**

Under our Constitution the condition of being a boy does not justify a kangaroo court.

—*In re Gault*, 387 U.S. 1 (1967)

Introduction

As discussed in Chapter 12, the idea of a juvenile court, separate in principle from adult criminal courts, had its beginnings in Chicago in 1899. The juvenile court ideal, which inspired juvenile justice system workers in this country for over one hundred years, was, however, disgraced by the actions of a corrupt Pennsylvania judge in the 2000s. In 2009, former Luzerne County, Pennsylvania, juvenile court judge Mark Ciavarella, 61, was convicted by a federal jury of twelve counts of racketeering and conspiracy for accepting cash payoffs totaling nearly $1 million to place juvenile offenders into privately owned detention facilities. Following Ciavarella's conviction, the Pennsylvania Supreme Court quickly dismissed thousands of juvenile convictions that he had issued, saying that Ciavarella had run his courtroom with "complete disregard for the constitutional rights of the juveniles" who came before him, including the right to legal counsel and the right to intelligently enter a plea.[1]

Ciavarella's conviction strongly contrasts with the idealistic perspective of Roscoe Pound, the dean of American jurisprudence, who called the juvenile court "the most significant advance in the administration of justice since the Magna Carta."[2] Many contemporary advocates of the **juvenile court** continue to insist that the informal setting of the court and the parental demeanor of the judge enable wayward youths to be saved or rescued from possible lives of crime.

Critics eventually challenged these idealistic views of the juvenile court, claiming that the juvenile court had not succeeded in rehabilitating youthful offenders, in bringing justice and compassion to them, or even in providing them with their due process rights.[3] Some investigators even accused the juvenile court of substantially harming the juveniles who appeared before it.[4]

Today three different positions have emerged concerning the role of the juvenile court. One position continues to support the *parens patriae* philosophy, or the state as parent, and holds to "the best interest of the child" standard for decision making.

A second position proposes that the justice model (see Chapter 12) replace the *parens patriae* philosophy as the basis of juvenile court procedures. In the 1980s, proposed procedural changes such as decriminalization of status offenses, determinate sentencing, mandatory sentencing, and opening up of juvenile proceedings and records struck at the very heart and core of traditional juvenile court proceedings.[5] Barry C. Feld is one of the most articulate spokespeople for this position, arguing that an integrated criminal court with a youth discount (juveniles would receive lesser sentences than adults for similar violations of the law) would provide youthful offenders with greater protections and justice than they currently receive in the juvenile justice system and with more proportional and humane consequences than judges currently inflict on them as adults in the criminal justice system.[6]

In sum, significant changes are clearly sweeping through the almost 110-year-old corridors of the juvenile court. In the early 2010s, what is actually taking place is that all three positions are represented: For minor offenses, as well as for status offenses in most states, the "best interest of the child" position is the guiding standard of juvenile court decision making; for offenders who commit more serious delinquent acts, the principles of the justice model are increasingly used in adjudicatory and disposition hearings; and repetitive or violent youthful offenders are commonly transferred quickly to the adult court and handled as adults. Perhaps the question is not whether the traditional juvenile court will change but whether the court will survive.

Juvenile Court

The concept of the juvenile court was rapidly accepted across the nation—thirty-one states had instituted juvenile courts by 1905, and by 1928, only two states did not have a juvenile court statute. In Cook County, the amendments that followed the original act brought the neglected, the dependent, and the delinquent together under one roof. The "delinquent" category comprised both status offenders and actual violators of criminal law.

Reformers further advocated that the juvenile judge sit at a desk rather than on a bench and that he occasionally "put his arm around [the delinquent's] shoulder and draw the lad to him."[7] But the sympathetic judge was instructed not to lose any of his judicial dignity. The

juvenile court
Any court that has jurisdiction over matters involving juveniles.

constitutionalists
The name given to a group of twentieth-century reformers who advocated that juveniles deserve due process protections when they appear before the juvenile court.

Kent v. United States
A 1966 U.S. Supreme Court decision on the matter of transfer; the first decision in which the Supreme Court dealt with a juvenile court case.

1. Youths should be given the same care as that provided by a good parent.

2. The aim of the court is to restore, help, and forgive.

3. Youths should not be treated as criminals.

4. The rights of youths are the rights to shelter, protection, and proper guardianship.

FIGURE 14–1
The Ideals of the Juvenile Court

goals of the court were defined as investigation, diagnosis, and prescription of treatment. Lawyers were deemed unnecessary because these civil proceedings were not adversary trials but informal hearings in which the best interests of the youths were the chief concern.

In short, the juvenile court was founded on several basic ideals: that the court should function as a social clinic designed to serve the best interests of youths in trouble; that youths who were brought before the court should be given the same care, supervision, and discipline as would be provided by a good parent; that the aim of the court is to help, to restore, to guide, and to forgive; that youths should not be treated as criminals; and that the rights to shelter, protection, and proper guardianship are the only rights of youths.[8] See Figure 14–1.

Changes in Legal Norms

In the twentieth century, the group known as the **constitutionalists**, one of the most formidable foes of the juvenile court, contended that the juvenile court was unconstitutional because under its system the principles of a fair trial and individual rights were denied. A series of decisions by the U.S. Supreme Court in the 1960s and 1970s demonstrated the influence of the constitutionalists on juvenile justice.

Figure 14–2 shows fourteen of the most important U.S. Supreme Court cases involving juveniles and juveniles rights. The earliest of those cases—including *Kent v. United States* (1966), *In re Gault* (1967), *In re Winship* (1970), *McKeiver v. Pennsylvania* (1971), and *Breed v. Jones* (1975)—differentiated juvenile case processing from adult criminal case processing and established juvenile rights that continue to be recognized today.

Important recent cases include *Roper* v. *Simmons* (2005), weighing the issue of the death penalty for juveniles, which the Court ultimately ruled unconstitutional. Following *Simmons*, the 2010 case of *Graham* v. *Florida*[9] held that the Eighth Amendment's ban on cruel and unusual punishments prohibits the imprisonment of a juvenile for life without the possibility of parole as punishment for a crime not including homicide; and the 2012 case of *Miller* v. *Alabama*[10] held unconstitutional a mandatory sentence of life without parole for the crime of murder committed by a juvenile because it violates the Eighth Amendment's prohibition on cruel and unusual punishment. Some of the most significant early cases are briefly discussed in the following sections.

In re Gault
A 1967 U.S. Supreme Court case that brought due process and constitutional procedures into juvenile courts.

In re Winship
A 1970 case in which the U.S. Supreme Court decided that juveniles are entitled to proof beyond a reasonable doubt during adjudication proceedings.

McKeiver v. Pennsylvania
A 1971 U.S. Supreme Court case that denied juveniles the right to trial by jury.

Breed v. Jones
A 1975 double jeopardy case in which the U.S. Supreme Court ruled that a juvenile court cannot adjudicate a case and then transfer the case to the criminal court for adult processing of the same offense.

▲ This family court building is located in the Bronx, New York.

■ What does this text mean when it says that "the language of juvenile justice reflects a gentler application of criminal law than the one used in the adult model"?

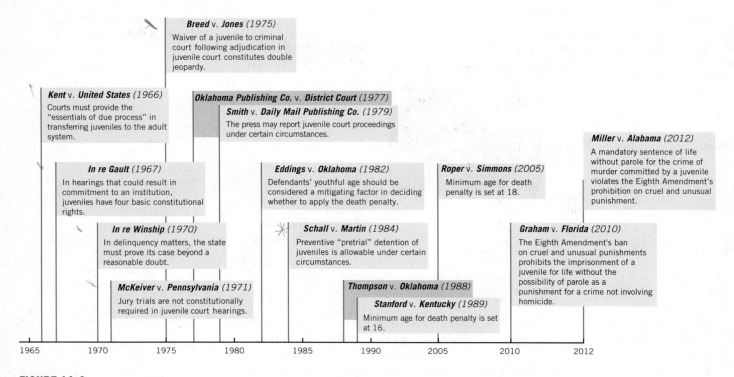

FIGURE 14–2

Timeline of U.S. Supreme Court Decisions of Special Relevance to Juvenile Justice

Source: Adapted from Howard N. Snyder and Melissa Sickmund, *Juvenile Offenders and Victims: 2006 National Report* (Washington, D.C.: National Center for Juvenile Justice, Office of Juvenile Justice and Delinquency Prevention, 2006), p. 101.

Kent v. United States (1966)

transfer

The process of certifying a youth over to adult criminal court. It takes place by judicial waiver and legislative waiver.

Kent is the first decision in which the U.S. Supreme Court dealt with a juvenile court case dealing with the matter of **transfer** (see Juvenile Law 14–1). The juvenile judge did not rule on the motions of Kent's counsel and held no hearings, nor did he confer with Kent, Kent's mother, or Kent's counsel. The judge instead entered an order saying that after full investigation he was transferring jurisdiction to the adult criminal court; he made no findings and entered no reasons for the waiver.

On appeal, the U.S. Supreme Court, holding that the juvenile court proceedings were defective, found that during a transfer hearing, Kent should have been afforded an evidential hearing; that he should have been present when the court decided to waive jurisdiction; that his attorney should have been permitted to examine the social worker's investigation

---

Juvenile Law 14–1
Kent v. United States

Morris A. Kent Jr., a sixteen-year-old youth living in Washington, D.C., was on juvenile probation and was charged with three counts each of housebreaking and robbery and two counts of rape. His mother retained an attorney who had Kent examined by two psychiatrists and a psychologist. The attorney then filed a motion for a hearing on the question of waiver, together with a psychiatrist's affidavit that certified that Kent was "a victim of severe psychopathology," and recommended hospitalization for psychiatric observation. Counsel contended that psychiatric treatment would make Kent a suitable subject for juvenile court rehabilitation. His counsel also moved for access to juvenile court probation records.

■ *What did Supreme Court Justice Fortas mean when he said that "there may be grounds for concern that the child receives the worst of both worlds"? Do you agree with his criticism of the juvenile court?*

Source: Kent v. United States, 383 U.S. 541, 86 S.Ct. 1045, 16 L.Ed.2d 84 (1966).

of the youth, which the court used in deciding to waive jurisdiction; and that the judge should have recorded a statement of reasons for the transfer. Justice Abe Fortas, in the decision, stated:

> There is evidence, in fact, that there may be grounds for concern that the child receives the worst of both worlds; that he gets neither the protection accorded to adults nor the solicitous care and regenerative treatment postulated for children.[11]

The Court decided that withholding Kent's record essentially meant a denial of counsel. The Court also held that a juvenile has a right to be represented by counsel, that a youth charged with a felony has a right to a hearing, and that this hearing must "measure up to the essentials of due process and fair treatment"; finally, a juvenile's attorney must have access to his or her social or probation records.[12]

In re Gault (1967)

In May 1967, the U.S. Supreme Court reversed the conviction of a minor in *In re Gault*. This influential and far-reaching decision represented a new dawn in juvenile court history because, in effect, it brought the light of constitutional procedure into juvenile courts—no longer could due process and procedural safeguards be kept out of the adjudication proceedings. Juvenile Law 14–2 gives the facts of this case.

In *Gault*, the U.S. Supreme Court overruled the Arizona Supreme Court for its dismissal of a writ of *habeas corpus* that had sought Gerald Gault's release from a training school.[13] Justice Fortas, for the Court majority, ruled on four of the six issues raised in the appeal:

1. Notice, to comply with due process requirements, must be given sufficiently in advance of scheduled court proceedings so that reasonable opportunity to prepare will be afforded, and it must "set forth the alleged misconduct with particularity."

2. The due process clause of the Fourteenth Amendment requires that in respect of proceedings to determine delinquency which may result in commitment to an institution in which the juvenile's freedom is curtailed, the youth and his parent must be notified of the youth's right to be represented by counsel retained by them; if they are unable to afford counsel, counsel will be appointed to represent the youth.

3. The constitutional privilege against self-incrimination is as applicable in the case of juveniles as it is with respect to adults.

4. No reason is suggested or appears for a different role in respect of sworn testimony in juvenile courts than in adult tribunals. Absent a valid confession adequate to support the determination of the juvenile court, confrontation and sworn testimony by witnesses available for cross-examination are essential for a finding of "delinquency" and an order committing Gerald to a state institution for a maximum of six years.[14]

Juvenile Law 14–2
In re Gault

Gerald Gault, a fifteen-year-old Arizona boy, and a friend, Ronald Lewis, were taken into custody on June 8, 1964, on a verbal complaint made by a neighbor. The neighbor had accused the boys of making lewd and indecent remarks to her over the phone. Gault's parents were not notified that he had been taken into custody, he was not advised of his right to counsel, he was not advised that he could remain silent, and no notice of charges was made either to Gerald or to his parents; additionally, the complainant was not present at either of the hearings. In spite of considerable confusion about whether or not Gerald had made the alleged phone call, what he had said over the phone, and what he had said to the judge during the course of the two hearings, Judge McGhee committed him to the State Industrial School "for the period of his minority (that is, until age 21) unless sooner discharged by due process of law."

■ *What due process rights did this case grant juveniles? What due process rights did juveniles still lack after this decision?*

Source: *In re Gault*, 387 U.S. 1, 18 L.Ed.2d 527, 87 S.Ct. 1428 (1967).

Web Extra 14–1
OJJDP PowerPoint presentation: "Juvenile Offenders in Court"

Library Extra 14–1
OJJDP publication: *Juvenile Offenders and Victims: 2006 National Report* (Chapter 6)

Justice Fortas, in delivering the Court's opinion, recalled other cases that had provided juveniles with due process of law. In both *Haley* v. *Ohio* (1948) and *Gallegos* v. *Colorado* (1962), the Supreme Court had prohibited the use of confessions coerced from juveniles; in *Kent,* the Court had given the juvenile the right to be represented by counsel.[15] Justice Fortas concluded his review of legal precedent with the sweeping statement that juveniles have those fundamental rights that are incorporated in the due process clause of the Fourteenth Amendment to the U.S. Constitution

The *In re Gault* decision affirmed that a juvenile has the right to due process safeguards in proceedings in which a finding of delinquency can lead to institutional confinement. The decision also established that a juvenile has the right to notice of the charges, right to counsel, right to confrontation and cross-examination, and privilege against self-incrimination. However, the Court did not rule that juveniles have the right to a transcript of the proceedings or the right to appellate review.

In choosing not to rule on these two latter rights, the Court clearly did not want to turn the informal juvenile hearing into an adversarial trial. The cautiousness of this decision was underlined by a footnote stating that the decision did not apply to preadjudication or postadjudication treatment of juveniles.

In re Winship (1970)   PBARD - Not- P.L.

beyond a reasonable doubt
A legal standard establishing the degree of proof needed for a juvenile to be adjudicated a delinquent by the juvenile court during the adjudicatory stage of the court's proceedings.

In *Winship*, the Supreme Court decided that juveniles are entitled to proof **beyond a reasonable doubt** during the adjudication proceedings[16] (Juvenile Law 14–3 presents the facts of this case). In ruling that "preponderance of evidence" is not a sufficient basis for a decision when youths are charged with acts that would be criminal if committed by adults, the *Winship* decision not only expanded *Gault* but also reflected other concerns of the justices. The Court desired both to protect juveniles at adjudicatory hearings and to maintain the confidentiality, informality, flexibility, and speed of the juvenile process in the prejudicial and postadjudicative states. The Court obviously did not want to bring too much rigidity and impersonality to the juvenile hearing.

McKeiver v. *Pennsylvania* (1971)

During the 1969 through 1971 sessions, the Supreme Court heard three cases together (*McKeiver* v. *Pennsylvania*, *In re Terry*, and *In re Barbara Burrus*) concerning whether the due process clause of the Fourteenth Amendment guaranteeing the right to a jury trial applies to the adjudication of a juvenile court delinquency case.[17] The decision, which was issued in *McKeiver* v. *Pennsylvania*, denied the right of juveniles to have jury trials. Juvenile Law 14–4 summarizes the facts of these three cases.

The Supreme Court gave the following five reasons for its ruling:

1. Not all rights that are constitutionally assured for the adult are to be given to the juvenile.

2. The jury trial, if required for juveniles, may make the juvenile proceedings into a fully adversarial process and will put an end to what has been the idealistic prospect of an intimate, informal protecting proceeding.

double jeopardy
A common law and constitutional prohibition against a second trial for the same offense.

Juvenile Law 14–3
In re Winship

The *Winship* case involved a New York boy who was sent to a state training school at age 12 for taking $112 from a woman's purse. The commitment was based on a New York statute that permitted juvenile court decisions on the basis of a "preponderance of evidence," a standard that is much less strict than "beyond a reasonable doubt."

■ *What is the actual difference between "preponderance of evidence" and "proof beyond a reasonable doubt"? What was the importance of this difference in this case?*

Source: In re Winship, 397 U.S. 358, 90 S.Ct. 1968, 25 L.Ed.2d 368 (1970).

Juvenile Law 14–4
Application of the Due Process Clause of the Fourteenth Amendment to Juveniles

MCKEIVER V. PENNSYLVANIA

Joseph McKeiver, age 16, was charged with robbery, larceny, and receiving stolen goods, all of which were felonies under Pennsylvania law. This youth was found delinquent at an adjudication hearing and was placed on probation after his request for a jury trial was denied.

IN RE TERRY

Edward Terry, age 15, was charged with assault and battery on a police officer, misdemeanors under Pennsylvania law. His counsel's request for a jury trial was denied, and he was adjudicated a delinquent on the charges.

IN RE BARBARA BURRUS

Barbara Burrus and approximately forty-five other youths, ranging in age from eleven to fifteen years old, were the subjects of

juvenile court summonses in Hyde County, North Carolina. The charges arose out of a series of demonstrations in the county in late 1968 by African American adults and youths protesting school assignments and a school consolidation plan. These youths were charged with willfully impeding traffic. The several cases were consolidated into groups for hearing before the district judge, sitting as a juvenile court. A request for a jury trial in each case was denied, and each juvenile was found delinquent and placed on probation.

■ *Some states now permit jury trial for juveniles. How can they grant a jury trial with this Supreme Court decision?*

Source: *McKeiver v. Pennsylvania*, 403 U.S. 528, 535 (1971); *In re Terry*, 215 Pa. Super 762 (1970); and *In re Barbara Burrus*, 275 N.C. 517, 169 S.E.2d 879 (1969).

3. A jury trial is not a necessary part even of every criminal process that is fair and equitable.

4. The jury trial, if injected into the juvenile court system, could bring with it the traditional delay, the formality, and the clamor of the adversary system.

5. There is nothing to prevent an individual juvenile judge from using an advisory jury when he or she feels the need. For that matter, there is nothing to prevent individual states from adopting jury trials.[18]

A number of states do permit jury trials for juveniles, but most adhere to the constitutional standard set by the Supreme Court. Surveys of states report that juveniles choose jury trials in only about 1 to 3 percent of cases.[19] The significance of the *McKeiver* decision is that the Court indicated an unwillingness to apply further procedural safeguards to juvenile proceedings, especially during the preadjudicatory and postadjudicatory treatment of juveniles.

Breed v. Jones (1975)

The question of transfer to an adult court, first considered in the *Kent* case, was taken up again in the *Breed* v. *Jones* decision.[20] This case raised the issue of **double jeopardy**, questioning whether a juvenile could be prosecuted as an adult after an adjudicatory hearing in the juvenile court. The increased use of transfers, or the **binding over** of juveniles to the adult court, makes this decision particularly significant today (see Juvenile Law 14–5).

The U.S. Supreme Court ruled that Breed's case did constitute double jeopardy—a juvenile court cannot adjudicate a case and then transfer the case over to the criminal court for adult processing on the same offense. The significance of *Breed* is that **prosecutors** must determine which youthful offenders they want to transfer to the adult court before juvenile court adjudication; otherwise, the opportunity to transfer, or certify, those youths is lost.[21]

Today nearly every state has defined the specific requirements for transfer proceedings in its juvenile code (discussed in more detail later in this chapter). At present, when a transfer hearing is conducted in juvenile court, due process law usually requires (1) a legitimate transfer hearing, (2) a sufficient notice to the juvenile's family and defense attorney, (3) the right to counsel, and (4) a statement of the court order regarding transfer.

Some evidence exists that youths who have counsel may get more severe dispositions than those without counsel.[22] For example, studies reported in 1980 and 1981 that juveniles

▲ Washington, DC sniper Lee Boyd Malvo makes a court appearance.
■ **Did Malvo deserve to be treated as an adult for purposes of the law?**

✴**binding over**
The process of transferring (also called certifying) juveniles to adult criminal court. Binding over takes place after a judicial hearing on a juvenile's amenability to treatment or his or her threat to public safety.

prosecutor
The representative of the state in court proceedings. Also called *county's attorney, district attorney,* or *state attorney.*

Juvenile Law 14–5
Breed v. *Jones*

In 1971 the juvenile court in California filed a petition against Jones, who was then seventeen years old, alleging that he had committed an offense that, if committed by an adult, would have constituted robbery. Jones was detained pending a hearing. At the hearing, the juvenile judge took testimony, found that the allegations were true, and sustained the petition. At the dispositional hearing, Jones was found unfit for treatment in the juvenile court, and it was ordered that he be prosecuted as an adult offender. At a subsequent preliminary hearing, Jones was held for criminal trial. An information hearing was held against him for robbery, and he was tried and found guilty. Counsel objected that Jones was being subjected to double jeopardy, but the defendant was committed to the California Division of Juvenile Justice.

■ *What is double jeopardy? Why is it important for juveniles and adults in the legal process?*

Source: *Breed* v. *Jones*, 421 U.S. 519, 95 S.Ct. 1779 (1975).

Library Extra 14–2
OJJDP publication: *Juvenile Court Statistics 2000*

with counsel were more likely to receive an institutional disposition than those without counsel.[23] When it exists, there are two possible explanations for this positive relationship between counsel and punitive dispositions: First, the juvenile judge is punishing youths who choose to be represented by counsel; second, the youths who have committed more serious crimes are the ones requesting counsel and are the ones most likely to be adjudicated to training school or transferred to adult court. Although the former may have been true in the past, the latter is typically true today.

Juvenile Courts Today

The structure of the juvenile court varies from one jurisdiction to another. Special and separate juvenile courts in some urban areas devote their total effort to the legal problems of children. Juveniles in smaller cities and rural areas are often tried by judges of the adult courts. A separate statewide court exists in several states, and only juvenile judges sit on cases in the various districts of those states. In other parts of the country, juvenile offenders are handled exclusively by family court judges who hear both juvenile and domestic relations cases.

More typically, juvenile courts are part of a circuit, district, county, superior, common pleas, probate, or municipal court. This broad-based trial court may be either the highest court of general trial jurisdiction or the lower trial court in which lesser criminal and limited-claim civil matters are heard.

Nationally, juvenile courts today are affected by a movement toward a single trial court, inclusive of all courts in which initial trials take place. For example, in a massive court reorganization in Cook County, Illinois, 208 courts became the circuit court for Cook County. The juvenile court of the District of Columbia was absorbed into the new single-trial court for the District.

A variety of personnel serve the juvenile court (Table 14–1). These include the judge, who heads up the court; the defense attorney and the prosecutor, who, respectively, defends the client and tries the case; referees, who are assistants to the judge; probation officers, who investigate and supervise cases; and the nonjudicial support personnel, who do everything from providing client services to keeping the court running smoothly. The numbers and qualifications of these persons vary widely from court to court.[24]

The Judge

Juvenile court judges have an enormously important and difficult job. The most traditional role of the juvenile court judge is to decide the legal issues that appear before the court. The judge must determine, according to Leonard P. Edwards, "whether certain facts are true, whether a child should be removed from a parent, what types of services should be offered to the family and whether the child should be returned to the family and the community or placed permanently in another setting."[25]

TABLE 14–1
Personnel in Juvenile Court

Personnel	Role
Juvenile judge	Most important role is to decide the legal issues that appear before the court.
Referee	Some states use these individuals as primary hearing officers, while disposition, if necessary, is left to the judge.
Defense attorney	Can be an adversarial advocate for the child, a surrogate guardian or parent to the child, and an assistant to the court with responsibilities to the children.
Prosecutor	Is expected to protect society, but, at the same time, to ensure that children appearing before the court receive their constitutional rights.
Probation officer	Acts as intake officer, assesses the needs of children, writes reports, and supervises youth.
Nonjudicial support personnel	These include volunteers, staff from agencies providing services to the court, and paid workers who perform routine administrative functions.

The juvenile court judge also has the following responsibilities:

1. To set juvenile justice standards within the community and within the criminal and juvenile justice systems

2. To make certain that juveniles appearing before the court receive the legal and constitutional rights to which they are entitled

3. To ensure that the systems that detect, investigate, resolve, and bring cases to court are working fairly and efficiently

4. To make certain that there are an adequate number of attorneys of satisfactory quality to represent juveniles in court

5. To know how cases that do not reach the juvenile court are being resolved

6. To monitor the progress of the child, the family, and the supervisory agency to make certain that each complies with the terms of the court's orders

7. To be an advocate within the community on behalf of children and their families

8. In some communities, to oversee the juvenile probation department and court staff.[26]

Juvenile judges are chosen by a variety of methods. In some states, the governor appoints candidates chosen by a screening board. In other states, judges are chosen through partisan elections, and in still other states, judges run for office without party affiliation. The legislature appoints judges in a few states. A dozen states have adopted the **Missouri Plan**, which involves (1) a commission being appointed to nominate candidates for judge vacancies; (2) an elected official, generally the governor, making judicial appointments from the list submitted by the commission; and (3) nonpartisan and uncontested elections being held (usually every three years) to give incumbent judges an opportunity to run on their records.[27]

Juvenile judges wield considerable power and, not surprisingly, a few do abuse their power as they become despots or dictators in "their courts," and some, as recently happened in Pennsylvania, engage in extreme corruption.[28] But many juvenile judges rise to the challenge and do a remarkable job. They scrupulously observe procedural safeguards and due process rights for juveniles. They are always seeking better means of detention and reserve the use of training schools as a last resort. They are extremely committed to the work of the juvenile court and sometimes even pass up promotions to more highly paid judgeships with greater prestige. The end result is that these judges change the quality of juvenile justice in their jurisdictions.

Missouri Plan
Adopted by a dozen states, this plan involves a commission being appointed to nominate candidates for judge vacancies.

The **National Council of Juvenile and Family Court Judges**, located in Reno, Nevada, has done much to upgrade the juvenile court judiciary. This organization has sponsored research and continuing legal education efforts. It also maintains a research facility, the National Center for Juvenile Justice, in Pittsburgh, Pennsylvania. The council publishes quarterly the *Juvenile and Family Journal*; monthly, the *Juvenile and Family Law Digest*; and eight times per year, the *Juvenile and Family Court Newsletter*.

The Referee

Juvenile courts frequently employ the services of a referee, who may or may not be a member of the bar. In the state of Washington, a referee is called a *commissioner*; in Maryland, a *master*. California uses both referees and commissioners. Although a number of states use only judges in the juvenile court, other states use referees, masters, and commissioners as the primary hearing officers. All perform similar functions for the courts.

Referees generally have a fundamental grasp of juvenile law, some basic understanding of psychology and sociology, and even some experience or training in social work. In some courts, referees hear cases at the fact-finding and detention hearings and may even adjudicate cases at the discretion of the judge. If a judicial disposition is necessary, it usually is left to the juvenile judge. The use of referees appears to be on the increase in some urban areas where the caseload pressures are great.

The Defense Attorney

Defense attorneys, or *respondents*, have been part of the juvenile court structure ever since the *Gault* decision stated that juveniles have the right to be represented by an attorney. Whether they are public defenders, court-appointed attorneys, or privately retained attorneys, defense attorneys presently play an increasingly important role in juvenile trials.[29] Yet, Barry C. Feld found that nearly half of the juveniles who appeared before the juvenile courts for delinquency and status offense referrals in Minnesota, Nebraska, and North Dakota were not represented by counsel. Equally serious, Feld found that many of the juveniles who were placed out of their homes in these states also did not have counsel.[30]

Defense attorneys typically have at least three roles from which to choose. They can be (1) an adversarial advocate for the child, (2) a surrogate guardian or parent to the child, or (3) an assistant to the court with responsibilities to the children.[31] Defense attorneys from public defenders' offices tend to do a better job of representing the rights of youth than do private and court-appointed counsel, primarily because public defenders appear in juvenile court day after day, thereby gaining valuable experience, whereas private attorneys appear only occasionally. Other studies have not found juveniles to be penalized or to fare worse in juvenile courts because they were represented by counsel.[32]

guardian ad litem
A lawyer who is appointed by the court to take care of youths who need help, especially in neglect, dependency, and abuse cases, but also occasionally in delinquency cases.

A **guardian ad litem** is usually a lawyer who is appointed by the court to take care of youths who need help, especially in neglect, dependency, and abuse cases, but also occasionally in delinquency cases. In delinquency cases, a *guardian ad litem* may be appointed if there is a question of a need for a particular treatment intervention, such as placement in a mental health center, and the offender and her or his attorney are resisting placement.[33]

The Prosecutor

The prosecutor, or *petitioner*, is expected to protect society and, at the same time, to ensure that children appearing before the court are provided with their basic constitutional rights. In urban courts, prosecutors typically are involved in every stage of the proceedings, from intake and detention through disposition. Prosecutors are particularly involved before the adjudication stage because witnesses must be interviewed, police investigations must be checked out, and court rules and case decisions must be researched. Prosecutors also play a role in detention decisions and represent the local or state government in all pretrial motions, probable-cause hearings, and consent decrees. Prosecutors are especially involved in deciding whether juveniles should be waived to the adult court or kept in the juvenile court. In states in which certain offenses are excluded from juvenile court jurisdiction, prosecutors may send juveniles who commit those offenses to the adult court. Prosecutors further represent the county or state at the adjudication hearing and at the disposition of the case. In some urban courts, prosecutors may be involved in plea bargaining with the defense counsel. Prosecutors in some states are permitted to initiate appeals for the limited purpose of clarifying a given law or procedure. Moreover, prosecutors represent the state or county on appeals and in *habeas corpus* proceedings. Some critics contend that the prosecutor in some juvenile courts has come to dominate juvenile court proceedings.[34]

The Probation Officer

Probation officers have some of the most demanding jobs of any court personnel, because their functions involve developing interfaces between the probation department and community agencies that service children, and managing cases from intake through aftercare. Probation officers act as intake officers, assess the needs of youths, write reports such as predisposition reports, and supervise youths in both probation and aftercare in some jurisdictions. The officer may be given an intensive probation caseload, may be responsible for youths who are on house arrest and are monitored with electronic equipment, or may be charged with intake or secure-detention responsibilities. In addition, the probation officer is expected to be a treatment agent as well as an agent of social control.[35]

Probation officers appear to have four different orientations to their clients. First, probation officers oriented to the enforcer role perceive themselves as enforcement officers who are charged with regulating juvenile behavior. Second, probation officers oriented to the detector role attempt to identify problematic juveniles in advance on the basis of previous rule infractions. Third, probation officers oriented to the broker role refer juveniles to appropriate community services and programs—a common practice today. Finally, probation officers oriented to the educator, mediator, and enabler role are more likely to instruct and assist youthful offenders in dealing with the problems that impede their successful adjustment to the community.[36] Many of these probation officers have undergraduate backgrounds in sociology, psychology, and social work. Numerous other probation officers with these backgrounds go on to get master's degrees in social work or criminal justice to further their careers in the criminal justice system.

probation officer
An officer of the court who is expected to provide social history investigations, supervise individuals who have been placed on probation, maintain case files, advise probationers on the conditions of their probation, and perform any other probationary services that the judge may request. Probation officers also inform the court when persons on probation have violated the terms of their probation.

Nonjudicial Support Personnel

Nonjudicial support personnel include volunteers, staff from agencies providing services to the court, and paid workers who perform routine administrative functions. Personnel from social service agencies also frequent the court as they make contact with youths and their families, but they have the job of writing reports to the courts summarizing the characteristics of youths as well as the progress youths are making. Finally, the court employs secretaries, clerks, bailiffs, legal researchers, and court administrators to perform the routine but necessary tasks of processing youths through the system.

Pretrial Procedures

The types of cases that are under the jurisdiction of the juvenile court vary widely among and even within states, but they generally include those involving delinquency, neglect, and dependency. In 2008, juvenile courts handled an estimated 1,653,000 delinquency cases. Between 1960 and 2008, juvenile court delinquency caseloads increased more than 300 percent.[37] Juvenile courts also may deal with cases involving adoption, termination of parental rights, appointment of guardians for minors, custody, contributing to delinquency or neglect, and nonsupport.

Pretrial procedures in the juvenile justice system (Figure 14–3) include the detention hearing, the intake process, and the transfer procedure, all of which take place before the adjudication stage of juvenile court proceedings.

Detention Hearing

Legislative acts that govern the juvenile court normally require that the police either take a youth to an intake officer of the court or a detention facility or release the youth to his or her parents. At a **detention hearing**, the criteria for detention are based on the need to

detention hearing
A hearing, usually conducted by an intake officer of the juvenile court, during which the decision is made as to whether a juvenile will be released to his or her parents or guardians or be detained in a detention facility.

FIGURE 14–3
Pretrial Processes

Procedure	Description
Detention Hearing	The criteria for detention are based on the need to protect the youth and to ensure public safety. This decision is usually made within 48 to 72 hours.
Intake Process	This is a preliminary screening process to determine whether a court should take place (and, if so, what action), or whether the matter should be referred elsewhere.
Transfer Procedure	All state legislatures have passed laws permitting juveniles to be transferred to adult court. Judicial waiver and legislative waiver are the two basic mechanisms for transferring youthful offenders to the adult court.

detention center
A facility that provides custodial care for juveniles during juvenile court proceedings. Also called juvenile halls and detention homes, detention centers were established at the end of the nineteenth century as an alternative to jails for juveniles.

shelter care
A facility that is used primarily to provide short-term care for status offenders and for dependent or neglected youths.

jail
A police lockup or county holding facility for adult offenders. Jails have few services to offer juveniles.

home detention
House arrest. This form of detention is used in some jurisdictions, and an adjudicated juvenile remains at home under the supervision of juvenile probation officers.

attention home
An innovative form of detention facility, found in several locations across the nation, that is characterized by an open setting.

bail
The money or property pledged to the court or actually deposited with the court to effect the release of a person from legal custody. Juveniles do not have a constitutional right to bail as do adults.

protect the youth and to ensure public safety. The decision to detain must be made within a short period of time, usually 48 to 72 hours, excluding weekends and holidays. Urban courts, which have intake units on duty 24 hours a day for detention hearings, frequently act within a few hours.[38]

In some states, intake officers of the juvenile court, rather than juvenile judges, conduct detention hearings. Such a procedure represents a progressive move because having the same judge preside over both the detention hearing and the adjudication hearing is a poor practice. Some states still require that the juvenile judge be responsible for the policies and operations of the detention facility; juvenile judges also are usually required to decide whether a youth who was admitted to detention a few days earlier must remain locked up to preclude inappropriate or overly long detention.

In 2008, the offense profile of detained delinquency cases was as follows: drug-law violations, 11 percent; person cases, 26 percent; public-order cases, 28 percent; and property cases, 35 percent.[39] Juveniles who are held in detention may be assigned to one of several different types of placements. The **detention center** (detention hall or detention home) physically restricts youths for a short period, whereas **shelter care** is physically nonrestrictive and is available for those who have no homes or who require juvenile court intervention. A third type of placement is **jail** or police lockup. A fourth is **home detention**; in-home detention restricts a juvenile to his or her home and is normally supervised by a paraprofessional staff member. Finally, **attention homes** offer services and staff support in a nonrestrictive setting.

Five states have legislated a hearing on probable cause for detained youths, and appellate cases in other states have moved in the direction of mandating a probable cause hearing to justify further detention. Courts in Alaska and Georgia have ruled that a youth is entitled to counsel at a detention hearing and to free counsel if the youth is indigent. The supreme courts of Alaska and California and an appellate court in Pennsylvania all have overturned cases in which no reason or inadequate reason was stated for continuing detention. Finally, courts in Baltimore, the District of Columbia, and Nevada have ruled that a juvenile who is in detention is entitled to humane care. The appeals court in the District of Columbia stated that there is a statutory obligation to provide a juvenile with care "as nearly as possible equivalent to that which should have been given him by his parents."[40]

Court decisions have differed concerning **bail** for a juvenile. Decisions have found that juveniles have a constitutional right to bail; that juvenile act procedures, when applied in a manner consistent with due process, provide an adequate substitute for bail; or that juveniles do not have a constitutional right to bail. Nine states (Arkansas, Colorado, Connecticut, Georgia, Massachusetts, Nebraska, Oklahoma, South Dakota, and West Virginia) have enacted laws granting juveniles the right to bail; on the other hand, Hawaii, Kentucky, Oregon, and Utah deny juveniles the right to bail.

The U.S. Supreme Court decision in the *Schall* v. *Martin* (1984) case represents an example of a fundamental change that seems to be occurring in detention practices.[41] The plaintiffs originally filed a lawsuit in federal district court claiming that the New York Family Court Act was unconstitutional because it allowed for the preventive detention of juveniles:

> The District Court struck down the statute as permitting detention without due process and ordered the release of all class members. The Court of Appeals affirmed, holding . . . the statute is administered not for preventive purposes, but to impose punishment for unadjudicated criminal acts, and that therefore the statute is unconstitutional.[42]

The Supreme Court, however, reversed the decision of the appeals court. Justice William H. Rehnquist, in writing the opinion for the majority, declared that the "preventive detention under the statute serves the legitimate state objective held in common with every State, of protecting both the juvenile and the society from the hazards of pretrial crime."[43] Some experts believe that the Court's ruling may encourage a significant expansion of preventive, or secure, detention for juveniles.

Intake Process

Intake essentially is a preliminary screening process to determine whether a court should take action—and if so, what action—or whether the matter should be referred elsewhere. Larger courts usually handle this function through a specialized intake unit, and probation officers or other officers of the court screen incoming cases in smaller courts.[44]

Between 1985 and 2008, the likelihood that a delinquency case would be handled informally decreased. The largest increases of petitioned cases between 1985 and 2008 were seen in drug cases (221 percent) followed by public-order cases (189 percent) and person offenses cases (137 percent). Table 14–2 shows the offense profile of delinquency cases for 2008.

Intake procedures follow **complaints** to authorities against youths. Juvenile law varies from state to state regarding who is permitted to sign such a complaint. Typically, most complaints are filed by the police, although they may be initiated and signed by a victim or by the youth's parents. In some states, parents, victims, probation staff, social services staff, neighbors, or anyone else may go directly to the court to file a complaint. Complaints also may be brought by school officials and truant officers.

After the intake officer receives the complaint, he or she must first decide whether the court has statutory jurisdiction. If the statutory guides are unclear, the intake officer should seek the advice of the prosecuting attorney. Once legal jurisdiction has been established, the second step is to conduct a preliminary interview and investigation to determine whether the case should be adjudicated nonjudicially or petitioned to the court. This evaluation procedure varies from jurisdiction to jurisdiction, principally because so many juvenile courts have failed to provide written guidelines, so the intake officer usually has broad and largely unregulated discretion in making the intake decision.

▲ A juvenile makes an appearance before a judge with an attorney at her side.
■ **What is the role of juvenile defense counsel?**

– intake
The first stage of juvenile court proceedings, in which the decision is made whether to divert the juvenile being referred or to file a formal petition in juvenile court.

– complaint
A charge made to an intake officer of the juvenile court that an offense has been committed.

TABLE 14–2
Offense Profile of Delinquency Cases, 2008

Most Serious Offense	Nonpetitioned	Petitioned
Person	23%	26%
Property	40	35
Drugs	10	11
Public order	27	28

Note: Details may not total 100% because of rounding.

Source: Charles Puzzanchera and Melissa Sickmund, *Juvenile Court Statistics 2008* (Pittsburgh, PA. National Center for Juvenile Justice, 2011), p. 36.

Options for the Disposal of Cases

The intake unit, especially in larger urban courts, may have up to five options for the disposal of cases: (1) outright dismissal of the complaint, (2) informal adjustment (chiefly diversion to a nonjudicial agency), (3) informal probation, (4) consent decree, and (5) filing of a petition.

Outright dismissal of the complaint takes place when legal jurisdiction does not exist or when the case is so weak that the intake officer questions the feasibility of petitioning the youth to the juvenile court. **Informal adjustment** means that the intake officer requires restitution from the youth, warns him or her, and then dismisses the case or diverts the youth to a social services agency. The diversion agency supervises such referrals and generally reports to the intake unit on the youth's progress; status offenders and juveniles charged with minor offenses typically are dealt with under this option.

Informal probation, which has been under increased criticism since the 1970s, involves the casual supervision of a youth by a volunteer or probation officer who reserves judgment on the need for filing a petition until the intake officer (or other designated person) sees how the youth fares during the informal probation period. See Juvenile Law 14–6 for more information on informal sanctions.

A **consent decree** is a formal agreement between the youth and the court in which he or she is placed under the court's supervision without a formal finding of delinquency. Consent decrees provide an intermediate step between informal handling and probation; the consent decree is used less often than the other options that are currently open to the intake officer. The consent decree, it should be noted, comes after the petition but before the adjudication hearing.

If none of these options is satisfactory, the intake officer can choose to file a petition. Unfortunately, the broad discretionary power given intake workers has often been abused. For example, Duran Bell, Jr., and Kevin Lang's study of intake in Los Angeles County revealed the importance of extralegal factors, especially cooperative behavior, in reducing the length of detention and the effect of age in increasing the length of detention.[45]

Research is needed to determine which approach to intake will result in the greatest services to youths and the least misuse of discretion, but until a systematic examination of the intake process is done, the principles of being fair and of doing the least harm possible to youths should guide the intake screening process.

Transfer Procedure

All state legislatures have passed laws permitting juveniles to be transferred to **adult court** (Table 14–3). **Judicial waiver**, the most widely used transfer mechanism, involves the actual decision-making process that begins when the juvenile is brought to intake. Predictably,

---

informal adjustment
An attempt to handle a youthful offender outside of the formal structures of the juvenile justice system.

informal probation
An arrangement in which, instead of being adjudicated as a delinquent and placed on probation, a youth is informally assigned to the supervision of a probation officer.

consent decree
A formal agreement between a juvenile and the court in which the juvenile is placed under the court's supervision without a formal finding of delinquency.

adult court
Criminal courts that hear the cases of adults charged with crimes and to which juveniles who are accused of having committed serious offenses can be waived (transferred). In some states, adult criminal courts have jurisdiction over juveniles who are accused of committing certain specified offenses.

judicial waiver
The procedure of relinquishing the processing of a particular juvenile case to adult criminal court; also known as certifying or binding over to the adult court.

Juvenile Law 14–6
Informal Sanctions

Informal processing is considered when decision makers (police, intake workers, probation officers, prosecutors, or other screening officers) believe that accountability and rehabilitation can be achieved without the use of formal court intervention.

Informal sanctions are voluntary; consequently, the court cannot force a juvenile to comply with an informal disposition. If the court decides to handle the matter informally (in lieu of formal prosecution), a youthful offender agrees to comply with one or more sanctions such as voluntary probation supervision, community service, and/or victim restitution. In some jurisdictions, before juveniles are offered informal sanctions, they must agree that they committed the alleged act.

When informally handled, the case is usually held open pending the successful completion of the informal disposition. Upon successful completion of these arrangements, the charges

against the offender are dismissed. But if the offender does not fulfill the court's conditions for informal handling, the case is likely to be reopened and formally prosecuted.

Informal handling is less common than in the past but is still used in a large number of cases. According to *Juvenile Court Statistics 2001–2002*, 42 percent of delinquency cases disposed in 2002 were handled informally, compared with more than half in 1987.

■ *What is your opinion of informal sanctions? What do you see as their strengths and weaknesses?*

Source: Howard N. Snyder and Melissa Sickmund, *Juvenile Offenders and Victims: 2006 National Report* (Washington, D.C.: National Center for Juvenile Justice, Office of Juvenile Justice and Delinquency Prevention, 2006).

TABLE 14–3
Juvenile Transfer Procedures by State

Most states have multiple ways to impose adult sanctions on offenders of juvenile age

State	Judicial waiver			Prosecutorial discretion	Statutory exclusion	Reverse waiver	Once an adult always an adult	Blended sentencing	
	Discretionary	Presumptive	Mandatory					Juvenile	Criminal
Number of states	45	15	15	15	29	24	34	14	18
Alabama	■				■		■		
Alaska	■	■			■			■	
Arizona	■			■		■	■		
Arkansas	■			■		■			■
California	■	■		■	■	■	■		■
Colorado	■	■		■				■	■
Connecticut			■					■	
Delaware	■		■		■	■	■		
Dist. of Columbia	■	■		■			■		
Florida	■			■	■		■		■
Georgia	■		■	■	■		■		
Hawaii	■						■		
Idaho	■				■		■		■
Illinois	■	■	■		■		■	■	■
Indiana	■		■		■		■		
Iowa	■				■	■	■		■
Kansas	■	■					■	■	
Kentucky	■		■			■			■
Louisiana	■			■	■		■		
Maine	■	■					■		
Maryland	■				■	■	■		
Massachusetts					■			■	■
Michigan	■			■			■	■	■
Minnesota	■	■			■		■	■	
Mississippi	■				■	■	■		
Missouri	■				■		■		■
Montana				■	■	■		■	
Nebraska				■		■			■
Nevada	■	■			■	■			
New Hampshire	■	■					■		
New Jersey	■	■	■						
New Mexico					■			■	■
New York					■	■			
North Carolina	■		■				■		
North Dakota	■	■	■				■		
Ohio	■		■				■	■	
Oklahoma	■			■	■	■	■		■
Oregon	■				■	■	■		
Pennsylvania	■	■			■	■	■		

(Continued)

TABLE 14–3 (Continued)
Juvenile Transfer Procedures by State

Most states have multiple ways to impose adult sanctions on offenders of juvenile age

State	Judicial waiver			Prosecutorial discretion	Statutory exclusion	Reverse waiver	Once an adult always an adult	Blended sentencing	
	Discretionary	Presumptive	Mandatory					Juvenile	Criminal
Rhode Island	■	■	■				■	■	
South Carolina	■		■		■				
South Dakota	■				■	■	■		
Tennessee	■					■	■		
Texas	■						■	■	
Utah	■	■					■		
Vermont	■			■	■	■			■
Virginia	■		■			■	■		■
Washington	■				■		■		
West Virginia	■		■						■
Wisconsin	■				■	■	■		■
Wyoming	■			■		■			

Note: Table information is as of the end of the 2009 legislative session.

Source: Patrick Griffin, Sean Addie, Benjamin Adams, and Kathy Finestine, *Trying Juveniles as Adults: An Analysis of State Transfer Laws and Reporting* (Washington, D.C.: Juvenile Offenders and Victims, National Report Series Bulletin, September 2011), p. 3.

the mechanisms used vary by state. For every one thousand petitioned delinquency cases, about nine are judicially waived to criminal court.[46] In some states, intake personnel, juvenile prosecutors, or judges make the decision based, in part, on the age or offense criteria. In other states, a court other than the juvenile court makes the decision. For example, the prosecutor or judge in the adult court may decide where a juvenile is to be tried.[47] The decision is determined by the requirements of the state and the way the intake officer, prosecutor, or judge interprets the youth's background. Typically, the criteria used include the age and maturity of the child; the child's relationship with parents, school, and community; whether the child is considered dangerous; and whether court officials believe that the child may be helped by juvenile court services.

Prosecutorial Discretion

Prosecutorial discretion occurs in states with concurrent jurisdiction statutes. These laws give prosecutors the authority to decide whether to try juveniles in either juvenile or adult court. Table 14–4 reveals that some states allow prosecutors to file certain categories of cases in juvenile or criminal court. Age is one factor taken into consideration by the states in setting up these statutes. It also indicates that three states, Florida, Nebraska, and Vermont, permit charges to be filed in either juvenile or adult court for any criminal offense, but most states specifically mention in their juvenile codes precisely which offenses may be tried in either court.

Statutory Exclusion

statutory exclusions
A legislative mandate which requires that juveniles accused of committing certain designated offenses be tried in adult criminal court.

Some states have a **statutory exclusion** of certain offenses from juvenile court, thereby automatically transferring perpetrators of those offenses to adult court. Table 14–5 shows that the states that exclude offenses from juvenile court primarily focus on "safety" crimes such as murder and other offenses against a person. The statutes also, however, spell out the minimum age that youths must reach before they may be transferred to adult court.

TABLE 14–4
Prosecutorial Discretion in Juvenile Cases by State and Offense

Some states allow prosecutors to file certain categories of cases in juvenile or criminal court.

State	Any criminal offense	Certain felonies	Capital crimes	Murder	Certain persons offenses	Certain property offenses	Certain drug offenses	Certain weapon offenses
Arizona		14						
Arkansas		16	14	14	14			
California		14	14	14	14	14	14	
Colorado		14		14	14	14		
Dist. of Columbia				16	16	16		
Florida	16	16	NS	14	14	14		14
Georgia			NS					
Louisiana				15	15	15	15	
Michigan		14		14	14	14	14	
Montana				12	12	16	16	16
Nebraska	16	NS						
Oklahoma		16		15	15	15	16	15
Vermont	16							
Virginia				14	14			
Wyoming	13	14		14	14	14		

Notes: An entry in the column below an offense category means that there is at least one offense in that category that is subjected to criminal prosecution at the option of the prosecutor. The number indicates the youngest possible age at which a juvenile accused of an offense in that category is subjected to criminal prosecution. "NS" means no age restriction is specified for an offense in that category. Table information is as of the end of the 2009 legislative session.

Source: Patrick Griffin, Sean Addie, Benjamin Adams, and Kathy Finestine, *Trying Juveniles as Adults: An Analysis of State Transfer Laws and Reporting* (Washington, D.C.: Juvenile Offenders and Victims, National Report Series Bulletin, September 2011), p. 6.

Other variations on waiver also exist, some very subtle. One such variation is a state legislature lowering the age over which the juvenile court has jurisdiction. For example, if a state's age of juvenile court jurisdiction is eighteen, the legislature may lower the age to sixteen. This approach focuses entirely on the age of the juvenile but ignores the offenses committed.

Yet other state legislatures have specified that juveniles of specific ages who commit specific crimes are to be tried in adult court. For example, until recently, Indiana statutes stated that any child age 10 or older who committed murder would be tried as an adult. This method of legislative waiver focuses as much on the offense as it does on the age of the offender.

Another method of waiver is one in which the statutes simply state that anyone who commits a specific crime may be tried in adult court. No reference is made to the age of the offender. This approach is attractive to those who believe that any youth who violates the law should receive punishment proportionate to the harm that he or she has caused.

Reverse Waiver and Blended Sentencing

In *reverse waiver*, some state laws permit youths who are over the maximum age of jurisdiction to be sent back to the juvenile court if the adult court believes the case is more appropriate for juvenile court jurisdiction. For a reverse waiver, defense counsel and prosecutors attempt to make their case for their desired action. Some evidence and testimony are allowed, and arguments are presented. When each side has had a chance to present its case and to rebut the opponents' arguments, the judge makes the decision.[48]

A *blended sentence* is a sentence imposed by a juvenile court that blends a juvenile disposition and an adult sentence for certain serious youthful offenders. Some states permit juvenile court judges at the disposition hearing in the delinquency court to impose both an adult and a juvenile sentence concurrently. This option may be given to juveniles who have

TABLE 14–5
Statutory Exclusion by Age and State

Many states exclude certain serious offenses from juvenile court jurisdiction

State	Any criminal offense	Certain felonies	Capital crimes	Murder	Certain person offenses	Certain property offenses	Certain drug offenses	Certain weapon offenses
Alabama		16	16				16	
Alaska					16	16		
Arizona		15		15	15			
California				14	14			
Delaware		15						
Florida				16	NS	16	16	
Georgia				13	13			
Idaho				14	14	14	14	
Illinois		15		13	15			15
Indiana		16		16	16		16	16
Iowa		16					16	16
Louisiana				15	15			
Maryland			14	16	16			16
Massachusetts				14				
Minnesota				16				
Mississippi		13	13					
Montana				17	17	17	17	17
Nevada	16*	NS		NS	16			
New Mexico				15				
New York				13	13	14		14
Oklahoma				13				
Oregon				15	15			
Pennsylvania				NS	15			
South Carolina		16						
South Dakota		16						
Utah		16		16				
Vermont				14	14	14		
Washington				16	16	16		
Wisconsin				10	10			

*In Nevada, the exclusion applies to any juvenile with a previous felony adjudication, regardless of the current offense charged, if the current offense involves the use or threatened use of a firearm.

Notes: An entry in the column below an offense category means that there is at least one offense In that category that is excluded from juvenile court jurisdiction. The number indicates the youngest possible age at which a juvenile accused of an offense in that category is subject to exclusion. Ns" means no age restriction is specified for an offense in that category. Table Information is as of the end of the 2009 legislative session.

Source: Patrick Griffin, Sean Addie, Benjamin Adams, and Kathy Finestine, *Trying Juveniles as Adults: An Analysis of State Transfer Laws and Reporting* (Washington, D.C.: Juvenile Offenders and Victims, National Report Series Bulletin, September 2011), p. 6.

received a direct file, mandatory or a prosecutorial waiver, to the adult court. In these cases, the juvenile is given both sentences but is first given the juvenile disposition. If the juvenile fulfills the requirements of this disposition satisfactorily, the adult disposition is suspended. If the juvenile does not fulfill the conditions of the juvenile disposition, the juvenile is then required to fulfill conditions of the adult disposition. Connecticut, Kentucky, and Minnesota are among the states adopting this sentencing authority.

In some states, the juvenile may be required to fulfill the juvenile disposition until he or she reaches the age of majority; at this point, the juvenile must begin to fulfill the adult sentence minus the time already spent fulfilling the juvenile disposition. In Texas, the juvenile court may impose a juvenile sanction that extends beyond the extended age of juvenile court jurisdiction, at which time the transfer of the youthful offender to an adult correctional facility is required. Under this form of expanded sentencing authority, the juvenile court judge or jury can impose a sentence of up to thirty years, depending on the seriousness of the offense. Legislation in 1995 added several offenses for which a juvenile may receive a determinate, fixed term of forty years.[49] See Figure 14–4 for the types of blended sentencing.

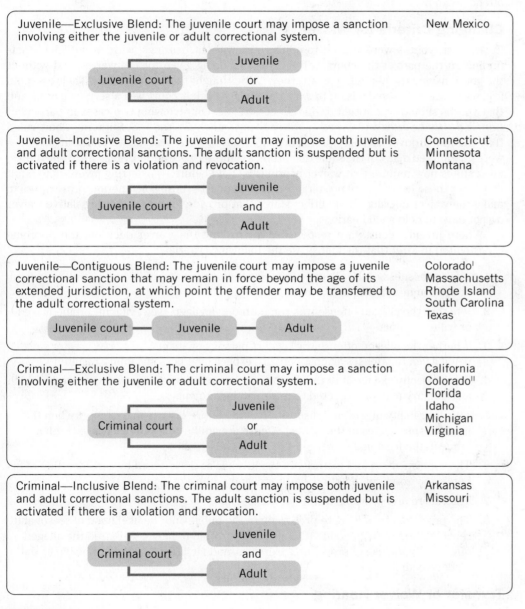

FIGURE 14–4
Blended Sentencing Options in Juvenile Cases

Note: Blends apply to a subset of juveniles specified by state statute.
I Applies to those designated as "aggravated juvenile offenders."
II Applies to those designated as "youthful offenders."

Source: Adapted from Office of Juvenile Justice and Delinquency Prevention, *1999 National Report Series* (Washington, D.C.: U.S. Department of Justice, 1999), p. 19.

Another common way for the adult criminal court to levy juvenile sanctions is through the creation of youthful offender programs. Otherwise known as "intermediate" or "third systems," these systems provide a mechanism that allows states to impose strict, adult sanctions on juveniles or young adults convicted of violent offenses, while maintaining a rehabilitation focus.

Since Colorado enacted the first program of this type, at least eleven other states have followed suit. These youthful offender-type programs are viewed in these states as one last chance before being sent to an adult facility.[50] See the discussion later on these youthful offender camps.

Changing Criteria for Waiver

In the past, youths were waived to adult court without hearings, without sufficient fact-finding on the part of the court, without reasons being given for the waiver, and without the youth having the benefit of an attorney. Critics fought these procedures. Their essential argument was that the decision to waive juveniles to adult court was a serious matter and that youths should be entitled to due process rights. On reviewing two cases in particular, *Kent* v. *United States* and *Breed* v. *Jones* (see Chapter 5), the U.S. Supreme Court ruled that traditional juvenile court procedures for waiver were inadequate and that juveniles were guaranteed many of the same due process rights as were adults. Since *Kent* and *Jones*, most states now require that waiver hearings be held before transferring juveniles to adult court. Yet these hearings are not required in all states, because some permit prosecutors to make the waiver decision. In addition, states that provide for mandatory legislative waiver do not have to hold such hearings.

Where juvenile courts are responsible for making the waiver decision, the Supreme Court stated in *Kent* that they must use the following criteria:

1. The seriousness of the alleged offense to the community and whether the protection of the community requires waiver
2. Whether the alleged offense was committed in an aggressive, violent, premeditated, or willful manner
3. Whether the alleged offense was against persons or against property, greater weight being given to offenses against persons, especially if personal injury resulted
4. The prosecutorial merit of the complaint, that is, whether there is evidence on which a grand jury may be expected to return an indictment
5. The desirability of trial and disposition of the entire offense in one court when the juvenile's associates in the alleged offense are adults who will be charged with a crime in the [criminal court]
6. The sophistication and maturity of the juvenile as determined by consideration of his home, environment, emotional attitude, and pattern of living
7. The record and previous history of the juvenile
8. The prospects for adequate protection of the public and the likelihood of reasonable rehabilitation of the juvenile (if he [or she] is found to have committed the alleged offense) by the use of procedures, services, and facilities currently available to the juvenile court.[51]

Transfer or Waiver Hearing

Once a prosecutor has decided that a juvenile is beyond the help of the juvenile court and has reviewed the legal sufficiency of the case, the prosecutor files a motion to send the youth to adult court; this motion requires a probable-cause hearing by juvenile judge. These hearings are required for both a mandatory judicial waiver and a discretionary judicial waiver. The judge begins either hearing by explaining the nature of the hearing and making certain that the youth and his or her parents understand the youth's rights and the consequences of the outcome. All interested parties should be present at this hearing.[52]

In the probable-cause hearing, everything said should be under oath. The prosecutor presents the state's case against the juvenile, affirming the identity of the juvenile and of witnesses and reviewing the affidavit, petition, and jurisdiction requirements—both of the age of the offender and of the geographical region from which the offender comes. The defense attorney then challenges the evidence of the prosecutor and may present witnesses; both the prosecutor and the defense attorney cross-examine the witnesses on the legal facts of the case. Both attorneys then summarize their cases at the conclusion of testimony.[53]

If the judge believes that probable cause has been established, he or she then determines whether the case satisfies the state's legally sufficient requirements for mandatory judicial waiver. If it does, the youth is transferred to criminal court. If probable cause is not established and the prosecutor's motion is denied, the National Council of Juvenile and Family Court Judges recommends the dismissal of the case. Some courts, in practice, refer the youth back to the probation department.[54]

In the judge's review of the case, the youth's dangerousness to self and others, the youth's sophistication and maturity in understanding the nature and consequences of his or her behavior, and the youth's amenability to further treatment are all evaluated. Whether to waive or retain also is based on whether the youth had a history of violent crimes, was a gang member, tested antisocial, had co-offenders, engaged in premeditated offenses, and had experienced trauma in childhood and adolescence. Very important is the availability of alternative treatments, including out-of-state placements. The youth's attorney plays a critical role in helping to evaluate the youth and in presenting alternatives that can benefit the youth. The judge must decide, if the youth is in detention, whether to continue detention or release the youth. The decision the judge finally makes should be based on clear and convincing evidence.[55]

Waiver to Criminal Court

Once the waiver decision is made, the juvenile's case is transferred to the adult court prosecutor. Prosecutors in some states may decide to send the case back to the juvenile court because the case may not meet the standards of legal sufficiency, such as probable cause. The prosecutor may confer with a judge about any legal questions the prosecutor believes the judge might have about the case before making a decision. In some states, the prosecutor takes the case to a grand jury; in other states, the prosecutor sets a date for an arraignment. There, the legal process starts all over again with the same people present, with the result that some juveniles are put on informal or formal probation and the others tried in adult court. The case now usually is tried in front of a jury, and the youth has the potential of receiving the same sentence as an adult.[56]

Evaluation of Waiver

Although waivers are still relatively infrequent, they are an important issue in juvenile justice. Significantly, juveniles waived to adult court are not always the most serious and violent offenders. Examinations of waiver have found that little consensus exists today on which criteria should be used in making the waiver decision. Furthermore, although remanded youth are receiving severe penalties, waiver generally does not result in more severe penalties than juvenile offenders would have received in juvenile court.

Several states have attempted to develop a process that would identify those juveniles unfit for retention in juvenile court. For example, using such criteria as age, offense, and prior record, Minnesota has codified the transfer procedures to be followed by judges and prosecutors. Given the adult courts' massive caseload and their limited judicial experience with sentencing youths, little evidence exists that adult judges know what to do with juveniles appearing before them.

Finally, even when waiver does occur, some evidence exists that waiver may have the effect not of deterring crime by juveniles, but of increasing it.[57] Richard E. Redding summarized the recent OJJDP-funded research on juvenile transfer by saying that transferred juveniles are more likely to offend, that they have a greater likelihood of rearrest, and that the process of transfer is found to increase recidivism.[58]

▲ Scott Dyleski, age 16, appears behind a protective glass barrier in Judge David Flinn's courtroom in Martinez, California, on October 27, 2005. Dyleski was charged as an adult with first-degree murder in the death of Pamela Vitale, the wife of well-known attorney Daniel Horowitz. Convicted in 2006, he was sentenced to life in prison without possibility of parole.

■ **Are such lengthy sentences appropriate for juvenile offenders who commit crimes like Dyleski's?**

Juvenile Trial Proceedings

The trial stage of juvenile court proceedings is divided into the adjudicatory hearing, the disposition hearing, and judicial alternatives. There is usually also a (statutory) right to appeal.

Adjudicatory Hearing

—adjudication

The court process wherein a judge determines if the juvenile appearing before the court committed the act with which he or she is charged. The term *adjudicated* is analogous to convicted in the adult criminal justice system and indicates that the court concluded that the juvenile committed the act.

Adjudication is the fact-finding stage of the court's proceedings. The adjudicatory hearing usually includes the following steps: the youth's plea, the presentation of evidence by the prosecution and by the defense, the cross-examination of witnesses, and the judge's finding. The number of cases in which the juvenile was adjudicated delinquent rose steadily from 1985 to 2000, but then leveled off and began a small decline around 2008—except for property cases, which began declining in the late 1990s[59] (see Figure 14–5).

The steps followed in the adjudicatory hearing serve as protections to ensure that youths are provided with proof beyond a reasonable doubt when they are charged with an act that would constitute a crime if it had been committed by an adult and that the judge follows the rules of evidence and dismisses hearsay from the proceedings. Hearsay is dismissed because it can be unreliable or unfair, inasmuch as it cannot be held up for cross-examination. The evidence must be relevant and must contribute to the belief or disbelief of the act in question.

On the other side of the ledger, most states now spell out their procedural requirements very carefully. For example, all juveniles now have the right to a hearing, which is likely to be much more formal than in the past. Written petitions are required, and these may be amended if necessary. Hearsay is prohibited, and the case must be proved beyond

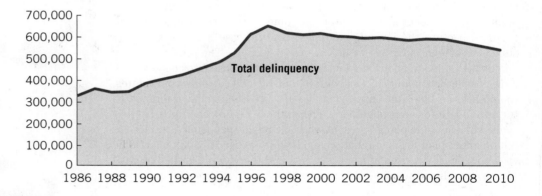

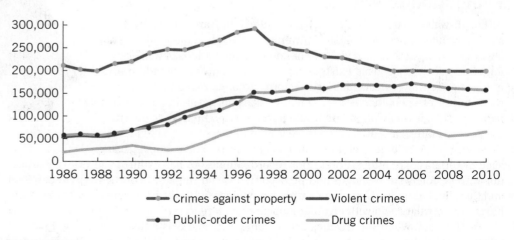

FIGURE 14–5

Adjudicated Cases in Juvenile Court

Source: Adapted from Charles Puzzanchera, Benjamin Adams, and Melissa Sickmund, *Juvenile Court Statistics 2008* (Pittsburgh, Penn.: National Center for Juvenile Justice, 2011), p. 46.

ADJUDICATORY HEARING
This is the fact-finding stage of the court's proceedings and usually includes the youth's pleas, the presentation of evidence by the prosecution and defense, the cross-examination of witnesses, and the judge's finding.

DISPOSITION HEARING
The traditional purpose is to administer individualized justice and to set in motion the rehabilitation of the delinquent. Accordingly, the judge is not limited by constitutional safeguards as much as he or she was at the adjudication hearing.

JUDICIAL ALTERNATIVES
These alternatives available to juvenile courts vary significantly from one court to another, but most courts have a variety of choices.

RIGHT TO APPEAL
Juveniles do not have a constitutional right to make an appeal of their cases to a higher judiciary, but nearly all states permit the right to appeal by statute.

FIGURE 14–6
Trial Proceedings in Juvenile Court

a reasonable doubt. Youths have the right to protect themselves against self-incrimination, and they may cross-examine witnesses and victims. Attorneys and prosecutors are likely to be present. Finally, some state codes call for a separation of the adjudication and disposition hearings.

If an attorney has not been appointed or retained by the juvenile by this point in time, one will be appointed by the court and, hopefully, the date of the hearing reset to allow the attorney time to talk with the youth, review the case, and prepare the defense. Some courts may assign a public defender to the youth, allow the defender a couple of minutes to read the documents and talk with the youth, and go immediately into the adjudication hearing. (See Figure 14–6.)

The National Council of Juvenile and Family Court Judges recommends that a script be used by the judge to ensure that the due process rights of the juvenile are maintained. These due process rights are given to the juvenile as a result of the *Kent, Gault, Winship, Breed* v. *Jones*, and *McKeiver* cases, discussed earlier in this chapter. Exhibit 14–1 is an example of a possible script.

If the youth's attorney and the prosecutor have agreed on a plea bargain, the agreement is presented to the judge at this time. If the judge accepts the plea bargain, the judge will issue a predisposition at this time, a process called a *sequential hearing*, and immediately assign a disposition in the case that will likely parallel those the juvenile may already have experienced earlier in his or her career. If the judge rejects the plea bargain, the adjudicatory hearing continues.

Prosecutors in most juvenile courts begin the adjudication proceedings by presenting the state's case. The arresting officer and witnesses at the scene of the crime testify, and any other evidence that has been legally obtained is introduced. The defense attorney then cross-examines the witnesses. Defense counsel also has the opportunity at this time to introduce evidence that is favorable to his or her client, and the youth may testify in his or her own behalf; the prosecutor then cross-examines the defense witnesses. The prosecution and the defense present summaries of the case to the judge, who reaches a finding or a verdict.

Ten states provide for a **jury trial** for juveniles, but jury trials are seldom demanded. Statutory provisions often close juvenile hearings to the general public, although this decision

jury trial
The court proceeding in which a panel of the defendant's peers evaluate evidence and render a verdict. The U.S. Supreme Court has held that juveniles do not have a constitutional right to a jury trial, but several jurisdictions permit juveniles to choose a jury trial.

Exhibit 14–1
Legal Rights of Juveniles

Juvenile Delinquency Court Judge: "I am now going to advise you of your legal rights:"

1. A petition has been filed against you, and it says that you (explain the offense).
2. Do you understand what you are charged with?
3. You have the right against self-incrimination. This means that you do not have to say anything about your part in the charges or even whether you were anywhere near where the charges happened if you do not want to. If you do choose to talk about it, what you say can be used against you. Do you have any question about what this means?
4. You have the opportunity to either admit to the charges if they are true or to deny the charges if they are not true. If you deny the charges, there will be a trial to determine whether or not the charges are true. At the trial, you have the right to:
   - Confront witnesses [who] testify against you, which means your attorney gets to ask them questions to try and show that the charges are not true. Do you have any questions about what this means?
   - Compel witnesses, which means the court can require a person who your attorney thinks can help you show [that] the charges are not true to come to court and tell what they know. However, you are not required to bring any witnesses. Do you have any questions about what this means?
   - You can choose to testify or not to testify at the trial. You can remain silent and not say anything if you want. If you decide not to testify, your choice will not be held against you. Do you have any questions about what this means?
   - If you admit the charges, or if I find you are guilty at the trial, by law I can (explain what dispositions can be imposed). Do you have any questions about what this means?

5. Do you admit or deny the charges? Are the charges true or not true?
   If the youth denies the charge, proceed to set the trial date and deal with all pretrial issues.
   If the youth admits the charges, then ask:
   - Do you understand that in saying the charges are true, you are giving up your right to a trial, which means you are also giving up your right to confront witness[es], make witness[es] testify for you, and to remain silent about the charges?
   - Has anyone made any threats or promises to you to get you to do this?
   - Have you taken any drugs, medicine, or alcohol within the last twenty-four hours? (If the youth answers yes, the judge must explore further to determine if the drug currently impairs the youth, which would mean [that] the plea should not be accepted.)
   - Are you admitting these charges to benefit yourself and nobody else?
   - At the time you did this, did you know those things were wrong?
   If the youth's answers support a plea of admit, the judge should ask the parent, custodian, or [person acting] in loco parentis whether they know of any reason that the judge should not accept the plea.

If the judge accepts the plea, the judge should call on the youth to explain what happened in detail. If the youth's explanation indicates that he or she is not really admitting to the offense, the judge should consider withdrawing the acceptance of the plea and setting the case for trial.

CRITICAL THINKING QUESTIONS

■ *How are the juvenile's due process rights protected by such a script? Do you believe that most youthful offenders appearing before the court in an adjudicatory hearing have any understanding of what the script means?*

Source: *Juvenile Delinquency Guidelines* (Reno, NV: National Council of Juvenile and Family Court Judges, 2005), Appendix.

varies from one jurisdiction to the next. The right to a speedy trial has been provided by state court decisions and by statutes that limit the amount of time that can elapse between the filing of a complaint and the actual hearing.[60]

In sum, the typical adjudication hearing has come a long way since the *In re Gault* decision. Although some judges and defense attorneys are exemplary in the support they give to the due process protection of juveniles during this stage of the court's proceedings, other judges and defense attorneys fall short in living up to either the spirit or the letter of post-*Gault* juvenile law. This is particularly true of defense attorneys who lack knowledge of juvenile court procedures or the juvenile law itself. Significantly, largely because of the changing standards for transfer to the adult court, the prosecutor has become a prominent figure at these proceedings.

Disposition Hearing

—**bifurcated hearing**
A split adjudication and disposition hearing, which is the present trend of the juvenile court.

Once a youth has been found delinquent at the adjudicatory stage, some juvenile court codes still permit judges to proceed immediately to the disposition (sentencing) hearing. However, the present trend is to hold a **bifurcated hearing**, or a split adjudicatory and dispositional hearing, because a split hearing gives the probation officer appointed to the case an opportunity to prepare a social study investigation of the youth.

The disposition stage of the court's proceedings normally is quite different from the fact-finding stage, especially when it is held at a different time. The traditional purpose has been to administer individualized justice and to set in motion the rehabilitation of the delinquent; therefore, the judge is not limited by constitutional safeguards as much as he or she was at the adjudication hearing. Rules of evidence are relaxed, parties and witnesses are not always sworn in, and hearsay testimony may be considered.[61] The starting point of the disposition hearing is usually the written social study of the juvenile prepared by the probation officer, a report that examines such factors as school attendance and grades, family structure and support, degree of maturity and sense of responsibility, relationships with peers, participation in community activities, and attitudes toward authority figures. In this final stage of the proceedings, juveniles are permitted to have legal counsel, and the *Kent* decision ensures the right of counsel to challenge the facts of the social study.

The factors that influence judicial decision making at the dispositional stage can be separated into formal and informal factors (Table 14–6). The three most important formal factors are (1) the recommendation of the probation officer and the information contained in the social study investigation, (2) the seriousness of the delinquent behavior and previous contacts with the court, and (3) the available options. The recommendation of the probation officer in the social study report is usually followed by the juvenile judge. The seriousness of the delinquent behavior and previous contacts with the court probably have the greatest impact on judicial decision making at this stage. Terence Thornberry confirmed that seriousness of the current offense and the number of previous offenses have the greatest impact.[62] M. A. Bortner's examination of disposition decision making in a large Midwestern county revealed that the youth's age, his or her prior referrals, and the detention decision surfaced as the most important influences.[63] Studies of the juvenile courts in Colorado, Pennsylvania, and Tennessee also indicated that prior decisions by juvenile court personnel were related

---

TABLE 14–6
Factors That Influence Judicial Decision Making

Formal

1. The recommendation of the probation officer and the information contained in the social study investigation
   a. The recommendation of the probation officer is usually followed by the juvenile judge.

2. The seriousness of the delinquent behavior and previous contacts with the court
   a. This has the greatest impact on judicial decision making at this stage. Studies of the juvenile courts in Colorado, Pennsylvania, and Tennessee also indicated that prior decisions by juvenile court personnel were related more strongly to disposition than any other factor.

3. The available options
   a. The most desirable placement may not be available in that jurisdiction, or the desired placement may have no space for the youth.

Informal

1. The values and philosophy of the judge
   a. Some judges work from a legal model, some from an educational model, and some from a medical model, and the model that a particular judge emphasizes will, of course, affect his or her handling of juvenile delinquents.

2. The social and racial background of the youth, as well as his or her demeanor

3. The presence or absence of a defense counsel

4. The potential political repercussions of the delinquent acts.

Sources: Terence P. Thornberry, "Sentencing Disparities in the Juvenile System," *Journal of Criminal Law and Criminology* 70 (Summer 1979); Lawrence Cohen, "Delinquency Dispositions: An Empirical Analysis of Processing Decisions in Three Juvenile Courts," Analytic Report 9 (Washington, D.C.: U.S. Government Printing Office, 1975); Rubin, *Juvenile Justice.* See also Joseph B. Sanborn, "Factors Perceived to Affect Delinquent Dispositions in Juvenile Court: Putting the Sentencing Decision into Context," *Crime and Delinquency* 42 (January 1996).

more strongly to disposition than any other factor.[64] Finally, the juvenile judge is influenced by the options that are available—the most desirable placement may not be available in that jurisdiction, or the desired placement may have no space for the youth.

The informal factors that sometimes influence judicial decision making at the disposition stage are the values and philosophy of the judge; the social and racial background of the youth, as well as his or her demeanor; the presence or absence of a defense counsel; and the potential political repercussions of the delinquent acts. In terms of the values and philosophy of the judge, some judges work from a legal model, some from an educational model, and some from a medical model, and the model that a particular judge emphasizes will, of course, affect his or her handling of juvenile delinquents.[65] Ruth D. Peterson found that racial, ethnic, gender, and age factors affected the disposition of older adolescents in New York's state courts. Race and ethnicity did not significantly influence disposition decisions in New York City, but outside the city, minority youths tended to become targets of stereotypes and to receive harsh treatment.[66]

Judicial Alternatives

The alternatives that are available to different juvenile courts vary significantly. Large urban courts have all or most of the following eleven alternatives at their disposal, but rural courts may have only a few:

1. *Dismissal.* Dismissal is certainly the most desired disposition for juveniles. The fact-finding stage may have shown the youth to be guilty, but the judge can decide, for a variety of reasons, to dismiss the case.

2. *Restitution.* Also usually very desirable is restitution, where youths may be required to work off their debt with a few hours each week, but their lives are not seriously interrupted.

3. *Outpatient psychiatric therapy.* Whether in the court clinic, in the community mental health clinic, or with a private therapist, outpatient therapy is a treatment-oriented decision and is often reserved for middle-class youths to keep them from being sent to "unfitting" placements.

4. *Probation.* As the most widely used disposition, probation seems to be a popular decision with delinquents and a good treatment alternative for the court. Probation is sometimes set for a specific length of time, usually a maximum of two years. The judge can direct the probation officer to involve the youth in special programs, such as alternative schools, speech therapy, or learning disability programs.

5. *Foster home placement.* Foster home placements are more restrictive, inasmuch as youths are removed from their natural homes. These placements are used most frequently for status offenders and dependent and neglected youths.

6. *Day-treatment program.* Day-treatment programs are a popular alternative with juveniles because the youths who are assigned to these programs return home in the evening, but these programs are few in number and are available in only a few states.

7. *Community-based residential program.* Different types of community-based residential programs, such as group homes and halfway houses, are available to many judges. These residential facilities may be located in the community or in a nearby community, but they are not as desirable as community-based day-treatment programs because youths are taken from their homes to live in these facilities.

8. *Institutionalization in a mental hospital.* Institutionalization may be seen as appropriate for a youth's needs but requires a psychiatric evaluation; after the evaluation, the doctor may recommend that the court initiate proceedings for commitment to a mental hospital.

9. *County or city institution.* Some county or city institutions are available to a few judges across the nation. Placement in these facilities may be deemed appropriate for a youth who needs more security than probation offers but who does not require long-term placement in the state training school.

Library Extra 14–3
OJJDP publication: *Juvenile Drug Court Programs*

Web Extra 14–2
Juvenile Detention Alternatives Initiative from the Annie E. Casey Foundation

Web Extra 14–3
National Institute of Mental Health's Child and Adolescent Mental Health Center website

Library Extra 14–4
OJJDP Juvenile Justice Bulletin: "Alternatives to the Secure Detention and Confinement of Juvenile Offenders"

10. *State or private training school.* The state or private training schools are usually reserved for youths who have committed serious crimes or for whom everything else has failed. In some states, state training schools include minimum-security (forestry camps, farms, and ranches), medium-security, and maximum-security institutions.

11. *Adult facility or youthful offender facility.* In a few states, if the youth has committed a serious offense and is seen as too hard core for a juvenile correctional institution, he or she is placed in an adult facility or a youthful offender facility.

Right to Appeal

Although juveniles do not yet have a constitutional right to make an **appeal** of their cases to a higher judiciary, practically all states grant them the right to appeal by statute. The states are following the lead of the U.S. Supreme Court, which pointed out in *Gault* that juveniles should have the same absolute right to appeal as do adults under the Equal Protection Clause of the Constitution. Since that ruling, most state legislatures have passed laws granting juveniles the right to appeal; state courts have also ruled that state statutes granting the right to appeal for juveniles must be applied uniformly to all juveniles, a decision that effectively undermines the past practice in which some courts gave judges the discretion to determine which juvenile cases could be appealed. The common practice today is to give juveniles the same rights to appeal that adults have.[67]

The right to appeal is limited for the most part to juveniles and their parents. States may appeal in some circumstances, but this right is seldom exercised, and few cases have come before the courts. Another issue of appeal concerns the type of orders that may be appealed—although states generally permit the appeal of final orders, what is "final" varies from state to state. Most state statutes call for the case to be appealed to an appellate court, but a few states call for a completely new trial. Other common statutory rights of juveniles at appeal are the right to a transcript of the case and the right to counsel.[68]

Organizational factors limit the use of the **appellate review** of juvenile court decisions. Many juveniles lack counsel at trial who can make a record and obtain a transcript, and even more juveniles lack access to appellate counsel. In addition, juvenile public defenders' caseloads frequently preclude the luxury of filing appeals; many public defenders neither authorize their clients to file appeals nor advise their clients of the possibility of an appeal. The only study that compared rates of appeals by criminal defendants and juvenile delinquents found that convicted adults appealed more than ten times as often as did juveniles.[69]

Juvenile Sentencing Structures

Determinate sentencing (fixed sentences for specified offenses) is a new form of sentencing in juvenile justice, and in some jurisdictions it is replacing the traditional form, **indeterminate sentencing** (sentencing at the judge's discretion). In addition, increasing numbers of juvenile courts are using a blended form of sentencing.

Criticism of the decision-making outcomes of juvenile courts has increased since the 1970s. Early on, the criticism focused on the arbitrary nature of the decision making that violated the due process rights of juveniles; more recently, this criticism has been based on the belief that the juvenile court is too "soft" on crime. This latter criticism, especially, has led to a number of attempts to change sentencing and other juvenile procedures.

One of the first efforts at reform was the **Juvenile Justice Standards Project**, jointly sponsored by the Institute of Judicial Administration and the American Bar Association. Officially launched in 1971 by a national planning committee under the chairmanship of Judge Irving R. Kaufman, the project proposed comprehensive guidelines for juvenile offenders that would base sentences on the seriousness of the crime rather than on the needs of the youth. The guidelines represented radical philosophical changes and still are used by proponents to attempt to standardize the handling of juvenile lawbreakers.

The belief that disparity in juvenile sentencing must end was one of the fundamental thrusts of the recommended standards. To accomplish this goal, the commission attempted to limit the discretion of juvenile judges and to make them accountable for their decisions, which would then be subject to judicial review. Also important in the standards was the

appeal
The review of juvenile court proceedings by a higher court. Although no constitutional right of appeal exists for juveniles, the right of adjudicated juveniles to appeal has been established by statute in some states.

appellate review
The review of the decision of a juvenile court proceeding by a higher court. Decisions by appellate courts, including the U.S. Supreme Court, have greatly affected the development of juvenile court law and precedent.

determinate sentencing
A model of sentencing that provides fixed terms of sentences for criminal offenses. Terms are generally set by the legislature rather than determined by judicial discretion.

indeterminate sentencing
In juvenile justice, a sentencing model that encourages rehabilitation through the use of general and relatively unspecific sentences. Under the model, a juvenile judge has wide discretion and can commit a juvenile to the department of corrections or youth authority until correctional staff make the decision to release the juvenile. This type of sentencing is used with juveniles in most jurisdictions other than those that have mandatory or determinate sentencing.

Juvenile Justice Standards Project
A project jointly sponsored by the Institute of Judicial Administration and the American Bar Association that proposes that juveniles' sentences be based on the seriousness of the offense committed rather than on the needs of the youth.

▲ Two teen girls in a holding cell in Marietta, Georgia. A recent report by Congress found that the nation's juvenile detention centers have become warehouses for mentally ill youths.

■ **Why are those children locked up?**

felony
A criminal offense punishable by death or by incarceration in a state or federal correctional institution, usually for one year or more.

mandatory sentencing
The requirement that individuals who commit certain offenses be sentenced to a specified length of confinement if found guilty or adjudicated delinquent.

provision that certain court procedures would be open to the public, although the names of juveniles still would remain confidential.

In the first part of the twenty-first century, juvenile court judges remain quite concerned about these proposed standards. Their basic concerns are that these standards attack the underlying philosophy and structure of the juvenile court and that these standards would limit their authority. They see the influence of the hard-liners behind this movement toward standardization and feel that the needs of youths will be neglected in the long run; they also challenge the idea that it is possible, much less feasible, to treat all youths alike.

Nevertheless, the adoption of the standards has been taking place across the nation. New York State was the first to act on them through the Juvenile Justice Reform Act of 1976, which went into effect on February 1, 1977. The act orders a determinate sentence of five years for class A **felonies**, which include first-degree kidnapping, first-degree arson, and murder, and the initial term can be extended by at least one year. The juvenile, according to the act, should be placed in a residential facility after the first year; then, if approved by the director of the division, the confined youth can be placed in a nonresidential program for the remainder of the five-year term, but the youth must remain under intensive supervision for the entire five-year term.

In 1977, the state of Washington also created a determinate sentencing system for juveniles in line with the recommendations of the Juvenile Justice Standards Project. In the 1980s, a number of states stiffened juvenile court penalties for serious juvenile offenders, either by mandating minimum terms of incarceration (Colorado, Kentucky, and Idaho) or by enacting a comprehensive system of sentencing guidelines (Arizona, Georgia, and Minnesota).[70]

In 1995, the Texas legislature introduced such "get-tough" changes in the juvenile justice system as lowering the age at which waiver could occur to fourteen years old for capital, first-degree, and aggravated controlled substance felony offenses and greatly expanding the determinate sentence statute that was first enacted in 1987. Under determinate sentences, any juvenile—regardless of age—can be sentenced for up to forty years in the Texas Youth Commission, with possible transfer to the Texas Department of Corrections. Finally, prosecutors can choose to pursue determinate sentence proceedings rather than delinquency proceedings, but they first must obtain grand jury approval.[71] Daniel P. Mears and Samuel F. Field's examination of the determinate sentencing statute for Texas found the increased proceduralization and criminalization of juvenile courts did not eliminate consideration of age, gender, or race/ethnicity in sentencing decisions.[72]

In the 1990s, nearly every state enacted **mandatory sentencing** for violent and repetitive juvenile offenders. The development of graduated, or accountability-based, sanctions was another means that states used in the 1990s to ensure that juveniles who are adjudicated delinquent receive an appropriate disposition by the juvenile court. Several states have created a blended sentencing structure, which is a mechanism for holding juveniles accountable for their offenses for cases involving repeat and serious juvenile offenders. This expanded sentencing authority allows criminal and juvenile courts to impose either juvenile or adult sentences—or at times both—in cases involving juveniles.[73]

Delinquency across the Life Course: The Impact of Transfer on Juveniles

The process of transferring juveniles to the adult court has generated considerable debate in juvenile justice circles and has raised a number of questions: Who should be transferred? What are the consequences in terms of criminal sanctions, as compared to juvenile court sanctions? What effect does the prison system have on juveniles? What are the consequences of transfer to the individuals involved? The answers to these questions help determine how transfer affects delinquents across the life course.

One finding is that transferred offenders, especially violent offenders, are significantly more likely to reoffend than those who have not been transferred.[74] L. Lanza-Kadace and colleagues conducted a Florida study that included 950 young adult offenders (half were transferred to the adult system in 1995 or 1996, and the other half remained in the juvenile justice system).[75] They found the following:

- Overall, 49 percent of the transferred offenders reoffended, compared with 35 percent of the retained offenders.

- For violent offenders, 24 percent of the transferred offenders reoffended, compared with 16 percent of the retained offenders.

- For drug offenses, 11 percent of the transferred offenders reoffended, compared with 9 percent of the retained offenders.

- For property offenses, 14 percent of the transferred offenders reoffended, compared with 10 percent of the retained offenders.[76]

Richard E. Redding proposed that juveniles tried as adults have higher recidivism rates because of the stigmatization and other negative effects, the sense of resentment and injustice juveniles feel about being tried and convicted as adults, the learning of criminal mores and behaviors in prison, and the decreased focus on rehabilitation and family support in the adult system.[77] What Redding does not mention is that juveniles are more likely to be victimized, including sexually assaulted, in the adult system than they are in the juvenile system (something that is discussed in Chapter 16).

It can be argued that at least juveniles who commit a violent crime before they are eighteen years old can no longer be executed—but as this book goes to press, they also cannot be placed in prison for life. The sentence of life without parole is an option that has been used in most states to deal with convicted adult as well as juvenile offenders. Sometimes, juveniles as young as thirteen or fourteen years old receive what amounts to being sentenced to die in prison. An organization known as the Equal Justice Initiative has documented seventy-four cases where children fourteen years of age or younger have been given this sentence.[78] In November 2009, the U.S. Supreme Court agreed to hear two cases that challenged the constitutionality of life sentences for juveniles. One of the cases involves thirty-four-year-old Joe Sullivan, a Florida prisoner who was sent away for life for raping an elderly woman when he was thirteen. The other case involves Terrance Graham, now age 22, who was convicted of armed robberies that were committed when he was sixteen and seventeen years old. Bryan Stevenson, one of the defense attorneys appearing before the Court, told reporters that his basic argument is "to say to any child of 13 that you are only fit to die in prison is cruel," and cruel and unusual punishment, and is prohibited by the U.S. Constitution.[79]

On June 25, 2012, the Supreme Court continued to limit how severely states may punish juvenile offenders, saying it is unconstitutional to mandate life in prison without parole for youthful offenders convicted of murder. The decision came in the robbery and murder case of Evan Miller and Kuntrell Jackson, who were fourteen when they were convicted and sentenced to life without parole.[80]

Delinquency and Social Policy: Excellence in Juvenile Courts

The meaning of excellence in the juvenile court is one of the topics that merits discussion among policy makers. The National Council of Juvenile and Family Court Judges provides its answer to this question, taking a somewhat broader approach and identifying the functions of the court and its judges (see Figure 14–7).

Excellence in Juvenile Courts

Applies to the entire system
- Juvenile justice systems must have adequate staff, facilities, and program resources.

Applies specifically to judges
- Judges should engage in judicial leadership and encourage system collaboration.
- Status should be the same as other judges and judges should have multiple-year or permanent assignment.
- Judges should make certain that cases are diverted to alternative systems whenever possible and appropriate.
- Judges should make certain that victims have access to services they need.
- Judges should make certain that court depositions are individualized and that they include graduated sanctions and incentives.
- Judges should ensure that effective post-dispositions are provided to each youth.
- Judges should ensure accountability among courtroom participants.
- Judges should ensure that an adequate information system is available to evaluate performance.
- Judges are responsible for ensuring that all court staff are adequately trained.

Applies to other staff members
- All members of the court team should treat youths, families, crime victims, witnesses, and others with respect, dignity, courtesy, and cultural understanding.
- Youths charged in the delinquency court should have qualified and adequately compensated legal representation.
- Staff should encourage family members to participate in the development and implementation of the youth's intervention plan.

Applies to the court
- Delinquency courts and juvenile abuse courts should have integrated one-family–one-judge case assignments.
- Courts should render timely and just decisions, and trials should conclude without continuances.

FIGURE 14–7
Excellence in Juvenile Courts

THE CASE

The Life Course of Amy Watters, Age 16

In Florida, the state where Amy lives, juvenile court jurisdiction extends to a person's nineteenth birthday. As a consequence of her involvement in the transportation and sale of controlled substances, Amy found herself facing formal processing by the juvenile court. At a hearing before a judge specializing in juvenile matters, Amy was adjudicated delinquent, placed on probation, and ordered to participate in a work program in the community. In Amy's case, the program was located at the local Society for the Prevention of Cruelty to Animals, and Amy had to report to the facility three days a week immediately following school. Her job was to clean the animals' cages and to follow instructions from the staff members there.

Amy loved animals, so she found the work rewarding. However, some of her old street friends soon began hanging around the facility, and would talk to Amy when she left the building to go on break. One of them, a fifteen-year-old girl named Skyler, asked Amy to bring her a dog that she had taken a liking to—an eight-month-old border collie that had been found wandering in a nearby neighborhood. Skyler told Amy that her parents didn't want her to have a dog, and wouldn't fill out the paperwork and pay the needed fees to adopt a dog. So, one day when no one seemed to be looking, Amy grabbed the collie and hurried it out a side door, giving it to Skyler.

Unbeknownst to Amy, however, a series of security cameras covered the kennels, and Amy's actions were caught on camera and digitized. Soon, her probation officer paid her a visit, and asked Amy if she knew that it was a crime in Florida to steal a dog.

Because Amy's boyfriend, CJ, was already nineteen at the time of his arrest, he was treated as an adult and taken before a state criminal court judge. CJ, who did not have any money, and whose parents were poor, was provided with a public defender to represent him; but he held true to his word that he would not implicate anyone else in the crimes with which he had been charged. After a month spent in jail for lack of bail money, CJ's attorney convinced him to plead guilty to charges involving the sale and distribution of a controlled substance. Because his criminal activities occurred on school grounds, however, he was also charged with violating the state's Drug-Free School Zone statute. Upon entering a plea of guilty, he received a five-year sentence, and was immediately taken to a prison within the state to serve his time. Federal drug trafficking proceedings against CJ were being contemplated by federal prosecutors. If found guilty under federal law, he could be ordered to spend additional time in prison—this time in a federal confinement facility.

How would Amy have been treated differently in court had she been an adult? What is likely to happen to CJ?

Learn More on the Web:

- The Self Report Method for Measuring Delinquency and Crime: https://www.ncjrs.gov/criminal_justice2000/vol_4/04b.pdf.
- Getting the Juvenile Justice System to Grow Up: www.time.com/time/nation/article/0,8599,1887182,00.html

Follow the continuing Amy Watters saga in the next chapter.

SUMMARY

This chapter has examined the juvenile court. Key points are as follows:

- The juvenile court concept, as originally formulated, was built on the idea of *parens patriae*, that is, the state acting as substitute parent in keeping with the best interests of the child.

- Another ideal underlying the juvenile court concept is that youths are malleable and that their personalities are not yet fully formed, offering the opportunity for reformation and rehabilitation.

- The classic purposes of the juvenile court have come under scrutiny as policy makers, facing public outcry over what some see as an increasingly violent and dangerous juvenile population, have been forced to rethink the proper role of the court.

- The resolution of the current debate, whatever its outcome, will have long-term repercussions for American juvenile justice.

- Beginning in the 1960s, important U.S. Supreme Court decisions accorded juveniles a significant number of due process rights. As a consequence, the typical juvenile court hearing today has many of the trappings of an adult criminal trial.

- Noteworthy decisions of the 1970s show that the Supreme Court has been unwilling to transform the activities of the juvenile court completely into an adversarial battleground like proceedings in adult criminal court.

- The pretrial procedures of the juvenile court consist of the detention hearing, the intake process, and the transfer procedure.

- The adjudicatory hearing is the fact-finding stage in juvenile court. The judge, the defense attorney, and the prosecutor are typically present at the adjudicatory hearing, especially in larger jurisdictions; witnesses are cross-examined, and proof beyond a reasonable doubt must be established.

- Once a youth is found delinquent, the judge then determines the most fitting disposition. Available judicial alternatives may range from dismissal to placement in a state or private training school.

- Juvenile court sentencing structures have expanded in many jurisdictions; having gone beyond the indeterminate sentence model, today they include various forms of determinate sentencing.

- The due process revolution in the area of juvenile justice took place because of a number of cases: *Kent* v. *United States* (juveniles deserve certain procedural rights at the time of trial; *In re Gault* (juveniles have certain due process rights when the finding of delinquency might lead to institutional confinement); *In re Winship* (juveniles entitled to proof beyond a reasonable doubt); *McKeiver* v. *Pennsylvania* (denied the right of juveniles to have jury trials); and *Breed* v. *Jones* (juveniles are protected from double jeopardy). The 2005 U.S. Supreme Court case of *Roper* v. *Simmons* precludes execution of anyone who commits a crime while under the age of eighteen years old. The 2010 case of *Graham* v. *Florida* held that the Eighth Amendment's ban on cruel and unusual punishments prohibits the imprisonment of a juvenile for life without the possibility of parole as punishment for a crime not including homicide; and the 2012 case of *Miller* v. *Alabama* held unconstitutional a mandatory sentence of life without parole for the crime of murder committed by a juvenile because it violates the Eighth Amendment's prohibition on cruel and unusual punishment.

KEY TERMS

adjudication, p. 372
adult court, p. 364
appeal, p. 377
appellate review, p. 377
attention home, p. 362
bail, p. 362
beyond a reasonable doubt, p. 356
bifurcated hearing, p. 374
binding over, p. 357
Breed v. *Jones*, p. 353
complaint, p. 363
consent decree, p. 364
constitutionalists, p. 352
detention center, p. 362

detention hearing, p. 361
determinate sentencing, p. 377
double jeopardy, p. 356
felony, p. 378
guardian ad litem, p. 360
home detention, p. 362
In re Gault, p. 353
In re Winship, p. 353
indeterminate sentencing, p. 377
informal adjustment, p. 364
informal probation, p. 364
intake, p. 363
jail, p. 362
judicial waiver, p. 364

jury trial, p. 373
juvenile court, p. 352
Juvenile Justice Standards Project, p. 377
Kent v. *United States*, p. 352
mandatory sentencing, p. 378
McKeiver v. *Pennsylvania*, p. 353
Missouri Plan, p. 359
National Council of Juvenile and Family Court Judges, p. 360
probation officer, p. 361
prosecutor, p. 357
shelter care, p. 362
statutory exclusion, p. 366
transfer, p. 354

JUVENILE DELINQUENCY VIDEOS

Intake Process 1

The first part of the *Intake Process* video shown an interaction between a juvenile offender and an intake officer. The juvenile has a history of delinquent behavior, but the intake officer focuses discussion on the personal successes and potential positive future for the youth. What motives might the intake officer have for leading the discussion in this manner? Based on what is displayed in the video and described in the readings, discuss the steps of the juvenile intake process. What are the goals of the intake process?

Intake Process 2

In the second part of the *Intake Process* video, the intake of two juvenile brothers is shown. Describe the differences between the two brothers in regards to prior records, behaviors, and specific individual needs. Both brothers were detained prior to their hearings. Do their individual histories and personal needs validate this decision by the court? Does the decision by the court act in the children's best interest? Why or why not?

REVIEW QUESTIONS

1. What are the three positions concerning the role of the juvenile court described in this chapter?
2. What were the most important U.S. Supreme Court cases concerning the rights of juveniles during the court process? What did each contribute?
3. What are the three important hearings that take place during pretrial procedures, and why are they important?
4. How is the transfer procedure different from one state to another?
5. What takes place during the trial stage of juvenile court proceedings?
6. How have juvenile sentencing structures changed in many jurisdictions?

DISCUSSION QUESTIONS

1. What is your opinion of the interesting present-day view of the constitutional perspective in Sheldon Richman's article "Phoney-Baloney Constitutionalist"? (It is available at http://www.ff.org/comment/'com0305n.asp.)
2. Should transfer to adult court be limited to violent juvenile offenders? Explain your response.
3. Only ten states currently allow jury trials for juvenile offenders. Do you think jury trials should be allowed for all juveniles? What do you see as the benefits and liabilities of doing so? Explain your response.
4. Do you think the structure of the juvenile court should be changed? Why or why not?
5. How should the juvenile justice system deal with status offenders?
6. How should juveniles who commit serious crimes be handled?

GROUP EXERCISES

1. Poll the students to determine who supports the *parens patriae* philosophy, who advocates the justice model, and who favors the abolition of juvenile courts. Moderate a discussion between the groups.
2. Divide the class into two groups: those who agree with the U.S. Supreme Court's ruling in *Kent* v. *United States* (1966) and those who disagree. Moderate a discussion between the groups.
3. Divide the class into two groups: those who agree with the U.S. Supreme Court's ruling in *In re Gault* (1967) and those who disagree. Moderate a discussion between the groups.
4. Divide the class into two groups: those who agree with the U.S. Supreme Court's ruling in *In re Winship* (1970) and

those who disagree. Moderate a discussion between the groups.
5. Divide the class into two groups: those who agree with the U.S. Supreme Court's ruling in *McKeiver* v. *Pennsylvania* (1971) and those who disagree. Moderate a discussion between the groups.
6. Divide the class into two groups: those who agree with the U.S. Supreme Court's ruling in *Breed* v. *Jones* (1975) and those who disagree. Moderate a discussion between the groups.
7. Invite a local juvenile court judge to address the class regarding his or her role in the juvenile court process.

NOTES

1. Details for this story come from Michael Rubinkam, "Pa. Judge Guilty of Racketeering in Kickback Case," AOL News, February 18, 2011, http://www.aolnews.com/2011/02/18/former-pa-judge-mark-ciavarella-guilty-of-racketeering-in-kick (accessed April 10, 2011).
2. G. Larry Mays, "Transferring Juveniles to Adult Courts: Legal Guidelines and Constraints," paper presented at the Annual Meeting of the American Society of Criminology, Reno, NV, November 1989.
3. Barry Krisberg, *The Juvenile Court: Reclaiming the Vision* (San Francisco: National Council on Crime and Delinquency, 1988); Arnold Binder, "The Juvenile Court: The U.S. Constitution, and When the Twain Shall Meet," *Journal of Criminal Justice* 12 (1982), pp. 355–66; and Charles E. Springer, *Justice for Children* (Washington, D.C.: U.S. Department of Justice, 1986).
4. Lisa Aversa Richette, *The Throwaway Children* (New York: Lippincott, 1969); Patrick Murphy, *Our Kindly Parent— The State* (New York: Viking Press, 1974); Howard James, *Children in Trouble: A National Scandal* (New York: Pocket Books, 1971); and William Ayers, *A Kind and Just Parent* (Boston: Beacon Press, 1997).
5. Dean J. Champion, "Teenage Felons and Waiver Hearings: Some Recent Trends, 1980–1988," *Crime and Delinquency* 35 (October 1985), pp. 439–79.
6. Barry C. Feld, *Bad Kids: Race and the Transformation of Juvenile Court* (New York: Oxford University Press, 1999).
7. Ibid.
8. Frederic L. Faust and Paul J. Brantingham, eds., *Juvenile Justice Philosophy* (St. Paul, Minn.: West, 1974).
9. *Graham* v. *Florida*, U.S. Supreme Court, No. 08–7412 (decided May 17, 2010).
10. *Miller* v. *Alabama*, U.S. Supreme Court, No. 10-9646 (decided June 25, 2012).
11. *Kent* v. *United States*, 383 U.S. 541, 86 S.Ct. 1045, 16 L.Ed.2d 84 (1966).
12. Ibid.
13. *In re Gault*, 387 U.S. 1, 18 L.Ed.2d 527, 87 S.Ct. 1428 (1967).
14. Ibid.
15. *Haley* v. *Ohio*, 332 U.S. 596 (1948); and *Gallegos* v. *Colorado*, 370 U.S. 49, 82 S.Ct. 1209 (1962).
16. *In re Winship*, 397 U.S. 358, 90 S.Ct. 1968, 25 L.Ed.2d 368 (1970).
17. *McKeiver* v. *Pennsylvania*, 403 U.S. 528, 535 (1971); *In re Barbara Burrus*, 275 N.C. 517, 169 S.E.2d 879 (1969); and *In re Terry*, 438 Pa., 339, 265A.2d 350 (1970).
18. *McKeiver* v. *Pennsylvania*.
19. Barry C. Feld, "Violent Youth and Public Policy: A Case Study of Juvenile Justice Law Reform," *Minnesota Law Review* 79 (May 1995), pp. 965–1128.
20. *Breed* v. *Jones*, 421 U.S. 519, 95 S.Ct. 1779 (1975).
21. H. Ted Rubin, *Juvenile Justice: Policy, Practice, and Law* (Santa Monica, Calif.: Goodyear Publishing, 1979).
22. See Charles Thomas and Ineke Marshall, "The Effect of Legal Representation on Juvenile Court Disposition," paper presented at the Southern Sociological Society in Louisville, KY, April 8–11, 1981. Also see S. H. Clarke and G. G. Koch, "Juvenile Court: Therapy or Crime Control and Do Lawyers Make a Difference?" *Law and Society Review* 14 (1980), pp. 263–308.
23. Thomas and Marshall, "The Effect of Legal Representation on Juvenile Court Disposition."
24. For a more expansive examination of juvenile court personnel, especially the juvenile court judge, see Ted. H. Rubin, *Behind the Black Robes: Juvenile Court Judges and the Court* (Beverly Hills, Calif.: Sage Publications, 1985); Ted. H. Rubin, "The Juvenile Court Landscape," in *Juvenile Justice: Policies, Programs, and Services*, edited by Albert R. Roberts (Chicago: Dorsey Press, 1989); and Leonard P. Edwards, "The Juvenile Court and the Role of the Juvenile Court Judge," *National Council of Juvenile and Family Court Judges* 43 (1992), p. 4.
25. Edwards, "The Juvenile Court and the Role of the Juvenile Court Judge," p. 25.

26. Ibid., pp. 25–28.
27. Larry J. Siegel and Joseph J. Senna, *Juvenile Delinquency: Theory, Practice, and Law*, 7th ed. (Belmont, Calif.: Wadsworth, 2000), p. 559.
28. See Stephanie Chen, "Pennsylvania Rocked by 'Jailing Kids for Cash' Scandal," http://eee.cnn.com/2009/CRIME/02/23/pennsylvania.corrupt.judges.
29. See Floyd Feeney, "Defense Counsel for Delinquents: Does Quality Matter?" paper presented at the annual meeting of the American Society of Criminology, Montreal (November 1987).
30. Barry C. Feld, "Criminalizing Juvenile Justice: Rules of Procedure for Juvenile Court," *Minnesota Law Review* 69 (1984), pp. 191, 199.
31. Rubin, *Juvenile Justice*, p. 194.
32. Joseph B. Sanborn, Jr., "Remnants of *Parens Patriae* in the Adjudication Hearing—Is a Fair Trial Possible in Juvenile Court?" *Crime and Delinquency* 40(4) (1994), pp. 599–615.
33. Siegel and Senna, *Juvenile Delinquency*, p. 561.
34. For other examinations of the prosecutor's role in the juvenile court, see John H. Laub and Bruce K. MacMurray, "Increasing the Prosecutor's Role in Juvenile Court: Expectation and Realities," *Justice System Journal* 12 (1987), pp. 196–209; and Charles W. Thomas and Shay Bilchik, "Prosecuting Juveniles in Criminal Courts: Legal and Empirical Analysis," *Journal of Criminal Law and Criminology* 76 (1985), pp. 438–79.
35. Lori L. Colley, Robert C. Culbertson, and Edward J. Latessa, "Juvenile Probation Officers: A Job Analysis," *Juvenile and Family Court Journal* 38 (1987), pp. 1–12.
36. Ann Strong, *Case Classification Manual, Module One: Technical Aspects of Interviewing* (Austin: Texas Adult Probation Commission, 1981).
37. Charles Puzzanchera, Benjamin Adams, and Melissa Sickmund, *Juvenile Court Statistics 2008* (Pittsburgh, Penn.: National Center for Juvenile Justice, 2011), p. 36.
38. Brenda R. McCarthy, "An Analysis of Detention," *Juvenile and Family Court Journal* 36 (1985), pp. 43–59. For other discussions of detention, see Lydia Rosner, "Juvenile Secure Detention," *Journal of Offender Counseling, Services, and Rehabilitation* 12 (1988), pp. 77–93; and Charles E. Frazier and Donna M. Bishop, "The Pretrial Detention of Juveniles and Its Impact on Case Disposition," *Journal of Criminal Law and Criminology* 76 (1985), pp. 1132–52.
39. Charles Puzzanchera and Melissa Sickmund, *Juvenile Court Statistics 2005* (Pittsburgh, Penn.: National Center for Juvenile Justice, 2008).
40. *Creek* v. *Stone*, 379 F.2d 106 (D.C. Cir. 1967).
41. *Schall* v. *Martin* (1984), United States Law Review 52 (47), pp. 4681–4696.
42. Ibid., p. 4681.
43. Ibid.
44. Duran Bell, Jr., and Kevin Lang, "The Intake Dispositions of Juvenile Offenders," *Journal of Research on Crime and Delinquency* 22 (1985), pp. 309–28. See also Randall G. Sheldon and John A. Horvath, "Intake Processing in a Juvenile Court: A Comparison of Legal and Nonlegal Variables," *Juvenile and Family Court Journal* 38 (1987), pp. 13–19.
45. Bell and Lang, "The Intake Dispositions of Juvenile Offenders."
46. Griffin, Addie, Adams, and Finestine, *Trying Juveniles as Adults: An Analysis of State Transfer Laws and Reporting,*
47. Samuel M. Davis, *Rights of Juveniles: The Juvenile Justice System*, 2d ed. (New York: Clark Boardman, 1986), Section 4-2; see also Melissa Sickmund, "How Juveniles Get to Juvenile Court" *Juvenile Justice Bulletin* (Washington, DC: Office of Juvenile Justice and Delinquency Prevention, 1994).
48. Davis, *Rights of Juveniles*, pp. 24–26.
49. *Juvenile Justice Reform Initiatives in the States 1994–1996,* http://wwwl.ojjdp.gov/pubs/reform/ch2_k.hml (accessed on April 30, 2012).
50. Ibid.
51. See *Juvenile Delinquency Guidelines: Improving Court Practice in Juvenile Delinquency Cases* (Reno, NV: National Council of Juvenile and Family Court Judges, Summer 2005), p. 51.
52. Ibid, p. 106.
53. Ibid.
54. Ibid., p. 107.
55. Ibid., p. 108.
56. Ibid., p. 110.
57. Griffin et al., *Trying Juveniles as Adults: An Analysis of State Transfer Laws and Reporting.*
58. Richard E. Redding, "Juvenile Transfer Laws: An Effective Deterrent to Delinquency?" *OJJDP Juvenile Justice Bulletin* (August 2008), 5–6. For an article that considers transfer and sentencing guidelines, see Brian D. Johnson and Megan C. Kurlychek, "Transferred Juveniles in the Era of Sentencing Guidelines," *Criminology* 50 (May 2012), pp. 525–64.
59. Howard N. Snyder and Melissa Sickmund, *Juvenile Offenders and Victims: 2006 National Report* (Washington, D.C.: National Center for Juvenile Justice, Office of Juvenile Justice and Delinquency Prevention, 2006).
60. For example, in the laws of Pennsylvania, Act No. 333 (Section 18a) requires a hearing date within ten days after the filing of a petition.
61. Rubin, *Juvenile Justice*.
62. Terence P. Thornberry, "Sentencing Disparities in the Juvenile Justice System," *Journal of Criminal Law and Criminology* 70 (Summer 1979), pp. 164–71.
63. M. A. Bortner, *Inside a Juvenile Court: The Tarnished Idea of Individualized Justice* (New York: New York University Press, 1982).
64. Lawrence Cohen, "Delinquency Dispositions: An Empirical Analysis of Processing Decisions in Three Juvenile Courts," *Analytic Report 9* (Washington, D.C.: U.S. Government Printing Office, 1975), p. 51.
65. Rubin, *Juvenile Justice*. See also Joseph B. Sanborn, "Factors Perceived to Affect Delinquent Dispositions in Juvenile Court: Putting the Sentencing Decision into Context," *Crime and Delinquency* 42 (January 1996), pp. 99–113.

66. Ruth D. Peterson, "Youthful Offender Designations and Sentencing in the New York Criminal Courts," *Social Problems* 35 (April 1988), pp. 111–30. See also Christina De Jong and Kenneth C. Jackson, "Putting Race into Context: Race, Juvenile Justice Processing, and Urbanization, *Justice Quarterly* 15 (September 1998), pp. 487–504; and Barry C. Feld, "Social Structure, Race, and the Transformation of the Juvenile Court," paper presented at the Annual Meeting of the American Society of Criminology, Washington, D.C., November 1998.

67. Davis, *Rights of Juveniles*.

68. Ibid.

69. Feld, *Bad Kids*.

70. Martin L. Forst, Bruce A. Fisher, and Robert B. Coates, "Indeterminate and Determinate Sentencing of Juvenile Delinquents: A National Survey of Approaches to Commitment and Release Decision-Making," *Juvenile and Family Court Journal* 36 (Summer 1985), pp. 1–12.

71. Daniel P. Mears and Samuel H. Field, "Theorizing Sanctioning in a Criminalized Juvenile Court," *Criminology* 38 (November 2000), pp. 983–1020.

72. Ibid.

73. Feld, "Violent Youth and Public Policy: Minnesota Juvenile Justice Task Force and 1994 Legislative Reform," paper presented at the Annual Meeting of the American Society of Criminology, Miami, FL, 1994. See also Feld, "Violent Youth and Public Policy: A Case Study."

74. Richard Redding, "Juvenile Transfer Laws: An Effective Deterrent to Delinquency?" *Juvenile Justice Bulletin* (Washington, D.C.: Office of Juvenile Justice and Delinquency Prevention, 2008).

75. L. Lanza-Kadace, F. Lane, D. M. Bishop, and C. E. Frazier, "Juvenile Offenders and Adult Felony Recidivism: The Impact of Transfer," *Journal of Crime and Justice* 28 (2005), pp. 59–77.

76. Ibid.

77. Redding, "Juvenile Transfer Laws."

78. "Death in Prison Sentences for 13- and 14-Year-Olds," http://www.cji.org/eji/childrenprison/deathinprison.

79. Associated Press, "High Court Looks at Life in Prison for Juveniles," http://www.msnbc.msn.com/id/33789880/ns/politics-more_politics/?gt1=43001 (accessed January 2, 2010).

80. Jesse J. Holland, "U.S. Supreme Court Ruled Out Mandatory Life without Parole for Juveniles," Associated Press, June 25, 2012.

15 Community-Based Corrections

Chapter Objectives

After reading this chapter, you should be able to:

1. Define community-based corrections.
2. Summarize the philosophy and objectives of community-based corrections.
3. Explain how community-based programs are administered.
4. Explain how probation is used in juvenile corrections, including its role, operations, emphasis, and use of volunteers.
5. Summarize the effectiveness of prevention programs in this nation.
6. Describe the use of house arrest and electronic monitoring.
7. Describe the various types of residential and day-treatment programs in juvenile corrections.

Our society is fearful of our kids. I think we don't know how to set limits on them. They begin to behave in severely outrageous ways, and nobody stops them.

—David York, Cofounder of Tough Love International

Introduction

From 1969 to 1973, Dr. Jerome Miller was head of the Massachusetts Department of Youth Services. Miller closed the reform schools in Massachusetts and replaced them with a few small, secure units and a diverse array of community-based services.

Miller creatively and courageously acted to change Massachusetts from large state schools to one of community-based programs. He described and implemented several principles:

1. Reform the "deep end" first. Eliminate large rural institutions and replace them with small urban-based alternative for the "worse kids." If the least deserving youth are treated with fairness and decency, the rest of the system will follow.

2. Ensure that the funds follow the youth to the community, otherwise the alternatives to institutions will become supplements, only increasing costs and capacity and unnecessarily isolating more youth.

3. Stay partially connected to the youth. Seek to understand and respect the uniqueness of each person and his or her life story.

4. Develop a diversity set of alternative responses to youths' behavior and conduct a meaningful and dynamic process for matching youth and programs.

5. Seize the moment. True reform is much more a matter of messy increments through risk-taking, creative fun management, and manipulation of personnel rules and staff appointments than master planning and smooth administration.

6. Building broad coalitions. Seek support not only from the usual child advocacy and juvenile reform groups, but also rely on groups such as the League of Women Voters.[1]

Miller's accomplishments in converting Massachusetts from the heavy use of state-run confinement facilities to community-based programs and services for juveniles is well remembered today. Miller's principles continue to inspire those who are working toward implementing an impressive array of alternative programs for juvenile offenders in communities across the nation, and which prevent the unnecessary institutionalization of many young offenders.

This chapter examines juvenile corrections in the community. The fundamental forms of **community-based corrections** are probation, residential and day-treatment programs, and aftercare. These services are alternatives to institutional placement, and help to keep juvenile delinquents out of training schools, jails, and adult prisons. The ongoing search for solutions to the problem of juvenile crime, the popularity of deinstitutionalization in juvenile justice, and the emphasis in the past twenty years on short-term behavioral control probably best explain why there are so many programs for juvenile offenders. Probation, day-treatment, and residential programs are examined in this chapter, while aftercare is discussed in the next chapter.

community-based corrections
A corrections program that includes probation, residential and day-treatment programs, and parole (aftercare). The nature of the links among community programs and their social environments is the most distinguishing feature of community-based corrections. As frequency, duration, and quality of community relationships increase, the programs become more community based.

The Philosophy Underlying Community-Based Corrections

Three somewhat diverse philosophies guide today's community-based corrections for juveniles: (1) reintegration, (2) a continuum of sanctions, and (3) restorative justice and peacemaking.

Reintegration

Community-based programs have traditionally rested on a **reintegration philosophy**, which assumes that both the offender and the community must be changed. Under this philosophy, the community is as important as the client and plays a vital role in facilitating the reabsorption of offenders into social life. Consequently, the task of corrections involves the construction (or reconstruction) of ties between offenders and the community through maintenance of family bonds, employment and education, and placement in the mainstream of social life.

reintegration philosophy
This philosophy assumes that both the officer and the receiving community must be brought together in formal programs.

More Intrusive to Offenders

Intensive probation

House arrest

Electronic monitoring

Residential facilities

Less Intrusive to Offenders

Prevention programs

Diversion programs

Probation

Day treatment programs

Community restitution

Drug courts

FIGURE 15–1
Continuum of Sanctions

Continuum of Sanctions

Advocates for a more effective juvenile justice system are increasingly calling for a range of punishment options, providing graduated levels of supervision in the community. Under this initiative, judges are able to exercise discretion by selecting the punishment that best fits the circumstances of the offense and the youth from among a range of sentencing options. Intermediate sanctions are thought to allow juvenile judges to match the severity of punishment with the severity of the offense. Juvenile institutions, then, are treated as backstops, rather than backbones, of the juvenile corrections systems.[2]

Providing justice through a **continuum of sanctions**, ranging from diversion programs to placement in community correctional facilities, is one of the exciting innovations in juvenile corrections today. Intermediate sanctions can be grouped from those that are less intrusive in the lives of offenders to those that are most intrusive. The basic aim behind intermediate sanctions, which are also known as alternative sanctions, is to escalate punishments to fit the offense. These sanctions typically are administered by probation departments and include such sanctions as intensive probation, community service, house arrest, and electronic monitoring. But they also involve sentences that are administered independently of probation, such as day-treatment programs, drug courts, and residential care (see Figure 15–1).

Restorative Justice

The concept of **restorative justice** has recently been coupled with intermediate sanctions. Humanistic in its treatment of offenders, restorative justice has as its focus the welfare of victims in the aftermath of crime. In bringing criminal and victim together to heal the wounds of violation, the restorative justice philosophy advocates alternative methods to incarceration, such as intensive community supervision. The most popular of the restorative strategies are victim–offender conferencing and community restitution. In many states, representatives of the victims' rights movement have been instrumental in setting up programs in which victims/survivors confront their victimizers.[3]

Restorative justice processes pay attention not only to the harm inflicted on the immediate victims of a crime, but also to the ways that the crime has harmed the offender and the community. Thus, the focus of restorative justice programs is on victim healing, offender reintegration, and community restoration. The emphasis on victim healing has persuaded some to consider restorative justice to be a victim-centered approach. Yet the emphasis on providing offenders an opportunity to make amends and to increase their awareness of the consequences of their actions has persuaded others to regard restorative justice as offender focused. It is the third emphasis, community restoration, that brings victim healing and offender reparation together.

The Administration of Community-Based Corrections

Comprehensive state-sponsored, locally sponsored, and privately administered programs are the three basic types of organizational structures in community-based initiatives.

In California, Indiana, Kansas, Michigan, Minnesota, and Oregon, state governments sponsor residential and day-treatment programs under **community corrections acts**. The Minnesota Community Corrections Act, which has become a model for other community corrections acts, provides for a state subsidy to any county or group of counties that chooses to develop its own community corrections system. The costs for juvenile offenders who are adjudicated to a training school are charged back to the county, and these costs are subtracted from the county's subsidy. Counties in Minnesota have been understandably reluctant to commit youths to training schools because of the prohibitive costs and therefore have established and encouraged a wide variety of residential and day-treatment programs. See Figure 15–2 for a map of community corrections acts across the United States.

The deinstitutionalization movement in Maryland, Massachusetts, North Dakota, South Dakota, Utah, and a number of other states has also led to the development of a wide network of residential and day-treatment programs for youths. In Massachusetts, the Department of Youth Services administers some of these programs, but more often the juvenile court sponsors them, or state or local agencies contract services for those youths from private vendors in the community. Whoever administers these community programs, the most innovative and effective ones attempt to provide a continuum of care for youthful offenders.

Private delivery of correctional services to youthful offenders originated in the early days of juvenile justice in America. Most of these programs were church- or business-backed, but were phased out in the early to mid-1900s. In 1972, the private sector reentered the field of juvenile corrections. Privatization, or placing the control of juvenile correctional facilities in the hands of the private sector, has expanded significantly in the past few decades. Privately run programs are emerging as a result of budget problems that prevent local or state agencies from supplying the services in an efficient manner. Privatization has become big business and has sparked the interests of investors from all walks of life. Those operating in the private sector receive payment for offering programs through federal, state, or local funding, from insurance plans, or from the juvenile's parents.

Federal grants provide the funding for many community programs. SafeFutures, a relatively new program funded by the Office of Juvenile Justice and Delinquency Prevention (OJJDP), appears to be a model worth replicating in communities across the nation. SafeFutures seeks to improve the service delivery system by creating a continuum of care responsive to the needs of youths and their families at all points along the path toward juvenile reintegration. This coordinated approach of prevention, intervention, and treatment is designed both to serve the juveniles of a community and to encompass the human service and the juvenile justice systems.

SafeFutures urban sites are located in Boston, Massachusetts; Contra Costa County, California; Seattle, Washington; and St. Louis, Missouri. The other two sites are Imperial County, California (rural), and Fort Belknap Indian Community, Harlem, Montana (tribal government). A national evaluation is being conducted to determine the success of the continuum of services in all six sites.

continuum of sanctions
The failure to respond to one sanction will result in a more serious or demanding sanction.

restorative justice
A sentencing model that builds on restitution and community participation in an attempt to make the victim "whole again."

community corrections acts
Legislative initiatives that enact statutory provisions in support of residential and day-treatment programs for juvenile offenders. The Minnesota Community Corrections Act has become the model for other states because it provides a state subsidy to any county or group of counties that chooses to develop its own community corrections system.

Library Extra 15–1
OJJDP Juvenile Justice Bulletin: "Planning Community-Based Facilities for Violent Juvenile Offenders as Part of a System of Graduated Sanctions"

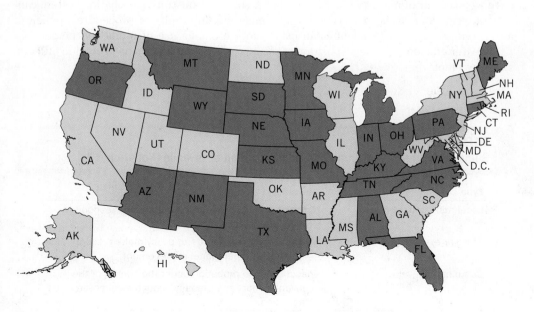

FIGURE 15–2
Community Corrections Acts in the United States

Note: The dark color indicates states with a community corrections act and the light color indicates those states without.

Source: National Committee on Community Corrections (Washington, D.C.: Center for Community Corrections, n.d.).

Probation

Probation permits juvenile offenders to remain in the community under the supervision of a **probation officer**, subject to certain conditions imposed by the court. Probation, which many consider to be the brightest hope of corrections, has several different connotations in the juvenile justice system: It is a legal system in which an adjudicated delinquent can be placed, an alternative to institutionalization, and a subsystem of the juvenile justice system.

The word *probation* is used in at least four ways in the juvenile justice system. It can refer to (1) a disposition of the juvenile court in lieu of institutionalization, (2) the status of an adjudicated offender, (3) a subsystem of the juvenile justice system (the term's most common use), and (4) the activities, functions, and services that characterize this subsystem's transactions with the juvenile court, the youthful offender, and the community. The probation process includes the intake phase of the juvenile court's proceedings, preparation of the social investigation for the disposition stage, supervision of probationers, and obtaining or providing services for youths on probation.

About 400,000 youth are placed on formal probation each year, which amounts to more than 60 percent of all juvenile dispositions. The use of probation has increased significantly since 1993 when around 224,500 adjudicated juveniles were placed on probation.[4]

The Administration of Probation

Two questions about the organization of probation services have been debated for some time: (1) Should probation administration be controlled by the judicial or the executive branch of government? (2) Should this control be centralized in the state or in a local administration? In fact, both forms of organization exist in various jurisdictions throughout the United States (Table 15–1).

Locally Administered Probation Departments

In those states in which probation is a local responsibility, the state is responsible only for providing financial support, setting standards, and arranging training courses. The locally based approach is applicable to one-third of juvenile probation departments in the United States.

One of the most persuasive arguments for the local administration of probation is that citizens and agencies in the community tend to readily support programs that are open to their participation and are responsive to local needs. Another supporting argument says small operations are more flexible, adjust more quickly to change, and are less encumbered by bureaucratic rigidity. Yet three arguments against local administration have won the ear of many policy makers: (1) A state administrative probation system can set statewide standards of service, thereby ensuring uniformity of procedures, policies, and services. (2) A large agency can make more effective use of funds and personnel. (3) Greater efficiency in the disposition of resources is possible when all probation officers are state employees.

TABLE 15–1
Summary of the Organization and Administration of Juvenile Probation

Type	Advantage
Local administration	Citizens and agencies of the community respond to local needs and problems.
State or executive	Allows uniform standards of policy making, recruitment, training, and personnel management.
Combination	Places juvenile probation under the control of the juvenile court and funds it through local government agencies.

State or Executive Administered Probation Departments

Assignment of probation to the executive branch on a statewide basis allows for the establishment of standards, including those pertaining to recruitment, training, and personnel management. Coordination with the state department of corrections is also facilitated. The most significant disadvantage is the development of a large probation bureaucracy involving echelons of decision makers shoveling memorandums from out-basket to in-basket with little contact with the real world from which most juvenile offenders come. Firm leadership with a grasp of sound management procedures, however, holds the potential to prevent this dismal prospect from manifesting.

Combination Approach

Juvenile probation is under the control of the juvenile court and is funded by city or county government in fifteen states and the District of Columbia. The other thirty-five states organize and administer juvenile probation in a variety of ways, and fourteen use a combination of approaches. The best strategy for the administration of juvenile probation appears to be placing it under the control of the juvenile court and funding it through local government agencies while, at the same time, providing revenue support or staff from the state to those agencies meeting standards established at the state level.

Private contractors have been used in juvenile probation, especially in providing intensive probation and aftercare services. For example, in January 2011, the Nebraska Department of Health and Human Services (DHHS) transferred case management functions in the eastern and southeastern service areas of the state to private contractors, who are known as family permanency specialists. Action by the Nebraska DHHS came as part of the Nebraska Families Matter reform, which is an initiative to partner with the private sector to improve services and outcomes for children and their families.[5]

To bring about greater uniformity in the administration of local probation, several states offer either revenue or manpower support to local systems if they comply with state standards. Michigan, for example, assigns state-funded probation officers to work with local probation officers. Usually, though, states make direct payments to local governments to defray part of the costs of probation services. In New York State, for example, a local community that is willing to meet state staffing standards is reimbursed up to 50 percent of its operating costs for probation services.

Other states, such as California, Nevada, Oregon, and Washington, have developed **probation subsidy programs** that encourage a decreased rate of commitment of offenders by counties to state institutions. The money saved by the state is returned to the counties. California initiated this program after a study indicated that many offenders committed to state correctional institutions could safely remain in the community under good probation supervision. With the closing of state-run training schools in California, which is currently under way, the plan is for county probation departments to assume the type of supervisory responsibility they did with the passing of the original probation subsidy programs.

probation subsidy program
Used in states such as California, Nevada, Oregon, and Washington, these programs encourage a decreased rate of commitment of juvenile offenders to state institutions by reimbursing the community for confining or working with youths locally.

The Function of Probation Services

The four basic functions of juvenile probation are (1) intake, (2) caseload management, (3) investigation, and (4) reports to the court. At the intake stage of the court proceedings, the probation officer decides whether or not to file a petition on a child referred to the court. The management of a caseload is an important responsibility of a probation officer. Investigation involves compiling a social history or study of a child adjudicated to be delinquent in order to assist the judge in making the wisest disposition. Supervision, initiated when the judge places a youth on probation, focuses primarily on risk control and crime reduction. We take a closer look at these four functions in the following sections.

Intake

During the **intake** stage of court proceedings (which were discussed in Chapter 14), the probation officer carefully screens referrals to the court. Both state statutes and the office of the state's prosecutor are helpful in determining whether or not any case referred to the court actually falls under its jurisdiction.

intake
At this stage of the processing of a juvenile offender, the probation officer conducts a preliminary investigation that includes an interview during which the youth is advised of his or her legal rights and the officer decides on the next step for the youth.

At intake, the probation officer also conducts a preliminary investigation, which includes an interview during which a youth is advised of his or her legal rights. If parents or guardians have not already been contacted, the probation department gets in touch with them to discuss the status of the child and to advise them of their right to have an attorney. The intake probation officer may need to interview the family, witnesses, victims, arresting officers, peers, or neighbors to obtain sufficient information with which to make a sound determination on the necessity of filing a court petition for detention of the child. The probation officer also may need to contact the school and other agencies that have worked with the child. If the youth has been in court before or is already on probation, the intake officer must also familiarize himself with the previous reports.

Casework Management

The probation officer maintains a file on each probationer for whom he or she is responsible. Within this file are court documents that spell out the requirements of probation, chronological entries of contacts between the officer and the probationer and others whose relationship with the probationer might be important, items of correspondence, and periodic reports made to the courts or to officials of the agency.

Commonly, probation officers divide probationers into several categories, based on their needs or on the risk they pose to the community. Some offenders are placed on minimum supervision status and are required only to mail in a report once a month or even less frequently. Offenders on medium supervision status must visit their probation officers at least once a month. Offenders on maximum or intensive supervision status must see their officers several times a month.

Probation officers' caseloads are typically so large that maintaining contact with probationers is difficult. Studies in adult probation seeking to link caseload size to recidivism go back forty years or more. Since the late 1970s, five major studies have sought to identify the impact of caseload sizes on recidivism, and three of the five studies found evidence supporting the contention that smaller caseloads were associated with lower recidivism rates. More recently, John L. Worrall and colleagues' analysis of the relationship between probation caseloads and property crime rates in California counties found that over a nine-year period, as probation loads increased, so did property crime.[6] Although similar studies in juvenile probation are lacking, it stands to reason that this would also be true with juveniles.

supervision
The surveillance, monitoring, casework services, and counseling or guidance services provided to a youthful offender who has been placed on probation. Supervision is provided by juvenile probation officers.

surveillance
The observation of probationers by probation officers; intended to ensure that probationers comply with the conditions of probation and that they do not break the law.

Supervision, Investigation, and Surveillance

The length of time a juvenile must spend on probation varies among states. The maximum length in some states is until the juvenile reaches the age of majority, which is usually age 16 or 17. Other states limit juvenile probation to a specific duration. In Illinois, it is limited to five years; in New York, two years; in Washington, D.C., one year; and in California, six months.

Once a youth has been placed on probation, the probation officer is required to provide the best possible **supervision**, which includes surveillance, casework services, and counseling or guidance. **Surveillance** involves careful monitoring of the minor's life within the community. To accomplish this, the officer must establish personal contact with the minor and must learn whether the youth is attending school or is working each day, whether adequate guidance is being received from parents, and whether the child is obeying the terms of probation. At the same time, the probation officer must determine if the youth is continuing to break the law.

▲ Police and probation officers talk with young members of the Crips street gang outside a Los Angeles high school. Good juvenile probation practice is mission-driven, performance-based, and outcome-focused.
■ **What does that mean?**

A popular means of probation for some departments has been team probation. Officers are divided into teams, and each team takes responsibility for a particular caseload and makes decisions on what community resources are needed by clients within that caseload. New probationers are interviewed by a member of the team, and their needs are plotted on a needs-assessment scale. The members of the teams are usually specialists in "needs subsystems," dealing with such problems as drug abuse, alcoholism, mental illness, or runaway behavior, and these specialists link the probationer with whatever services in the community are needed.

Concerns for public safety in the 1980s led many probation departments to develop classification systems or to use the Wisconsin system or community assessment centers to place probationers under intensive, medium, or minimum supervision. Under the **Wisconsin system**, a risk/needs assessment is conducted for each probationer at regular intervals. The risk scale was derived from empirical studies that showed certain factors to be good predictors of recidivism: prior arrest record, age at first conviction, the nature of the offense for which the probationer was convicted, school or employment patterns, and so forth. The needs assessment focuses on such indicators as emotional stability, financial management, family relationships, and health. The scores derived from the risk/needs assessment are used to classify probationers by required level of supervision—intensive, medium, or minimum. Reassessment of cases takes place at regular intervals, and the level of supervision may be increased or reduced.[7]

The most widely used risk/needs assessment of human behavior is the Problem Severity Index, a screening tool that gives intake officers and others clues about the types of problems the offenders might have. Once a problem area(s) is identified, the juvenile is assessed using diagnostic tools in an attempt to identify the problem more specifically. Clinicians then can combine various diagnostic measures to develop protocols for treatment. Risk assessment today is used to classify offenders, to predict future behavior for reducing recidivism, and for intervention planning.[8] An examination of risk assessments distinguishes between risk assessments that are developed to *predict* behavior and those developed to enable workers to *manage* behavior.[9]

The use of risk/needs assessments in juvenile probation raises the issue of how effective they are in predicting juveniles' behaviors. The fact of the matter is that it is very difficult to predict behavior, especially for juveniles. Thus, whatever predictive techniques or classification systems are used in juvenile justice, the results are far less than desirable in forecasting juvenile behavior.[10]

Accountability models began to be formulated in the 1980s for supervising juvenile probationers. For example, Dennis Maloney, Dennis Romig, and Troy Armstrong developed what they called the **balanced approach to juvenile probation**. Its purpose is "to protect the community from delinquency, to impose accountability for offenses committed, and to equip juvenile offenders with the required competencies to live productively and responsibly in the community."[11] One of the popular features of this balanced approach is the equal attention it gives to the community, the victim, and the juvenile offender. Juvenile probation departments in Oregon, Texas, and Wisconsin have implemented this accountability model in supervising juvenile probationers.[12]

The formulation of the balanced approach to juvenile probation has led to the development of the **restorative justice model**. This model, as suggested earlier, gained impetus in the 1970s and 1980s from the victim's movement, from youthful offenders' experiences with reparative sanctions, and from the rise of informal neighborhood programs and dispute resolution programs in the community.[13] The purpose of the integrated, balanced, and restorative justice model is to reconcile "the interests of victims, offenders, and the community through common programs and supervision practices that meet mutual needs."[14]

The Washington State Legislature has been funding evidence-based programs in the Washington State juvenile courts since 1999. The state-funded evidence-based programs are:

- Aggression Replacement Training (ART)
- Coordination of Services (COS)
- Functional Family Therapy (FFT)
- Family Integrated Transitions (FIT)
- Multi-Systemic Therapy (MST).

Reports to the Court

If a juvenile court uses the bifurcated hearing (separation of adjudicatory and disposition stages), a **social study report** is ordered by the judge when a youth is found delinquent at the

Wisconsin system
A system of supervision for youthful offenders that involves a risk/needs assessment conducted at regular intervals to see what level of supervision is appropriate for each individual offender.

balanced approach to juvenile probation
A philosophy of juvenile probation that strives to protect the community from delinquency, to impose accountability for offenses committed, and to equip juvenile offenders with the required competencies to live productively and responsibly in the community.

restorative justice model
A model of juvenile justice that works to reconcile the interests of victims, offenders, and the community through common programs and supervision practices that meet the needs of all parties.

social study report
A report ordered by a judge during the fact-finding stage of the court's proceedings.

fact-finding stage of the court proceedings. Probation officers usually are given up to sixty days to make their investigation, but if the court combines the adjudicatory and disposition stages, the social study must be completed before a youth appears in front of the judge. The judge is not supposed to read this social study *until* the child is found to be delinquent.

The social study report details the minor's personal background, family, educational progress, present offense, previous violations of the law, and employment. Also included are the description of the offender's neighborhood; the family's ability to pay court and institutionalization costs; the minor's physical and mental health; the attitude of the family, the police, neighbors, and the community toward the minor; and the attitude of the minor toward the offense in question and toward himself or herself. The social study concludes with the probation officer's diagnoses and treatment plan for the youth. An important plan is the probation officer's recommended course of action. In this report, the officer recommends whether the juvenile should remain in the community. If the judge agrees with the officer's recommendation, the conditions of probation are imposed and the offender enters probation.

The Work of Juvenile Probation Officers

The probation officer does not have an easy job. He or she is sometimes asked to supervise youths on aftercare as well as those on probation. The officer may be given a large caseload, may be responsible for youths who are on house arrest and are monitored with electronic equipment, or may be charged with intake or secure detention responsibilities. In addition, the probation officer is expected to be a treatment agent as well as an agent of social control.[15]

Duties of the Juvenile Probation Officer

The juvenile probation officer plays an important role in the justice process, beginning with intake and continuing throughout the period in which a juvenile is under court supervision. Probation officers are involved at four stages of the court process. At *intake*, they screen complaints by deciding to refer the juvenile to an agency for service, or refer the case to the court for judicial action. During the *predisposition* stage, they participate in release or detention decisions. At the *postadjudication* stage, they assist the court in reaching its dispositional decision. During *postdisposition*, they supervise juveniles placed on probation. Exhibit 15–1 lists some of the questions probation officers must answer as they handle juvenile offenders' cases.

Exhibit 15–1
Questions Facing Probation Officers

To make the decision of whether to revoke probation, modify the conditions of probation, or place a juvenile outside the home, probation officers consider some questions:

1. Is the juvenile a danger to self or others?
2. Is the juvenile exceeding the limits in the home, community, and school?
3. Is the family amenable to services?
4. How can the scarce resources be used wisely with this juvenile?
5. What other consequences (e.g., community service) can be imposed without court intervention?

To make the decision on what to do with a juvenile on an informal adjustment agreement who is not following home rules and who is violating curfew, failing urine tests, or failing to attend a substance abuse program, probation officers consider several questions:

1. Does the juvenile show any remorse for his or her actions?
2. Does the juvenile want to change or make an adjustment to the contract?

3. Have all other options been utilized?
4. Is the charge worth sending to the court to get compliance? (For example, is a simple misdemeanor worthy of the expense of court action?)

To answer the question of what to do with a juvenile who is already adjudicated delinquent with the charge of possession with intent to deliver a controlled substance, probation officers consider these questions:

1. Does use of evaluation/treatment help?
2. Does a forty-eight-hour lockup work?
3. Have we tried all other services and consequences?

CRITICAL THINKING QUESTIONS

■ *Which questions do you think would have the most influence on probation officers in these three scenarios? Why?*

Source: "Decisions Facing Probation Officers," courtesy of Juvenile Court Services of Black Hawk County, Iowa.

Their general duties are as follows:

- Provide direct counseling and casework services.
- Interview and collect social service data.
- Make diagnostic recommendations.
- Maintain working relationships with law enforcement agencies.
- Use community resources and services.
- Direct volunteer case aides.
- Write predisposition or social investigation reports.
- Work with families of children under supervision.
- Provide specialized services, such as group therapy.
- Supervise specialized caseloads involving children with special problems.
- Make decisions about the revocation of probation and its termination.

Risk Control and Crime Reduction

In the 1990s, as juvenile probation continued to face the criticism that it allowed probationers to escape punishment, reduced risk and increased surveillance models received major emphasis. Restitution and intensive supervision were the most widely used of these short-term behavior control models, but house arrest and electronic monitoring also gained some attention.

Restitution

Restitution, a disposition that requires offenders to repay their victims or the community for their crime, began to be used widely in probation during the 1970s and 1980s. Indeed, by 1985, formal programs were known to exist in more than four hundred jurisdictions; more than thirty-five states now have statutory authority to order monetary or community service restitution.[16] Part of the reason for the skyrocketing growth of restitution programs is that the OJJDP has spent some $30 million promoting the use of restitution in eighty-five juvenile courts across the nation.[17] OJJDP followed this initiative with the National Restitution Training Program in 1983 and the Restitution Education, Specialized Training, and Technical Assistance (RESTTA) Project in 1985. These initiatives are directly responsible for most of the growth of restitution programs.[18]

Three broad types of restitution obligations can be ordered by the juvenile court: (1) straight financial restitution, (2) community service, and (3) direct service to victims. Community service is the most common type, probably because it is the easiest to administer. Direct service is the most rare, largely because of victims' reluctance to have contact with offenders. However, the three program types frequently blend together. For example, a local jurisdiction may organize work crews and even enter into recycling, janitorial, and other service contacts with public or private agencies in order to provide youthful offenders with jobs so that they can pay restitution. The most common goals of restitution programs are holding juveniles accountable, providing reparation to victims, treating and rehabilitating juveniles, and punishing juveniles.[19]

When it comes to making restitution and community service work, probation officers are key players, and in many jurisdictions it is up to a juvenile probation officer to do some or all of a number of responsibilities:

- Determine eligibility for participation.
- Calculate appropriate amounts.
- Assess the offender's ability to pay.
- Develop a payment/work schedule.
- Monitor performance.
- Close the case.[20]

restitution
A court-ordered repayment to a victim; often used together with community service as a condition of juvenile probation.

▲ Young offenders paint fences as part of their sentence to community service.

■ **What are the responsibilities of juvenile probation officers who work with offenders sentenced to community service?**

intensive supervision programs (ISPs)
A form of probation supervision involving frequent face-to-face contact between the probationer and the probation officer.

Juvenile courts have instituted job skills preparation classes to help juveniles with ordered restitution to find and hold jobs. The private and public sectors sometimes provide jobs in which youths required to make restitution can earn money and compensate victims. Juveniles failing to complete their restitution payments may have their probation term extended.

With community work restitution, probationers generally are required to work for a certain number of hours at a private nonprofit or government agency. Sites where the work may be performed include public libraries, parks, nursing homes, animal shelters, community centers, day care centers, youth agencies, YMCAs and YWCAs, and local streets. In large departments, restitution programs provide supervised work crews in which juveniles go to a site and work under the supervision of an adult. For a description of community service in Hennepin County (Minneapolis), Minnesota, see Exhibit 15–2.

Intensive Supervision

In the early 1980s, **intensive supervision programs (ISPs)** began to be used in adult probation as a response to the emerging issues of prison crowding, cost escalation, and society's hard-line response to crime. The phrase *intensive probation supervision* was used because these programs (1) were operated or administered by probation departments, (2) involved increased contacts, and (3) generally emphasized external controls and surveillance.[21]

Juvenile justice soon followed adult justice, as so frequently happens, and ISPs were implemented in juvenile probation. Georgia, New Jersey, Oregon, and Pennsylvania have experimented with or have instituted statewide ISPs for juveniles.[22] Indeed, by the end of the 1980s, juvenile judges across the nation were commonly placing high-risk offenders on small caseloads and assigning them frequent contact with a probation officer.

In one example, the Juvenile Court Judges' Commission in the Commonwealth of Pennsylvania developed such a project in the 1980s because of its concern with the increasing number of commitments to training schools.[23] The standards adopted for this project included a caseload size of no more than fifteen, a minimum of three contacts per week with the youth, a minimum of one contact per week with the family or guardian, and a minimum of six months and a maximum of twelve months of intensive services.[24] Thirty-two counties in Pennsylvania had established ISPs using these standards within ten years of the commission's recommendation.[25]

An integrated social control (ISC) model of intensive supervision recently has been developed that utilizes the major causal factors identified in delinquency theory and research. This model integrates the central components of strain, control, and social learning theories. It builds on the belief that the combined forces of inadequate socialization, strains between educational and occupational aspirations and expectations, and social disorganization in the

---

Exhibit 15–2
Community Service Sanctions

In Hennepin County (Minneapolis), Minnesota, youthful offenders quickly discover themselves placed by the juvenile judge on a Saturday work squad for a specified amount of community service. First-time offenders usually find that they are sentenced to forty hours. Every Saturday, these youths are required to be at the downtown meeting place at 8:00 a.m. From there, five trucks are sent out with ten youths and two staff members in each truck. The coordinator of the program, who is on the staff of the probation department, then assigns each youth to a specific work detail. These details include:

- Recycling bottles and cans
- Visiting patients at a nursing home
- Doing janitorial work
- Cleaning bus stops
- Planting trees or removing barbed wire fences at a city park
- Working at a park reserve.

Source: Information gained during an on-site visit to the Hennepin County Probation Department, Minneapolis, Minnesota, and updated during a phone call to a staff member at the department.

neighborhood leads to weak bonding to conventional values and to activities in the family, school, and community. Weak bonding, in turn, can lead juveniles to delinquent behavior through negative peer influence.[26]

The evaluation of ISPs in adult probation has received encouraging results in the prevention of recidivism.[27] Two national evaluations of these programs in juvenile probation, however, have discovered that "neither the possible effectiveness nor the possible ineffectiveness of these programs had been carefully examined. As a result, their status in this regard, including their impact on recidivism, was essentially unknown."[28]

House Arrest and Electronic Monitoring

House arrest, or home confinement, is a program of intermediate punishment whereby youths are ordered to remain confined in their own residences during evening hours, after curfew, and on weekends.[29] Those receiving house arrest may be allowed to leave during the day for doctors' appointments, school, employment, approved religious services, or other approved activities. Electronic monitoring equipment, a contemporary aspect of technocorrections (see Exhibit 15–3), may be used to verify probationers' presence in the residence in which they are required to remain.

Electronic monitoring was developed when a New Mexico district court judge read a comic strip in which the character Spiderman was tracked by a transmitter affixed to his wrist. At the judge's request, an engineer designed an electronic bracelet to emit a signal picked up by a receiver placed in a home telephone. The design of the bracelet was such

house arrest
A program of home confinement whereby youths are ordered to remain confined in their residences during evening hours, after curfew, and on weekends.

electronic monitoring
The use of electronic anklets and bracelets to verify probationers' presence in the place where they have been ordered confined.

Exhibit 15–3
Technocorrections in Juvenile Justice

People generally think of electronic systems as a technological method to keep tabs on offenders in the community. However, use of the technology is expanding into a variety of applications. For example, at Bryan Adams High School in East Dallas, Texas, students who have been chronically truant are being monitored with a global positioning system, which tracks their whereabouts 24/7 via a court order. The court is using the electronic monitoring (EM) technology in an attempt to keep truants in school.

The use of EM to track criminal offenders who are granted community release should also expand as systems become more sophisticated. Some of the services provided by EM systems including the following:

- *Identity verification devices* can recognize different parts of the body to ensure that the reporting person is the offender.
- *Programmed contact devices* call the juvenile probationer at scheduled or random times and use various technologies to determine the identity of the person who answers (voice verification or a device worn by the probationer to insert in a verifier box attached to the phone, or a camera for visual verification).
- With *global positioning systems*, the juvenile probationer wears a transmitter that sends signals to a satellite and back to a computer monitor, pinpointing the offender's whereabouts at all times. This expensive technology, which is generally used for high-risk offenders, can determine when an offender leaves an area where he or she is supposed to be (inclusion zone) or enters an area where he is not allowed to be (exclusion zone) as ordered by a judge.
- *Remote alcohol detention devices* require users to blow into the device to measure blood alcohol content. This may be used alone or with other devices listed above. The proba-

tioner is required to blow into a device called an Alco-Sensor, which transmits the results to a computer that records the amount of alcohol consumed. These devices may be attached to automobile ignitions in order to prevent driving after consuming alcohol.[30] Another system is known as Tattle Tail, which can detect alcohol or drug use by the offender. It senses these substances through a person's perspiration.

- *Ignition interlock devices* are linked to the electronic systems of automobiles. The driver expels deep lung air into the device. The vehicle will not start if the driver's blood alcohol content registers above a level that is safe for driving.
- *Victim notification systems* alert the victim when the offender is approaching his or her residence. A transmitter is worn by both the offender and the victim, and the receiver is placed at both residences.
- *Field monitoring devices*, or drive-by units, are employed by probation or parole officers or other authorities. These are portable handheld devices or devices placed on a vehicle with a roof-mounted antenna. When within two hundred to eight hundred feet of an offender's ankle or wrist transmitter, the portable device can detect the transmitter's radio signals.
- *Group monitoring units* permit supervisors to monitor several offenders in the same location, in order to verify attendance of multiple offenders at a day reporting program or to monitor offenders confined in a residential setting.

Sources: Sam Merton, "For Whom the Bell Tolls," *Dallas Observer,* June 16, 2008, http://www.dalas.observer.com/2008-06-26/news/for-whom; Secure Trac Systems, Omaha, Nebraska, http://www.isecuretrac.com/Services.aspx?-p-EMManagement; Massachusetts Probation Service, "The Electronic Monitoring Program Fact Sheet," http://www.mass.gov/courts/probation/elmofactsheet.pdf (all cites accessed May 8, 2012).

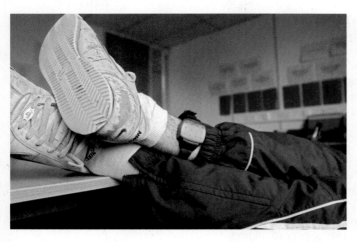

▲ Seen here is a youthful offender's remote location monitoring ankle bracelet.

■ **What are the different kinds of electronic monitoring that can be employed in the supervision of juvenile offenders?**

that if an offender moved more than 150 feet from his or her home telephone, the transmission signal would be broken. Authorities then would know that the offender had left his or her residence.[31]

More than 150,000 offenders, or approximately 20 percent of those on community-based supervision in the United States, are monitored at home.[32] Electronic monitoring equipment is being provided by some twenty private companies. Internationally, about 20 percent of 50,000 offenders in England and Wales who are under pre- or postrelease supervision receive electronic monitoring. In Sweden, about 25 percent of all inmates are placed on electronic monitoring.[33] The use of electronic monitoring in juvenile justice has gradually gained acceptance. For example, according to a November 1988 survey, only eleven juvenile programs used electronic monitoring.[34] Today, electronic monitoring programs are used in juvenile justice programs throughout the United States. These programs have the following goals:

- To increase the number of juveniles safely released into existing home confinement programs
- To reduce the number of juveniles returned to juvenile detention for violating home-confinement restrictions
- To reduce the number of field contacts required of home confinement officers
- To provide a reasonably safe alternative for lower-risk offenders
- To provide for early reunification with the juvenile's family
- To allow the juvenile to return to school.[35]

The Role of Volunteers in Probation

Throughout the second half of the nineteenth century, volunteers were widely used to provide probation services, but they largely disappeared at the beginning of the twentieth century and did not reappear until the late 1950s. Indeed, only four courts were using volunteers in 1961; but today more than two thousand court-sponsored **volunteer programs** are in operation in this country. The use of volunteers has become a valuable tool in helping offenders adjust to community life.

volunteer program
The use of unpaid adult community members to assist probation officers in a variety of ways.

The National Information Center on Volunteers in Court has identified several areas in which volunteers can work effectively with juvenile offenders. A volunteer can provide a one-to-one support relationship for the youth with a trustworthy adult; can function as a child advocate with teachers, employers, and the police; can be a good role model; can set limits and teach prosocial values; can teach skills or academic subjects; and can help the youth to develop a realistic response to the environment.

In addition to these areas of direct contact, volunteers can assist in administrative work. They can help recruit, train, and supervise other volunteers; can serve as consultants to the regular staff; can become advisers to the court, especially in the policy-making area; can develop good public relations with the community; and can contribute money, materials, or facilities.

Volunteers can improve the morale of the regular probation staff, because they are usually positive and enthusiastic about the services they provide. Because many volunteers are professionals (physicians, psychiatrists, psychologists, and dentists), they can provide services that the probation department may not have the financial resources to obtain. Finally, their contributions can reduce the caseload of the regular staff.

Several criticisms have been leveled at volunteer programs: The programs tend to attract a high ratio of middle-class persons, and they often create more work than they return in service. Volunteers cannot handle serious problems and sometimes in fact can harm their clients. Parents may resist the volunteer as an untrained worker. Although inappropriate volunteers clearly can do a great deal of damage, proper screening, training, and supervision can do much to ensure that volunteers provide high-quality probation services.

Juvenile Probation Programs

Juvenile probation usually offers a number of programs for probationers. Table 15–2 lists the types of programs to which probation officers can refer youths at the intake stage or later in the juvenile court process. Some jurisdictions, of course, have more of these programs than do others.

Of the programs listed in Table 15–2, the most common are (1) restitution programs, in which youths are assigned to a work crew to fulfill their community service sanctions; (2) volunteer programs in which volunteers are trained to work with probationers; (3) mentoring programs in which youths individually or in a group are assigned mentors, especially to work with them on their school assignments; (4) youth courts or teen courts, in which juveniles themselves are given a voice on what happens to their peers; after-school study programs for youths doing below-average school work; (5) drug or alcohol counseling, conducted individually or in groups; and (6) sex offender programs for youthful sex offenders.

The safe houses in Minneapolis and St. Paul, Minnesota, which provide a haven for female prostitutes, provide an example of a notable probation program. Safe houses program staff are particularly eager to involve adolescent females who have run away from home and ended up as prostitutes. When interviewed, adolescent residents of the safe houses, who were on probation for having committed prostitution, revealed that these facilities and their staff represent a hope for them to escape from street life and the inevitable drug use that accompanies street life.[36] With the downturn of the economy in the early twenty-first century in the United States, these types of programs have become more essential for dealing with increasing numbers of teenage runaways, homeless juveniles, juveniles with mental health issues, and juveniles "strung out" on drugs.

The Rights of Probationers

The U.S. Supreme Court has ruled on two cases concerning probation revocation: *Mempa v. Rhay*[37] and *Gagnon v. Scarpelli*.[38] The Court held in the *Mempa* case that the Sixth Amendment's right to counsel applies to the sentencing hearing that takes place after a probation violation has been reported.

Gagnon v. Scarpelli involved an offender whose probation was revoked in Wisconsin without a hearing. Scarpelli, who had been sentenced to fifteen years of imprisonment for armed robbery, had his sentence suspended and was placed on probation for seven years. He was given permission to reside in Illinois, where he was subsequently arrested for burglary.

TABLE 15–2
Some Programs Utilized by Local Probation Departments

4-H programs	Self-improvement classes	Day school
Social skills development	Youth courts	Evening care
School-based probation	Teen courts	Community service
Truancy programs	Drug courts	Volunteer work
After-school study programs	Positive peer groups	Big Brothers Big Sisters
Sports programs	Reintegration programs	Volunteers in probation
After-school counseling	Faith-based initiatives	Drug counseling
Writing a paper	Treatment courts	Sex offender programs
Curfew requirements	Job training	Aggression replacement training
Restorative programs	Alcohol counseling	Runaway programs
Restitution programs	Mentoring programs	

His probation at that point was automatically revoked without a hearing. Scarpelli appealed the revocation, claiming that his failure to receive a hearing and to have counsel represent him at such a hearing violated his due process rights. Although the Supreme Court held that the right to counsel should be decided on a case-by-case basis, the Court did agree on the need for a hearing prior to revocation of probation.[39]

These two adult cases have influenced what takes place during a probation revocation hearing in juvenile court, because in many jurisdictions the juvenile probationer has the same basic rights as an adult. The juvenile has the right to a hearing, the right to five-day notification of the probation revocation hearing, the right to be represented by an attorney, the right to confrontation, and the right to see the reports detailing his or her violations.

"Reasonable efforts" is the standard that most juvenile judges adhere to at the probation revocation hearing. According to this standard, the probation officer must show that reasonable efforts have been made to provide appropriate services and programs to the probationer. It, therefore, provides clear and convincing evidence of the youth's refusal or inability to profit from these services and shows that he or she cannot be allowed to remain free in the community.[40]

The Effectiveness of Probation

Studies of probation in the 1960s and 1970s demonstrated that juvenile probation was more effective than any other method for the rehabilitation of youthful offenders. For example, drug researcher Douglas Lipton and colleagues' work reviewed the studies of adult and juvenile probation and arrived at the following conclusions: (1) Evidence exists that a large proportion of offenders now incarcerated could be placed on probation without any change in the recidivism rates; (2) probationers have a significantly lower violation rate than do parolees; and (3) intensive probation supervision (a fifteen-ward caseload) is associated with lower recidivism rates for youths under age 18.[41]

A major problem in understanding the effectiveness of probation today, however, is that probation has changed so much since these early evaluation studies. Today's risk reduction programs, such as restitution, intensive supervision, and house arrest, are still being evaluated. Evidence suggests that restitution and intensive supervision studies are returning some positive results, but it is too early to draw any firm conclusions from these studies about the present effectiveness of juvenile probation.

day-treatment program
A court-mandated, community-based corrections program that juveniles attend in the morning and afternoon. They return home in the evening.

There are two positive themes that can be used to improve the effectiveness of juvenile probation: (1) to implement as much as possible the successful probation practices in adult probation and (2) to examine juvenile probation practices across the nation and to utilize those that might be helpful in your jurisdiction. For example, juvenile probation officers with the Department of Juvenile Justice in Florida play a major role throughout the juvenile justice process because they work with youth from the time they are arrested to the time they transition back into the community. The strength of this approach to juvenile probation is providing a continuum of contact and services, so that juvenile probation officers continue their supervision of those with whom they have worked in the past, as they are processed through the juvenile justice system.[42]

A social worker talks with a homeless girl.
■ **What kinds of services are likely to be of greatest interest to marginalized young women?**

Day-Treatment Programs

Day-treatment programs, in which youngsters spend each day in the program and then return home in the evenings, have been widely used in community-based juvenile corrections. These court-mandated programs are popular because they are more economical than residential placements, do not need to provide living and sleeping quarters, make parental participation easier, require fewer staff members, and are less coercive and punishment oriented.

Nonresidential programs generally serve male juveniles, although California has operated two programs for girls and several coeducational ones. Nonresidential programs have been used widely by the California Treatment Project, the New York Division for Youth, and the Florida Division of Youth Services. Nonresidential programs in New York, which are called STAY, are similar to many other nonresidential programs in that they expose youths to a guided-group interaction experience.

Day-treatment programs, similar to diversion programs, were used less in the 1980s and early 1990s than they were in the 1970s, but two of the most promising programs—the nationwide Associated Marine Institute (AMI) and Project New Pride—continue to thrive. The AMI is described here.

Associated Marine Institute

The original Associated Marine Institute was a privately operated program funded jointly by state funds and private donations. Its programs were tailored to the geographical strengths of each community, using the ocean, wilderness, rivers, and lakes to stimulate productive behavior in youths referred by the courts or by the Division of Youth Services. Of the forty schools and institutes of the AMI, twenty-five were nonresidential. The fourteen- to eighteen-year-old male and female trainees in the nonresidential programs lived at home or in foster homes.[43]

The Marine Institutes, which constituted most of the schools, set individual goals for the training period in a dozen categories, including diving, ship-handling skills, ocean science, lifesaving, first aid, and such electives as photography and marine maintenance. In a nationally broadcast television program, in which he announced his crime bill, President Bill Clinton said, "These [AMI] programs are giving young people a chance to take their future back, a chance to understand that there is good inside them."[44]

Today AMI has been renamed AMIkids and operates fifty-six programs in eight states. The reorganization and new name reflect the fact that organization now includes many different types of programs across the nation that formerly operated independently. Rather than just operating marine programs, today's AMIkids programs provide probation services including community service, wilderness programs, substance abuse counseling, and varied after-school programs. They also volunteer their services to veterans, homeless people, and senior citizens and participate in shoreline cleanups and other types of community service built around President Obama's call for community service.[45]

Residential Facilities or Group Homes

The group home, the group residence, and the group foster home are all used in juvenile corrections in this country. The term **group home** generally refers to a single dwelling owned or rented by an organization or agency for the purpose of housing offenders. Although it is not part of an institutional campus, this facility provides care for a group of about four to twelve children, and staff are viewed as houseparents or counselors rather than as foster parents. The administrative, supervisory, and service responsibility for the group home rests with the parent agency or organization. Usually indistinguishable from nearby homes or apartments, the group home reaches out to the community for resources and service.

The terms *group residence* and **halfway house** are used in some parts of the country to identify a small facility serving about thirteen to thirty-five youths. It usually houses two or more groups of youths, each with its own child care staff. This residence tends to use agency rather than community services, and its architecture and large size differentiate it from nearby homes and apartments.

Group homes fulfill several purposes in juvenile corrections. First, they provide an alternative to institutionalization. Dependent, neglected, and other noncriminal youths, especially, are referred to them. Second, group homes may be used as short-term residences. The communities in which they are located provide the youths with the resources to deal with such problems as family conflict, school difficulties, and peer interactions. Third, group homes can be used either as a "halfway-in" setting for offenders who are having difficulty keeping to the conditions of probation or as a "halfway-out" setting for juvenile offenders who are returning to the community but do not have adequate home placement.

group home
A placement for youths who have been adjudicated by the court that serves a group of about thirteen to thirty-five youths as an alternative to institutionalization; also called *group residence, halfway house,* or *attention home.*

halfway house
A residential setting for adjudicated delinquents, usually those who need a period of readjustment to the community following institutional confinement.

Group home programs tend to vary from home to home because they have been developed to meet varying needs for different populations and communities, and standard guidelines do not exist. Consequently, group homes often reflect the personal philosophies of their founders or directors. Intake criteria, length of stay, treatment goals, target population serviced, quantity and quality of staffing, services offered, physical facilities, location in relation to the rest of the city, and house rules are extremely diverse in group homes in this country. This diversity need not be a problem, however, if additional support services are available. One of the most important studies of juvenile justice found a significant reduction in recidivism in Massachusetts when community-based programs had an integrated network of services.[46]

Many group homes are treatment oriented. Group therapy often is used as a treatment modality. These group sessions are largely supportive; they do not probe very deeply, and discussion usually is limited to problems as they arise. Guided group interaction (GGI) is probably the most popular treatment method; the members of the group are expected to support, confront, and be honest with one another so that they may be helped in dealing with their own problems. The role of the therapist in GGI is to help the members develop a more positive and prosocial group culture. Some group homes deliberately avoid a comfortable climate, and staff may even try to arouse anxiety. The treatment philosophy behind this is that without a relaxed atmosphere, youths are more likely to become unsettled and thereby more receptive to personality change.

One of the most innovative programs is the House of Umoja (HOU) project, which was founded in 1968 in Philadelphia, Pennsylvania. When she became aware that one of her six sons had joined a gang, Muslim Sister Falaka Fattah (born Frances Brown) and her husband, David Fattah, took the bold step of inviting the gang to become a part of their family. Sister Falaka saw possible solutions to the violence of gangs in "the strength of the family, tribal concepts, and African value systems." She and her husband created an African-style extended family in which members of the gang could find alternative values to those of their street-life culture. Residents are required to be drug free and are encouraged to maintain good grades. Since its establishment, three thousand adolescents belonging to seventy-three different street gangs have passed through the HOU doors. The success of the Umoja concept led to its duplication in Bridgeport, Connecticut, and Portland, Oregon. The principles of this resident program are part of the National Center for Neighborhood Enterprise's highly successful Violence-Free Zone initiative that has since been instituted in five cities.[47]

Yet innovative programs still are not typical of group homes across the nation. In too many group homes, vacancies are hard to find and many even have long waiting lists. Staff are notoriously underpaid, believe that they have not been properly trained, and have high rates of turnover.[48] Residents also typically have longer stays than they would have in training schools, and this raises real questions about whether group homes are a less punitive placement than juvenile institutions. The evaluations of residential programs further make it difficult to support the conclusion that residential programs in the community result in lower rates of recidivism than do institutional programs. Nevertheless, a convincing case can be made that residential programs are at least as successful as training schools, with far less trauma to youths and usually at less cost to the state.

Wilderness Programs

Outward Bound
A wilderness-type survival program that is popular in many states as an alternative to the institutionalization of juveniles.

wilderness programs
Sometimes called survival programs, these venues expose youth who have been entered into them to participate in forest, mountain, and ocean training. The best known is Outward Bound.

Outward Bound is perhaps the best-known wilderness, or survival, program. All outdoor **wilderness programs**, whether they take place in the mountains, canoe country, the forest, the sea, or the desert, believe that the completion of a seemingly impossible task is one of the best means to gain self-reliance, to prove one's worth, and to define oneself as a person.

Outward Bound programs were first used in England during World War II. The first Outward Bound school in the United States was the Colorado Outward Bound School, which was established in 1962 and accepted its first delinquents in 1964. This program, situated in the Rocky Mountains at an altitude of 8,800 feet, consists of mountain walking, backpacking, high-altitude camping, solo survival, rappelling, and rock climbing. Other Outward Bound programs soon followed in Maine, Minnesota, North Carolina, Oregon, and Texas. A similar program, a Homeward Bound school, was opened in 1970 in Massachusetts. Several

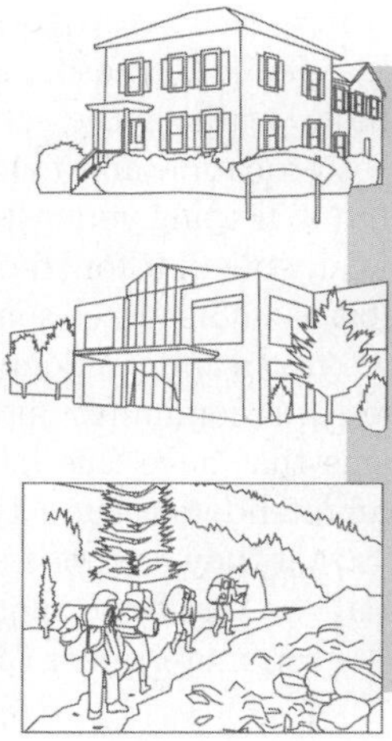

FIGURE 15–3
Three Types of Community Programs

Group Home
Residential placement into which juveniles are assigned, either while on probation or when released from a training school

Day-Treatment Programs
Nonresidential programs that do not provide living and sleeping quarters

Wilderness Programs
Use the wilderness, desert, sea, and urban areas in order to allow participants to gain self-reliance, to prove one's worth, and to define one's personhood

community-based wilderness programs that begin and end in the community but include sessions in a nearby wilderness area are also in operation.[49]

Today, Outward Bound has twelve regional schools: Alabama, Baltimore, California, Hurricane Island, New York City, North Carolina, Northwest, Omaha, Philadelphia, Rock Mountain, Thompson Island, and Voyageur. They offer 750 wilderness courses serving adults, teens, and youths. Courses include rock climbing, kayaking, dogsledding, sailing, rappelling, backpacking, and more. Over ten thousand students have so far participated in wilderness courses. Outward Bound also offers multiyear partnerships with 150 schools across the United States. It encourages over thirty thousand students and four thousand teachers to reach high levels of achievement and to discover their potential.[50]

Figure 15–3 summarizes the three types of community programs just discussed.

Improving the Effectiveness of Community-Based Programs

Increasing numbers of studies demonstrate empirically that many community-based correctional programs reduce recidivism and are less expensive than confinement. It would appear, however, that improving the effectiveness of community-based corrections ultimately requires overcoming community resistance to the presence of such programs, and obtaining greater citizen involvement.

To break down community resistance and to obtain greater citizen involvement in community-based programs, departments of juvenile corrections must develop and implement effective action plans. These plans need to include a well-developed vision for the establishment of programs and for deciding which juvenile offenders will be placed in community facilities.

Careful planning is necessary to gain greater public support for community-based programs.

Advocates of keeping the community informed as soon as a site for a program is chosen claim that to do otherwise is dishonest. Opponents of this approach argue that advance information will permit the community to mobilize resistance against the proposed community program. They claim that the community is more likely to accept an already established and successful program than one that exists only on the drawing board.

Widespread controversy also exists over the selection of youths to be placed in community-based programs. One approach is conservative: If the wrong youth is put in the wrong place at the wrong time and commits a serious or violent crime, such as rape or murder, the adverse publicity may destroy the best-planned and implemented program. Therefore, to preserve the viability of community-based programs, only juveniles most likely to be helped should be kept in the community. The opposite approach argues that all but the hard-core recidivist should be retained in the community, for it is there that the youth's problems began in the first place. Advocates of this position believe that institutionalization will only make more serious criminals out of confined youths. Some of these supporters even propose leaving many of the hard-core or difficult-to-handle youths in the community.

The quality of staff is a key factor in the effectiveness of probation and community-based correctional programs. Staff who care and are committed to helping youngsters; staff who have skill in working with difficult youth; and staff who can stay in it for the long run can have a lifetime of success with youthful offenders. (Exhibit 15–4 discusses some of the characteristics of effective—as well as ineffective—probation officers and residential staff.)

Finally, improving the continuum of services for juveniles in a community usually requires a strong deinstitutionalization emphasis. The programs that have this integration of services are more likely to have positive effects on youthful offenders assigned to them. Another advantage of these continuum-of-service programs is that they are not as likely to experience the fragmentation and duplication of services that are found so frequently in other programs in the juvenile justice system. Exhibit 15–5, describing Project CRAFT, illustrates a continuum of service programs for juveniles.

Delinquency Across the Life Course

One of the underlying themes of this book is that committed corrections professionals can have an exciting and worthwhile career while, at the same time, making a difference in the lives of the youth with whom they work. Such professionals can become a vital force in youths' live, if they:

- See themselves as persons of integrity.
- Treat youth with dignity and respect.

Exhibit 15–4
Communication with Clients

Probation officers and residential staff who relate well and do an effective job with clients tend to have certain characteristics in common:

1. They are genuine in their relationships with probationers and do not hide behind a professional role; that is, they attempt to avoid barriers that would isolate them from their clients. Furthermore, they try to be honest with their clients and expect the juveniles to be honest in return.
2. They respond to others with respect, kindness, and compassion. Because they are caring persons, they are able to listen and reach out to others.
3. They are not gullible or easily hoodwinked by probationers, because they know what life on the streets is like.
4. They are able to encourage others to pursue positive experiences; they also have an uncanny knack of knowing what to say and do when others fail.
5. They have a good understanding of themselves and have a reasonable idea of their own problems, shortcomings, and needs. They know, in addition, their biases, prejudices, and pet peeves.
6. They are very committed to their jobs, for the job to them is much more than a paycheck. Moreover, their enthusiasm does not wane following the first few weeks or months as probation officers.

Probation officers who continually have problems with clients also have certain characteristics in common:

1. They do not keep their word. Either they promise more than they are capable of delivering or they simply fail to follow through on what they have said they would do.
2. They become bored with their jobs, chiefly because they see little meaning in working with youths whom they regard as losers who will always be marginal citizens.
3. They either have unreal expectations for probationers or are inflexible in interpreting the terms of probation.
4. They permit their personality problems to affect their performance on the job, which often results in a lack of warmth, a preoccupation with self, or a sharp, biting response to others. Not surprisingly, these personality traits alienate them from both probationers and other probation staff.
5. They seem to be unable to respond to lower-class youths who do not share their own middle-class values, so they become judgmental and moralistic in dealing with clients.
6. They are unwilling to pay the price of changing their own lives in order to influence or alter the lives of juvenile offenders. They are also willing to recommend that youths become involved in programs, such as Project CRAFT (see Exhibit 15–5).

Exhibit 15–5
Project CRAFT

Project CRAFT is a community restitution and apprenticeship-focused training program. This vocational training program for high-risk youths is sponsored by the Home Builders Institute (HBI), the educational arm of the National Association of Home Builders (NAHB). Project CRAFT offers pre-apprenticeship training and job training for adjudicated juveniles referred to the program. It was started in 1994 by HBI in Bismarck, North Dakota; Nashville, Tennessee; and Sabillasville, Maryland. It has been replicated in five sites in Florida (Avon Park, Daytona Beach, Fort Lauderdale, Lantana, and Orlando), in Texas, and in Connecticut.[51] This program works in partnership with private facilities, juvenile judges, juvenile justice system personnel, educational agencies, and other human service agencies.[52] Although the initial sample size was small, an early study indicates that 15 percent of youths recidivate during their first year after release, 10 percent recidivate their second year, and 1 percent recidivate their third year after release; these data compare favorably with an untreated sample with a 50 percent recidivism rate over three years.[53]

Project CRAFT has been teaching court-involved youth ages 15 to 19 marketable construction trade skills that help them find jobs, instill a sense of confidence and excitement about the future, and provide them with viable career options. Once graduates earn their industry-recognized pre-apprenticeship certification, Project CRAFT staff helps them find jobs, continue their education, or join the military.

Journey-level trades instructors teach the HBI's Pre-Apprenticeship Certificate Training (PACT) curriculum in electric wiring, carpentry, landscaping, facilities maintenance, plumbing, and painting. Some of their accomplishments are as follows:

- HBI Project CRAFT Avon Park Youth Academy students have installed solar panels on academy buildings to reduce its carbon footprint.
- Students at HBI Project CRAFT Baltimore have renovated Family League of Baltimore City office space into a state-of-the-art conference room and built a bench for a presiding Baltimore City juvenile judge.
- HBI Project CRAFT Okeechobee Girls Academy is the only juvenile justice residential program in Florida that provides career and technical education to young women.

Source: http://www.hbi.org/Programs/PreApprenticeship/Project/CRAFT.asp (accessed on May 12, 2012).

- Model positive behaviors to both youth and staff.
- Refuse to accept unethical behavior from fellow staff members.
- Work to create a positive workplace.
- Are committed to making a difference.
- Become proactive leaders, anticipating and preventing problems before they occur.
- Remember the importance of accountability, attention to detail, and following the schedule.
- Listen to others.
- Go the second mile for individual youth, especially if they show signs that they want to change.

How do the authors know that good people can make a difference in youngsters' lives? There is evidence of this in some of the *Voices of Delinquency* stories. There are people whom the authors have met whose lives were affected by individuals who cared and supported them during their troubled years. And one of the authors was heading for reform school and perhaps a life of crime before an adult intervened to change his life!

Delinquency and Social Policy for Community-Based Corrections

Community-based corrections has the following advantages over residential placement for juveniles:

- Long-term institutional care is extremely expensive, sometimes costing $50,000 to $100,000 a year per resident.
- It is very difficult for large impersonal institutions to provide quality care for youngsters.

- Institutional care can harm youngsters and cause them to increase their commitment to lives of crime.
- Juveniles are not always safe in long-term institutions, and there is a long and sad legacy of juvenile victimization in institutional settings.
- The recidivism rate has always been very high for wards after their release from long-term institutional care.

It can be argued that some juveniles need confinement in a closed facility to protect themselves as well as society. But many policy makers today support a policy of deinstitutionalization. They are working to retain institutional care for the few juveniles who cannot safely remain in the community while ensuring that the remainder of juvenile offenders remain in the community benefitting from some form of community care.

The Case

The Life Course of Amy Watters, Age 16½

As a consequence of failing to meet the requirements of her probation, Amy was brought back to juvenile court. The no-nonsense judge before whom she appeared asked a few questions, and ordered her to be sent to a residential facility for serious juvenile offenders, where she was to be held for six months. During that time, the judge told Amy that she had to participate in and successfully complete a drug-education program that the facility offered. While there, the judge said, Amy would be expected to attend an on-site school (she was in the tenth grade), and to maintain at least a C average in the courses she took. Any sign of further misbehavior, the judge told Amy, could result in her being held at the facility until she turned nineteen. Soon after the hearing concluded, Amy was taken to a state-run residential facility for girls.

Would the judge have made a better decision by allowing Amy to continue on probation? Why or why not?

Learn More on the Web:
- Models for Change—Community-based Alternatives: http://www.modelsforchange.net/about/Issues-for-change/Community-Based-Alternatives.html

Follow the continuing story of Amy Watters in the next chapter.

SUMMARY

This chapter examined community-based corrections for juveniles, including probation. Among the most important issues discussed in this chapter include the following:

- Today more delinquents are treated in the community than are adjudicated to training schools, because juvenile judges remain supportive of the least restrictive or soft-line approach for minor offenders.

- Community-based corrections include probation, residential and day-treatment programs, and aftercare.

- Clients placed on probation or in aftercare are more likely to participate in intensive supervision programs than in the past.

KEY TERMS

balanced approach to juvenile probation, p. 393
community-based corrections, p. 387
community corrections acts, p. 389
continuum of sanctions, p. 389
day-treatment program, p. 400
electronic monitoring, p. 397
group home, p. 401
halfway house, p. 401

house arrest, p. 397
intake, p. 391
intensive supervision programs (ISPs), p. 396
Outward Bound, p. 402
probation, p. 390
probation officer, p. 390
probation subsidy programs, p. 391
reintegration philosophy, p. 387

restitution, p. 395
restorative justice, p. 389
restorative justice model, p. 388
social study report, p. 393
supervision, p. 392
surveillance, p. 392
volunteer program, p. 398
wilderness programs, p. 402
Wisconsin system, p. 393

JUVENILE DELINQUENCY VIDEOS

Juvenile Probation and Parole 1

In the first *Juvenile Probation and Parole* video, a juvenile comes before an administrative review committee to discuss the possibility of being granted parole. The youth must "convince" the committee that his time in the facility has changed his behavior for the better and that as such he deserves a chance to be released back into the real world. Listen to the questions the committee is asking the youth in regards to his past criminal history, time in the facility, and future plans. What importance do these questions have in determining the status of the juvenile? Does the youth's gang involvement have an impact in the decision of the committee? What is the decision of the committee? What programs are suggested for the youth to engage in? Why?

Future Soldiers Program

The *Future Soldiers Program* follows a youth offender through a specialized treatment program aimed at training youths in military fashion to promote discipline and set future goals for military service. What are other goals of the Future Soldiers Program? The video displays the admissions process for entering the Future Soldiers Program. What are some of the questions asked by the committee? Why are these important factors in assessing whether a juvenile will be able to handle the intense program? Based on the video and the readings, compare and contrast the Future Soldiers Program to other treatment models. For which types of juveniles might the Future Soldiers Program be more effective?

REVIEW QUESTIONS

1. What is the purpose of probation?
2. What are the three basic functions of probation services?
3. What are the various forms of risk control being used today? How does each work?
4. What are the three types of residential and day-treatment programs? How does each function?

DISCUSSION QUESTIONS

1. What are the job responsibilities of a probation officer?
2. Given their notoriously heavy caseloads, is it responsible to blame probation officers when a juvenile probationer reoffends? Are probation officers made into scapegoats by the media? Explain your responses.
3. What are the differences between probation and aftercare services?
4. Of the programs discussed in this chapter, which do you believe is the most effective for helping offenders reintegrate into the community?
5. How effective are community-based corrections programs? What can be done to improve the effectiveness of community-based corrections?

GROUP EXERCISES

1. Invite a local probation officer to address the class regarding his or her role in the juvenile justice process.
2. Have the students clip newspaper articles related to residential and day-treatment programs for juvenile offenders in your state. Discuss them in class.
3. Have the students compare recidivism rates for juveniles who have completed the Outward Bound and Associated

Marine Institute programs and compare them to the recidivism rates for juvenile offenders on conventional probation. Discuss their findings in class.
4. Have the students research how many juvenile offenders are currently electronically monitored and the annual cost of such monitoring compared to the cost of conventional supervision.

NOTES

1. Joseph Heinz, Theresa Wise, and Clemens Bartollas, *Successful Management of Juvenile Residential Facilities: A Performance-Based Approach* (Alexandria, Va.: American Correctional Association, 2010), pp. 35–36.
2. Patricia M. Harris, Rebecca D. Petersen, and Samantha Rapoza, "Between Probation and Revocation: A Study of Intermediate Sanctions Decision-Making," *Journal of Criminal Justice* 29 (2001), p. 308.
3. Ibid., p. 175.
4. Howard N. Snyder and Melissa Sickmund, *Juvenile Offenders and Victims: 2006 National Report* (Pittsburgh, PA: National Center for Juvenile Justice, 2006), pp. 174–75.

5. See Nebraska Department of Health and Human Services, "Families Matter," http://dhhs.ne.gov/children_family_ services/Pages/familiesmatter.aspx (accessed May 19, 2012).

6. John L. Worrall, Pamela Schram, Eric Hays, and Matthew Newman, "An Analysis of the Relationships between Probation Caseloads and Property Crime Rates in California Counties," *Journal of Criminal Justice* 32 (2004), pp. 231–41.

7. Joan Petersilia, *The Influence of Criminal Justice Research* (Santa Monica, Calif.: Rand, 1987), p. 72.

8. K. Heilbrun, C. Cottle, and R. Lee, "Risk Assessment for Adolescents," *Juvenile Justice Fact Sheet* (Charlottesville: Institute of Law, Psychiatry, and Public Policy, University of Virginia, 2000).

9. Ibid.

10. C. Cottle, R. Lee, and K. Heilbrun, "The Prediction of Criminal Recidivism in Juveniles: A Meta-Analysis," *Criminal Justice and Behavior* 28, no. 3 (June 2001), pp. 367–94.

11. See Dennis Maloney, Dennis Romig, and Troy Armstrong, "The Balanced Approach to Juvenile Probation," *Juvenile and Family Court Journal* 39 (1989), pp. 1–49.

12. Ibid., p. 10. See also Gordon Bazemore and Mark S. Umbreit, *Balanced and Restorative Justice: Program Summary* (Washington, D.C.: Office of Juvenile Justice and Delinquency Prevention, 1994).

13. Bazemore and Umbreit, *Balanced and Restorative Justice,* p. 5.

14. Ibid., p. 7.

15. See Lori L. Colley, Robert C. Culbertson, and Edward J. Latessa, "Juvenile Probation Officers: A Job Analysis," *Juvenile and Family Court Journal* 38 (1987), pp. 1–12.

16. Anne L. Schneider, "Restitution and Recidivism Rates of Juvenile Offenders: Results from Four Experimental Studies," *Criminology* 24 (1986), p. 533.

17. William G. Staples, "Restitution as a Sanction in Juvenile Court," *Crime and Delinquency* 32 (April 1986), p. 177.

18. OJJDP Model Program Guide, *Restitution/Community Service,* http://www.dsonline.com/mpg_non_flash/ restitution?community? service.htm.

19. Patrick Griffin and Patricia Torbet, eds., *Desktop Guide to Good Juvenile Probation Practice: Mission-Driven, Performance-Based, and Outcome-Focused* (Pittsburgh, Pa.: National Center for Juvenile Justice, 2002), p. 85.

20. Ibid., pp. 85–86.

21. Ted Palmer, *The Re-Emergence of Correctional Intervention* (Newbury Park, Calif.: Sage Publications, 1992), p. 80.

22. Emily Walker, "The Community Intensive Treatment for Youth Program: A Specialized Community-Based Program for High-Risk Youth in Alabama," *Law and Psychiatry Review* 13 (1989), pp. 175–99.

23. Cecil Marshall and Keith Snyder, "Intensive and Aftercare Probation Services in Pennsylvania," paper presented at the annual meeting of the American Society of Criminology, Baltimore, MD, November 7, 1990, p. 3.

24. Bernadette Jones, "Intensive Probation, Philadelphia County, November 1986–February 1989," paper presented at the annual meeting of the American Society of Criminology, Baltimore, MD, November 1992), p. 1 of Appendix.

25. Marshall and Snyder, "Intensive and Aftercare Probation Services in Pennsylvania," p. 3.

26. Barry Krisberg et al., *Juvenile Intensive Supervision: Planning Guide* (Washington, D.C.: Office of Juvenile Justice and Delinquency Prevention, 1994), p. 7.

27. For a review of these studies in intensive supervision programs for adults, see Larry Siegel and Clemens Bartollas, *Corrections Today* 2d ed. Belmont, CA.: Wadsworth, 2013), p. 94.

28. Palmer, *The Re-Emergence of Correctional Intervention,* p. 82.

29. J. Robert Lilly and Richard A. Ball, "A Brief History of House Arrest and Electronic Monitoring," *Northern Kentucky Law Review* 13 (1987), pp. 343–74.

30. Griffin and Torbet, *Desktop Guide to Good Juvenile Probation Practice,* p. 79.

31. Richard A. Ball, Ronald Huff, and Robert Lilly, *House Arrest and Correctional Policy: Doing Time at Home* (Newbury Park, Calif.: Sage Publications, 1988), pp. 35–36.

32. Jennifer Lee, "Some States Track Parolees by Satellite," *New York Times,* January 31, 2002, p. A3.

33. Ralph Gable and Robert Gable, "Electronic Monitoring: Positive Intervention Strategies," *Federal Probation* 69 (2005), pp. 21–25.

34. Joseph B. Vaughn, "A Survey of Juvenile Electronic Monitoring and Home Confinement Program," *Juvenile and Family Court Journal* 40 (1989), pp. 4, 22. For a description of another program, see Michael T. Charles, "The Development of a Juvenile Electronic Monitoring Program," *Federal Probation* 53 (1989), pp. 3–12.

35. Vaughn, "A Survey of Juvenile Electronic Monitoring."

36. One of the authors and his wife interviewed willing residents of these safe houses.

37. *Mempa* v. *Rhay,* 339 U.S. 128, 2d Cir. 3023 (1968).

38. *Gagnon* v. *Scarpelli,* 411 U.S. 778 (1973).

39. Ibid.

40. Information gained from an interview with a juvenile probation officer in Iowa.

41. Douglas Lipton et al., *The Effectiveness of Correctional Treatment: A Survey of Evaluation Studies* (New York: Praeger, 1975), pp. 59–61.

42. Florida Department of Juvenile Justice, *Florida Juvenile Justice Probation and Community Intervention,* http:// www.djj.state.fl.us/services/probation (accessed May 21, 2012).

43. Information on the Associated Marine Institute was supplied in a 1995 phone conversation with Magie Valdés.

44. Unpublished mimeographed statement circulated by AMI, n.d.

45. For additional information on AMIkids, see Jasmine Ouhrt, "New Name, Same Mission: AMI Lakeland is now AMIkids," http://www.theledger.com/article/20090725/ NEWS/907255003?Title=New-Name-Same-Mission- AMI-Lakeland-Is-Now-AMIKids. Also see Links on AMIkids on Facebook. http://www.facebook.com/posted .php?id=108818992527.

46. B. Krisberg, J. Austin, and P. Steele, *Unlocking Juvenile Corrections* (San Francisco: National Council on Crime and Delinquency, 1991).

47. For the House of Umoja, see http://www.volunteersolutions .org/volunteerway/org/1236595.

48. One of the authors has had a number of former students who were employed in group homes, and they consistently make these criticisms.

49. Joshua L. Miner and Joe Boldt, *Outward Bound USA: Learning Through Experience* (New York: Morrow, 1981).

50. For Outward Bound USA, see http://www.outwardbound.org.

51. For more information on Project Craft in Florida and Connecticut, visit Project Craft, http://www.hbi.org/page .cfm?pageID=129.

52. Robin Hamilton and Kay McKinney, "Job Training for Juveniles: Project CRAFT," *OJJDP Fact Sheet* (Washington, DC: Office of Juvenile Justice and Delinquency Prevention, 1999), p. 1.

53. Steve V. Gies, "Aftercare Services" (Washington, D.C.: OJJDP, September, 2003), pp. 18–20, http://www.ncjrs.gov/ pdffiles1/ojjdp/201800.pdf.

Chapter Objectives

After reading this chapter, you should be able to:

1. Describe the various types of institutional placements in juvenile corrections.

2. Describe the kinds of experiences juveniles have in institutional placements.

3. Summarize the rights of confined juveniles.

4. Summarize how aftercare is used in juvenile corrections, including its objectives, operations, and emphases.

5. Summarize the problem of sexual violence during juvenile institutionalization and efforts to address it.

Juveniles may be committed to a facility as part of a court-ordered disposition or they may be detained prior to adjudication or after adjudication while awaiting disposition or placement elsewhere.

—OJJDP, *Juveniles in Corrections*

Introduction

An investigation exposes a lawsuit and barbaric conditions at a for-profit youth facility in Mississippi. The story behind this exposé concerns a young man named Michael McIntosh who was housed at the Walnut Grove Youth Correctional Facility near Jackson, Mississippi.[1] When his father went to visit his son, he was not at the facility. The father then launched a search that lasted for six weeks, but failed to find his son. Finally, a nurse told the father to check the area hospitals. After a number of frantic phone calls, the father found Mike in a hospital in Greenwood, hours away. When he went to the hospital, the father was shocked at what he saw. His son, Mike, could not see or talk or use his right arm. "He's got this baseball-size knot on the back of his head," the father told reporters, "He's got cuts all over him, bruises. He has stab wounds. The teeth in the front are broken. He's scared out of his mind. He doesn't have a clue where he's at—or why."

A later Southern Poverty Law Center (SPLC) investigation of Walnut Grove Youth Correctional Facility turned up a youth riot in which several youths were stabbed, including Michael, who, in addition to a fractured nose, cuts, and stab wounds, had suffered irreparable brain damage. A dozen youths were hospitalized, including some who were thrown from an upper floor to the ground.

Further investigation revealed that a female guard had apparently endorsed the disturbance by allowing inmates to enter into a fight. She was fired, but not charged with any crime. Her involvement in the resident's misbehavior was determined not to be unusual, as other guards frequently instigated or incited youth-on-youth violence.

Violence by youths and guards was not the only problem at Walnut Grove. Some guards were found to have gang affiliations; medical and mental health care were grossly inadequate; the use of drugs and others contraband proliferated; the facility was cited for a lack of effective educational and rehabilitative programs; and staff members were cited for the wild overuse of pepper spray on passive youths. To make matters worse, an investigation by the U.S. Department of Justice (DOJ) found that sexual abuse, including brutal youth-on-youth rapes and brazen sexual misconduct by prison staff who coerced residents into these behaviors, was "among the worst that we [DOJ] had seen in any facility anywhere in the nation."[2]

The initial investigation turned into a federal civil rights lawsuit, with the American Civil Liberty Union (ACLU) and Jackson-based civil rights attorney Robert McDuff as co-counsels. It was settled in March 2012 with a sweeping consent decree designed to end the barbaric, unconstitutional conditions and the rampant violations of federal and state law that were documented separately by both the SPLC and the DOJ.

The juvenile justice system often is accused of being too lenient, yet youths who are believed to be dangerous or who show little sign of mending their ways frequently find themselves locked up behind its walls. The facilities in which these youths are placed are divided into two general categories: temporary care facilities and correctional facilities. Detention homes, shelters, reception centers, and jails are temporary care facilities; boot camps, ranches, forestry camps, and training schools are longer-term correctional facilities. Table 16–1 lists the number of these various types of short- and long-term facilities.

The primary differences between these two categories of facilities are the absence of correctional programs and the shorter lengths of stay in temporary care facilities. Temporary care facilities frequently house both males and females in the same general location, whereas correctional facilities often separate them. Juveniles waived to adult court can also be sentenced to adult prisons, or they can be placed in mental health facilities. Although a large variety of residential placement options are available to judges in juvenile court, this chapter focuses on the training school because of the length of time it holds youths and because of the special role it plays in juvenile justice.

Investigations of juvenile training schools have repeatedly reported the type of abuse illustrated by the story that opened this chapter. Beginning in the 1970s and continuing in the 1980s, through the 1990s, and into the post-2000 decade, a series of investigations reported similar stories of institutionalized youths being abused and victimized within the very facilities that were originally designed to help them.

Exhibit 16–1 provides examples of victimization in the 2000s, but there is also good news out of California about juvenile institutionalization. While acknowledging what is inhumane

TABLE 16–1
Number of Juvenile Facilities in the United States, by Type

Facility operation	Total	Detention center	Shelter	Reception/ diagnostic center	Group home	Ranch/ wilderness camp	Training school	Residential treatment center
				Facility type				
Number of facilities	2,458	734	167	64	661	85	210	847
Operations profile								
All facilities	100%	100%	100%	100%	100%	100%	100%	100%
Public	47	86	31	67	22	52	89	29
State	19	20	4	59	11	12	73	16
Local	27	66	26	8	10	40	15	13
Private	53	13	69	33	78	48	11	71
Facility profile								
All facilities	100%	30%	7%	3%	27%	3%	9%	34%
Public	100	55	4	4	13	4	16	21
State	100	31	1	8	16	2	32	28
Local	100	72	7	1	10	5	5	17
Private	100	7	9	2	40	3	2	46

Source: Sarah Hockenberry, Melissa Sickmund, and Anthony Sladky, *Juvenile Residential Facility Census, 2008: Selected Findings* (Washington, D.C.: U.S. Department of Justice, Juvenile Offenders and Victims: National Report Services Bulletin, 2011), p. 3.

Exhibit 16–1
Juvenile Corrections

Child advocates have harshly condemned the conditions under which youth offenders are housed in institutional care. California juvenile facilities, according to a recent report, are failing their children. Juveniles have little chance of leaving institutionalized settings improved, and some are worse off than when they arrived.[3] Another report documented the violence, sexual abuse, and lack of accountability in juvenile facilities in the state of Texas.[4] In March 2007, responding to the reports of sexual abuse of youths at the Texas Youth Commission institutions, Texas Governor Rick Perry placed the Texas Youth Commission under conservatorship to guide reform of the agency. Similarly, the Connecticut Juvenile Training School has been a headache for state authorities since its opening in 2001. Its high-security perimeter fence, thick steel doors, and small cells with slits for windows make it feel more like a prison than a rehabilitation facility for juveniles. The problems increased as of 2010 when Connecticut raised the maximum age for juvenile offenders from fifteen to seventeen years old, moving many of the 250 to 300 sixteen- and seventeen-year-olds who now go to adult prisons each year into juvenile facilities.[5]

The U.S. Department of Justice has filed lawsuits against facilities in eleven states for supervision that is either abusive or harmfully negligent. Although the DOJ does not have the power to shut down juvenile correctional facilities, through litigation it can force a state to improve its facilities and protect the civil rights of jailed youths.[6] In a recent nationwide survey, the Associated Press contacted each state agency that oversees juvenile correctional centers and asked for information on the numbers of deaths as well as the numbers of allegations and confirmed cases of physical, sexual, and emotional abuse by state members since January 1, 2004. According to this survey, more than thirteen thousand claims of abuse were identified in juvenile correctional facilities around the nation from 2004 through 2007—a disturbing number given that the total population of detained youths was about forty-six thousand at the time the states were surveyed.[7]

In the midst of the bad news about juvenile institutionalization, there is what some consider a ray of hope from California. In the past decade, under a strategy known as juvenile justice realignment, the state of California has closed eight of its eleven juvenile facilities and successfully turned the responsibility for nonviolent offenders over to the state's counties. Governor Jerry Brown wants to complete the transformation soon by phasing out the three remaining state facilities that hold one thousand more-serious offenders. State spending on the system has dropped by half, from nearly $500 million to just above $245 million today, and the state has cut its juvenile population from about ten thousand in the mid-1990s to about one thousand today. Some critics are concerned, however, that without a state juvenile system to hold violent offenders prosecutors may try more young people as adults. The state can prevent this, however, by monitoring and penalizing counties that overprosecute juveniles and by funding extended custody in local facilities for those juveniles who have committed more serious crimes.

The Department of Corrections and Rehabilitation's Division of Juvenile Facilities, the former California Youth Authority, continues to remain under a consent decree due to previously identified abusive conditions, systemic mismanagement, and ineffectual services (*Farrell* v. *Cate,* 2004). As state legislators have realized, the closure of the state juvenile facilities would eliminate the state's obligation under the *Farrell* litigation, resulting in a potential $500 million budget reallocation to assist counties with the realignment plan and reduce the state's current budget deficit.

CRITICAL THINKING QUESTIONS

■ *Is the California realignment plan a positive development? How might juvenile institutions be reformed without closing them?*

Sources: Christopher Murray, Chris Baird, Ned Loughran, Fred Mills, and John Platt, *Safety and Welfare Plan: Implementing Reform in California* (Sacramento: California Department of Corrections and Rehabilitation, Division of Juvenile Justice, 2006); David W. Springer, *Transforming Juvenile Justice in Texas: A Framework for Action* (Austin, Tex.: Blue Ribbon Task Force Report, 2007); "Connecticut Juvenile Training School to Close," *New England Psychologist*, October 2005, http://www.masspsy.com/leading/0510_ne_CT.html; and Catherine McCracken and Selena Teji, An Update: *Closing California's Division of Juvenile Facilities: An Analysis of County Institutional Capacity* (San Francisco: Center on Juvenile and Criminal Justice, October 2010), http://www.cjcj.org/files/An_Update_Closing_Californias_Division_of_Juvenile_Facilities.pdf, accessed April 26, 2012.

and at times brutal in some training schools, this chapter presents examples of effective models of juvenile institutionalization as well as principles and strategies that can help all training schools become more effective.

Library Extra 16–1
OJJDP National Report Series publication: *Juveniles in Corrections*

The Short-Term Confinements of Juveniles

Juvenile offenders are placed in jails, detention centers, and shelter care facilities for short-term confinement. In this section, we briefly discuss each of these types of short-term facility.

Jails

The degrading conditions of nineteenth-century **jails** motivated reformers to establish houses of refuge. Even in those early times, it was commonly agreed that jails were not a place for juveniles. Overcrowded conditions and idleness fostered a lawless institutional society, one in which the juvenile was frequently a victim.

jail
A facility that provides temporary care and custody for juveniles during juvenile court proceedings. Also called *juvenile hall* and *detention home.*

Still, partly because so few alternatives were available, large numbers of juveniles continued to be confined in county jails and police lockups. Estimates varied, but between five hundred thousand and one million youths were locked up in jails each year during the 1970s.[8]

The numbers appeared to decline in the 1980s and 1990s, chiefly because of the Juvenile Justice and Delinquency Prevention Act (JJDPA) of 1974. This act provided restrictive criteria governing the confinement of juveniles in adult facilities. Congress amended the JJDPA in 1980, requiring participating states to remove all juveniles from adult jails and lockups by the end of 1985 if they wanted to receive federal funding for juvenile justice. The 1985 deadline for the *jail-removal mandate* was extended to 1988 and then again was amended in 1989 because so few states had achieved full compliance.[9] Over the years, the number of youths in adult jails was finally dramatically reduced. At the same time, with an increasing number of states sending juveniles to adult court, the percentages of youths in adult jails began to increase.

According to data published in 2006, an estimated 7,083 youth younger than eighteen years old were held in adult jails on June 30, 2004. These inmates accounted for 1 percent of the total jail population in 2004. In 2004, 87 percent of the jail inmates younger than eighteen were held as adults; this proportion was greater than the 80 percent in 2000 and the 76 percent in 1994.[10]

Several reasons exist why jail removal of juveniles continues to remain a distant goal. First, juveniles who are transferred to adult court and are waiting for criminal trials make up an increasingly large category of youths confined in jail. Second, many states continue to resist full compliance with the JJDPA jail-removal mandate. The claim is frequently made that the states lack the necessary resources and alternatives to implement the mandate.[11] Third, the belief is widely held that physically separating juveniles from adult inmates is sufficient to protect juveniles against the harmful effects of jail confinement. Such separation is typically based on a "sight and sound" criteria, where juveniles are sufficiently separated from the adult population so that they are unable to see or hear adult inmates.

Even though progress has been slow, a number of states have taken a strong stand against the jailing of juveniles. California and Utah have made it unlawful to send a youthful offender to an adult jail.[12] Illinois, Missouri, North Carolina, Tennessee, and Virginia enacted legislation in the 1980s either prohibiting the jailing of minors or restricting the number of admissions to jails.[13]

Detention Centers

Library Extra 16–2
OJJDP National Report Series publication: *Juvenile Residential Facility Census*

detention center
A short-term confinement facility in which juveniles are held awaiting resolution of their case.

Established at the end of the nineteenth century as an alternative to jail for juveniles, **detention centers**, also called *juvenile halls*, are intended to be temporary holding centers. The court administers the majority of juvenile detention centers, although state agencies, city or county governments, welfare departments, and juvenile courts also manage these facilities. The governments of Connecticut, Delaware, Vermont, and Puerto Rico assume responsibility for administering juvenile detention centers. Georgia, Maryland, Massachusetts, New Hampshire, and Rhode Island operate regional detention facilities.

The traditional detention center has sparked many horror stories, and on more than one occasion, former residents have described to the authors the toxic environment of these facilities. Fortunately, detention in the United States has experienced marked improvement in the past two decades. A nationwide movement to develop standards for detention and more innovative detention programs has provided the impetus to improve detention practices in the United States.

Attention homes were initiated in Boulder, Colorado, and have spread to other jurisdictions. Their stated purpose is to give juveniles *attention* rather than *detention.* These facilities have no fences, locked doors, or other physical restraints. They also provide more extensive programming and involvement between residents and staff. Home detention, as previously discussed, is a nonresidential approach to confinement. It was first used in St. Louis, Newport News, Norfolk, and Washington, D.C., and is now being used throughout the nation.

shelter care facility
A facility that is used to provide short-term care for status offenders and/or dependent or neglected youths.

In spite of the overall improvement, detention practices still exhibit many disturbing features in the United States. The most serious concerns are that over half offer no treatment programs and that an increasing number of detention centers have turned to mechanical restraints and isolation to control their populations.[14]

Shelter Care Facilities

▲ A resident in the Hennepin County Home School spends time with horses. Riding horses and canoeing are two of the activities that make this placement very different from most institutional settings.

■ **How do such activities further the treatment goals of institutions that employ them?**

Shelter care facilities were developed in the early 1970s to provide short-term care for status offenders and for dependent or neglected children. Although only twenty-three public shelters existed in 1975, they quickly increased in number because of the funding mandate of the JJDPA, which requires that noncriminal youths be placed in such facilities.

The length of stay in these nonsecure facilities with no locked doors varies from overnight to a few days. Occasionally, a juvenile must stay several weeks because of difficulty in scheduling court-required family therapy sessions or because of hearing delays in the juvenile court. Delinquent youths may be placed in shelter care facilities if the county has no detention center and the juvenile judge is reluctant to detain the youth in the county jail, or if a judge decides to reward a delinquent youth's positive behavior in detention by transferring him or her to the more open shelter care situation. Shelter care facilities do permit residents to enjoy home visits on weekends and field trips into the community during the week.

The openness of these settings, not surprisingly, creates problems with runaways and makes it difficult to control contraband drugs among residents. Another problem for staff is that these facilities have their share of disciplinary problems among residents, who often have difficulty controlling their attitudes and actions.

The Long-Term Confinement of Juveniles

Reception and diagnostic centers are generally short-term facilities. Boot camps can be longer-term facilities; while ranches and wilderness programs generally hold their charges for a relatively long periods of time. In this country, training schools are the main forms of long-term juvenile correctional institutions (see Table 16–2). Juveniles also may be transferred to mental health placements or sentenced to youthful offender facilities and adult prisons.

Boot Camps

Boot camps received increased attention in juvenile justice in the late 1980s and 1990s. Emphasizing military discipline, physical training, and regimented activity for periods that typically range from 30 to 120 days, the intent of these programs is to shock youthful offenders to prevent them from committing further crimes. Boot camp programs generally are designed for offenders who have failed with lesser sanctions such as probation. The Orleans Parish program, established in 1985, was the first boot camp for juveniles in the country. This program accepts anyone who is sentenced by a juvenile judge, but most programs generally exclude sex offenders, armed robbers, and violent offenders.[15]

The rationale for juvenile boot camps is consistent with the juvenile justice system's historical emphasis on rehabilitation, usually incorporating explicit assumptions about the needs of delinquent youths and providing remedial, counseling, and aftercare programs necessary to address these needs.[16] All of the programs employ military customs and courtesies, including uniformed drill instructors, a platoon structure, and summary punishment of participants, including group punishment under some circumstances. Although there are differences in emphasis, with Denver creating the most militaristic environment, juvenile boot camp programs generally have discovered that they must tailor their environment to participants' maturity levels.[17]

Boot camps for juveniles are generally reserved for midrange offenders, such as those who have failed with lesser sanctions like probation but who are not yet hardened delinquents. The shock aspect of the boot camp experience includes incarceration as suggested by the environment within which the program takes place.[18] A few programs limit themselves to youths who are nonviolent, have committed their first serious offense, or are being confined for the first time.[19]

boot camp
A military-style facility used as an alternative to prison in order to deal with prison crowding and public demands for severe punishment.

TABLE 16–2
Types of Juvenile Placements

Type	Goals	Characteristics
Boot camps	Shock treatment	Short- or longer-term facilities that emphasize military-style discipline.
Reception and diagnostic centers	Evaluation and placement	Short-term facilities used to evaluate juveniles for possible placement in other facilities.
Ranches and wilderness camps	Minimum security	Medium-term facilities that involve informal contact with staff and a less secure placement than training schools.
Public and private training schools	Longer and more secure institutional placement	These are larger physical facilities involving longer terms of stay and sometimes violent residential life.

▲ Corrections officers demand the attention of a new recruit on the first day of orientation at the Greene County Impact Incarceration Program in Illinois. The program, a military-style boot camp for first-time juvenile offenders who have been convicted of felonies, is supposed to shock residents into conforming their behavior to the requirements of the law.

■ **How successful have such programs been?**

Web Extra 16–1
OJJDP PowerPoint presentation: "Juvenile Offenders in Correctional Facilities"

reception and diagnostic center
A facility where juveniles who have been committed to correctional institutions frequently are first sent. This type of center diagnoses youths' problems and develops individualized treatment plans.

Three programs—located in Cleveland, Denver, and Mobile—were funded through the Office of Juvenile Justice and Delinquency Prevention (OJJDP), which launched a three-site study of boot camps for youthful offenders in 1991. The program guidelines of these three experimental programs identified six key components to maximize their effectiveness: education and job training and placement, community service, substance abuse counseling and treatment, health and mental health care, individualized and continuous case management, and intensive aftercare services. The 1994 evaluation of the three sites found that the sites were unable to implement the program guidelines fully. Each program "experienced considerable instability and staff turnover" and was unable to "implement and sustain stable, well-developed aftercare services."[20]

Boot camps for juveniles include some type of work detail; most allocate more than half the day to educational and counseling activities, and most include some form of drug and alcohol counseling. In addition, most of the boot camp programs assign graduates to a period of intensive community supervision.[21]

A fair assessment may be that the quality of boot camps depends largely on how much they tailor their programs to participants' maturity levels and how effective they are in implementing and sustaining effective aftercare services. Doris MacKenzie and colleagues completed a study of twenty-six juvenile boot camps, comparing them with traditional facilities (the experiences of 2,668 juveniles in twenty-six boot camps were compared to 1,848 juveniles in twenty-two traditional facilities).[22] They found that, overall, juveniles in boot camps perceived their environments as more positive or therapeutic, less hostile or dangerous, and more structured than how juveniles in traditional facilities perceived their environments. Moreover, this study revealed that, over time, youths in boot camps became less antisocial and less depressed than did youths in traditional facilities.[23]

Almost all other follow-ups on juvenile boot camps have found recidivism rates to be slightly higher or about the same as those of traditional juvenile facilities.[24] Charges of abuse in boot camps have taken place in almost all states with boot camps. In a 2007 federal report that examined the cases of ten adolescents who died while at programs in six states, it was found that there was "significance evidence of ineffective management" and "reckless or negligent operating practices." The report revealed evidence that teenagers were forced to eat their own vomit, were starved, and were required to wallow for hours in their own excrement.[25]

The disappointing recidivism results, combined with the charges of abuse, have prompted Arizona, Florida, Georgia, Maryland, and South Dakota to shut down or reevaluate the "get tough with juveniles" approach popularized in the early 1990s. Arizona removed fifty juveniles from a boot camp in which a juvenile died. Maryland shut down one boot camp and suspended the military regimens at its other two facilities after reports of systematic assaults. In Maryland, the charges of abuse led to the ouster of the state's top five juvenile justice officials.[26] In March 2006, Florida closed all of its boot camps after charges of abuse and the beating to death of a juvenile by boot camp staff.

Panaceas die hard in juvenile corrections, and this highly publicized approach of the past two decades will likely continue to be used in some states across the nation. The recent criticisms and disappointing recidivism data probably will result in fewer new programs being established and more scrutiny of the existing programs.

Reception and Diagnostic Centers

The purpose of **reception and diagnostic centers**, which include both publicly and privately administered ones, is to determine which treatment plan suits and which training school is the best placement for each adjudicated juvenile. Exhibit 16–2 discusses a faith- and character-based juvenile facility in Indiana.

A few of the larger states have reception and diagnostic centers, but for most states, this diagnostic process takes place in one of the training schools. Although staff are more

Exhibit 16–2
Indiana Implements a Faith- and Character-Based Housing Program

During the 2005 session, the Indiana General Assembly passed a new law, House Bill 1429, that permits the Indiana Department of Corrections (IDOC) to operate faith-based transitional dormitories at any facility operated by the agency. Before the bill was signed into law, IDOC began developing curricula for pilot programs, named Purposeful Living Units Serve (PLUS), at three facilities, one of which was a juvenile one—the Plainfield Juvenile Correctional Facility. Since the opening of the three pilot sites, this program has expanded to sixteen facilities. The PLUS program is available at female and male facilities, juvenile and adult facilities, and at all security levels.

The juvenile PLUS program takes sixteen weeks to complete. In addition to their appropriate treatment program, those in the PLUS program participate in additional programming from a faith- or character-based perspective. The PLUS curriculum focuses on helping students integrate the core values of respect, responsibility, honesty, tolerance, and compassion into the education they are already receiving. PLUS program staff members, along with volunteer members, assist the students in this reflection process.

The following topics are used with juvenile participants from a faith or character perspective: religious/cultural diversity, community service projects, mentoring from a community volunteer, and victim impact/restorative justice. The major goals of PLUS are:

* Better behavior, which is measured by fewer conduct reports
* Better adjustment as measured by fewer grievances
* Restitution in the form of community service
* Smoother transition back to home
* Reduced recidivism rates.

CRITICAL THINKING QUESTIONS

■ *What do you think of using a faith- or character-based juvenile facility in juvenile corrections?*

Source: Stephen T. Hall, "Indiana Implements a Faith- and Character-Based Housing Program," *Corrections Today* (March 2008), pp. 62–67.

concerned about short-term diagnosis than long-term treatment, youths frequently receive more attention during this period than at any other time during their confinement. A psychiatrist usually will evaluate the youth and will see him or her several times if the youth is confined for a violent crime. A clinical psychologist, or a person with skills in administering psychological tests, frequently will subject the youth to a battery of tests to determine intelligence, attitudes, maturity, and emotional problems. A social worker, meanwhile, completes a case study of each youth. Equipped with background material from the court, which sometimes takes a week or two to arrive at the reception center, the social worker primarily investigates the youth's family background. Academic staff identify any learning problems and determine the proper school placement. A physical and dental examination also is frequently administered. Finally, cottage or dormitory supervisors evaluate the youth's institutional adjustment and peer relationships. A case conference on each resident is held once all the reports have been prepared, the needs and attitudes of the youth are summarized, and recommendations are made as to the best cottage or institutional placement.

Although previously staff had evaluated residents over a period of four to six weeks, this process has been condensed today to an average length of stay of thirty-four days.[27] The youth is then transferred to the approved institutional placement, and the diagnostic report goes with him or her. It is not uncommon for this report to receive little attention, so the youth often must repeat a similar process in the admitting institution.

Library Extra 16–3
OJJDP Juvenile Justice Bulletin: "Psychiatric Disorders of Youth in Detention"

Ranches and Wilderness Camps

Ranches and **wilderness camps** are minimum-security institutional placements that are normally reserved for youths who have committed minor offenses or who have been committed to the department of youth services or private corrections for the first time.

In these camps, residents typically do conservation work in a state park, cutting grass and weeds, cleaning up, and doing general maintenance. Treatment programs generally consist of individual contacts with social workers and the child care staff, group therapy, and an occasional home visit. Residents may be taken to nearby towns on a regular or weekly basis to make purchases and to attend community events.

Only about 20 percent of these facilities have one or more confinement features other than locked sleeping rooms. They contrast with detention homes and long-term secure facilities, roughly 90 percent of which have one or more confinement features beyond locked

ranch
A public or private juvenile correctional institution that, like a forestry camp, is usually less secure than a training school and that has a more normal atmosphere.

wilderness camp
A correctional facility where residents usually do conservation work in state parks, including cleaning up, cutting grass and weeds, and doing general maintenance.

sleeping rooms. Unlike in the past, when ranches and camps tended to be populated by white youths, today's ranch and camp residents are 76 percent minority offenders; 12 percent of the residents are female. Also, in keeping with today's concerns, it is important to note that 68 percent of secure facilities screen all incoming youth on their first day for suicide risk, and another 17 percent screen selected youths.[28]

Residents are typically more positive about a placement at a wilderness camp or ranch than about placement in a training school. They like the more relaxed security, the more frequent community contacts, the shorter stays, and the better relations with staff. Yet some youths cannot handle these settings. They may be too homesick or too victimized by peers, so they repeatedly run away until they are transferred to more secure facilities.

Training Schools

In 2008, there were a total of 2,458 juvenile facilities, holding 81,015 offenders for relatively long periods of time. Of these, 1,150 were public facilities, holding 56,157 juvenile offenders; and 1,300 were private facilities, holding 24,757 offenders.[29] Table 16–3 lists the numbers of juveniles facilities and the number of children in custody in each state.

The number of residents held in the 2008 census put 25 percent of facilities at or over their capacity. The largest facilities were the most likely to be crowded. Overall, the juvenile offender custody population dropped 12 percent from 2006 to 2008. In fact, forty-five states held fewer juvenile offenders in 2008 than in 2006.[30]

The cost of juvenile confinement is significant (Figure 16–1). A 2006 report, *Implementing Reform in California*, revealed the skyrocketing average cost of juvenile institutional care in that state. It costs California $115,129 per year to institutionalize a resident, which is greater than the cost in five other states for which data were available, and the average length of stay in a juvenile facility is more than two years (Figure 16–2), which was nearly three times as long as the average of the nineteen states that participated in a nationwide survey. Note that California is one of only six states that have an extended age of jurisdiction that goes beyond the age of twenty. California's length of stay for a juvenile offender goes up to twenty-four years of age, and this has contributed to the lengthy stay for those sentenced to juvenile facilities in California.[31]

California, Texas, Illinois, Michigan, New York, and Ohio are among those states that have several training schools. Smaller states have one training school for boys and another for girls, and Massachusetts and Vermont have no training schools. Although coeducational institutions gained some acceptance in the 1970, and North Carolina even converted all of its training schools into coeducational facilities, that trend seems to have passed.

Organizational Goals and Security Levels

Organizational goals vary among training schools. David Street, Robert D. Vinter, and Charles Perrow's classic study of several public and private training schools identified three

FIGURE 16–1

Cost per Youth per Year of Confinement in Selected States, 2005

Source: Christopher Murray, Chris Baird, Ned Loughran, Fred Mills, and John Platt, *Safety and Welfare Plan: Implementing Reform in California* (Sacramento: California Department of Corrections and Rehabilitation, Division of Juvenile Justice, 2006), p. 5.

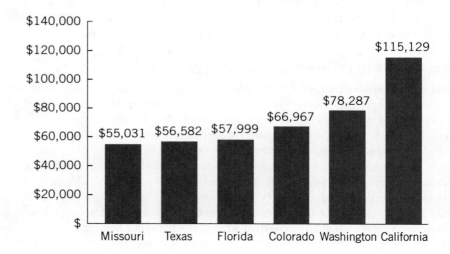

TABLE 16-3
Juveniles Facilities and the Number of Children in Custody, by State

State	Juvenile facilities			Juvenile offenders			State	Juvenile facilities			Juvenile offenders		
	Total	Public	Private	Total	Public	Private		Total	Public	Private	Total	Public	Private
U.S. total	2,458	1,150	1,300	81,015	56,157	24,757	Missouri	68	63	5	1,226	1,196	30
Alabama	56	13	43	1,328	632	696	Montana	16	8	7	161	114	30
Alaska	18	8	10	249	178	71	Nebraska	16	4	12	773	438	335
Arizona	40	16	20	1,488	1,198	240	Nevada	23	17	6	1,052	841	211
Arkansas	32	11	21	836	286	550	New Hampshire	8	2	6	157	86	71
California	215	117	98	13,309	12,056	1,253	New Jersey	49	39	10	1,564	1,428	136
Colorado	56	13	43	1,688	853	835	New Mexico	19	15	4	409	397	12
Connecticut	12	3	9	303	180	123	New York	169	40	129	3,157	1,470	1,687
Delaware	7	6	1	256	239	17	North Carolina	52	22	30	1,014	557	457
Dist. of Columbia	10	3	7	236	174	62	North Dakota	9	4	5	85	73	12
Florida	118	37	81	5,895	2,210	3,685	Ohio	87	66	21	3,871	3,521	350
Georgia	40	26	14	2,692	2,168	524	Oklahoma	46	16	29	923	626	276
Hawaii	8	3	5	130	118	12	Oregon	47	25	22	1,437	1,106	331
Idaho	28	15	13	683	540	143	Pennsylvania	152	34	118	5,034	1,263	3,771
Illinois	42	28	14	2,440	2,141	299	Rhode Island	10	1	9	291	168	123
Indiana	76	37	39	2,422	1,561	861	South Carolina	33	13	20	1,258	794	464
Iowa	66	15	51	1,060	297	763	South Dakota	23	7	14	507	233	261
Kansas	41	17	24	973	682	291	Tennessee	48	30	18	1,151	836	315
Kentucky	39	29	10	944	873	71	Texas	109	85	24	5,831	5,192	639
Louisiana	43	17	26	1,294	909	385	Utah	35	18	17	770	384	386
Maine	7	2	5	215	189	26	Vermont	4	1	3	48	24	24
Maryland	35	14	21	787	615	172	Virginia	61	56	5	2,114	2,022	92
Massachusetts	58	18	40	961	343	618	Washington	37	31	6	1,382	1,302	80
Michigan	82	37	45	2,659	1,252	1,407	West Virginia	26	11	15	565	376	189
Minnesota	76	21	55	1,332	697	635	Wisconsin	69	20	49	1,395	884	511
Mississippi	16	14	2	413	351	62	Wyoming	21	2	19	247	84	163

Notes: "State" is the state where the facility is located. Offenders sent to out-of-state facilities are counted in the state where the facility is located, not the state where they committed their offense.

Totals include 8 tribal facilities (holding 101 juvenile offenders) located in Arizona, Montana, Oklahoma, and South Dakota.

Source: Sarah Hockenberry, Melissa Sickmund, and Anthony Sladky, *Juvenile Residential Facility Census, 2008: Selected Findings* (Washington, D.C.: U.S. Department of Justice, Juvenile Offenders and Victims: National Report Services Bulletin, 2011), p. 2.

FIGURE 16–2
**Average Length of Stay in Months
In a Juvenile Facility, 2005—Males**

Source: Christopher Murray, Chris
Baird, Ned Loughran, Fred Mills, and
John Platt, *Safety and Welfare Plan:
Implementing Reform in California*
(Sacramento: California Department
of Corrections and Rehabilitation,
Division of Juvenile Justice, 2006),
p. 2.

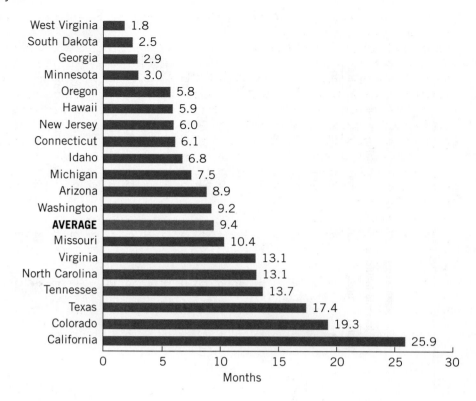

Library Extra 16–4
OJJDP Juvenile Justice Bulletin: "Planning
Community-Based Facilities for Violent
Juvenile Offenders as Part of a System of
Graduated Sanctions"

basic organizational goals: obedience/conformity, reeducation/development, and treatment. They found that staff in obedience/conformity institutions kept residents under surveillance and emphasized rules. They were also punitive with residents and did not become involved with them. Although staff in reeducation/development institutions demanded conformity, hard work, and intellectual growth, they were more willing to give additional rewards for conformity to positive behavior and to develop closer relationships with residents. Staff in treatment-oriented training schools were much more involved with residents as they worked with, helped, and permitted residents to become more emotionally involved with them.[32]

The philosophy of *parens patriae* has encouraged administrators at training schools to claim rehabilitation as their official goal, but the overall objective for most training schools is to provide a safe, secure, and humane environment. The actual goal depends on the security level of the training school. States that have only one training school for boys and one for girls must enforce all security levels in the one facility, but states with several training schools have the option of developing minimum-, medium-, and maximum-security institutions.

Security features and size vary by the types of facilities. Over 38 percent of facilities said that at least some of the time residents are locked in their sleeping rooms. Seventy-six percent of public facilities and 62 percent of state facilities reported that they locked residents in sleeping rooms. Few private facilities locked residents in sleeping rooms (5 percent). Among facilities that locked youth in sleeping rooms, most did this at night (85 percent) or when a youth was out of control (77 percent).[33]

The Lighthouse Youth Center at Paint Creek in southern Ohio is one of the most widely hailed minimum-security institutions in the nation. This privately operated facility has the capacity to hold thirty-three residents but generally has a population of twenty-six or twenty-seven. Juveniles who have committed serious offenses from the southern counties of the state are typically committed to this facility. The facility features a comprehensive and integrated therapeutic approach that emphasizes accountability, social learning, and positive peer culture. The center also includes a school where youth can receive a high school diploma or GED. It has a choir and a choir director, a horticulture program, a pottery program, and a family therapy program and also offers intensive aftercare services to those residents returning to the community.[34]

The physical design of medium- and maximum-security training schools varies from fortresslike facilities with individual cells to open dormitories with little privacy to the homelike atmosphere of small cottages. Maximum-security training schools usually have one or two fairly high fences and sometimes even a wall. The interiors in maximum-security schools are characterized by bleak hallways, locked doors, and individual cells covered by heavy screens or bars; the youths' daily lives are constrained by rules.

Medium-security training schools usually are designed as dormitories or cottages. Similar to maximum-security institutions, medium-security training schools usually have the perimeter security of a six- or seven-foot-high fence. The atmosphere in medium-security institutions is more relaxed, and residents can move around more freely than they can in maximum-security training schools.

Institutional security is the primary emphasis in medium- and maximum-security training schools. Administrators' jobs typically depend on their success in preventing runaways. The account of a runaway incident from a maximum-security facility, for example, may receive statewide media coverage. If a runaway commits a violent crime, then even more pressure is placed on institutional administrators and their staff. Fortunately, the federal courts' recent involvement in juvenile institutions has eliminated some of the past abuses that sometimes took place to punish those who attempted to run away and those who actually did but were caught and returned.

Programs

The programs in medium- and maximum-security training schools are much more adequate than those in jails or detention homes and more varied than those in camps and ranches. Most of the larger training schools have a full-time nurse on duty and a physician who visits one or more days a week. Such services as the removal of tattoos are sometimes made available if residents desire them.

Most medium- and maximum-security training schools provide educational programs for residents. These may be accredited by the state for granting high school diplomas, and most offer classes to prepare for a GED test. In addition to the regular academic courses, training schools usually offer basic skills classes consisting of a review of the necessary techniques for reading, writing, and arithmetic; some programs have laboratories and programmed instruction as well. Classes are usually small, and pupils are permitted to progress according to their own rate of learning. The Indiana Boys School is an example of one training school that focuses on the learning disabilities of residents, because Indiana correctional officials believe that learning disabilities are closely linked to delinquent behavior.

Well-equipped male training schools offer vocational training in automobile repair, printing, welding, carpentry, woodworking, barbering, machine shop skills, drafting, and food service. Training schools for girls generally are more limited and offer training programs in sewing, food service, secretarial skills, and beauty care.

As a rule, vocational training does not help residents secure jobs after release for several reasons: They have difficulty gaining admission to the necessary labor unions; they lack the necessary credentials, such as a high school education; or they simply choose not to pursue the skills they learned. Yet some residents leave the institution and acquire excellent jobs with their acquired skills.

Recreation has always been popular in training schools. Some staff emphasize it because they believe that a tired youth is a well-behaved one or, in the words of one recreation leader, "If we wear them out during the day, they won't fool around at night." Other staff advocate a heavy dosage of recreation because they believe that teaching residents a competitive sport builds self-respect and self-confidence. Still other staff know that juveniles like to play, and recreation is simply a good way for them to entertain themselves and to work off excessive energy. Male residents can compete in softball, volleyball, flag football, basketball, and sometimes even boxing. Cottages usually compete against one another, and the institution may even have a team that competes with other institutions or with teams in the surrounding community. Nonathletic recreational activities include movies, building model cars, painting, decorating the cottages (especially at Christmas), and playing ping-pong, pool, checkers, and chess. Female residents also have recreational possibilities such as softball, volleyball, and basketball. In addition to the nonathletic recreational activities to which the boys have access, girls perform in talent shows or dramatic productions, and occasionally, they have dances with boys from nearby training schools.

Religious instruction and services are always provided in state training schools. Larger training schools usually have a full-time Protestant chaplain and a part- or full-time Roman Catholic chaplain. Smaller training schools contract for the services of clergy from a nearby community. Religious services generally include Sunday mass and morning worship, confession, baptism, instruction for church membership, choir, and the participation of community groups. Yet, few residents have much interest in organized religion, and they are usually quite resistant to compulsory attendance at these religious services.

The most widely used treatment modalities are transactional analysis, reality therapy, psychotherapy, behavior modification, guided group interaction, positive peer culture, and drug and alcohol treatment. The errors-in-thinking modality, models to deactivate gangs, and law enforcement education are new forms of treatment recently implemented in a number of private and public training schools across the nation.

Volunteers are an important adjunct to institutional programs, and an institution that has an active volunteer program can greatly enrich the stay of its residents. Some states have better developed volunteer programs than others and have volunteer coordinators in their major institutions. Confined offenders frequently are receptive to services rendered by unpaid volunteers who do not represent authority figures, but who can present the needs of youth and become their advocates in the community. Among the many services that volunteers provide for institutionalized youths are the following:

1. Education—tutoring and supplying books
2. Entertainment—arranging choral programs and other means of entertainment provided by community groups
3. Chaperones—escorting selected youths to community events
4. Counseling—providing one-to-one contact with offenders
5. Family service—contacting and reassuring parents on the progress of their children
6. Financial aid—providing money for youths' canteen accounts
7. Gifts—supplying Christmas and birthday remembrances
8. Job-finding—assisting youths in locating community jobs while they wait to be released or in securing permanent jobs after release
9. Letter writing—helping youths to correspond with family and friends
10. Recreation—playing basketball, softball, and other sports with residents

Finally, prerelease activity-related programs are an important component of institutional activities. These programs typically occur more in minimum- than in medium- or maximum-security facilities. In some training schools, residents are transferred to another cottage or to another location to begin a formal program of community reintegration, including exposure to experiences designed to prepare them for a full return to the community. Techniques of interviewing for a job, instruction in reading the help-wanted section of a newspaper, and assistance in money management are important elements of these programs.

Home furloughs, afternoon trips off campus, and permission to work in the community are typical of the privileges given to residents of prerelease cottages or to those who are just a step or two away from release. Home furloughs are probably the most widely used. Some staff believe that reintegrating youths gradually to the community after a long absence of perhaps several years will help ease the shock of release. Home visits also provide opportunities for residents to interview for jobs and visit with family members. Some training schools permit trips off campus for several hours with parents. This enables parents and children to spend time together away from the institution and possibly to shop for clothing or to eat in a restaurant. Community jobs generally are reserved for those youths who are only two or three months from release and who need financial resources before they return to community living. Staff members are very careful in choosing the residents who are

Library Extra 16–5
NIJ publication: *National Study Comparing the Environments of Boot Camps with Traditional Facilities for Juvenile Offenders*

permitted to work in the community. Prerelease programs usually have a positive impact on residents, but home visits, especially, result in a high percentage of runaways.

Social Control of Institutional Residents

Until the past ten years or so, most training schools still employed cottage parents. These individuals often were a retired couple who were attracted to this work because of their interest in young people. Cottage parents sometimes provided a strong parental model for the youth placed in their care. The cottage parents system was continued so long simply because institutional administrators felt that cottage parents created more of a homelike atmosphere for confined delinquents than did staff members who worked eight-hour shifts and lived in the nearby community. But the appearance of increasingly difficult-to-handle delinquents and efforts to develop more efficient institutional management techniques resulted in the replacement of cottage parents with staff members who are commonly called *youth supervisors*, *youth leaders*, *cottage supervisors*, *group supervisors*, or *group-care workers*.

The emerging nature of this role has left a number of questions unanswered: How much of a homelike atmosphere should these supervisors establish in the cottages? How involved should they become with residents? Are they to be only custodial agents, or do they also have treatment responsibilities? What are they to do if residents refuse to cooperate? What personal fulfillment can they expect to achieve in their jobs? Although encumbered by these and other questions, the role of youth supervisor is well established in juvenile correctional settings in this country. For a list of typical rules that residents are expected to follow in residential facilities, see Exhibit 16–3.

The youth supervisors wake residents in the morning, see to it that their charges wash and dress for breakfast, supervise the serving of breakfast in the cottage or escort residents to a central dining facility, and conduct a brief room inspection. They also ensure that those youths enrolled in the academic and vocational programs go to school and that those who work on the grounds, in the kitchen, or in the community go to their jobs. In medium- and maximum-security training schools, residents are usually escorted to their particular assignments, but on many honor farms, and in conservation camps and ranches, they are permitted movement without staff supervision.[35]

Exhibit 16–3
Rules of Youth Conduct

1. You will not be allowed to fight with peers or staff.
2. You will follow the direct orders of staff.
3. You will treat others with courtesy by avoiding the use of profanity, disrespectful language, or physical gestures.
4. You will avoid sexually inappropriate language or gestures towards staff and other youth.
5. You will avoid horseplay, rowdy-rough play, body punching, shadow boxing, verbal taunting, running, [and] wrestling, which could lead to more serious behavior.
6. You will avoid destroying, defacing, or altering state property or the property of others.
7. You will avoid the use of and/or passing of any form of tobacco, alcohol, and drugs.
8. You will avoid the use of and/or possession of contraband.
9. You will avoid leaving trash on tables, chairs, or floors by placing it in proper receptacles.
10. You will maintain personal grooming, hygiene, and clothing at all times throughout the institution. Appropriate dress includes shirttails in pants, pants zipped and uncuffed (not pegged), belt fastened, shoes tied, and socks on.
11. You will refrain from borrowing, lending, buying, trading, betting, selling, and gambling with peers, staff, or visitors.
12. You will play radios only in acceptable areas and at acceptable times.
13. You will not enter any office or restricted areas without staff permission.
14. You will avoid interfering with staff members' duties.
15. You will report any injury or any change in a medical condition to a staff member immediately.
16. You will not steal.
17. You will adhere to all movement instructions.
18. You will not spit.
19. You will not use any phone without staff supervision.
20. You will not use the restroom without permission.

CRITICAL THINKING QUESTIONS

■ *Do you believe all these rules are necessary? What rules would you substitute? How would you feel if restricted by these rules?*

Source: The Ohio Department of Youth Services, Training Institution, Central Ohio, 1990.

Cottage parents typically remain in the cottage to prepare lunch and to take care of other cottage tasks, but youth supervisors are generally assigned duties that keep them occupied until they pick up their residents for lunch. These duties may include school patrol, inspection of the rooms of residents on restriction, and outside patrol of the recreation field.

Residents are met at the academic area and escorted back to the cottage for lunch, after which they are returned to school or to other assigned duties. The afternoon shift of supervisors picks up the youths in school and brings them back at the end of the day. If the institution has an active group program and youth supervisors are involved, they usually hold several group meetings a week after school. Guided group interaction, positive peer culture, and transactional analysis are the most popular group modalities used in these sessions. Time generally is structured after school because many administrators believe that problems arise when youths have a great deal of free time, but in some institutions the period from the end of school until the evening meal is a free one.

After the evening meal, especially during warmer weather, residents are permitted to engage in outside recreational activities. They may participate in organized activities or may choose to throw a football, shoot a basketball, pitch a softball, or talk with a friend. Staff must at this time be particularly alert, because runaways often take place during these outside activities. Following a shower and a little television, residents are usually sent to their rooms and lights are out around 10 P.M.

The night shift, normally consisting of one person, takes over at 11 or 11:30 P.M. This person's job basically is to make certain that youths do not escape from the cottage during the night and to be available if a problem such as an illness or escape attempt occurs. The youth supervisor generally spends the greater part of the eight-hour shift sitting at a desk in the staff office and responding to a periodic phone check on cottage security.

As part of their daily tasks, youth supervisors also intervene in conflicts among residents, respond to emergency situations, search residents and residents' living quarters, orient new residents, advise residents concerning personal or institutional progress, and assign tasks to residents and monitor their performance.

Differences Between Public and Private Training Schools

In a recent year, little more than half (53 percent) of juvenile facilities holding offenders were private, but public facilities held over two-thirds (69 percent) of the juvenile offenders. Compared with public facilities, private facilities hold a smaller share of delinquents and a larger share of status offenders.[36] Public facilities hold more than three-quarters of those confined for homicide, robbery, aggravated assault, weapons possession, and technical violations of probation or aftercare. Nevertheless, as noted in the *Juvenile Offenders and Victims: 2006 National Report*, "public and private facilities had fairly similar offense profiles."[37]

David Shichor and Clemens Bartollas's examination of the patterns of public and **private juvenile placements** in one of the larger probation departments in southern California, however, revealed that few offense differences existed between juveniles sent to public and private facilities. Although juveniles placed in private facilities had more personal problems and those in public institutions were somewhat more delinquent, placements in private facilities included delinquents with serious offenses.[38]

Second, privately administered training schools are probably better known to the public than are state facilities because of their public solicitation of funds. Boys' Town in Nebraska and Glen Mills School in Pennsylvania (near Philadelphia) are two private institutions that are well known to the public.[39] Private training schools also have avoided most of the scathing critiques faced by public training schools during the past two decades.

Third, proponents of private training schools claim that they are more effective than public training schools because they have a limited intake policy that allows them to choose whom they want to admit; they have more professional staff; they have better staff–client ratios; they are smaller; and they are more flexible and innovative.

Gaylene Styve Armstrong and Doris Layton MacKenzie examined forty-eight residential juvenile correctional facilities in nineteen states (sixteen private and thirty-two public facilities). Using both self-report surveys and data from facility records, they found that private

Library Extra 16–6
NIJ Research in Brief: "Resources for Juvenile Detention Reform"

private juvenile placement
A training school that operates under private auspices. The county or state generally pays the school a per diem rate for the care of youths committed to these facilities.

facilities had a more extensive admission process, had a higher percentage of juvenile delinquents incarcerated for property offenses, were smaller, and held a higher percentage of males than female offenders. Yet they found that there were no significant differences between private and public juvenile facilities in terms of the quality of their environments.[40]

The advantage of private over public rehabilitation programs may have been more true in the past than in the present. The increased use of interstate compacts for children has resulted in some private schools taking as many children as they can get. Indeed, some private institutions exploit the inadequate licensing procedures of the states to warehouse youths as cheaply as possible and thereby reap good profits.[41] It is also true that private training schools are smaller than public ones, but even so, half of the private institutions hold one hundred or more children each; these are still too large to effectively rehabilitate juveniles. It is probably accurate to say that private institutions offer greater flexibility of programs because private institutions are relatively free from political processes and bureaucratic inertia. Yet Bartollas and Shichor's comparison of the attitudes of staff and residents at a state training school for adolescent males in the Midwest and at a private facility in the same state found that the enforcement of excessive rules in the private placement created a rigid cottage structure and living environment.[42] Moreover, Shichor and Bartollas found that private placements in southern California do not always provide the services of professional treatment personnel that they purport to provide.[43] Perhaps the old adage is true after all: The best institutions are private ones and the worst institutions are also private ones.

▲ The Glen Mills School, which has been at its present location in Concordville, Pennsylvania, for over one hundred years, is the oldest existing residential school for court-adjudicated male delinquents in the country.

■ **How large a role does residential placement play in the juvenile justice system?**

Facilities for Females

The social roles in training schools for girls are generally based on a family or kinship social structure:

- Rose Giallombardo's examination of three training schools for girls in various parts of the United States found that aggressive girls tended to adopt the male sexual roles ("butches") and put pressure on new residents to adopt the female sexual roles ("fems").[44]

- Christopher M. Sieverdes and Bartollas's study of six Southeastern coeducational training schools also revealed the presence of the family social structure in the girls' cottages. This study further divided the seven social roles found in these living units into aggressive, manipulative, and passive roles.[45]

- Alice Propper examined three coeducational and four girls' training schools scattered through the East, Midwest, and South, five of which were public and two of which were private Catholic facilities. In contrast to previously held assumptions, she found little overlap between pseudo-family roles and homosexual behavior; participation in homosexuality and make-believe families was just as prevalent in coeducational as in single-sex institutions, and homosexuality was as prevalent in treatment- as in custody-oriented facilities.[46]

In sum, similar to institutions for adolescent males, those for adolescent females also provide an environment in which strong girls take advantage of weaker ones and where aggression is the dominant force in the living environment.

Rights of Institutionalized Youths

The rights of juveniles is a major issue in juvenile justice. Proponents of due process rights of children within the juvenile justice system challenge whether institutionalized youths have sufficient legal protection. They argue that confined juveniles ought to receive three

FIGURE 16–3
The Three Major Rights of Juveniles

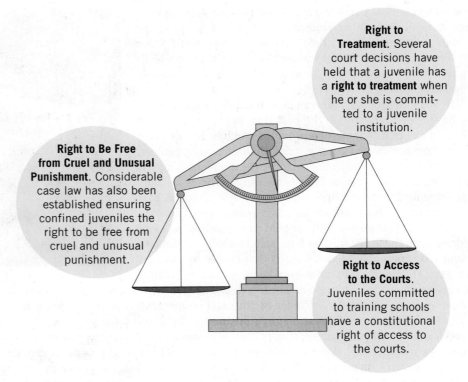

basic rights: the right to treatment, the right to access to the courts, and the right to be free from cruel and unusual punishment (Figure 16–3). The rights of confined offenders have been examined by the federal courts and are supported by the Civil Rights of Institutionalized Persons Act.[47] Some of the rights accorded to institutionalized juveniles, either by court decision, or by law, are discussed in what follows.

Right to Treatment

right to treatment
The entitlement of a juvenile who has been committed to a training school to receive any needed services (e.g., therapy, education).

Several court rulings have found that a juvenile committed to a training school has a **right to treatment**. In the District of Columbia case of *White* v. *Reid* (1954), the federal District Court for the District of Columbia ruled that juveniles could not be held in institutions that did not provide for their rehabilitation.[48] In a Rhode Island case, the *Inmates of the Boys' Training School* v. *Affleck* (1972) decision also stated that juveniles have a right to treatment because rehabilitation is the true purpose of the juvenile court.[49] In *Nelson* v. *Heyne* (1973), Indiana's Seventh Circuit agreed with the district court that inmates of the Indiana Boys' School have a right to rehabilitative treatment.[50]

In what some regard as a landmark Texas case, the 1973 case of *Morales* v. *Turman*, the U.S. District Court for the Eastern District of Texas held that a number of criteria had to be followed by the state of Texas in order to ensure that proper treatment would be provided to confined juveniles. These criteria included minimum standards for assessing and testing children committed to the state; minimum standards for assessing educational skills and handicaps and for providing programs aimed at advancing a child's education; minimum standards for delivering vocational education and medical and psychiatric care; and minimum standards for providing a humane institutional environment.[51] A settlement agreement, approved by the court, established a three-member Morales Consultant Committee to investigate the Texas Youth Commission (TYC). Between 1984 and 1989, that committee examined thirty-three issues that the settlement agreement identified. Each year between 1985 and 1989, the consultant committee provided reports to the TYC, detailing changes that needed to be made in the state's juvenile facilities, and in each of those years, the TYC responded with its own written reports. By 1989, the committee found TYC to be in total compliance with the settlement agreement.[52]

Right to Access to the Courts

As mentioned in an earlier chapter, the 1967 U.S. Supreme Court case of *In re Gault* recognized a juvenile's right to counsel. In a famous sentence taken from that decision, Justice Fortas declared that "under our Constitution, the condition of being a boy does not justify a kangaroo court." The *Gault* case held that children require safeguards in juvenile court, and that access to counsel is one of the most important ways of ensuring that their rights are met. Eventually a number of other cases were decided that provided juveniles with a hearing before being transferred to the adult criminal court and required that evidence of a crime be proven beyond a reasonable doubt. One important right not granted to children, however, was the right to trial by jury.

Right to Be Free from Cruel and Unusual Punishment

Some courts have applied the Eighth Amendment, barring **cruel and unusual punishment**, to juvenile institutions to forbid the use of corporal punishment in any form, the use of Thorazine and other medications for the purpose of control, and the use of extended periods of solitary confinement.[53] The *Pena* v. *New York State Division for Youth* decision held that the use of isolation, hand restraints, and tranquilizing drugs at Goshen Annex Center was punitive and antitherapeutic and, therefore, violated the Eighth Amendment.[54] In the case of *Inmates of the Boys' Training School* v. *Affleck*, the court also condemned such practices as solitary confinement and strip cells, and it established minimum standards for youths confined at the training school.[55] In the *Morales* v. *Turman* decision in Texas, the court found instances of physical brutality and abuse, including staff-administered beatings and tear gassings, homosexual assaults, excessive use of solitary confinement, and the lack of clinical services.[56] In *Morgan* v. *Sproat*, a Mississippi case, the court found that youths were confined in padded cells with no windows or furnishings and only flush holes for toilets and were denied access to all programs or services except a Bible.[57] Finally, in *State* v. *Werner*, the court found that residents were locked in solitary confinement; were beaten, kicked, slapped, and sprayed with mace by staff; were required to scrub floors with a toothbrush; and were forced to stand or sit for prolonged periods without changing position.[58] In each of these cases, the courts condemned these cruel practices.

cruel and unusual punishment
Inhumane punishments against which a guarantee is provided by the Eighth Amendment to the U.S. Constitution. Accordingly, juveniles in correctional custody must not be treated with unnecessary harshness.

Web Extra 16–2
Juvenile Justice Trainers Association

Juvenile Aftercare

Release is the prime goal of a confined youth. The days, weeks, months, and sometimes years spent in confinement are occupied by thoughts and fantasies of release or even escape. The entire juvenile justice system is focused on release. Staff are responsible for guiding residents throughout their confinement, with punishment, education and vocational training, and rehabilitative techniques being used in an effort to guarantee that a resident's return to the community will be permanent and positive.

Parole, or **juvenile aftercare**, as it is usually called, is concerned with the release of a youth from an institution when he or she can best benefit from release and can make an optimal adjustment to community living. A major concern in juvenile justice in the past 40 years has been the development of a workable philosophy and concept of aftercare. A number of objectives for juvenile aftercare or parole have been developed through the years:

juvenile aftercare
The supervision of juveniles who are released from correctional institutions so that they can make an optimal adjustment to community living.

1. Release residents from confinement at the most favorable time for community adjustment.
2. Prepare youths for their successful community completion of aftercare.
3. Reduce the crimes committed by released juveniles.
4. Reduce the violent acts committed by released offenders.
5. Increase the confidence of the community in the system of parole.
6. Alleviate overcrowding of training schools.
7. Monitor youthful offenders as they refrain from trafficking in or abusing drugs.
8. Discourage the return of youths to street gangs.

The achievement of these objectives requires extensive planning and research. For example, determining the most favorable time for release requires far more knowledge than is presently available. Many new and innovative techniques for prediction can be devised, and research must enable releasing authorities to compare the costs of leaving juveniles in institutions with the possible harm to society if they are released.

There is some question whether any method is effective in knowing when to release an institutionalized youth. For example, a study of 16,779 juveniles in Florida released from community programs to the community found that there was no consistent relationship between length of confinement and recidivism. The length of confinement, this 2008 study found, was only significant for male offenders released from high-risk facilities.[59]

Once a youth is adjudicated to a state training school, the state normally retains jurisdiction until his or her release. The authority to make the decision about when to release a youth from a training school is usually given to institutional staff, although a number of states give other agencies and boards the authority to parole juveniles. Often the cottage staff will review the progress of each youth at designated intervals, and when the staff recommend release, the recommendation is reviewed by a board made up of staff from throughout the institution. If this board concurs, the recommendation must be approved by an institutional coordinator at the youth authority or youth commission.

Characteristics of Those on Aftercare

Unlike adult corrections, an area in which the publication, *Probation and Parole in the United States,* provides information on those on probation and parole each year, information regarding the characteristics of the aftercare population is not readily available.[60]

Howard N. Snyder has developed a portrait of juveniles returning to the community (Table 16–4). He reports that nearly one hundred thousand juvenile offenders are released annually from juvenile facilities across the country. These youths have spent a considerable proportion of their adolescent life in custody. Most are male, minority, and nonviolent offenders. About half live in single-parent families and about one-fourth have a sibling. In addition, about one-fourth have a father who has been incarcerated. Most have not completed eighth grade, which can be compared to one-fourth of similarly aged youth across

TABLE 16–4
A Portrait of Youths Returning to the Community

Number of Returnees	About one hundred thousand a year.
Gender	Mostly male. The majority of females have a history of physical or sexual abuse.
Race/Ethnicity	Mostly minority.
Offense Background	Most are nonviolent offenders.
Age	Mostly older.
Family Background	About half live in single-parent households; one-fourth have a father who has been incarcerated, and about 10 percent are parents themselves.
Educational Background	Most have not completed eighth grade and have high rates of learning disabilities.
Mental Health	Two-thirds of these youth have a mental health disorder.
Previous Custodial Experience	Most have spent the majority of their adolescence in custody.
Economic Background	The majority will be returning home to an impoverished family and neighborhood.

Source: Howard Snyder, "An Empirical Portrait of the Youth Reentry Population," *Youth Violence and Juvenile Justice* (2004), pp. 39–55; and Laura S. Abrams and Susan M. Snyder, "Youth Offender Reentry: Models for Intervention and Directions for Future Inquiry," *Children and Youth Services Review* 12 (December 2010), pp. 1787–95.

the nation. The prevalence of the presence of a learning disability is higher than that in the general adolescent population. Excluding alcohol, two-thirds indicate regular drug use. Two-thirds of youths adjudicated to training school have a mental health disorder, with the rate for females being higher. The majority of females leaving a correctional facility have a history of physical or sexual abuse. Finally, a majority of these juveniles will be returning home to an impoverished family and neighborhood.[61]

In Abram and Snyder's more recent 2010 study, they reported that the vast majority of this population is made up of older (81 percent) members of an ethnic minority group (36.6 percent non-Hispanic white, 39.4 percent African American, and 19.8 percent Hispanic). The majority came from single-parent homes (56 percent) or did not live with a parent (26 percent) prior to confinement and approximately one out of eleven were parents themselves.[62]

Administration and Operation of Aftercare Services

Aftercare is the responsibility of the state and is administered by the executive branch in forty-four states. In four states, aftercare is under the organization of the probation department and is administered by probation officers, and in four other states, other means of organizing and administering aftercare are used.[63]

The aftercare or probation officer (probation officers in many jurisdictions have aftercare youths as part of their caseloads) who is responsible for the case sometimes corresponds with or may even visit the institutionalized youth in training school. In many states, a youth cannot be released until the aftercare officer approves the home placement plan submitted by the institutional home worker, which usually involves a visit to the home by the officer to make certain that the home is a good placement. At other times, the aftercare officer must locate an alternate placement, such as a foster home, group home, or halfway house.

Bert Burraston and colleagues' 2012 study examined the reduction of juvenile recidivism with cognitive training, a program that helps individuals examine their principles and beliefs more clearly, and an automated cell phone coaching program.[64] In this study of the recidivism of seventy juvenile offenders, the results suggest that cognitive training supplemented with a cell phone coach is an effective and cost-efficient intervention for reducing recidivism.[65]

An **interstate compact** is sometimes initiated when a youth has no acceptable home placement within his or her own state. The institutional social worker usually contacts the appropriate agency in another state where the youth has a possible placement and submits an interstate compact for the transfer of the youth to that state after release from training school. The state of original jurisdiction retains authority over the youth and is kept advised of the juvenile's status.

Part of the problem in juvenile aftercare is that youthful offenders usually are sent back to the same communities (and the same families) and are exposed again to the same problems they could not deal with effectively earlier. Most of their friends are still around, and it is not long before a friend suggests that they commit another crime together. If the returnee is determined, he or she may be able to say, "Hey, get out of my face. I don't want to hear that business." But if the young person cannot find a job—and jobs are scarce for delinquent youths, who frequently are school dropouts—or is under financial pressure, it becomes harder and harder not to return to crime.

Most youths on aftercare status are placed on supervision in the community for a year or more after their release. The aftercare officer, who is expected to monitor the behavior of youths under supervision, provides each youth with a list of rules; these rules usually resemble those given to adult parolees and pertain to such matters as obeying parents, maintaining a satisfactory adjustment at school or at work, being home at a certain time every night, avoiding contact with other delinquents, avoiding use or possession of any narcotic, and reporting to the aftercare officer as requested.

Risk Control and Crime Reduction

The current emphasis in aftercare is on short-term behavior control. The OJJDP has developed an intensive aftercare program that incorporates the principles of preparing youths for release to the community, facilitating youth–community interaction and involvement, and monitoring youths' reintegration into the community.[66]

interstate compact
The procedure for transferring a youth on probation or aftercare/parole from one state to another.

Similar to juvenile probation, intensive supervision programs (ISPs) are being increasingly used—as of 1992, there were over eighty aftercare ISPs in the United States.[67] The most noteworthy of these intensive programs are the ones in the thirty counties of Pennsylvania; "Lifeskills 95", the Violent Juvenile Offender Research and Development Program in Boston, Memphis, Newark, and Detroit; the Skillman Intensive Aftercare Project; the Michigan Nokomis Challenge Program; the PARJO program in New York; and OJJDP's Intensive Aftercare Program (IAP).

There has also been a focus on developing an integrated theoretical framework for guiding intensive supervision of chronic juvenile offenders. Based largely on combinations of social control, strain, and social learning theories, the IAP model focuses on the reintegrative process[68] (Figure 16–4 shows the program elements of this model). The underlying assumptions of this model are that chronic and serious delinquency are related to weak controls produced by social disorganization, inadequate socialization, and strain; that strain is produced by social disorganization independent of weak controls; and that peer group influences intervene as a social force between youths with weak bonds and/or strain on the one hand and delinquent behaviors on the other.[69]

This IAP model was initially implemented in Clark County (Las Vegas), Nevada; Arapaho, Douglas, and Jefferson counties and metropolitan Denver, Colorado; Essex, Newark, and Camden counties, New Jersey; and the city of Norfolk, Virginia. The participation of the New Jersey counties ended in 1997, but the other three programs have carried through on preparing high-risk offenders for progressively increased responsibility

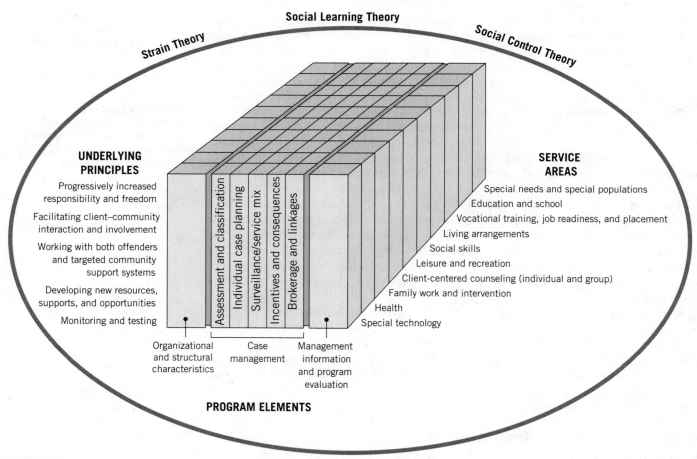

FIGURE 16–4
Intervention Model for Juvenile Aftercare

Source: David Altschuler et al., *Reintegration, Supervised Release, and Intensive Aftercare* (Washington, D.C.: Office of Juvenile Justice and Delinquency Prevention, 1999).

and freedom in the community. These programs' well-developed transition components, which begin shortly after a youth is adjudicated to an institution and continue through the early months of community adjustment, are particularly striking (see Table 16–5 for these transition components). The results of the first five years of implementation (1995–2000) revealed a dramatically improved level of communication and coordination between institutional and aftercare staff as well as the ability to involve parolees in community services almost immediately after institutional release.[70]

In-house detention and electronic monitoring programs still have not received the attention that they deserve in juvenile aftercare.[71] Juvenile aftercare also emphasizes drug and alcohol urinalyses (sometimes called "drug drops") and continues to use boot camp programs as a means of releasing juveniles early from training schools.

TABLE 16–5
Transition Components of Intensive Aftercare Programs

Transition Component	Intensive Aftercare Programming Site		
	Colorado	Nevada	Virginia
Early parole planning	Initial plan complete at 30 days after institutional placement; final plan complete at 60 days prior to release.	Initial plan complete at 30 days after institutional placement; final plan complete 30 days prior to furlough.	Initial plan complete 30 days after institutional placement; final plan complete 30 days prior to release.
Multiple perspectives incorporated in plan	Case manager, institutional staff, youth, parents, and community providers all routinely involved.	Parole officer, institutional community liaison, institutional staff, and youth; parent participation limited.	Parole officer, institutional case manager, youth, interagency "Community Assessment Team," and parent.
Parole officer visits to institution	One to two times per week; routine.	Once per month; routine since spring 1997.	One to two times per month; routine.
Treatment begun in institution and continued in community	Via community providers. Includes multifamily counseling, life skills training, individual counseling, and vocational skills training; done routinely.	Via an institution—community liaison and parole officers. Includes life skills and drug/alcohol curriculums; done routinely until liaison vacancy.	Via one provider at Hanover only. Drug/alcohol treatment; sporadic use; state policy discourages contract services by community providers for institutionalized youth.
Youth prerelease visits to community	Supervised day trips to community programs, beginning 60 days prior to release.	Not allowed.	Not allowed.
Preparole furlough	Overnight/weekend home passes, beginning 30 days prior to release.	Thirty-day conditional release to community, prior to official parole.	Not allowed.
Transitional residence	Not part of the design, but occurs for some youth.	Not part of the design.	Two group homes in Norfolk; 30- to 60-day length of stay; used for most youth.
Transitional day programming	Two day-treatment programs in Denver; used for almost all youth during the first few months after release.	One day-treatment supervision/treatment program; used for most youth.	Day treatment used for youth who do not go to group homes.
Phased supervision levels on parole	Informal system: contact once per week during the first few months, down to once per month later.	Four-phase system: contact four times per week during furlough; three times per week next 90 days; two times per week next 60–90 days; once per week next 30–60 days.	Four-phase system: group home; contact five to seven times per week next 60 days; three to five times per week next 60 days; three times per week last 30 days.

Source: Richard G. Wiebush, Betsie McNulty, and Thao Le, *Implementation of the Intensive Community-Based Aftercare Program* (Washington, D.C.: Office of Juvenile Justice and Delinquency Prevention, 2000), p. 2.

revocation of aftercare
The cancellation of parole and return of the offender to an institution. It takes effect if a juvenile on aftercare commits another offense or violates the conditions of parole.

Web Extra 16–3
OJJDP Model Programs Guide

▲ A teenager in jail.

■ **Why should jailed juveniles be separated from adults who may be held in the same facility?**

Library Extra 16–7
OJJDP Juvenile Justice Bulletin: "Aftercare Services"

In both traditional and intensive aftercare, if a rule is violated or a law is broken, a youth may be returned to a training school. Although guidelines for the **revocation of aftercare** for juveniles have not been formulated by court decisions, revocation of a youth's aftercare status is no longer based solely on the testimony of the aftercare officer, who could be influenced by personality clashes or prejudice toward the client. Today most jurisdictions have formal procedures for the revocation of aftercare. The aftercare officer may initially investigate the charge; if the finding is that the youth did commit the offense, the officer will report the parole violation to the supervisor. The supervisor may review the case and make the decision, or a revocation committee may examine the violation. The aftercare officer may be required to submit a written recommendation for revocation but is not allowed to testify, and the youth is permitted to speak in his or her own defense.

Juveniles in Adult Prison

Juveniles who end up in prison have usually been transferred to the adult court and been given a prison sentence. They soon discover that adult correctional institutions are a world apart from nearly all training schools: Prisons are much larger, some containing several thousand inmates, and can cover acres of ground; life on the inside is typically austere, crowded, and dangerous; and the violent and exploitative relationships that are found in adult correctional institutions make this disposition a hard one for juveniles, who are particularly vulnerable to sexual victimization and physical assault.[72]

Variations on the practice of confining juveniles in adult institutions exist among the states. In some jurisdictions, judges have no alternative but to place juveniles in adult institutions if the law requires it, but judges in a few states (under special circumstances) can place youths in either juvenile or adult institutions. In yet other states, judges can refer juveniles back to juvenile court, but they are then transferred to adult institutions when they come of age.[73]

In October 2000, Indiana stopped sending juveniles convicted of adult crimes into the general prison population. Those with lesser offenses are now held at the medium-security Plainfield Correctional Facility or at the minimum-security Medaryville Correctional Facility, but Indiana juveniles who commit violent or serious offenses are sent to Wabash Valley, a maximum-security facility.[74]

In 2002, an estimated 4,100 new court commitments involving juveniles younger than age 18 were sent to adult state prison. Between 1985 and 2002, the annual number of new court commitments to state prisons involving juveniles younger than age 18 increased 22 percent, with new commitments overall increasing 114 percent.[75]

Thirteen states permit the transfer of juveniles to adult facilities: California, Colorado, Hawaii, Indiana, Kentucky, Massachusetts, New Jersey, New York, Rhode Island, South Carolina, Texas, Washington, and Wisconsin. The court has authority to make such transfers in one-third of these states, the commitment agency has authority in one-third, and the transfer decision is a joint agreement between two authorities (e.g., agency and court or juvenile and adult agency) in one-third. The reasons for such transfers include age of the offender, seriousness of the offense, failure to benefit from the program, and poor institutional adjustment. A violent attack on a staff member by an older resident with an initial serious offense, for example, would be the type of case most likely leading to a transfer from a juvenile facility to an adult prison.[76]

Prevention of Delinquency

It might be said that speaking of the prevention of delinquency when this chapter has considered the confinement of youthful offenders seems to be out of line. Yet there are a number of juvenile facilities that have been selected as model juvenile facilities, and these facilities provide a much different quality of life to residents. These programs may not prevent delinquency, but they can do much to reduce the likelihood that youths will continue a life of crime. These facilities are the Hillcrest Training School in Cincinnati, Ohio; Hennepin County Home School in Minnetonka, Minnesota; and Hogan Street Regional Youth Center in St. Louis, Missouri.

Hillcrest Training School

Hillcrest operates 118 treatment beds for adjudicated male delinquent youth placed by the Hamilton County Juvenile Court. There are also twelve assessment beds for girls and twelve assessment beds for boys. Aftercare services are provided for boys and girls who have completed the program.

The program primarily serves youth who have committed felony offenses. The age of youth in residence ranges between twelve and eighteen.

Education

The Hillcrest educational program is a "Special Needs Independent Charter School." Students have their educational needs met through a challenging multidisciplinary curriculum designed to consider current credit needs, academic skill deficiencies, vocational interests, and cognitive self-management strategies for the classroom. The educational program supports each student's return to his or her community school. College scholarship funds are available for deserving students.

Cognitive-Behavioral Treatment

The Hillcrest Training School treatment program consists of three tracks:

- Youthful offenders who have sexually abused others
- Youthful offenders who have abused alcohol and other drugs
- Youthful offenders who have disruptive behavior disorders.[77]

Hennepin County Home School

The Hennepin County Home School combines features of camps and ranches. Except for a fourteen-bed security unit, it is an open facility, located in a beautiful 160-acre wooded site approximately seventeen miles from downtown Minneapolis. The 164-bed facility is coeducational and holds youths who range in age from thirteen to seventeen, with an average age of fifteen. The school receives no status offenders; instead, the population is made up of those who have committed a variety of property and personal offenses. The typical resident has had at least five prior court involvements, and far more than half the residents have been involved in some type of out-of-home placement before their commitment to the Hennepin County Home School.[78]

The institution comprises three Juvenile Male Offender cottages, two Juvenile Sex Offender cottages, one cottage for female offenders, and one Beta cottage for short-term restitution offenders.

The residents remain in the Beta program for three to eight weeks and in other cottages for as long as a year. Each resident of the Juvenile Sex Offender cottages would have received an indeterminate sentence, while residents of the other cottages would have received a determinate sentence. The institution's sophisticated treatment program uses such modalities as an educational program that focuses on those with learning disabilities, family therapy, transactional analysis, behavior modification, and reality therapy. Horseback riding and canoeing are favorite recreational activities.

Residents are typically more positive about a placement at a wilderness camp or ranch than about placement in a training school. They like the more relaxed security, the more frequent community contacts, the shorter stays, and the better relations with staff. Yet some youths cannot handle these settings. They may be too homesick or too victimized by peers, so they repeatedly run away until they are transferred to more secure facilities.[79]

Hogan Street Regional Youth Center

The Missouri Division of Youth Services won the 2008 Annie C. Casey Innovations Award in Children and Family System reform. Hogan Street Regional Youth Center is a Missouri Division of Services facility that serves some of the most serious offenders committed to youth services. Located in St. Louis, Missouri, Hogan Street Regional Youth Center is a secure residential treatment center for serious juvenile offenders with a capacity of thirty-five youth. It is designed exclusively for boys between fourteen and sixteen years old. The average length of stay is one year.

The facility is designed to be a welcoming place with a family atmosphere, much like a college dorm. As with the other thirty-two Missouri sites, Hogan House is committed to maintaining ties to the family. Youths, whenever possible, are within fifty miles of home. They are placed in treatment groups of ten to twelve. They receive educational services, vocational guidance, and a variety of counseling services. It is designed as an open-dorm model with a limited number of individual rooms for prerelease students and youth not functioning well in the group setting.

There is an expectation that staff will develop prosocial relationships with residents, treat them with respect, and use the best practices approach of "social learning," to promote positive change.

What Makes These *Model* Facilities?

A number of features distinguish these model programs:

- *Strong leadership.* Staff are role models who are passionate about youth service.
- *Open to outside reviews.* These facilities are open to all outside reviewers.
- *Organized within a framework that small is better.* Smallness and consistency of staff lead to residents identifying with and building trust quicker with staff.
- *Facilities are safe.* These facilities make safety their first priority.
- *Staff are dedicated.* Staff at all levels are committed to helping youth succeed.
- *Staffing is at an adequate level and competent.* For the population that these facilities serve, this means no more than a one-to-eight staff ratio.
- *Administrators and staff have strong pro-youth philosophy.* Youth are taught that they have strengths and are given tools to meet their needs legally.
- *Programming meets youth needs.* All three facilities have strong educational, vocational, life skills, family involvement, health, psychological services, and transition programs.
- *Family connections are built or strengthened.* These facilities make working and partnering with family a priority.
- *Community involvement is stressed.* All three place a high value on not isolating youth from the communities from which they came. This means bringing community agencies and advocates into the facilities and creating opportunities for youth to practice learned skills in their community at school and work and in recreation.[80]

Delinquency Across the Life Course: *Juvenile Victimization*

Juvenile victimization is one of the most troubling aspects of juvenile institutionalization. Institutionalization is a painful process for most youthful offenders, though it is clearly more painful for some than for others. Juvenile victimization can be such a painful experience that it can have lifelong effects.

Many studies of training schools for boys reflect an inmate society in which the strong take advantage of the weak. In their study of the State Industrial School for Boys in Golden, Colorado, Gordon E. Barker and W. Thomas Adams found two types of residential leaders: One held power through brute force and the other ruled through charisma. According to these researchers, residents were involved in an unending battle for dominance and control.[81]

Howard W. Polsky studied a cottage in a residential treatment center in New York; the staff in Cottage Six were unable to keep residential leaders from exploiting peers. The social hierarchy the researchers identified in this cottage had a pecking order; those at the bottom of the status hierarchy found life so debilitating that most of them ended up in mental hospitals.[82]

Sethard Fisher studied a small training school in California and identified victimization and patronage as two of the major behaviors taking place. He defined *victimization* as "a predatory practice whereby inmates of superior strength and knowledge of inmate lore prey on weaker and less knowledgeable inmates."[83] *Patronage* referred to youths' building of "protective and ingratiating relationships with others more advantageously situated on the prestige ladder." Fisher also saw victimization as being made up of physical attack, agitation, and exploitation.[84]

Clemens Bartollas, Stuart J. Miller, and Simon Dinitz's *Juvenile Victimization: The Institutional Paradox,* examined the culture that end-of-the-line delinquents established in a maximum-security institution in Columbus, Ohio. In this training school, dominant youths exploited submissive ones in every possible way. Ninety percent of the one hundred fifty residents were involved in this exploitation matrix; 19 percent were exploiters who were never themselves exploited, 34 percent were exploiters and victims at different times, 21 percent were occasionally victims and never exploiters, and 17 percent were chronic victims. Ten percent of the residents were neither victims nor exploiters.[85]

In a fifteen-year follow-up evaluation of this training school, Miller, Bartollas, and Dinitz found that the negative youth culture described in the 1976 study still thrived and that the strong still victimized the weak. Staff members were more disillusioned than they were at the time of the first study. They also were more fearful of victimization from residents.[86]

Martin Forst, Jeffrey Fagan, and T. Scott Vivona, relying on data collected in both juvenile facilities and adult correctional facilities, found that 1.7 percent of youth in training schools reported having been sexually attacked while in the facility and 8.6 percent (five times as many) of juveniles in adult correctional facilities reported such victimization while incarcerated during the previous twelve months.[87]

Following the passage and signing of the Prison Rape Elimination Act (PREA) of 2003, three major government-sponsored research effectors have provided additional insights about the conditions and scope of sexual victimization of confined juveniles. The first drew on a nationally representative sample of 7,073 youths held in 203 facilities and found that 3.6 percent (1 in every 28) of juveniles in residential facilities reported having been sexually victimized at least one time.[88] A second study based on the administrative records data collected by the Bureau of Justice Statistics as part of the PREA-mandated study of sexual violence incidence and prevalence in U.S. correctional institutions found that in 2004 the rate of sexual victimization reported by authorities in juvenile institutions was more than 5 percent of confined juveniles.[89] The third study was conducted during 2007 in twelve facilities—located in six states and including nine male facilities, one female facility, and two coeducational facilities. According to the study, 19.7 percent of responding youth reported at least one incident of sexual victimization during the previous twelve months of confinement.[90]

In sum, although many exceptions to the lawless environment described in these studies exist, an environment in which the strong take advantage of the weak, the fact is that the quality of life for male residents in too many training schools is extremely problematic. Even more troubling is the high rate of staff involvement in the sexual victimization of residents. Exhibit 16–4 describes sexual victimization in juvenile facilities.

Delinquency and Social Policy: How to Make Juvenile Facilities Better

A number of recommendations for the management of a juvenile facility are offered below. These recommendations have been tested in the field and are intended to offer a humane and effective juvenile facility.

Exhibit 16–4
Sexual Victimization in Juvenile Facilities

In a 2010 report, *Sexual Victimization in Juvenile Facilities*, the Bureau of Justice Statistics (BJS) conducted the first nationally representative survey of sexual abuse in residential juvenile facilities. This BJS study surveyed 26,550 adjudicated youth held in state-operated and large local or privately operated juvenile facilities; overall 91 percent of the youth in these facilities were male and 9 percent were female. It was found that an estimated 12 percent of youth in state facilities and large nonstate facilities (representing 3,220 youth nationwide) reported one or more incidents of sexual victimization by another youth or facility staff member in the previous months or since admission.

- About 2 percent of institutionalized youth (700 nationwide) reported an incident involving a peer and, alarmingly, 10.3 percent (2,730) reported an incident involving facility staff.
- About 4.3 percent of institutionalized youth (1,150) reported having sex or other sexual activity with facility staff as a result of some type of force; 6.4 percent of youth (1,710) reported contact with facility staff without force or threat.
- Approximately 95 percent of all institutionalized youth reporting staff sexual misconduct said they had been victimized by female staff. In 2008, 42 percent of staff in state juvenile facilities were female.
- Rates of sexual victimization varied among youth: 9.1 percent of institutionalized females and 2.0 percent of institutionalized males reported unwanted sexual activity with other youth.

- Youth with a sexual orientation other than heterosexual reported significantly higher rates of sexual victimization by another youth (12.5 percent) compared to heterosexual youth (1.3 percent).
- Youth who had experienced any prior sexual assault were more than twice as likely to report sexual victimization in the current facility (24.1 percent), compared to those with no sexual assault history (10.1 percent).
- Among youth victimized by another youth, 20 percent said they had been physically injured, and 5 percent reported they had sought medical attention for their injuries.
- Among youth victimized by staff, 5 percent reported a physical injury, and fewer than 1 percent had sought medical attention.

CRITICAL THINKING QUESTIONS

■ *If a juvenile facility must be safe for residents, then this BJS report, as well as other recent ones, is a serious indictment of this nation's policy of juvenile institutionalization. How can juveniles be better protected from each other as well as others?*

Source: Allen J. Beck, Paige M. Harrison, and Paul Guerino, *Sexual Victimization in Juvenile Facilities reported by Youth, 2008–2009* (Washington, D.C.: U.S. Government Printing Office, Bureau of Justice Statistics, 2010), p. 1.

Recommendations for Juvenile Facility Management

- *Pursue excellence in the facility.* Successful administrators set high standards. They not only expect excellence, they demand it.
- *A meaningful institutional program requires a carefully thought-out plan of action or strategy.* Administrators must determine where they want to go (their vision) and understand how it is possible to get there (implementing the vision).
- *Management should be proactive.* An anticipatory and preventative approach is fundamental in maintaining institutional control.
- *Professionalism should be held up as a goal to all staff.* Staff development and training are important steps in staff seeing themselves as professionals.
- *Cleanliness and orderliness of the facility are absolute necessities.* Cleanliness shows that the staff are in control.
- *The institutional environment must be safe for youths and staff.* If an institution is not a safe environment, little positive can be accomplished.
- *Both residents and staff must be treated with dignity and respect.* The norm for staff is that they treat residents as they would want their own sons or daughters to be treated.
- *Good programming by committed staff must be available for those youths who want to make positive changes in their lives.* Treatment programs must be delivered effectively to those interested residents, especially those with addictions and anger management.
- *An effective system of accountability for both staff and youths is necessary.* Sufficient consequences are required for inappropriate behavior, especially when rules are broken.

- *The services that are promised must be delivered to youths when they are scheduled to be delivered.* It is important for the system to be predictable and trusted to do what was promised.

- *Facilities, as much as possible, should have the following characteristics.* They should be as close as possible to juveniles' families, smaller with personalized services, family friendly, and managed in a caring manner.

- *The administrator must be a model of integrity in every way, both inside and outside the facility.*

- *Accreditation is an important process in a juvenile residential facility offering humane confinement and mission effectiveness.* [91]

The Case

The Life Course of Amy Watters, Age 17

Amy was taken to a state-run residential facility for girls. On arrival at the facility, she was interviewed, given a battery of written tests, and assigned to live in a small cottage that was also home to five other girls. All of the girls were around the same age as Amy, although they were of different ethnic backgrounds and came from different parts of the state.

Amy seemed to have no trouble fitting in, and she soon became friends with her roommates. The cottage had individual beds, lockers for clothes, and a small cosmetics area in the shared bathroom for each girl to keep her personal items in. There was only one television, however, so when the girls weren't attending classes or participating in other programs, they had to agree on what programs they wanted to watch. Lights went out at 10:00 P.M., and came on again at 6:00 A.M. Breakfast was at 7:00 A.M., and the girls were required to attend. The school day started at 8:00 in the morning, and went until 4:00 in the afternoon. Amy soon learned, however, that the curriculum differed quite a bit from the public schools she had previously attended; it contained options allowing the girls to learn trades. Amy selected a couple of beautician courses, and soon found herself learning hairdressing and the art of makeup application. She even received training in how to give pedicures and manicures—something she very much enjoyed. When they had nothing else to do, the ladies who taught the course allowed Amy and her friends to practice what they had learned on each other, and the time spent giving and receiving beauty treatments made the girls feel good about themselves. One of the teachers, a middle-aged woman whom the girls called Mrs. Woods, took a special interest in Amy, and told her about how enjoyable a career as a beautician could be. She also encouraged Amy to think seriously about her future, and advised her to avoid getting back in with the wrong crowd when she went home. Soon, Amy began to think about attending beauty school when she was released, and started figuring out ways of paying for it.

Before she knew it six months had passed and Amy was released back into her father's care.

Epilogue: Amy made good on her plan to become a cosmetologist. She found a part-time job working in a local eatery and, with supplementary funds provided by her father, was able to attend a local beauty college. After a few months she became licensed as an esthetician, and took on full-time work as a beauty specialist in a spa associated with a large retail store where she specialized in performing microdermabrasions (a peeling away of the outer layer of the skin to allow for healthy new skin to grow). She never saw CJ again, but was soon able to afford her own apartment. The distance between Amy and her father, Simon, grew, and she rarely saw him once she was on her own. More importantly, she stayed away from drugs, and began dating a clean-cut young man who had recently received a two-year degree in criminal justice from the local Palm Beach State College. It appeared as though Amy had finally gotten her life on the right track.

What aspects of the residential placement setting that Amy experienced might have helped turn her life around? What role did trade training likely play? How important might the personal attention she received from Mrs. Woods have been?

Learn More on the Web:
- Census of Juveniles in Residential Placement Databook: http://www.ojjdp.gov/ojstatbb/ezacjrp
- Pathways to Desistance Study: http://www.pathwaysstudy.pitt.edu
- PACE Center for Girls: http://www.pacecenter.org

SUMMARY

This chapter examines juvenile corrections and aftercare. Among the most important issues discussed in this chapter are the following:

- Under a federal jail removal mandate, juveniles are not allowed to be housed in adult jails within sight or sound of adult prisoners.
- Long-term juvenile institutions consist of wilderness camps and ranches, boot camps, and training schools.
- Although the proportion of juveniles who are sent to long-term facilities is small, these institutions of last resort are an integral part of society's efforts to exercise control over juveniles who break the law.

- Training schools tend to be quite expensive, but the length of time residents spend there, the programs that are offered, and the nature of the peer subcultures that exist within them tend to vary from state to state and even from training school to training school.
- Aftercare (or parole, as it is called in some states) has much in common with probation. Indeed, in some jurisdictions, the same officer is responsible for both a probation and an aftercare caseload.
- Juveniles who are transferred to adult court may be sentenced to spend time in an adult prison.

KEY TERMS

boot camp, p. 415
cruel and unusual punishment, p. 427
detention center, p. 414
interstate compact, p. 429
jail, p. 413

juvenile aftercare, p. 427
private juvenile placement, p. 424
ranch, p. 417
reception and diagnostic center, p. 416
revocation of aftercare, p. 432

right to treatment, p. 426
shelter care facility, p. 414
wilderness camp, p.417

JUVENILE DELINQUENCY VIDEOS

Disproportionate Minority Confinement and Contact (DMC)

Disproportionate Minority Confinement and Contact (DMC) discusses the overrepresentation of nonwhite juveniles within the justice system. DMC calls for proper precautions to be taken to keep these juveniles out of the system to provide them the opportunity for a better future. How can DMC be detrimental to the goals of the justice system? Based on the readings in this chapter as well as this video, what steps can be taken to decrease the proportion of nonwhite juveniles within institutions? What theories of crime might explain the disproportionate number of minorities within the justice system? Discuss.

Life Inside

Life Inside follows youths as they give a "tour" of a juvenile institution. The juveniles interviewed give their perspective on how the institutions function as well as giving a personal account of future plans. Based on the interviews in the video, how did the juvenile institutions have an impact on the goals of the youths?

What are some of the programs that juvenile institutions offer and what are the goals of these programs? Using information from the video as well as the readings, discuss whether the institution in the video focuses on retribution or rehabilitation. Why? What would be different if the center operated through the some other treatment model?

The Professional Perspective

The Professional Perspective interviews the superintendent of a juvenile facility. Discuss the differences between the juveniles' perspective of the happenings within the institution from the *Life Inside* video and the perspective of the superintendent. How do the points of view differ? How are the perspectives similar? The superintendent speaks about recruiting and retaining staff members within the institution. According to the superintendent, what characteristics make up a good staff member for an institutional environment? Discuss the impact a staff member can have on the lives of institutionalized juveniles.

REVIEW QUESTIONS

1. What is the jail removal mandate? How does it impact the short-term confinement of juveniles?
2. What are the main types of juvenile institutions? How do these types differ?
3. What are the main types of programs that take place during an institutional stay?
4. What is aftercare? Why is this transition to the community so important?

DISCUSSION QUESTIONS

1. What are the various kinds of juvenile correctional facilities discussed in this chapter? What type of facility do you think would be the most effective at reforming delinquents? Why?
2. How effective are training schools? What can be done to make training schools more effective?
3. Many states today are moving to institutionalize fewer juvenile offenders, and to shift the financial burden of housing those who are institutionalized to local governments. Why is this happening? How will it impact juvenile corrections?

GROUP EXERCISES

1. Invite the director of a local juvenile correctional facility to speak with the class, or arrange for an online session where the class can interact with him or her. Prepare questions for the director prior to the interaction.
2. What's the philosophy behind boot camps? Do you think that they work to reform offenders? How can they be improved?

NOTES

1. Brandon Artiles, "Vigil Coincides with Landmark Decision," MS News Now, February 27, 2012, http://www.msnewsnow.com/story/17027287/vigil-coincides-with-landmark-decision (accessed November 19, 2012).
2. Booth Gunter, "Investigation, Lawsuit Exposes Barbaric Conditions at For-Profit Youth Prison in Mississippi," Southern Poverty Law Center, May 3, http://www.splcenter.org/get-informed/news/splc-investigation-lawsuit-expose-barbaric-conditions-at-for-profit-youth-prison-I (accessed July 5, 2012).
3. Christopher Murray, Chris Baird, Ned Loughran, Fred Mills, and John Platt, Safety and Welfare Plan: Implementing Reform in California (Sacramento: California Department of Corrections and Rehabilitation, Division of Juvenile Justice, 2006).
4. David W. Springer, Transforming Juvenile Justice in Texas: A Framework for Action (Austin, Tex.: Blue Ribbon Task Force Report, 2007).
5. "Juvenile School Would Grow," Hartford Courant, February 10, 2008; Alison Leigh Cowan, "New Connecticut Law May Save a Troubled Prison for Juveniles," New York Times, July 30, 2007; Christine Stuart, "Juvenile Injustice," CT News Junkie, July 19, 2006; and Nan Shnitzler, "Connecticut Juvenile Training School to Close," New England Psychologist, October 2005, http://www.masspsy.com/leading/0510_ne_CT.html.
6. Holbrook Mohr, "13,000 Abuse Claims in Juvie Centers," Associated Press, March 2, 2008.
7. Ibid.
8. Rosemary, "Gender Issues in Juvenile Justice," Crime and Delinquency 29 (1983), 390.
9. Howard N. Snyder and Melissa Sickmund, Juvenile Offenders and Victims: A National Report (Pittsburgh, Pa.: National Center for Juvenile Justice, 1995), p. 72.
10. Ibid., p. 236.
11. Charles E. Frazier and Donna M. Bishop, "Jailing Juveniles in Florida: The Dynamics of Compliance to a Sluggish Federal Referral Initiative," paper presented at the annual meeting of the American Society of Criminology, Baltimore, MD, November 1990, p. 4.
12. Ira M. Schwartz, Linda Harris, and Laurie Levi, "The Jailing of Juveniles in Minnesota: A Case Study," Crime and Delinquency 34 (1988), p. 146; David Steinhart, "California's Legislature Ends the Jailing of Children: The Story of a Policy Reversal," Crime and Delinquency 34 (1988), pp. 169–70.
13. David Steinhart and Barry Krisberg, "Children in Jail," State Legislature 13 (1987), pp. 12–16.
14. Dale G. Parent, "Conditions of Confinement," in Juvenile Justice, Vol. 1., No. 1 (Spring/Summer 1993), pp. 2–7. For other criticisms of detention practices, see Ira M. Schwartz and William H. Barton, eds., Reforming Juvenile Detention: No More Hidden Closets (Columbus: Ohio State University Press, 1994).
15. Roberta C. Cronin, Boot Camps for Adult and Juvenile Offenders: Overview and Update, Final Summary Report (Washington, D.C.: National Institute of Justice, 1994), p. 37. See also Mark Jones and Steven Cuvelier, "Are Boot Camp Graduates Better Probation Risks?" paper presented at the annual meeting of the American Society of Criminology, New Orleans, LA, November 1992; and Thomas W. Waldron, "Boot Camps Offer Second Chance to Young Felons," Corrections Today 52 (1990), pp. 144–69.
16. Jean Bottcher, "Evaluating the Youth Authority's Boot Camp: The First Five Months," paper delivered to Western Society of Criminology, Monterey, CA, February 1993; Institute for Criminological Research and American Institute for Research, Boot Camp for Juvenile Offenders: Constructive Intervention and Early Support—Implementation Evaluation Final Report (New Brunswick, N.J.: Rutgers University Press, 1992).
17. Cronin, Boot Camps for Adults and Juvenile Offenders.
18. Anthony W. Salerno, "Boot Camps: A Critique and a Proposed Alternative," Journal of Offender Rehabilitation 20 (1994), p. 149.
19. Ibid., p. 37.
20. Michael Peters et al., Boot Camps for Juvenile Offenders: Program Summary (Washington, D.C.: Office of Juvenile Justice and Delinquency Prevention, 1997), pp. 3, 35.
21. Ibid.

22. Doris Layton MacKenzie et al., "The Impact of Boot Camps on Traditional Institutions of Juvenile Residents: Perceptions, Adjustment, and Change," *Journal of Research in Crime and Delinquency* 38 (August 2000), pp. 279–313.

23. Ibid., p. 279.

24. Brent Zaehringer, "Juvenile Boot Camps: Cost and Effectiveness vs. Residential Facilities," Koch Crime Institute White Paper Report, http://www.hrf.uni-koeln.de/sitenew/content/e/filejuvbootcamps.pdf.

25. For this report, see Diana Jean Schemo, "Report Recounts Horrors of Youth Boot Camps" *New York Times*, December 11, 2007, http://www.nytimes.com/2007/10/11/washington/1report.htm.

26. Alexandra Marks, "States Fall Out of (Tough) Love with Boot Camps," *Christian Science Monitor*, December 27, 1999, p. 1.

27. For the classification system in California, the most highly developed in the nation, see Murray et al., *Safety and Welfare Plan*, pp. 12–18.

28. For the most recent data on ranches and camps, see Snyder and Sickmund, *Juvenile Offenders and Victims: 2006 National Report* (Pittsburgh, Pa.: National Center for Juvenile Justice, 2006), pp. 208, 221–27; Sarah Hockenberry, Melissa Sickmund, and Anthony Sladkey, *Juvenile Residential Facility Census, 2008: Selected Findings*, Juvenile Offenders and Victims: National Report Series Bulletin (Washington, D.C.: U.S. Department of Justice, July 2011).

29. Sarah Hockenberry, Melissa Sickmund, and Anthony Sladkey, *Juvenile Residential Facility Census, 2008: Selected Findings*, Juvenile Offenders and Victims: National Report Series Bulletin (Washington, D.C.: U.S. Department of Justice, July 2011).

30. Ibid., p. 6.

31. Murray et al., *Safety and Welfare Plan*, p. 2.

32. David Street, Robert D. Vinter, and Charles Perrow, *Organizations for Treatment: A Comparative Study of Institutions* (New York: Free Press, 1966).

33. Hockenberry et al., *Juvenile Residential Facility Census, 2008*, p. 4.

34. "Youth Center at Paint Creek Provides Opportunities," *Lighthouse Views*, Winter 2008, p. 1.

35. Experiences of one of the authors in several juvenile institutional systems have revealed these activities of youth supervision.

36. Synder and Sickmund, *Juvenile Offenders and Victims: 2006 National Report*, p. 197.

37. Ibid, p. 198.

38. David Shichor and Clemens Bartollas, "Private and Public Juvenile Placements: Is There a Difference?" *Crime and Delinquency* 36 (April 1990), pp. 286–99.

39. Glen Mills, for example, was featured in Bill Howard, "Florida Tries to Clone Preppy Glen Mills," *Youth Today: The Newspaper on Youth Work* 5 (July–August, 1996), pp. 1, 12, 13.

40. Gaylene Styve Armstrong and Doris Layton MacKenzie, "Private versus Public Juvenile Correctional Facilities: Do Differences in Environmental Quality Exist?" *Crime and Delinquency* 49 (October 2003), pp. 542–63.

41. Shichor and Bartollas, "Private and Public Juvenile Placements."

42. Clemens Bartollas and David Shichor, "Juvenile Privatization: The Expected and the Unexpected," paper presented at the annual meeting of the American Society of Criminology, Baltimore, MD, November 1990.

43. Shichor and Bartollas, "Private and Public Juvenile Placements," pp. 286–99.

44. Rose Giallombardo, *The Social World of Imprisoned Girls: A Comparative Study of Institutions for Juvenile Delinquents* (New York: Wiley, 1974).

45. Christopher M. Sieverdes and Clemens Bartollas, "Social Roles, Sex, and Racial Differences," *Deviant Behavior* 5 (1982), pp. 203–18.

46. Alice Propper, *Prison Homosexuality: Myth and Reality* (Lexington, Mass.: D.C. Heath, 1981).

47. Civil Rights of Institutionalized Persons Act (CRIPA), 42 U.S.C. §§ 1997–1997J.

48. *White* v. *Reid*, 125 F. Supp. 867 (U.S.D.C., D.C. 1954).

49. *Inmates of the Boys' Training School* v. *Affleck*, 346 F. Supp. 1354 (D.R.I. 1972).

50. *Nelson* v. *Heyne*, 355 F. Supp. 451 (N.D. Ind. 1972).

51. *Morales* v. *Turman*, 364 F. Supp. 166 (E.D. Tex. 1973).

52. Frances Paula Reddington, *In the Best Interests of the Child: The Impact of Morales v. Turman on the Texas Youth Commission*, Ph.D. dissertation, College of Criminal Justice, Sam Houston State University, Huntsville, Texas, 2005.

53. See *Lollis* v. *N.Y. State Department of Social Services*, 322 F. Supp. 473 (S.D.N.Y. 1970) and N. N. Kittie, *The Right to Be Different: Deviance and Enforced Therapy* (Baltimore, Md.: Johns Hopkins University Press, 1971), for more information on this subject.

54. *Pena* v. *New York State Division for Youth*, 419 F. Supp. 203 (S.D.N.Y. 1976).

55. *Inmates of the Boys' Training School* v. *Affleck*.

56. *Morales* v. *Turman*.

57. *Morgan* v. *Sproat*, 432 F. Supp. 1130 (S.D. Miss. 1977).

58. *State* v. *Werner*, 242 S.E.2d 907 (W. Va. 1978).

59. Kristin Parsons Winokur, Alisa Smith, Stephanie R. Bontranger, and Julia L. Blankenship, "Juvenile Recidivism and Length of Stay," *Journal of Criminal Justice* 36 (2008), pp. 126–37.

60. Lauren E. Glaze and Thomas P. Bonczar, *Probation and Parole in the United States, 2009* (Washington, D.C.: Bureau of Justice Statistics, 2010), Tables 17–19.

61. Howard N. Snyder, "An Empirical Portrait of the Youth reentry Population," *Youth Violence and Youth Justice* 2 (January 2004), pp. 39–55.

62. Laura S. Abrams and Susan M. Snyder, "Youth Offender Reentry: Models for Intervention and Directors for Future Inquiry," *Children and Youth Services Review* 32 (December 2010), pp. 1787–95.

63. Patricia McFall Torbet, *Organization and Administration of Juvenile Services: Probation, Aftercare, and State Delinquent Institutions* (Pittsburgh, Pa.: National Center for Juvenile Justice, 1988).

64. Steve V. Gies, "Aftercare Services," OJJDP (Washington, D.C.: U.S. Department of Justice, 2003), 1.

65. Bert Burraston, David Cherrington, and Stephen Bahr, "Reducing Juvenile Recidivism with Cognitive Training and a Cell Phone Follow-Up: An Evaluation of the Real Victory Program," *International Journal of Offender Therapy & Comparative Criminology* 56 (2012), pp. 61–80.

66. D. M. Altschuler and T. L. Armstrong, *Intensive Aftercare for High-Risk Juveniles: A Community Care Model* (Washington, D.C.: Office of Juvenile Justice and Delinquency Prevention, 1994).

67. Ted Palmer, *The Re-Emergence of Correctional Intervention* (Newbury Park, Calif.: Sage, 1992), p. 82.

68. David M. Altschuler and Troy L. Armstrong, *Intensive Aftercare for High-Risk Juveniles: Policies and Procedures* (Washington, D.C.: Office of Juvenile Justice and Delinquency Prevention, 1994).

69. For more extensive examination of these intensive aftercare programs, see Betsie McNulty, Richard Wiebush, and Thao Le, "Intensive Aftercare Programs for Serious Juvenile Offenders: Preliminary Results of Process and Outcome Evaluation," paper presented at the Annual Meeting of the American Society of Criminology, Washington, D.C., November 1998.

70. Richard G. Wiebush, Betsie McNulty, and Thao Le, *Implementation of the Intensive Community-Based Aftercare Program* (Washington, D.C.: Office of Juvenile Justice and Delinquency Prevention, 2000).

71. For an example of a house detention component of an aftercare program, see W. H. Barton and Jeffrey A. Butts, "Visible Options: Intensive Supervision Program for Juvenile Delinquents," *Crime and Delinquency* (1990), pp. 238–56.

72. Melissa Sickmund, *Juveniles in Corrections: National Report Series Bulletin* (Washington, D.C.: Office of Juvenile Justice and Delinquency Prevention, 2004).

73. Donna Hamparian et al., "Youth in Adult Court: Between Two Worlds," *Major Issues in Juvenile Justice Information and Training* (Columbus, Ohio: Academy for Contemporary Problems, 1981).

74. Vic Rychaert, "15 Youths Doing Time with State's Meanest," *Indianapolis Star*, April 30, 2001.

75. Snyder and Sickmund, *Juvenile Offenders and Victims*.

76. Kelly Dedel, "National Profile of the Organization of Juvenile Correctional Systems," *Crime and Delinquency* 44 (1998), pp. 507–25.

77. Interview with staff at Hillcrest in 2010.

78. A basic description of this program is included in a brochure developed by the Hennepin County Home School (n.d.). See also the Web page of the Hennepin County Home School.

79. Interviews with superintendent of this facility in 2010.

80. Joseph Heinz, Theresa Wise, and Clemens Bartollas, *Successful Management of Juvenile Residential Facilities: A Performance-Based Approach* (Alexandria, Va.: American Correctional Association, 2010), pp. 124–25.

81. Gordon E. Barker and W. Thomas Adams, "The Social Structure of a Correctional Institution," *Journal of Criminal Law, Criminology and Police Science*, 49 (1959), pp. 417–99.

82. Howard W. Polsky, *Cottage Six: The Social System of Delinquent Boys in Residential Treatment* (New York: Russell Sage Foundation), pp. 69–88.

83. Sethard Fisher, "Social Organization in a Correction Residence," *Pacific Sociological Review* 5 (Fall 1961), p. 89.

84. Ibid., pp. 89–90.

85. Clemens Bartollas, Stuart J. Miller, and Simon Dinitz, *Juvenile Victimization: The Institutional Paradox* (New York: Sage Publications, 1976), pp. 131–50.

86. Stuart J. Miller, Clemens Bartollas, and Simon Dinitz, *Juvenile Victimization Revisited: A Fifteen-Year Follow-Up at TICO* (unpublished manuscript).

87. Martin Forst, Jeffrey Fagan, and T. Scott Vivona, "Youth in Prisons and Training Schools: Perceptions and Consequences of the Treatment–Custody Dichotomy," *Juvenile and Family Court Journal* 40 (1989), pp. 1–14.

88. Andrea Sedlack, "Sexual Assault of Youth in Residential Placement," presentation at Bureau of Justice Statistics Workshop, Washington, D.C., January 18, 2005.

89. Allen J. Beck and Timothy A. Hughes, *Sexual Violence Reported by Correctional Authorities, 2004* (Washington, D.C.: Bureau of Justice Statistics, 2005).

90. Cited by Richard Tweksbury, "What We Know About Sexual Violence in Juvenile Corrections," paper presented at the 2007 Winter Conference, Grapevine, TX.

91. Heinz et al., *Successful Management of Juvenile Residential Facilities*, pp. 43–44.

academic performance Achievement in schoolwork as rated by grades and other assessment measures. Poor academic performance is a factor in delinquency.

adjudication The court process wherein a judge determines if the juvenile appearing before the court committed the act with which he or she is charged. The term *adjudicated* is analogous to convicted in the adult criminal justice system and indicates that the court concluded that the juvenile committed the act.

adjudicatory hearing The stage of juvenile court proceedings that usually includes the youth's plea, the presentation of evidence by the prosecution and by the defense, the cross-examination of witnesses, and a finding by the judge as to whether the allegations in the petition can be sustained.

adolescence The life interval between childhood and adulthood; usually the period between the ages of twelve and eighteen years.

adult court Criminal courts that hear the cases of adults charged with crimes and to which juveniles who are accused of having committed serious offenses can be waived (transferred). In some states, adult criminal courts have jurisdiction over juveniles who are accused of committing certain specified offenses.

aftercare The supervision of juveniles who are released from correctional institutions so that they can make an optimal adjustment to community living; also, the status of a juvenile conditionally released from a treatment or confinement facility and placed under supervision in the community.

Age of onset The age at which a child begins to commit delinquent acts; an important dimension of delinquency.

alcohol A drug made through a fermentation process that relaxes inhibitions.

alternative school A facility that provides an alternative educational experience, usually in a different location, for youths who are not doing satisfactory work in the public school setting.

amphetamine A stimulant drug that occurs in a variety of forms.

appeal The review of juvenile court proceedings by a higher court. Although no constitutional right of appeal exists for juveniles, the right of adjudicated juveniles to appeal has been established by statute in some states.

appellate review The review of the decision of a juvenile court proceeding by a higher court. Decisions by appellate courts, including the U.S. Supreme Court, have greatly affected the development of juvenile court law and precedent.

arrest The process of taking a person into custody for an alleged violation of the law. Juveniles who are under arrest have nearly all the due process safeguards accorded to adults.

Attention Deficit/Hyperactivity Disorder (ADHD) A cognitive disorder of childhood that can include inattention, distractibility, excessive activity, restlessness, noisiness, and impulsiveness.

attention home An innovative form of detention facility, found in several locations across the nation, that is characterized by an open setting.

autonomic nervous system The system of nerves that govern reflexes, glands, the iris of the eye, and activities of interior organs that are not subject to voluntary control.

bail The money or property pledged to the court or actually deposited with the court to effect the release of a person from legal custody. Juveniles do not have a constitutional right to bail as do adults.

balanced and restorative model An integrative correctional model that seeks to reconcile the interests of victims, offenders, and communities through programs and supervision practices.

balanced approach to juvenile probation A philosophy of juvenile probation that strives to protect the community from delinquency, to impose accountability for offenses committed, and to equip juvenile offenders with the required competencies to live productively and responsibly in the community.

behavioral modification A technique in which rewards of punishments are used to change a person's behavior.

beyond a reasonable doubt A legal standard establishing the degree of proof needed for a juvenile to be adjudicated a delinquent by the juvenile court during the adjudicatory stage of the court's proceedings.

bifurcated hearing A split adjudication and disposition hearing, which is the present trend of the juvenile court.

binding over The process of transferring (also called certifying) juveniles to adult criminal court. Binding over takes place after a judicial hearing on a juvenile's amenability to treatment or his or her threat to public safety.

biological positivism The belief that juveniles' biological characteristics and limitations drive them to delinquent behavior.

birth order The sequence of births in a family and a child's position in it, whether firstborn, middle, or youngest child.

blocked opportunity The limited or nonexistent chance of success; according to strain theory, a key factor in delinquency.

boot camp A military-style facility used as an alternative to prison in order to deal with prison crowding and public demands for severe punishment.

born criminal An individual who is atavistic, who reverts to an earlier evolutionary level and is unable to conform his or her behavior to the requirements of modern society; thus, an individual who is innately criminal.

Breed v. Jones A 1975 double jeopardy case in which the U.S. Supreme Court ruled that a juvenile court cannot adjudicate a case and then transfer the case to the criminal court for adult processing of the same offense.

broken home A family in which parents are divorced or are no longer living together.

brother–sister incest Sexual activity that occurs between brother and sister.

bullying The hurtful, frightening, or menacing actions undertaken by one person to intimidate another (generally weaker) person, to gain that person's unwilling compliance and/or to cause him or her to be fearful.

capitalism An economic system in which private individuals or corporations own and control capital (wealth and the means of production) and in which competitive free markets control prices, production, and distribution of goods.

child abuse The mistreatment of children by parents or caregivers. Physical abuse is intentional behavior directed toward a child by the parent or caregiver to cause pain, injury, or death. Emotional abuse involves a disregard of a child's psychological needs. Sexual abuse is any intentional and wrongful physical contact with a child that entails a sexual purpose or component, and such sexual abuse is termed *incest* when the perpetrator is a member of the child's family.

child savers A name given to an organized group of progressive social reformers of the late nineteenth and early twentieth centuries who promoted numerous laws aimed at protecting children and institutionalizing an idealized image of childhood innocence.

chronic youthful offender   A juvenile who engages repeatedly in delinquent behavior. The Philadelphia cohort studies defined chronic offenders as youths who had committed five or more delinquent offenses. Other studies use this term to refer to a youth involved in serious and repetitive offenses.

citation   A summons to appear in juvenile court.

clearance by arrest   The solution of a crime by arrest of a perpetrator who has confessed or who has been implicated by witnesses or evidence. Clearances can also occur by exceptional means, as when a suspected perpetrator dies prior to arrest.

club drug   A synthetic psychoactive substance often found at nightclubs, bars, raves, and dance parties. Club drugs include MDMA (Ecstasy), ketamine, methamphetamine (meth), gamma hydroxybutyrate (GHB), phencyclidine (PCP), and Rohypnol.

cocaine   A coca extract that creates mood elevation, elation, grandiose feelings, and feelings of heightened physical prowess.

Cognitive-Behavioral Therapy (CBT)   Therapy based on the assumption that the foundations for criminal behavior are dysfunctional patterns of thinking.

cognitive theory   A perspective on human development that says children develop cognitive abilities through interaction with the physical and social worlds.

Cognitive Thinking Skills Program (CTSP)   A cognitive-behavioral intervention program designed to improve offenders' thinking processes.

cohort   A generational group as defined in demographics, in statistics, or for the purpose of social research.

cohort studies   Research that usually includes all individuals who were born in a specific year in a particular city or country and follows them through part or all of their lives.

commitment   A determination made by a juvenile judge at the disposition stage of a juvenile court proceeding that a juvenile is to be sent to a juvenile correctional institution.

commitment to the social bond   The attachment that a juvenile has to conventional institutions and activities.

community-based corrections   A corrections program that includes probation, residential and day-treatment programs, and parole (aftercare). The nature of the links among community programs and their social environments is the most distinguishing feature of community-based corrections. As frequency, duration, and quality of community relationships increase, the programs become more community based.

community corrections acts   Legislative initiatives that enact statutory provisions in support of residential and day-treatment programs for juvenile offenders. The Minnesota Community Corrections Act has become the model

for other states because it provides a state subsidy to any county or group of counties that chooses to develop its own community corrections system.

complaint   A charge made to an intake officer of the juvenile court that an offense has been committed.

conduct norms   The rules of a group governing the ways its members should act under particular conditions; the violation of these rules arouses a group reaction.

conflict theory   A perspective that holds that delinquency can be explained by socioeconomic class, by power and authority relationships, and by group and cultural differences.

consent decree   A formal agreement between a juvenile and the court in which the juvenile is placed under the court's supervision without a formal finding of delinquency.

constitutionalists   The name given to a group of twentieth-century reformers who advocated that juveniles deserve due process protections when they appear before the juvenile court.

containment theory   A theoretical perspective that strong inner containment and reinforcing external containment provide insulation against delinquent and criminal behavior.

continuum of sanctions   The failure to respond to one sanction will result in a more serious or demanding sanction.

control theory   Any of several theoretical approaches that maintain that human beings must be held in check, or somehow be controlled, if delinquent tendencies are to be repressed.

cottage system   A widely used treatment practice that places small groups of training school residents into cottages.

crack   A less expensive but more potent form of cocaine.

crime control model   A correctional model supporting discipline and punishment as the most effective means of deterring youth crime.

crime index   A now-defunct but once-inclusive measure of the UCR Program's violent and property crime categories, or what are called *Part I offenses.*

cruel and unusual punishment   Inhumane punishments against which a guarantee is provided by the Eighth Amendment to the U.S. Constitution. Accordingly, juveniles in correctional custody must not be treated with unnecessary harshness.

culture conflict theory   A perspective that delinquency or crime arises because individuals are members of a subculture that has conduct norms that are in conflict with those of the wider society.

cultural deviance theory   A theory wherein delinquent behavior is viewed as an expression of conformity to cultural values and norms that are in opposition to those of the larger U.S. society.

culturally defined goals   In Merton's strain theory, the set of purposes and interests a culture defines as legitimate objectives for individuals.

cultural transmission theory   An approach that holds that areas of concentrated crime maintain their high rates over a long period, even when the composition of the population changes rapidly, because delinquent "values" become cultural norms and are passed from one generation to the next.

cyberbullying   The use of the Internet and related technologies to harm other people, in a deliberate, repeated, and hostile manner.

cycle of alienation   The process of police–juvenile interaction that further alienates youth who are already only loosely bound to the wider society.

day-treatment program   A court-mandated, community-based corrections program that juveniles attend in the morning and afternoon. They return home in the evening.

Deinstitutionalization of Status Offenders (DSO)   The removal of status offenders from secure detention facilities.

delinquent sibling   A brother or sister who is engaged in delinquent behaviors; an apparent factor in youngsters' involvement in delinquency.

desistance   The termination of a delinquent career or behavior.

detention   The temporary restraint of a juvenile in a secure facility, usually because he or she is acknowledged to be dangerous either to self or to others.

detention center   A short-term facility that provides custodial care for juveniles during juvenile court proceedings. Also called juvenile halls and detention homes, detention centers were established at the end of the nineteenth century as an alternative to jails for juveniles.

detention hearing   A hearing, usually conducted by an intake officer of the juvenile court, during which the decision is made as to whether a juvenile will be released to his or her parents or guardians or be detained in a detention facility.

determinate sentencing   A model of sentencing that provides fixed terms of sentences for criminal offenses. Terms are generally set by the legislature rather than determined by judicial discretion.

determinism   A philosophical position that suggests that individuals are driven into delinquent or criminal behavior by biological or psychological traits that are beyond their control.

Developmental Life-Course (DLC) theory   A framework suggesting that four key factors determine the shape of the life course: location in time and place, linked lives, human agency, and timing of lives.

differential association theory   The view that delinquency is learned from others and that delinquent behavior is to be expected of individuals who have internalized a preponderance of definitions that are favorable to law violations.

differential identification theory A modification of differential association theory that applies the interactionist concept of the self, allows for choice, and stresses the importance of motives.

differential opportunity structure The differences in economic and occupational opportunities open to members of different socioeconomic classes.

dispositional hearing The stage of the juvenile court proceedings in which the juvenile judge decides the most appropriate placement for a juvenile who has been adjudicated a delinquent, a status offender, or a dependent child.

Disproportionate Minority Confinement (DMC) The court-ordered confinement, in juvenile institutions, of members of minority groups in numbers disproportionate to their representation in the general population.

disruptive behavior Unacceptable conduct at school. It may include defiance of authority, manipulation of teachers, inability or refusal to follow rules, fights with peers, destruction of property, use of drugs in school, and/or physical or verbal altercations with teachers.

diversion programs Dispositional alternatives for youthful offenders that exist outside of the formal juvenile justice system.

double jeopardy A common law and constitutional prohibition against a second trial for the same offense.

drift theory The theoretical perspective that juveniles neutralize the moral hold of society and drift into delinquent behavior.

dropout A young person of school age who, of his or her own volition, no longer attends school.

drug addiction The excessive use of a drug, which is frequently characterized by physical and/or psychological dependence.

due process rights The constitutional rights that are guaranteed to citizens—whether adult or juvenile—during their contacts with the police, their proceedings in court, and their interactions with the public schools.

Ecstasy A form of amphetamine (MDMA) that began to be used by adolescents in the United States in the 1980s and 1990s and is now rather widespread.

electronic monitoring The use of electronic anklets and bracelets to verify probationers' presence in the place where they have been ordered confined.

emerging gang Any youth gang that formed in the late 1980s and early 1990s in communities across the nation and that is continuing to evolve.

emotional abuse A disregard for the psychological needs of a child, including lack of expressed love, withholding of contact or approval, verbal abuse, unrealistic demands, threats, and psychological cruelty.

emotionality An aspect of temperament. It can range from a near absence of emotional response to intense, out-of-control emotional reactions.

escalation of offenses An increase in the frequency and severity of an individual's offenses; an important dimension of delinquency.

evidence based The use of scientific research as the basis for determining the best practices in a field.

father–daughter incest Sexual activity that occurs between a father and his daughter. Also refers to incest by stepfathers or the boyfriend(s) of the mother.

family size The number of children in a family, a possible risk factor for delinquency.

father–son incest Sexual activity between father and son. Also refers to incest by stepfathers or the boyfriend(s) of the mother.

family therapy A counseling technique that involves treating all members of a family; a widely used method of dealing with a delinquent's socially unacceptable behavior.

felicific calculus A method for determining the sum total of pleasure and pain produced by an act; also the assumption that human beings strive to obtain a favorable balance of pleasure and pain.

felony A criminal offense punishable by death or by incarceration in a state or federal correctional institution, usually for one year or more.

feminist theory of delinquency A theory that adolescent females' victimization at home causes them to become delinquent and that this fact has been systematically ignored.

fingerprinting A pretrial identification procedure used with both juveniles and adults following arrest.

focal concerns The values or focal concerns (trouble, toughness, smartness, excitement, fate, and autonomy) of lower-class youths that differ from those of middle-class youths.

free will The ability to make rational choices among possible actions and to select one over the others.

gang A group of youths who are bound together by mutual interests, have identifiable leadership, and act in concert to achieve a specific purpose that generally includes the conduct of illegal activity.

gang unit A specialized unit established by some police departments to address the problem of gangs.

gender The personal traits, social positions, and values and beliefs that members of a society attach to being male or female.

gender ratio of crime The comparison of rates of criminal offending by gender.

gender role A societal definition of what constitutes either masculine or feminine behavior.

group home A placement for youths who have been adjudicated by the court that serves a group of about thirteen to thirty-five youths as an alternative to institutionalization; also called *group residence, halfway house,* or *attention home.*

guardian ad item A lawyer who is appointed by the court to take care of youths who need help, especially in neglect, dependency, and abuse cases, but also occasionally in delinquency cases.

Guided Group Interaction (GGI) A treatment modality based on the assumption that youths can confront their peers and force them to face the reality of their behavior more effectively than staff can. GGI is the most widely used treatment modality in juvenile corrections.

halfway house A residential setting for adjudicated delinquents, usually those who need a period of readjustment to the community following institutional confinement.

heroin A refined form of morphine that was introduced around the beginning of the twentieth century.

hidden delinquency Any unobserved or unreported delinquency.

home detention House arrest. This form of detention is used in some jurisdictions, and an adjudicated juvenile remains at home under the supervision of juvenile probation officers.

house arrest A program of home confinement whereby youths are ordered to remain confined in their residences during evening hours, after curfew, and on weekends.

house of refuge An institution that was designed by eighteenth- and nineteenth-century reformers to provide an orderly, disciplined environment similar to that of the "ideal" Puritan family.

human agency The active role juveniles take in their lives; the fact that juveniles are not merely subject to social and structural constraints but also make choices and decisions based on the alternatives that they see before them.

incest Any intrafamily sexual abuse that is perpetrated on a child by a member of that child's family group and that includes not only sexual intercourse but also any act designed to stimulate a child sexually or to use a child for sexual stimulation, either of the perpetrator or of another person.

incidence of delinquency The frequency with which delinquent behavior takes place.

indeterminate sentencing In juvenile justice, a sentencing model that encourages rehabilitation through the use of general and relatively unspecific sentences. Under the model, a juvenile judge has wide discretion and can commit a juvenile to the department of corrections or youth authority until correctional staff make the decision to release the juvenile. This type of sentencing is used with juveniles in most jurisdictions other than those that have mandatory or determinate sentencing.

informal adjustment An attempt to handle a youthful offender outside of the formal structures of the juvenile justice system.

inhalant A volatile liquid that gives off a vapor, which is inhaled, producing short-term excitement and euphoria followed by a period of disorientation.

in loco parentis The principle according to which a guardian or an agency is given the rights, duties, and responsibilities of a parent in relation to a particular child or children.

In re Gault A 1967 U.S. Supreme Court case that brought due process and constitutional procedures into juvenile courts.

In re Winship A 1970 case in which the U.S. Supreme Court decided that juveniles are entitled to proof beyond a reasonable doubt during adjudication proceedings.

insight-based therapy Treatment designed to encourage communication of conflicts and insight into problems, with the goal of symptoms relief, change in behavior, and personality growth.

institutionalized In Merton's theory, culturally sanctioned methods of attaining individual goals.

intake At this stage of the processing of a juvenile offender, the probation officer conducts a preliminary investigation that includes an interview during which the youth is advised of his or her legal rights and the officer decides on the next step for the youth.

intensive supervision programs (ISPs) A form of probation supervision involving frequent face-to-face contact between the probationer and the probation officer.

interstate compact The procedure for transferring a youth on probation or aftercare/parole from one state to another.

jail A facility that provides temporary care and custody for juveniles during juvenile court proceedings. Also called *juvenile hall* and *detention home*.

judicial waiver The procedure of relinquishing the processing of a particular juvenile case to adult criminal court; also known as certifying or binding over to the adult court.

jury trial The court proceeding in which a panel of the defendant's peers evaluate evidence and render a verdict. The U.S. Supreme Court has held that juveniles do not have a constitutional right to a jury trial, but several jurisdictions permit juveniles to choose a jury trial.

just deserts A pivotal philosophical underpinning of the justice model that holds that juvenile offenders deserve to be punished and that the punishment must be proportionate to the seriousness of the offense or the social harm caused.

justice model A contemporary model of imprisonment based on the principle of just deserts.

juvenile A youth at or below the upper age of juvenile court jurisdiction in a particular state.

juvenile aftercare The supervision of juveniles who are released from correctional institutions so that they can make an optimal adjustment to community living.

juvenile court Any court that has jurisdiction over matters involving juveniles.

juvenile court officer A probation officer who serves juveniles (the term is used in some but not all probation departments).

juvenile delinquency An act committed by a minor that violates the penal code of the government with authority over the area in which the act occurs.

Juvenile Justice and Delinquency Prevention (JJDP) Act of 1974 A federal law that established a juvenile justice office within the then-existing Law Enforcement Assistance Administration to provide funds for the prevention and control of youth crime.

Juvenile Justice Standards Project A project jointly sponsored by the Institute of Judicial Administration and the American Bar Association that proposes that juveniles' sentences be based on the seriousness of the offense committed rather than on the needs of the youth.

juvenile officer In some police departments, a police officer who has received specialized training to work effectively with juveniles and who is tasked primarily with such work.

Kent v. United States A 1966 U.S. Supreme Court decision on the matter of transfer; the first decision in which the Supreme Court dealt with a juvenile court case.

labeling theory The view that society creates the delinquent by labeling those who are apprehended as different from other youths when in reality they are different primarily because they have been tagged with a deviant label.

learning disability (LD) A disorder in one or more of the basic psychological processes involved in understanding or using spoken or written language.

mandatory sentencing The requirement that individuals who commit certain offenses be sentenced to a specified length of confinement if found guilty or adjudicated delinquent.

marijuana The most frequently used illicit drug; usually smoked, it consists of dried hemp leaves and buds.

masculinity hypothesis The idea that as girls become more boylike and acquire more masculine traits, they become more delinquent.

McKeiver v. Pennsylvania A 1971 U.S. Supreme Court case that denied juveniles the right to trial by jury.

Miranda v. Arizona The landmark 1966 U.S. Supreme Court ruling that suspects taken into

police custody must, before any questioning can take place, be informed that they have the right to remain silent, that anything they say may be used against them, and that they have the right to legal counsel.

Missouri Plan Adopted by a dozen states, this plan involves a commission being appointed to nominate candidates for judge vacancies.

mother–son incest Sexual activity that occurs between a mother and her son. Also refers to incest by stepmothers or the girlfriend(s) of the father.

National Council of Juvenile and Family Court Judges Located in Reno, Nevada, this organization works to improve the juvenile court judiciary through sponsored research and continuing education.

National Crime Victimization Survey (NCVS) An ongoing survey of crime victims in the United States conducted by the Bureau of Justice Statistics to determine the extent of crime.

neglect A disregard for the physical, emotional, or moral needs of children. Child neglect involves the failure of the parent or caregiver to provide nutritious food, adequate clothing and sleeping arrangements, essential medical care, sufficient supervision, access to education, and normal experiences that produce feelings of being loved, wanted, secure, and worthy.

neutralization theory A theory examining how youngsters attempt to justify or rationalize their responsibility for delinquent acts.

Office of Juvenile Justice and Delinquency Prevention (OJJDP) A federal agency that works to provide national leadership, coordination, and resources to prevent and respond to juvenile delinquency and victimization.

opportunity theory A perspective that holds that gang members turn to delinquency because of a sense of injustice about the lack of legitimate opportunities open to them.

orthomolecular imbalance A chemical imbalance in the body, resulting from poor nutrition, allergies, and exposure to lead and certain other substances, which is said to lead to delinquency.

Outward Bound A wilderness-type survival program that is popular in many states as an alternative to the institutionalization of juveniles.

parens patriae A medieval English doctrine that sanctioned the right of the Crown to intervene in natural family relations whenever a child's welfare was threatened. Under *parens patriae*, the state assumed the parental role over juvenile lawbreakers. The philosophy of the juvenile court is based on this legal concept.

petition A document filed in juvenile court alleging that a juvenile is a delinquent and asking that the court assume jurisdiction over the juvenile or asking that an alleged delinquent be waived to criminal court for prosecution as an adult.

petitioner   In the juvenile justice system, an intake officer (prosecutor) who seeks court jurisdiction over a youthful offender.

police discretion   A police officer's ability to choose from among a number of alternative dispositions when handling a situation.

police interrogation   The process of interviewing a person who has been arrested with the express purpose of obtaining a confession.

Positive Peer Culture (PPC)   A total system for building positive youth subcultures. Its main goal is to turn around negative peer cultures and to mobilize the power of the peer group in positive ways.

Positive Youth Development (PYD)   A comprehensive way of thinking about adolescence that challenges the traditional deficit-based perspective by pointing out that youths can sometimes thrive even in the presence of multiple risk factors.

positivism   The view that just as laws operate in the medical, biological, and physical sciences, laws govern human behavior and these laws can be understood and used.

power-control thesis   The view that the relationship between gender and delinquency is linked to issues of power and control.

pretrial identification practices   The procedures such as fingerprinting, photographing, and placing juveniles in lineups for the purpose of identification prior to formal court appearance.

prevalence of delinquency   The percentage of the juvenile population who are involved in delinquent behavior.

primary deviation   According to labeling theory, the initial act of deviance that causes a person to be labeled a deviant.

private juvenile placement   A training school that operates under private auspices. The county or state generally pays the school a per diem rate for the care of youths committed to these facilities.

probation   A court-ordered nonpunitive juvenile disposition that emphasizes community-based services and treatment and close supervision by an officer of the court. Probation is essentially a sentence of confinement that is suspended as long as the probationer meets the conditions imposed by the court.

probation officer   An officer of the court who is expected to provide social history investigations, supervise individuals who have been placed on probation, maintain case files, advise probationers on the conditions of their sentences, perform any other probationary services that a judge may request, and inform the court when persons on probation have violated the terms of that probation.

probation subsidy program   Used in states such as California, Nevada, Oregon, and Washington, these programs encourage a decreased rate of commitment of juvenile offenders to state institutions by reimbursing the community for confining or working with youths locally.

problem-oriented policing   A contemporary policing strategy through which police agencies place more emphasis on addressing the fundamental circumstances that create juvenile crime rather than focusing exclusively on incidents of delinquency.

process of becoming deviant   In labeling theory, the concept that the process of acquiring a delinquent identity takes place in a number of steps.

progressive era   The period from around 1890 to 1920, when a wave of optimism swept through American society and led to the acceptance of positivism.

prosecutor   The representative of the state in court proceedings. Also called *county's attorney, district attorney,* or *state attorney.*

psychoanalytic theory   A theory based on Sigmund Freud's insights, which have helped to shape the handling of juvenile delinquents. They include these axioms: (1) The personality is made up of three components—id, ego, and superego; (2) a normal child passes through three psychosexual stages of development—oral, anal, and phallic; and (3) a person's personality traits are developed in early childhood.

psychopath   An individual with a personality disorder, or a hard-core juvenile delinquent/adult criminal; also called a *sociopath.*

radical criminology   A perspective that holds that the causes of crime are rooted in social conditions that empower the wealthy and the politically well organized but disenfranchise the less fortunate.

radical nonintervention   A policy toward delinquents that advises authorities to "leave the kids alone whenever possible."

ranch   A public or private juvenile correctional institution that, like a forestry camp, is usually less secure than a training school and that has a more normal atmosphere.

reaction formation   The psychological strategy for dealing with frustration by becoming hostile toward an unattainable object.

reception and diagnostic center   A facility where juveniles who have been committed to correctional institutions frequently are first sent. This type of center diagnoses youths' problems and develops individualized treatment plans.

recidivism   The repetition of delinquent behavior by a youth who has been released from probation status or from training school.

rehabilitation model   A correctional model whose goal is to change an offender's character, attitudes, or behavior so as to diminish his or her delinquent propensities. The medical, adjustment, and reintegration models are variants of this model because they are all committed to changing the offender.

reinforcement theory   A perspective that holds that behavior is governed by its consequences, especially rewards and punishments that follow from it.

reintegration philosophy   This philosophy assumes that both the officer and the receiving community must be brought together in formal programs.

rejection by parents   The disapproval, repudiation, or other uncaring behavior directed by parents toward children.

reliability   The extent to which a questionnaire or interview yields the same answers from the same juveniles when they are questioned two or more times.

representing   The use by criminal street gangs of secret handshakes and special hand signs.

residential program   A program conducted for the rehabilitation of youthful offenders within community-based and institutional settings.

resiliency   The capacity to regain personal power and develop a strong core sense of self in the face of poverty, severe family hardship, and community devastation.

respondent   The defense attorney in the juvenile court system.

restitution   A court-ordered repayment to a victim; often used together with community service as a condition of juvenile probation.

restorative justice model   A model of juvenile justice that works to reconcile the interests of victims, offenders, and the community through common programs and supervision practices that meet the needs of all parties.

revocation of aftercare   The cancellation of parole and return of the offender to an institution. It takes effect if a juvenile on aftercare commits another offense or violates the conditions of parole.

right to treatment   The entitlement of a juvenile who has been committed to a training school to receive any needed services (e.g., therapy, education).

routine activities approach   The contention that crime rate trends and cycles are related to the nature of everyday patterns of social interaction that characterize the society in which they occur.

running away   The act of leaving the custody and home of parents or guardians without permission and failing to return within a reasonable length of time; a status offense.

school search   The process of searching students and their lockers to determine whether drugs, weapons, or other contraband is present.

search and seizure   The police procedure used in the investigation of crimes for the purpose of gathering evidence.

sedative   A drug that is taken orally and affects the user by depressing the nervous system, causing drowsiness.

self-report study   A study of juvenile crime based on surveys in which youths report on their own delinquent acts.

sentencing circles   A form of restorative justice that incorporates principles of ancient, aboriginal tribal justice to address the harm suffered by crime victims and their families, the responsibilities of offenders, and the role of community.

sex-role socialization   The process by which boys and girls internalize their culture's norms, sanctions, and expectations for members of their gender.

shelter care facility   A facility that is used to provide short term care for status offenders and/or dependent or neglected youths.

social capital   The resources that reside in the social structure itself—norms, social networks, and interpersonal relationships that contribute to a child's growth.

social contract   An unstated or explicit agreement between a people and their government as to the rights and obligations of each.

social control theory   A perspective that delinquent acts result when a juvenile's bond to society is weak or broken.

social development model   A perspective based on the integration of social control and cultural learning theories that proposes that the development of attachments to parents will lead to attachments to school and a commitment to education as well as a belief in and commitment to conventional behavior and the law.

social disorganization theory   An approach that posits that juvenile delinquency results when social control among the traditional primary groups, such as the family and the neighborhood, breaks down because of social disarray within the community.

social injustice   According to many conflict-oriented criminologists, social injustice is found in apparent unfairness in the juvenile justice system arising from poor youths being disproportionately represented, female status offenders being subjected to sexist treatment, and racial minorities being dealt with more harshly than whites.

social interactionist theory   A theoretical perspective that derives its explanatory power from the give-and-take that continuously occurs between social groups and between individuals and society.

socialization   The process by which individuals come to internalize their culture; through this process, an individual learns the norms, sanctions, and expectations of being a member of a particular society.

social process theory   A theoretical approach to delinquency that examines the interactions between individuals and their environments, especially those that might influence them to become involved in delinquent behavior.

social structure   The relatively stable formal and informal arrangements that characterize a society, including its economic arrangements, social institutions, and values and norms.

social study report   A report ordered by a judge during the fact-finding stage of the court's proceedings.

sociobiology   An expression of biological positivism that stresses the interaction between biological factors within an individual and the influence of the person's particular environment; also the systematic study of the biological basis of all social behavior.

soft determinism   The view that delinquents are neither wholly free nor wholly constrained in their choice of actions.

specialization   The repeated involvement of a juvenile in one type of delinquency during the course of his or her offending.

station adjustment   One of several disposition options available to a police officer whereby a juvenile is taken to the police station following a complaint, the contact is recorded, and the juvenile is given an official reprimand and then released to his or her parents or guardians.

status frustration   The stress that individuals experience when they cannot attain their goals because of their socioeconomic class.

status offender   A juvenile who commits a minor act that is considered illegal only because he or she is underage.

status offense   A nondelinquent/noncriminal offense; an offense that is illegal for underage persons but not for adults. Status offenses include curfew violations, incorrigibility, running away, truancy, and underage drinking.

statutory exclusions   A legislative mandate which requires that juveniles accused of committing certain designated offenses be tried in adult criminal court.

strain theory   A theory that proposes that the pressure the social structure exerts on youths who cannot attain cultural success goals will push them to engage in nonconforming behavior.

supervision   The surveillance, monitoring, casework services, and counseling or guidance services provided to a youthful offender who has been placed on probation. Supervision is provided by juvenile probation officers.

supervision and discipline   The parental monitoring, guidance, and control of children's activities and behavior.

surveillance   The observation of probationers by probation officers; intended to ensure that probationers comply with the conditions of probation and that they do not break the law.

symbolic interactionist theory   A perspective in social psychology that analyzes the process of interaction among human beings at the symbolic level and that has influenced the development of several social process theories of delinquent behavior.

taking into custody   The process of arresting a juvenile for socially unacceptable or unlawful behavior.

theory of differential oppression   The view that in the United States, authority is unjustly used against children, who must adapt to adults' ideas of what constitutes "good children."

training school   A correctional facility for long-term placement of juvenile delinquents; may be public (run by a state department of corrections or youth commission) or private.

trait-based personality model   A theory that attributes delinquent behavior to an individual's basic inborn characteristics.

transfer   The process of certifying a youth over to adult criminal court. It takes place by judicial waiver and legislative waiver.

Uniform Crime Reporting (UCR) Program   The Federal Bureau of Investigation's program for compiling annual data about crimes committed in the United States.

utilitarianism   A doctrine that holds that what is useful is good and that the aim of social or political action should be the greatest good for the greatest number.

validity   The extent to which a research instrument measures what it says it measures.

vandalism   The act of destroying or damaging, or attempting to destroy or damage, the property of another without the owner's consent or destroying or damaging public property (except by burning).

violence   A forceful physical assault with or without weapons. It includes many kinds of fighting, rape, other attacks, gang warfare, and so on.

volunteer program   The use of unpaid adult community members to assist probation officers in a variety of ways.

wilderness camp   A correctional facility where residents usually do conservation work in state parks, including cleaning up, cutting grass and weeds, and doing general maintenance.

wilderness programs   Sometimes called survival programs, these venues expose youth who have been entered into them to participate in forest, mountain, and ocean training. The best known is Outward Bound.

Wisconsin system   A system of supervision for youthful offenders that involves a risk/needs assessment conducted at regular intervals to see what level of supervision is appropriate for each individual offender.

Name Index

A

Aaltonen, M., 295n.38
Abadinsky, H., 292nn.3, 5, 26, 26
Abbott, E., 210n.7
Abram, K. M., 288, 295n.66
Abrams, L. S., 428, 429, 440n.62
Achcroft, J., 349n.68
Ackley, E., 270n.71
Acoca, L., 180nn.42, 43
Acosta de Brenes, E., 127n.39
Adams, A., 102n.8
Adams, B., 37, 366, 367, 368, 372, 384nn.37, 46
Adams, W. T., 434, 441n.81
Addie, S., 366, 367, 368, 384n.46
Addington, L. A., 237n.17
Adler, F., 180n.59, 270n.71
Afanasyer, V., 155n.56
Ageton, S., 210n.4
Ageton, S. S., 50n.37, 128n.72, 129nn.84, 85, 295n.43
Agnew, R., 57, 75n.25, 88, 89, 92, 103nn.45, 46, 48, 49, 50, 53, 127n.28, 128n.62, 158n.141, 165, 180nn.51, 52, 55, 68
Aichhorn, A., 63, 77n.73
Ajken, I., 295n.51
Akers, R. L., 110, 126nn.11, 14, 127n.31, 128n.79, 294n.38
Akos, P., 237n. 26
Alexander, J. F., 158n.122
Alinsky, S., 95
Allen, E., 161, 179n.17
Alltucker, K. W., 50n.49
Alper, B. S., 326nn.39, 40
Altschuler, D. M., 38, 68, 294nn.36, 430, 441nn.66
Amedeo, S., 198, 212n.77
Anderson, A., 55, 75n.19
Anderson, C. A., 192
Anderson, E., 80
Anderson, E. A., 181n.77
Anderson, J., 269n.10
Anderson, K., 157n.98
Aniwar, S., 55, 75n.16
Annie E. Casey Foundation, 11, 211n.12
Antaramin, S., 210n.6
Antonaccio, O., 239n.83
Archer, M., 97, 104n.95
Armstrong, D. P., 50n.57
Armstrong, G., 348n.22
Armstrong, G. S., 424, 440n.40
Armstrong, T., 325n.28, 393, 408nn.11, 12, 441nn.66, 68
Arneklev, B. J., 128n.78
Arthur, M., 157n.115
Artiles, B., 439n.1
Arum, R., 231, 239nn.90, 91
Asgeirsdottir, B. B., 349n.54
Atkins, C., 243
Atkinson, D., 296n.81
Augustus, J., 299–300, 325n.6
Austin, J., 24n.28, 408n.46
Ayers, W., 383n.4

B

Bachman, J. G., 275, 276, 277, 278, 283, 294nn.2, 7, 348n.13
Bahr, S., 441n.65
Bahr, S. J., 271n.101
Baird, C., 413, 418, 420, 439n.3
Bales, W., 239n.79
Ball, R. A., 408nn.29, 31
Ballard, D., 157nn.116, 117, 158n.119, 296n.73
Banfield, E., 112
Banks, R., 237n.19
Barker, G. E., 434, 441n.81
Barkley, G., 5
Barksdale, D., 243, 252
Barlowe, D. B., 325n.15
Baron, S. W., 97, 103n.53, 104nn.86, 88
Bartels, M., 76n.43
Bartollas, C., 25n.81, 39, 181n.83, 311, 325n.11, 326n.74, 407n.1, 408n.27, 424, 425, 435, 440nn.38, 41, 42, 43, 45, 441nn.80, 85, 86
Bartollas, L. D., 243
Barton, W. H., 439n.14, 441n.71
Baskin, J. R., 176, 182nn.110, 111
Batani-Khalfani, A. S., 269n.14
Bates, J. E., 214n.141
Bauzer, R., 349n.27
Bazemore, G., 157n.106, 296nn.83, 84, 325n.28, 408nn.12, 13, 14
Beach, S., 76n.56
Bearch, L. R., 25n.64, 75n.10
Beattie, I. R., 231, 239nn.90, 91
Beaver, K. M., 76n.44, 238n.43
Beccaria, C., 53–54, 75nn.4, 8
Beck, A. J., 25n.70, 436, 441n.89
Beck, A. T., 66, 77n.100
Becker, H., 131, 132–133, 135, 155nn.9, 10
Beger, R. R., 181n.83
Belknap, J., 165, 180nn.40, 41
Bell, D., Jr., 364, 384nn.44, 45
Bell, R., 296n.80
Belshaw, S., 89, 103n.51
Belyea, M. J., 212n.63
Benning, J. J., 216, 237n.2
Benson, M. L., 128n.77
Benson, P., 157n.114
Bentham, J., 54, 75nn.4, 7,9
Beres, J., 303, 325nn.12, 13
Bergseth, K. J., 157n.110
Bergsmann, I. R., 213n.108
Berlin, L. J., 214n.141
Bernard, B., 157n.114
Bernard, T. J., 88, 97, 102n.8, 103n.44, 103n.65, 104nn.91, 92
Bernburg, J. G., 134, 155nn.27, 28
Berry, G., 269n.10
Beyer, M., 164, 180nn.35, 36
Bilchik, S., 327, 384n.34
Binder, A., 383n.3
Bishop, D. M., 75n.23, 181nn.85, 86, 87, 317–319, 322, 326nn.51, 52, 55, 57, 75, 384n.38, 385nn.75, 76, 439n.11

Simpson, J., 128n.71, 156n.83, 179n.11, 180nn.62, 63, 64, 65
Sladky, A., 412, 419, 440nn.28, 29, 30
Slater, M. D., 64, 77n.79
Slawson, J., 75n.31
Slowkowski, J., 294n.1
Smart, C., 160, 179n.2
Smith, A., 440n.59
Smith, C., 260, 270n.76, 271n.89, 295n.60
Smith, C. A., 129n.100, 211n.25, 214nn.121, 135, 271n.113
Smith, D., 50n.36
Smith, D. A., 179n.11
Smith, J. D., 330, 348n.11
Smith, L., 270n.68
Smith, M. H., 237n.8
Snodgrass, J., 108
Snyder, H. N., 6, 8, 24nn.25, 29, 50n.46, 214n.123, 307, 326n.58, 334, 343, 349nn.56, 60, 63, 64, 66, 354, 364, 384n.59, 407n.4, 428, 439nn.9, 10, 440nn.28, 36, 37, 61, 441n.75
Snyder, K., 408nn.23, 25
Snyder, M., 237n.17
Snyder, S. M., 428, 429, 440n.62
Snyder, T. D., 219
Sommers, I., 176, 182nn.110, 111
Soohill, K., 51n.67
Souse, C., 213n.118
Spelman, E. V., 161, 174, 179n.15, 181nn.75, 76, 98, 102, 103
Spergel, I. A., 247, 264, 271nn.94, 104, 105, 106, 107, 108
Spitzer, S., 155n.58
Spoth, R. L., 295n.49
Spracklen, K. M., 296n.85
Spring, J. H., 216, 237n.8
Springer, C. E., 383n.3
Springer, D. W., 413, 439n.4
Spruance, L. M., 325nn.31, 32, 33, 34
Staff, J., 222, 238n.34, 239n.92
Stafford, M. C., 238n.40
Stanton, W., 78n.105
Staples, W. G., 408n.17
Stapleton, W. V., 350nn.75, 76
Stark, R., 102nn.16, 19
Steele, P., 408n.46
Steffensmeier, D., 161, 179nn.17, 24
Steinhart, D., 439nn.12, 13
Steinmetz, 213n.94
Stephens, R. D., 238n.70, 269n.33, 350n.74
Stephenson, R. M., 180n.54
Stern, K., 76n.61
Stern, S. B., 210n.2
Sterne, R. S., 210n.9
Stevens, J., 64, 77n.84
Steward, E., 76n.56
Steward, L., 325n.29
Stewart, E. L., 102n.20, 128n.62
Stinchcombe, A. L., 216, 237n.4
Stoddard-Dare, P., 60, 76n.57
Stouthamer-Loeber, M., 49n.27, 50nn.52, 53, 77n.85, 210n.4, 211n.16, 211n.25
Straus, M. A., 197, 212n.74, 213n.94
Strauss, J., 181n.80
Street, D., 440n.32
Streit, J., 213n.107
Strodtbeck, F. L., 75n.23
Strong, A., 384n.36
Stuart, B., 146, 157n.104
Stuart, C., 439n.5
Sullivan, D., 156nn.63, 64
Sullivan, J., 379

Sun, F., 158nn.141, 142
Sutherland, E. H., 58, 75n.32, 76n.47, 96, 107–109, 118, 126nn.3, 4
Suttles, g. d., 271n.91
Swaim, R. C., 77n.79
Sykes, G. M., 127n.20, 349n.30

T

Tajima, E. A., 213n.118
Tangri, S. S., 115, 127n.45
Tannebaum, F., 155nn.3, 4
Tannebaum, J., 63
Tannenbaum, F., 131–132, 135
Tapia, M., 155n.18
Tappan, P., 77n.77
Tate, L., 299 illus
Tauscher, S., 130
Taylor, C. S., 260, 269n.3, 270n.75
Taylor, D. W. T. J., 349n.68
Taylor, I., 75nn.29, 30, 127n.32, 156n.82
Taylor, J., 126n.8
Taylor, T. J., 269n.25, 271n.103
Teague, R., 213n.110
Teji, S., 413
Teplin, L. A., 288, 295n.66
Terry, E., 357
Terry, R. M., 181n.83, 348nn.20, 21
Thomas, C., 383nn.21, 22
Thomas, C. W., 24nn.36, 38, 75n.23, 384n.34
Thompson, W. E., 127n.40
Thornberry, T., 210n.2, 239n.93
Thornberry, T. P., 24nn.24, 43, 49nn.16, 17, 50n.38, 75n.23, 103n.47, 119, 120–121, 123, 128n.72, 129nn.87, 88, 99, 100, 201, 210n.2, 211n.25, 214nn.120, 121, 135, 223, 238n.47, 265, 271n.112, 113, 114, 115, 116, 295n.60, 375, 384n.62
Thorne, B., 163, 180nn.30, 33, 34
Thornton, W. E., 168
Thornton, W. E., Jr., 180nn.57, 61
Thrasher, F., 77n.77, 241, 247, 269nn.7, 8
Thurston, J. R., 216, 237n.2
Tibbetts, S. G., 50n.55
Tifft, L., 156nn.63, 64
Tittle, C., 50n.36
Tittle, C. R., 76n.54, 127n.62, 128n.78, 155n.16
Tobias, J. J., 77n.77
Tobin, K., 51nn.71, 72, 129n.100
Toby, J., 210n.9, 238n.36
Tomkins, S. S., 75n.24
Tonry, M., 102nn.17, 19
Torbet, P., 408nn.19, 20, 30
Torbet, P. M., 440n.63
Tracy, P. E., 36
Tracy, S. K., 269n.29
Travis, J., 99
Tremblay, R. E., 66, 68, 69
Triplett, R. A., 96, 104n.85, 133–134, 135, 155nn.20, 21, 23, 24
Truman, J., 219
Tseloni, A., 75n.11
Tuell, J. A., 320
Turk, A. T., 142, 143, 157n.81
Turner, J. H., 156n.66
Tweksbury, R., 441n.90
Tzoumakis, S., 66, 78n.102

U

Umbreit, M., 157n.106, 408nn.12, 13, 14
Unnever, J. D., 158n.143

Subject Index

Note: The locators followed by "illus", "b", "t" and "f" refer to illustrations, boxes, tables and figures cited in the text.